PICTURING EXTRATERRESTRIALS

PICTURING
EXTRATERRESTRIALS
ALIEN IMAGES IN MODERN CULTURE
JOHN F. MOFFITT

Prometheus Books
59 John Glenn Drive
Amherst, New York 14228-2197

Published 2003 by Prometheus Books

Inquiries should be addressed to
Prometheus Books
59 John Glenn Drive
Amherst, New York 14228–2197
VOICE: 716–691–0133, ext. 207
FAX: 716–564–2711
WWW.PROMETHEUSBOOKS.COM

07 06 05 04 03   5 4 3 2 1

Library of Congress Cataloging-in-Publication Data

Moffitt, John F. (John Francis), 1940–
    Picturing extraterrestrials : alien images in modern culture / John F. Moffitt.
        p. cm.
    Includes bibliographical references and index.
    ISBN 1–57392–990–5 (alk. paper)
    1. Human-alien encounters. 2. Life on other planets in art. 3. Popular Culture I. Title.

BF82050 .M64 2002
704.9'49001942—dc21

                                                                    2002018950

Printed in Canada on acid-free paper

TO ALL TRUE BELIEVERS . . . PRESS ON, REGARDLESS!

Exspectavimus lucem, et ecce tenebrae.

—Isa. 59:9

"Nothing exists except atoms and empty space; everything else is opinion."

—Democritus

"And there is no new thing under the sun [*nihil sub sole novum*]."

—Eccles. 1:9

"The soul never thinks without a picture."

—Aristotle

"And, as imagination bodies forth
The form of things unknown, the poet's pen
Turns them to shapes, and gives to airy nothing
A local habitation and a name . . .
How easy is a bush suppos'd a bear!"
    —William Shakespeare, *A Midsummer Night's Dream*, 5.1.7

"A wise man proportions his belief to the evidence."

—David Hume

"Like other wares, art is dependent upon producers and consumers."

—Rudolf Wittkower

"Follow the money!"

—"Deep Throat," circa 1972

"It takes work to be skeptical; you have to know something."

—Carl Sagan

"We weren't born believing in UFOs!"

—"Brenda," an abductee in 1992

Contents

6: PREMODERNIST RELIGIOUS TRANSPORTS, POSSESSION, AND POETIC INSPIRATION

7: THE INCUBUS AS PROTO-ET: THE CASE OF HENRY FUSELI'S *NIGHTMARE*

8: HERE COME THE FLYING SAUCERS!

9: THE FALTERING HISTORY OF UFOLOGY

10: NOTHING NEW IN OUTER SPACE

11: SOME MUNDANE CONTEXTS FOR OUTLANDISH BELIEFS

12: PICTURING AND THE MODERN REINVENTION OF OCCULTISM

13: AN ETIOLOGY OF THE MODERNIST EXPERIENCE

14: MORE STRICTLY MUNDANE CONTEXTS FOR ETs, AND SOME CONCLUSIONS

List of Illustrations

1. Martin Cannon, "Extra-Terrestrials among Us" (paperback book-cover: George C. Andrews, *Extra-Terrestrials among Us*, St. Paul, Minn.: Fate, 1993).
2. Constantinopolitan artist, "Head of Christ" (*Mandylion*; circa 500). Genoa, S. Bartolomeo degli Armeni.
3. Warner Sallman, "Head of Christ" (1940; unauthorized Mexican copy, circa 1960, "El Divino Redentor").
4. Ted Jacobs, "Head of an Extra-Terrestrial" (paperback bookcover: Whitley Strieber, *Communion*, New York: Bantam, 1987. Trademark [TM] Walker & Collier Inc.).
5. "How a Member of the Kingdom of Heaven Might Appear" (as depicted on the Heaven's Gate Web page in 1997). (Author's collection.)
6. "The Virgin of Guadalupe Appears to Juan Diego at Tepeyac in 1531" (anonymous Mexican chromolithograph, circa 1985).
7. Fritz Erler, "Adolf Hitler, Architect of the Millenarian Reich" (1939; present location unknown). (Author's collection.)
8. Joe Nickell, "Alien Time Line" (from *Skeptical Inquirer* 21, no. 5, September/October 1997).
9. *The Day the Earth Stood Still* (1951): *alienus* as peacemaker (with title, as published in *Newsweek*, 7 July 1997).
10. *Alien Nation* (1988): *alienus* as buddy (with title, as published in *Newsweek*, 7 July 1997).

11. *Species* (1995): *alienus* as gorgeous nymphomaniac man-killer (with title, as published in *Newsweek*, 7 July 1997).
12. *Men in Black* (1997): *alienus* as comedic illegal immigrant (with title, as published in *Newsweek*, 7 July 1997).
13. *Alien* (1979): *alienus* as reptile parasite and woman-chaser (with title, as published in *Newsweek*, 7 July 1997).
14. *Predator* (1987): *alienus* as standard slime-ball, big-game man-hunter (with title, as published in *Newsweek*, 7 July 1997).
15. *E.T.: The Extraterrestrial* (1982): *alienus* as household-pet (with title, as published in *Newsweek*, 7 July 1997).
16. Barney Hill, "UFO Crew Man" (pencil-drawing, 1966, as reproduced in John G. Fuller, *The Interrupted Journey*, New York: Dell, 1967).
17. "Betty Hill with an Extraterrestrial" (video-still from the 1975 NBC TV–movie *The UFO Incident*). (Author's collection.)
18. "An Extraterrestrial" (video-still from the 1975 NBC TV–movie *The UFO Incident*). (Author's collection.)
19. "Epiphany of the Extraterrestrial" (video-still from the 1977 Steven Spielberg movie *Close Encounters of the Third Kind)*. (Author's collection.)
20. Mike Rogers (?), "The Humanoid ET Abductors of Travis Walton" (1976; as reproduced in *World Almanac Book of the Strange*, New York: Signet, 1977).
21. Betty Andreasson, "Entity in the Examination Room" (pencil-drawing, circa 1979, as reproduced, with enhancements, in Ronald E. Fowler, *The Andreasson Affair*, New York: Bantam, 1980).
22. Betty Andreasson, "Entities Moving through a Closed Door" (pencil-drawing, circa 1979, as reproduced, with enhancements, in Ronald E. Fowler, *The Andreasson Affair*, New York: Bantam, 1980).
23. Greco-Roman Relief, "Three Maenads" (circa 100 C.E.) Florence, Uffizi.
24. "St. Mark" (full-page [8 × 10 in.] author-portrait from the *Gospel Book of Ebbo*, circa 830). Épernay, Bibliothèque Municipale.
25. Vincent van Gogh, *Self-Portrait* (1889). Paris, Musée de l'Impressionisme.
26. Henry Fuseli, *The Nightmare* (1781). Detroit, Institute of Art.
27. Giotto di Bordone, "The Adoration of the Magi" (circa 1304). Arena Chapel, Padua.
28. "The Airship Seen Hovering over Oakland in November 1896" (from the *San Francisco Call*, November 22, 1896).
29. Myron, *Diskobolos* (as a "Frisbee Thrower"), (circa 450 B.C.E.) Rome, Terme.

Introduction

This is a book about a provocative topic—those "extraterrestrials" said to dwell among us earthlings (fig. 1)—that has boldly established itself in recent U.S. history and, especially, in the American mass-consciousness. Being anomalous, even aberrant, it has been typically ignored by ivory-tower historians, especially those dedicated scholars chronicling the heroic evolution of modern art, the "serious" kind now prestigiously enshrined in most public museums. Nonetheless—although it has not previously been recognized—the "alien invasion" phenomenon especially calls for the attention of a properly trained art historian. As it turns out, the "evidence" testifying to the physical presence among us of a now-standard ET iconographic type—the macrocephalic, bug-eyed, and gray alien—is largely visual. As shown here, finally its actual art-historical progression can be charted (see especially figs. 4, 5, 16–22). The only other "documentation" for the ashen and pop-eyed ETs cohabiting with us is strictly verbal, and that "proof" is quoted here in abundance.

The way they (meaning the ETs) get here—and they seem to do so with ever-increasing ease—is by means of their so-called UFOs (unidentified flying objects). Regarding them, first there is an incident, a "sighting," the perception of an anomalous event, and then that incident is interpreted by other people. Perhaps the most wide-ranging yet, this book is also an interpretation of the various contexts informing a phenomenon—

The UFO Experience—just half a century old. UFO beliefs have come into being and now flourish in a culture with a modernist ideology, specifically the kind called "New Age," that is congenial to their existence and prolix exegesis. Among other things, I will propose a new title for these putative outer-space vehicles: "MFOs" (misidentified fugitive observations). Again the viewer has been alerted to a skeptical perspective.

Put into the larger, cultural perspective, our subject—the artistic portrayal of extraterrestrial (otherworldly) entities—very much belongs to the present moment: the figurative millenarian end of our historical evolution. Chronologically speaking, besides being literally "postmodernist," the ET phenomenon so prominent in the popular consciousness is also to be metaphorically designated as being equally "millenarian" and "New Age." Although largely the product of homegrown American imaginations, these awe-inspiring "alien" biological entities are said to come from "outer space"—and never across our terrestrial borders. As such, these otherworldly beings are correctly called *extraterrestrials*. But please always keep in mind that the literal synonym to "extraterrestrial" is "supernatural."

Caveat lector. Our extraterrestrial subject is, most likely, wholly apocryphal. In this case, that adjective designates (according to Webster)—and as derived from the Greek, αποκρυφοσ, "the hidden or spurious"—"writings or statements of doubtful authorship or authority." Thus our subject matter becomes a particularly American, postmodernist *apocrypha* of the specifically anthropomorphic sort, for that is the way in which the ETs now appear depicted in their abundant apocryphal portraiture. As much as possible, I have endeavored to track down the contemporary written testimony substantiating the authenticity of the apocryphal ET phenomenon, and necessarily incorporating, in the larger sense, the UFO experience. What follows is a detective-like investigation, in the course of which I unearth the evidence abundantly attesting not to ETs, but instead to massive mental manipulation and often-zestful commercial exploitation.

Quoted here *in extenso*, the first-person documentation defining the UFO experience permits these anomalies to speak for themselves, and in ways likely unfamiliar to the reader of a book like this, that is, a scholarly work (as you see, this one does have copious notes, or "documentation"). Where possible, the eyewitness testimonies are presented in the form of, and are treated as, transcripts. As such, they are here presented as forensic evidence, and they will be handled as such. As is required, this is detective work. Consequently, I must also present the writs submitted by the opposition, those nonbelievers (skeptics) who do not accept the canonic interpretation of the phenomenon presented by the True Believers. In effect, this book is implicitly cast in the legal format of a trial. Both sides do have an equal say, and each has its own eloquent advocates to defend the respective points of view. You, dear readers, are the jury. I am, as it were, the district attorney.

In order to put the phenomenon of extraterrestrial portraiture into a wider public context and thus enhance its significance as a cultural artifact, I have compared it to many complementary historical phenomena. Side issues explored here in some detail include the modernist allegorization of big business (as personified here by "Betty Crocker"); the traditional imagery generated by the religious visionary experience; the meaning of angels and demons in their nocturnal visitations; the astral imagery conventionally acknowledging epiphanies of divinity; the narrative and iconographic conventions of a now mostly obsolete belief system called "witchcraft"; the clinical invention of "hysteria" by French doctors and the coeval alliance forged between avant-garde artists and the occult during the 1890s; the effects of a millenarian psychology; the now conventional role of visual spectacle and psychological manipulation in modernist mass movements; the complementary role of the postmodernist infotainment industry; the workings of archetypal myth; and so forth. As treated here, the widely pictured extraterrestrials, and the UFO experience which directly spawned them, are symptoms. Accordingly, the cultural patterns embracing them, their macrocosmic matrix, are to be additionally treated as a fitting subject of forensic medicine, an "autopsy."

Not really a detective, and certainly not a physician, I am instead an art historian, and one much published in the appropriate scholarly venues—which are, however, not the kind that would deign to publish an art-historical inquest of extraterrestrial portraiture, however serious (or ironic) its intentions. I have interpreted my professional endeavor: "art history" (previously earthbound for me); often this specifically means that my task is to illustrate the actual workings of "history" (meaning anything that happened the day before yesterday) by means of its time-specific imagery (aka "art"). Besides time-specific, the kind of imagery that interests me most is also decidedly culture-specific. However, unlike many other art historians, I am usually not all that much interested in "the Good, the True, and the Beautiful," which is the way that art used to be emotionally defined. Instead, besides treating my various subjects like objective forensic evidence, I am much more fascinated by what art actually *illustrates*, namely, the way that given cultures really do work. Thus, for these kinds of exclusively modernist materials, it often proves more useful if one bothers to examine what most art historians will not deign to look at, namely, "the bad, the patently false, and the faked beautiful"—kitsch, in short.

A case is additionally made here that the extraterrestrials, such as they represent a wholly modernist phenomenon, perhaps embody something pernicious and patently false that is particularly inherent (or endemic) to our postmodernist culture. That is also on trial here. Hopefully, the allegation of inauthenticity should not offend fundamentalist subscribers to ancient biblical prophecy, some of which is also quoted here. Nonetheless, those who do believe—often fervently—in the reality of visitors from outer space, the kind of investigators proudly calling themselves "UFOlogists," will no doubt be offended by this scholar's labored autopsy of their postmodernist extraterrestrial culture. According to this meticulous inquest, its origins are strictly terrestrial. (Sorry.) No matter. Kitsch is absolutely essential to understand what really happens in our postmodernist culture, especially the kind driven by manipulative marketing and knee-jerk mass consumption, and a poignant case in point is the *ex nihilo* pictorialization of alleged "alien" visitors deriving from places with extraterrestrial zip codes.

Caveat lector. Therefore, dear reader, if you are either a rigid Fundamentalist or, especially, if you actually believe that you are a card-carrying abductee (i.e., that you have actually been abducted by extraterrestrials), then perhaps this book is not really for you. This has been written for people with "inquiring minds" (but if you are a devoted reader of the *National Enquirer*, don't bother). As for myself, I cheerfully confess straightaway to having seen neither UFOs nor ETs. (Sorry.) Nonetheless, the colorful, even lurid, details supporting these apocryphal beliefs—also the committed fervor of their ardent True Believers—make for a fascinating excursion into the great beyond.

History is an invaluable tool in the arsenal of rational inquiry into the essentially irrational. Historical analysis distances participants from events that they have probably observed at least at secondhand—by newspapers, books, movies, television, and so on—and in which, on occasion, they may have even directly participated. Such distancing allows the removed observers, perhaps even the emotionally involved participant, to obtain a less emotional, or rational and contextual, perspective, seeking better understanding in assessing extraordinary claims. That is, should the dazzled onlookers actually have any genuine desire to understand what is really going on, as opposed to passively consuming what they have been told is happening.

Although passing as a detective story, what follows is pure scholarship—in this instance, exercising the investigative mechanisms to determine the truth about things the hard way, by exhaustive research. Nonetheless, I hope the sheer delight I had in rooting out these odd beliefs is somehow communicated to the reader. For this writer, scholarship is fun; if it is not, then please don't bother with it. Reading, particularly the kind devoted to nonfiction, should be—besides informative in useful and often surprising ways—entertaining. Although irony is a staple of postmodernist discourse, so, too, is political correctness. In the United States, all belief systems are granted equal validity by constitutional law. Besides that, it is just not politically correct to approach anybody's belief system with irony—even if they torment you with dire forebodings, even wish to inspire terror in you. But irony is politically correct when it is employed to attack consumerist manipulations and profiteering, and that is my larger target. Since the UFO experience is also treated here as big business, where possible, I shall cite the actual dollar figures (and their published sources).

I will soon quote authority figures who implicitly urge you to become *terrorized* by what they believe to be happening: alien abductions. Theirs is certainly not an entertaining point of view. I will also cite known instances where people have actually become terrified, have unquestionably experienced great personal suffering, have sometimes had their mental health permanently damaged by these (induced) experiences. Even worse, there are even people who have committed suicide because of these beliefs, sometimes en masse. Because of this heavy burden of induced seriousness, and because (as I must confess) it outrages me, at times I have deliberately adopted a jocular tone. Long ago, William Congreve (1670–1729) observed that "humour has charms to soothe the overcommitted breast." Much later, in a postmodernist context, we may call that approach "gallows humor"—or just whistling in the darkness.

Either way, I hope what follows captures your interest. It certainly did mine.

John F. Moffitt
Las Cruces, NM
(not all that far from Roswell)

Chapter 1

A Preamble to Modernist Apocryphal Portraiture

OVERTURE TO AN AUTOPSY OF THE EXTRATERRESTRIAL NEW AGE

Caveat lector! Although this is indeed a book mostly about extraterrestrials, in no way is this a *catalogue raisonné*. (See figs. 1, 4, 5, 15–22.) Chronologically sequenced and minutely descriptive listings of the extraterrestrials' every known visitation among awestruck earthlings do already exist; there is in fact a plethora of such publications, many of which I cite in what follows, with many, many more being listed elsewhere.[1] There even exist scholarly studies that show that, rather than being a New Age phenomenon, human interest in extraterrestrial life-forms and customs has a continuous history, in fact one extending back over two millennia to the ancient Greeks.[2] This book is, however, different from all the rest—quite. To my knowledge, the phenomenon of the strictly modern picturing of extraterrestrials has never before been seriously treated from an art-historical perspective, that is, discussed both as a historically embedded phenomenon and as "art" (of the admittedly marginalized sort). Besides situating the modernist extraterrestrials within a much wider world of art-historical phenomena than has been customary (decidedly so!), this book also places them alongside the real world of pertinent American, even worldwide, historical events, a plethora of phenomena exerting influences both physical and emotional.

23

In the wider sense, this is really a book about a much more challenging subject: a hidden world lurking within postmodern culture.

A consistently applied tactic in this book is to pose questions. Often provocative, they ask the reader to question his or her beliefs, if any, regarding modern culture and its beliefs, particularly the kind propagated by the commercial mass media. This is appropriate: the best postmodernist cultural pursuits pursue similar inquisitorial goals. Certainly belief in extraterrestrials calls for some severe challenges. At times, a healthy measure of irony also seems indispensable when dealing with such apocryphal materials; sometimes (but all too rarely) laughter heals psychic wounds. Particularly questioned here is the orthodox modernist ideology of the worth of individual revelation, an ever weirder notion from the strictly postmodernist, meaning skeptical, cultural perspective, which stridently questions the worth of individual authorship. Since we are all postmodernists, if only for strictly chronological reasons, then this, too, must be our perspective. Provocation hopefully leads to critical thinking, and vice versa: recontextualization in short. No thought; why bother? No matter; never mind.

But first we need briefly to establish the overwhelming importance of our subject, the awesome "fact" of any number of extraterrestrials lurking among us, with their portraiture being a necessary offshoot of their increasingly close encounters with our merely mundane selves. First, we need to quote a reputable authority calling our attention to the gravity of the problem, one of world-historical significance. Our designated, heavily credentialed expert is John E. Mack, M.D., professor of psychiatry at the Harvard Medical School. As he has stated, in print and for the record:

> The idea that men, women, and children can be taken against their wills from their homes, cars, and schoolyards by strange humanoid beings, lifted onto spacecraft, and subjected to intrusive and threatening procedures is so terrifying, and yet so shattering to our notions of what is possible in our universe, that the actuality of the phenomenon has been largely rejected out of hand or bizarrely distorted in most media accounts. This is altogether understandable, given the disturbing nature of UFO abductions and our prevailing notions of reality. The fact remains, however, that for thirty years, and possibly longer, thousands of individuals who appear to be sincere and of sound mind and who are seeking no personal benefit from their stories have been providing, to those who will listen, consistent reports of precisely such events. *Population surveys suggest that hundreds of thousands and possibly more than a million persons in the United States alone may be abductees* or

"experiencers," as they are sometimes called. The abduction phenomenon is, therefore, of great clinical importance if for no other reason than the fact that abductees are often deeply traumatized by their experiences. At the same time *the subject is of obvious scientific interest*, however much it may challenge our notions of reality and truth.[3]

As you see, "the fact remains" that this is a really, *really important* phenomenon: *the subject is of obvious scientific interest*! For this alarming insight, you need not just take *my* word for it—Dr. Mack is the guy with the awe-inspiring credentials and institutional affiliation; he has even profitably published a book on those spine-tingling close encounters with "aliens" (*que no son los trabajadores mejicanos indocumentados*), the kind that abduct people, just folks, like you and me.[4] Another heavily credentialed expert is Mack's colleague, M.I.T. physicist David E. Pritchard (with a Ph.D. from Harvard); his conclusion, outdoing even Mack's, has it "that as many as one percent of the overall population—two and a quarter million citizens of the United States—might possibly be abductees," and Dr. Pritchard is somewhat conservative since others would even boost the figures to *3.7 million potential American abductees*![5] Look out: a Holocaust is coming! Fear and loathing has left Las Vegas, and now occupies the entire Republic: You have been warned!

Budd Hopkins, a celebrated UFOlogist (alas, no Ph.D.) who has profitably published several paperbacks ("Soon to be made into a major movie!") documenting the gruesome experiences recounted by his huge harvest of abductees, provides statistics even more expansive and terrifying: "3.7 million Americans might qualify as probable abductees [and] *at a minimum*, 560,000 Americans might be abductees."[6] Good Lord! Given the alarming conclusions reached by such prestigious and well-situated (and well-published) professionals, most likely *you* may be one of them, too. Given their statistics, if you have never been contacted, interviewed, briefed, threatened, kidnapped, prodded, or fondled by the little gray folk, then it must be your fault and not theirs; you probably suffer from alien b.o. (or worse). The American moguls of UFOlogy appear quite effective in terrorizing the general population (and making them change their underwear more frequently). This is serious: Have you already forgotten about the self-inflicted holocaust performed by the Heaven's Gate UFO cult early in 1997?

There is, on the other hand, another way of actually justifying these awesome figures. In 1990, yet another lurid account of alien abduction was published. Raymond Fowler's *The Watchers* details the ongoing extraterrestrial visitations of one Betty Andreasson (whose earlier adventures with ETs are discussed in chapter 5). In order to fortify his case, Fowler briefly considers alternative explanations, quickly noting in passing that merely "4 percent of the American population have been described as *fantasy-prone personalities*."[7] Although this is an argument we shall later (in chapter 11) give much greater exposure than did Fowler, we may now mention the fact that if the combined North American (United States and Canada) population comprises approximately 330 million people, then 4 percent of that figure would yield a thronging 13 million "fantasy-prone personalities." Viewed in this manner, we are necessarily surprised that the UFO experts will *only* allow that there may be "3.7 million potential American abductees." According to our figures, instead there should really be 13.2 million potential "experiencers." Again, you have been warned!

Obviously, yet another well-intentioned book dealing with menacing extraterrestrials endlessly alighting among us is called for. In providing one, I am (perhaps ironically) responding to John Mack's expressed reason for publishing *his*: "It is my hope that, if nothing else, this book will encourage at least some of the skeptics who have criticized my methods and hypotheses to immerse themselves in the primary data of this field, namely the experiences of those who have undergone the abduction encounters."[8] Okay, Dr. Mack, you have gotten what you hoped for, and explain why that "primary data" needs to be quoted here *in extenso*.

IDENTIFYING AN AUDIENCE CULTURE FOR ETs

What follows here is a somewhat novel art-historical exercise. Here modernism is often discussed as a *social history* of "audience culture," the kind that wants to see these otherworldly creatures pictured, over and over again. Obviously, the extraterrestrials only persist as recognizable visual phenomena due to zealous attention paid to them by their audience culture. No audience culture: no attention, not even any recognition. The term "audience culture" and some of its applications were initially suggested to me by Norman Klein.[9] As eventually embraced by art historians, the application is now officially called *Rezeptionsgechichte*, "reception theory."[10] Simply stated, it asks, "Who actually enjoyed it, how so, and why?" In short, who *encouraged* it? In the specific case of Dr. Mack's awesome postmodernist revelations, we do have a specific answer—and that may be taken to be representative in a generic way of most of our other published ET/UFO research materials. In short, in

1993 John Mack received a *quarter-of-a-million-dollar* ($250,000) advance on royalties from his publisher, Scribner's, for his soon-to-be-best-selling *Abduction: Human Encounters with Aliens*.[11] Ergo, what accounts for or "encourages" this particular phenomenon—the mass celebration of "alien abductions"—is, in part, *profitability*. As the historical records show, there *is* money to be made here: that is, if the author emphatically states that his account is "true," and Mack's book was, of course, labeled "nonfiction" by its amply remunerated publisher. To the contrary, the royalty advance given to the author of *this* book—me, who deals with "alien abductions" as mostly "fiction"—was zip, null, zero, goose egg, nothing, *nada*. And those are the actual dollar figures attached to (a) terrorism and (b) scholarship.

To get a handle on this interpretive approach, *Rezeptionsgechichte*, the kind now focusing on a consumerist mass audience, to which certain manufacturers now eagerly pander, let us briefly imagine that, rather than the corpus of extraterrestrial portraiture, our focus was instead directed at the audience culture that enshrined the art and thought of Norman Rockwell (1894–1978). His art was, and is, certainly accessible to the masses; so is extraterrestrial portraiture. There is no way you would mistake either for avant-garde art: Rockwell's artworks always look "real," and its content is always immediately legible and literally populist, just as you would expect of an artist who rose to widespread popular acclaim in the 1930s. In fact, relentlessly celebrating American notions of democracy and family values, Rockwell's highly finished, often sentimental and folklorish art formally looks very much like the contemporary art of the Third Reich, but it is much more witty and self-deprecating. He, too, was a kind of *völkisch Künstler*, "an artist of and for the people," and the audience culture for this popular, and populist, artist seems not very different from the kind that presently celebrates the much more rudimentary, but obviously emotionally effective, graphic materials depicting extraterrestrials. Art appreciation, particularly for the more intellectually challenging kinds of vanguard art, seems particularly a matter of education and its latent complement: social *class*, itself typically based on either inherited wealth or innate poverty.

Viewed from the standard avant-garde aerie, say a loft in SoHo, an affluent Ivy League supporter of the austere virtues attributed to rigorously vanguard art expression would guess (since the issue has yet to be adequately researched) that the audience culture for Rockwell (also Roswell) necessarily consists of people very different from him or her. So viewed (probably pejoratively) by the self-styled "intellectuals," Rockwell's fans seem mostly to include white folks, the kind who mainly live in trailer parks, who drink mass-produced beer and copiously consume discounted cigarettes, who maybe have only a high school diploma, and who support themselves in repetitive blue-collar occupations and eagerly peruse the *National Enquirer* ("for inquiring minds"). In sum, rather than patronizing the ballet or performance art, it may be assumed that these simple folks would much rather view talk shows and football games on TV. Most likely, this is also the audience culture that so eagerly consumes TV shows melodramatically portraying "unexplained phenomena," the sort often accounted for in completely different ways—that is, as readily explainable—by scientists and psychologists: in print, and not on TV. Maybe not. We confess ignorance: Norman Rockwell is not discussed by either academic art historians or mainstream art critics. Neither are the extraterrestrials.

In our case, however, the targeted audience culture is the one that created extraterrestrials, and we recognize that there are other audiences with different physiognomies and psychic needs, like the thronging one for Rockwell or, conversely, avant-garde art (which does, surprisingly, have its own self-designated audience culture). Without *that* audience—and especially without the mass media which had, in turn, shaped it and its distinctive taste—most likely we never would have even heard of the extraterrestrials. Before postmodernism, ever more ubiquitous since around 1975 and corresponding to an era of multinational capitalism, there was what I call "orthodox modernism," historically paralleling the era of European hegemony and colonialism. According to Klein, back then, in the orthodox-colonialist period, "The distinctions between high and low culture were laid out as firmly as lines on the spectrum: art that is not self-critical belongs to the culture industry; art that claims to be self-critical is generically fine art, though it may not be free of the coloration of mass culture." Since then, in postmodernism, there is acknowledged a change in values, mainly "due to the shift in information systems—how culture is delivered."[12] Now, in a multinational capitalist era, we wish to know who our cultural providers are, and what's in it for them to deliver to us "this" over "that." In this case, we ask the culture industry: Why UFOs and ETs?

The postmodern cultural audience experience is largely one of pre-sold "pseudoevents" (to be discussed at length in chapter 3). Its operations are, obviously, most easily seen in the "blockbuster" movie phenomenon (discussed in chapters 5, 9, 13, 14), likewise at the slightly more elitist "blockbuster" museum exhibition (from King Tut to Vincent van Gogh), where a mass audience *objet d'art* only becomes viable because of its *marketing* campaign. It was, in fact, in the early cinema that a leveling of the distinctions between high and low culture occurred for the first time in post-Renaissance Europe, that historical-geographical entity that also eventually brought us, after 1492, Euro-American culture. That second, derivative entity—Euro-American culture—is perhaps now better labeled "pop culture," and ever more that is what passes for *Kultur* throughout the postmodernist global village. In the postmodernist age of instant infotainment, the "buzz" about the cultural artifact, however so designated—vanguard art works included, along with the extraterrestrials—is what makes it "happen." No buzz, no audience; the two are inseparable. An example: a book dealing with urban paranoia was recently lauded on a popular daytime talk show (e.g., *Oprah*), and the publishers immediately ordered a new press run of a quarter-*million* copies.

It seems as though we are really not choosing, that the selection made available has been decided for us by marketers and scarcely disinterested promoters: movie moguls, television producers, and paperback publishers at one extreme, and academic theorists, art critics, and art historians at the other. We bear witness to one or the other, televised football games or live performance art, evidently according to our stereotyped market identification, Joe Sixpack or Ivory Tower vanguard. In the postmodern postcapitalist international marketplace, everything—culture included—is reduced to its logical *reductio ad absurdam*, demographics. Lowbrow or highbrow, whether consumer of mainstream mass-produced diversions or hard-core connoisseur of vanguardist singularity and high moral purpose, besides desperately seeking status signifiers, we are collectively entertaining ourselves to mass self-distraction.[13] A point of quantitative fact: entertainment is probably the biggest export item now produced by the United States of America; earlier, in 1992, film and television was already worth *$3.7 billion* to Europe alone, being second (then) only to the aerospace industry, whose "Star Wars" schemes were also eagerly exported by USA Inc.[14]

My guess: the political and moral collapse of the USSR owed far more to Hollywood than to the Pentagon. But not a guess is the fact, as later shown here, that American films and television have now become the major vehicles for propagating in a postmodernist, transglobal "visual culture" the popular imagery of lurking ETs and their high-tech UFO vehicles. The "world-as-a-text" ideal celebrated by Renaissance humanists has now been replaced by the "world-as-a-picture" championed by the postmodernist theoreticians, producing what Guy Debord labeled back in 1967 the "Society of the Spectacle."[15] In this spectacular society the image matters more than the object, in fact, much more so than mere objective truth. Now, capital has commodified all aspects of everyday life. Presently, in a postmodernist (or post-text) age, "visual-izing" has now become all but compulsory, and the voyeuristic results are as much consumer-driven as technology-driven. Consumption of visual images is, for the most part, a collective experience, as it is in a cinema, and movies are also taken to be a more "democratic" medium than is the written text, an elitist artifact now becoming ever more obso-lescent. For its providers, capitalist speculators, their needy task is enti-tled "capturing eyeballs" (but rarely minds). And, as nearly all observers recognize, that distinctively postmodernist (also postliterate) consumer is a *passive* one: we watch television, do not listen to it, and think even less about it. Accordingly, and as is also widely acknowledged, television has mostly "dumbed down" Western society. As I would additionally sug-gest, a major symptom of that encroaching ignorance, so warranting its book-length autopsy, is the fact of an endless postmodernist picturing of extraterrestrials within our *société du spectacle*.

As a self-critical postmodernist, Klein states that now "we must imagine a mass-produced modernism that is also without clearly defined self-critical features [and] the resistance to self-criticism can be summed up in the phrases: 'It's only entertainment,' or, 'I just enjoyed it, that's all.'" Now we recognize that "a mass-produced modernism exists parallel to the fine arts, owing nothing substantial to 'genuine culture.'" Now we recognize that "mass culture has an even broader role; it is the industri-alization of entertainment that has in turn become the industrialization of information, in the service of international business interests." In this case, the crucial factor is what I call here the infotainment industry. Like Klein, now we recognize that "we live in a world that is over stimulated, and desensitized at the same time—a world dominated by the narratives and politics of an audience-centered economy, particularly in the U.S."[16] Stuck in among other kinds of postmodern industrialized information there is even the history of art, especially the stimulating sort made in response to the appalling real-life events of our catastrophic century. As we have often been told, another appalling real-life event of our age is frequent visitations by the extraterrestrials.

What follows is a contextual study that reads at times like an exer-cise in cultural anthropology. The various contexts, describing ever-diminishing parameters around the extraterrestrials, function like the diagrams found in any number of old, leather-bound folio volumes belonging to the esoteric tradition. According to this truly ancient scheme, the extraterrestrials represent the *microcosm* ("little world"). What surrounds the extraterrestrials are a series of corresponding, ever-larger, *macrocosms*, those "bigger worlds" functioning like the intricately carved, husklike motifs of Chinese ivory puzzles. Once laboriously unraveled, some interesting configurations often emerge. We shall especially be looking for some hidden (*occulta*) correspondences: between art and life, between myth and reality, between artifact and spirit.

Emanuel Swedenborg described these linkages long ago, stating the truth of them so forcefully that innumerable future adherents would believe in occult correspondences similar to those existing between *Heaven and Hell* (1758), the title of his most influential treatise. For the True Believers, such correspondences provide an ongoing confirmation of ancient wisdom. This Swedish seer recognized how, unlike contemporary modern materialists, who live in what he called a "world that primarily focuses on worldly things only," "the ancient people behaved differently. As far as they were concerned, a knowledge of correspondences was the finest of all knowledges. . . . The nature of correspondence [is that] the whole natural world corresponds to the spiritual world." In short, "Man is both a heaven and an earth in smallest form; on the model of the greatest, he has a spiritual world and a natural world within him." Swedenborg's conclusions need italics: "*Anything that occurs in his natural world* (his body, its senses, and its actions), *occurs from his spiritual world* (his mind, its discernment, and its intention) and is called a correspondent. . . . All this has to do with *the correspondence* of the inner or spiritual realm of man [i.e., the microcosm] with his outer or natural realm [or macrocosm]."[17] That is an excellent point: then as now, it is mostly in your mind. Likewise, academic postmodernist theory states that the world itself is nothing but culturally engineered "signs" and "simulacra."

For our purposes, the principal macrocosm of the extraterrestrials' world is, of course, the often hermetically sealed inner world of psychic perception and projection, humanity itself, particularly the kind desperately seeking spiritual succor. This is, therefore, "the whole natural world [that] corresponds to the spiritual world" of the extraterrestrials. As we shall see in greater detail, extraterrestrials are just one small component of a convoluted cultural macrostructure, postmodernism in short. Nevertheless, the extraterrestrials are a particular component that so perfectly fits into the larger cultural matrix that, had they not been born—for instance, in July 1947 at Roswell, New Mexico—then they would have needed to be "invented." After all, just as Swedenborg explained long ago, it is all a product of our collective imagination: "this mind, its discernment, and its intention." In order to demonstrate a perhaps novel argument, the world of popular culture and folk beliefs will at times be viewed almost as an anthropologist might scrutinize the curious clan rites of some obscure tribe situated in a peculiar outback, one still largely unknown to the rest of the ordinary workaday world. One purpose of the cultural autopsies that follow is to demystify some familiar dogmas routinely taught by the mass media, with which you, too, are all too familiar. Viewed from our expansive cultural perspective, the *Lebenslauf* (life and works) of the extraterrestrials serve as a handy sort of map to guide us through some rather tangled psychic forests belonging to bourgeois and lowbrow, postmodernist cultural game preserves.

One reason why ETs are not often treated by "serious" scholars is their lowly place of origin and their designated habitat; rather than belonging to high culture (embracing the Good, the True, and the Beautiful), they are the inhabitants of American pop culture.[18] That populist *sub*-cultural phenomenon is strictly modernist. The single physical fact attesting to a strictly modernist invention of pop culture is easily identified: the invention of *leisure*. Previously, leisure was an option only available to the aristocracy. Nonaristocrats had none of that; a century and a half ago, the average workweek in the United States was seventy-five hours. Obviously, then, people did not have the leisure time, to say nothing of the means (i.e., money), to become absorbed in the kind of emotional diversions documented in these pages. Modern *Homo ludens*—leisure man, who is fervently devoted to pop culture—only emerges in force around 1890, when the frontier was declared closed in America and the country was settled from coast to coast. A new mood emerged; discarding the primitive settler virtues holding that "idleness debases," there were new affirmations of "the right to be lazy" and the proclamation of a "gospel of relaxation."

This ethical transformation set the stage for a century and more of trends, crazes, manias, and unneeded luxuries; "fads" in short. In the beginning, there were music halls, café concerts, nickelodeons, wax museums, beer halls, and dressing up like celebrities ("Gibson Girl" or "Gibson Man"). Those became all the rage in the 1890s, and it would take many monographs to detail all the fads, now mostly forgotten, subsequently produced by a century and more of pop culture. Only two early manifestations need be cited here, as they are particularly relevant to the evolution of our subject. The first "best-seller list" was published in 1895; a "best-seller" is the kind of book that launches nationwide spin-off clones and crazes. By 1905, entertainment was becoming big business in the cities; the newest fad in 1905 was the nickelodeon, where there were exhibited what we now call "movies." As is implicitly argued here, UFOs and ETs, and the best-selling books and blockbuster movies chronicling their endless close encounters, constitute yet another modernist fad spawned by pop culture.

Pop culture has been labeled a throwaway culture, here today and gone tomorrow. Something is popular when it is deliberately created to respond to the values of the teeming majority, the *populus*, and what is implicitly understood by that majority is whatever it is that does not require special knowledge or experience on their part. Pop culture, since it is the modernist equivalent of "folk culture," never strives for the "shock of the new"; convention and underlying continuity are its guiding principles. Unlike elite high culture, its creators are seldom known to their audiences. These mostly unsung creators try to satisfy as many people as possible; equally important, they mean to offend as few as possible. So doing, they garner the maximum profits from their eager audiences. Pop culture is nearly exclusively responsive to the marketplace; thus it will only produce that which will sell well. Most of all, the thronging audience for pop culture seeks to be entertained. Thrills and terror sell as well as does buffoonish comedy. ETs provide thrills and terror for millions of postmodernists.

Another macrostructure looming large in this investigation is the esoteric tradition, of which Swedenborg was an early and influential spokesman—and of which extraterrestrials are an essential, but rarely so acknowledged, component. Whereas true believers would call such beliefs "spiritual science," others might just call it "occultism" (from the Latin *occulere*, to cover over, hide, conceal). Simply put, for Colin Wilson (among innumerable subscribers), "The fundamental tenet of 'occultism' is that the mind possesses *hidden powers* that can influence the external world."[19] Alas, whatever its occasional nomenclature, now mostly New Age, such plebeian esoterica occupies a bizarre outback largely ignored by accredited scholars in general and by art historians in particular, maybe because it remains defiantly hidden (*occulta*) to them because of their myopic elitist interests. (At times, academic specialization strikes one as another way of expressing *tribalism*, just as urban youth packs express themselves in drive-by shootings.) Nevertheless, *occultism*, although it rarely calls itself such, does loom very large in our collective consciousness. As we shall see in due course, it was this pervasive esoteric mass mentality that had, in effect, created the conditions for the surprisingly widespread acceptance of the curious activities so emotionally described by subscribers to the extraterrestrials and their various earthly apparitions.

The so-called UFO experience is a warped kind of democratic expression; the principle of equal opportunity to formerly privileged "visions" also applies to contemporary art, and in a way is historically unprecedented. It is notorious, for instance, that the highly praised German avant-garde artist Joseph Beuys (1921–1986) repeatedly asserted that "everyone is an artist." Coincidentally, published research indicates that he, too, subscribed to occultist principles, namely the kind generated by the Anthroposophical cult.[20] Beuys's magnanimous claim, although now shared by many other vanguard artists, goes completely against the grain of old-style fine art assumptions: only those few favored with innate talent, "genius" if you will, were formerly granted the prestigious title of "artist" (*Künstler*), and then only after undergoing years of rigorous professional training. Similarly, with its new title, *New Age*, formerly elitist occultism has likewise become democratic, even populist, and this is quite to the contrary of old-style esotericism, which for centuries had defiantly kept its spiritual secrets literally "occult" from the ignorant masses. The New Age, promising instant enlightenment to all comers, has its own democratic and national point of invention: it was brought to the world by the same culture that gave us "fast food" (*Eilspeise*).[21] Just as, for instance, Beuys had hoped to make "*Jedermann ein Künstler*," so, too, the hucksters of New Age enlightenment wish to market their spiritual gifts to all applicants. As summed up by Henry Gordon:

> The idea now being sold is that inside *every* human being there is a wonderful and talented personality. And this personality will grow and flourish if the individual just looks inward and ignores any consideration for others. Just do whatever you feel like doing. This will help you expand your conscious and will make you more "self-aware"—whatever that means. . . . This movement has spread out to encompass a huge variety of subjects, and to draw in a much wider audience than would be interested only in the occult. The New Age has now become a generic term for those interested in metaphysics, spiritualism, alternative medicine, and a hodgepodge of faddish ideas.[22]

In 1987 there appeared a best-selling book describing a writer's close encounter with outer-space aliens, Whitley Strieber's *Communion* (examined in chapter 5); also appearing the same year, with similar content, was longtime UFOlogist Budd Hopkins's *Intruders: The Incredible Visitations at Copley Woods*. In short, the ETs had arrived in force as an important commercial phenomenon. Recognition of the all-pervasive appeal of occultism in the larger sense around the time of extraterrestrials' greatest popularity occurs in *Time*, whose December 7, 1987, cover story is, quite appropriately, "The New Age." The full-color cover photo shows a well-known media figure, who, face wreathed in a knowing Cheshire cat smile, offers up to the needy public a handful of sparkling beads and refulgent rock crystals. The caption makes the vital connection between culturally site-specific *imago* and *motto*: "OM . . . The New Age, Starring Shirley MacLaine, Faith Healers, Channelers, Space Travelers, and Crystals Galore."

The article within ("New Age Harmonies") proves to be a well-written and thought-provoking piece of pop anthropology authored by Otto Friedrich. The all-pervasive New Age is rightly acknowledged to be, besides highly popular (and thus commercially successful), "a combination of spirituality and superstition, fad and farce, about which the only thing certain is that it is *not* new." The case of Ms. MacLaine as occult authoress demonstrates the economic viability of heightened consciousness within high-tech materialist capitalism; her five books of "self-exploration" have sold at last count (back in 1987) eight *million* copies. As Friedrich points out, "New Age fantasies often intersect with mainstream materialism, the very thing that many New Age believers profess to scorn." Big business sponsors meditational seminars; according to one corporate spokesman, "The principle here is to look at the mind, body, heart, and spirit."[23] Nevertheless, as the student of historical occultism well knows, this has essentially been "the principle" since time immemorial.

Although the term "New Age" seems to have been circulating since the age of the beatniks, to the average American it remained obscure until the Reagan era, also appropriately known as the age of "Star Wars." Whatever its chronology, and perhaps it initially emerged in the Renaissance (as *tempus novus*), New Age adherents typically described their obscure pursuits as "being into metaphysics"; that sounded good, as though the speaker was something between a scientist and a philosopher, instead of, more likely, being balefully ignorant of both academic disciplines. Whatever its rationales, back in 1987 the *symptoms* of New Age credulity apparently represented an essentially harmless anthology of mass illusions. Besides UFOs and ETs (the latter already made into pop icons by Steven Spielberg, and which are now said commonly to reside in New Mexico), by my reckoning, the outward, indeed omnipresent, "paranormal" New Age manifestations mostly included such diverse buzzwords, artifacts, and obsessions as the following:

> "channeling" (that is, to various occult "powers," for which Ms. MacLaine's ubiquitous rock crystals are often recommended), astrology, telepathy, precognition, telekinesis, ESP (extrasensory perception), psychic auras and "remote viewing" of distant places (all steadfastly invisible to you and me), divining rods, dowsing and water-witching, "other dimensions" (i.e., beyond the merely mundane), good vibes, energy vibrations (of which love is the highest, goodest vibe), faith healing, color and sound therapy, fortune-telling, karma, palmistry, pre-

cognition and déjà vu, numerology, acupuncture, transmigration of souls (à la Swedenborg), self-healing, New Age music ("like, I tapped into a radio station on Mars"), transcendental meditation, "harmonic convergence," bio-feedback, transmigrations of (kindred) souls, out-of-body and/or near-death experiences, Atlantis and the Bermuda Triangle (neither recognized by professional cartographers), Lemuria (ditto), all facets of "Pyramidology," prophecies by Nostradamus and the *I Ching* (particularly as mistranslated into English), tarot decks, neopaganism—replete with postmodernist witches, druids, goddess-worshipers, Vikings and rune-readers, ghosts and poltergeists, "cryptozoology" (i.e., Big Foot and the Loch Ness Monster), solar energizers, angels and/or other ethereal messengers and spiritual guardians (70 percent of Americans believe in angelic beings), Dianetics (aka Scientology), herbal teas, temple bells, colored candles, gem elixirs, holistic massage, rhythmic chanting, and pricey seminars ("Aspects of Zen Practice," "Internal Kung Fu," "Holistic Systemic Thinking," "Jungian Symbolism in Astrology").

Weird beliefs are like pornography—difficult to define, but perfectly obvious when you see them (or buy into them). Whatever you call it, there is money in it for someone. Like the exotic *divertissements* listed above, UFO publications and movies are a commercial product. So are cigarettes. One carries a scary message signed by the surgeon general; the other carries a scary message and labels itself "nonfiction"—but "non" it's not.

Ten years later, the roster of mass media esoterica was about the same, but the psychic slant had gotten worse: pure paranoia. According to one of the more useful mass media surveys (from *Newseek*, July 8, 1996), presently "aliens and UFOs are the most prominent paranormal obsessions." The magazine conducted a poll then: 48 percent of Americans were shown to believe that UFOs are real and 29 percent accepted that we have "made contact with aliens." Another 48 percent thinks there is "a government plot" to cover the whole thing up, that is, UFOs and ETs. Twenty years ago a Gallup poll found that only 30 percent of American college graduates believed that flying saucers visited earth in some form; today, 42 percent of college graduates accept the credulous premise—further proof that the quality of higher education in the United States has surely diminished by (at least) half.[24] However, besides UFOlogy (quickly dismissed by *Newsweek* as "belief in little green men from distant planets"), also big today are such quintessential therapies as shamanic journeying ("soul-traveling through upper and lower worlds to learn 'healing' lessons") and hands-on-healing ("using meditation, crystals or 'subtle energies' to influence the body's health"). A 1996 Gallup poll shows that 96 percent of American adults believe in God, 90 percent in heaven, 79 percent in miracles, and 72 percent in angels. Whether or not, as some anthropologists believe, religion and "alternate religions" expounding belief in God and other kinds of otherworldly (aka extraterrestrial) beings do have a biological basis, unquestionably such "belief-systems are fundamental to the human psyche."[25]

Here is further statistical *proof* that the extraterrestrials are very much upon our collective minds. According to a more recent (April 1998) survey, 70 percent of women and 48 percent of men in America believe in the paranormal, largely meaning anything now refuted by real scientists. More interesting, and more specific, are the results of a recent (May 1998) investigation of the World Wide Web, that cyberspace where the more technologically advanced (and, hence, supposedly more rational) citizens congregate. Under the heading "Science: Alternative: Paranormal Phenomena," the Yahoo! search-engine will find for you a listing of more than 1,000 such sites. This quest yields a complete *catalogue raisonné* of all the New Age *folies du jour*—and the extraterrestrials lead the pack, by a metaphorical mile! Here are the results, arranged in quantitative (not qualitative) rankings: "Extraterrestrial Life" (423); "Astrology" (156); "Witchcraft" (114); "Magick" (87); "Divination" (82); "Mysticism" (71); "Ghosts" (43); "Cryptozoology" (33); "Parapsychology" (23); "Voodoo" (18); "Crop Circles" (16); "End of the Millennium" (16); "Near-Death Experiences" (16); "Astral Projection" (12); "Loch Ness" (11); "Kirlian Photography" (10); "Reincarnation" (8); "Alchemy" (7); "Dowsing" (7); "Spiritism" (7); "Remote Viewing" (7); "Biorhythm" (6); "Healings" (5); "Hollow Earth" (5); "Spontaneous Human Combustion" (5); "Bermuda Triangle" (2); and so on.[26] A local friend of mine, much more adept in cyberspace flight than I am, just ran a search for me (using "Infoseek"); individual Web pages devoted to "extraterrestrials" number 5,160, and the ones lurking under the rubric "UFOs" (also necessarily including mention of their dreadful ET pilots) reach the dizzying figure of 45,530 different sites! To me, these are scary figures.

Carl Sagan has quoted from a 1995 publication from California (where else?) which, by calling itself a primer for what passes for "Critical Thinking for a New Age," so also defines the term "oxymoron." According to this *summa theologia* for New Age enthusiasts,

> There's no such thing as objective truth. We make our own truth.
> There's no such thing as objective reality. We make our own reality.
> There are spiritual, mystical, or inner ways of knowing that are superior

to our ordinary ways of knowing. If an experience seems real [to you], it is real. If an idea feels right to you, it is right. We are incapable of acquiring knowledge of the true nature of reality. Science itself is irrational or mystical. It's just another faith or belief system or myth, with no more justification than any other. It doesn't matter whether beliefs are true or not, as long as they're meaningful to you.[27]

There you have it: something like an underground Magna Carta for the much remarked "dumbing down" of America, and Europe, too.

Likewise, here you see the usually hidden physiognomy of postmodernist culture. The academic theorists tell us that all reality is socially constructed, that it only represents a mutually agreed upon illusion.[28] Rather than "reality," theory becomes the illusive cultural leveler. Highbrow postmodernism or lowbrow New Age: "We make our own reality," likewise ridiculing yours all the while. Besides defensive but eager credulity and a seemingly insatiable lust for distraction, the single common denominator among all these wildly diverse contemporary pursuits, gauche encounters as it were, is money: some people are making a pile from this global postmodernist audience culture. But this kind of willful, even joyous, irrationality is nothing new; among various not-so-recent authors to be quoted here, another had told once adoring crowds: "A new era of the magical explanation to the world is rising, an explanation based on will rather than knowledge. There is no truth, in either the moral or the scientific sense."[29] His name was Adolf Hitler (see fig. 7). Poor chap; the media has since treated this celebrity rather unfairly. As diehard American skinhead advocates would now hasten to remind us, he loved dogs (*German* shepherds especially), delighted in the company of drooling infants, was sensible in his diet (only vegetables, thank you), eschewed tobacco (not in my presence!), had an exemplary sex life (celibacy, thank you), profoundly respected the British Empire, and, perhaps most commendable—no couch potato he!—Hitler never watched television. All rather New Age, wouldn't you say?

Brief mention should be made at the outset of the physical evidence attesting to extraterrestrials' posthumous fame—and their literal evaluation. In short, they are presently *famous*. Their enduring worth, their very *celebrity*, justifies our plodding study of them and their great operations among the earthlings. In our world, particularly in America, the only real indicator of the true worth of anything, or anybody, is the monetary value actually attached to that person or thing. In the postmodern world, "celebrity" has a market value: the more celebrated a person or thing, the greater its/his/her evaluation. Other than dollars (pounds-sterling, yen, francs, deutschmarks, Euros, and so on), all the rest is mere prattle. Another random example: anyone interested in reading a book with this kind of scholarly intention tacitly agrees that poets must be valued for their sensitivity and intellectual insights. Nonetheless, inarticulate—likely antisocial, too—basketball players actually get the celebrity, and all the cash that automatically accompanies their mass-media celebrations (and scholars don't). Also instantly made celebrities are "alien abductees"; surely you, too, have seen them on television talk shows and documentaries dealing with the UFO experience.

Some relative figures: the average NBA player pulls in $2.4 *million* per annum. On the other hand, a university instructor with a Ph.D. in the humanities and/or fine arts (typically on part-time status) is lucky to cobble up $25,000 a year. One professional endeavor is literally valued *one hundred times* better than the other. So why the gross disparity? Simple: one trade is far more *entertaining* than the other, and is peopled with acknowledged *celebrities*.

Among other points discussed here, brief mention should be made of the fact that "fine art" (*les beaux-arts*) is often worshipped today by the educated elite, particularly in such consecrated sanctuaries as galleries and museums. Nonetheless, the producers of those beaux-arts, the artists, are grossly underpaid. Since I myself have produced bunches of it, meaning art of the obviously avant-garde sort, as an engaged art-producer (*artifex*) even I find that kind of devout audience culture response really weird. But I wouldn't be so aghast in the case of, for example, mass production of plaster statuettes of the Madonna and Child (neither a pop singer). As I can affirm, but only in my *artifex* capacity, making art is *fun*. Likewise, playing golf is fun, or at least so I've been told. The unasked question is: Why are these activities so *revered*, particularly by those people who do *not perform* as either artists or golfers? The answer is provided by John Walker, a British author of a useful book titled *Art in the Age of Mass Media* (1994):

> Even *the concept of "art" itself*—the concept which enables us to distinguish works of art from non-art objects—*can be regarded as a social institution*. A satisfactory history of European art, therefore, ought to include a history of the [imposed] concept "art" as well as a history of artists, works and patrons. . . . The "fine arts" gained their specific character by *contrast with* mechanical, applied or *useful*, *arts* and crafts. . . . Appreciation of the fine arts is primarily associated with the upper classes, and appreciation of the mass media with the lower classes. Of course, a person's opportunity to enjoy a variety of types and levels of culture increases dramatically with the possession of wealth

and leisure. . . . Even marketing and advertising agencies recognize that the public can be sub-divided, according to such factors as income, employment, psychology, tastes and lifestyle.[30]

In short, reverence for, or ignorance of, "art" is all a matter of one's respective audience culture, mass or merely elitist, each in any case being determined mostly by class. Today, exhibitions of "real" art of different sorts have become an unacknowledged component of the info-tainment industry: today, museum attendance actually exceeds that recorded for live football contests. Even contemporary art, including the unquestionably popular sort depicting the outer-space folk, proves acceptable to the masses—but the self-designated elitist masses must draw the line at ET portraiture. Even so, vanguard contemporary art—as opposed to the first modernist artworks created nearly a century ago by then usually excoriated vanguard pioneers—now has even become incorporated within a system of entertainment, business sponsorship, publicity, and tourism. An example: the prestigious "Documenta" exhibitions in Kassel, which attract tens of thousands of middle-class tourists to this German town.

In 1992, with specific reference to the Documenta events, Belgian artist Jan Vercruysse published a critical reaction to the postmodernist hype typically surrounding these vanguard affairs. "Our culture," he then observed, "is sliding into a culture of spectacle. Media and spectacle-oriented performance and events with reference to art create a *negative* energy, turning art into an 'art event,' a spectacle to be consumed for and by everyone. The attention for art roused by the spectacle is bad since it is not founded on content, but on the effect of its media existence. I contest the idea that all these media operation 'serve' art, resulting in an increase of real interest for art from more and more people."[31] Nonetheless, as exclusively known to us in artistically rudimentary form, the plentiful depictions of extraterrestrials constitute another ubiquitous cultural "spectacle," but this is one wholly founded upon its understood content, and this has unquestionably resulted in a real hunger for extraterrestrial portraiture "from more and more people."

All in all, whether it is finally judged by history to have been either a dwarf star or a giant nova in the modern cultural constellation, an in-depth discussion of the odd case of extraterrestrial portraiture and, especially, its distinctive audience culture casts useful astral light upon some curious workings of the larger world in which we all live. Additionally, these revelations will particularly illuminate still dimly perceived operations in the world of the popular culture, a postmodernist macrocosm which delights in, and even thrives upon, bizarre esoterica. And, for these purposes, "esoterica" can pertain to ideas, even the lowly graphic materials illustrating such commonly shared beliefs. In the mostly unmentionable case of the extraterrestrials, it actually became both at once. Since their microworld remains mostly tenaciously hidden to the average inhabitant of the academic ivory tower, even also to most of their awed celebrants, what emerges here should prove illuminating to readers. If that actually proves to be the case, art history finally becomes useful, rather than merely intellectually decorative: useful like a trip to your friendly family physician for a cultural mammogram.

PORTRAITURE AND TELEVISION:
HOW WE PICTURE EARTHLINGS AND EXTRATERRESTRIALS

As is it now practiced, perhaps one of the most interesting aspects of the scholarly discipline called "art history" is the topics it still will not deign worthy of serious scrutiny. As presently overlooked by "serious" scholarship, a significant case in point is what we may call "extraterrestrial (ET) portraiture." Therefore, rather than investigating a prestigious ("upper-class") example of medieval or Renaissance portraiture in painting or sculpture, which is the sort of thing I usually do, I have instead perversely decided to investigate the historical contexts informing that commonly disparaged iconographic staple of late- to post-modernist mass culture, the myriad depictions of "extraterrestrials" (ETs), or outer-space and/or otherworldly "aliens" (see fig. 1). "Extraterrestrial" literally means (of course) "not of this world," that is, of the planet earth. As will be shown here, such otherworldly beings, albeit as known by different nomenclature, prove to comprise a standard iconographic fixture in the history of art. Our immediate subject is "portraiture," *apocryphal* in this case, which, as was mentioned earlier, means hidden or spurious, particularly referring to writings or statements of doubtful authorship or authority.

Richard Brilliant additionally provides us with a concise definition of the standard artistic genre putting them into our mass consciousness: "Simply put, *portraits* are art works, intentionally made of living or once living people by artists, in a variety of media, and for an audience, [and they are made] by means of the established or invented schema whose recognizable content shapes the identity of the subject and conveys it to the beholder." The Latin root of "portraiture" is *protrahere*, to draw forth, sometimes even *ex nihilo*, out of thin air as it were. Brilliant's next observation is particularly germane to this argument: if certain portraits are "replicated in vast number (e.g., on postage stamps) . . . significant consequences in reception may occur."[32]

Due to such mass replication, currently we *all* know—you, too—that the "classic" alien, an ET, is small in stature, hairless, usually pale gray in color, has a proportionately oversized, triangular-shaped and somewhat bulbous head, and large, dark, and reflective, wrap-around eyes. In short, his (its) distinctive physiognomy makes him (it) look something like a cat-faced *homunculus* (see fig. 1).[33] That image presently constitutes what Brilliant would concisely call "the established or invented schema" of ET portraiture and, as he adds, in this specific case we all should know how "they all have two eyes—slanted of course, no nose, two ears, a pointed chin, no hair, spindly limbs, etc."[34] The physiological rationale, largely unspoken, explaining this diminutive figure suggests that the ET is the "evolved" human of the future—all brains (and much "spirit") and scarcely any body, since technology will (supposedly) release us from physical labor and the kind of usable carcass that goes with it.

Now we may make brief reference to some scientific research proving that we are *all* infected with this exotic iconography, a point which UFOlogists stoutly deny. Back in 1987, Dr. Charles L. Gruder (chair of the psychology department, University of Illinois–Chicago) reported the results of an interesting experiment. He asked a number of students "to draw a UFO and draw an [ET] alien." The pictorial results looked just like the illustrations in currently best-selling books dealing with the aliens intruding in our midst, most notably Budd Hopkins's *Intruders* (1987). According to Gruder, "It isn't surprising, because how do people know what a UFO should look like?" The UFO drawn by the students in fact recreated the glowing, saucer-shaped craft depicted in Steven Spielberg's movie *Close Encounters of the Third Kind* (1977), and who missed seeing that cinematic feast? More to the immediate point, Gruder noted that Hopkins "mentioned a particular shape of a head [designating an ET], or the fact that the mouth was a line, and I found that most of those [student drawings] were humanoids. Of the 23 drawings, 18 were human-like; of these, one-third had big heads, one-third had a line for a mouth."[35] As an art historian, my task will be to specify the actual historical sources of this distinctive extraterrestrial iconography which, in fact, first appeared two decades before the publication of Hopkins's best-seller.

Highbrow or lowbrow, whether depicting mere mortals or the extra-terrestrials, *portraiture* as such has much inherent power over the mundane mind. This is a psychological factor long since recognized, both by the consumers of portraiture and its makers. A particularly celebrated member of the second group was Leonardo da Vinci (1452–1519; see fig. 35); as he remarked in his writings (only published long after his death),

> And if the poet claims that he can inflame men to love . . . the painter has the power to do the same, and indeed more so, for he places before the lover's eyes the very image of the beloved object, [and the lover] often engages with it [the portrait], embracing it, and talking with it; which he would not do were the same beauties placed before him by the writer, and so much the more [does painting] conquer the minds of men, to love and fall in love with a painting [even] when it does not portray any living woman [or divinity]. And once it happened to me that I made a painting which represented a female saint, which was bought by someone who loved it, and he wanted me to remove the symbols of that saint, so that he could kiss it without impropriety. But in the end his conscience overcame his sighs and his passion, and he had to remove it from his house.[36]

More important for what follows—a serious study of postmodernist extraterrestrial portraiture—is the historical evidence demonstrating that portraiture is itself often employed as an essential stimulus for a forthcoming realistic perception of supernatural beings. Long before they were so commonly labeled "ETs," supernatural beings were said to visit with earthlings; these proto-ETs customarily received the names belonging to those divinities—superterrestrial beings par excellence—which were held in especially high regard by the perceiver's culture. The exact terminology given to identify the visionary experience—for instance, "I saw X" versus "I saw Z"—is, of course, culture-specific and, like fashion, cultures change in time. As the document which follows indicates, the prior existence of human-made portraiture is often essential to consummation of the visionary experience. Here is how Saint Teresa de Avila (1515–1582) recorded her first vision of Christ, a startling event triggered by, even specifically shaped by, her prior viewing of a contemporary portrait of the Savior:

> It was during mass on the feast of St. Paul, when Jesus Christ [first] deigned to appear before me, complete in his very holy human incarnation, indescribably beautiful and majestic—as he is depicted in paintings of him resurrected. . . . Though imaginary, I never saw this vision with the eyes of my body or any other, only with the eyes of my soul. . . . Had I spent years trying to envisage such beauty, I could never have succeeded; its whiteness alone and brilliance were such that they surpassed anything we on earth could imagine. It is a brilliance that does not

dazzle, but a suave whiteness; a splendor so innate that it induces inde-
scribable and untiring pleasure in the beholder; it is a translucence that
allows the soul to see this beauty so divine; it is a light infinitely different
from those on earth and, next to it, the sun's rays became so dull that I
did not wish ever to open my eyes again. . . . Sometimes I thought that
what I could see was nothing more than a painting, but on many other
occasions it was obviously Jesus Christ himself. Much depended on how
clearly he wanted to reveal himself to me. Sometimes, when the clarity
was not very strong, it did seem to me that I might be looking at a
painting, but a painting quite different from those here on earth, even
the very best. I have seen many excellent ones, and am in a position to
say that they are as different from one another as a living person is different from his own portrait: however lifelike it is, one cannot help but
see it [the portrait of a mere earthling] as something inanimate.[37]

Repeatedly fascinated by human folly (like Erasmus, in *Moriae
encomium*, 1509), I have become an art historian particularly interested
in what may be called the iconography of the fantastic, mostly the kind
associated with what we now call "occultist" movements.[38] You are forewarned that here I will align the extraterrestrial portraiture phenomenon
with the occultist one. I also often understand my job title—"art historian"—to make me a scholar who interprets, even "diagnoses" if you
will, significant cultural symptoms through the images produced by, and
so characterizing, various historical cultures. Moreover, in practice I typically prefer the term "image" over "art," and this is because the latter,
art, has for some time—since the Renaissance—become increasingly
overinflated, grossly emotionalized, choked with class prejudice and
debased by status-seeking and "prestige" (Latin: *praestigium*, an illusion
or delusion). This is an observation, particularly as it relates to modernist imagery, which is shared by others.[39] To the contrary, an express
concern with "images," an emotionally neutral term, allows one to
manipulate *any* sort of graphic material, especially that lowly sort associated with mass culture. As may be argued, the only really significant
iconography is that "artless" kind so deeply embedded in its given culture that it can—as a typology—be easily "read" by the majority of its
viewers. So read, it provokes a generally predictable emotional reaction—like "art" used to do, for instance in the Christian Middle Ages.
But, as many now recognize, we postmodernists no longer have even "a
valid conception of what a work of art is."[40]

Contemporary populist graphic material, especially as it includes ET
portraiture, proves especially useful in identifying cultural symptoms
establishing a distinctively modernist pathology.[41] In either case, high or

low, I treat imagery—iconography, even "art," if you wish—as the means to acquire greater *iconological* understanding of larger cultural transactions.[42] A case in point, even though it is haughtily overlooked in the art historical literature, is that omnipresent modernist portraiture of extraterrestrial entities (see fig. 1). Doggedly pursuing his pictorial *corpus delicti*, this art historian ever more seemed to become a detective working at the Bureau of Missing Persons. While admittedly not necessarily of any great "aesthetic significance," this ubiquitous iconographic corpus does urgently require study, in this instance a detailed historical autopsy, for it has recently demonstrated its own dramatic, even fatal, consequences. Viewed clinically by a figurative forensic surgeon, extraterrestrial portraiture, posited (as it were) upon an *abductio ad absurdum*, potentially becomes of great diagnostic value: it concretely illustrates the actual workings of a much remarked upon postmodernist phenomenon, the "dumbing down" of America and Europe.[43] Granted that larger cultural significance, then the only compelling reason for an art historian *not* to study ET portraiture must be social in nature: class prejudice.

Nonetheless, even if you yourself have never been personally abducted by aliens, you *do* know exactly what they look like, and that is because you have repeatedly, actually, "seen" the wholly codified, bug-eyed, outer-space waifs: "illustrated" anonymously, and endlessly reproduced either on TV or in the tabloid newspapers. Sheer *quantity* defines cultural significance; *quality* is, however, something else, a confounding *Je ne sais quoi* that we shall leave to the elitists. The factor particularly defining the extraterrestrials as representing a particularly characteristic postmodernist phenomenon is *visual celebrity*. In the broadest sense, obviously "portraiture" is the essential weapon of visual celebrity.

Americans eagerly seek celebrity; they like to be in its physical presence, perhaps even hope to become one themselves—however briefly—by appearing on television. Whatever (or whomever) its subject, "celebrity" is wholly wrought by *publication*, and its universal visualization precludes the necessity of a wholly literate audience culture. However, as *pure image* visual celebrity potentially commands the attention of the entire terrestrial population, including the statistical majority of near illiterates. Another definition of a celebrity is strictly commercial: a *celebrity* is someone who can get a seven-figure book deal, without writing a line. According to the party-line of the UFOlogists (which statements you will find in the prologues to all of their paperback publications), alien abductees do *not* actively seek money and publicity. Instead, they are shy and reticent folk; they fear ridicule because of their bizarre, seemingly unbelievable stories. That's what they tell you, but you know better, that is, if you watch a lot of television. If they abhor celebrity, then why is that *you* have seen them on TV? These video celebs include the likes of Betty Hill, Betty Andreasson, Travis Walton, and Whitley Strieber (and their influential stories are related in chapter 5), among many, many other ET-encountering celebrity-seekers.

A complementary case in point about strictly visual celebrity, one known to everybody, concerns the late Princess Di (née Diana Spencer). She, poor thing, was a bulimic and compulsive shopper who consulted astrologers and employed a personal psychic; she is a "New Age" icon who still posthumously shares with ETs, albeit in superior measure, the media-generated, postmodernist trait of universal visual celebrity. Times have changed. In former times, say the Middle Ages, the *only* universal visual celebrity—meaning an anthropoid being whose portraiture was universally identifiable by the earthling masses (*Homines terrestres*)—was Jesus Christ (see fig. 2). He was even called a "spaceman" (*Homo coelestis*) and he was then usually perceived in the cultural context of an "icon" (*eikon*).[44] Not even the reigning monarch then enjoyed such visual celebrity, for only the very rich handled the coin of the realm bearing his embossed portrait. All that changed with Gutenberg's invention and, with the exponential rise of the mass media, historical cultures subsequently became ever more visual in their collective representation.[45] In all cases, ancient or modern, real or apocryphal, the iconic status of visual celebrity requires what Hans Belting calls "general consensus."[46]

Nevertheless, we must admit that, according to academic consensus, the currently commonplace portraiture of extraterrestrials is not "art." So what is it? I will answer by reversing the moron's cliché: I may not know much about what I like, but I do know about art. Leaving aside for the moment sticky matters of aesthetic evaluation, for the purposes of some radical redefinition we will consider extraterrestrial portraiture as the tangible representation of a series of *pseudoevents*. By taking this tack, we leave behind matters narrowly considered as art history and instead venture into the fuzzier territory of undifferentiated social phenomena. In this case, the wider, essentially anthropological, context relating to the extraterrestrials' earthling audience is the contemporary setting of what Deborah Root calls our omnipresent "cannibal culture." For theory-ridden postmodernist academics, the key buzzword is "appropriation," and, says Root, "The world has increasingly come to be imagined as a vast warehouse of images." The cultural ideas, likely wholly misunderstood, that come with these images can likewise be feasted upon, cannibal-like; they are all acquired in the great shopping mall we call the world, its history, its peoples, all likely wholly misunderstood by postmodernist image consumers. And the way that we acquire our (mis)understanding of these diverse phenomena is the mass media. And, of course, we are all manipulated by the mass media to some degree or another. As Root points out with wit and intelligence, ours is a world in which "the museum collapses into the shopping mall, where cultural difference becomes another commodity to be bought and sold. The mall has become the true axis of Western culture. Here, as elsewhere, commodification works by repetition and the recognition this fosters. . . . In contemporary capitalist culture celebrities are marketable. . . . The sites where this cultural consumption takes place can be some of the most cherished institutions in Western culture: art galleries, libraries, museums, universities." Besides exotic artworks, particularly characteristic of this new cannibal culture is the New Age, "a vast smorgasbord of interests, from crystal power, to the channeling of ancient extraterrestrials, to a revival in goddess-worship [and] the trappings of Native spiritual philosophies and the ceremonies and regalia that go along with these." Regardless of the diversity of exotic paraphernalia, states Root, at bottom it all "tends to be a middle-class phenomenon."[47]

What has so decisively shaped our bourgeois-cannibalistic postmodernist age, especially including its vague perceptions of what passes for art, is a ubiquitous home appliance—the television set. Seemingly beneath the interests, or even express contempt, of the art historian, it has, since around 1960, universally shaped the human spirit, including its aesthetic responses and especially its imagination (or lack thereof). The situation now, at the beginning of a new millennium, is simply this: American children spend nearly twice as much time watching TV as they do in school. As Flo Conway and Jim Siegelman, two appalled students of mass communications and the social sciences, have observed, television in particular, the chosen medium of mass distraction in the post–Cold War era, has significantly contributed to the common phenomenon of "*snapping*, a term which designates the sudden, drastic alteration of personality in all its many forms." Television "may be our culture's primary contributor to snapping in everyday life [since] it has become the predominant purveyor of news, the molding force of public opinion, and the principal source of our collective images, dreams, hopes, amusements, and desires." Like trendy New Age pseudoreligions, "TV stills the mind through repetition. . . . Its incessant transmission of information physically trains an individual to hear and observe without stopping to think."

Television is of course absolutely essential to bourgeois, postmodernist, cannibal culture: "Advertisers have long known that its rapid-fire kaleidoscopic manner of consumption may make television viewers more vulnerable to their suggestions."[48] TV unleashes a titanic flood of sound-bites and picture bombs. Particularly, it effortlessly produces endless individual images embracing a stunning range of stylistic expressions. The result is pictorial glut: the average postmodernist couch potato likely experiences more images per diem than earlier peoples did throughout their entire life. Contemporary artists suffer from this glut: they cannot, in short, compete with the home appliance. Among other cultural results, postmodernist art suggests that, once again, artists have for the most part packed it in, have retreated from the challenge; they have become mere accomplices of the omnipresent TV set, similarly producing reams of eye-catching, glossy, and essentially empty, repetitive imagery. Among other idle visual diversions, ETs are big on TV.

This response is however vastly different from the one produced by the last time pictorial artists were collectively challenged by a mechanical competitor, the photographic camera. A professional staple of the average painter's paid employment had been portraiture; by the mid-nineteenth century that option was denied to the average painter with a bourgeois clientele (aristocratic patrons remained faithful however to the prestige associated with oil paints). At the end of the same century, with the introduction of a cheap box camera, the Kodak Brownie, the very purpose, even further existence, of landscape painting was likewise biologically challenged. But a century ago, vanguard painters responded differently: they evolved technical languages with formal vocabularies—Fauvism, Cubism, Futurism, Expressionism, and so forth—strictly inherent to their chosen artistic media. To the contrary, with scarcely a whimper of noncompliance, postmodernists appear to have wholly surrendered to the cybernetic age of seductive virtual reality. Picasso, and even Joseph Beuys, would be appalled.

Even more ominous is the fact reported by our snapping experts that, in an apparently universal fashion, "television teaches an individual to experience scenes of terror, anger, shock, and tragedy—purely as entertainment." Like cigarette smoking (especially its secondhand smoke), the full, probably largely detrimental, effects of television on impressionable minds and bodies have not yet been fully assessed. Preliminary scientific studies do, however, show that

> as the nervous system adapts to great daily doses of experience received with no initiative or effort, the child may, in fact, become physically passive and intellectually lazy. Furthermore, reading tests of young television watchers confirm that their imaginations may have become permanently stunted. Educators report that heavy TV watching destroys

the natural ability of children to form mental images from what they read or hear. With too much TV, the growing child's basic capacity of imagination, like an unused muscle, never reaches a level adequate for performing even the most elementary creative acts.[49]

That last comment tells why art historians, particularly those who fashionably bewail the apparent intellectual impoverishment of post-modernism and its arts, should turn on their own TV sets. Whether in the Middle Ages, the Renaissance, or (even) in the postmodernist age, the artist was/is shaped by the popular culture she/he lived/lives in, electronic in our case. So are the artists—from hack draftsmen to movie directors—who have been commissioned by media moguls to visually recreate the visitations by extraterrestrial biological entities described by their earthling "experiencers." If you don't know that, the profound effect wrought by the ambient *vox populi* (Latin for mass opinion, even mass ignorance), then you fail to treat this or that artist's work as a cultural artifact. So doing, you just see it as "art," and then the result is that you only see its colorful surface, not its underlying meaning as a cultural device. Arguably, television has decisively shaped the mentalities of receptive audiences numbering millions and millions since the 1970s; this conclusion particularly applies to all those still collectively amazed by the legend of extraterrestrial visitations.

This attitude (admittedly skeptical) exploring novel and wide-ranging contextual approaches may lead us toward some useful, new, and more wide-ranging perceptions of the ET phenomenon. That, too, is a cultural artifact. Our aim is the revelation of certain preexistent and widespread cultural phenomena that have made such a thing both possible and (even) important. As previously stated, and in different ways, the ET phenomenon—regardless of whatever the ETs themselves may actually signify—must take into account the nature of its audience, of its committed promoters and of its avid consumers, even the odd experiencer. Thus, the ET phenomenon, formerly ignored as an object of art-historical interest, must itself be interpreted within the timeless context of crowd psychology. The lone seer is one thing; the heterogeneous crowd-audience is perhaps something quite different. This critical distinction was perhaps best summarized by poet Friedrich Schiller: "Anyone, taken as an individual, is tolerably sensible and reasonable; taken as a member of a crowd, he at once becomes a blockhead." Certainly the study of crowd psychology—and of its manipulation—is nothing new. Just as Charles Mackay observed way back in 1852, in his classic study *Extraordinary Popular Delusions and the Madness of Crowds*,

In reading the history of nations, we find that, like individuals, they have their whims and their peculiarities; their seasons of excitement and recklessness, when they care not what they do. We find that whole communities suddenly fix their minds upon one object, and go mad in its pursuit: that millions of people become simultaneously impressed with one delusion, and run after it, till their attention is caught by some new folly, more captivating than the first. . . . Men, it has been well said, think in herds; it will be seen that they go mad in herds, while they only recover their senses slowly, and one by one.[50]

The generic "city" provides the context of promotion by the mass media of the ET phenomenon and, particularly, it is the lair of the bulk of their adoring audiences and media producers. It is particularly in the teeming metropolis where, stated Mackay so long ago, "men [and women] think in herds." The urban setting, and its highly specialized psychological conditionings, are essential to a general understanding of the ET phenomenon, indeed to the very meaning of modernism itself, even including its orthodox and postmodern variants. Thus, according to Mackay,

The popular humors of a great city are a never-failing source of amusement. . . . But, like all other earthly things, [any particular fashion] has its season, and passes away as suddenly as it arose, never again to be the pet and idol of the populace. A new claimant drives it from its place, and holds undisputed sway, till, in its turn, it is hurled from its preeminence, and a successor appointed in its stead. . . . These are the whimsies of the mass, the harmless follies by which they unconsciously endeavor to lighten the load of care which presses upon their existence.[51]

DOCUMENTATION: HOW WE PROVE
THE EXISTENCE OF EXTRATERRESTRIALS

What are the research materials of the historian? Like the district attorney, we study physical evidence: artifacts found—or not found—at the site of the alleged transaction. Like the D.A., we gather the written documents attesting to what "really" happened and study the credibility of eyewitness testimony supposedly certifying that the event did (or did not) take place as so described. The art historian also examines the strictly pictorial evidence, in this case extraterrestrial portraiture. However, since the photographic evidence is either missing or (oops!) has been shown to have been faked, our art-historical documentation is limited to handmade or computer-generated portraiture and that, of course, is wholly of human manufacture. Not one piece of evidence from these diverse fields certifies, or negates, by itself the actuality of the alleged event. The diverse bits of evidence must be laboriously examined as a whole, and in context.

Dr. John Mack states that skeptics must "immerse themselves in the primary data" of the abduction experience. (Spot on, John.) Accordingly, and just as any reputable scholar must do, I will now industriously examine the art-historical "primary documents" explicitly establishing both a now-standard iconographic format of extraterrestrial portraiture—the bug-eyed space-waif—and its now-identifiable historical sources. The current acceptance of this now-standardized physiognomy—currently enjoying precedence over previous ET archetypes (see fig. 8, Nickell's "Alien Time Line")—historically replicates the medieval installation of successive "authentic" portraits of Christ, each of which, states Hans Belting, "needed publicity to establish its cult." All such replications were then marketed as representing a "*Copie authentique de la Saint Face*" (see fig. 2). The most "authentic" of all was the kind called by Byzantine theologicans the *theographos typos*, "a figure painted by God"; hence, the intervention of the self-expressive earthling artist was absolutely undesirable.[52] Their point was well taken: only by removing all mediation by a human agent could credibility, meaning absolute verisimilitude, be guaranteed.

The surviving documentary evidence has ensured that the iconography of a postmodernist extraterrestrial portraiture has become as conventionalized as a Byzantine icon (*theographos typos;* see fig. 1). This documentation entirely consists of eyewitness reports produced by those unfortunate earthlings, citizens of the United States of America for the most part, who have been involuntarily "abducted" by extraterrestrial aliens, evidently for largely malignant purposes. One particularly earnest researcher, David M. Jacobs (with a Ph.D. according to the paperback cover), produced a thick monograph in 1992 (in paperback by 1993); this had been "based on the testimony of some sixty individuals [mostly women, with a female-male ratio of 3:1] with whom I have explored more than 300 abduction experiences." Beginning in 1980, all of these unfortunate "abductees" had been interviewed by Jacobs *under hypnosis.* To his credit, Jacobs does admit that "it is easy for a hypnotist to ask—consciously or inadvertently—leading questions that steer the abductee [or he] can put pressure on the subject to invent details"[53] (and much more will be said about these dubious means of eliciting information in chapter 14). In the event, as derived from Jacobs's hypnotically induced investigations, the following, absolutely standard, iconographic tableau of the mostly loathsome otherworldlings has repeatedly emerged. According to Dr. Jacobs's summary:

> They are small—about three and one-half to four feet tall. These Small Beings are usually gray, tan, pale white (not Caucasian), or "colorless." They have bald, bulbous craniums. Their immense eyes are dark, with no pupils or corneas. They either have no nose or it is so slight that it is unnoticeable, and their small, slit-like mouth does not move. They have no ears. Their bodies are very thin. They either wear nothing or what appears to be form-fitting clothing.[54]

John E. Mack (M.D. on the paperback cover) extends the canonical mode of portraiture even further. He does so on the basis of "seventy-six abductees (ranging in age from two[!] to fifty-seven; forty-seven females and twenty-nine males, including three boys eight and under[!]) fulfilling my quite strict criteria for an abduction case." And the unimpeachable results are these:

> By far the most common entity observed are the small "grays," humanoid beings three to four feet in height. The grays are mainly of two kinds—smaller drone or insect-like workers, who move or glide robotically outside and inside the ships and perform various specific tasks, and a slightly taller leader or "doctor," as the abductees most often call him. Female "nurses," or other beings with special functions, are observed. The leader is usually felt to be male, although female leaders are also seen. Gender difference is not determined so much anatomically as by an intuitive feeling that abductees find difficult to put into words.
>
> The small grays reported have large, pear-shaped heads that protrude in the back, long arms with three or four long fingers, a thin torso, and spindly legs. Feet are not often seen directly, and are usually covered with single-piece boots. External genitalia, with one exception (Joe, in [Mack's] chapter 8), are not observed. The beings are hairless with no ears, have rudimentary nostril holes, and a thin slit for a mouth which rarely opens or is expressive of emotion. By far the most prominent features are huge, black eyes which curve upward and are more rounded toward the center of the head and pointed at the outer edge. They seem to have no whites or pupils, although occasionally the abductee may be able to see a kind of eye inside the eye, with the outer blackness appearing as a sort of goggle. The eyes, as we will see in the case examples, have a compelling power, and the abductees will often wish to avoid looking directly into them because of the overwhelming dread of their own sense of self, or loss of will, that occurs when they do so. In addition to boots, the aliens usually wear a form-fitting, single-

piece, tunic-like garment, which is sparsely adorned. A kind of cowl or hood is frequently reported.

The leader or doctor is reported as slightly taller, perhaps four and a half or five feet at most, and has features similar to the smaller grays, except that he may seem older or more wrinkled. He is clearly in charge of the procedures that occur on the ship. The attitude of the abductees toward the leader is generally ambivalent. They often discover that they have known one leader-being throughout their lives and have a strong bond with him, experiencing a powerful, and even reciprocal, love relationship. At the same time, they resent the control he has exercised in their lives. Communication between the aliens and humans is experienced as telepathic, mind to mind or thought to thought, with no specific common learned language being necessary.[55]

The taxonomic definition first published by Jacobs in 1992 and extended in 1994 by Mack, both being authoritatively based on those obviously unimpeachable eyewitness reports, is now complemented by a recently published (1996), and now apparently definitive (and pseudo-ornithological), *Field Guide to Extraterrestrials*:

> The popular image of extraterrestrials is of short human-like beings with lightbulb-shaped heads, almond-shaped black eyes, and fragile bodies. . . . Generally speaking, the Grays are three and a half feet tall and possess the characteristic grayish white skin. They have large, hairless, fetus-like heads with narrow jaws that taper to a "V." Their black eyes have no pupils or eyelids and wrap around the head to the temple. They have no nose, just small nostril holes, and a thin, lip-less slit for a mouth. Their torsos are rather scrawny; their arms and legs are long and thin. And their hands have three non-tapering fingers. . . . The ubiquitous small humanoids known as the Grays have smooth, pale, hairless skin, which can be either pasty-looking or translucent. Often witnesses can't tell if they are seeing the aliens' naked skin or their tight-fitting clothing. This confusion can, for instance, lead an observer to describe an alien with silvery skin or clothing as a robot.[56]

Also of obvious interest to all these earnest researchers is the matter of what the extraterrestrials actually *do*. Dr. Mack gives us a useful *précis* (all the details being substantiated by the transcripts quoted in the next chapter), and the literally breathtaking results are these:

> The abductee is usually undressed and is forced naked, or wearing only a single garment such as a T-shirt, onto a body-fitting table where most of the procedures occur. The experiencer may be the only one undergoing the procedures during a particular abduction, or may see one,

two, or many other human beings undergoing similar intrusions. The beings seem to study their captives endlessly, staring at them extensively, often with the large eyes close up to the humans' heads. The abductees may feel as if the contents of their minds have been totally known, even, in a sense, taken over. Skin and hair, and other samples from inside the body, are taken with the use of various instruments that the abductees can sometimes describe in great detail.

Instruments are used to penetrate virtually every part of the abductees' bodies, including the nose, sinuses, eyes, ears, and other parts of the head, arms, legs, feet, abdomen, genitalia, and, more rarely, the chest. Extensive surgical-like procedures done inside the head have been described, which abductees feel may alter their nervous systems. The most common, and evidently most important procedures, involve the reproductive system. Instruments that penetrate the abdomen or involve the genital organs themselves are used to take sperm samples from men and to remove or fertilize eggs of the female. Abductees report being impregnated by the alien beings and later having an alien-human or human-human pregnancy removed. They see the little fetuses being put into containers on the ships, and during subsequent abductions may see incubators where the hybrid babies are being raised (as do Catherine, Jerry, and Peter, among my cases). Experiencers may also see older hybrid children, adolescents, and adults, which they are told by the aliens or know intuitively are their own. Sometimes the aliens will try to have the human mothers hold and nurture those creatures, who may appear quite listless, or will encourage human children to play with the hybrid ones as, for example, Catherine is made to do.

Needless to say, all of this is deeply disturbing to the abductees, at least at first, or when the material first surfaces [under hypnosis]. Their terror may be mitigated somewhat by reassurances the aliens give that no serious harm will befall them, and by various anxiety-reducing or anesthesia-like means they use. Those involve instruments that affect the "energy" or "vibrations" (words that abductees often use) of the body. These processes may greatly reduce the abductees' fear or pain, and even bring about states of considerable relaxation. But in other cases they are incompletely successful, and terror, pain, and rage break through the emotion-extinguishing devices used. As I will document in detail in several case examples, the traumatic, rape-like nature of the abduction material may become altered [i.e., the stories change] as the abductees reach new levels of understanding of what [they are helped to believe] is occurring, and as their relationship to the beings themselves changes in the course of our [i.e., Mack's plus the hypnotized patient's] work.

In sum, the purely physical or biological aspect of the abduction phenomenon seems to have to do with some sort of genetic or quasi-genetic engineering for the purpose of creating human-alien hybrid offspring. We have no evidence of alien-induced genetic alteration in the strictly biological sense, although it is possible [to believe, if so inclined] that this has occurred.[57]

Well, there you have it: the currently canonical ET icon (fig. 1), and it is presently as canonical as was once a Byzantine icon (fig. 2). In either case, the justification is essentially that one put forth by seventh-century theologians, and their argument (as summarized by Hans Belting) held that "if Christ [himself an extraterrestrial entity since his *Anastasis*] is real, there is no alternative to his portrait [and] the image thus takes on the status of a confession of faith."[58] The idea was earlier (first century C.E.) fixed by Dion Chrysostomus in his *Twelfth (Olympic) Oration*: "Since we imagine the gods in the shape of the cult images we see around us, the artist's responsibility is great, for it is he who determines exactly how we will imagine the gods placed in our midst."[59] Therefore, then and now, we have an abundance of extraterrestrial portraiture.

NOTES

1. See, especially, the extensive listings in George M. Eberhart, ed., *UFOs and the Extraterrestrial Contact Movement: A Bibliography* (Metuchen, N.J.: Scarecrow Press, 1986; 2 vols.); Ronald D. Story, ed., *The Encyclopedia of Extraterrestrial Encounters: A Definitive, Illustrated A–Z Guide to All Things Alien* (New York: New American Library, 2001); for introductory interpretations, see Thomas E. Bullard, *UFO Abductions: The Measure of a Mystery*, Vol. 1: *Comparative Study of Abduction Reports* (Bloomington, Ind.: Fund for UFO Research, 1987); James R. Lewis, ed., *The Gods Have Landed: New Religions from Other Worlds* (Albany: State University of New York Press, 1995; what might be called an anthropological approach). For another way to assess the quantity (if not quality) of such publications, go to "amazon.com" on the Internet and search for "UFOs"; innumerable titles will appear (and I must confess that I have not read them all).

2. See Steven J. Dick, *Plurality of Worlds: The Origins of the Extraterrestrial Life Debate from Democritus to Kant* (Cambridge: Cambridge University Press, 1982); Karl S. Guthke, *The Last Frontier: Imagining Other Worlds, from the Copernican Revolution to Modern Science Fiction* (Ithaca, N.Y.: Cornell University Press, 1990); Michael J. Crowe, *The Extraterrestrial Life Debate, 1750–1900* (Mineola, N.Y.: Dover, 1999).

3. John E. Mack, foreword to *Secret Life: Firsthand Documented Accounts of UFO Abductions*, by David M. Jacobs (New York: Fireside, 1993), p. 1 (emphasis mine).

4. John Mack, *Abduction: Human Encounters with Aliens* (New York: Scribner's, 1994); my references shall be to the revised paperback edition (New

York: Ballantine, 1995), which was made in defensive response to criticisms following the first edition.

5. For Pritchard's reasons for arriving at these inflated figures, see C. D. B. Bryan, *Close Encounters of the Fourth Kind: Alien Abduction, UFOs, and the Conference at M.I.T.* (New York: Knopf, 1995), pp. 235–36; for the maladroit Roper poll giving rise to these horrifying statistics, see pp. 44–46; for a detailed critique of same, see L. Stires, "3.7 Million Americans Kidnapped by Aliens?" in *The UFO Invasion: The Roswell Incident, Alien Abductions, and Government Coverups*, ed. Kendrick Frazer (Amherst, N.Y.: Prometheus Books, 1997), pp. 203–206.

6. Bryan, *Close Encounters*, p. 46.

7. R. Fowler, *The Watchers: The Secret Design behind UFO Abduction* (New York: Bantam, 1990), p. xxi (emphasis in original).

8. Mack, *Abduction*, pp. 435–36.

9. R. Klein, "The Audience Culture," in *Theories of Contemporary Art*, ed. Richard Hertz (Englewood Cliffs, N.J.: Prentice-Hall, 1985; 2d ed. [with different essays], 1993), pp. 251–57.

10. For an innovative exposition of this methodology, particularly emphasizing the viewer's emotive and/or interpretive participation, see John Shearman, *Only Connect: Art and the Spectator in the Italian Renaissance* (Princeton: Princeton University Press, 1992; with further bibliography).

11. For this figure, see *Publishers Weekly*, 18 April 1994.

12. Klein, "The Audience Culture."

13. See further Neil Postman, *Amusing Ourselves to Death: Public Discourse in the Age of Show Business* (New York: Penguin, 1986).

14. Nicholas Mirzoeff, *An Introduction to Visual Culture* (London and New York: Routledge, 1999), p. 3 (also suggesting some of the observations immediately following).

15. G. Debord, *La Société du Spectacle* (Paris: Gallimard, 1992, reprint).

16. Emanuel Swedenborg, *Heaven and Hell*, ed. G. F. Dole (New York: Swedenborg Foundation, 1984), pp. 80, 82 (emphasis mine).

17. Klein, *The Audience Culture*.

18. For what immediately follows, I borrow from Charles Panati's invaluable historical survey, *Panati's Parade of Fads, Follies, and Manias. The Origins of Our Most Cherished Obsessions* (New York: Harper, 1991). Alas, Panati's exhaustive catalogue discusses neither ETs nor UFOs.

19. Colin Wilson, *The Mammoth Book of the Supernatural* (New York: Carroll and Graf, 1991), p. 446.

20. On this artist, and the particular sources for his occult beliefs, see J. F. Moffitt, *Occultism in Avant-Garde Art: The Case of Joseph Beuys* (Ann Arbor: University of Michigan Research Press, 1986).

21. For a balanced survey, pro and con, of the standard New Age apocrypha, see Hana Umlauf et al., *The World Almanac Book of the Strange* (New York: Signet, 1977).

22. Henry Gordon, *Channeling into the New Age: The "Teachings" of Shirley MacLaine and Other Such Gurus* (Amherst, N.Y.: Prometheus Books, 1988), pp. 25, 45.

23. Otto Friedrich, "New Age Harmonies," *Time*, 7 December 1987, pp. 62–72.

24. For much (much) more proof, see Peter Sacks, *Generation-X Goes to College: An Eye-Opening Account of Teaching in Postmodern America* (Chicago: Open Court, 1996).

25. Michael Shermer, *Why People Believe Weird Things: Pseudoscience, Superstition, and Other Confusions of Our Time* (New York: Freeman, 1997), p. 275.

26. Listing given in *Skeptical Inquirer* (May/June 1998): 12.

27. In Carl Sagan, *The Demon-Haunted World: Science as a Candle in the Dark* (New York: Ballantine, 1997), p. 246.

28. For a wonderful deconstruction of such postmodernist dogma, see Alan Sokal and Jean Bricmont, *Impostures Intellectuelles* (Paris: Editions Odile Jacob, 1997); for a parody of such academic "lit-crit," see H. M. S. Phake-Potter, *Postmodernist Deconstruction for Dummies: A Survivor's Guide to Building Your Academic Career*, ed. J. F. Moffitt (Philadelphia: Xlibris, 2002).

29. Adolf Hitler, as quoted in Sagan, *Demon-Haunted World*, p. 261.

30. John A. Walker, *Art in the Age of Mass Media* (Boulder, Colo.: Westview, 1994), pp. 6–7, 11 (emphasis mine).

31. Vercruysse, as quoted in ibid., p. 70.

32. R. Brilliant, *Portraiture* (Cambridge: Harvard University Press, 1991), pp. 8, 38.

33. For Renaissance descriptions of the canonical, meaning pre-ET, *homunculi*, see Klaus Völker, ed., *Künstliche Menschen: Dichtungen und Dokumente über Golems, Homunculi, Androiden und liebende Statuen* (Munich: DTV, 1971), pp. 31–59.

34. Brilliant, personal communication, 5 October 1997.

35. Gruder research, as reported in Philip J. Klass, *UFO-Abductions: A Dangerous Game* (Amherst, N.Y.: Prometheus Books, 1989), p. 183.

36. J. P. Richter, ed., *The Literary Works of Leonardo da Vinci* (Oxford: Oxford University Press, 1939), p. 64; see also Shearman, *Only Connect*, chap. 3, "Portraiture and Poets."

37. Saint Teresa, as quoted in Victor Stoichita, *Visionary Experience in the Golden Age of Spanish Art* (London: Reaktion, 1995), p. 45 (in his chap. 3, "Visions and Paintings").

38. See Moffitt, *Occultism in Avant-Garde Art*; J. F. Moffitt, *Alchemist of the Avant-Garde: The Case of Marcel Duchamp* (Albany: State University of New York Press, 2003; in press). Both of these artists, however, belong to the realm of "serious" scholarship.

39. For cogent arguments to this effect, see Suzi Gablik, *Has Modernism Failed?* (New York: Thames & Hudson, 1985).

40. Ibid., p. 117.

41. For a rather extreme view from a clinical psychologist, see Louis A. Sass, *Madness and Modernism: Insanity in the Light of Modern Art, Literature, and Thought* (New York: BasicBooks, 1992); for firsthand reports validating this appraisal, see Jon E. Lewis, ed., *The Permanent Book of the Twentieth Century: Eye-Witness Accounts of the Moments That Shaped Our Century* (New York: Carroll & Graf, 1994).

42. For this interpretive technique, including exemplary demonstrations, see E. Kaemmerling, ed., *Ikonographie und Ikonologie: Theorien—Entwicklung—Probleme* (Cologne: DuMont, 1979).

43. See Paul Fussell, *BAD, or the Dumbing of America* (New York: Touchstone, 1991).

44. For this standard Latin terminology, see Hans Belting, *Likeness and Presence: A History of the Image before the Era of Art* (Chicago: University of Chicago Press, 1996), p. 93 (translation mine). On this pictorial category, the actual basis of ET portraiture, see further Moshe Barasch, *Icon: Studies in the History of an Idea* (New York: New York University Press, 1992; for the theoretical contexts); Helmut Fischer, *Die Ikone: Ursprung, Sinn, Gestalt* (Freiburg: Herder, 1995; for the technical and historical contexts).

45. For the historical evolution of the mass media and their role in art history, see Juan Antonio Ramírez, *Medios de masas e historia del arte* (Madrid: Cátedra, 1981; an excellent introduction worthy of translation).

46. Belting, *Likeness and Presence*, p. 30.

47. Deborah Root, *Cannibal Culture: Art, Appropriation, and the Commodification of Difference* (Boulder, Colo.: Westview, 1996), pp. viii, 17–18, 87.

48. Flo Conway and Jim Siegelman, *Snapping: America's Epidemic of Sudden Personality Change* (New York: Delta, 1979), pp. 13, 190.

49. Ibid., p. 191; for further evidence of brain decay among the TV generation, see Postman, *Amusing Ourselves to Death*, pp. 83 ff.; Sacks, *Generation-X Goes to College*, esp. pp. 142 ff.

50. Charles Mackay, *Extraordinary Popular Delusions and the Madness of Crowds* (New York: Page, 1932; facsimile reprint of the 1852 edition), pp. xix–xx.

51. Ibid., pp. 619–31.

52. Belting, *Likeness and Presence*, pp. 53–55, 220–21.

53. Jacobs, *Secret Life*, pp. 15, 321 (now an associate professor of modern history at Temple University, and [alas] not a trained psychologist, Dr. Jacobs's 1973 dissertation dealt with UFOs in the popular imagination).

54. Ibid., p. 88; for many more structural details, see pp. 221–28: "Anatomy of an Alien." If nothing else, Jacobs's bibliography, and mine, too, documents the fact that a great many functionally literate people take this nonsense seriously. Jacobs's acknowledged mentor-model is the lucrative paperback reportage of Budd Hopkins; among other titles, see his *Missing Time* (New York: Berkley, 1983). Since Hopkins had previously enjoyed minor success as an abstract expressionist painter, he also has an art-historical context.

55. Mack, *Abduction*, pp. 2, 22–23.

56. Patrick Huyghe, *The Field Guide to Extraterrestrials* (New York: Avon, 1996), pp. 5, 7.

57. Mack, *Abduction*, pp. 23–24.

58. Belting, *Likeness and Presence*, p. 155.

59. Dion, in Barasch, *Icon*, p. 41.

Chapter 2

Eyewitness Accounts of Close Encounters with Postmodernist ETs

MORE DOCUMENTATION, THE KIND "PROVING" THE FACT OF EXTRATERRESTRIAL VISITATIONS

As perhaps you were not aware, there are some pretty strict rules governing the credibility of your qualifications to earn the prestigious title "abductee" or "experiencer" (an alternate designation favored by Mack and some other experts in the field). According to Mark Rodeghier, director of investigations at the J. Allen Hynek Center for UFO Studies (CUFOS) in Chicago:

> In order to qualify as an "abductee," a person must be (a) taken against his or her will; (b) from terrestrial surroundings; (c) by non-human Beings. The Beings must take a person: to (d) an enclosed place; (e) non-terrestrial in appearance; that is (f) assumed or known to be a spacecraft by the [abductee] witness. In this place, the person must either be: (g) subjected to a physical examination; (h) engaged in communication, verbal or telepathic, or (i) both.[1]

The specifications seem perfectly clear. If you possess these qualifications, the Chicago branch of CUFOS is eagerly awaiting your phone call. Another support group is "Abductees Anonymous" (whom you could have contacted at their Web site: http://www.CyberGate.com/~ufoline).

And another agency expecting a similar response is the Federal Bureau of Investigation. In 1987, Philip Klass published a statement in which he offered to pay any "victim" of an "abduction" by extraterrestrial aliens the sum of $10,000, "providing the alleged abduction is reported to the Federal Bureau of Investigation and FBI investigation confirms that the kidnapping really occurred." His press release also cautioned that "anyone who knowingly reports a spurious kidnapping to the FBI is vulnerable to a $10,000 fine and up to five years in prison."[2] Even though Klass's bank account remains unaffected by his generous offers, and in spite of the *several hundred thousand* abductees said to be hiding in the American underbrush, we do know that the FBI is actively researching the ominous matter. Our authority is a popular TV series, *The X-Files*, assuring us that Agents Fox Mulder and Dana Scully are on the job and looking after our collective welfare (well, sort of). The movie *The X-Files: Fight the Future* premiered in the summer of 1998, and grossed *$187 million*.[3] And another one who has cashed in on the FBI connection is a credulous Brit, Nicholas Redfern, who published in 1998 a mass-market paperback book, *The FBI Files: The FBI's UFO Top Secrets Exposed*.[4] And, yes, there really were FBI files on UFOs, even a few on their "alien" crew members, but all these are just typical (and obligatory) bureaucratic follow-ups on reported sightings. However, after perusing these, American taxpayers should only feel chagrin at the time wasted by their civil servants in generating these voluminous, but wholly inconclusive, memoranda.

It is my assumption (admittedly pure intuition) that the kind of people who would most likely read a book like this, the kind self-designated as being both "scholarly" and "skeptical," are most likely not to be very well read in the abundant primary (and mostly paperback) literature lending credence to the idea of plentiful extraterrestrial visitations among mere earthlings. Therefore, I will now proceed to quote literally (*verbatim*) a few of the more standard accounts of the earthlings' close encounters with their otherworldly intruders. Remember Dr. Mack's piqued injunction that "the skeptics who have criticized my methods and hypotheses [must] immerse themselves in the primary data." The forthcoming exposure—a full Mackian immersion—will give an extraterrestrially unsophisticated, but evidently otherwise erudite, reader the complete picture. This tableau delineates in full detail the narrative style and quirky content typifying all the essential historical documents substantiating the postmodernist paperback publishing phenomenon of alien abductions.

Happily, the strictly narrative aspects of this new and unquestionably popular literary genre have been carefully analyzed by a competent Canadian literary scholar, Professor Terry Matheson, who respectfully treats the lucrative publishing phenomenon as "a modern, secular myth," a kind of populist "storytelling" or "fabrication, a form of 'making things up.'" In the event, once treated as *a literary genre*, then the commercially successful narratives of UFO abductions do reveal themselves to closely conform, as they must, to recognized *genre conventions*. As Matheson reveals, "All books dealing with UFO abductions present their readers with something akin to a historical text, in that they maintain that they are describing real events in the past." Nonetheless, by their very nature, the abductees' anecdotes must remain "forever beyond unequivocal verification or refutation." Undaunted, "abduction authors are fond of emphasizing the high degree of *consistency* that can be found within the abductees' various recollections [even though] such consistency can be used as evidence *against* the stories' literal truth." Besides being described as persons of undoubted "sincerity," the abductees must additionally be presented by their ghostwriters as being "publicity shy," and "it goes without saying that the abductees are all given glowing character references."

Matheson goes on to say that a given author additionally will "impress upon us that, unlike his critics, he was free from personal bias or prejudice regarding the subject of UFOs at the time the experiences [he records] occurred." All such narrations make a great show of "objectivity"; that display is "itself a strategy, part of a shrewd attempt to appear fair-minded in order to win the reader over to the thesis the authors have favored all along." Resort to "unsupported speculation is a most successful strategy" in such apocryphal texts, and scrupulously avoided is any examination of "the issue of human personality and social context, even the possible presence of a psychological component, as they relate to the [purported] abduction phenomenon." These authors "divide all people into two groups: those who believe the subject to be important and worthy of study, and those who, out of lack of information or mere indifference, simply ignore the phenomenon," so showing themselves to be insensitive louts, if not outright Luddites. Accordingly, "the task of debunking is likened to laughing at rape victims." In sum, and in all cases, "the problem here is that the *only* proof is in the form of the anecdotal information supplied by the alleged abductees themselves." Additionally, a standard implication is that "abductees (and their authors) have not benefited financially from their stories." Nonetheless, just as Matheson points out, such claims are "manifestly untrue: there is a great deal of money to be made in abductions," much of which gets "made into motion pictures and 'made-for-TV' movies, for which all concerned were presumably remunerated."[5]

This is it. Regardless of its potential literary value (or nonvalue), what shall now be extensively quoted is the UFOlogists' *evidence*, what passes for *proof* that anything at all really happened. They, in close collaboration with their commercial paperback publishers, have printed out reams and reams of their "essential documentation." Its sheer quantity (which is considerable) is taken to attest to, besides an inherent *consistency* characterizing the test results (or repetitiousness, if you wish), the intrinsic validity of their earnest UFOlogical research and the obvious significance of their meticulously exhumed case studies. Nonetheless, that argument is easily disposed of, even by an intelligent UFOlogist; as Jacques Vallée remarked way back in 1965, "The investigator of the UFO phenomenon is rarely concerned with such reports of contacts [with aliens], which follow an easily recognizable pattern[:] all criteria of imagination and fraud are met by these 'consistent' stories."[6] In 1987 another researcher, Thomas E. Bullard, went much further, determining that the inevitable narrative pattern comprises eight "consistent" features, some of which may, however, be omitted: (1) *capture*: the witness is caught and taken aboard a UFO; (2) *examination*: ETs subject the witness to a physical, and sometimes mental, examination; (3) *conference*: the abductee converses for a while, typically through "telepathy," with the ETs; (4) *tour*: the ETs allow the abductee to see various parts of their high-tech UFO; (5) *otherworldly journey*: the abductee goes on a voyage in the UFO; (6) *theophany*: the abductee has a religious experience after receiving profound messages from the ETs; (7) *return*: the abductee is returned to Mother Earth and allowed to depart from the UFO; (8) *aftermath*: abductee reports after-effects, mostly psychic and perhaps even including discovery of "implants."[7]

This pattern had been discerned by Bullard following his intense scrutiny of endless publications "documenting" the minutiae attending over 300 alien-abduction cases; many more such, of course, have been published since 1985, when he finished his 402-page manuscript. One can only hope that the national arboreal resources have not suffered terminal trauma as a result of the UFOlogists' as-yet unchecked publishing feats. No matter; evidently the forests will regenerate by themselves, as the human race cannot—unless, so we are told, we can confront and resolve the pressing problem of the extraterrestrials in our midst. However dire their predictions, the case made by UFOlogists for the credibility, the very authenticity of all those diverse reports of close human encounters with aliens and extraterrestrials, intelligent creatures from outer space, essentially stands—or falls—on the basis of what follows.

In this case, most of the essential documents have been gathered, carefully transcribed and published by indefatigable researcher David M. Jacobs, Ph.D. Since he is a figure often recurring in what follows, I will let journalist C. D. B. Bryan quickly draw us a sketch of this interesting personality (whom you have perhaps already seen on TV): "Jacobs is [in 1992] in his early fifties, a pink-cheeked, mustached, portly man in a carefully tailored charcoal-gray suit. He wears his tightly curled gray hair in a modified Afro, but he would not be out of place in mutton chops. He exudes an air of self-confidence which, I later learn, [some people] read as self-importance. . . . Being a historian, he has also developed an academician's fervor for [any] facts that support his point of view."[8] He also has a certain literary strategy, which Terry Matheson shows to reflect a certain "core narrative which had been circulating throughout North America for almost three decades."[9]

As fervently presented by Dr. Jacobs, his eyewitness documents may also be read like the published transcripts of a sensational courtroom drama. Jacobs uses the abbreviation "DJ" to indicate the hypnotist's probing, even leading, queries, and the abbreviation "R" to indicate the hypnotized abductee's obedient, sometimes emotionally overwrought, response to these industrious extraterrestrial inquisitions. We may begin by citing six interviews of the sort typically conducted by David Jacobs, and these we may call his model "cases," with these providing eyewitness accounts of melodramatic close encounters with aliens and extraterrestrials. In the next section, we will give narrative résumés of nine more cases. Since these texts constitute the prima facie evidence for the historical validity of the postmodernist ET apparition phenomenon, they need to be examined in detail. Particularly, the eyewitness testimony (as provided by various people designated as "R") needs to be quoted *in extenso*, so allowing the abused victims to make their case by providing the aghast reader with all the horrific details attached to their alleged close encounters with these industrial-strength alien abusers of a cowering gaggle of American adults.

In the first example, case one, R felt "nervous" because her ET was evidently "angry with me for something." As DJ asks with commendable insight, "At this time, were you in the middle of your *anorexia* problem, or at the end of it, or just beginning?" It was, in fact, "Toward the end," and the bony respondent perceives that ET is "concerned about the weight, but he's more concerned about other stuff, too." Regarding that "other stuff," as it turns out, "it's not really the fact that I'm real skinny; it's just that I think that he knows that my period stopped." In fact, this cyclic event had gone missing for rather a long time: "I guess it was about eight months. Maybe a little bit more than that. Not fully a year." But R's interlocutors also include the "Taller Being" and the "Small Beings," and R knows that "they're talking about me." When DJ asks about their specific topic of conversation, he is informed that "they know that I stopped menstruating, and they think that I'm also so skinny, they think that I'm sick or something." But the ETs are not just solicitous; instead, "The taller [ET] guy seems annoyed again because I've lost weight." Her spunky explanation to him is "And I just said, 'Because I want to be thin.'" His reasonable retort to her holds that "I have to start eating, because my body doesn't function right if I don't." But it all works out in the end (more or less): "But after he says that, he just starts looking at me again. And [then] everything is pretty okay. I get those same feelings again, and I get the feeling he's not really mad at me."[10]

In case two, R tells DJ that the taller ET "told me that I had to get undressed. He seemed kind of annoyed that I wasn't already." An argument arises between the tall ET and the smaller ETs, and R "felt, like, he was mad at them. He said something to them; he just was unhappy." DJ wonders whether they were "annoyed with you?" No, says R, in fact, "he was mad at them. He said something to them; he just was unhappy." Addressing his alien underlings, the tall one says, "This isn't the way this is supposed to be done." Turning then to a properly befuddled R, he again reminds her that she was "supposed to be undressed already, or why wasn't I undressed already, or something like that." His will prevailed: "They just took my clothes off when I was lying there. He came back after a few minutes. He looked at me again, and he said, 'This will be over in a minute.' I started to feel scared again, too."[11]

In case three, the close encounter gets rather more intimate: "Then he [the ET] looked between my legs." R's brusque retort to him is "That's not nice; you shouldn't do that." But ET explains that he is merely curious, something like a obsessive inquirer, "I'm not going to hurt you, I just want to look inside." His method of insider inquiry is literally illuminating; according to R, "So this light came on somewhere. There's this big light between my legs. And I could just see this big light, kind of burning my eyes." His interest now definitely piqued, DJ wants specific information, so he asks, "The light was not focused on your eyes, though, is that correct?" And the emphatically specific reply has it that "the light was focused *between* my legs. Then he stuck something in it [the inguinal region], and it really hurt. It just really hurt, and I couldn't move." Ever desirous of the explicit detail, DJ needs to know what the "instrument" wielded by ET was actually shaped like. R really doesn't remember, but she concludes (presumably with a psychic shudder) that "whatever it was, it fit, but it hurt. It just ripped right through in there. It just ripped me right through; it felt like I was ripping. I know there was some blood there. It felt kind of dripping and wet."[12]

Case four actually takes place, so we are told, within a UFO. As any plucky Hollywood heroine would do in such a locale, now R is "trying to get away." Just as Sigourney Weaver showed us on the giant silver screen (for instance in *Alien*), one's proper duty is "to try to run." So instructed, R believes that "down there is a hall or something; there's a passageway, and I start to run away." R was convinced that "I'd see something they [the ETs] wouldn't want me to see, and then I'd be able to do something. They would take me out; they would let me get out if I did something that I wasn't supposed to do. I could get away. So I was running." Excited by her kinetic tale, DJ asks, "How far do you get?" Unfortunately for R, "I don't get that far. I get a little ways. I'm trying to run, and I can't. Then I'm up against the wall, because I can't move. I'm pressing against something. They [the ETs] say, 'Don't be afraid.'" One of them accompanies R, and "He's walking beside me, in front of me a bit, and I try the other thing, to go backward, instead of running forward to resist it backward, but it's even harder to do that. And I push, kind of kick backward. And kicking against it, I can't do that either. Just with my right foot, I tried to kick." DJ inquires about what she was trying to kick, and the reply is right out of *Star Wars*. In effect, R's intention was to "kick the force, or whatever it is. It's, like, I'm on a [nameless object, one which is] moving along, and I can't even control it."[13]

Case five describes a rapelike anatomical examination performed by the aliens. At some point in their tedious gynecological inquiry, R states that "I got a second wind. Then I got up, and I don't think they wanted me to do that." Her bold resolve to retain anatomical independence "took every ounce of will that I had. I got up off the table. I just kind of pushed past them. They're not physically strong, but there's some other kind of control they have to use, and I think I was really fighting it." She was especially piqued that ET was "preparing to look up inside of me, but I think I decided I had just about enough of it." DJ asks if she was indeed able to stand up, and she bravely responds, "Mm-hmm. It was kind of wobbly, but I just had to put forth all of my energy and my will to move." Evidently, if one shows some resolve, the ETs will retreat: "They don't really attack you that much. They just kind of backed off a little. They tried to stand in my way, then they backed off." Ever plucky, R exits the examination sector, but only to find herself in another palestra within the UFO. This was "another control kind of area, where they had the window and the machinery. And there was something in the middle of the room. It was, like, a big round thing sticking up that was luminous. It was lit up. And there was a little bar that went around it." Even here she was again assailed: "I found myself being cornered into it. A couple of ones [more ETs] had left their areas in this room, and they started cornering me, like you corner a cat or a rabbit. But I got my back against it [the bar or railing]. And I just got my shoulders pinned up against it."

Case five continues with R seeming to be trapped in the choreography of an alien ballet, and she "kept inching around the rail, but they kept moving in. I kept inching around and around this rail because they were coming at me initially from one side, but then they just surrounded the thing." As was inevitable, R is again captured. But now attention shifts from her groin to her head; a determined ET "was sticking something into my head, like, up in here." Typically, the effect was nasty, something like a trip to the dentist: "It wasn't like somebody was trying to drill something into your head, but you could feel something sticking in, and the initial sting." The after-effects were, however, better than those produced by any dentist you may know: "It felt like there was a flash of light in my head. But then I started to feel kind of soothed and tingling all over, like I had just been drugged. I couldn't really tighten any of my muscles. Then they put their hands over me, and I just started floating again. They floated me up, and back into the examining room. I couldn't move really; I felt like Jell-O." The last word has it that the ETs have given up dentistry and have instead reverted to gynecology: "They were busy putting my feet up in stirrups, little raised areas. And he [the taller ET] start[ed] doing this very intense pelvic procedure."[14]

Case six presents us with a post-pelvic kind of close encounter. According to the dazzled recollection of Ms. R, as a Taller Being magnanimously states, "That's it for now. That's it for now." Now they even "helped me put my nightgown on." Ever the stickler for the telling graphic detail, DJ asks if they also put on her panties. R's eloquent reply, "Uh-huh. They helped me put them on." But she also notes that the ETs are clumsy oafs: "I think they put that nightgown on backward. Not backward, inside out. I think that's what they did, because I remember the next morning thinking that I was stupid; I must have been awfully tired because I put my nightgown on inside out. I think that's what *they* did." DJ returns to his preferred article of intimate clothing: "Did they put your underpants on in the correct way?" Happily, "Um-hmm. They did that all right." Overall, R seems rather satisfied with this sort of intense voyeuristic inspection, doting attention, as it were, paid to her by, besides DJ, also ET: "But I didn't mind it. I don't really want to go back. I liked him. It was a really nice experience." In fact, as she concludes, her bizarre experience was rather like a blind date with a happy ending: "And he held my hand and he walked down the steps with me. We walked out into the woods and into the field. You know, I think we walked pretty far, just slowly. And I don't think we said anything, but I was really enjoying the feelings—like I was taking a midnight stroll with a lover."[15]

EVEN MORE DOCUMENTATION, WITH EVEN CLOSER ENCOUNTERS WITH THE ETs

As reported here, we see that the level of intimacy and perceived spiritual bonding of the earthlings with the extraterrestrials often becomes quite striking, even emotionally intimate. Moreover, frequently their close encounters get *really* close, even corporeally so. As was formerly said by vaudevillians (with certain grammatical license), "You ain't seen nothing yet!"

A case in point is case seven. In this episode, the aliens attached headgear to R and began their so-called mindscan procedures. Once that was done, the senior ET scopes her out with his eyes. His ocular abilities are striking, like Svengali's, and R gets really rattled: "He's looking in my eyes, and I can't see. I can't see. I can't see anything because he's in my eyes. How can he be in my eyes? He's in my eyes. This is making me crazy. I can't stand this. How can he be in my eyes?" Indeed, this fellow seems to be endowed with what we may call *Augengewalt* ("eye power" in German, or just *Oy gevalt!* in Yiddish). According to R's over-the-top recollection, "He's in my eyes. He's flooding my eyes. He's completely penetrating me; every bit of me is in my eyes. He's in my eyes. I can't do anything about it. He's spreading into my brain. He's spreading into my brain—totally. He is invading me. He's in my brain. Oh, God. He's in my mind. He's everywhere. He's absolutely everywhere. I can't stand it. I can't stand it. I can't stand it!" As was further explained by David Jacobs's eyeball-ravaged respondent,

> And he's making me feel things. He's making me feel things. He's making me feel things in my body that I don't feel. He's making me feel feelings, sexual feelings. He's making me feel things. It must be that he's making me feel them because I don't feel them. And he's in my brain. I wouldn't feel them. He's making me feel them. He's making me feel things. And he's there. He's everywhere. He's in my brain, and he is everywhere in my body too, somehow. That's very confusing. But it's not so black. But my body is changing. My body is getting tense in a different way. He's making my body do things and then they take the [mindscan] thing off

my head. Somebody takes the thing off my head. That's good, because it was uncomfortable and heavy. I didn't like that. And I can see more now. And he's still there, but it's not everywhere. But my body is, I have funny feelings. I'm not used to these feelings. I don't understand, between my legs. I don't understand why this [place between my legs] is feeling this way.

Here is a literal transcription of R's overwhelmed response to the ET's cease-less scopic ravishments: "Oh no. Oh God, no, no, no, no. No—oh God, no."

As the R of case seven also informs us, her eye-zapper looks very much like a demonic character pictured in Fuseli's *Nightmare* (fig. 26), namely, "He's absolutely out of it. His mouth is hanging slack, and his hands are loose at his side, kind of like an ape. And his eyes are glazed over, cloudy, unfocused." Certainly, he is an effective, albeit unwelcome, sort of ravisher: "He's making my body respond sexually. I mean, I didn't know what it was at that time, what a sexual response was. I knew it was very strange. It had pleasurable parts to it, but it wasn't a pleasurable sit-uation, obviously." Yes, this R is reluctant, in fact, she fears alien preg-nancy: "I have the idea that I've just ovulated, or I'm about to ovulate or something. And that's connected. I don't want this to happen. But it does." He may be ugly, but this ET is a veritable stud; after he "climbs on top of me," R recalls how "the guy who was looking in my eyes sort of zaps me. There's a sort of jolt of power or something, and all of a sudden I'm really sexually excited. Overwhelmingly, sexually excited. And this guy climbs on top of me, and he's moving and it doesn't make any sense, but it feels like he starts to climax and doesn't finish, or he gets to the point of coming [i.e., ejaculation], but what's the point of that? What's the point of that?"

And R concludes case seven by telling us just what "the point" really was. After the ET had done his loathsome thing, his alien cohorts "just pull him off, and they stick something up [me] where he was [inside her vagina], a metal thing it feels like. And then they're moving [it] very fast. Oh, I know from other times what's about to happen," and she proceeds to describe how the Beings took an egg from her ovaries.[16] Ladies and gentlemen, there you have it: a first-person account of the original ET blind date from hell!

For a change, the victim (R) belonging to case eight is a male, and this unfortunate person was made the reluctant subject of a gender-spe-cific but dreadful "sperm extraction procedure." At the start of the pro-cedure, it appears that he was given Prozac: "I just feel kind of like a baby, a little. Very safe, calm. I get the feeling these [ET] guys are guys who were busy doing something down there." Doped up, he perceives that "they hook up a machine on a tube, with a suction cup end. So now they put it on my penis," and, not surprisingly, "That's where sexual feeling comes." The next stage is perhaps predictable; the conniving ET "touches me somehow. That's when I ejaculate. At least, that's the way I see it. And I think, while one little guy hooks up the machine, the other one pumps my stomach for some reason. That seems to be the procedure." R's emotional reaction to this genital invasion seems odd (to me at least): "When he looks into my eyes, I get this bonding feeling." Now that the terrestrial and the extraterrestrial have achieved their male "bonding," the next step is just a matter of mechanics: "When the machine's all hooked up and ready, he strokes me or something. It feels pleasurable. And I ejaculate into the machine." Once the ETs have their seminal harvest in hand, "Then they take it [the sperm extraction machine] away. They wheel this thing away." The climax to this ejaculative event is more male bonding, the kind with decided homoerotic flavor. In the sentimental finale, the ET "either bends down, or waits a little, and he looks back into my eyes. I think he looks back into my eyes for a short time. Then I get this feeling of 'Till we meet again,' or something [similar]. A real close, ongoing relationship that will continue. Then he gets up and leaves, and I lie there for a while."[17] And one wonders if R, spent, then lit up a cigarette.

Case nine reverts to form, since R is now a female, and this unfortunate was made the reluctant subject of a gender-specific, but equally atrocious, "fetal extraction procedure." This procedure will be of particular interest to the medical community since no account of it appears as yet in the professional literature. As explained by R, "My legs are up, and I'm getting snipped, but internally. Something's snipping. Something burned, burned. A fluid burns me, burns. There's a fluid put on me, and it burns me. It's put inside of me. It burns me. [She cries.]" According to R, the adroit ET clinicians are mostly "pressing and there's snipping." DJ asks R to describe their "instruments," and the description of their devices has it that they are "Very tiny, tiny, long; very long, little, bitty scissors things, but very, very tiny." Since this is an emotionally searing experience for R, once again, "She cries,"and DJ does the manly thing: "I comfort her." Soothed, she returns to describe the surgical procedure: "They're not taking eggs out of me. They're just snipping; it's like they're snipping. They're releasing; they're snipping. It's like they're cutting threads or something." The dénouement to all this snipping and pressing is that "they removed something out of me. They removed, like, a, like, a little baby or something. And they removed the sac or something. They removed the [unintelligible word] but it's tiny, it's real tiny. It's not a baby." Evidently "an embryo," the extracted bit is then "placed in this cylinder, like a silver cylinder. I don't know, tube, silver, probably three inches wide by . . . [gestures with her hand to indicate the length]." The ever inquisitive DJ asks how long this process took, and the reply is "Pretty long. I can't fucking believe this!" (Neither can I, but, admittedly, I wasn't there.) The case ends on a dramatic note when we find that we are in what appears to be a baby factory: "God! It's like they've got other babies there. They're in like drawers in the walls. It's, like, little drawers that pull out, and there's babies, like, little, little somethings in these drawers that pull out, like in a lab or something."[18]

Case ten gives a similarly gripping account of yet another fearsome "fetal extraction." Earthling physicians will be interested to know how such procedures are actually done. It seems that one deftly employs "this long metal thing, like a needle. But I don't know what context [it is in]. I think he stuck that thing inside me, and I thought it was going to hurt." According to R, the point of insertion, or mode of entrance, is "vaginally." But to what purpose? R's "impression is that he is putting something inside of me," and, for some unaccountable reason, left within her was "a little round thing." Overall, R's impression is that "I feel like I'm going to have a baby, and that I want to have a baby." DJ inquires, "Do you think that might be related to seeing that thing put inside you?" R's final response is "I don't know. I don't know why, all of a sudden, I would want to have a baby."[19] So be it: *de gustibus non disputandum*.

Case eleven deals with the same procedure as performed by yet another intrusive ET gynecologist. Once again, "He puts something inside me." When DJ asks, "Do you feel whether this is going in just a little way, or a long way, or . . . ?" the emphatic retort is "It's all the way in." In this case, the preferred operative mode is the mysterious "belly-button procedure." Although never described in any meaningful way, the distinguishing characteristic of the BBP is that "it hurts." In any event, "It feels like they put something in." As was solicitously explained to R by a tall ET, "He said I was implanted." The climax of the implantation narrative is terse, succinct. DJ asks, "What do you say when they say that?" R's reply, "I don't remember saying anything."[20]

Case twelve addresses a typically postmodernist concern, a gender issue, and such as this pertains to the sexual identity of extraterrestrials. As it appears, in short, they have little or none. DJ inquires about the ET infesting yet another bedeviled R, asking her, "Do you think it's female, or does that apply?" The answer has it that "it's more like a she than a he; more like a nonsex than either." Pestered for a more detailed exposition of her perception of latent femininity, the reply is that it is due to "the nonmasculine quality of its personality. Maybe it's the unconditional warmth, or something. I don't know. I don't think men are so unconditional, maybe that's why I'm picking this up." As we are informed, since ETs are nurturing and attentive, they must then be "unconditional" in their emissions of "warmth," that is, as opposed to *conditional*, which notoriously is the way of male terrestrials (or so we are repeatedly told by female earthlings). As R further develops her thesis, the sensitive ET "wants me to look into its eyes, then it links up with me in that caring way, and then it touches my forehead—and I feel quite calm and at peace." Whereas the emotional element is evident, it must not understood in a base sense: "I don't mean physically. I do feel such a strong emotional [lacuna]. Emotional isn't really the right word, but bond. I trust. I, to a degree, [feel] love, I think, because I so much need what is being given [i.e., 'trust' and 'love']."

Ever verging upon voyeurism, DJ insists upon the presence of at least "a slight sexual component." The R in case twelve eagerly seizes upon his suggestion: "Wait a minute; let me get ahold of this. There is, yeah, if you want to say that, willing surrender [which] is sexual; it's there." Next comes a startling revelation, the matter of an askew chronological context. According to DJ's query, "Is this a little bit confusing to a ten-year-old girl?" Whence we learn that this particular "repressed memory" is being opportunely retrieved some twenty-five years later! R's response has it, vaguely, that "it's not a child's emotion. But who analyzes like that? It's just something new." Whatever the emotion was, "It's desirable, good, beautiful, and shocking and traumatic, without having as much intensity as those words imply because I can't analyze it; it's just there." Whatever it was, it did, however, "have a slightly sexual component, which [being ten years old] I don't recognize at the time. But, in another way, it can never leave. It's there, as a perfect experience—and you always try to recapture those, don't you? I don't think I'd want to give it up."[21] And those of us who may have had a "perfect experience" can sympathize with that "beautiful and shocking" conclusion.

Case thirteen returns to the now-familiar motif of ocular enchantment. DJ encourages R to picture the ET as he "comes over and he sort of stares into your eyes. Do you have those same feelings of liking him?" She ("Patti") replies, "Yeah, kind of liking him. Not being really threatened by him. Kind of sympathizing with his purposes, whatever they would be." DJ prods furthers, asking her, "Patti, do any of these emotions seem sort of bordering on romantic feelings, or anything approaching that?" Patti, now definitely with the program, responds, "Yeah, I really do. Because he's definitely the dominating one." Encouraged, DJ goes even further, "Do you feel that you've sort of given yourself over to him?" Dreamily, she responds, "Um-hmmm. Like possession, in a way." DJ returns to his favorite line of inquiry, now suggesting, "Does this have a sort of sexual component to it?" The indicated answer is (of course) "Yeah. In a way. It's not unpleasant, though. It's, like, you are meant to do this."[22] According to my conclusion, as you inquire, so shall ye reap.

Case fourteen brusquely describes a ritual disrobement, a quick strip-tease performed for the delight of ET voyeurs. DJ starts the narrative rolling by asking what the ETs actually told Ms. R to do. Her answer is, quite simply, "I'm told to undress. I don't want to." No doubt picturing the scene in his mind's eye, DJ asks, "Do they help you get undressed then?" Her reply, "They're sort of pulling my clothes." He next queries, "What are you wearing?" and the answer is "A nightgown." DJ then eagerly demands, "And what happens next?" In short, "They force me to take my clothes off, and they make me get on the table."[23] Alas, once the lady gets stripped to the buff, the rest of the torrid tale is left to our imagination.

It only gets better, and case fifteen is really inflammatory. In this case, absolutely nothing is left to our ever laboring imaginations. In fact, had it not been presented to an awestruck public in the guise of "non-fiction," in this case the kind providing a supposedly objective relation of activities perpetrated by otherworldly "aliens," it would instead be better labeled "pornography." Here's how the libretto proceeds in case fifteen, which serves as our last example illustrating David Jacobs's unique contribution to postmodernist culture and literature. As he tells it, as deftly directed by voyeur extraterrestrials, the R starring in case fifteen is instructed to "climb up on him," and "he" is another earthling. As you have already guessed, thereafter the two terrestrial prisoners of the ETs are made to copulate.

Unfortunately, the male half of the human odd couple is a nonpar-ticipant. Responding to DJ's explicit query, "Does he respond genitally?" R recalls, "He doesn't do anything. I don't do anything, after I get there. Then it's, like, they [the ETs] don't even know what's going on, [don't know] what to tell me to do, or something." Queried explicitly by DJ regarding her exact posture in relation to her comatose partner, R explains, "I sit up. I kind of straddle him." The ETs cheer the limp pair on, giving them blow-by-blow instructions; one of them "tells me to kiss him or something. It seems strange; I didn't think they would know that word ['kiss'], or whatever. I don't really want to. Then I think I could fool them, because they don't really know what they're talking about." The directions provided by the ETs get even more explicit: "They told me they wanted me to touch his penis, but I didn't want to. Like, I was sup-posed to scoot down below. You know? Down low on the table. I didn't want to." Following much bantering by the ETs about whether R should actually be made to "scoot down below" (apparently an euphemistic ref-erence to fellatio), the dénouement is decidedly limp.

According to R's befuddled recollection, "Maybe he gets an erection. But he doesn't have any other signs, and I'm just sitting on top of the guy. I don't even know how he could breathe; I'm just sitting on his stomach. But he's not really excited. It seems like I know that he does have an erection, at some point. There's no other part of his body that responds, so it's not even like an erection. Do you know what I mean?" To that query DJ brightly replies, "Now, after he does have an erection, what happens then?" And the less than surprising answer is that he ejaculates. Undaunted, DJ presses on, regardless, "After he ejaculates, what happens directly after that, within a few seconds?" According to R, "I have the black feeling ['Mindscan?' Jacobs wonders to himself]. It seems like I get kind of stimu-lated for the first time. I wasn't before. But then I feel. I don't know. It's not, like, he just kind of winds down. I don't remember much. . . . I get a little worried, because I think, God, I might get pregnant by this guy. I remember thinking that." DJ's final question is "Where were you in your [menstrual] cycle?" and the dismal final reply is "Right in the middle."[24]

And so on and so forth. For one kind of case-specific interpretation for each one of these often lurid banalities, the reader is directed to Dr. Jacobs's books. As you might expect, he takes all this very seriously, and he really *cares* about these wretched sufferers and their truly awful mis-adventures. Besides being a very *simpático* kind of guy, Dr. Jacobs is unquestionably sincere, very much so. However, for a probably superior brand of hermeneutics, work out your own earthbound interpretations for each one of these fifteen carefully transcribed narratives (but if you can't, see chapters 11 and 14). The same goes for Dr. Mack, and the thir-teen case studies recounted in his *Abduction: Human Encounters with Aliens*, from which I will cull three examples. Either way, these are *the* historical records, actual transcripts, which are constantly being cited as constituting valid evidence for abduction and human encounters with aliens. Alas, there isn't much else. This is the sworn testimony serving to certify such anomalous experiences as being *real*, further specifying that these garbled and artificially retrieved memories specifically recall the facts of genuine alien visitations inflicted upon these unquestionably troubled earthling respondents. Since they say (with just a little help from Dr. Jacobs) that it *really* happened, then it did—of course. *Quod erat demonstrandum.*

MORE OF THE SAME: THE HOPKINS AND MACK TRANSCRIPTS

David Jacobs is not the only indefatigable archivist of the extraterrestrials and their typically egregious close encounters with typically impotent earthlings. There are several of these story collectors and they, too, often succeed in presenting their epistles to the people in the canonical commercial paperback format. The other, perhaps more famed (for being seen more frequently on TV), entrepreneur of ET encounters and alien-abduction apocrypha is Budd Hopkins, also acknowledged to be the venerable pioneer in gathering such accounts. By his own admission, he had been "fascinated by UFOs since 1964." Like Jacobs, Hopkins also conforms to a certain literary strategy, wherein, as Terry Matheson shows, he resorts to "unsupported speculations as a most successful strategy," complemented by "the same array of predictable rhetorical devices[:] announcement of the author's skepticism, arguments from consistency, glowing assessments of the abductees," and so on.[25] In Philip Klass's admittedly biased opinion, this is the fellow who created a "Hopkins Syndrome": "While Hopkins was not the first to discover 'covert UFO-abductions,' in my opinion he has become the 'Typhoid Mary' of this tragic malaise."[26] For a more neutral approach, we must turn to journalist C. D. B. Bryan's quick biosketch:

> Hopkins is the dean of the UFO abduction investigators, with about fifteen hundred [!!] cases to his credit. He is the author of *Missing Time* (1981) and *Intruders: The Incredible Visitations at Copley Woods* (1987); *Intruders* has just been made into a two-part television miniseries broadcast by CBS the month before [i.e., in May 1992]. He is also a talented painter and sculptor, whose works are part of the permanent collections of the Whitney, the Guggenheim, the Hirshhorn, the Brooklyn Museum, and the Museum of Modern Art. Hopkins is a tall, gentle, silver-haired man with expressive features; his topic today is "Acquisition"—how the aliens acquire their abductees. But before he gets into that, he suggests that UFO abductions may be more common [and more cinematic] than UFO sightings and that they are "the most portentous phenomenon science has yet to face"—a pronouncement P. T. Barnum himself would have been proud to have produced.[27]

Now we must read some of the momentous Hopkins transcripts. He introduces his 1981 epic *Intruders* with a meretricious justification for what follows, tales which some readers might just find the sort of thing which, he admits, "will almost certainly strain your credulity to the breaking point." Still, says Hopkins, there is a significant historical precedent, the kind that puts our compliant acceptance for what ensues within an appropriate postmodernist mode of political correctness: "One historical example of our inability to comprehend and believe a chilling truth is [the fact] that by the end of 1943, when a sizable portion of the world's population had read or been told of Hitler's systematic liquidation of the Jewish people, this ongoing horror was simply not believed."[28] So, not believing what follows is just like complacently allowing for a future Holocaust, with ETs supplanting Nazis. Okay, I'm convinced; how about you? But you might demur, noting that the historical evidence for the Holocaust (*Shoah*) is both abundant and undeniable, also adding (a bit perversely) that only the reverse holds true for the ubiquitous alien abduction legend.

Since the Hopkins transcripts are formatted so much like the Jacobs transcripts, both being extruded under hypnosis, we may follow the same prosaic layout: "DJ" (now standing for Delirium Jockey) is answered by "R" (It *Really* Happened to Me). Rather than referring to "cases," these otherworldly transactions are referred to as successive "episodes," and four of these extraterrestrial epiphanies will surely suffice.

Episode one begins with a profound question posed by DJ, namely, "What do you watch on TV?" The earth-shaking answer is "*Bob Newhart Show*. Then *Mary Tyler Moore*. Reruns." Actually, this information is useful to have in hand; it directly informs us about the intellectual interests and conceptual capacities of the kind of people who are most susceptible to alien infestation. In short, their lives are conceived of, and are then enacted as "reruns." In this instance, and following hours of comedic reruns, R ("Kathie"), slumped in a funk on a couch, describes how she feels: "Tired. And heavy. And tender. I feel like someone's touching me. My eyes are shut. I'm still on the couch. It's really nice, in a way. Just when I first started to feel it, I jumped, but I never opened my eyes. And after a moment, I wasn't afraid anymore. It's real nice." DJ helpfully defines this "touching" as being more like "a caress," and R agrees that it goes "Just on and on. Feels good. My face: stroking my face and my shoulder, real gentle. Real tender. And they rub, somebody [an ET] rubs the small of my back, real easy." Further pressed by DJ for details, we find that she feels "kinda funny, but not bad. Peaceful, but tingly all over. Real warm and nice. Real tingly. Just Okay. My legs feel funny. I feel like I'm being pulled apart. But it doesn't hurt."[29]

The action warms up a bit in episode two, when R begins to "feel some poking; thumping on my chest, under my left breast. It's kind of like somebody thumped you. Hmmm. I'm asleep, but I can't think. I think I'm asleep; I feel fine. It's real tingly." These are the kind of ETs who go for the pectorals. According to R's recollection, as much olfactory as optical, "Now somebody poked me under my left breast. This time my right breast and my ribs, by my heart. I can smell burning matches again. It smells like burning matches and it stinks." Ignoring the sulfuric stink, DJ gets to the meat of things, "Did they poke you through your nightgown?" As R responds, "I don't think I have any clothes on. I don't know. I don't feel any [on me]. I feel cold. They're doing something with my chest." Although she cannot tell DJ just who these tactile folks are, she knows it is happening: "Whoever's touching me; I feel touching. I feel cold touches on both sides of my chest, underneath my breasts and alongside of them, and fingers or something cold touching me."[30]

In episode three we learn that all this icy-fingered cuddling "makes my stomach hurt." Moreover, "I just can't move, and it feels like I'm being squeezed, and I just don't want it. It feels like my legs are being pulled off my body, from the waist down." Additionally, "I'm laying down, but my legs are floating. I feel like I'm being pulled, really hard. And I just, I don't like it." And for poor R (Kathie) it only gets worse: "I'm hot from the waist down, and cold from the waist up, and my [trails off]. I feel like I have [trails off]. I feel like I'm getting one of those gyno- [trails off]. [One of] those [unintelligible, but obviously one of those recurrent gynecological exams]. The cramps [are] really bad." DJ asks about the *locus classicus* of her inner turmoil, and she states that it is "where my uterus is, down low, like I'm going to have my period. It's hard; it hurts. It's like a toothache. [There's] a lotta pressure. Oh! Oh, it feels like someone's pushing on me real hard, wriggling and pushing, right in there. Ooh!" In fact, what is doing all this wriggling is "a finger," and "It feels like it's in me." Naturally, DJ has to ask where it has been inserted, namely, "In your vagina, or where?" and the reply is "No. In my [trails off] real low. Right above my bladder and stuff. Just right in there. It feels real tight. I can't move." In sum, her apparently ET-provoked principal symptom is "Kinda burning sensation from the waist down. Can't move."[31]

In episode four, providing the essential dénouement, the symptomology becomes more pronounced: "I can't move my legs. I feel half numb. I can feel something big, too big, but it doesn't hurt." Next a botanical metaphor is added to the litany of distress: "I feel like a flower opened up. It doesn't hurt. It doesn't hurt. No, not at all. I'm just [trails off]. It's too weird; it feels wide open. Too much." Confronted by such anatomical blooming, DJ asks, just as one should, "What part of your body feels wide open?" The perhaps expected riposte is "All my female stuff. It doesn't hurt. I can feel it; but I can't feel pain. It feels real. It feels good, in a way. It's strange." Like DJ David Jacobs, DJ Budd Hopkins knows how to pose a sensational question; in this instance he asks, "Is there any sensation at your clitoris, that you're being touched there in any way?" She states, "Not there." He persists, "More outside, or more inside, or where?" She responds, "More inside." DJ now asks, "Do you feel like there's anything in you?" There is indeed; in fact, it is "Something very large." Questioned as to whether this outsized object is "a part of a person, or an instrument," R's reply is less than enlightening: "I don't know."

Undaunted, DJ Hopkins does know how to track down a sensation, however fugitive; as he now queries, "Do you feel it way up inside you, or down near the mouth of your vagina, or where?" Accordingly, now R concurs; indeed, it is "All through it [the vaginal tract]. Everything." On a roll, Hopkins aims another shot at her groin: "Kathie, you've had pelvic examinations. Is it like that? Or is it different? Or is it partly alike and partly different?" So directed, her response goes where it had just been led: "Sort of like when the doctor puts the thing in [the vagina] and spreads it real far. Only a lot wider. A lot more." DJ Hopkins keeps pushing his questioning in the pelvic direction: "Kathie, would you describe the feeling as sexual feeling, the way you feel when you're touched in a nice way, sexually? Or just more neutral, the way you might feel when you're getting your shoulders rubbed? Is there any way you can describe your feelings?" Her bland response is that the "feelings" are "Slow. Gentle-like." Ever pushy, Hopkins's last query is "Tell me what's happening, Kathie." And her final response is an emphatic "No!"[32] Indeed, enough *is* enough.

Imagine this: the Budd Hopkins text goes on and on like this, and for 318 pages (including the endnotes). And just think, the four-part episodic adventure just quoted had been presented to the gullible public as constituting a real encounter with aliens, those pesky ETs. On the other hand, and as an earthling gynecologist might now say, "Hmm, sounds to me more like a classic case of menopausal hot flashes." Regarding this "talented painter and sculptor, whose works are part of the permanent collections of the Whitney, the Guggenheim, the Hirshhorn, the Brooklyn Museum, and the Museum of Modern Art," the art historian must make a professional observation. Before I found myself coping with extraterrestrial portraiture, I had never heard of Budd Hopkins, and presently I can find no references to him in the standard literature dealing with the New York art scene. Perhaps the turn to literary (versus plastic) creativity, Hopkins's best-selling alien-abduction oeuvre, represents a brilliant midlife career move.

The other towering authority in the alien-abduction business is, of course, Dr. John E. Mack, who, he says, "was introduced to the abduction phenomenon in January 1990 by Budd Hopkins," and he also cites with appreciation the "pioneering" archival work of David Jacobs. Naturally, he hews to the same literary conventions (and fallacies) as do his equally well-paid predecessors.[33] However, Mack's credentials to look into people's skulls for anomalous experiences are much better than the other two; he is, after all, a Pulitzer Prize–winning author, a properly credentialed psychiatrist (M.D.), and a tenured staff member of the medical faculty at Harvard University. Nonetheless, his criteria seem (to me, at least) not particularly onerous: "Taking seriously an observation by an abductee is [judging] whether what has been reported was *felt* to be real by the experiencer and was communicated sincerely." Perhaps his methodology is also a bit slack: "The experiencer may *at first* call what is happening a dream. But careful questioning [by Mack] will reveal that the experiencer has *not* fallen asleep at all. . . . The investigator [Mack] seems to play an important part in enabling the abductee to bring forth and realize the [assigned] significance of the [opportunely retrieved] information." (I understand that "careful questioning," albeit applied less gently, was also a specialty of the KGB and Gestapo.) Here is how Mack gets his subjects: "A possible abductee comes to see me, either referred through the UFO network . . . or self-referred upon learning of my work through the media." Above all, Mack is impressed by the "*consistency* of reports conveyed with extreme intensity of feeling by sincere individuals of sound mind." Mack's conclusion: "No plausible alternative explanation for the reports of abductions experiences, which are sometimes corroborated by physical evidence, has been discovered."[34]

Although I have myself not yet seen any *credible* accounts of that ever-elusive corroboratory physical evidence, I have found the "plausible alternative explanation" which Dr. Mack seems to have missed. It is short and definitely to the point. According to Michael Shermer:

> We can expect consistencies in the stories since so many of the abductees go to the same hypnotist[s], read the same alien encounter books, watch the same science fiction movies, and in many cases even know one another and belong to "encounter" groups (in both senses of the word). Given the shared mental states and social contexts, it would be surprising if there was not a ["consistent"] core set of characteristics of the abduction experience shared by the abductees. And what are we to do with the shared *absence* of convincing physical evidence?[35]

Journalist C. D. B. Bryan provides us with a quick verbal portrait of UFOlogist Mack in 1992, when he was sixty-three years old, and already cruelly dubbed "the media's latest official 'Harvard crazy': Timothy Leary *cum* Wilhelm Reich":

Mack has the stooped posture of a tall, thin academician whose failing eyesight has left him permanently bent from having spent so much time straining to decipher his handwritten lecture notes. Mack's visage is furrowed and darkened by the anguish of contemplating nuclear holocausts, his studies of suicide—*real* and, for his participation in a conference on people who believe they have been abducted by alien crews from UFOs, perhaps *academic*—along with the inevitable wounds and distresses that have surfaced in forty years of psychiatric practice. He runs his long, thin fingers through his thick, dark hair and says, "Welcome to this extraordinary event!" Mack at first speaks too fast to allow accurate transcription. . . . Mack remarks upon the "politics of mindset," "the politics of ontology." He has a way of answering one question with another: "Does the alien abduction phenomenon require that we create a new scientific paradigm? Is consciousness, and all that consciousness perceives, but itself the play of some divine or cosmic technology?" He lets these questions hang in the air and sits down.[36]

Mack brings a new, "divine or cosmic" wrinkle to the ET enterprise initially shaped by Hopkins and Jacobs. He also has a profound sense of mission: "This work has led me to challenge the prevailing worldview." In short (and I will return to consider his spiritual agenda in chapter 11), "I devote more attention [than does the typical UFOlogist] to the transformational and spiritual growth aspects of the abduction experience. . . . I believe that this [positive] feature of the phenomenon has either been neglected or has been viewed as incompatible with the traumatic dimension of an abduction as it has most often been described." Among putative positive signs of "personal growth and transformation" purportedly arising from one's very close encounters with an extraterrestrial, Mack cites "ego death" (versus the merely corporeal sort); the wholesome fact that "abductees sometimes liken the alien beings to angels, or other 'light beings' (including the 'grays')"; that the self-described abductees "experience themselves as returning to their cosmic source or 'home,' an inexpressibly beautiful realm beyond"; that they eagerly participate in "past life experiences"; that they report "separateness of consciousness"; that their alien encounters "lead abductees to open up to other realities beyond space/time"; and so forth.[37]

In spite of all this heavy New Age speculation, Mack also gives just what the readers of this kind of sensationalist literature really want: sensational details. I will now provide you with three examples of this exciting stuff, so enjoining the reader to go out and purchase Mack's paperback—then you can savor the provocative rest at your leisure. Given his more accomplished literary style, alas, we must depart from our standard format, "DJ" (Doctor in Jeopardy) as answered by "R" (Ready to Respond). Either way, here is exactly how Mack tells his more titillating tales. We only need quote from three examples of these prose narratives, and these we'll call "cases."

In case one, the reluctant heroine is Jerry. According to Mack's straightforward account, when the aliens stripped off her pajamas, not surprisingly, Jerry felt embarrassed. As she eloquently declared later, "It's, like, they think they're doctors or something. I don't think they're doctors." That was a sound conclusion; Mack is a doctor. Nonetheless, when lying on her back, Jerry recalled that she then felt somehow more "relaxed" and less afraid. Then one of the ETs put his hands over her eyes. Next he pressed something, which Jerry said "looks like a tube," through the wall of her abdomen above the umbilicus. With the alien instrument still deep within her earthling abdomen, the ET took his hands away from her eyes. Inexplicably, now Jerry felt more relaxed, also sleepy. Next, she noted that one of her alien oppressors was holding a shiny, horseshoe-shaped object with a handle on it. At this point, some other ETs bent her knees upward and apart. Crying, she told Mack, "He's going to cover my eyes again. Why is he doing this? I don't think I want to know. I don't want to know what they did." She threatened the ETs that she would tell her mother. Nonplused, they said that she wouldn't. As Jerry claimed, "She [Mom] wouldn't let them do this if she was here." But the ETs insisted that she would not tell Mom because she, Jerry, would not remember her close encounter. They were wrong; thanks to hypnosis, she did "remember" and, thanks to Dr. Mack, we all got to read about it.

At this point, Mack asked her if it was "Okay for you to remember now?" She said that it was, but exclaimed, "It's not fair!" Mack of course, agreed with this point. He was also sympathetic to her conjecture that the dastardly ETs "tried to make me think it was just a nightmare. What do they think, I'm just an animal or something?" Indeed, she was treated in a beastly manner, and Jerry's fear mounted once again as she felt "pressure inside her vagina." Then she cried and moaned, sobbing, "I just want my mom," as she felt "something round inside," a "cramped and pinched feeling." "Why are they doing this?" Jerry cried out. "I'm not going to let them do this again!" Mack, being a sensitive guy, "encouraged her to express her emotions." Accordingly, she became even more histrionic: "Why won't this end? Stop it!!" she cried. Mack takes Jerry on her word, accepting in good faith that, in truth, "something had been placed deep within her body, beyond the vagina, perhaps through the cervix."[38] Also implicit is Mack's consistent belief that the vagina stuffers were none other than ETs.

The hero of case two is a lad named Peter. His adventures had a properly exotic setting: Hawaii. Peripatetic Peter was "there to learn about the future," he said (and which revelation should have told Mack straight away that his patient was a space cadet). As he recounted his tale to Dr. Mack, Peter said he saw three "beings" (that is, ETs). The first one, placed directly in front of him, had a "really big forehead" and seemed older than the other two. The one on the left was an alien female. The third being, a male, was an alien as well. The ET's outsized forehead was knotted with a kind of split in the center. Peter assured Mack that "he's the same one that oversaw all the operations. I feel like he's smarter; I mean, he's definitely the boss." The female being was said by Peter to be "his teacher": "She's going to be my guardian, or something. She's gonna watch for me. She's, there's something that's going to transpire." Then Peter arrived at a sudden awareness of forthcoming alien nastiness. As he then exclaimed, "Oh, my God . . . we're gonna *fuck*!" According to Mack's breathless commentary, "Fear, not desire, filled Peter at this point." As Peter himself exclaimed fearfully, "I'm going to breed with her. I'm getting that *that* [i.e., 'breeding'] is what this was all about." All of this data was communicated to him mainly by the old one, whom Peter also called "Mr. Know-It-All" and "Bubblehead." "I didn't want to know this," he recalled. "It just kind of blew me away."

As he told Dr. Mack, Peter was shocked to be told that the babies he saw upon entering the spaceship were *his* "alien or hybrid babies." He concluded that his mission was to be "breeding with aliens. That's what my sperm has been doing." As described in Mack's sizzling prose, "Peter's fear grew again, as he considered the implications of what he was discovering. He realized that he had repeatedly made love with an alien female." Peter's confessional statement also sizzles, like an overdone steak: "It feels like she's my real wife; I want to say on a soul level. She's the person that I'm really connected to, and she's the one I'm going to be there with, or be with, or something." Once again, this vital information was, or so we are told, communicated to Peter by "Bubblehead" and the alien woman herself. However dubious to a skeptic like me, Peter felt its "truth" with great conviction; so did Mack.

According to Dr. Mack, "as he spoke of this, Peter experienced his 'consciousness being separated from my physical body, like up here, looking down at myself sitting at this table.' This was all becoming 'too much' for Peter." It is also just a bit too much for me, as is Peter's next outburst, "It's not even about making love or sex," but "*breeding* with her." Peter's anguished declamation continues, "Oh, God, John; my hunch is that this woman is a human also, and that they've been taking her eggs and my semen and putting them together and breeding them up there." As Peter finally stated to Mack, "I don't think I can put into words the depth of how shocking, about how much I've been taken aback by what I just saw. The most frightening thought for me is that she may be an alien and I'm seeing her as a human—and that *I'm making love with an alien!*"[39] This final trope is scarcely surprising; as I recall, during the 1950s a popular line of films shown at drive-in theaters was called something like *I Made Love to An Alien*.

In case three, once again, the angst-ridden, ET-bedeviled heroine is the ever-intrepid Jerry. By putting her under hypnosis—or "relaxation," as Mack calls it—Jerry was actually made to believe that "an embryo was placed inside her body." Jerry believed that this particular implantation episode was relatively brief: "Those are the quick ones." She was given information by the aliens showing how they take DNA from a human male, and the ETs combine it with an egg. After combining the male and female "germ substance," she said, "the aliens alter the embryo in some way, perhaps adding a genetic principle of their own." This altered embryo is then reinserted into the female body, for "gestation." Reprising the account of her previous abduction experience (case one), again Jerry described how the ETs separated her legs "like in a regular gynecologist's office," but, because she had been paralyzed by an alien downer, no stirrups were needed. After assuming the supine position, next a long tube was inserted in her vagina and she felt "a pinch." Being a certified veteran of such exotic close encounters, she knew this was one of the times that an embryo had been deftly inserted into her, "because I've been through this before and I recognize the routine." The ET leader had taken an embryo out of one of the drawers in a handy cabinet and brought it over to her. As she explains, "The other way" (when they remove a fetus from her body) is "worse than putting it in," for then she feels painful cramping.

Jerry expounded "intense embarrassment" as she told Mack the gruesome details. The leader pushed her legs into a "pulled-up-and-apart" position to "check me, and he brings a light, this really bright light, and I'm thinking: What are they going to do? I don't like this. It's just, really, it's okay to, you know, poke at me and everything, but I don't like that. That's my private area [i.e., genital parts], and I don't think they should be doing anything there, and [once again, *faute de mieux*] I don't think my mom would like that." At first, they were "just looking" inside her vagina, but then "they put something in there," that was "kinda like when I get older, the gynecologist, you know, kinda like that." This procedure was painful, and Jerry, a creature of habit, screamed in terror for her mother. But "that doesn't stop 'em." It was "over real quick," and after all this looking and "checking," Mack summarizes the finale of the story, "The being who performed it looked up to the leader and said 'no,' or gave some sort of negative response to a question of his. Jerry interpreted this [negative response] to mean she was not yet ready for their reproductive procedures." According to Dr. Mack's professional conclusion, "This vaginal examination seemed to Jerry to be part of an overall 'checking' the beings did."[40] Such breathtaking accounts also clearly call for some "checking," and the place to start is the reporter's brain.

Imagine this: the John Mack text goes on and on like this, 455 pages of it, including an extensive bibliography. Although I may be accused of ungentlemanly behavior, I would like to mention a couple of details, quantifiable facts, not included in Mack's best-seller for they only surfaced soon after its publication. For his high-minded literary endeavor in composing his book *Abduction*, we saw how Dr. Mack had received an advance payment of $250,000 from his publisher, Scribner's (and the numbers corresponding to his subsequent royalty payments are not yet made public).[41] I wish briefly to put this not inconsiderable sum into some sort of professional perspective. Put simply, my own experience in publishing several scholarly books with reputable university presses is this: I have been lucky to get back $2,000 in royalties, *in toto*. After factoring in my previous expenses (travel, materials), and by making a guesstimate of the hours I had actually devoted to researching and writing each book manuscript, it appears that my compensation—as wages per hour—works out to a mind-boggling figure of *minus* $2.50. The conclusion to be drawn inevitably from one's comparative study is this: since mature scholarship in the humanities pays far less than flipping burgers at McDonald's (in effect, you get no pay at all), then a complete career shift (180 degrees) to alien-abduction research is clearly indicated. It will only work, however, if said "research" is presented to a commercial publisher and opportunely labeled as representing "nonfiction"—and you must never admit the possibility (explored later in chapters 11 and 14) that your "experiencers" are only experiencing "fantasy proneness."[42] Were you to own up to that possibility, two results can be expected: (1) your colleagues will think you are a fool, or (2) your publisher will take back his $250,000.

Here is another revelation later surfacing about Dr. Mack's unquestionably earnest labors with his pathetic "experiencers." *Time* magazine assigned an investigative reporter, James Willworth, to look into Mack's claims. As was later reported (*Time*, April 25, 1994), one of Mack's abductees, Donna Bassett, was actually a researcher who had successfully "infiltrated" herself into his support group. (But I think that is disgraceful behavior. Don't you?) In the event, by carefully reading the abundant pop literature dealing with UFO abductions, Ms. Bassett was enabled to "recall under hypnosis" her very own childhood experiences with an ET playmate. As she got more proficient, at one of the later hypnotic sessions, which took place in a bedroom of Mack's house, Bassett told the good doctor how she "recalled" being lifted up into a flying saucer. This picturesque incident, she stated, took place in 1962, during the Cuban missile crisis. Once beamed up into the UFO, she (as she told Mack) saw President Kennedy and Premier Krushchev. Since the Russian leader was crying from chagrin, Bassett (as she told Mack) sat in his lap, put her arms around his neck and gave him a warm hug, reassuring him that the dreadful crisis would be soon resolved and the world would be a better place for it. According to *Time*, "Hearing her tale, Mack became so excited that he leaned on the bed too heavily, and it collapsed."[43] Crash! Sorry, John; facts are facts, and it is all now a matter of public record.

EASTER BUNNY AND TOOTH FAIRY; UFO HISTORIAN AND ET ARCHIVIST DAVID JACOBS

Since perhaps you were about to ask "Why bother?" I must repeat the major point I made before laboriously presenting all of these carefully transcribed "eyewitness reports." Don't forget: Dr. Mack told all potential skeptics that we *have "to immerse [our]selves in the primary data of* this field, namely the experiences of those who have undergone the abduction encounters, and draw [our] own conclusions about what is taking place here."[44] Okay, we've done that. My main reason (i.e., "Why bother?"), however, is to point out that, again and in short, *this is it*. What you have just read—and in case you are still with us, have actually bothered to get this far—represents the UFOlogists' *evidence*, what passes for *proof* that *anything* at all *really* happened. However dire their predictions, typically so, the case made by UFOlogists for the credibility belonging to their fearful argument rests wholly on this kind of eyewitness testimony. All the *evidence* and/or *proof* presented by UFOlogists attesting to the very authenticity of all those diverse reports of dreadfully close human encounters with aliens and extraterrestrials, intelligent creatures from outer space, essentially stands—or falls—on the basis of what was just quoted. That is why it had to be presented to you in detail, with all of its incoherent, mostly tiresome, anecdotal minutiae.

As the extraterrestrial *aficionado* will now no doubt accuse this scholarly district attorney: Foul play! You, sir, have quoted these statements out of context. But you, dear reader, can test the validity of that forthcoming accusation for yourself: purchase all those ubiquitous paperbacks, and you, too, can read all about it—original context *and* dire conclusions—all by yourself, at your leisure. However, be forewarned: it's an irksome experience (and so is root-canal work). I do however confess to selectivity, which may seem like "decontextualization" to purist ET advocates. Admittedly, I did opt for the more sensational bits, and I now leave the more boring bits (*der langweiligere Scheiß*), constituting the greater majority, for your close inspection, at your leisure (whenever).

Using similar methodology and evidence, mostly anecdotal, I shall now *prove* for you the physical reality of three mythic figures in American culture with whom, of course, you are also quite familiar. My own empirical experience—with, however, accompanying physical evidence (available upon request)—has *proven* the existence of (a) Santa Claus, (b) the Easter Bunny, and (c) the Tooth Fairy. In this case, clearly I am not "quoting out of context."

As a child, on the morning of each and every December 25, I would find—also "experience"—a bulging red sock, white-topped, pinned up alongside the fireplace that had been filled with a variety of goodies for "Master Jackie" (me). Who was the corporeal agent of such largesse? According to a card in an envelope (Hallmark©—but still written proof!), the potlatch provider was—so signed—"Santa Claus." Case one closed. In the springtime, on a fixed date, my cousins and I would prowl the greensward and encounter *eggs*, neatly painted and then internally *hard boiled* by an extraterrestrial caloric-energy source. Inscriptions found in the vicinity named the disguised ET ovum agent as "Easter Bunny"—and the disguise element is obvious even to a diehard skeptic: rabbits don't lay chicken eggs! Case two closed. A bit later, when one's dental tribulations began, after loosing either molar or fang, I would deposit the same under my rumpled pillow and, lo and behold, in the morning I would find a "quarter" (a monetary unit used at the time) magically substituted for the gory dontological relic! According to a card in an envelope (written proof!), the money-eyed messenger was—so signed—"The Tooth Fairy." Case three closed.

However, since the Jacobs transcripts constitute such invaluable evidence, especially for UFOlogists, the historian must place this especially indefatigable archivist in his own biohistorical context. In short, Dr. Jacobs was not always such a committed True Believer; he used to be a scholar, a conscientious historian of American popular culture and its characteristic mental manipulations. Back in 1982 (or thereabouts), he wrote an essay on the UFO experience for an anthology of scholarly studies that was first published in 1983. The title of this collection, *The

Occult in America, indicates exactly where Jacobs *then* thought such apocrypha really fit best. As he then pointed out, and this observation still holds true decades later, "The evidence for the existence—to say nothing of the origin—of the [extraterrestrial] phenomenon was [and still is wholly] anecdotal . . . no one had [or has since] produced artifacts." But I can produce artifacts proving the existence of (a) Santa Claus, (b) the Easter Bunny, and (c) the Tooth Fairy.

For Jacobs, that is, back in 1982, the whole UFO argument was fatally flawed by "its lack of verifiability, lack of predictability, and the poor quality of anecdotal data, [all] inappropriate for scientific scrutiny." As was already recognized by many other skeptics back in 1982, Jacobs stated that the phenomenon was largely "a function of hypnosis and had no basis in external objective reality." Such unsubstantiated, literally otherworldly, explanations then clearly put the extraterrestrial explanation, as he put it, squarely "into the realm of the occult," a kingdom of unchecked subjectivity where "rational explanations and methodology were less necessary." Then as now, "extraordinary claims required extraordinary evidence, and the UFO proponents did not [and still do not] have it."[45] But, what the hell, isn't everybody entitled to a change of heart?

Given my job title, *art* historian, my professionally particularized question is this: What are the identifiable sources and provenance of the currently canonical ET icon (fig. 1)? Besides the vivid verbal descriptions so recently provided by all those unfortunate earthling "abductees," what is the real (art) historical pedigree of extraterrestrial portraiture? Is its source really "outer space" (i.e., *theographos typos*), such as is assumed by all those UFOlogists who so intently (and often profitably) study the popular phenomenon, or does this portraiture instead represent a wholly earth-born iconography, such as this scholarly art historian means to prove, and specifically date? More important—and regardless of what it is actually labeled—what is the larger significance of all this apocryphal portraiture?

As it turns out, the real context is our wholly mundane world of inchoate spiritual longings, mass culture, visual celebrity, and (especially) commercial exploitation. Albeit never invested with extraterrestrial significance, a useful case in point by which to illustrate these hidden operations is provided (in the next chapter) by the thoroughly mundane, but nonetheless wholly apocryphal portraiture of Betty Crocker. This model pop cultural exemplar illustrates the origins of, and some novel functions applied to iconic portraiture of celebrity "personalities" in our age of mass-produced imagery. And that completely commercialized topic, as you will soon see to your further surprise, also logically embraces the specific pictorial image of Jesus Christ that is likely most familiar to you (which is *not* fig. 2).

NOTES

1. Mark Rodeghier, as quoted in C. D. B. Bryan, *Close Encounters of the Fourth Kind: Alien Abduction, UFOs, and the Conference at M.I.T.* (New York: Knopf, 1995), p. 13.

2. Philip J. Klass, *UFO-Abductions: A Dangerous Game* (Amherst, N.Y.: Prometheus Books, 1989), pp. 6, 163.

3. For this figure, see *Entertainment Weekly*, 5 February 1999.

4. See N. Redfern, *The FBI Files: The FBI's UFO Top Secrets Exposed* (London: Pocket Books, 1998).

5. Terry Matheson, *Alien Abductions: Creating a Modern Phenomenon* (Amherst, N.Y.: Prometheus Books, 1998), pp. 13–14, 31, 38, 72, 117–18, 127, 132, 164, 223, 243.

6. Jacques Vallée, *Anatomy of a Phenomenon: UFOs in Space—A Scientific Appraisal* (1965; reprint, New York: Ballantine, 1972), pp. 134–35.

7. Thomas E. Bullard, *UFO Abductions: The Measure of a Mystery*, vol. 1, *Comparative Study of Abduction Reports* (Bloomington, Ind.: Fund for UFO Research, 1987), pp. 48ff.

8. Bryan, *Close Encounters of the Fourth Kind*, p. 17.

9. For Jacobs's literary tactics and conventions, see Matheson, *Alien Abductions*, pp. 229–49.

10. David M. Jacobs, *Secret Life: First-Hand Documented Accounts of UFO Abductions* (New York: Fireside, 1993), pp. 233–36; Jacobs here gives the name of this anorexic respondent, likewise those belonging to nearly all the rest to be quoted here. (But I won't bother.)

11. Ibid., pp. 229–30.

12. Ibid., p. 245: "Name omitted upon request, 1970."

13. Ibid., pp. 263–65.

14. Ibid., pp. 265–68.

15. Ibid., pp. 209–10.

16. Ibid., pp. 202–205.

17. Ibid., p. 123.

18. Ibid., pp. 120–22.

19. Ibid., pp. 113–14.

20. Ibid., pp. 111–12.

21. Ibid., pp. 105–106.

22. Ibid., pp. 103–104.

23. Ibid., p. 90.

24. Ibid., pp. 198–202 (there is no mention of any pregnancy resulting from this oh-so-very close encounter).

25. For Hopkins's literary tactics and conventions, see Matheson, *Alien Abductions*, pp. 131–59.

26. Klass, *UFO-Abductions*, p. 215, with extensive references to Hopkins and his indefatigable abductive mission given in chapters 7–9, 17.

27. Bryan, *Close Encounters of the Fourth Kind*, p. 15.

28. Budd Hopkins, *Intruders: The Incredible Visitations at Copley Woods* (New York: Ballantine, 1988), p. xi.

29. Ibid., pp. 169–70 (I have here removed Hopkins's melodramatic stage-directions, e.g., "moans," "pauses," "sighs," and so on).

30. Ibid., pp. 96–97.

31. Ibid., pp. 162–63.

32. Ibid., pp. 171–73 (*genug noch*).

33. For Mack's literary tactics and conventions, and his *fallacies*, see Matheson, *Alien Abductions*, pp. 251–78.

34. John Mack, *Abduction: Human Encounters with Aliens* (New York: Scribner's, 1994), pp. ix, 1, 3, 8, 18, 25 (emphasis mine); see also pp. 28–29 for more of Mack's emphasis on the "consistency" argument.

35. Michael Shermer, *Why People Believe Weird Things: Pseudoscience, Superstition, and Other Confusions of Our Time* (New York: Freeman, 1997), p. 97.

36. Bryan, *Close Encounters of the Fourth Kind*, pp. 11–12, 417.

37. Mack, *Abduction*, pp. 16, 31, 33–34.

38. Ibid., p. 114.

39. Ibid, pp. 313–14.

40. Ibid., pp. 120, 124–25.

41. A smaller figure (a mere $200,000) is given by Philip Klass, in Kendrick Frazer, ed., *The UFO Invasion: The Roswell Incident, Alien Abductions, and Government Coverups* (Amherst, N.Y.: Prometheus Books, 1997), p. 209.

42. See Joe Nickell, "A Study of Fantasy Proneness in the Thirteen Cases of Alleged Encounters in John Mack's *Abduction*," in ibid., pp. 237–44.

43. *Time*, as quoted in ibid., pp. 235–36, 247.

44. Mack, *Abduction*, pp. 435–36.

45. David Jacobs, "UFOs and the Search for Scientific Legitimacy," in *The Occult in America: New Historical Perspectives*, ed. H. Kerr and C. L. Crow (Urbana: Illinois University Press, 1986), pp. 218–31.

Chapter 3

Betty Crocker
An Art-Historical Inquest

THE INVENTION OF BETTY CROCKER

Betty Crocker represents a characteristic example of modernist apocryphal portraiture—so too do the plentiful, and thoroughly conventionalized, depictions coming slightly later that portray the extraterrestrials lurking among us (figs. 1, 4, 5, 15–22). Even though they do admittedly serve somewhat different cultural purposes, a revelation of the pertinent material contexts informing the unquestionably terrestrial invention of the Betty portraiture allows for a more objective examination of the historical functions of equally modernist and apocryphal depictions of extraterrestrial biological entities (EBEs).

As you may know, Betty Crocker has accomplished much in her amazingly active professional life, being especially famed as the authoress of innumerable mass-circulation how-to cookbooks. Alas, this Betty Crocker, who for nearly eighty years has graced store aisles and bookshelves—and the American consciousness—has never actually existed.[1] This essential fact of noncorporeality is worth mentioning: a clerk at a bookstore, where I was acquiring some research materials for this unlikely project, had a dim childhood memory of having seen her at a General Mills outlet, one of the many Betty Crocker Kitchens, in St. Louis, Missouri. Evidently not. But that act of remembering, of an apparent witnessing, is not surprising: we have all seen portraits of Betty Crocker at various times. Hers is an inescapable presence, like that of a movie star, or even the famous extraterrestrials celebrated in the mass media for their various, frequently profitable epiphanies in unlikely places, most notoriously Roswell, New Mexico. Betty Crocker is, in short, that quintessential modernist product, a celebrity (from the Latin, *celebritas,* for "multitude" as much as "fame").

For a wholly fictitious woman, Betty Crocker has certainly acquired an enviable measure of celebrity. Her face is almost as recognizable as that of Princess Di (who, however, we think may have once been a real person). Even though, perhaps surprisingly, she has not yet made her appearance with Oprah or on the *Larry King Show,* during World War II, Betty Crocker selflessly served a bellicose nation at the request of the United States Department of State. Then, her major contribution to the war effort was a patriotic radio show, *Our Nation's Rations.* According to *Fortune* magazine, in April 1945 she was the second-best-known woman in America; first place was reluctantly granted to Eleanor Roosevelt. Now invested with the status of an American folk icon, albeit wholly of commercial lineage, the incorporeal Betty has gone on to "write" numerous (*200* plus!) best-selling cookbooks (many *millions* of copies!), narrate films, record recipes on cassette tapes, and become a one-woman cottage industry, even something of a prototypal feminist icon. It is amazing how, upon occasion, absolute nonexistence can become invested with the widely scrutinized trappings of tangible substance. The old name for this miraculous feat was *transubstantiation.* For wholly material reasons we now understand why Betty Crocker merits a scholarly scrutiny previously denied her.

After her modest beginnings, Betty Crocker's corporate endeavors have now grown to embrace more than mere recipes, and her name appears on over two hundred General Mills products. Each year at least thirty new Betty Crocker products are introduced to a seemingly insatiable market. For their conducted tours, the Betty Crocker Kitchens annually receive visitors from every state in the Union and from many foreign countries: an estimated 1.5 *million* visitors. Today, women in battalion strength help maintain the Betty tradition. Highly trained home economists operate her various kitchens, constantly testing products and creating new recipes. A team of specially trained correspondents answer mail, *600,000* letters annually, and some eager telephonic consumers go so far as to insist on talking "with Betty herself." Crowned "America's First Lady of Food," unquestionably Betty Crocker is known to almost every woman in the United States. And yet, for all that, she never existed.

It started way back in 1921. The Washburn-Crosby Company of Minneapolis, later to be absorbed by General Mills, was then receiving hundreds of requests weekly from homemakers seeking advice on baking problems. To give company responses a more personal touch, the management created "Betty Crocker," initially not yet a woman but rather a signature that would appear on outgoing letters. Why that name, the one that was to exert such momentous aftereffects? The surname Crocker was selected to honor a recently retired company executive, William G. Crocker, and because Crocker was the name of the first Minneapolis flour mill. The prefix "Betty," the cozy diminutive of Elizabeth, was chosen merely because it sounded "warm and friendly." An in-house handwriting contest among female employees was held to arrive at a distinctive Betty Crocker signature. The winning entry, with nicely rounded letters, was penned by a secretary (otherwise unnamed) back in 1921. (Even though it still appears on all Betty Crocker products, my guess is that the loyal scribe was never made privy to any royalties for her widely reproduced calligraphic efforts.) It was an earlier marketing decision which had however forced the initial corporeal epiphany of Betty Crocker.

Successfully marketed since 1880, Gold Medal Flour officially became a General Mills product in 1929, and a picture puzzle ad was run in a national magazine to publicize the name of the new conglomerate corporation. By 1931, General Mills was in fact to become the largest milling consortium in the world. When solved, the jigsaw puzzle produced a rustic village scene depicting outback customers gleefully carrying sacks of Gold Medal Flour out to their vehicles. The seductive prize for laboriously working out the hucksterish picture was a small pin cushion in the form of a miniature Gold Medal Flour sack. Although gaining this prize must now be ranked considerably below winning the state lottery, seventy-five years ago the essentially unexpected response half-buried the General Mills office force: more than 30,000 people had sent in the completed puzzle! Extra personnel had to be hired to sort out heaps of mail, and a corner of the mill was requisitioned for their hectic work area. Unexpectedly, along with submission of their puzzle solutions, hundreds of women additionally felt moved to include chatty little questions: "How do you make a one-crust cherry pie?" "What's a good recipe for apple dumplings?" "How long do you knead bread dough?"

The beleaguered advertising staff was perplexed, but rose brilliantly to the occasion. Recipes from laboratory personnel and home economists, as well as from office personnel and their wives, were feverishly collected. These in hand, each letter industriously received a "personal" reply: "In answer to your inquiry about a one-crust pie, I suggest you try [insert recipe]. Sincerely, X." "Sincerely," but from whom? "X" just wouldn't do; you need the implied presence of a person to establish the chummy fiction of sincerity. Management knew the answer: somehow the routine letter needed the signature of a person, a given woman. The advertising department again excelled, came up with a crucial surname, "Crocker," honoring that popular, recently retired, secretary-director of the company, William G. Crocker. Now that they had the properly Anglo-Saxon cognomen, all they needed was a first name, something cozy and familiar-sounding, for instance "Betty." Now forgotten, but then famous, was Betty Boop, a cute cartoon songbird but likewise wholly fictitious. Accordingly, the new corporate riposte was "In answer to your inquiry about a one-crust cherry pie, I suggest you try [a, b, and c]. Sincerely, *Betty Crocker*." Now "sincerely" had a persona to lend it psychic authority.

A cultural phenomenon was in the works. Confiding American home-makers immediately took so credulously to Betty Crocker that soon management realized that rather a bit more than her signature was required. *Vox populi:* the people had spoken! After the invention of that elegant, but wholly disembodied signature, the next step was to make "Betty" speak. In 1924, the pre–General Mills, Washburn-Crosby Company had picked up a bankrupt local Minneapolis radio station for a song, changed its name to WCCO, and Betty Crocker's voice—that of a paid actress, of course—debuted on the electronic ether in the first cooking program ever to reach out to the hungering American masses. It was an overnight success. Beginning as a regionalist essay, the "Betty Crocker Cooking School of the Air" would eventually become a nationwide phenomenon, running uninterrupted on the NBC network for twenty-four years. Within months, the program was beamed from thirteen stations, each with its own region-alist "Betty Crocker" reading from the same company-composed script. Its significant cultural legacy, still with us, includes Julia Child and count-less other galloping gourmets of the mass media. Still, there are those dis-gruntled types (probably all hopelessly "Eurocentric") who would say that "American food has been drained of flavor and nourishment, crammed with additives, and disguised by fancy packaging."[2] If you share this tasteless opinion, which is also obviously unpatriotic, then perhaps you might think that General Mills, a recognized pioneer in packaged human food (like Ralston-Purina for the quadrupeds), might have made its own special contribution to the national degustation syndrome.

THE INVENTION AND EVOLUTION OF BETTY CROCKER'S VISAGE

Although most American housewives believed Betty Crocker was a real person ("Why, I just heard her on the radio!"), still, no one had yet seen her picture. She was merely that ubiquitous warm feminine presence on the airwaves, at first just one, soon thirteen mini-Bettys, then more and more. Although everyone likely had their own mental image of the Betty of the airwaves, nobody actually knew what she looked like because, no surprise this, she never really existed. In fact, no portraits of her existed until 1936, in the bleak heart of the Depression era. In that momentous year, to celebrate the fifteenth birthday of the Betty Crocker name, a portrait was officially commissioned from a successful New York commercial illustrator, Neysa McMein.* Departing from standard procedures for routinely discharging a lucrative portrait commission, Ms. McMein did not use a single model. Instead, she requested that all the women working in the company's Home Service Department be assembled for her calculating ocular inspection. That order complied with, as the company propaganda proudly stated later, the proficient commercial artist then artfully "blended their features into an official likeness."[3]

As the art historian recognizes, this iconic image, an institutionally designated "official likeness," has a prestigious generic antecedent: the *state portrait*. According to Marianna Jenkins in her fundamental monograph on the subject, "The state portrait is intended to symbolize an immaterial entity like the State," whose functions are now, centuries later, effectively taken up by the multinational corporation. In the broadest sense,

> the classification [of state portraiture] embraces those works that depict people of great political power or achievement in their public character. The primary purpose is not the portrayal of an individual as such, but the evocation through his [or her] image of those principles for which [the official portrait] stands. . . . Of course it may happen that formulas used for this purpose will be adopted for persons of lesser political and social distinction, for the prestige accruing to them will inevitably tempt the merely ambitious and pretentious.[4]

Whatever their rank (or gender), those worthies portrayed in generic state portraiture represent

> the earthly embodiments of abstract principles [and] effort has been made to stress this fact, even at the expense of personal characterization. They are large in scale and austerely monumental in conception, with the result that they are admirably adapted to purposes of public display. In every case, the figure is posed in a ceremonious attitude

---

*Regrettably, General Mills Inc. would not permit me to reproduce Betty's portrait for this volume.

PICTURING EXTRATERRESTRIALS

which seems to spring from a sense of inborn authority. In the treatment of the faces realism has been tempered with idealism, and any revelation of personal feeling is conspicuously lacking. The commanding note struck by the calculated poses is therefore reinforced by the suggestion that the subject is both physically and spiritually a remote and superior being. The formulas and methods of procedure embodied in these works were developed in the sixteenth century, but they are still being perpetuated, and it would often seem that they have acquired symbolic import betokening supreme power as invested in individuals or the states [or corporations] whose aspiration they serve or personify. . . . Political needs and public taste demanded a type of portrait expressly designed to depict great people in their official character; and full realization of those needs coincided with movements in both art and aesthetics that enabled painters to produce that very rare thing—a solution that was not only impeccable but enduring.[5]

Betty Crocker, albeit a composite, an artificial hybrid, now became, in the year 1936, something like a living, breathing, sentient corporate image, one now endowed with a visage. The initial Betty Crocker physiognomy made her into a motherly type, and this rather gaunt and stern-faced version reigned unaltered for nineteen years—until the company finally got around to updating the iconic portrait. Instead of having aged the twenty years that had actually transpired in her concocted life span, in her 1955 portrayal Betty actually appeared younger. And she has continued to grow more youthful and "contemporary" with each succeeding reissue of her likeness. Such is the power of art and artifice. In both her official 1965 portrait and in a more recent one, painted in 1980, she is represented as a modern, hence professional, woman. Perhaps the culture-specific update process is even more apparent in her latest official icon, arrived at with computerized assurance in 1996. Unquestionably, the extended series of Betty Crocker state portraiture has produced "a solution that was not only impeccable but enduring."[6]

Betty's icon is thoroughly malleable; it faithfully conforms to the everywoman image of the moment, so "allowing all women to more readily identify with her."[7] All of this is revealed in a General Mills publication ingenuously describing "The Betty Crocker Portraits":

In celebration of the fifteenth anniversary of the Betty Crocker name in 1936, a portrait was commissioned from Neysa McMein, a prominent New York artist [sic: I've never heard of her; neither have you]. In her rendition, McMein blended the features of several Home Service Department members into a motherly image, which remained the official likeness of Betty Crocker for nearly twenty years.

In 1955, six well-known artists, including Norman Rockwell, were invited to paint fresh interpretations of Betty Crocker. About 1,600 women [which ones, and why were *they* chosen?] from across the country evaluated the finished works. The one they chose, by illustrator Hilda Taylor [*nota bene*: not expensive Norman, just another *inconnue*], was a softer, smiling version of the original image. In 1965 and again in 1968, the portrait was updated by Joe Bowler, a noted magazine illustrator. Both Bowler versions were dramatic departures from the earlier two—Betty Crocker was changing with the times.

The fifth portrait, painted in 1972 by Minnesota artist Jerome Ryan, depicted a more businesslike Betty Crocker, symbolizing American women's newly significant role outside the home. The 1980 version, however, has a softened image with more casual coiffure and clothing, allowing all women to more readily identify with her. In 1986, New York artist Harriet Perchik portrayed Betty Crocker as a professional woman, approachable, friendly, competent, and as comfortable in the boardroom as she is in the dining room.

For her seventy-fifth anniversary in 1996, a national search [but as based on which premises?] found seventy-five women of diverse backgrounds and age who embody the characteristics of Betty Crocker. The [idealized, hence wholly imaginary] characteristics that make up the [likewise fictional] spirit of Betty Crocker are: (1) enjoys cooking and baking; (2) committed to family and friends; (3) resourceful and creative in handling everyday tasks; and (4) involved in her community. A computerized composite of the seventy-five women, along with the 1986 portrait of Betty served as inspiration for the painting by internationally known [but not to me!] artist John Stuart Ingle. The portrait was unveiled on March 19, 1996, in New York City.

In all eight of her portraits, Betty wears a red dress, jacket or sweater, with white at her neck. Over the years, her hairstyles and clothes have reflected the changing fashions of American women. Through it all, the goal has been to present an image of Betty Crocker to which modern women can relate, an image that recalls the promise of thoroughly tested products and up-to-date recipes.[8]

A shrewd colleague, one who works in marketing and public relations in Philadelphia, has suggested an inherent flaw in the "youthing" of Betty Crocker. As he recently put it to me, "There are two kinds of icons: those that reflect the value of the product, and those that reflect the image of the consumer. Traditional Betty was a wisdom figure—she represented the value of the product (knowledge, experience, skill). But the latest Betty is clearly designed to represent an image of the consumer. The problem with this is that women don't want to *be* Betty Crocker— they want Betty to work *for* them." And he points out the physical evidence for his *aperçu*: "That's probably why you don't see the new Betty much—even though you *think* you have. Look at the packages and ever more (since 1954) now you'll only find the signed spoon logo, not Betty. Regarding her digitized 1996 transformation, as one commentator noted, 'This is not Betty Crocker. This is Betty Rodríguez, who married a Crocker.'"9 My reply to him: "Just think: few medieval women imagined themselves to be literally comparable to the Virgin but, unquestionably, they wanted Mary to work for them. Imagine this: Betty Crocker as the post-medieval *mediatrix*" (see figs. 6, 33, 34).

We should now quote the documentary evidence serving to substantiate this claim for an understood intercessor function. Proof for Betty's incarnate tangibility is provided by many epistles actually addressed to her by adoring disciples. Here is one written to her in 1954 from the Kimana Swamp in Kenya by no less than Mrs. Ernest Hemingway (and I quote verbatim from letters published by General Mills):

> Dear Betty Crocker: We are on safari in Africa. How the women who live on remote farms in Kenya find the time and energy to devote to the finer points of baking while dealing with invading lions, leopards and locust plagues is remarkable. But they complain that the lightness and texture of the cakes they bake need improvement. The flour used here is simply ground wheat, not so fine nor white as [is] General Mills Soft-silk cake flour. Could you possibly tell us, if it is not a trade secret, what might be done to improve the quality of Kenya flour? Your assistance would be extremely welcome, both for its intrinsic value and as a gesture of American kindness.10

Betty's timely riposte (a document of interest to more than mere art historians) reads as follows:

> Your letter arrived this morning, just after we heard over the radio of your fortunate escape from two airplane crashes. . . . There isn't much your friends can do in their own kitchens to improve their [Kenyan vs. General Mills] flour, but they can refine the flour some by putting it through a sifter, fine strainer or through loosely woven silk cloth. Any cloth with an open texture will do, though it might take more than one sifting. Flour in our mills is sifted many times through silk and other fine meshes. Rich cakes won't be so successful with their [Kenyan] flour, but I have enclosed some recipes for a few that should work [which "Betty" proceeded to transcribe].11

Much later, in 1990, an unnamed woman writing from Chicago (evidently not a celebrity spouse) invoked Betty's succor: "I live on the 50th floor of an apartment building. Do I need to use the high altitude directions on the cake mix package?" As usual, Betty's response was immediate and directly addressed the supplicant's needs: "High altitude directions apply to elevations of 3,500 to 6,500 feet. You are safe in Chicago to use the regular cake mix directions." And another supplicant, calling telephonically from Arizona in 1990, addressed the Minneapolis Mediatrix in this chummy way: "Hi, Betty. I just found a Betty Crocker Angel Food cake mix in our civil defense bomb shelter. It must be over 20 years old. Is it okay to use?" The response was again immediate, wonder-working, and the grateful recipient called in again: "Hello, Betty. On your advice, I went ahead and made the Angel Food cake mix that we found in our bomb shelter. It rose just beautifully! You were right. It worked after all these years because it was stored in a cool, dry place." *Mirabile dictu*!

MARKETING BETTY: THE MODERN MECHANICAL IMAGE AND THE TURN TO "STYLE"

Since we now know the exact dates determining Betty's progressive corporealization—1921 as a signature, 1924 as a voice, and, definitively, 1936 when she acquired a face—she can be historically situated within the age of industrial capitalism. More specifically, the period of the 1920s and 1930s saw the first maturity of a new concept, *populist consumer democracy*, propelled by mass production increasingly dependent upon the marketing of stylish goods. In commercial parlance, another word for "style" is "design." The term used in the Italian Renaissance, *disegno*, referred to either pictorial composition or, more narrowly, drawing itself. By the 1830s however, and as specifically due to the Industrial Revolution, the term *design* was beginning to acquire its modern connotation: the superficial application of decoration to the surface of an industrial— meaning mass-produced and mass-consumed—product. A century before the timely iconographic invention of Betty, as an historian of modern design observes, "the application of art and style" to the surfaces of manufactured goods had become "important to their marketing."[12]

Accordingly, separation of form from substance increasingly became a characteristic feature of nineteenth-century industrialism and its mass productivity. Obviously, deceitful *packaging* still is the predominant trait now, in the postindustrial era, or "postmodernism." That compulsive trend toward fictional embodiments is still with us: image-making and mongering is the ruling obsession of populist consumer democracy.[13] And that is why, among other commercial phenomena, we have Betty Crocker, pure image: there is nobody there. As we just saw, recently on General Mills products, as a matter of fact, even "she" is not there. Now typically there is only her elegant cursive signature; the corporate packaging now avoids the motherly face and matronly presence, replacing them with a highly abstracted spoon logo incorporating the disembodied calligraphic rubric. Broadly viewed, this is the *post*modernist multinational corporate approach, perhaps best exemplified by the anti-anthropomorphic "Swoosh" emblem of the sporty products brought to you by Nike Inc.

Nonetheless, as a necessary technical (and psychological) antecedent to all that lifelike Betty portraiture, which is itself necessarily naturalistically modeled and colored, from the 1840s onward we need cite the proliferation of polychrome lithographs, either colored by hand or machine-tinted ("chromolithography"). Today, the best known of these are those appearing under the commercial imprimatur of Currier & Ives, a partnership operating since 1857.[14] Designating their cultural mission to be the "Publisher of Cheap and Popular Pictures," they provided the most popular pictorial art form before the cinema. Lithos and chromos were skillfully executed on an industrial scale by industrious, mostly anonymous, artists. The kind vended by Currier & Ives had prices ranging from fifteen cents to three dollars. For the lesser classes, these mass-produced, thus inexpensive, colored images took the place of oil paintings, prestigious handmade artifacts naturally always made inaccessible to all the less-than-aristocratic and, therefore, unmoneyed classes. Suitable for framing, many of these early colored lithographs were reproductions of critically acclaimed paintings, the kind then called "high art."

Now the emergent bourgeoisie could show their professed allegiance with *Kultur* in their own overstuffed parlors. Their visitors felt envy, the desired effect, and they in turn purchased some of their own. Envy multiplied pictorial consumption, mainly because Americans now wished to display their allegiance to newly laudable principles of "cultivation" and "taste."[15] Chromos transported the visual trappings of *high* art into that democratized, emerging *low* consumer marketplace. Once chromolithography became invested with cultural values, naturally it became a usefully seductive tool of the emerging advertising industry. Late-nineteenth-century advertising and packaging eagerly employed the colorful mass medium. Alluring images depicting genre scenes, historical narratives, and people, especially women, either sultry or maybe just maternal, were emblazoned on packages of soap, cigarettes, food—the stuff of daily life. Feminine logos also appeared on sacks of flour, disposable venues where Betty was eventually to find her favored domain.

All this happened in a larger, but easily forgotten, international context: the visual, often horrifying material innovations signaling the new, or early modernist, age, gearing up since 1890. Their effects are even more pronounced now, over a century later. Since Betty Crocker appears to us in graphic form, art, she may be situated (however marginally) within the history of modern art. Customarily, that term, *art*, is used only in reference to elitist culture. Elitist Betty is not, but she was shaped in a world that did have that elitist minority. She is one of the many decidedly nonartistic components flowing from the cultural context of formally and psychologically innovative *fin-de-siècle* Symbolist and post-Symbolist art and literature. From their artistic innovations, especially abstract painterly imagery and the stream-of-consciousness novel, all the rest of avant-garde modernist expression naturally flowed (as discussed further in chapter 12). The effects of strictly material changes in art production, and a new artistic consciousness, were, however, manifested even earlier. Of particular historical significance here is the rise of the so-called mass media, a phenomenon unfortunately little discussed for its strictly *art*-historical consequences, which are considerable.[16] And Betty is certainly a product of the mass media. In the media, it is the images, not the facts, that shape public opinion. Since the art historian deals exclusively with visual images, perhaps he or she is the best qualified to explain that emotional sculpting of public consensus through mass-produced imagery.

Whether Betty or the ETs, we are dealing with visualized artifacts made known universally through postmedieval technology. The benchmark invention is, of course, the printing press with movable type, another epochal product of the Renaissance. Besides potentially leading to an unprecedented democratization of the intellect, by such wholly mechanized means a more or less artistic image, the printed illustration could now be put in the hands of a virtually unlimited audience. This mass audience culture also included professionally ambitious artists, and now they could instantly become apprised of the most prestigious look enjoying critical fame at that moment in distant European capitals. Another result was that art imagery began to be ever more evaluated as an available corpus of predigested and premarketed technical solutions and iconographic formulas. The eventual consequence was that, today, a formalist (versus narrative) critical evaluation has become predominant. But that observation only applies to the elitist minority. The silent majority, to whom Betty belongs, only evaluates narrative resonance and efficiency; in fact, this group loathes any sort of formal ambiguity.

In short, the printing press marked the beginning of a slow process of changing culture values operating during an extended "Age of Mechanical Reproduction." The result was, according to Walter Benjamin (writing in 1936), that the work of art lost a magical "aura" it had once enjoyed, that is when art works were all handmade, and, moreover, "originated in the service of a ritual: first the magical, then the religious kind."[17] Following universal acceptance of the printing press, the mechanically reproduced, increasingly "aura-less," art-image was issued in series. The momentous result—since the artisan's hand no longer intervened—was an image which *never changed*. Unchanging, the printed image became implicitly timeless and anonymous. Therefore, also implicitly, the momentary and nervous fluctuations of the artist's hand eventually became in themselves prestigious emblems. In an age of industrial reproduction, the independent creator's manual markings stood for nonmechanical and spontaneous individuality; thus they became valued visual signs, representing an individual "style," with *style* itself connoting "artistic freedom." Hence the inevitable trend toward "formalism" in self-designated vanguard art.

The first illustrated newspaper, the *Nieuwe Tijdingen*, began to appear in Antwerp after 1605. The intimate text-image linkage belonging to such cheaply sold, illustrated ephemera began to create stereotypes of codified meaning and ever more banal imagery. Most often the editorial-izing purpose ordering the appearance of visual imagery was sheer pro-paganda, to shape and direct mass consciousness. The *New York Mirror* was founded in 1823, followed in 1836 by *Le Siècle* and *La Presse* in France, and, in England, the *Penny Magazine* (1832) and the *Illustrated London News* (1842). Soon afterward there came another innovation, the "penny papers," largely subsidized by advertisers, also adding their own spate of visual propaganda (and *propaganda* is still the word connoting commercial "advertising" in Spain). In practice, the near total commer-cialization of the popular press led to yet another effect, an overt linkage of the instruments of ideological expression with commercial enterprise. Accordingly, themselves requiring large capital investment, newspapers increasingly tended to align themselves to the capitalist establishment.

Another significant effect of the acceleration of iconographic accu-mulation, sheer pictorial glut, was increasing boredom, thus inspiring a search, initially undertaken by only a very few vanguard artists, for alter-native means of pictorial expression. This feverish pursuit of visual het-erogeneity is, of course, one of the hallmarks of modernist avant-garde art, but its roots go back further. Early signs of this movement, and within the popular press itself, include the first signs of the comic book, particularly Rudolphe Töpffer's *Docteur Festus* (1829), *M. Cryp-togramme* (1830), and *M. Jabon* (1833).[18] In his unquestionably popular publications, Töpffer installed an important pre-Surrealist iconographic innovation: textless drawings with only the most vague narrative significance. Without the symbiosis of Töpffer's sketchy graphic material, the accompanying text itself signifies nearly nothing. Töpffer's *trouvaille*— that images rather than text provided a new and compelling, mostly graphic, modern way to convey a story, where the artful pictures are "read" as a text used to be—achieved something like its mass media apotheosis a century later. In October 1936, Henry Luce founded a new magazine, *Life*. Within a few weeks of its debut, *Life* was selling a million copies a week. *Life* was mainly dedicated to "picture essays," also known as photojournalism. Although *Life* recently ceased publication, its spawn are still thriving in, and industriously pandering to, a subtextual postmodernist mass audience culture. A typical mass-circulation publication, *People* for instance, exclusively caters to a voyeuristic postmodernist obsession with visual celebrities.

New mechanical innovations exacerbated the iconographic surfeit: lithographic presses appeared after 1796; the first cast-iron press appeared in 1798; in 1811, Andrew Bauer produced the first steam-powered press. More so than earlier graphic means, lithography encouraged amateurism due to its immediacy of execution: you just "drew" (even blotted) upon the stone. Another consequence of the proliferation of spontaneous lithographic imagery was that cultural habits of perception shifted to an appreciation of looser and more disconnected imagery and more unpremeditated conceptualization on the part of artists. This new mode was even enjoyed occasionally by the nonelitist mass audience. This important shift in visual taste occurred just as railways began to be commonly utilized by the ordinary public and, as it turns out, such unparalleled means of speedy democratic locomotion had their own unique, impressionistic, visual effects. In 1830, the Rev. Edward Stanley described these new speedy perceptions in *Blackwood's Magazine* for his many, as yet immobile, readers:

> In the rapid movement of these engines there is an optical deception worth noticing. A spectator observing their approach, when at extreme speed, can scarcely divest himself of the idea, that they are not enlarging and increasing in size rather than moving. I know not how to explain my meaning better, than by referring to the enlargement of objects in a phantasmagoria [an early special effects spectacle]. At first the image is barely discernible, but as it advances from the focal point, it seems to increase beyond all limit. Thus an engine, as it draws near, appears to become rapidly magnified, and as if it would fill up the entire space between the banks, and absorb everything within its vortex.[19]

As a sort of contemporary illustration to that perceptual novelty, one might well cite William Turner's well-known painting of *Rain, Steam, Speed* (1844).

The core idea here is perception altered by conditions of modern speed, sheer mechanical acceleration. The issue is unquestionably central to modern art, as may be demonstrated by another observation made, in this case however, some eighty-five years later. In a statement published in *Les Soirées de Paris* in 1914, the Cubist painter Fernand Léger recognized the existence of a "new visual state imposed by the evolution of new [and largely mechanical] means of production." Then he proceeded to describe the results in strictly painterly terms:

> *If pictorial expression has changed, it is because modern life has necessitated it.* The existence of modern creative people is much more intense and more complex than that of people in earlier centuries. The thing that is imagined is less fixed; the object exposes itself less than it did formerly. When one crosses a landscape by automobile or express train, it becomes fragmented; it loses in descriptive value but gains in synthetic value. The view through the door of a railroad car or the automobile windshield, in combination with the speed, has altered the habitual look of things. A modern man registers a hundred more sensory impressions than an eighteenth-century artist. The composition of the modern picture, its variety, its breaking up of forms, are the result of all this. It is certain that the evolution of the means of locomotion and their accelerated speed have a great deal to do with *the new way of seeing*.[20]

Unquestionably however, the single most important mechanical invention affecting the professional life of the early modernist painter was the camera and its photographic image.[21] In the modern photograph— from the Greek, *photo-graphein*, or "light-drawing"—it is not the hand which "draws" the image. Therefore, effectively that image has been created automatically and by chance, without the intervention of human reason, as the Surrealist spokesman André Breton might have said. The process itself is however not altogether modern: the camera, as a "camera obscura," had been known to practicing artists long before the photographic image of the mid-nineteenth century. During the Renaissance the *camera obscura* was a device indispensable for the correct elaboration of "perspective vistas" which were, of course, still drawn laboriously by the artist's hand. The strictly modern innovation of the nineteenth century was mechanical, a way to "fix" the automatically acquired image with silver salts upon a glass plate; soon after, the tin-type or, eventually, paper print and celluloid film stock, made their tardy mechanized entrance.

The newly mechanized imagist developments following along with the Industrial Revolution—our "photography"—were largely due to two Frenchmen, Joseph Nicéphore Niepce (1765–1833) and Louis Jacques Mandé Daguerre (1791–1851). The first negative photograph on paper was achieved in 1816, and by 1822 the procedures for photoengraving had been worked out. In 1839, William Henry Fox Talbot (1800–1877) announced his discovery of the photographic negative, permitting infinite, and amazingly cheap, identical repetition of the same image. For early commercial photographers, necessarily limited in their subject matter by long time exposures, favored themes were dusty still lifes, urban architectural scenes, slumbering landscapes, and stiffly posed portraits. The laborious and painstaking manual craft of the painter could not compete economically with the mechanical expediency—or cheapness—of the photographer's efficiently mechanized production. Moreover, standard narrative genres which had long remained the exclusive province of the painter—portraits, still lifes, and landscapes—were now largely denied to him as a viable way of earning a living. The centuries-old craft of the painter was now professionally challenged, drastically so.

In an even broader sense, "art-less naturalism" became conceptually, symbiotically identified with the photographic image, an industrial artifact commonly consumed by the commonly excoriated lower classes. Since the artistic painter could no longer economically compete with the photographer on the naturalistic front, then he must necessarily seek other pictorial means by which to make his mark, and also thereby (perhaps) to find his own market. The most obvious alternative for the ambitious, would-be fine artist was, therefore, to produce a personal *style* as much "antinaturalistic" as it was self-consciously "arty." As is equally obvious, that did become the general look characterizing progressive or avant-garde art expression around 1890. For economic reasons, most photographs were black and white, a monochromatic *grissaille*. Additionally, they were servile to external perspective configurations, for being mechanically monocular. The resulting physical product, the photographic print, was wholly flat, or devoid of any surface effects. Therefore, it also logically followed, albeit with perhaps irrational applications, that the avant-garde alternative to the insurmountable photographic challenge ideally must be antithetical: antiperspectival, brightly colored, and heavily textured. And so it was. But that was the elitist solution. In form as well as in content, the Betty Crocker portraiture represents the very antithesis of modern elitist representation. Form follows function: a commercial product cannot afford to be elitist.

This antithetical consciousness was early, circa 1910 to 1912, expressed clearly in paintings characteristic of the "classic" phase of Cubism, where prominent are the appearance of a collapsed and arbitrarily planarized space, coarseness of technique (*facture*) and a similarly radical antifinish proclaimed by introduction of collage effects employing discarded industrial products or alternative materials. The originally dull, monochromatic, and often muddy Cubist palette was soon however, in the "synthetic" phase of about 1913 onward, to be rejected for more primary, expressionistic hues laid on in thick impasto. Even though all of this makes perfect *economic* sense, there were also any number of other relevant cultural developments and psychic effects accounting for the dramatic transfiguration of pictorial expression beginning around 1890. This was inevitable, since the artist's psyche had been drastically affected by the modernist world rising around him. Some of these psychic effects will be discussed later (in chapters 12 and 13) in order to explain the marginalized but complementary modernist phenomena producing extraterrestrial portraiture.

BETTY CROCKER'S INVENTION AS A HISTORICAL ARTIFACT OF CORPORATE CULTURE AND "STYLING"

Betty Crocker's name is attached to all manner of commercial products; besides flour and baking products, she also, since 1946, endorses a surprising range of household appliances. General Mills deals with the marketing of each of these in an artful way, and has created for them what are now known as "multipurpose styling divisions."[22] A pioneer in this development, now a standard feature in all multinational corporate enterprise, was a German company, Allgemeine Elektricitäts-Gesellschaft (AEG), founded in 1883. AEG commissioned architect-designer Peter Behrens (1869–1940) to create a uniform corporate look for them between 1907 and 1914, a *Bild* (image) leading to *Bildung* (education): visually induced mental formation for consumers. The results of pioneering Behrens's *design equals education* endeavors are now illustrated in every standard art-historical textbook. Behrens created what he called an "artistic context" for all facets of the corporate effort, from its towering buildings to its mass-produced products, down even to its publicity flyers. In short, nearly single-handedly, Behrens invented what we now refer to as the "corporate image."[23] And the post-Behrens "Betty Crocker" *Bild equals Bildung* is the corporate image of General Mills, Inc.

As such, Betty Crocker represents an instrument of corporate *public relations*, a term coined in 1922 by Edward Bernays, and the main thrust since has been to present an image of the corporation as being benignly directed and populated by fictitious creatures called "just folks."[24] The timely invention of Betty Crocker is also the result of calculated "consumer engineering," an all-too-revealing term contemporaneously coined by package designer Egmont Arens to describe any brilliantly conceived modernist, complex, and coordinated merchandising effort. Typically, pictorial imagery, a particular tactic, is central to the larger strategies governing such marketing campaigns. By employing "styling" (including Betty Crocker) as a new business tool, it was increasingly accepted in a post-Freudian age that the merchandiser must speak directly to the consumers' unconscious, to their primal urges. As we have seen, Betty Crocker's correspondents seem to want desperately to *believe* that she really exists; some telephone and insist on "talking with her." The purposes and techniques for all this mental manipulation were made clear by Arens in a book coauthored with Roy Sheldon bearing a telling title, *Consumer Engineering* (1932). Interestingly, this publication appeared just before the official debut of the first Betty Crocker portraiture. That *Bild-zum-Bildung* sequence is what had already been given to her devoted fans: a real "personality" upon which to focus their mass adulation.

This was an age obsessed with personality. Even obviously inanimate artifacts had to be invested with anthropomorphic potential. Emily Post published a thick volume in 1930 called *The Personality of a House*, in which it was authoritatively stated, "Its personality should express your personality, just as every gesture you make—or fail to make—expresses your gay animation or your restraint, your old-fashioned conventions, your perplexing mystery, or your emancipated modernism—whichever characteristics are typically yours." But Emily was not the only one obsessed with the physical environment expressive of the personality *manqué*. Some years earlier, in 1913, Elsie de Wolfe, another American evangelist of good taste, published her own primer on *The House in Good Taste*, proclaiming:

> If you are both sincere, if your purpose is to have the best things you [or your husband] can afford, the house will express the genius and character of your [hired] architect and the personality and character of yourself. . . . A woman's environment will speak for her life, whether she likes it or not. How can we believe that a woman of sincerity of purpose will hang fake [i.e., inexpensive] "works of art" on her walls, or satisfy herself with [merely] imitation velvets or silks? . . . A house is a dead-give-away.[25]

As Russell Lynes wryly observes, "Such remarks set a great many women to wondering just what their personalities *were*: mysterious? emancipated? old-fashioned?"[26] Then it was a burning question, perhaps it still is.

In the very same year that Betty's face was invented for the adoring American masses, there was published a famous (or infamous) book explaining how one could systematically acquire a marketable, but wholly synthetic or styled, personality. When Dale Carnegie's *How to Win Friends and Influence People* was first published in 1936, it provided an evidently needful technical guide for human relations. "When dealing with people," Carnegie told his millions of readers, "we are not dealing with creatures of logic. We are dealing with creatures of emotion, creatures bristling with prejudices and motivated by pride and vanity." Success in "dealing with people [involves skills] in human engineering," he argued, so making an ongoing appeal to those raw emotions already exploited by Arens and other "human engineers."[27] Using anecdotes extrapolated from his own *mittelamerikanische* life, and more drawn from the lives of other "successful" people, Carnegie amassed a catalogue of manipulative techniques for what he called "handling people," for neutralizing and circumventing conflict. Mainly, these were to be opportunistically utilized for getting what you want from others.

In order to "make a good impression," Carnegie offered the following maxims of mental manipulation: "Actions speak louder than words, and a smile says, 'I like you. You make me happy. I am glad to see you.' An insincere grin? No. That doesn't fool anybody. We know it is mechanical and we resent it. I am talking about a real smile: a heart-warming smile, a smile that comes from within, the kind of smile that will bring [you] a good price in the market place." Dale didn't mince words. In order to achieve this "real" smile, the kind "that will bring a good price in the market place," Carnegie counseled, "You don't feel like smiling? Then what? Two things. First, *force* yourself to smile. If you are alone, force yourself to whistle or hum a tune or sing. Act as if you were already happy, and that will tend to make you happy. Everybody in the world is seeking happiness, and there is one sure way to find it. That is by controlling your thoughts."[28] In this passage, and throughout most of his unquestionably successful best-seller, Carnegie advised the instrumental cultivation of a marketable self. The idea of a marketable self is certainly what lies behind the opportune invention of Betty Crocker. As the populist Carnegie instructed his essentially clueless followers, in short, what you should be doing is practicing social manipulation: "human engineering."

Put another way, the Carnegie desideratum is "self-fashioning," to use the term currently employed by academic scholars to describe a phenomenon first set in place during the Renaissance by books of social etiquette like Baldessare Castiglione's *Libro del Cortegiano* (1527).[29] The self-fashioning of a personable, warm, maternal, and wholly fictitious

Betty Crocker is definitely an industrial product of the same neurotic psychological milieu that produced the historical success of Dale Carnegie's meretricious manual, and that of Emily Post's *Etiquette: The Blue Book of Social Usage* (1922). In turn, that social gospel goes back to a precedent set centuries before by Castiglione—about whom we imagine that homespun Dale and Emily had never heard. No matter; Dale Carnegie is now recognized as the great American popularizer of "the techniques of false *personality*."[30] Even viewed in the most charitable fashion, we must recognize that the real essence of Betty Crocker is likewise "false personality," likewise the kind specifically designed to ensure success in the marketplace. Although the best known, and the most life-like, Betty Crocker is only one among many other anthropomorphic American corporate trademarks; other notable capitalist nonentities include "Aunt Jemima" (invented in 1893), "Joe Camel" (incarnated in 1913), "Mr. Peanut" (1916), and "Elsie the Cow" (1939).[31] In short, "personality," however ersatz, has itself become a marketable product, another potentially vendible commodity. And, to carry out your manipulative designs, it is very useful if you present the public with their portrait—and that icon is preferably realistically rendered.

BETTY'S STATUS AS A MODERNIST CELEBRITY AND PSEUDOEVENT

As so affirmed in the official General Mills propaganda, Betty Crocker is (literally) "a celebrity." As the anonymous corporate scribes explain, "In late 1989, Donnelly Marketing conducted a survey of 2,500 households asking, 'How much more (or less) likely would you be to purchase a particular product/service if it were endorsed by [fill in the blank]?' Of the 34 'celebrities' rated (including, Alan Alda, Bill Cosby, Walter Cronkite, James Garner, Bob Hope, and Jane Pauley [but omitting any Nobel Laureates]), Betty Crocker ranked first in the 25–49 and the 50–64 age groups, and second to Walter Cronkite in the 65+ group."[32] Most impressive for Betty, but most appalling as a sign of the collective mental health of America in 1989. And it only gets worse in the twenty-first century. So just what is a "celebrity" these days; what is their real cultural significance?

As defined (in italics) by cultural historian Daniel J. Boorstin, "*The celebrity is a person who is known for his [or her] well-knownness. . . .* Celebrity is made by simple familiarity, induced and re-enforced by public means. The celebrity therefore is the perfect embodiment of *tautology*: the most familiar is the most familiar."[33] Another comment explains the unquestionable success of Betty Crocker in her function as a fabricated celebrity, for all such "are nothing but ourselves seen in a magnifying mirror." "In the creation of a celebrity somebody always has an interest[:] they are made to order, can be made to please, comfort, fascinate, and flatter us. . . . 'The idol,' said James Russell Lowell, 'is the measure of the worshipper.' Celebrities are made by the people." Put otherwise, they are urgently summoned by the *vox populi*. As Boorstin also observes, "The celebrity in the distinctive modern sense could not have existed in any earlier age, or in America before the Graphic Revolution," beginning with those cheap chromos and now culminating in television, a nearly inescapable medium. He cites as the first verbal evidence Ralph Waldo Emerson's mention, in 1848, of "the *celebrities* of wealth and fashion."[34] Although rarely lauded as such, since 1848, celebrities have become the distinguishing hallmark of modernism.

However, the historical phenomenon immediately leading to the slightly later invention of Betty Crocker was the "star system." Even though geographically situated in southern California for the most part, like Ms. Crocker in Minneapolis, celebrities' "hallmark was simply and primarily their prominence in popular consciousness." Boorstin observes how these Hollywood star-celebrities were, like Ms. Crocker, provided by their professional publicists with "a definable, publicizable personality . . . which could become a nationally advertised trademark."[35] As so frequently portrayed in the movies, significantly most of those stars were themselves apocryphal: even their very names—like "Betty Crocker"— were contemporaneous inventions, pure fiction. The list of such invented, apocryphal people is nearly endless, including the likes of "Fred Astaire" (Frederick Austerlitz), "Theda Bara" (Theodosia Goodman), "Jack Benny" (Benny Kubelsky), "Joan Crawford" (Lucille Le Sueur), "Tony Curtis" (Bernard Schwartz), "Kirk Douglas" (Issur Danielovich Demsky), "Judy Garland" (Frances Gumm), "Hedy Lamarr" (Hedwig Kiesler), and so forth.

Above all, what is most useful about a celebrity, somewhat real or wholly imaginary, is the capacity to be made into a *trademark*. By that functional definition—"trademark"—Betty Crocker represents the purest form, the very essence and apotheosis of *celebritas*. Chronologically, she belonged to the high Industrial Age, the age of orthodox modernism; now morphed into a disembodied scribble on a spoon, she admits her own aesthetic obsolescence. *Au contraire*, the reigning apocryphal celebrity of the postindustrial—meaning postmodernist—age is the extraterrestrial (figs. 1, 4, 5, 15–22). In Boorstin's view, the *celebrity*, whether male or female, "is the human pseudoevent." Properly speaking, a pseudoevent, animate or inanimate, must possess the following four characteristics:

1. It is not spontaneous, but comes about because someone has planned, planted, or incited it. Typically, it is not a train wreck or an earthquake, but an interview.

2. It is planted primarily (but not exclusively) for the immediate purpose of being reported or reproduced. Therefore, its occurrence is arranged for the convenience of the reporting or reproducing media. Its success is measured by how widely it is reported. The question "Is it real?" is less important than "Is it newsworthy?"

3. Its relation to the underlying reality of the situation is ambiguous. Its interest arises largely from this very ambiguity. Concerning a pseudoevent, the question "What does it mean?" has a new dimension. While the news interest in [for instance] a train wreck is in *what* happened and in the real consequences, the interest in an interview is always, in a sense, in *whether* it really happened and in what might have been the motives. Did the statement *really* mean what it said? Without some of this ambiguity, a pseudoevent cannot be very interesting.

4. Usually it is intended to be a self-fulfilling prophecy.[36]

Boorstin then goes on to tell us just which characteristics of pseudoevents, or "celebrities," make them overshadow spontaneous, or *real*, events or persons. As should be common knowledge, legitimate questions do exist concerning what might constitute a "spontaneous or real event" in the context of the contemporary and/or postmodernist *Weltanschauung*. Among other sensitives, I am not able to provide a definitive answer to that potent question, but it may be mentioned that already in 1967 Guy Debord was addressing that conundrum, concluding that we only exist in a hollow "World of Spectacle," that being visual for the most part.[37] Nevertheless, the reader is encouraged to ponder the applicability of the term *pseudoevent*—a situation having its own very real psychological causes and effects—when considering the overtly public nature of much of today's celebrity mongering, the effects of which are invented in, and then widely disseminated by, the mass media. Lately, in the real world, the quintessential "pseudoevent" is manifested by any scheduled presidential press conference, with sound bites and, especially, photo-ops. In the "other world" (literally so) of postmodernist popular culture, the classic pseudoevent is figured in the expanding portraiture of the extraterrestrial (figs. 1, 4, 5, 15–22).

Again by Boorstin's reckoning, there are eight factors that make *celebrities*, anthropomorphic pseudoevents, inevitably superior to their "real" counterparts:

1. Pseudoevents [as "celebrities"] are more dramatic.
2. Pseudoevents [as "celebrities"], being planned for dissemina-

tion, are easier to disseminate and to make vivid. Participants are selected for their newsworthy and dramatic interest.

3. Pseudoevents [as "celebrities"] can be repeated at will, and thus their impression can be reinforced.

4. Pseudoevents [as "celebrities"] cost money to create: hence *somebody* has an interest in disseminating, magnifying, advertising, and extolling them as events worth watching or worth believing. They are, therefore, advertised in advance, and re-run, in order to get their money's worth.

5. Pseudoevents [as "celebrities"], being planned for intelligibility, are more intelligible and hence more reassuring.

6. Pseudoevents [as "celebrities"] are more sociable, more conversable, and more convenient to witness. Their occurrence is planned for our convenience.

7. Knowledge of pseudoevents [as "celebrities"]—of what has been reported, or what has been staged, and *how*—becomes the test of being "informed" of what has been reported in the news media. Pseudoevents [especially as "celebrities"] begin to provide that "common discourse" which some of my old-fashioned friends have hoped to find in the Great Books.

8. Finally, pseudoevents [as "celebrities"] spawn other pseudoevents [as "celebrities"] in geometric progression. They dominate our consciousness simply because there are more of them, and ever more.[38]

But none of this is strictly modern; two millennia ago, Cicero stated that the pursuit of celebrity—"Glory" itself—is the prime impulse for all human endeavor: *"Gloria est frequens de aliquo fama cum laude"* (*Rhetorica* 2.166). If not opting for philosophical profundity or warlike prowess, then the postmodernist tribal subcultures now vicariously settle for the outer trappings of visual celebrity (i.e., *Gloriaque fama*). So we learned again, in September 1997, from the commercial feeding frenzy subsequent to the violent demise of Princess Di, the foremost visual celebrity of her time. Like uncountable portraits of Jesus Christ, past or present (figs. 2, 3), the late Diana was a biological entity unlikely to have ever been actually seen in the flesh by her thronging devotees. Both ethereal creatures seemed to have descended from a higher plane, one well beyond our mundane existence; we experienced both wholly through the mass media. Even though we may doubt that even 0.001 percent of the entire planetary population had ever actually beheld Di with their very own eyes, we do know that nearly everybody would instantly recognize her endlessly reproduced portraiture, and that each would respond instantly with a pronounced *emotional reaction* to that iconic image. Such is the intrinsic power of celebrity portraiture.

Although with considerably less fervor, the same holds true for our Betty Crocker portraiture—instant recognition and instant emotional response. As to the "why," that seems answered by a journalist decrying the posthumous, and singularly egregious, Diana spectacle: "Evidently many scores of millions of people lead lives of such anesthetizing boredom, emotional aridity, and felt insignificance that they relish any opportunity for vicarious involvement in larger events. . . . The media turn the world into an echo chamber and establish for the promptable masses the appropriate 'reaction' to events. Mass hysteria is a riveting spectacle, whether it occurs at a Nuremberg [Nazi] rally or a rock concert."[39] The internationally distributed, rather mawkish, Princess Di devotional syndrome is admittedly exaggerated in an outlandish fashion. However, the bottom line is that, like Betty Crocker and the ETs, her image-mongering is commercially based, emotionally fed, and propelled by market forces and the mass media.

Nonetheless, Betty Crocker evokes a kindlier, gentler vision, site specific to the bucolic mid-American heartland. It's a pity that Norman Rockwell never painted her *völkisch Bild*, a nostalgic folk icon incarnating and encouraging a mythic national legend, *eine Bildung*. The instructional interaction between the lifestyle imputed to the celebrity and popular consumption patterns of "the imitative fan," mostly women, was observed with smarmy approval (no irony here!) in 1939 by Margaret Farrand Thorp:

> One obvious way to resemble your ideal is to dress as she does. . . . [Publicists] will fill in for you all the little intimate details that make a personality real, that make identification close and exciting. . . . The imitative fan is almost always feminine but sometimes she wants to establish a sense of intimate friendship with a male adored one. There are two good channels for that, food and house furnishing. No issue of a fan magazine is complete without a favorite recipe of Clark Gable or Tyrone Power or some other of the [star-ridden] galaxy. . . . Interior decoration offers further possibilities for sympathetic magic.[40]

We may leave the last word on the essentially disembodied "visual celebrity," including that function as currently attached to Betty Crocker, to Stuart Ewen:

> We are constantly addressed by alluring images; they speak the universal language of the eye. Each is the product of deliberate creation. Each has been selected for its particular appeal, its particular purpose. Each offers a point of view. Yet as we look, we rarely reflect upon what

Kenneth Burke called a "rhetoric of motives." We are educated, from infancy, to *look*; we are not encouraged to see and interpret simultaneously. Our eyes imbibe images, with little critical resistance, as if they offer an ordained glimpse of some distant, yet accessible *reality*. . . . In capitalist societies, where the power of commercial images has become ubiquitous, the tendency toward aestheticization may be among the most profound arenas for what Georg Lukacs described as the "phenomenon of reification." For Lukacs, reification was the process by which the social relations of a modern exchange society assume the apparent status of universal truth, stamping their "imprint upon the whole consciousness of man." As relations among people are drawn, more and more, into a web of commodity exchange, "the reduction of all objects for the gratification of human needs to commodities" takes on a "ghostly objectivity," establishing a common discourse for survival, and for aspiration.[41]

BETTY CROCKER'S 1936 STATE PORTRAIT AS AN ART-HISTORICAL TOPOS

We recall how, in an apparent act of artistic egalitarianism, Neysa McMein did not employ a single woman to sit for the first corporate portrait of Betty Crocker. Instead, in the momentous year 1936, all the women in the General Mills Company's Home Service Department were ordered to assemble, and the artist, just as the company proudly stated, had artfully "blended their [individual] features into an official [collective] likeness." The same (literally) synthetic procedure was hewed to six decades later, but now a high-tech, postmodernist procedure was employed: "A computerized composite of the seventy-five women, along with the 1986 portrait of Betty, served as inspiration for the painting by internationally known artist John Stuart Ingle." Knowing that fact, itself resting upon unimpeachable documentary evidence as it were, speeds the art historian into a paroxysm of gratuitous erudition. In short, McMein's, likewise Ingle's, procedure reveals—as was likely unrecognized by either of them—the presence of a venerable art-historical *topos*, a commonplace, even cliché if you will.

Here is the famous story—"famous" that is to us art historians—that initially propelled this unparalleled iconological investigation of Betty Crocker's portraiture. In this case, the artistic hero is Zeuxis of Herakleia, professionally active around 395 B.C.E. Although none of his paintings survived antiquity, not even in copies, his fame was eternally assured by an account of his most famous work given (75 C.E.) by Pliny the Elder (*Historia Naturalis* 35, 61):

He was so attentive to precision of detail that, when he was about to make a picture [of "Helen"] for the people of Akragas, which they were going to dedicate in the temple of Hera at public expense, he made an inspection of the virgins of the city, who were nude, and selected five in order that he might represent in the picture that which was the most laudable feature of each woman [*elegerit, ut quod in quaque laudatissimum esset pictura redderet*].[42]

A point of contextual clarification belongs here: like Betty Crocker, Helen was a personage never actually viewed by the painter, Zeuxis in this case.

The synthetic feat embodied in the artistry of Zeuxis was also immortalized for later generations by Cicero, writing slightly earlier (circa 40 B.C.E.). Such as the story was told in much greater detail by the Roman rhetorician (*De Inventione* II, 1), once the painter had been commissioned to create a state portrait of Helen:

Zeuxis immediately questioned them as to which were the most beautiful virgins which they had in the city. . . . "I beg you to provide me," he said, "with the most beautiful of these virgins, while I paint the picture which I promised you, in order that the truth may be transferred to the mute image from the physical model." Thereupon, by a resolution of the public council, the citizens of Kroton gathered the virgins into one place and gave the painter the power to choose whichever ones he wanted. And so he chose five, whose names many poets have handed down to posterity because they were approved by the judgment of him who is supposed to have had the most reliable judgment about beauty. For he did not believe that it was possible to find in one body all the things he looked for in beauty, *since nature has not refined to perfection any single object in all its parts. Consequently Zeuxis selected the best feature of each* of the virgins whom he had chose to serve as models for his painting.[43]

In short, the composite image represents the essence of the classical aesthetic: an artful assemblage of "the most laudable features" of a multitude of individuals, and these are selected according to the artist's unique insight into the true meaning of "beauty." Alas, beauty is never found whole in any single individual; it must be deduced from the many, each of whom can only partake of it *in partibus*. Given that we are discussing a *cultural ideal*, obviously Zeuxis was not the only ancient practitioner of the synthetic composite approach to portraiture. Another name for this commonplace approach is idealization (see figs. 34, 35). All this was concisely explained (circa 190 C.E.) by the Greek physician

Galen (*De Temperamentis* I, 9): "Modellers and sculptors and painters, and in fact image-makers in general, paint or model beautiful figures by observing an ideal form in each case, that is, whatever form is most beautiful—in man, or in the horse, or in the cow, or in the lion—*always looking for the mean within each genus.*"[44]

By the second century of the Christian era this was commonplace; as explained much earlier (circa 450 B.C.E.) by Xenophon (*Memorabilia* III, 10): "In making a likeness of beautiful forms, since it is not easy to find one man [or woman] who is completely faultless in appearance, *you take the most beautiful features from each of many models* and thus you make the whole body appear beautiful." But such "beauty" is not just skin deep; its purpose is to "imitate" underlying (subcutaneous) ethical character (*ethos*): "You imitate [or represent] the character of the soul, the character which is the most persuasive, the sweetest, the most friendly, the most longed for, and the most beloved," states Xenophon, "and likewise grandeur and liberality, as well as lowliness and illiberality, moderation and thoughtfulness, as well as insolence and vulgarity— these too are revealed through the expression of the face and through the attitudes of the body, both stationary and in movement."[45]

As we see, the specific technical name for the *topos* illustrated by Zeuxis's legendary portraiture is, according to its ancient culture-specific terminology, "imitation." In our modernist example, we are dealing with an *imitation* of Betty Crocker, the kind that has deliberately represented her, as Xenophon said, with "the character which is the most persuasive, the sweetest, the most friendly, the most longed for, and the most beloved." By their own admission, such was also the goal of the hucksters at General Mills, in their case to market a synthetic image "allowing all women to more readily identify with [Betty Crocker] as a professional woman, approachable, friendly, competent, and as comfortable in the boardroom as she is in the dining room." The operative term in turn comes from the Latin *imitatio*, itself a literal translation of the Greek *mimesis* (μιμεσισ). As designated millennia later by the spokespersons of General Mills, the "spirit of Betty Crocker" represents the following approved ethical values: "(1) enjoys cooking and baking; (2) committed to family and friends; (3) resourceful and creative in handling everyday tasks; and (4) involved in her community." Illuminating various complementary contexts restoring the forgotten cultural heritage embodied in Betty Crocker's once ubiquitous portraiture, the evidence presented here shows its real impetus in *imitatio*, a plastic artistic corollary to literary *ekphraseis*, the rhetorical and wholly verbal descriptions of famous artworks. Although the notion of "imitation"—or *mimesis*—is truly ancient, it was eagerly contracted for the emerging purposes of Renaissance humanism.[46]

In his standard history of literary criticism, William Wimsatt traces the origin of the interpretive term to Plato's passing use of *mimesis* (μιμεσισ) in *The Republic* (Book III), where it was observed that certain poems, dramas, actually imitate what happened. Unfortunately, these are the most dangerous, for their mimed passions may prove contagious to the audience, later to be called consumers (a point a postmodernist critic like Stuart Ewen would likely agree with). In Book X, *mimesis* appears in another pejorative aspect, and the painter, acting as a mere imitator, is denied the status of a creator, and since even "the tragic poet is an imitator," he, too, is "twice removed from the truth."[47] Aristotle also treated *mimesis*. In the *Meteorology* (IV, 3), he makes the famous observation that "Art imitates Nature" (*hé techné mimeitai tén physin*), specifically in the sense of "filling out what nature leaves undone" (*Politics* VII, 17). As put in the *Physics* (II, 8), "Art finishes the job when nature fails, or imitates the missing parts." For later generations however, the most important statement on *mimesis* appears in Aristotle's *Poetics* (I, 2): the object of poetic imitation must specifically be "men in action," their characters, deeds, and passions (i.e., *éthé-praxeis-pathé*).[48]

As practiced in the Renaissance, imitation meant, according to Sem Dresden, "a kind of homage paid to the model, which at the same time proved that the imitator [from Ms. McMein to Mr. Ingle in this instance] was capable of something similar"; moreover, "the theory of divine inspiration was [then] nearly always coupled with *imitatio*."[49] The idea of the *exemplar*, an instructive aesthetic model, is a specifically Roman contribution to Hellenic idea of *mimesis*. Its most influential spokesman was Horace, and it was he who spoke of "those Greek models which you must have at hand and engage yourself with, day and night" (*Ars poetica*, 268–69: "*vos exemplaria Graeca nocturna versate manu, versate diurna*").[50] As is commonplace knowledge, beginning in the Renaissance, legion are those ambitious artists who did intend to emulate those *exemplaria Graeca*, indeed even to surpass the works of the Ancients in general—just as contemporary testimonies do attest. As John Shearman puts it, back then it was acknowledged by artists and critics that "a successful Imitation requires recognition of the model or text that is to be *over*-reached"; it was largely a matter of professional competitiveness.[51] Nowadays however, the ethical exemplars are homegrown, not ancient, are not "men in action," but are instead wholly "visual celebrities," like Betty Crocker. As we may further believe, in such modernist capitalist trademark figures wholly absent is any authentic theory of divine inspiration. To the contrary, as I shall argue (particularly in chapter 11), the idealized postmodernist portraiture of extraterrestrials (figs. 1, 4, 5, 15–22) does very much partake of traditional perceptions of the divine.

AN UNLIKELY PAIRING: BETTY CROCKER AND JESUS CHRIST

Since our goal is to illuminate the historical genesis of a particular icono-graphic archetype—*Betty Crocker* in this instance—the complementary, likewise specifically modern, depiction of the Christian Savior provides a helpful case in point. Again, if I were to ask you, "What does Betty Crocker look like?" you would probably know (even if you won't admit it); and, likewise, if I were instead to ask you, "What does Jesus look like?" you would know that, too, and perhaps would likely have no qualms admitting that iconographic familiarity. In short, you would most likely conjure up in your mind's eye a distinctly handsome looking chap, about thirty years old, with long and flowing golden locks, a neatly trimmed, silky beard, noble mouth, broad forehead, aquiline nose, high cheekbones, and baby-blue eyes. That image, by the way, conforms to a now discredited, generic racial type that used to be happily called (that is, before 1945) an Aryan, and as Voltaire observed long ago: "If God made us in His own image, we have certainly returned the favor." My guess to the contrary, since I am a trained historian (and a skeptic), is that, as possibly portrayed circa 30 C.E. by an itinerant Roman-era artist skilled in "veristic" portraiture, and given the known ethnic background of the Savior, the historical Christ would have instead most likely looked like a youthful Yasir Arafat.[52] But that is certainly not the way Jesus is usually portrayed today, and the omnipresent modernist icon does not even remotely look like a Byzantine *eikon* (fig. 2), which did, nonethe-less, constitute *the* iconographic standard for well over a thousand years.

The historical source of the Christological image most likely now tenaciously lodged in your head can be specifically traced to an oil painting, logically called *Head of Christ*, that was executed in 1940 by one Warner Sallman (1892–1956), a devoutly Christian, commercial artist of the Protestant-Evangelical persuasion (see fig. 3).[53] Whereas the physiognomy characterizing Sallman's modernist *eikon* is risibly anachronistic, the rudimentary compositional format he employed—showing a spiritualized figure *en buste* and as viewed in "dramatic close-up," just like most of our Betty Crocker icons—has functionally signaled "devotional painting" for centuries.[54] No matter; the reason you do know this particular image is because of its universal distribution and mass mechanical reproduction since 1940: perhaps one *billion* copies at last count (the one illustrated here is an unauthorized Mexican knock-off). Sallman's copyrighted icon has been endlessly reproduced, on calendars, postcards, bookmarks, stickers, even night-lights; unquestionably, sheer quantity defines another instance of modernist visual celebrity. Nonetheless, according to recent art-historical research, Sallman's inspiration was strictly terrestrial.

From an old issue of *Ladies' Home Journal* (1922), the ambitious Sallman clipped out a black-and-white reproduction of Léon Lhermitte's *The Friend of the Humble* (1892). Sallman then scrapped all the French Salon painter's historical *bricolage*; all that was retained by the skilled American plagiarist was the glowing, goldy-locked hero viewed *en buste au profile*, and the enduring result was, according to one adverse critic (among many), "the pretty picture of a woman with a curling beard." Sallman was, however, an artist of his time, just as was Hans van Meegeren, the notorious faker of Vermeer.[55] Both artists, whether Dutch or American, cast their imagined extraterrestrial Savior into the modernist mold of a *visual celebrity*.[56] In both cases (Betty's too), the ideological model was provided by Hollywood. Here we see the cinematographer's halo, the rigid studio pose, the amber-glazed lighting: an image right out of the contemporary world of celebrity publicity stills. This standard rendition of Christ is a "close-up," a movie star pin-up, sheer Garboesque glamour. Now you know why, and when, the modernist Christ got to look the way he does—and he does so in spite of historical recollections, long since published, that had been produced by such verifiable eyewitnesses as (Saints) Matthew, Mark, Luke, John, and Paul.

Although likewise made into something like a devotional icon (*en buste*), we now know the cultural sources presently providing us with a familiar physiognomy called Betty Crocker. Initially invented in 1936, she has nothing to do with the New Testament. From our explorations of various historical conditions calling for her epiphany, we now recognize that she probably owes far more to the absolutely secular cultural milieu that gave us such post-biblical heathen scriptures as Egmont Arens and Roy Sheldon's *Consumer Engineering* (1932) and Dale Carnegie's *How to Win Friends and Influence People* (1936). Nonetheless, as we also have shown (but as you never would have guessed on your own), the various state portraits of Betty Crocker demonstrate that the classical art of *mimesis* still thrives, so proven by commentaries on similarly synthetic portraiture (as quoted here) written by the likes of Pliny and Cicero, Galen and Xenophon.

Well, there you have it. The currently canonical Betty Crocker icons, and they are still as canonical as was once a rigidly hieratic Byzantine icon of the Pantokrator (fig. 2), with that archetype now being superseded by Sallman's smarmy modernist devotional image (fig. 3). In either case, Betty or Jesus, the justification is still essentially the one put forth by seventh-century theologians, and their argument (as summarized by Hans Belting) had held that if Christ, himself an extraterrestrial entity since his *Anastasis*, "is real, there is no alternative to his portrait [and] the image thus takes on the status of a confession of faith." As we saw, the idea was earlier (first century C.E.) fixed by Dion Chrysostomus in his *Twelfth (Olympic) Oration*: "Since we imagine the gods in the shape of the cult images we see around us, the artist's responsibility is great, for it is he who determines exactly how we will imagine the gods placed in our midst."

Therefore, then and now, we have an abundance of mass-produced cult images, the apocryphal portraiture of "the gods [and goddesses] placed in our midst" by the postmodernist mass media. Now called "celebrities,"[57] the lastest postmodernist icons will be found by you in the populist likes of *People* magazine, and their "responsibility is great, for it is [they] who determine exactly how we will imagine the [celebrities] placed in our midst." The same point is proven by a novel and in-depth, art-historical case study of extraterrestrial portraiture, a pictorial genre which we will now reveal to have been invented in its now-definitive format slightly later than was the canonical Betty Crocker state portraiture, namely in the mid-1960s.

NOTES

1. For actual facts attending "The Invention of Betty," see especially "The Story of Betty Crocker," an anonymously written six-page feuilleton sent to me by General Mills in June 1998. Also useful to what follows is the information provided in Hannah Campbell, *Why Did They Name It . . . ?* (New York: Ace, 1964), pp. 19–20; Charles Panati, *Panati's Extraordinary Origins of Everyday Things* (New York: Harper, 1987), p. 409; Harvey A. Levenstein, *Paradox of Plenty: A Social History of Eating in Modern America* (Oxford: Oxford University Press, 1993), pp. 33–34, 115–16, 132–33; Karel Ann Marling, *As Seen on TV: The Visual Culture of Everyday Life in the 1950s* (Cambridge: Harvard University Press, 1994), chap. 6, "Betty Crocker's Picture Cook Book: The Aesthetics of Food in the 1950s." For the general context, wholly commercial, see T. J. J. Lears, *Fables of Abundance: A Critical History of Advertising in America* (New York: Basic-Books, 1994), including a brief reference to Betty Crocker, p. 384.

2. John and Karen Hess, *The Taste of America* (New York: Penguin, 1977; cover-blurb); the text inside thoroughly documents their digestive jeremiad: *d'accord!*

3. "The Story of Betty Crocker."

4. M. Jenkins, *The State-Portrait: Its Origin and Evolution* (New York: College Art Association, 1947), p. 1.

5. Ibid., p. 46.

6. Ibid., p. 6.

7. "The Story of Betty Crocker," p. 6.

8. Ibid., pp. 2, 4 (my interpolations).

9. E-mail from J. G. O'Boyle, March 27, 1998 (whom I thank for getting me started with Betty).

10. "The Story of Betty Crocker," p. 5.

11. Ibid.

12. Arthur J. Pulos, *American Design Ethic: A History of Industrial Design to 1940* (Cambridge: Harvard University Press, 1983), p. 12.

13. On this all-pervasive phenomenon, see D. J. Boorstin, *The Image: A Guide to Pseudo-Events in America* (New York: Colophon, 1964).

14. See Harry T. Peters, *Currier & Ives, Printmakers to the American People* (Garden City, N.Y.: Anchor, 1942); however, since their pictures were hand-colored, technically this firm did not produce "chromolithographs."

15. For the historical evolution of American pretensions to "cultivation" and "taste," see the classic study by Russell Lynes, *The Tastemakers* (New York: Universal Library, 1954).

16. Juan Antonio Ramírez, *Medios de masas e historia del arte* (Madrid: Cátedra, 1981).

17. Walter Benjamin, "The Work of Art in the Age of Mechanical Reproduction," reprinted in his *Illuminations* (London: Tiranti, 1970), pp. 219–53.

18. For Töpffer's considerable, but mostly unsung, contributions to modern art, see E. H. Gombrich, *Art and Illusion: A Study in the Psychology of Pictorial Representation* (Princeton: Princeton University Press, 1960), pp. 336–42, 348–56.

19. Edward Stanley, in Francis D. Klingender, *Art and the Industrial Revolution* (London: Paladin, 1972), p. 129.

20. Fernand Léger, in Charles Harrison and Peter Wood, eds., *Art in Theory, 1900–1990: An Anthology of Changing Ideas* (Oxford: Blackwell, 1992), p. 157; my emphasis.

21. Although for what follows my major inspiration remains Ramírez, *Medios de masas*, see also Van Deren Coke, *The Painter and the Photograph* (Albuquerque: University of New Mexico Press, 1972); Aaron Scharf, *Art and Photography* (Harmondsworth, U.K.: Penguin, 1974).

22. For this, and much more, see Stuart Ewen, *All-Consuming Images: The Politics of Style in Contemporary Culture* (New York: BasicBooks, 1988; perhaps a better subtitle would be "A Primer of Postmodernism").

23. See T. Buddensieg and H. Rogge, *Industriekultur: Peter Behrens and the AEG* (Cambridge: Harvard University Press, 1984).

24. See Lynes, *Tastemakers*, pp. 291–93.

25. Emily Post and Elsie de Wolfe, as cited in ibid., p. 188.

26. Ibid., p. 241.

27. D. Carnegie, *How to Win Friends and Influence People* (1936; reprint, New York: Pocket Books, 1977), pp. 28, 72–74.

28. Ibid.

29. See Stephan Greenblatt, *Renaissance Self-Fashioning: From More to Shakespeare* (Chicago: University of Chicago Press, 1980); weirdly, Greenblatt makes no mention of Castiglione.

30. Ewen, *All-Consuming Images*, p. 84.

31. For these corporate character-logos, see Campbell, *Why Did They Name It?*, pp. 40–42, 62–63, 101–102; Panati, *Extraordinary Origins*, pp. 393, 407–408.

32. "The Story of Betty Crocker," p. 5.

33. For the modern visual "celebrity" as specifically representing "the human pseudoevent," see Boorstin, *The Image*, pp. 44–76, 154–61 ("Star"). For the role of the "celebrity" as a "commodity" in a postmodernist "Adcult," see James B. Twitchell, *Adcult USA: The Triumph of Advertising in American Culture* (New York: Columbia University Press, 1996), pp. 129–37, also illustrating the "state portraiture" of Betty Crocker.

34. Boorstin, *The Image*, pp. 22–23.

35. Ibid.

36. Ibid.

37. Guy Debord, *La Société du Spectacle* (1967; reprint, Paris: Gallimard, 1992).

38. Boorshin, *The Image*, pp. 49–50.

39. George F. Will, in *Newsweek*, 15 September 1997, 84.

40. Margaret F. Thorp, as in Ewen, *All-Consuming Images*, pp. 98–99.

41. Ibid., p. 156.

42. Pliny, as in J. J. Pollitt, ed., *The Art of Greece, 1400–31 B.C.* (Englewood Cliffs, N.J.: Prentice-Hall, 1965), p. 155.

43. Cicero, as in ibid., p. 156 (my emphasis).

44. Galen, in ibid., p. 89 (my emphasis).

45. Xenophon, in ibid., p. 161.

46. See R. W. Lee, *Ut Pictura Poesis: The Humanistic Theory of Painting* (New York: Norton, 1967), esp. pp. 9–16, "Imitation."

47. W. K. Wimsatt, *Literary Criticism: A Short History* (New York: Vintage, 1957), pp. 11–12.

48. Ibid., pp. 26–27; for a fuller account of historical applications of the term in literary practice, see the classic study by Erich Auerbach, *Mimesis: The Representation of Reality in Western Literature* (Garden City, N.Y.: Anchor, 1957).

49. S. Dresden, *Humanism in the Renaissance* (New York: McGraw-Hill, 1968), p. 177.

50. Horace, as in Lee, *Ut Pictura Poesis*, p. 17; Wimsatt, *Literary Criticism*, p. 82.

51. John Shearman, *Only Connect: Art and the Spectator in the Italian Renaissance* (Princeton: Princeton University Press, 1992), p. 53.

52. For a lost icon-archetype of the "Semitic" type depicting the Christian

Savior, see Hans Belting, *Likeness and Presence: A History of the Image before the Era of Art* (Chicago: Chicago University Press, 1996), pp. 134–39, figs. 80, 82.

53. For what immediately follows, see David Morgan ed., *Icons of American Protestantism: The Art of Warner Sallman* (New Haven, Conn.: Yale University Press, 1996), p. 43. On this venerable pictorial category, "icon," the actual basis of extraterrestrial portraiture, see Sixten Ringbom, *Icon to Narrative: The Rise of the Dramatic Close-Up in Fifteenth-Century Devotional Painting* (Doornspijk: Davaco, 1984); Moshe Barasch, "The Frontal Icon: A Genre in Christian Art," in his *Imago Hominis: Studies in the Language of Art* (New York: New York University Press, 1994), pp. 20–35; see further M. Barasch, *Icon: Studies in the History of an Idea* (New York: New York University Press, 1992); Robin Cormack, *Painting the Soul: Icons, Death Masks, and Shrouds* (London: Reaktion, 1997, for the theoretical contexts); Helmut Fischer, *Die Ikone: Ursprung, Sinn, Gestalt* (Freiburg: Herder, 1995, for the technical and historical contexts).

54. Morgan, *Icons of American Protestantism*.

55. For Van Meegeren, see Ian Haywood, *Faking It: Art and Politics of Forgery* (New York: St. Martin's, 1987), pp. 105 ff.

56. For the modern visual "celebrity" as representing "the human pseudo-event," again see Boorstin, *The Image*, pp. 44–76, 154–61 ("Star").

57. Ibid.

Chapter 4

Extraterrestrial Portraiture
An Art-Historical Inquest

AN EXTRAORDINARY POPULAR PHENOMENON: THE ETs AMONG US

As I assume you will all agree, the entire idea of extraterrestrials is extraordinary. As those of you with any sort of scientific training must further concur, extraordinary claims require extraordinary physical evidence to make them credible. Since our goal is to locate the historical genesis of a particular iconographic "archetype," the complementary, specifically modern (versus old style; see fig. 2), depiction of the Christian Savior provides a helpful case in point. Again, if I were to ask you, "What does an ET look like?" you *would* know (even if you won't admit it; see figs. 1, 5), and, likewise, if I were instead to ask you, "What does Jesus look like?"—you would know that, too; perhaps you would have no qualms admitting *that* iconographic familiarity.

However, even if we are actually enabled to manipulate real physical evidence attesting to the real presence of ETs among us, we must still recall Werner Heisenberg's recognition that nature never reveals itself to us as it is, but instead always through the questions *we* put to it. In short, and just as Albert Einstein observed in 1926, "It is the theory which decides what we can observe." In the particular case of the ETs, the "evidence" is *all* anecdotal, meaning just a corpus of verbal affirmations made after the fact by those troubled individuals who say it "really happened" to them. Worse, these distinctive narratives are nearly always produced as the result of hypnotic stimulus applied by a "researcher" who only pursues *these* kinds of fabulous stories. Before David Jacobs, another who did so successfully was a manic-depressive, best-seller horror-fiction writer, Whitley Strieber. This was the fellow who had received a whopping *million-dollar* advance from his New York publisher, William Morrow, for his best-seller autobiography(!), *Communion: A True Story* (1987), profitably reporting his "true story" of alien abductions and other egregious molestations. (see fig. 4).[1] We shall examine these scary anecdotes in greater detail in chapter 5.

But first it will be useful to point out that, in effect, we postmodernists cannot easily escape familiarity with such stories. In short, presently the ET/UFO legends represent an essential, and very profitable, component of the infotainment industry. The annual worth to them of such apocrypha is estimated to run into ten-digit dollar figures (but no specific sums are cited, for obvious reasons). Just as the environmentalists warn us, indeed, there is much pollution in the air; another kind is broadcast over the airwaves. Besides lucrative, the abundant media displays of alien close encounters are also omnipresent, inescapable. Here is the physical proof. I live in a typical, middling-sized town—Las Cruces, New Mexico; population 80,000—located in the Great American Outback. Las Crucens avidly consume the same television fare as do videophiliac citizens in the rest of the Republic. And here is a summary of exactly what we are provided, prime time only, and as advertised, day by day, in a typical week (April 25–May 1, 1998):

> SATURDAY: *X-Files, Star Trek, Earth: Final Conflict.*
> SUNDAY: *X-Files, Star Trek, The Outer Limits, Sci-Fi Files, Space Beyond, Earth 2, Sightings.*
> MONDAY: *Sci-Fi Files, Sightings* (Monday is an unusually sparse evening).
> TUESDAY: *3rd Rock from the Sun, Sightings, Alien Secrets: Area 51.*
> WEDNESDAY: *3rd Rock from the Sun, Star Trek: The Next Generation* (in Spanish), *Sightings, We Are Not Alone, The Sender* (movie: "A military man probes a possible alien encounter").
> THURSDAY: *Star Trek: The Next Generation* (in Spanish), *Stargate SG-1, Roswell, We Are Not Alone, UFOs: Have We Been Visited?, Enemy Mine* (movie: "An Earthian pilot crash-lands on a planet with a lizard-like warrior from the Dracon Empire"), *Alien Nation* (movie: "A police detective and his humanoid partner find a conspiracy of 'newcomers'"), *Alien Nation: Dark Horizon*

(movie: "A police detective and his humanoid partner unearth a plot to destroy aliens in near future Los Angeles").

FRIDAY: *Beyond Belief: Fact or Fiction?*, *Millennium*, *The Outer Limits*, *Unsolved Mysteries*, *Stargate SG-1*, *UFOs and Other Close Encounters*, *The Case of the UFOs*, *Spaceballs* (movie: "President Skroob pits evil Dark Helmet against Lone Starr and the half-man, half-dog Barf").

(Note: The show *ET*, which is listed every night, merely seems to refer to *Entertainment Tonight*; sorry.)

On a somewhat higher plane of mental contact, the printed word, a complete bibliography of the UFO and/or ET monographs plentifully published by commercial enterprises, and typically to their great profit, would itself probably be book length.[2] In this case, sheer *quantity* of documents also proves the current cultural importance attaching to ETs and their celebrated UFO transportation. Accordingly, it matters not that most of the authors recounting these apocryphal tales do shamelessly plagiarize from one another, so creating a collective symbiosis of mass credulity. In short, although admittedly successful in the capitalist-post-modernist mass media marketplace, *none* of the prolix testimony now attesting to the validity of these "sightings" would, needless to say, pass muster in any proper court of law.

Validity is not, however, what propels the infotainment industry's eager embrace of such apocrypha; financial incentive does. Nonetheless, rather than a mere shrug, even piqued expressions of moral heartburn, this omnipresent cultural detritus deserves serious analysis. So does "acid rain" and "global warming" and, most dreaded of all, "the coming plague."[3] The significance of the UFO/ET phenomenon was remarked upon by Jacques Vallée, a longtime investigator of the cultural "mythic" embeddedness of many such paranormal experiences:

> What interests me is that, with each new wave of sightings, the social impact becomes greater. Conventional science appears more and more perplexed, befuddled, at a loss to explain [it]. Pro-ET UFOlogists become more dogmatic in their propositions. More people become fascinated with space and with new frontiers in consciousness. More books and articles appear, changing our culture in the direction of a new image of man. Meanwhile, the phenomenon offers occasional rational elements to entice credible researchers, while offering an equal number of ludicrous elements so as to effectively deny itself, to annihilate evidence of itself.[4]

Given this, my perhaps not startling revelation is that the widely reproduced extraterrestrials seen by all of us have a strictly earthling—*inter*terrestrial, or merely mundane—origin (see figs. 1, 4, 5, 16–22). This opinion admittedly runs counter to the official position of contemporary UFOlogists, who implicitly concur with Cicero (106–43 B.C.E.), both affirming that all ET portraiture (whatever you may specifically call it) is *non humana manu factum, sed de coelo lapsum*, that is, "not of human artifice, rather fallen from the heavens."[5] After literally grounding, as it were, the inevitably airborne ETs, the broad conclusion then becomes that *all* such otherworldly apparitions, however they may be labeled, are experienced strictly according to the historical earthling culture in which they were/are experienced.[6] An example: no orthodox Buddhist seems ever to have enjoyed an airborne vision of Christ, and likely no orthodox Christian has ever spiritually benefited from a celestial sighting of Buddha. Put otherwise, a medieval inquisitor labeled a "demon" what a contemporary UFOlogist calls an "alien" (and "demons" will be further explained in chapters 7 and 10).

Here is a recently researched example illustrating the cultural specificity of UFO sightings. On the night of July 29, 1992, beginning at about 11 P.M., and lasting for a reported five-hour period, a variety of seemingly miraculous apparitional signs were seen glowing in the inky midnight sky above Klang, Malaysia. These luminescent effects were exclusively observed by nearly two hundred students and a female instructor at the Hishamuddin Secondary Islamic School. Including the word *Allah*—"god" in Arabic—a total of twenty-six skyborne nocturnal images were reported. The following night, July 30, the words *Allah* and *Mohammed* reportedly appeared while the students were collectively praying in a school field. Unlike the first episode, this time the calligraphy was much larger (but the reports do not specify whether the classic Kufic script was used). The images in both instances were reportedly formed either within, or upon, clouds. Twenty-six drawings of the images were made by students, so pictorially documenting their collective experience. Nonetheless, the logical and dispassionate (and strictly non-Islamic) verdict is that they all appear to have misperceived clouds in the night sky in a way uniquely reflective of their specific religious background and emotional attachments. Another strictly non-Islamic verdict, rendered in Mississippi rather than Malaysia, would be to call them "UFOs." Either way, however you may wish to label the physical phenomena generating the excited reports, this is a classic example of "mass wish-fulfillment."[7]

A further, rather specific, *revelatio* (or *apocalypsis*, "uncovering") argues that the initial and primary source for the earthly epiphanies of all specifically modernist ETs was/is textual. This additionally means that all we have is the verbalization of *emotional* experiences—and not objective reportage of any physical reality. In fact, such as it had been vividly verbalized by a surprising number of awed earthlings, conventional extraterrestrial portraiture antedates by two centuries (at least) the now canonical, strictly postmodernist, visual representations of the bug-eyed, outer-space waif (see fig. 4). That posttextual illustrative aspect—canonical texts inspiring canonical pictures—is typical of a well-known art-historical phenomenon, *ekphrasis* ("description"), a rhetorical technique arising from classical-era pedagogical practice. As a declamatory envisioning, ekphrasis became common in the Renaissance, when painters would attempt to recreate long-gone but still prestigious ancient artworks from their written descriptions.[8] This venerable practice will be shown to be, once again, essential in the creation of postmodernist extraterrestrial portraiture.

Particularly in the case of contemporary ET portraiture, the question of whether *any* of the UFOlogist writers of the abduction scriptures—also the postmodern ekphrastic artists illustrating these tales—had ever really seen their exotic, otherworldly subject matter remains moot. The "reality" of all such gauche encounters is, to put it mildly, a matter for your conscience, not mine.[9] No matter; according to my research, there are three historical stages in the evolution of ET ekphrastic artworks. Our current model (fig. 1), the iconographic canon codified in the testimony of David Jacobs's hypnotized eyewitnesses, is, as Patrick Huyghe observes, "the short Gray entity, [which] although ubiquitous today, was largely absent from the UFO scene prior to the 1960s."[10] As has not been done previously, I will here specify (in chapter 5) the date of its appearance in this definitive form as being late in 1966. Similarly forgotten today, a more diversified verbal model for previous ET formal heterogeneity was initially published by a once widely read European author around 1760, and his ekphrasis was further embroidered by an American follower in 1847, and many other complementary accounts followed in due course (as will be explained in chapter 10). Nonetheless, these authors were themselves only embroidering upon a truly ancient literary genre reporting extraterrestrial contacts. And at every stage of the historical evolution it seems there was an ekphrastic artist ready and able to lend his vocational talents to a vivid visualization of the initially verbalized ET.

THE HISTORICAL SIGNIFICANCE OF ALIEN VISITATIONS

Largely because extraterrestrial portraiture has never (to the best of my knowledge) been either superbly rendered with oils on canvas and put into an expensive gilt frame, or cunningly carved in Carrara marble, or expertly cast in bronze by any recognized modernist master, such ubiquitous imagery will never, of course, be called "art." In fact, extraterrestrial portraiture can never be labeled *art* just because its most avid consumers typically populate the lowest rungs of the social ladder. Mired as it were in the cultural pits, the patrons of ET ekphrasis represent the *wrong* social class to sponsor "significant" artworks. The acknowledged audience culture for extraterrestrial portraiture, its earthling consumers, are mostly lower-middle-class folk; stuck at the bottom of the economic hierarchy, the proletariat that avidly consumes TV and eagerly peruses the tabloid newspapers. Besides ETs, they are also enthusiastic consumers of all manner of "paranormal phenomena," particularly the kind lucratively broadcast by the mass media.[11]

This mass credulity is, of course, wholly unfamiliar cultural material for historians of art. Ourselves mostly members of the middling middle classes, typically we only deal with artifacts manufactured for the upper classes, *la haute bourgeoisie*, whose aristocratic manners, social affectations and pretensions are frequently mimicked by us, *la petite-bourgeoisie* art historians. As a sensitive colleague once remarked to me: "The people who claim that they see aliens [i.e., ETs] are always pathetic low-lifes with boring and ill-paid jobs," and obviously no self-respecting academic would dare identify with (or admit to) such a pathetic lifestyle. But she was wrong. It now turns out that most self-described "abductees" are solidly middle class ("bourgeois"), with women in the majority, and with most holding responsible professional positions.[12] In short, since they make as much money as do we notoriously underpaid college instructors in liberal arts studies, so must they be "as good as" we are! Besides monotonously catering to petty-bourgeois taste, we must also note that (and for reasons we cannot yet fully fathom) male, hyphenated Americans (African-, Mexican-, Asian-, Native-, etc.) are rarely invited to the alien séances. This unique experience seems therefore largely enjoyed by middle-class, *white* Americans, mostly females.[13] These are the demographic facts, such as they are known presently. In short, the UFO experience is not an equal-opportunity employer.

Another reason why such omnipresent imagery—extraterrestrial portraiture—is never analyzed by art historians is that it can never be manipulated as an "original"; in fact, it is only made tangible to the public such as it is repeatedly *reproduced* in the mass media. Thus it lacks pitifully that magical "aura" famously attributed by Walter Benjamin to the "real," or singularly made, "original work of art."[14] As we further understand—and this trait makes our widely published subject truly unique among postmodernist mass media visual celebrities—there are no authentic *color* photographs of ETs; the few published as such were later shown to be fakes. Accordingly, ET physiognomy is only made known to us visually in the medium of *grissaille* drawings, and the generally unartful results most resemble drawings produced from the graphic identity kits used by the police (see figs. 5, 16, 20–22). Whitley Strieber's artful portrait in oil paints is a rare exception (fig. 4). In all cases, verbal description ("ekphrasis") from self-identified eyewitnesses serves to produce a rudimentary, strictly descriptive, artistic visualization. Accordingly, to sound a positive note, ET portraiture also demonstrates that "ekphrastic" art-making certainly did not disappear with the extinction of Renaissance humanism.

Nonetheless, and *nota bene*, the larger postmodernist cultural significance of extraterrestrial portraiture lies precisely in their essentially disembodied physical manifestations. Being wholly visual, specifically graphic and thus functionally subtextual, this makes the populist genre both marginally literate and entirely media-generated. Treated now as a central (but unaccredited) postmodernist cult icon, the ET portrait tangibly illustrates significant trends in our contemporary cultural condition, particularly a postmodernist malaise mainly characterized by mass *dementia*, literally a "de-braining."[15] First coined in 1896, the term *dementia praecox*, strictly meaning "early senility," is now (since 1908) usually dubbed *schizophrenia*, pointing to a "divided brain," and that somewhat ambiguous syndrome in turn is often called the "modern condition" par excellence.[16]

Further treated as a quintessential simulacrum, the ET portrait acquires towering historical evidential status—that is, once it is opportunely recognized as constituting something like the core emblem of our postmodernist, specifically "New Age," mass culture.[17] Twenty years ago, a Gallup poll found that only 30 percent of American college graduates believed that flying saucers visited earth in some form; today, nearly 60 percent accept that credulous premise, further proof that the quality of "higher" education in the United States has surely diminished by (at least) half.[18] Treated accordingly as a diagnostic tool, by which to perform some timely forensic surgery upon postmodernist popular culture, this ubiquitous visual motif, extraterrestrial portraiture, serves a constructive purpose. If so, as mentioned previously, then art history finally becomes useful, rather than merely intellectually decorative.

Now we need a timely case in point to illustrate the extreme, even lethal, fascination exerted in some quarters by this ubiquitous postmodernist cult icon. This example additionally proves the absolute urgency propelling the present scholarly inquiry. A widely dramatized media event of recent memory (March 1997) in America was the Heaven's Gate holocaust of thirty-nine, mostly petty-bourgeois, True Believers led by one Marshall Herff Applewhite (aka "Do") in sunny southern California.[19] A much remarked feature on the esoteric map in California since the 1970s, the bunch had formerly been loosely called "The UFO People."[20] A quintessential postmodernist cultural phenomenon, this deeply occultist UFO sect was obsessed by science fiction, essentially the visual kind plentifully supplied by TV. Their favorite outer-galactic saga was *Star Trek*, and also avidly consumed was the paranoiac *X-Files* series, postulated upon scary alien-abduction episodes. As we recall the original media reportage, the Heaven's Gate folk had merely abandoned their "human vehicles" in order to be "beamed up" to a higher level and into a welcoming space vehicle (i.e., a UFO). Do asked his followers if they were ready to "walk out the door" of their lives and embark with him on an intergalactic voyage to a higher place. They were.

The Heaven's Gate UFO was, so they were informed, following in the slipstream of the portentous Hale-Bopp comet, for the rest of us merely another decorative feature in the night sky. As published on the Heaven's Gate Web site, the picture of a "Member of the Kingdom of Heaven" ready to welcome them into his UFO (fig. 5) looks (surprise!) just like the bug-eyed but cuddly ET universally broadcast into the popular mind by Mr. Steven Spielberg in 1977 in *Close Encounters of the Third Kind*, and again in 1982, with his immensely profitable movie *ET: The Extraterrestrial* (see figs. 15, 19). Affecting androgynous costumes and shaven heads, this was exactly what Do's deluded bunch wished to become: *extraterrestrials*. As both shown on the Heaven's Gate Web page in 1997, and as displayed iconlike in their main conference room, we have the "classic" alien: diminutive, smooth and hairless, pale gray in color, with a proportionately oversized, triangular shaped head and large, dark, and reflective eyes; in short, a cat-faced homunculus. This was the smiley-face EBE that guided them, voluntarily, to their postmodernist, occultist holocaust.

THE HISTORICAL PRECEDENTS FOR ALIEN VISITATIONS

The American continent seems particularly welcoming to such other-worldly apparitions. Let me cite some complementary manifestations. In

1988 there occurred a widely reported postmodernist subcultural event, one still surfacing with some frequency. Reports then began to be published about "sightings" of Elvis (Presley). But he had *died* on August 16, 1977, eleven years *earlier*. No matter; never mind. His initial posthumous epiphany was perceived at quintessential *völkisch* commercial sites: at a Michigan Burger King and a JCPenney store. The phenomenon initially represented pure tabloid mania, but eventually even the authoritative *New York Times* deigned to report that The King had been sighted in checkout line no. 2 at a supermarket in Vicksburg, Michigan. Like so much else in the history of human-generated imagery (i.e., *Kunstgeschichte*), Elvis also had his regionalized iconographic ancestors, and these may be even found south of the political border presently defining the United States of America.

So why are Americans—both Anglo-Saxons *and* Latinos—more prone to this esoteric condition than are their ethnic relatives remaining in Europe? In short, Americans (North and South) belong to "settler societies."[21] Such societies are transplanted; most of the immigrants came as isolated, mostly male, individuals. Additionally, they predominantly came from working-class backgrounds, the kinds typically alienated from conventionalized religions, the kind that had been typically supported by the women they left behind. The immigration experience literally represents a "sea-change," leading to expectations that they, and the new world they came to, would and should be markedly different from the one they had known. Besides for economic gain, these self-uprooted people were typically driven by utopian dreams of building a new and far improved society. Their reality was instead the adversity, isolation, and (often) lawlessness of pioneer life, the kind demanding pragmatic solutions and immediate results. A corollary effect was the appeal of spiritualism in settler societies, and the concrete results were a nonclerical, do-it-yourself religion, the kind offering immediate contact with the other world. Among the many post-Renaissance spiritual options made available for immediate consumption, occultism is the most "ready-made" (an American term turned into art in 1915 by another European transplant, Marcel Duchamp).

We may cite a Latino example, one ostensibly clothed in Catholic orthodoxy. Centuries earlier, in December 1531 to be precise, the Virgin of Guadalupe made her initial apparitional appearance at Tepeyac Mexico. to an unlettered *indio*, Juan Diego, and another national icon-idol—her miraculously imprinted *self*-portrait—entered the collective folk consciousness (see fig. 6).[22] In fact, on July 31, 2002—and as solely based on the dubious legend of his miraculous acquisition of the Virgin

Mary's *archeirpoeitic* (meaning "not made by human hands") portraiture—the Vatican dubbed him "Saint" Juan Diego: *Mirabile dictu!* Now we must again cite the historical documentation substantiating the fact of yet another extraterrestrial visitation, in fact, a uniquely portrait-generating apparition. According to an (undated) account written in Nahuatl called "This is the Great Miracle" (*Inin huey tlamahuitzoltzin*):

> This is the great marvel. It was our Lord God who worked it on behalf of the ever Virgin Saint Mary. This is it, so that you will grasp and hear how, by a miracle, she wished that her house be built, that her home be established, the one that they call the Lady Saint Mary in Tepeyac.
>
> This is how it happened. [She appeared to] a lowly man, a commoner. Was he not a man of great devotion, this humble digging-stick, this humble hod-carrier, a peasant who was walking at the hillock of Tepeyac? Was he not perhaps scraping for a small root [at the spot] where the precious Mother of God showed herself to him? She summoned him, and she said to him, "My youngest son, go into the great city [*altepetl*] of Mexico, tell him who has charge of [Christian] spiritual matters, the archbishop [Zumárraga], what I want; tell him that it is my will that here, at Tepeyac, they build me a home and that they erect my house for me in order that believing souls, the Christians, may come there to know me well and to pray to me. . . ."
>
> Our man returned again. He came away sad, and the sovereign Lady appeared to him again. And when our man saw her, he said to her, "Lady, I went to where you sent me, but the [Christian] ruler did not believe me. He just said to me that perhaps I dreamed it, or perhaps I was drunk; and he told me that for him to believe it, you should give me some sign to take back to him." And the sovereign Lady, the precious Mother of God, then said to him, "Do not be sad, my youngster. Collect and cut the flowers where they have bloomed." It was only by a miracle that these flowers bloomed there. When it is dry on the ground [at Tepeyac], flowers did not bloom anywhere.
>
> When our man cut them, he put them in the fold of his cloak. He went to Mexico City. He went to say to the priestly ruler, "O lord, here I bring the flowers that the heavenly Lady gave me in order that you may believe that what I come to tell you is the truth, and that it is her word and that it is her wish. In truth, she has said it to me herself." And when he extended his cloak, in order to show the flowers to the archbishop, he saw there, on our man's cloak, that there—by a miracle—the sovereign Lady was painted, was copied, and was expressed [in the form of a portrait] in order that the archbishop would now believe. They knelt down and wondered at it.
>
> And it is the very same image of the sovereign Lady, the one which was painted as a portrait upon this lowly person's cloak—and only by a

miracle, which is placed today as enlightenment for all the world [*cemanahuácatocatl*]. They come there to know her [by means of her portraiture] and to pray to her here. And it is she, who in her great compassionate motherhood helps them there. She gives them whatever they ask for. And in truth, whoever fully accepts her as his advocate, and who totally gives himself to her, by her love the precious Mother of God will make herself his intercessor. In truth, she will help him very much and she will show him that she loves him who goes to place himself under her shadow, under her shade.[23]

There you have it! The essential historical document saying it really happened. Nonetheless, a knowledgeable art historian might perhaps find the Mexican tale a bit fanciful, and may even view the actual artifact as just an opportune reprise of the medieval *Mandylion-Veronica* convention of heaven-sent portraiture, "made without manual intervention" (*acheiropoïeta*).[24] (For another acknowledged *Mandylion*, see fig. 2.) No matter. Both native American icons—Elvis and Guadalupe—are also now to be found commonly painted upon black velvet, and vended as such: *imaginería icónica*. Likewise endowed with a lively "mythic imagination," Europe also has had its UFO-like celestial apparitions, but they tend to be much less innovative (or more traditional) than is the kind imagined for the inventive and technologically obsessed New World.[25] More or less recent, but iconographically conventional, Old World examples include Guadalupe-like apparitions of the Virgin at Lourdes, France (1858); Knock, Ireland (1879); Fátima, Portugal (1917); Beauraing and Banneux, Belgium (1932–33); Amsterdam, Holland (1945–59); Garabandal, Spain (1961–65); Medjugorje, Bosnia (1981 to present); and so on.[26] By the way, although not to our surprise, the Fátima apparition has repeatedly been cited as representing "a UFO."[27]

SOME EXTRATERRESTRIAL VISITATIONS IN FIFTEENTH-CENTURY SPAIN

Such apparitions have been with us for a very long time, much longer in fact than the currently popular ET variations. Even the Virgin of Guadalupe (fig. 6) has her popular archetypes. Not surprisingly, the airborne American imagery of the Blessed Virgin Mary (BVM, not UFO) reported to have been seen hovering over Tepeyac in 1531 was earlier coined in Spain (see fig. 33). This means that the Guadalupe's perceptual, even iconographic, conventions strictly belong to the Old World country that produced the same Archbishop Zumárraga who was said to have opportunely sponsored the native Mexican Guadalupe icon. As a newly coined national icon, not surprisingly the Guadalupe usefully served evangelical colonial policies sponsored by Zumárraga's successors in a recently dubbed *Nueva España*. Just as David Jacobs and Budd Hopkins have so helpfully provided us with firsthand accounts of ET apparitions in postmodernist America, so has William Christian industriously assembled the corresponding documentation relating to the phenomenon as initiated previously, in fifteenth-century Spain. Any functional resemblance between the two kinds of apparitional sightings, BVM versus ETs, may be considered merely coincidental, that is, if you are so minded. In the event, here are some characteristic accounts of similar phenomena observed in late medieval Iberia that antedate both the Guadalupe (fig. 6) and Steven Spielberg's extraterrestrials (figs. 15, 19).

Our first example made its miraculous descent to earth in Lérida province in northeastern Spain; it happened in 1458 C.E.:

> And first he was asked what vision [*visió*] he said he saw in the last few days. The witness said that on last Thursday, after the hour of vespers, for the southern fields were in shadow, he went after the mules, which were near the Doria pool. Near the pool, in a small meadow above it, which he said he would point out, the witness suddenly perceived a thing before him [*esdevingué davant una cosa*], like a beautiful child [*semblant a un bell infant*], about three paces away from him. It [the mini-ET] was kneeling with its hands joined toward heaven, holding a beautiful cross with Our Lord who was crucified, *similar, he thought, to one exhibited [nearby] in Riner on the altar of Saint Sebastian*. It wore a very fancy red cape, which touched the ground all around it, as it was kneeling.

At the outset of this transcription, we learn something very important: the "vision" appearing to the witness looks very much like a work of art, in this case, most likely a polychromed sculpture of the Infant Jesus holding a crucifix. As the narration continues:

> As soon as the witness saw it [the mini-ET], it came toward him, and he stepped back two or three paces along the right bank of the pool. Then it spoke to him, "O son, come here and tell the people. . . ." But he could not listen to it any more for fear, and fled while it was still talking. When the witness was a little way off he heard it say [something garbled about] "weeks," and he heard nothing else. And, all frightened and shaken, he went back to his sowing. He told his mother what happened, and she went there right away but [oddly enough] she could not find anything.
>
> Asked if it [the mini-ET] seemed very big to him, he said it seemed

to be about the size of a child two to three years old [see fig. 15]. He was asked if he could tell if it was a man or a woman. He said he doesn't know, [or] if it wore anything on its head; since he was so afraid of it, he did not notice. The witness was asked how old he was. He said *he was about eight years old* [like the character in the Spielberg movie *E.T.*]. Asked if he knew more, he said no. Everything was read to him and he confirmed it.[28]

In this document I have put emphasis on the fact of the youth of the "experiencer," and especially on the alignment of what he said he had seen with what we know he actually did see: a small sculpture in a nearby church that most likely depicted Jesus at around the age of the uniquely priviledged vision-viewer. In a similar fashion, today we do know that all postmodernist "abductees" (few being church attendees) have seen ETs on TV (see figs. 9–15, 17–19).

Another report of 1430 also includes the commonplace bright-light motif, likewise standard in so many postmodern ET abduction reports (e.g., the Travis Walton incident, as recounted in chapter 5). As stated here, yet another apparition was observed in the Andalusian town of Jaén by one Juana Fernández, whose testimony was given "under oath." As she explained in an unusually vivid manner, on "last Saturday night, June 10 of the present year [1430], after the first sleep but before the rooster called. She got up to go into the yard of her house, because she had diarrhea [*pasyón en las tripas*] and had gotten up [for the same urgent reason] three times already." Certainly this frankly stated abdominal context is unique among all reports known to me regarding sightings of either the Mother of God or of (mere) extraterrestrials. As the report continues in a similarly vivid fashion:

> In these circumstances, she saw a sudden great brilliance near the back of the chapel of the church of San Ildefonso. At first, she thought it was a lightning bolt, but then she decided it could not be that, because the light was so strong, resplendent, and continuous. As she pondered this, between the doors of her compound she saw a lady coming with many other people from the direction of the pottery works, up the street toward the chapel. It appeared that the lady carried in her arms and at her breast an object, but she could not see what it was; and it seemed to her that the brilliance shone forth from her face and the object. They came as in a procession over the rubbish heap [*muladar*] near the chapel, and behind [the lady] came other people dressed in white. It seemed that some of them carried staves upright in their hands but, because the sill of the doors in her compound is low, she could not see whether they were crosses or scepters, or what they were. This bril-

liance did not seem like that of the sun, the moon, or candles; rather it was a brilliance she had never seen before.[29]

And we further hear, the Jaén incident vividly recalls another, and much better known, extraterrestrial encounter, the one which transpired near Damascus much earlier (and such as that momentous luminescent incident was documented in Acts 9:1–9):

> When this witness saw it, she fell down; paralyzed with fright, she began to tremble all over. And, because she was blinded, she turned toward the wall with her back to the light and stayed there a while. Then she got up and began to feel her way along the wall to her room. The [unparalleled] brilliance continued. Before, when she was looking, it appeared that the lady had stopped behind the chapel, hence she lost sight of her, because she could not see that from her house. But the brilliance remained. And, out of fear, this witness went to flee with her husband, and a child was with him, and she carried it and, trembling, she lay down beside her husband.[30]

When asked by the local inquisitor if the supernatural people "went in a procession or in a group," the answer was that, "because she was afraid, she did not notice, except that many people came dressed in white. Closest to the lady came two persons [of the ET sort], although she could not tell whether they were men or women, one on one side, one on the other." In fact, the supernatural "lady appeared to be taller than the others. Soon afterwards she heard matins ringing. It appeared to her that the [supernatural] lady and the other [ET] people came very slowly in procession."[31]

Another witness to the same extraterrestrial apparition, María Sánchez, reported a fact of great significance to my interpretation of the postmodernist ET phenomenon. This is, once again, the fact of prior *portraiture*—unquestionably human-made, meaning specifically of terrestrial origin—as playing an essential role in shaping the reported extraterrestrial apparition. According to Señora Sánchez, "Between eleven and twelve, when she got up to get water for her son who was sick, she saw a great light inside her houses, which seemed to be shining like gold in sunlight." The witness thought it was lightning; afraid, she got down on her knees on the ground. Looking out into the street, through a wide crack between the doors of her compound, she saw that a lady was passing in the street. She explained that the extraterrestrial apparition "was dressed in white clothes [decorated] with bright white flowers that stood out in the cloth." In fact, it seemed to her that the mantle the lady was wearing was lined with silks the color of sunflowers. Moreover, "she was carrying a baby boy on her right arm, as clasped by her left arm, and the child was wrapped in a cloth of white silk. She was more than a meter taller than the other persons, and the baby appeared to be about four months old and well fed." Next comes the essential art-historical component, prior portraiture:

> On her right side was a man [another *apparition*] *who appeared to be like the image [or depiction] of Saint Ildefonsus found in the altar of the [local] church* of San Ildefonso. He was wearing a stole around his neck and carried a book in his hand. He wore the stole as [local] priests do to say mass; he also carried a maniple in his hand, with the book with a white cover open in both hands, as if he was holding it in front of [the lady] so she could see it. On the other side of the lady walked a woman like a saint [*beata*], a little behind, and she did not know who she was.
>
> All the brilliance issued forth from the lady's face; and on seeing the lady and the brilliance she suddenly took fright. Afterward, she realized that it was the Virgin Saint Mary: she saw a crown [or halo] on the lady's head, *just as portrayed in the altar of the [local] church—segund está figurada en el altar de la dicha eglesia. She recognized her* [as the BVM] because of what she has said, and *because she was very similar to the image of Our Lady in the altar.* Saint Ildefonsus [the apparition] also had a crown [or halo] on his head and a tonsure wide and open like a monk's—*just as he [too] is portrayed in the [local] church.* After the lady came [other extraterrestrial] people, all dressed in white; she saw no crosses or candles, just the [supernatural] brilliance. After [the ET lady] had gone by, it was as bright in her houses and the street as when [the ET lady] was going by.[32]

The eyewitness reports compiled by William Christian describing Iberian apparitions occurring five hundred years ago even include some composed in an inquisitorial format. As such, they are formally rather like the ET-encounter interviews much more recently gathered by David Jacobs in order to be mass produced in paperback. Here is one typical example of the much earlier reportage, as transcribed in 1449 in Toledo province, and the inquisitorial query is signaled by "DJ" (District Judge in the case, not David Jacobs) and, as before, the humbled response is indicated by "R" (so replacing numerous repetitions of "Asked if . . ." with "DJ," and "She said that . . ." with "R.") In this case, the unhypnotized respondent (R) is one Inés (no last name given). This inquiry may begin with a question put by DJ, namely, "whether on that day, she [R] said anything, to anyone, of what she had seen." Including many picturesque details, the R explained that

on her way back to Cubas with her pigs, she walked with the shepherd
boys, and on the path she asked them if they had seen anything, and
they said no, and on the path she asked them, "Didn't you see at noon
today that woman who came to me when you were eating?" And they
said, "No, why do you ask?" And she said, "A very beautiful woman
came to me and asked me if I fasted on the days of Saint Mary. And I
told her I did." And they [the shepherd boys] said, "We didn't see anything; maybe it was just a traveling prostitute [*una mondaría*]." And
she told them, "I do not know who it was," and they did not pay much
attention and went off with their animals.

Then DJ asked what were "the clothes the Virgin Mary wore on that
Tuesday?" and we find that they were "the same that day as the day
before." Fashion conscious, DJ wonders "if the Virgin Mary wore an over-
skirt [or train, *falda*]?" and R explains that "the skirt [*saya*] was
rounded." DJ then asks if "she was afraid when she saw the lady?" and
R explains that "at first when she saw her she was afraid, but, as soon as
she spoke, she had no fear. And when she came up to her, she was afraid
again." This was a close encounter; R was only "a little way off" from the
Virgin Mary, and both persons, one a divinity and the other a humble
peasant, were "standing." The time of the momentous encounter "was
about noon." We also learn that R had "fasted that day" (so suggesting
that hypoglycemia may have contributed to her vision). Next DJ inquires
about another apparition, the one that "happened on the Sunday following." This time, "the Virgin Mary called to me and said, 'Get up,
daughter.'" Oddly, DJ questions, "Did she come with stockings or bare-
legged?" and we learn that "she came bare-legged [*descalza*]." Asked
what additional comments the Regina Coeli expressed, R says that "she
got up and said to the Virgin Mary, 'Give me, Lady, a sign, because they
do not believe me,' and the Lady replied, 'I can certainly believe that [*yo
bien lo creo esso*]!'" And when the BVM uttered this affirmation her
voice was "was very fine and beautiful" (and the inquiry carries on in a
similar manner, for various pages).[33]

Nonetheless, the much later case of the populist portraiture on black
velvet depicting Elvis in the Sky (and "clothed in the sun": *amictus sole*,
à la Rev. 12:1 ff.) is admittedly different, unique even. The late Mr.
Presley was (merely) a modernist performing artist catering to a mostly
secular and significantly unspiritualized audience. However, in all these
cases, whether BVMs or ETs, at least at present, the common denominator is mass media–generated, *visual celebrity* amplified within a consistently otherworldly ("extraterrestrial") context. I must also admit to
my professional, also personal, bias: I derive much more subjective sat-

isfaction, of the strictly aesthetic sort, from traditional depictions of the BVM (figs. 6, 33, 34) than I do from any of the postmodernist ET iconography that I presently feel impelled to investigate.

Whatever its label, unquestionably certain kinds of portraiture can transfigure the viewer. People often forget the emotional power exerted by iconic imagery (even) in our own modern, rampantly secular, age. The fact of an emotionalized neomedieval iconic potency may be illustrated by the rapt testimony of a modern German devotee placed before a portrait of another modernist visual celebrity, his godlike leader, Adolf Hitler (fig. 7):

> *Mein Führer!* Thus, on this day [Hitler's fiftieth birthday: April 20, 1939], I step before your picture. This picture is super-dimensional and nearly limitless. It is powerful, hard, beautiful, and sublime. It is [also] so simple, kind, modest, and warm. Yea, it is father, mother, and brother, all in one, and yet it is more. It carries within it the greatest years of my life. It embraces the quiet hours of reflection, the days full of worries and fears, the sun of faith and fulfillment, the victory which is forever the beginning of new duties and new fields. The more I attempt to comprehend it, the larger, brighter, and more endless it becomes—yet without once feeling strange or distant.[34]

With slightly different terminology, the same profound emotional reaction would be expressed by a contemporary American fundamentalist when placed before his tribal icon, the glamorous *Head of Christ* painted by Warner Sallman (fig. 3).

CHRONOLOGY AND CONTEXT FOR POSTMODERNIST ALIEN ICONOGRAPHY

Let us now return to consider the presently commonplace "alien/ET" iconographic image, the bug-eyed space waif (fig. 4), which, as it turns out, is one that seems to have been with us for only two decades. By this, I mean only twenty years old in its strictly *graphic* mode, and that is an envisioned image which I am now going to credit solely to (North) American ekphrastic inventiveness. In its diverse manifestations, all dating to the post–World War II and/or Cold War period, to one degree or another the apparitional ET had nearly always been portrayed in the humanoid mold; the space-waif version of the "aliens" merely represents the finalized version of an evolutionary cycle. Whereas modern ET iconography has been a mass media graphic staple for nearly a half-century, it was originally much more diversified—just as is verified by that recently published *Field Guide to Extraterrestrials*, a pioneering *catalogue raisonné des extraterrestres* listing no less than forty-nine iconographic types.[35] The initial heterogeneity belonging to post–World War II alien iconography is now usefully diagrammed for us in a comprehensive graphic presentation of the "Alien Time Line," recently published by Joe Nickell (fig. 8), apparently inspired by similar time lines now routinely attached to standard undergraduate art-history textbooks.[36]

Terminology is itself often revealing. It is interesting to note that, since the 1950s, unsolicited (human) immigrants into the United States have (also) been commonly called "illegal aliens." Interestingly, in Spanish they are merely known as *los indocumentados*, people without bureaucratic documentation. A decade before, at the outset of World War II, Americans became obsessed with "aliens," the kind with parents from Germany and Japan; the latter, "Orientals," got sent to concentration camps; the former, white people, were treated in a much more civil manner. We doubt however that native-born (white) American xeno-phobic types are aware that the word "alien" comes from the Latin *alienus*, meaning "the other," a stranger. Nor would they know that later, in the eighteenth century, the term *aliené* was used by French doctors to characterize the typically strange inmates of insane asylums, all of whom were evidently earthlings. Likewise, British paleopsychiatrists treating these unfortunate souls were commonly called "alienists."

Given such precedents, it is perhaps only natural that, presently, it is mainly the bohemian avant-garde artist who is self-identified by his martyred "social alienation," a standard mental state sometimes even leaving him "spaced out." *Alienation*, officially dubbed schizophrenia by the medical establishment since 1908, is also currently recognized as embodying the core symptomology of "the modern malaise," itself exces-sively given over to "acute self-consciousness and self-reference."[37] In short, long before the timely *inventio* of the postmodernist ETs, stereo-typed "aliens"—labeled "monsters" or "wildmen" in medieval texts and pictures—broadly reflected the fears and taboos characterizing different historical cultures confronting the "anti-social and/or anti-human," meaning the archetypal "not Me."[38]

In the case of the strictly late modernist, ET-portraiture phenom-enon, the movies have, of course, provided us with the widest broadcast, thus best-known, examples of the acceptable, meaning now officially canonized, iconographic spectrum. The cinematic contribution is nearly as venerable as the (purported) Roswell incident; in fact, Hollywood motion pictures with plots of alien visitation were being produced as early as 1949 (further discussed in chapters 9, 10, and 14). A more or less random cinematic selection includes the following iconographic typologies, all of which are unquestionably terrestrial or human-made (see figs. 7–10). The variant, "nearly human" type of the ET cinematic canon, serving however different emotional functions, is illustrated by *The Day the Earth Stood Still* (1951; *alienus* as peacemaker), *Alien Nation* (1988; *alienus* as buddy), *Species* (1995; *alienus* as gorgeous nymphomaniac man-killer), and *Men in Black* (1997; *alienus* as comedic illegal immigrant; (figs. 11, 12). Far more sinister, and *really* scary, iconographic variations contemporaneously appeared serially in *Alien, Aliens, Alien 3*, and *Alien Resurrection* (1979, 1986, 1992, and 1997; *alienus* as slimy and implacable, reptilian-insectoid, woman-hunter, i.e., pursuing the ever-pursuable Sigourney Weaver), with innumerable spin-offs, including *Predator* (1987; *alienus* as standard slime-ball, big-game man-hunter; figs. 13, 14).[39]

Viewed in terms other than New Age, for the most part these are monsters, mostly of the devilish sort, the kind of creature medieval folk would call a *diabolos*, devil. Before the movies came along, one of the most famous of these was named Leviathan, and he was really scary. According to one eyewitness account, "His eyes are like the eyelids of the morning. Out of his mouth go burning torches, and sparks of fire leap forth. Out of his nostrils a smoke goeth, as of a seething pot and burning rushes. His breath kindleth coals, and a flame goes forth from his mouth" (Job 41:18–21). Another one of these nasty creatures was called Behemoth. Our ancient abductee also described *him* with the proper measure of terror and awe: "Lo, now, his strength is in his loins, and his force is in the muscles of his belly. He moveth his tail like a cedar, his bones are as tubes of brass, his limbs are like bars of iron. His is the chief of God's works, made to be a tyrant over his peers" (Job 40:16–19). By the Middle Ages, all these beasts merged into *Satanas*, the CEO of the Devils; Satan's other diabolic names were *Azazel* ("Wasteland"), *Beelzebub* ("Lord of the Flies"), *Beelzeboul* ("Lord of Excrement"), *Belial* ("Worthless"), *Mastema* ("Enmity"), and *Satanel* (from "Adversary" or "Opponent").[40]

Nonetheless, standing out among these is the currently standard movie ET–type, the canonical core image, and as such our primary interest (see fig. 19). This was cinematically illustrated in a big way initially by Steven Spielberg's *Close Encounters of the Third Kind* (1977), portraying the *alienus* as the spiritualized, wispy and small, pale gray, hairless, macrocephalic, chinless, big-eyed waif. For its psychic aftereffects upon the paranoia of postmodernist UFOlogists, also noteworthy is the plot of the movie, built upon a conspiracy constructed by bumbling government bureaucrats to systematically conceal from the public vital information about UFO sightings. In his universally viewed cinematic extravaganza, Spielberg succeeded in both making canonical the look of the postmodern ET and also in providing a standardized explanation for why *we* never get to see them: it's all due to a "government cover-up." Subsequently, the benign iconographic type became absolutely canonized in Spielberg's *E.T.* (1982), portraying the *alienus* as adorable, dark brown, house pet and/or surrogate sibling (fig. 15).

The importance of Spielberg in disseminating ET iconography is universally recognized by those who worry about such things. More interesting is the conspiratorial spin that has been applied to Spielberg's ET sagas for some time by informed UFOlogists. One of these is Jenny Randles, who dominates UFOlogy in the United Kingdom, and she put her suspicions on record back in 1988:

> The possibility of an "education programme" to end the [UFO/ET] cover-up gradually was first mooted to me by a source [unnamed] in the House of Lords, when I gave a talk to a gaggle of Lords, Barons and MPs in 1980. I was told that the truth about the alien nature of UFOs was to be released slowly. The world must be prepared. Films such as Spielberg's *Close Encounters of the Third Kind* (and presumably his later one *E.T.*) had been financed by the right money being placed in the correct hands at the appropriate time. This made it seem quite innocent, but the idea [in financing the Spielberg ET epics] was to foster an acceptance of friendly, cuddly aliens and pleasant UFO connotations in society as a whole. . . . I have since learned that the same "myth" has entered the UFO community in the USA from similar leaked sources.[41]

Sic dixit Randles. My repeated phone calls to Mr. Spielberg in Hollywood, seeking to hear his riposte to this dire accusation, have not been answered.

Since Spielberg's alien-encounter movies have been seen by nearly everyone on the planet, we may briefly question how they are to be rated as "art." Whereas their literal worth as a lucrative commercial product is unmistakable, their aesthetic merits now seem questionable. The skeptical viewpoint is presented by science writer Martin Gardner:

> Alas, beneath the visual hanky-panky stretches a thin, hackneyed plot that was done to death in the science-fiction magazines and third-rate films of the fifties. This is easier to comprehend if you read Spielberg's ghost-written version, *Close Encounters*, issued by Dell paperbacks in 1977 as a movie tie-in. Here on the stark pages, uncontaminated by clanking sounds and flashing colors, you can savor the film's dull story,

cardboard characters, and dreary dialogue in all their pure, clean, adolescent banality. Both novel and movie, however, have one thing going for them that could make the film as whopping a success as *Star Wars*. More than any other sci-fi novel or movie, they reflect the extent to which UFOlogy has become a pop religion. Millions of Americans, disenchanted with science and politics, are longing for apocalypse—for a mystical explosion that will instantly solve the world's problems and start a new age of love. . . . For those who cannot believe in the Second Coming, or the Messianic hopes of orthodox Judaism, there are the UFOs! . . . The cast of mind of true believers in alien UFOs is remarkably similar to that of true believers in spiritualism in its heyday.[42]

As interpreted by the art historian, Spielberg's commercialized ETs constitute another example of ekphrastic art. As I shall show in the next chapter, they, too, have their identifiable sources in previously published, *textual* materials. Since Spielberg's *Close Encounters of the Third Kind* and *E.T.* were both international blockbuster movies, meaning they were seen by nearly all the *lumpenproletariat*, they truly fixed, indeed canonized, the Reagan era "classic alien" portrait. Due to the inherent verism of photography, movies made ETs palpably "real"—like Christ for earlier generations of easily dazzled earthlings (see figs. 2, 3). The current iconographic reality is like that verism attributed to a Byzantine icon-painter, Eulalios, by a contemporary epigramatist: "Either Christ Himself came down from Heaven and showed the exact cast of His features . . . or else the famous Eulalios had ascended into the sky itself and, with his eloquent [*eulalous*] hands, exactly delineated the appearance of Christ."[43] In either case, Eulalios or Spielberg, pictorial tangibility definitely enhances extraterrestrial credibility.

NOTES

1. For this whopping dollar-figure, see Philip J. Klass, *UFO-Abductions: A Dangerous Game* (Amherst, N.Y.: Prometheus Books, 1989), pp. 126, 141; for Strieber's bizarre mental state and active involvement with (and eventual estrangement from) Budd Hopkins, see especially chapters 13 ("Communion?") and 14 ("Rivals"); see also Keith Thompson, *Angels and Aliens: UFOs and the Mythic Imagination* (New York: Ballantine, 1993), pp. 202–209.

2. See the extensive bibliographies, also including many obscure author-funded mini-publications, compiled in George Eberhart and J. Gordon Melton, *UFOs and the Extraterrestrial Contact Movement: A Bibliography* (Metuchen, N.J.: Scarecrow Press, 1986); see also James Lewis, *The Gods Have Landed: New Religions from Other Worlds* (Albany: State University of New York Press, 1995).

3. On the latter, complemented by ecodisasters, see Laurie Garrett, *The Coming Plague: New Emerging Diseases in a World out of Balance* (New York: Penguin, 1995), a solidly researched, credible piece of work.

4. Jacques Vallée, as interviewed by Thompson, *Angels and Aliens*, p. 194; see also Vallée, *Confrontation: A Scientist's Search for Alien Contact* (New York: Ballantine, 1990).

5. Cicero, as in Hans Belting, *Likeness and Presence: A History of the Image before the Era of Art* (Chicago: University of Chicago Press, 1996), p. 55.

6. For the apocryphal historical parallels, see Patrick Harpur, *Daimonic Reality: A Field Guide to the Otherworld* (London: Arkana/Penguin, 1995).

7. Klang case, as in R. E. Bartholomew and G. S. Howard, *UFOs and Alien Contact: Two Centuries of Mystery* (Amherst, N.Y.: Prometheus Books, 1998), p. 220.

8. For an extensive bibliography on "ekphrasis," see J. F. Moffitt, "The Palestrina Mosaic with a 'Nile Scene': Philostratus and Ekphrasis; Ptolemy and Chorographia," *Zeitschrift für Kunstgeschichte* 60, no. 2 (1997): 227–47 (esp. note 6); for its strictly medieval applications, see Henry Maguire, *Art and Eloquence in Byzantium* (Princeton: Princeton University Press, 1981).

9. For the convincing (to me, at least) argument that ET encounters are essentially induced "false memories," see (inter alia) Klass, *UFO-Abductions*.

10. Patrick Huyghe, *The Field Guide to Extraterrestrials* (New York: Avon, 1996), p. 129.

11. For a deconstructive survey of many of these standard paranormal phenomena, see Kendrick Frazier, ed., *Encounters with the Paranormal: Science, Knowledge, and Belief* (Amherst, N.Y.: Prometheus Books, 1998); Martin Gardner, *The New Age: Notes of a Fringe Watcher* (Amherst, N.Y.: Prometheus Books, 1988); Terence Hines, *Pseudoscience and the Paranormal: A Critical Examination of the Evidence* (Amherst, N.Y.: Prometheus Books, 1994); Paul Kurtz, ed., *A Skeptic's Handbook of Parapsychology* (Amherst, N.Y.: Prometheus Books, 1992); Joe Nickell, ed., *Mysterious Realms: Probing Paranormal, Historical, and Forensic Enigmas* (Amherst, N.Y.: Prometheus Books, 1993); Joe Nickell, *The Outer Edge: Classic Investigations of the Paranormal* (Amherst, N.Y.: CSICOP, 1996); Joe Nickell, *Looking for a Miracle: Weeping Icons, Relics, Stigmata, Visions, and Healing Cures* (Amherst, N.Y.: Prometheus Books, 1998); James Randi, *Flim-Flam! Psychics, ESP, Unicorns, and Other Delusions* (Amherst, N.Y.: Prometheus Books, 1986); for their historical sources, see Ruth Brandon, *The Spiritualists: The Passion for the Occult in the Nineteenth and Twentieth Centuries* (London: Weidenfeld & Nicolson, 1983).

12. See David M. Jacobs, *Secret Life: Firsthand Documented Accounts of UFO Abduction* (New York: Fireside, 1993), pp. 327–28, listing the gender and occupations of his "abductees."

13. An exception to this seeming rule is Barney Hill, an African American male (discussed below), but his "abduction," as I will argue, seems to have been psychologically inflicted upon him by his wife, an imaginative (and domineering) Caucasian type.

14. W. Benjamin, "The Work of Art in the Age of Mechanical Reproduction,"

in *Art in Modern Culture: An Anthology of Critical Texts*, ed. F. Frascina and J. Harris (London: Phaedon, 1992), pp. 297–307.

15. For this perception, and its supporting anecdotal evidence, see Peter Sacks, *Generation-X Goes to College: An Eye-Opening Account of Teaching Postmodern America* (Chicago: Open Court, 1996).

16. See Louis A. Sass, *Madness and Modernism: Insanity in the Light of Modern Art, Literature, and Thought* (New York: BasicBooks, 1992).

17. For the unwelcome argument that "New Age" credulity is really old hat, see John F. Moffitt, *Occultism in Avant-Garde Art: The Case of Joseph Beuys* (Ann Arbor: University of Michigan Press, 1986), pp. 21, 72, 78, 181–83.

18. Sacks, *Generation-X Goes to College*, pp. 138–39.

19. For all the gruesome details of their mass demise, see New York Post Staff, *Heaven's Gate: Cult Suicide in San Diego* (New York: HarperCollins, 1997).

20. For an early study on them, see H. Hewes and B. Steiger, *UFO Missionaries Extraordinary* (New York: Pocket Books, 1976); for an academic discussion of the group, the last published before its sudden demise and instant celebrity, see Robert W. Balch, "Waiting for the Ships: Disillusionment and the Revitalization of Faith in Bo and Peep's UFO Cult," in Lewis, *The Gods Have Landed*, pp. 137–66.

21. I am repeating here observations made by Robert S. Ellwood, in Lewis, *The Gods Have Landed*, pp. 167–68.

22. For an objective historical approach, see C. M. Stafford Poole, *Our Lady of Guadalupe: The Origins and Sources of a Mexican National Symbol, 1531–1797* (Tucson: Arizona University Press, 1996); for her immediate prototypes, see William Christian, *Apparitions in Late Medieval and Renaissance Spain* (Princeton: Princeton University Press, 1981); no comparable scholarship seems to exist for the Elvis apparitions.

23. *Inin huey tlamahuitzoltzin*, as quoted in Poole, *Our Lady of Guadalupe*, pp. 40–41; Nahuatl text on pp. 245–46.

24. See Belting, *Likeness and Presence*, chap. 11, "The 'Holy Face': Legends and Images in Competition." For the contemporary art-historical context of the Guadalupe apparition in 1531, see Sixten Ringbom, *Les images de dévotion: XIIe–XVe siècle* (Paris: Monfort, 1995).

25. For a provocative look at the communality of apparitional phenomena, see Harpur, *Daimonic Reality*; Thompson, *Angels and Aliens*.

26. See Harpur, *Daimonic Reality*, pp. 102–11; Nickell, *Looking for a Miracle*, pp. 167–208.

27. See, for instance, Vallée, *Anatomy of a Phenomenon*, pp. 20, 25, 53, 87, 160–64, 179, 191.

28. Archival reports, as in Christian, *Apparitions*, p. 121 (my emphasis); Catalan text, p. 297.

29. Archival reports, as in ibid., pp. 47–49 (my emphasis); Castilian texts, pp. 258–62.

30. Ibid.

31. Ibid.

32. Ibid.

33. Inés, as in ibid., pp. 68–69; see also the complete Castilian text, pp. 269–76.

34. Anonymous SS celebrant, as in Joachim Remak, ed., *The Nazi Years: A Documentary History* (Englewood Cliffs, N.J.: Spectrum, 1969), p. 49.

35. Again see Huyghe, *Field Guide to Extraterrestrials*.

36. J. Nickell. "Extraterrestrial Iconography," *Skeptical Inquirer* 21, no. 5 (September/October 1997): 18–19, citing Huyghe's *Field Guide to Extraterrestrials* as his essential inspiration, but making no reference to either Gardner's or Janson's *kunstgeschichtlicher* time lines.

37. Sass, *Madness and Modernism*, pp. 8, 14, et seq.

38. For the historical texts and pictures, see R. Bernheimer, *Wild Men in the Middle Ages: A Study in Art, Sentiment, and Demonology* (New York: Octogan, 1970); J. B. Friedman, *The Monstrous Races in Medieval Art and Thought* (Cambridge: Harvard University Press, 1981).

39. These examples were so illustrated, and titled, in *Newsweek* (7 July 1997): 60–62; for *six* cinematic types, see also Kurt Andersen, "The Origin of Alien Species," *New Yorker*, 14 July 1997: 38–39; see also (of course) Huyghe, *Field Guide to Extraterrestrials*, also providing the bibliography for "sightings" antedating those seen in the cineplexes.

40. See Alice K. Turner, *The History of Hell* (New York: Harvest, 1995), pp. 63–65.

41. Jenny Randles, *The UFO Conspiracy: The First Forty Years* (London: Javelin, 1988), pp. 83–84.

42. M. Gardner, *Science: Good, Bad, and Bogus* (New York: Avon, 1983), pp. 347–49.

43. Xanthopoulous, in Maguire, *Art and Eloquence in Byzantium*, p. 12.

Chapter 5

It All Began with
Betty and Barney Hill

THE MASS MEDIA AND THE ALIEN TIME LINE

Returning to our handy diagram, the "Alien Time Line" (fig. 8), at the very beginning—in 1947—we see indicated that the "'Flying Saucer' craze begins" (as discussed further in chapters 8 and 9). The postmodernist art historian is however most interested in the year 1961, marking on the Alien Time Line the epochal "Betty and Barney Hill abduction," and illustrated here with the initial "classic alien portrait"— exactly as it had been reported by the Hills.[1] As observed by Joe Nickell, who designed this invaluable Alien Time Line, theirs was "the *first widely reported* alien abduction."[2] According to Terry Matheson, the indefatigable scholar of the postmodernist ET literary genre, as eventually told in John Fuller's best-selling book, *Interrupted Journey* (1966), the spine-tingling Hill saga "would provide a model for all later abduction authors. . . . What Fuller's book does for the abduction myth is set the pattern for future works of this type, for good *and* ill."[3]

Thomas E. Bullard, another painstaking student of the seemingly endless stream of UFO abduction literature, flatly states that the now canonical ET physical type (fig. 1) represents "the sort of beings made famous in the Hill case," additionally noting that "the Hill case set the style for hidden abduction memories to be released by hypnosis." In short, the Hill case "introduced the abduction idea to public awareness and their story spread throughout the culture to set the standard for *all* retellings to come . . . the general story affixed itself in collective memory. . . . Each [subsequent] story simply retells the Hill case, plus or minus a few details." And the rule is that, following publication of the Hill narrative in 1966,

> the standard, or core abduction story describes the physical capture of a witness by apparently alien beings, who carry him (or her) aboard a craft for physical examination and release him or her within an hour or two. Longer or shorter durations are possible. Related, but gradually less similar, types of experience may extend this core-narrative in the form of psychic abductions, voluntary entries, time-lapse cases, teleportation, contactee experiences and UFO-connected disappearances. This body of reports covers in the broadest possible sense *all* UFO encounters that might be called "abductions." This [post-Hill] continuum joins abductions to other sorts of UFO phenomena as well, since abductions and other close encounters share the same elements.[4]

This epoch-making event supposedly happened in the New Hampshire boondocks late at night, when the Hills saw a light-flashing flying saucer trailing their car. Their auto stalled; the spacecraft landed; its ET crewmen descended, nabbed the terrified couple, and hustled them into the saucer; then the ETs subjected them to a bumbling examination of their midde-aged reproductive organs. So said the Hills, and as aided by hypnotic regression. In the particular sense of "widely reported," that observation additionally, and most significantly, tells us we are now specifically dealing with a classic postmodernist, wholly media-generated, "pseudoevent" as defined in chapter 3.[5] Accordingly, the Hills themselves became "pseudopeople"—*tabloid celebrities*, people who have become "famous for being famous." As Patrick Huyghe further specifies:

> Not until the late 1960s, with the publicity surrounding the Betty and Barney Hill case, did UFO organizations begin to take seriously the reports of [ET] entities. . . . Now, of course, UFO organizations are interested in little else but the closest of all encounter stories—the abduction reports. Most of these are bedroom encounters with the black-eyed creatures and never even seem to involve a UFO or flying saucer. The craft have [since] become superfluous.[6]

Nonetheless, the *real* date of the "media event" as such—and thus of its attendant iconographic contributions—is 1966; 1961 is merely the year retroactively assigned by the Hills to their apocryphal close encounter, specifically alleged to have occurred on September 19. The year 1966 is when John Fuller's *Interrupted Journey*, describing in great detail the Hill encounter with ETs, was published. Enjoying best-seller status as a much-reprinted paperback (since 1967), it was later (1975) made into a television movie for millions of nonreaders (see figs. 17, 18). Such as their abductors were described by the Hills—*Achtung*: well after the fact and *under hypnosis*—the enduring iconographic result was what Joe Nickell labels "the little big-headed humanoid with large, wrap-around eyes."[7] The sensational Hill epic, a wholly media-generated pseudoevent, made the ET's career as an American visual celebrity, a star, an enduring media icon, like Elvis. Now we must quote the original historical document inspiring *all* subsequent, wholly ekphrastic, standard ET portraiture. What follows is the art historian's equivalent of a "slam dunk" (a reference to basketball, a game usually seen on TV, not Dante's *Inferno*, a world-class work of art).

BARNEY AND BETTY'S CLOSE ENCOUNTER IN A DERIVATIVE CONTEXT

The Hills were a biracial couple. Barney was black (African American) and a postal worker. Betty was white (Euro-American) and a social worker. Both were thoroughly bourgeois, just folks. As the apocryphal incident was initially reported by Barney Hill to his psychiatrist, on April 5, 1964, "I was sitting there out on that mountain road at night. I could actually see what I described as the Cheshire cat. This growing, one-beam eye, staring at me, or rather not staring at me, but being a part of me." Still under hypnosis, Barney then "sketched from memory what the man [*sic*, ET] might have looked like," and this maladroit bug-eyed *bozzetto* was published by Fuller in his paperback best-seller.[8] (See fig. 16.) Only afterward, when no longer under hypnosis, Barney recounted to John Fuller, probably early in 1966, the distinctive, now-canonical, features of his outer-space molestor. By then, however, he had significantly added many more colorful details. As a result, the following, now universal, alien tableau had finally emerged:

> The men [ETs] had rather odd-shaped heads, with a large cranium, diminishing in size as it got toward the chin. And the eyes continued around to the sides of their heads, so that it appeared that they could see several degrees beyond the lateral extent of our vision. . . . And something [else] that I remembered—[only] after listening to the tapes

[of the interviews made under hypnosis]—is the mouth itself. I could not describe the mouth before, and I drew the picture without including the mouth. But it was much like when you draw one horizontal line with a short perpendicular line on each end. . . . The texture of the skin, as I remember it from this quick glance, was grayish, almost metallic looking. I didn't notice any hair—or headgear for that matter. Also, I didn't notice any proboscis; there just seemed to be two slits that represented the nostrils. . . . So it looked as if the mouth had almost no opening and as if they had practically no nose.[9]

In sum, ETs are grayish (hence "Grays"), bubble-headed, mostly noseless and, best of all, they have huge, catlike and dark-colored, wraparound eyes. Above all, it is the oculus-motif which will prove central to all forthcoming, post-1966, canonical ET iconography (see figs. 1, 4, 17–22). As Betty Hill recalled them, again long after the supposed close encounter, by then the ETs directly reminded her of creatures familiar to her from her stressful job as a social worker:

In a sense, they looked like mongoloids, because I was comparing them with a case I had been working with, a specific mongoloid child, [having] this sort of round face and broad forehead, along with a certain type of coarseness. The surface of their skin seemed to be a bluish gray, but probably whiter than that. Their eyes moved, and they had pupils. Somehow, I had the feeling they were more like cats' eyes. . . . Their bodies seemed to be a little out of proportion, with a bigger chest cavity, broader chest.[10]

In this case, it was Betty who had recorded the *first* mental image of a now-canonical, "gray" and "cat-eyed," ET physiognomic perception.

Fuller's sensational tale, *The Interrupted Journey*, supposedly experienced by the Hills in 1961, also must be credited with inaugurating a now-standard literary format for subsequent alien-abduction narratives: the hypnotist's queries as followed by the mesmerized responses. As we did before (in chapter 2) in citing various close encounter stories published following the enviable marketplace success of *The Interrupted Journey*, we will again revert to the pattern of "DJ" (the doctor's judicious query) and "R" (the patient's response). In this instance, R is Barney, who gives us extremely vivid descriptions of his bug-eyed ET. As we see here, this is an alien creature which oddly metamorphoses from an Irishman into a Nazi, then briefly into a "bunny," then right back into the kind of ET with which we are now—over thirty-five years later—all too familiar.

As always, the essential first step is to get R deeply hypnotized. Once that desirable state of considerably altered consciousness was achieved, DJ announces into the tape recorder, "You're clear now. Relaxed . . ." Thereupon R queries, "What do they [the ETs] want? What do they want?" Initially, R's perception of them is positive: "One [alien] person looks friendly to me. He's friendly-looking. And he's looking at me—over his right shoulder. And he's smiling." DJ then asks, "What was his face like? What did it make you think of?" R's initial response has it that the alien face "was round. I think of—I think of—a red-headed Irishman." After mulling over that inaugural earthling-ethnic designation, R decides that this is "because [the] Irish are usually hostile to Negroes. And when I see a friendly Irish person, I react to him by thinking: I will be friendly. And I think this one that is looking over his shoulder is friendly."

As we further learn, the seemingly friendly Gaelic ET turns out to be facing a wall in the UFO, and DJ asks, "You saw him through this window? You said there was a row of windows?" According to R's hypnotically induced recollection, "There was a row of windows. A huge row of windows. Only divided by struts, or structures that prevented it from being one solid window. Or then [maybe] it would have been one solid window." Immediately following, now the ET acquires an "evil face"; in fact, "He looks like a German Nazi. He's a Nazi." As we all know (for we have all seen old Hollywood movies depicting such notoriously "evil" people), all "Nazis" wear uniforms. However, when DJ inquires into the details characterizing the Nazi-ET costume, the response is a sartorial novelty: "He had a black scarf around his neck, dangling over his left shoulder."

Unfazed, DJ wonders, "How could you see the figures [in the UFO] so clearly at that distance?" And the logical explanation is that R "was looking at them with binoculars." Regarding the extraterrestrial physiognomy belonging to the formerly Irish crew member, we are now told that "his eyes were slanted. Oh, his eyes were slanted! But not like a Chinese." Confronted with this new ethnic dilemma, next R cries out, "Oh, I feel like a rabbit." Given such a non sequitur, DJ naturally wonders, "What do you mean by that?" According to the rambling response:

> I was hunting for rabbits in Virginia. And this cute little bunny went into a bush that was not very big. And my cousin Marge was on one side of the bush, and I was on the other, with a hat. And the poor little bunny thought he was safe. And it tickled me, because he was just hiding behind a little stalk, which meant security to him, when I pounced on him, and threw my hat on him, and captured the poor little bunny who thought he was safe. Funny I thought of that, right out there on the field. I feel like a rabbit.

Well, since that wasn't much help, DJ then asks, "What was Betty doing all this time?" and "Did you make any outcry to her, the way you did to me?" And the less-than-illuminating response is "I can't remember. I don't know." But what R does remember is that, rather than Betty, the ET "creature is telling me something." Bizarrely, ET does not actually talk; R can only "see it in his face. No, his lips are not moving." When queried as to the actual content of this unprecedented, for being otherworldly, dialogue, R replies, "He's just telling me: Don't be afraid. I'm not a bunny. I'm going to be—I'm going to be safe. He didn't tell me I was that bunny." Besides the comforting rabbit remark, ET's further instructions included an injunction to "Stay there, and keep looking. Just keep looking, and stay there. And just keep looking." After observing that ET actually "didn't say it," and that R instead only does "know [that] he said it," his only resort is then to scream, "It's pounding in my head!" Then comes another deafening scream: "I gotta get away! I gotta get away from here!" DJ's professional comment is "All right. All right. Calm down."

After R settles down a bit, DJ again asks how he could "be sure he was telling you this?" And the answer is wholly ocular: "His eyes! His eyes. I've never seen eyes like that before." Besides the pseudo-Gaelic ET, there was also another ET, designated by R as "the leader"; he was the fey fashion plate with "the black, black shiny jacket and the scarf." DJ needs more commentary concerning the ocular equipment of the ET leader, and R replies, "I've never seen eyes slanted like that. They began to be round and [the eyes] went back like that, and like that. And they went up like that." Finally comes the moment of strictly art-historical significance, and this comes when R (Barney) makes a momentous plea: "Can I draw it?" Eager to accede, DJ says, "I'm giving you a pad and a pencil. You can open your eyes, and you can draw whatever you want. You can draw it now. Go ahead."[11] Barney then drew his rudimentary eyewitness portrait (fig. 16).

Well, there you have it: the archetypal confrontation between a rabbitlike, cowering human being and a flashily dressed, neo-Nazi ET. This also marks the epochal moment of the initial installation of a now-canonic, postmodernist mode of extraterrestrial populist portraiture.

Whether functioning as a chronicler of popular literature or graphic art, the historian should be particularly sensitive to the chronology and context of events defining the legendary Hill abduction event initially inspiring a now-classic ET iconographic type. As marked on Nickell's time line (fig. 8), "1961" was however only the year assigned to their "abduction" by the Hills—if indeed that gauche encounter ever did happen. This epochal event, establishing a now-standardized extraterrestrial art-historical topos, requires rigorous deconstruction. Besides recalling the chronological marker showing that their story was only *published* in September 1966 in *Look* magazine, with Fuller's book immediately following, a further fact is that, well before Betty Hill ever actually began "remembering" in her nightmares the infamous abduction episode, she was studying printed materials containing nearly identical extraterrestrial leitmotifs.

For instance, we do know that she had read in September 1961, in one sitting, Donald Keyhoe's paranoid paperback tome called *The Flying Saucer Conspiracy* (1955), among other materials put out by Keyhoe's organization, the National Investigations Commission on Aerial Phenomena (NICAP), cofounded by James and Coral Lorenzen.[12] Therein Keyhoe had described putative alien abductions in Venezuela where diminutive ETs aggressively abused their cowering earthling captives. Moreover, the underlying aggressor-alien invasion motif characterizing the famous Hill encounter broadly reflects instilled attitudes common during the Cold War; Barney himself had said that "it's right and proper to defend [yourself] against an aggressor at all times."[13] An avid (but apparently not a very discriminating) reader, Betty surely also studied Coral Lorenzen's sensational paperback exposé of *The Great Flying Saucer Hoax* (1962), reporting fleets of saucer- and cigar-shaped UFOs given to trailing cars along lonely country roads; supposedly they did so, just as the Hills were later led to believe, "to discover human reaction to their presence."[14]

On September 26, 1961, less than one week after the supposed ET encounter, Betty Hill wrote to NICAP's director, Donald Keyhoe, author of the sensational *Flying Saucer Conspiracy*—which she had just read. In this letter, whereas she described their UFO sighting, not only did she not mention anything about seeing ETs, *she made absolutely no mention whatsoever of the now-celebrated abduction.* This melodramatic episode was, in fact, not mentioned until *after* the NICAP experts responded to her inquiry.[15] Only then did she "dream" that she and Barney had been abducted! Certainly, the Lorenzen opus was well known to the NICAP UFOlogists who began lavishing welcome attention on the Hills after October 21, 1961. They then provided Betty with further reading materials, and cited by them as especially meritorious was the authority of "reports documented [*sic*] in the book by Coral Lorenzen, *The Great Flying Saucer Hoax*, William-Frederick Press, 1962."[16] Now Betty Hill, but not Barney, was thoroughly *au courant* with apocryphal UFO visitations in the outback. Moreover, it was in fact the

NICAP investigators who first raised the possibility that Betty's dreams were based on UFO reality. She obviously thought that was a swell idea. By mid-1962, Betty was giving lectures to local groups, describing the UFO incident and, more importantly, her abduction dreams, which, of course, she now presented to her rapt audiences as something that had really happened to her.

This is scarcely surprising. There was even something like a family tradition of seeing UFOs: Betty's sister, Janet, "saw" them as early as 1953 and repeatedly thereafter.[17] Accordingly, well before the alleged abduction encounter of 1961, and just as Barney himself confessed: "Yes, Betty did believe in flying saucers."[18] In fact, and just as John Fuller had ingenuously observed, "as Betty Hill's confidence [in her ET encounter] increased through her study of the NICAP materials [including Lorenzen's *Great Flying Saucer Hoax*], so did her willingness to reveal more of the details."[19] Barney also repeatedly complained about Betty's dogged insistence that he must subscribe to her beliefs, which, obviously, he finally did.[20] He additionally mentioned to his doctor how all this UFO bickering had aggravated his stomach ulcer and elevated his blood pressure to dangerous levels.[21] In fact, a stroke killed him in 1969. As he complained to his analyst, "I am mad with her. I say to myself, I believe Betty is trying to make me think this is a flying saucer."[22] In short, and as even Fuller recognized, "The reality or non-reality of the [ET] dreams was of course foremost in Betty's mind."[23] Put another way, she inflicted them upon her henpecked husband.

There is even more reason to doubt the famous Hill close encounter with the ETs, and this has to do with strictly modern and American popular culture. Most likely, Betty also saw a truly sleazy sci-fi movie, now a cult classic, called *Invaders from Mars* (1953), where a female abductee was (similarly) poked and prodded by aliens playing doctor; in fact, just as in Betty's account, the Hollywood aliens specifically insert a needle into an actress's navel (and amniocentesis has been a standard medical procedure since the Victorian era, when it was employed to draw off amniotic fluid in difficult pregnancies). Moreover, the crucial Hill story motif of amnesia with reversible memory, likewise communication by mental telepathy, had previously appeared in another bad movie, *Killers from Space* (1954).

Even more damning is the television angle. Long before publication of the Hills' best-selling gauche encounter, an episode of *The Outer Limits* TV show—entitled "The Bellero Shield"—had been aired on February 10, 1964.[24] Exactly twelve days *later*, the very same bug-eyed ET iconographic type as was featured in the televised drama then appeared for the very *first* time in Barney's hypnotized recollections; as he then admitted, "I've never seen eyes slanted like this before."[25] The art historian now insists upon the world-historical significance of "The Bellero Shield" ocular iconography, for this had (inadvertently) spawned a now-standard, worldwide ET portraiture.[26]

Only after watching the television dramatization, and at the hypnotist's specific suggestion, Barney then produced his crude pencil sketch (fig. 16) of a cat-faced homunculus wearing a billed cap and what he described as "a black scarf around his neck."[27] As may be added in passing, the cap and the scarf, and wrap-around sunglasses, are also standard accessories for menacing American motorcycle gangs (e.g., "Hell's Angels"), for which there are still many well-documented "sightings." Moreover, Barney confessed to feeling paranoid about such earthling hoodlums just before he was kidnapped by extraterrestrial thugs.[28] A lot of people were that way back then—paranoid—if only because they, too, had all seen the movie *The Wild One* (1954), with a menacing motorcyclist Marlon Brando decked out in a black leather jacket, sunglasses, and funky cap.

However, Barney's first fully detailed, verbal ET portrait, as given to Fuller early in 1966 (and as quoted above), had only emerged long *after* Betty's first hypnotic session, dated March 7, 1964. Interestingly, in earlier sessions, whereas Betty recalled many details of the alleged abduction, Barney did not. But her detailed tableau, for which we even have a transcription in her own handwriting, is to be dated even earlier; it is known that she had written it all out long before she had ever consulted with the hypnotist![29] Probably it dates even to late 1962, when Betty was telling the locals all the lurid details, which, of course, were also repeatedly passed on to Barney. According to her (undated) iconographic prescription:

> Their chests are larger than ours; their noses were larger (longer) than the average size. . . . Their complexions were of a gray tone; like a gray paint with a black base; their lips were of a bluish tint. [Their] eyes were very dark, possibly black. . . . They wore trousers and short jackets. . . . They were all wearing military caps, similar to the Air Force, but not so broad on the top. They were very human in their appearance, not frightening [etc.].[30]

Surprise: that is exactly the same tableau (fig. 16) that Barney was to dredge up a couple of years later due to persistent prodding from, first, the UFOlogists and, later, his hypnotizing psychiatrist. In short, another art-historical slam dunk.

No wonder that the Hills' psychiatrist, Dr. Benjamin Simon, who had worked with them between January and June 1964, thought their "memories"—unquestionably later to exert considerable pop-cultural influences, and also including all these postmodernist ET icons (figs. 1, 4, 15–22)—were really a classic example of a *folie à deux*, an involuntarily shared fantasy![31] More important is Simon's recollection of his interview with a magazine editor sent from New York to Boston late in 1966, when *Look* was about to publish the first account of the Hill story. The editor quickly asked him, "Doctor, do you really believe that the Hills were abducted [by aliens] and taken aboard a flying saucer?" Simon's reply was emphatic: "*Absolutely not!*"[32] No matter: everybody else was ready and eager to buy into the tall tale. Making no mention of Dr. Simon's crucial disclaimer, *Look* sailed ahead and published the discredited fantasy anyway; so did the editorial directors at Dial Press, the publishers of Fuller's best-selling *The Interrupted Journey*. Qualified psychiatrists may render a professional opinion but, when all is said and done, money talks, has the last word, and its voice is very, very loud.

The aftermath was rather pathetic, at least for the central players. As reported by British UFO enthusiast Jenny Randles:

> Transcripts of the sessions were later written up by New England journalist John Fuller as *The Interrupted Journey*. It proved one of the biggest sellers in UFO history and produced world headlines in the mid-1960s. Later [in 1975] a TV movie was based on the book, dramatizing the encounter as "The UFO-Incident" [figs. 17, 18]. Barney did not live to see that. He died from a stroke, whilst still young in 1969 [Barney was, you will recall, put to a lot of psychic stress, particularly by Betty]. Betty, however, continues in the role of a kind of UFO guru. She enjoys this [media attention] and has reported seeing countless lights which others, who have investigated, are certain can be explained as aircraft. Nevertheless, few question the sincerity of the original story.[33]

Admittedly, the "sincerity of the original story" may be allowed, but the matter of its *credibility* is altogether something else. In sum, all the distinctive narrative features of the epochal Hill abduction anecdote—compressed later to produce a single iconographic staple, the ET portrait *en buste* (fig. 16)—can all be shown to have their now identifiable, widely published antecedents. Skeptically viewed, the nearly universally celebrated Hill sighting, as first published to great acclaim late in 1966, just represents a *pasticcio* providing exotic motifs already ubiquitous in the contemporary pop culture milieu. Specifically, the crucial seedbed for all this popular cultural detritus, a *locus classicus* as it were, was Betty Hill's overheated imagination, unilaterally and obsessively cooking up this distinctive iconography since 1962. The result is a now-omnipresent repertoire of canonical extraterrestrial portraiture (figs. 1, 4, 5, 15–22), and its effects upon postmodernist international culture have been enormous. Perhaps this kind of deconstructive insight, and the tenacity to unmask the actual historical sources supplying all the essential pictorial components of the apocryphal event, required the professional eye and ethical commitment of an art historian. Certainly, the pullulating UFOlogists have not bothered to do the essential research.

THE UFO INCIDENT AND THE FABULOUSLY FAKED "ABDUCTION" OF TRAVIS WALTON

Here is another piece of art-historical evidence, posthumous in the case of Barney Hill. On October 20, 1975, the NBC television network aired a made-for-TV movie based on the Hills' hypnotically retrieved misadventures with the aliens. Called *The UFO Incident*, it starred Estelle Parsons as Betty, and the role of Barney Hill was played by James Earl Jones (who, two years later, became the voice of Darth Vader in another universally viewed space opera called *Star Wars*). *The UFO Incident* was repeated, again in prime time, on September 9, 1976 (and it still lurks in the wee hours for insomniac video voyeurs).

Although not previously so acknowledged, this cinematic artifact, *The UFO Incident*, is of considerable art-historical significance. Since no certified extraterrestrial aliens were registered with the Screen Actors Guild, artificial *alieni* had to be created for the TV movie. Accordingly, working from verbal descriptions given in Fuller's *Interrupted Journey*, and as additionally guided by Barney's maladroit pencil sketch, the creative "special effects" (F/X) artists at NBC created three-dimensional simulations of the Hill ETs (figs. 17, 18). The imaginative made-for-TV movie, meretriciously presented as a sort of "documentary," was watched by millions; if you missed it the first time, there were replays. The world-historical artistic result was, as Michael Shermer reports, "the stereotypical alien with a large, bald head and big, elongated eyes." And he adds that this is, of course, the very same biological oddity "reported by so many abductees since 1975."[34]

The UFO Incident also represented a most profitable enterprise for all concerned; the movie rights—of which the Hills received 40 percent, Fuller and Simon 30 percent each—must surely have been in the *half-million-dollar* range since Dr. Simon later told Philip Klass that "I'm not going to tell you the highest bid, and the *lowest* is $300,000."[35] And that revelation again proves a significant point: a sufficiently dramatic abduction by aliens will prove very good for your bank account and, obviously, it proves even better for the profit margins enjoyed by the manipulative managers of the American infotainment industry. If nothing else, the UFO experience represents great business for its entrepreneurs, and that is why—trust me!—it is not likely to go away any time soon. A case in point, as we shall see shortly, is the widely publicized "abduction" of Travis Walton late in 1975.

The iconographic impact of *The UFO Incident* was immediate; Philip Klass notes that a "rash of abduction reports followed in the wake of the NBC-TV movie," which he lists. A UFO organization compiled statistics showing that from 1947 to 1976, which includes the decade after publication of the celebrated Hill case (also the "contactees" discussed in chapter 8), there were only fifty abduction-type reports: less than two a year. In the two years immediately following the broadcast of *The UFO Incident*, there were reported over a hundred cases of abduction by aliens: fifty per annum, a *2,500 percent increase*. Klass's conclusion: "After viewing the movie, any person with a little imagination could now become an *instant celebrity* by claiming a UFO-abduction."[36]

In case any of those forthcoming and unfortunate "experiencers" managed to miss *that* movie (as I did), then the same classic Hill ET was also faithfully recreated for them slightly later with Steven Spielberg's cuddly version in *E.T.: The Extraterrestrial* (1982; fig. 15). Now for an art-historical lesson, the kind dealing with transmission of iconographic types. The huggable alien of the 1982 space opera blockbuster is a different breed than the emotionally distant one seen five years earlier in Spielberg's *Close Encounters of the Third Kind* (1977; fig. 19). In short, the ET devised in 1977 by Spielberg's clever F/X artists is a near knock-off from the 1975 *UFO Incident* (cf. figs. 17, 18)! It, too, looks like a bug-eyed, turtle-necked, fetuslike homunculus. Even if someone might have missed the TV epic, nearly everybody saw Spielberg's movies (me, too).

The extraterrestrially fertile year 1977 also brought us *Star Wars* (another blockbuster movie), and the first manned, interplanetary flight in the U.S. space shuttle *Enterprise*, and the launch of unmanned spacecraft *Voyager I* and *Voyager II* into outer space, not to mention a space probe of the planet Venus and the return of the *Pioneer II* spacecraft, bringing new data about the magnetic field of the sun. Back on earth however, President Carter was warning the locals that the energy crisis could bring on a "national catastrophe," to which Americans must respond with the "moral equivalent of war," by making "profound" changes in their petroleum consumption patterns.[37] This dreadful problem had been brought to us by other "aliens," the mostly Islamic members of OPEC.

The contributions made by the 1975 TV movie to the historiography of the burgeoning abduction-by-aliens movement were immediately perceivable. It also *proves* the point made here about the collusive role of, and instantaneous effects exerted by the mass media upon postmodernist American pop culture—and especially as it relates to the ubiquitous UFO Experience. On the evening of November 5, 1975, barely two weeks after the primetime showing of *The UFO Incident*, the most spectacular of all alien epiphanies was said to have occurred. On that date, six young woodcutters called the Navajo County Sheriff's Department in Heber, Arizona. Headed by crew chief Mike Rogers, they had been frantically trying to fulfill a contract Rogers had made with the U.S. Forest Service the year before to clear out underbrush to prevent forest fires. They reported that they had been working in nearby Sitgreaves National Forest in the mountainous and heavily forested, east-central part of the state. As their story went, their partner, Travis Walton, now missing, had been "zapped" by a hovering UFO emitting something like a bolt of lightning that allegedly blew the poor lad into the air, right up into the looming spacecraft!

Travis (born 1952) was to explain on national television and other media venues that he believed he had been in the UFO for the entire period of his "missing time," some five days, although he was conscious for only a few hours. He awoke in an all-metal room, which he took to be a "hospital." His shirt was pulled up, and a "thing," not attached anywhere, lay across his chest. He then saw three "aliens," about five feet tall, bald, dressed in "orangeish-brown coveralls," with "chalky white skin" and small features, except for big brown eyes. As Travis put it in his inevitable paperback exposé, *Ultimate Encounter: The True Story of a UFO Kidnapping*:

> They were very short, shorter than five feet, and they had very large bald heads, no hair. Their heads were domed, very large. They looked like fetuses. They had no eyebrows, no eyelashes. They had very large eyes—enormous eyes—almost all brown, without much white in them. The creepiest thing about them were those eyes. Oh, man, *those eyes*; they just stared through me.[38]

Anyone who has bothered to read Travis's true-confession book, *The Walton Experience* (1978), must concur with literary scholar Terry Matheson that his "abduction narrative is arguably the only one of its kind, that is, frankly, boring."[39] Viewed otherwise, but as seems perfectly logical, an amateur artist's ekphrastic rendering of the ET "humanoids" described by Travis faithfully conforms to the Hill model as recently broadcast to the world by the NBC TV movie (see fig. 20; cf. figs. 16–18). Travis reported that, frightened, he knocked the object off his chest and pushed away the "aliens," who left the room without saying anything. A "human" then entered, dressed in a blue uniform and a "clear, bubble-type helmet." About six feet tall, with "brownish-blond hair" and "golden-hazel eyes," the Aryan-type humanoid smiled silently at Walton's babbling. He led Walton to a smaller room down a hallway, where three other (ersatz) "humans" put over his face a clear, soft, form-fitting plastic mask. With a black ball attached to it, it was "like an oxygen mask," but without tubes. Walton passed out, and the next thing he remembered was waking up in a road in the woods, where he "saw this craft disappear straight up."

Not until five days later, on November 12, did Walton turn up, just a few miles away from the woodsy spot where he had last been seen by his friends. Then he told that chilling story of being taken aboard a flying saucer and given the seemingly inevitable physical examination. This was a truly newsworthy event! This was the first UFO incident in which the alleged abduction was reported to law enforcement authorities while the "victim" was still missing. That made it official, a matter of local government record. Even more important, it was the first alien-abduction episode for which there were six supporting witnesses, captained by Mike Rogers. Surely, this was the best substantiated of all UFO abduction stories to date. Best of all, young Travis, a handsome chap with curly hair and a roguish mustache, got on television! The local matriarch of UFOlogy, Coral Lorenzen, based in Tucson, quickly endorsed Walton's tale, calling it "one of the most important and intriguing in the history of the UFO phenomenon." Surely it was all of that, but not in the way she had hoped. In a book published in 1987, Philip Klass proved it was a hoax, more specifically, a scheme calculated to defraud the federal government.[40]

The ingenious, detective-like unraveling by Klass of the collective falsehood perpetrated by the Rogers gang may be quickly summarized. Travis's older brother, Duane, was interviewed during the "missing time." At that time, he showed no concern over his sibling's whereabouts or well-being; as he put it, "He's not even missing. He knows where he's at, and I know where he's at." He then also admitted that he had read science fiction, in fact, "as much as anybody"; presumably, so did his brother. Duane stated that he and his brother were actively competing to have a UFO experience. As he eagerly explained, once the craft was seen,

"We would immediately get directly under the object. We discussed this time and again. The opportunity [to board a UFO] would be too great to pass up, and who ever happened to be left on the ground—if one of us didn't make the grade—would try to convince whoever was in the craft to come back and get the other one." According to prescient Duane, by being zapped and abducted, "He's received the benefits of it." He sure did: Travis later sold the rights for his story, and yet another widely viewed movie resulted: *Fire in the Sky* (1993). Although the sum he actually received is not known to me, we may imagine, given the Hill precedent, that it was something around *a half-million dollars*.

Travis's story was supposedly given additional credence when it was reported that he had passed a lie detector test; as we were told, so did Duane. That test was administered in Phoenix by George J. Pfeifer, who was employed by Tom Ezell & Associates, and that is the mechanized questionnaire everyone heard about. It was arranged by the Aerial Phenomena Research Organization (APRO), the leader of which was Coral Lorenzen, hardly an objective sponsor. Also noteworthy was Klass's discovery of notations Pfeifer put on his charts, showing that he had allowed Travis to "dictate" some of the questions put to him; such practice is unheard of among reputable polygraphists. More interesting is the identity of the organization which paid for the test: the *National Enquirer*. There was, however, another lie detector test put to Travis, which is the one you did *not* get to hear about.

This polygraph examination was given to him on November 15, meaning before the APRO test, by Jack McCarthy. Besides being considered reputable and far more experienced in such matters than was Pfeifer, McCarthy had no affiliations with either the UFO enthusiasts or the *National Enquirer*. When Klass later asked McCarthy about his conclusions, as based on *his* test results, his reply was emphatic: "*Gross deception!*" But these findings were deliberately covered up: the *National Enquirer* asked McCarthy to sign a hastily typed "secrecy agreement," which he did. As it turned out, Travis's track record in veracity was already severely besmirched. In May 1971, young Walton had pleaded guilty to charges of burglary, stealing bank-roll checks, and forgery. His coconspirator was no less than Charles Rogers, the brother of Mike Rogers, the chief of the work crew which, in November 1975, all swore to Travis's melodramatic "zapping" by aliens. Another member of that dubious crew, Alan Dalis, would later plead guilty to three armed robberies arising from his hard-drug habit. In short, not an especially trustworthy bunch.

Besides celebrity, quickly forthcoming, there was also an immediate monetary incentive for Walton. Several weeks after Travis had flunked outright the McCarthy lie detector test, undismayed, the *National Enquirer* ran a large feature story describing his "abduction" by aliens: it sold an awful lot of copies. The *National Enquirer* was clearly pleased with the results. Besides publicizing the story, for which they bought the exclusive rights, the tabloid had (perhaps unwittingly) directly inspired it. Since 1973, the *National Enquirer* had been offering a "prize" of $100,000 for convincing evidence attesting to even one extraterrestrial visitor. Also offered was a consolation prize for the most impressive UFO story of the year; that would pay five to ten thousand dollars.

In 1976, the ante was upped to *one million dollars*—that is, before the award for dubious achievement was finally dropped, due to the lack of qualified candidates. But there were no lack of aspirants: as the zealous tabloid editors reported in 1985, "as of 1980, reports the *National Enquirer*, UFO sightings had increased to the rate of more than *1,000 a day* worldwide" (their emphasis).[41] And, lo and behold! the noble-minded tabloid paid Rogers and his five other helpers $5,000 for their story, which, of course, they all collectively affirmed to represent the truth, the whole truth, and nothing but the truth. (By the way, since Travis suffered no discernible physical after-effects, not even the odd scorch mark, for a million bucks, even a mere hundred grand—what the hell, even five thousand, I, too, would be willing to get a bit "zapped" in the Arizona woods.) Although I have no hard evidence to cite, I also suspect that the Rogers bunch got a fair share of the royalties from the forthcoming TV movie.

So how did the other woodcutters, as directed by Mike Rogers, specifically get into the act? Here the finger of guilt points directly to Rogers as the most likely mastermind of the lucrative scheme, and Walton appears merely the photogenic actor chosen as the best equipped to read Mike's inspired lines. Rogers later admitted to Klass that he had, in fact, eagerly viewed *The UFO Incident* on October 20 (figs. 17, 18); on November 5, Rogers reported that Travis had been "beamed up" into the same kind of spacecraft as was shown in the movie, and on November 12, Travis reported close encounters with the same kind of aliens (fig. 20) practicing the same kind of anatomy lessons as had been shown on TV just a fortnight earlier. Coincidence? Try this on for size.

Crew Chief Rogers was in dire straits with the U.S. Forest Service (and we recall that his brother was a convicted forger and burglar). Moreover, he was not a very competent contractor; in 1974, he had won a contract to thin out secondary growth on federal land, but his bid was half that of a much more experienced contractor. His bid for the 1,227-acre site was just $27.40 an acre, to be divided by Rogers and his six coworkers. Worse, by August 1975, the 200 working days had expired and he had completed less than 70 percent of the job. He had to request a time extension, for which he would be penalized one dollar an acre, or about $350. Worse, 10 percent of what his crew had already earned—$2,500—would be withheld until satisfactory compliance. The contract he had with the federal agency was now seriously behind schedule; in fact, it ran out on November 10, 1975, after which time the $2,500 would be used to pay another contractor.

By November 10, meaning just two days before Travis miraculously emerged from the woods to confirm the fact of his alien encounter, Rogers had completed only 37 percent of the remaining 353 acres. Rogers had defaulted on a previous contract; this was his last chance. On November 10, just after watching *The UFO Incident*, Rogers wrote a letter to the U.S. Forest Service attempting to explain why he was so delinquent on his contract. Among other whines, he stated that "I have had considerable trouble keeping a full crew on the job. The area is very thick [with under-brush] and the guys have poor morale because of this." What he did *not* state here was the fact that he was delinquent specifically because he was using his crew to work for other contractors who would pay Roger's crew more than they could earn on his own under-bid job.

Rogers had, however, figured a way out, evidently that very night. It turns out that Forest Service contracts have "Act of God" provisions. Should one of his crew be witnessed by the rest (Rogers included) as having been "abducted" by a "UFO," that feat would qualify as one of those unforeseeable "Acts of God." Given that dreadful occurrence, which was reported as fact, now the Rogers workcrew would be understandably too terrified to finish their arboreal chores, and Rogers would be given his desperately sought time extension, and without any monetary penalties. Klass's conclusion: "Rogers had resorted to deception and falsehood." My conclusion is that he had defrauded the U.S. government, and that is a federal crime. As I do know, had I been the one to have done so, I would now be cooling my heels in a federal prison. By virtue of his nimble imagination, Mike Rogers got off scot free. So did Travis Walton.

No matter; never mind. It did not matter one whit that the Travis Walton episode had been shown by Philip Klass to be thoroughly bogus as long ago as 1987. Money was still to be made from the fakery; in 1995 yet another book was published, again presenting Walton's tall tale as "nonfiction."[42] The arresting cover shows young Travis caught in the malicious light-beam: he looks properly stunned, like Saul-Paul on the off-ramp to Damascus. The clerk at the bookstore where I inspected this particularly egregious bit of postmodernist yellow journalism happily told me that she loved the inevitable made-for-TV movie. When I explained that it was "all crap," she was, naturally, disappointed. I said, "No matter, not to worry; there's even more bullshit in the works."

Due to his/her specific professional training and insights, the art historian specifically knows that a timely perception of an eclectic and synthetic vision—the one concocted by Betty Hill, apparently a person sincerely deluded, or the one attributed to Travis Walton, proven a deliberate hoax—likewise eventually exposes the evidence pointing to another kind of hoax germane to the art historian's professional endeavors. That other act of willful contrivance is called art forgery, and it represents the more elevated and aesthetic counterpart of counterfeiting: printing bogus pieces of colored paper with numbers and portraits of historical notables. As is learned in graduate school, once fakery is suspected, in order to (for example) specifically prove the fact of the forgery in modern times of an important antiquity, one has first to demonstrate the easy availability in contemporary print culture of illustrations depicting all the individual authentic motifs carefully chosen to appear in the clever hoaxer's modern iconographic assemblage.[43] That said, I must add that I do not think the Hills were in any way hoaxers, rather that they were sincerely, but merely, deluded by the *grands frissons délicieux* attending their intimate *folie à deux*. As for Travis, he was a visionary forger, which, as yet, is not recognized to be the kind of crime that sends the Secret Service snapping at your heels.

THE AWFULLY CLOSE ENCOUNTERS OF BETTY ANDREASSON

As we also observe from Nickell's time line (fig. 8), the bug-eyed, outer-space, waif-motif was opportunely recycled in 1967 for the "Betty Andreasson abduction." That alleged event happened, of course, just one year after the appearance of Fuller's best-selling paperback reportage of the apocryphal Hill encounter. We now know for a fact that this was a much discussed populist publication which was eagerly read by both Mrs. Betty Andreasson and by her own helpful hypnotist-accomplices. In their case, they had plenty of time to do so. This Betty's exotic memories were "suppressed" for over ten years, only emerging in time to get published much later in hardback (1979), again to be launched the following year as yet another hugely profitable paperback.[44] It seems significant that the initial Andreasson publication was expressly admitted by its amanuensis, Raymond Fowler, to have been directly shaped by Fuller's account of the Hill affair: "We recalled the classic UFO abduction case involving Betty and Barney Hill that was described in John Fuller's *The Interrupted*

Journey." Fowler also admits to having been Fuller's accomplice in his earlier, likewise lucrative, ventures into alien-kidnapping reportage, a matter of public record in any event.[45] The public loved it; to assuage their morbid fascination with Betty A.'s psychological, and even gynecological, violations by aliens, two more monographs from the adept scribe Fowler seemed desirable, meaning also profitable for the publisher.[46]

For the art historian, however, the greater superiority of the later Andreasson publication over Fuller's *Interrupted Journey* is that Fowler's book is copiously illustrated with skilled ekphrastic line drawings reformatting Betty A.'s original pencil sketches illustrating her dramatized "CE-III" (Close Encounters of the Third Kind; see figs. 21, 22). Our favorite artworks are the ones showing such art-historical novelties as extraterrestrial "Entities Moving through a Closed Door," as complemented by an ET ersatz gynecologist "Entity in the Examination Room." In short, under hypnosis Betty A. drew the same classic "Grays" that faithfully conform to the widely reproduced Hill prototype, to which she also added an imaginative "lemur" variant.[47] But that pictorial enhancement is not surprising; as we are told, art was her favorite subject in elementary school.[48]

Also not surprising is the fact of an orthodox iconographic conformity to a standard ET portraiture already decades old by the time Mr. Fowler so profitably put into print Betty's dazzled recollections. All we need to know about that feat of physiognomic replication is a standard description—as published long ago, in 1968—which Fowler quotes (in 1979) with evident approval: "The most commonly described alien [in 1968] is about three and one-half feet tall, has a round head, arms reaching to or below his knees, and is wearing a silvery space suit or coverall. They have particularly wide (wrap-around) eyes and mouths with very thin lips."[49] Do you have any doubts that Mr. Fowler kindly shared this bibliographical nugget with Betty? Also telling is the fact that Betty's "Gray" ETs are wearing cheesy uniforms copied right out of the popular *Star Trek* TV series. Do you doubt that she was an avid watcher? No matter: they belong to the cinematic stereotypes defining the conventionalized inhabitants of the Other World imagined by Hollywood (cf. figs. 15, 17–19).

The text in the awe-inspiring Andreasson-Fowler opus is worth quoting in extenso (especially since I presume my otherwise learned readers have not yet bothered to consult it firsthand). Its format hews to the now-classic question-and-hypnotized-response mode that is standard in the copious alien-encounter literature. In this instance, the hypno-inquisitor is to be labeled "DJ" (Delirium Joiner) and Betty's responses (also her daughter's), like those belonging to the rest of our alien perceivers, are signaled by an "R." Since the whole Andreasson family contributes, we may label their situation a *folie en famille*. One episode begins with an incident rather like the multiplication of the fishes and loaves recounted in the New Testament. According to Betty A.:

> The leader [of the ETs] put the book [the Bible] in his hand. And he waved his hand over it, and other Bibles appeared, thicker than the original. Then he passed it to those beside him, and they took the books, and each one was spontaneous. They somehow flipped it, page by page, and looked down. Each page was pure white, luminous white. And then they stopped—and I started to look in the little blue book.

R (Betty) next gives us the *locus classicus* of her initial encounter: "I'm in the living room still. I'm over near the TV, and I'm just looking over to the left." The inclusion of a functioning television set is, I believe, essential in providing the most likely source for what follows, another cinematic close encounter. So equipped, next she espies a being that "looks like it's a clay man. He looks like a clay man, talking to my mom. Some kind of man-creature." But, hark, he's not alone; in fact, "behind him, right behind him toward the right, there's one, a little one—and there're two after him, that are just exactly like triplets."

DJ then asks R to specify whether these diminutive gray folks are "things" or "men." By her steadfast reckoning, "They're men. They're really babies, but to me, I guess, they would be more man than woman. They look like clay. They look like they're smooth, watered-on clay." And, fortunately, "No, they didn't touch me." Now the whole Andreasson clan takes part in Betty's epiphany: "I was standing right there, watching them, and they knew that my other brothers, my brothers and my . . . Wait a minute! My one, two, three brothers were sitting there, and Grammie—she's over there. Oh! Where's Grampy?" As for the missing relative, we soon find out that "Grampy went out to look with Mom; he's looking out the window." Meanwhile, back in the kitchen, "My mom was standing there with her hand on something, and that clay form [ET] had his hand on the other part, like a book. The [ET's] clay hand is holding it on the right hand side." DJ asks, "Where did the book come from?" and the reply is just more befuddlement regarding the ET scriptures: "The book? I don't know. She must have had it. I don't know."[50]

Next comes a rambling description of the ETs who, of course, correspond to the classic iconographic pattern—"classic," that is, since about 1968: first verbal, then televised (figs. 16–18), and later appearing at your local cineplex (figs. 15, 19). In this part of the transcripts, R says, "I woke up and they were in the room. Mom was talking to them, and there was a book already in his hand." Next comes a description of the all-important television set. As we are told, it was on, emanating its endless pictorial prototypes. While that is not surprising in a family like this, what is odd is, according to Betty, that "the TV is . . . it's different. No picture, no sound— very, very dim like when you turn down the color—like you turned it down, so it's very gray and low." The misfunctioning family entertainment center prompts the alert DJ to inquire, "Becky, you are upset about something, aren't you?" In this case however, what is upsetting are "Those things [the ETs]. They're scary." DJ then gently reminds his compliant R that "you told us that, once before, you felt a very, very close relationship to them—that you like them." Indeed, this is the case: "Yes. They are very kind, and they don't mean any harm, but they are scary to look at. They look scary."

So, asks DJ, just what is it that makes them appear so "scary?" From the answer following, their dreadful aspect seems mostly due to a bad tailor, the kind who designed the costumes for *Star Trek*. As was explained by R, "They were wearing—it looked like pants and a tucked-in type of shirt, but it was tight-fitted. Something like a . . . what it reminded me of was something like a scuba-diving outfit that would be close to a person's skin." Moreover, just in case you might have missed the contemporaneous TV source for such sartorial splendor, we learn that the bottom of the legs of the skin-suit "ended near the shoe." Furthermore, the "pants went down like a skin-suit, and then there was a cut where it was. It stopped with one lighter shade, and it went into a darker shade, like a shoe or a boot would be."

Following this fashion statement, we get to the most important ET motif, the *eyes*. "They looked like marbles. It had big eyes." (Of course.) However, although "I didn't see any hair," the other striking observation was that ET's "head looked like a pear, an upside-down pear." Moreover, "Sideways, he didn't have a mouth. When he turned, he did; it was like a wrinkle in the clay: not a line, but like a line. And I can't see any nose." As always, the most striking alien feature is those ever chilling "black eyes. Like marbles. They looked scary." So, naturally, this apparition induces fear and trembling, and this is "because he scares me by the way he looks, but I can't do anything, [I] can't move. I'm not afraid of him, because there's a feeling that he's not going to hurt me. He scares me just by the way he looks."[51]

As eagerly guided by her hypnotically adept DJ, Betty is soon enjoined to tell us about much more exciting events. As we soon learn, she actually gets to ascend into the alien spacecraft! Obviously, dear reader, this is becoming a really compelling story, a much better adventure than any ever experienced by either you or me. Since we've never been in such a privileged place, that is, within a real, functioning UFO, Betty's unmatched description of the alien dreadnought needs to be quoted intact:

> We're in, like, a half-bubble, or quarter of a bubble, room. And he [the ET named "Quazgaa"] has withdrawn himself with the others, and they are standing over there, talking. I'm just looking at this room. Something goes down the sides of the bubble. Where the steps come up, it goes down. I feel very weightless and icky. My hands and my legs feel like they are asleep or something. And they are still talking over there, and they glance over at me once in a while. Oh, hurry up! And I'm crossing my arms now. I'm tired of just standing there. I feel weightless. Oh, my feet are pins and needles, or something; even my arms and my hands. He [Quazgaa] is still talking, and about two or three of them are leaving. That door whooshed open, and they are going in, and it's closing. He [Quazgaa] brought me over to where they were, and he is saying something to them about going and making himself ready. [She sighs.] Would they please bring me to the upper room?
>
> And so, the two—one went in front of me and one in back of me—we went over to the furthest right-hand end of the quarter bubble. And—whoosh!—another door opened. And you can't even see those doors. They just go up when they open [all as shown on *Star Trek*]. And there are stairs there, going around—somehow going around. They seem like they are floating up, but my waist feels so heavy there. And we are going up those stairs. Looks like I can see something down there. We're all going around the stairs and we are going up around, and this door goes down. The door goes down. It doesn't lead down. It disappears down, somehow. And now they are going into that room. And I see that, ah, box, or that desk and, ah, see something else there. It's, ah, red and black. It's black, outlined with red. And it's some kind of mirrors, I think. I don't know. Seems like there're, ah, in that circular room, big ripples like windows. They are leading me still [she sighs], and they are bringing me over to that further edge—are bringing me further over there. And now they're stopping and I'm standing there. And the two are withdrawing. They are saying I'll be all right here for a time.[52]

This rather incoherent tour of the UFO consumes various pages. Finally, we come to the best part of the whole story: Betty's gynecological exam by the voyeuristic ETs. This is the sort of lurid account that makes for a postmodernist best-seller (which is worth knowing, that is, just in case you, too, wish to reap similar fiduciary benefits). As DJ, Betty's amanuensis, solemnly comments, "The alien creatures' physical examination of Betty was one of the most emotion-packed portions of the case." Because this was obviously an extremely traumatic transaction, Betty again had to be put into a deep hypnotic trance in order to retrieve it in all its poignant details (so we will revert to the "DJ" and "R" format). Here is how her exam—a real event, of course—actually went. Ever observant to alien fashion modes, R noticed how "In that [medical examination] room, they seemed to be in different clothes: shiny, white-silver clothes." Besides having different raiment, her new gynecological inquisitors appeared to be dermatologically distinct: "Their skin seemed whiter; maybe it's because of the bright light in there. It didn't seem so clay-like, gray."

Costumed in their shiny outfits, the new set of albino ETs set about to their grim work. They first strap Betty on to a "long block-thing," and there she perceives bright "lights coming from the walls, and wires, *needle* wires." Next (and this is truly scary to relate), "They took those long silver needles—they were bendable—and they stuck one up my nose and into my head." (Ouch!) As to the purpose of all this needling about, "They said they were *awakening* something." At this point DJ reboots his own hypnotic powers: "Just relax, relax, just relax. You're going deeper and deeper into a beautiful place of peace, of quiet. Your whole body is relaxing as you go still deeper and deeper." Now, with her brain thoroughly anesthetized, next comes her description of the gruesome sound effects accompanying Betty's head job: "When they stuck that needle up my nose, I heard something break, like a membrane or a veil or something, like a piece of tissue, or something; they broke through." All the while there is much "penetrating: pushing." By the way, that needle went in through her *left* nostril, not the right one (and such trivial details do lend verisimilitude to an otherwise apocryphal narrative).

Once her nose has been properly drilled, Betty then brings us to the fun part, that is, the abominable alien abdominal (versus nasal) violation. At this point (or place), "they inserted another long silver thing through my belly-button, my navel. And when they did [that], they started talking with each other." DJ then brightly asks, "Did they tell you what the purpose was for the penetration of your navel? What was that examination for?" And the penetrating reply, which seems to posit a portentous metaphor, is that it was "something about *creation*, but they said there were some parts missing," and that anatomical lacuna "was because I had a hysterectomy, I guess." After Betty was finally awakened from her numbed hypnotic state, DJ gently inquires, "What do you think?" Her riposte is fitting, wholly appropriate; in short, "It's kind of unbelievable to me."[53]

We must, however, also observe that by 1979, the initial date of the multipartite Andreasson media-event, Steven Spielberg's movie cinematically illustrating the same Gray archetype, *Close Encounters of the Third Kind* (fig. 19), had already been seen—by nearly everybody—two years prior. Besides being inspired by the movies, Betty's graphic imagination was also decidedly fertilized by the fact that she was a devout Christian, in fact a declared Pentecostal-Baptist.[54] During one of the hypnotic episodes, she states that the ETs proclaim to her, "I have chosen you." You see, she is a designated *special* person. Given her intellectual formation, her properly awed response makes perfect contextual sense:

> Are you my Lord Jesus? I would recognize my Lord Jesus. Oh, it says, "I love you. God is love, and I love you," they said, or whatever it was. I say they, but it seemed like one. [She sighs and continues.] Oh, praise God, praise God, praise God! [She is crying.] I know, I know I am not worthy. Thank you for your Son. [Betty breaks into uncontrollable sobbing.] Thank you for your Son.[55]

And thank *you*, Betty, for sharing with us your wonderful, very special, adventures with the extraterrestrials.

Unfortunately, since I am not a gentleman, I feel constrained to mention some facts *not* reported in Fowler's best-selling paperback drama.[56] Although we are told that the close encounter actually occurred in 1967, it was not voiced until 1974; that is when brave Betty "went public." So, what happened that year? The *National Enquirer* began offering its $100,000 cash prize for convincing evidence of earthling contacts with extraterrestrial tourists: this is the same premium that brought Travis Walton out of the woods with *his* story. So, of course, this is when Betty "reluctantly" submitted her inspiring tale, previously latent, to appraisal by the tabloid. Alas, the editors of the première gazette "for inquiring minds" were not sufficiently impressed with Mrs. Andreasson's saga even to recommend that she receive the annual "best case" award, typically worth a mere $5,000. After much searching for a sympathetic audience, Betty finally got in contact with the Mutual UFO Network (MUFON). Under their eager direction, her first regressive hypnosis session was held on April 3, 1977, Raymond Fowler got into the act that June, and the rest is, as they say, history (or hysteria).

WHITLEY STRIEBER'S BEST-SELLING "COMMUNION" WITH THE ETs

One of the notable blockbuster publishing events of recent times is Whitley Strieber's *Communion: A True Story*. According to the gloating blurb (in uppercase type) printed on the cover of the paperback edition, this is "the controversial *New York Times* bestseller!" (See fig. 6.) Its original hardback publisher, William Morrow, knew when a good piece of business was in the offing; Strieber's advance on his forthcoming royalties was reported to be *one million* dollars (after taxes, around $600,000, still much more than you or I will ever make in one fell swoop).[57] Happily, the publishers quickly recovered their massive initial outlay. By late March 1986, *Communion* was in the number two position on the nonfiction [*sic*] best-seller lists of both the *New York Times* and the *Washington Post*, and shortly afterward it zoomed up to a prestigious (and profitable) number one slot.

This feat constituted a world-historical pseudoevent: this was the first time that a book on the UFO experience had ever achieved such distinction in the marketplace. Obviously, a lot of people bought into this story, both metaphorically and moneywise, and one only needs now invest the trifling sum of $4.95 to acquire the inevitable paperback (published by Avon). Mr. Strieber, already a best-selling author of horror fiction, now, in 1987, turned his horrific talents to "a true story"—and sold even more paperbacks. For those with the proper credentials in *belles-lettres* (and also a good literary agent), it would appear that alien abduction pays off big.

Strieber, born in 1945 in San Antonio, Texas, was initially a Roman Catholic but, as so often happens, "I was deeply conflicted about my Catholicism, wondering whether the tenets of my faith could be fitted to the picture I was forming of the world. . . . Still, my faith was a burning fire in me. I loved Christ and Mary especially, and used to pray with great fervor."[58] Already in 1958, he "discovered that there is a whole mythology of flying saucer technology, and a lot of it revolves around the concept of counter-rotating magnets." When he "was about thirteen, my interest in horror began," and "I would see my first horror movie, *The Creature from the Black Lagoon* [1954], which was shown at my summer camp."[59] Later, in 1971, he became a card-carrying member of the Gurdjieff Foundation, a notorious occultist operation founded upon the mystical deep thought of G. I. Gurdjieff and D. P. Ouspensky.[60] In fact, admits Strieber, "I spent fifteen years involved with the Gurdjieff Foundation."[61] As any accredited therapist will tell you, a keen interest in occultism will make people, ordinary folks, receptive to the complementary ET experience; so does, especially, actively reading about ETs and UFOs. Let's face it; both activities are wholly voluntary, and some of us will only think about such things under duress.

According to Strieber, late in 1985, "my brother had sent me for Christmas a book called *Science and the UFOs* by Jenny Randles," whom we have already encountered. Once Strieber had been put under hypnosis (and as is not at all surprising to me), "I realized that my [carefully retrieved] memories fitted in with the material described in *Science and the UFOs*."[62] Just to make sure, Strieber admits that by April 1986, "I read thousands of pages of material about the whole [ET and UFO] phenomenon."[63] Still, that was certainly not Strieber's first close encounter with the popular literature purveying such esoterica: "I have certainly read a book or two about them [maybe even dozens?]. Pressing myself, I thought maybe [uh-huh] I *could* remember seeing something years ago in *Look* magazine about somebody named Hill being taken aboard a flying disk. . . . I *must* have seen something about the story, though, because I remember it."[64]

Right: you, and nearly everybody else in the United States, "must have seen something about the story." And if you missed that particular cinematic close encounter, perhaps because you were doing anthropological work in the Congo, then you could scarcely have missed seeing Steven Spielberg's blockbuster movie of 1977, *Close Encounters of the Third Kind*. Surprise: neither could Strieber. Accordingly, he recalled one of his ET visitors as looking not quite "as naked as the creature who emerged in *Close Encounters*."[65] As, of course, they must.

Enough of such background material, presented here as forensic evidence. Let us get to the heart of the matter: Strieber's accounts of colorful, dramatic, and awfully close encounters with the extraterrestrials (which I assume, dear reader, you previously have not had the opportunity to peruse). As before, the inquisitor-hypnotist is again referred to as "DJ" (Delirium Joiner) and successful author Strieber is "R" (newly Rich raconteur).

In one session, DJ tells the compliant R to "look at it [the ET] very hard." He does, and "She's staring right back at me. She looks like a big bug." True to form, this alien pin-up conforms to the classic ET mold; she has "great big, black eyes. She's sort of brown. She has a little, tiny mouth. She's thin." Otherwise (and this information takes many lines of print to elicit), the buglike lady has no "antennae," "she's bald," additionally, she seems to have neither ears nor eyebrows. There is, however, a "little, bitty, tiny sort of two-holed nose." As for the mouth, "It's straight and sort of . . . it's straight and . . . for some reason, it's a little hard to look at." In short, "It's very slight. Just an opening." Following her rudimentary physical description, next comes a statement of her actions. *Mirabile dictu*, she makes a pass at R! Still, hers is a maladroit advance, or perhaps it was just half-hearted: "She sat there for a long time, then put a hand out, put it under my shirt and under my sweater and under me, and put it right up against my chest, on the side of my chest. And it felt sort of soft, and it's . . . it doesn't feel bad to be touched like that by that [ET] thing. And she takes her hand away." In spite of the admitted effect—"it doesn't feel bad to be touched like that"—R's immediate reaction is perhaps surprising: "I'm just scared to death. I'm totally coming out of it."

Aghast, R starts his car ("I was in the woods on a dirt road") and chugs along until "I see this weird white pickup." Sitting inside the parked truck are some people who are (imagine this!) even worse than Texans, namely, "two [ET] people in uniforms." Nonetheless, according to R's addled recollection, they *do* rather act like Texans: "He [an ET] says to me, 'Get out of here.' Then this lady on the other side [another ET] says, 'We don't want you here.' I say, 'Who are you?' She looks at me with a real mean look on her face. She's a [expletive deleted] real mean." R/Strieber concludes with an accurate summary of the real meaning of his hypnotically induced recollection, namely, "You know, I just can't tell what's going on here. I don't know what the hell happened."[66] Neither do I.

In another session, the hypnotized Strieber begins to recall what the art historian would call his most likely, perhaps even unavoidable, iconographic sources. In sum, "They were pictures." Put otherwise, "I think increasingly that they might be pictures out of my mind of my worst fears. . . . Maybe a [pictured] fear so terrible that I can't even make heads or tails of it [even] under hypnosis." After a tedious round of verbal foreplay between DJ and R, we eventually learn (but just as we expected), "that it [the ET] had a bald, rather largish head for someone that size. And that its eyes are slanted, more than an Oriental's eyes [cf. figs. 17–19]. And they're quite . . . there's a piercing glare, almost. There's a real fierce look to the whole face. I'm not sure, but at some point I almost thought it looks like a bug." The buggish alien also has, but just as it must, "a bald head." At this point DJ prods R, asking, "Have you ever seen an image like that before?" In spite of an evasive reply, we now discover that Strieber was—no surprise here!—familiar with the widely broadcast Barney and Betty Hill story:

> The only thing I ever remember reading about this was in *Look* magazine years and years ago. "The Incident," the John Fuller article [the one later made into a best-seller paperback and a TV movie: see figs. 16–19] about people [the Hills] who were picked up [by ETs in a UFO]. That's all [??] I've [ever?] read about it. And whether or not they [the copious media reportage of the Hill incident] had pictures drawn [for them], I just don't know.

Then DJ prods further, "Are you *sure* you haven't seen an image like that before? What about the book you have [referring to Randles, *The Sci-*

ence and the UFOs]?" and "What about the Hynek book [referring to J. Allen Hynek, *The UFO Experience*, 1972]? I think there's a drawing in that." (DJ was wrong; Hynek's book has no ET drawings.) Although pleading no knowledge of Hynek's paperback scriptures, R's response is to observe, and quite correctly, that "in our culture, there's so much media around. It's possible [that one had seen the ubiquitous ET pictures], but I don't [choose to] think so, because this [vision] is so damn real. It just seems impossible [*why?*] that it could be an image I picked up from somewhere. . . . Maybe the drawings [which he either did, or did not, see] were right. That's possible too."[67]

Since anything (or everything) seems possible, here is a transcription of yet another mind-numbing close encounter experienced by mesmerized Whitley Strieber. Once again, DJ states, "I want you to see her [the ET] very vividly, very vividly. I want you to see her face." He works manfully at his feat of induced visualization. The results are decidedly unattractive: "She's got bald . . . she's got a big [bald] head and her eyes have bulges. She's sort of brown-skinned, not like a black [African American] person, but like leather. Yellow-brown. And when she opens her mouth her lips are all—she hasn't got lips exactly—but it [the mouth] flops down. Her lips are floppy." Next he begins to speak rather oddly, in falsetto and as if he were angrily addressing the floppy-lipped ET, "You know, I'm not buying this. You can show me all that little insignia you want, and I'm still not buying this." Oddly, this bold rejoinder reminds me of a famous line, "I don' need no stinkin' badges," from *The Treasure of the Sierra Madre* (1949).

While this is mildly colorful stuff, much more is needed to put your book on the *New York Times* best-seller list. Here's how you do it. As DJ helpfully suggests, "What did she mean by saying can you get harder?" In this case the adjective "harder" is not referring to the difficulties attending most worthy intellectual efforts, instead to *sexual* activity (or dysfunction). As R vividly explains, "I was about half up. Hard. *Penis*. And she says, 'Can you get *harder?*' And the truth is, I could not. I didn't even know I was in that state [of erection]. And with her around, there's just no way." Pursuing the game plan, DJ deftly ripostes, "Was this [erection] natural, or somehow induced?" R doesn't know, but he does announce the presence of a previously unmentioned alien device, something placed inside him. As he recalls (well, sort of), "that [ET proctologist's] thing stayed in me. I don't even know when it went out. It was almost like it was alive. It was a big, gray thing with what looked like a little cage on the end of it, a little round nubbin about the size of the end of your thumb. And they shoved it into me—they showed me afterward—so they must have taken it out of me, but I don't remember them doing it."

Even though this makes for a striking literary device, R's anus insert immediately disappears from the narrative. Its derailment may be attributed to DJ's subsequent query, "One thing you mentioned was this message [from the ETs] that you were 'the chosen one.'" Isn't that strange; our intrepid ET contactee labels himself just as had been earlier reported in the Betty Andreasson book, and as first published in 1979! But R again turns defiant, just "because they say, 'You are our chosen one,' it's just bullshit. Like, they're trying to stroke me, you know." As we may infer, the macho Whitley has learned a lesson from Betty Andreasson's notorious gullibility. In the event, R has previously seen many "other [ET] people. There was a whole row of 'em. But that was a long time ago. They didn't know where they were or what they were doing. I was sittin' up in bed." Wondering about the chronology of this earlier close encounter, DJ queries, "How old were you?" And the astonishing answer is "Twelve."[68] Spot on, Whitley!

Typically, hypnotized recollections do tend to ramble, Whitley Strieber's included. For greater narrative coherence and dramatic effort, let us now turn to another close encounter as told by professional story-teller Strieber in his own writing, and when he was older (if not wiser) than twelve:

> Then I was lifted up and seemed suddenly to be in another room, or perhaps I simply saw my present surroundings differently. It appeared to be a small operating theater. I was in the center of it, on a table, and three tiers of benches were populated with a few huddled figures, some with round, as opposed to slanted, eyes. I was aware that I had seen four different types of [ET] figures. The first was the small robot-like being that had led the way into my bedroom. He was followed by a large group of short, stocky ones in the dark-blue coveralls.
>
> These had wide faces, appearing either dark gray or dark blue in that light, with glittering deep-set eyes, pug noses, and broad, somewhat human mouths. Inside the room, I encountered two types of creatures that did not look at all human. The most provocative of those was about five feet tall, very slender and delicate, with extremely prominent and mesmerizing, black slanted eyes [see fig. 4]. This being had an almost vestigial mouth and nose. The huddled figures in the theater were somewhat smaller, with similarly shaped heads but round, black eyes like large buttons.

As we see from this passage, when Whitley is not laboring under an externally induced hypnotic burden, he can write good quality, pulp-fiction prose. His narrative skills enable us, his breathless readers, to vividly picture in our mind's eye the very look of his horrid captors. As

we read next, Mr. Strieber also has a fine command of the essential ingre-
dients making for competent pornography of the masochistic sort.

> Soon I was in more intimate surroundings once again. There were
> clothes strewn about, and two of the stocky ones drew my legs apart.
> The next thing I knew I was being shown an enormous and extremely
> ugly object, gray and scaly, with a sort of network of wires on the end.
> It was at least a foot long, narrow, and triangular in structure. They
> inserted this thing into my rectum. It seemed to swarm into me as it if
> had a life of its own. Apparently its purpose was to take samples, pos-
> sibly of fecal matter, but at the time I had the impression that I was
> being raped, and for the first time I felt anger.
>
> Only when the thing was withdrawn did I see that it was a mechan-
> ical device. The individual holding it pointed to the wire cage on the tip
> and seemed to warn me about something. But what? I never found out.
> Events once again started moving very quickly. One of them took my
> right hand and made an incision on my forefinger. There was no pain at
> all. Abruptly, my memories end. There isn't even blackness, just
> morning. I had no further recollection of the incident.[69]

Well, there you have it: as told in his own words, such was the wretched
tale that made Mr. Strieber a huge chunk of cash, around a million dollars.
Even more amazing (to me at least) is the fact that you can get turgid stuff
like this put into print by apparently reputable publishers. Just imagine: if
your own personal account of some very special, and ever so close, encounters with the ETs is sufficiently gross, even you might also be allowed to sell
a million copies of your very own spiritual autobiography. Also noteworthy
about such often hysterical scribblings is the fact that, besides commonly
partaking of the bottomlessly banal, they are all basically boring.

CORAL LORENZEN: A LITERARY MATRIARCH FOR ALIEN ENCOUNTERS

Also noteworthy is the fact that, by the time of Betty Andreasson's since
endlessly replayed UFO abductions, as allegedly initiated in 1967, there
was already a decade-long history of alien-invasion movies, the most
famous being the *War of the Worlds*, which appeared in 1953 (others will
be discussed in chapter 9). In a somewhat stereotyped fashion, most of
these appeared for eager mass consumption with their own widely
viewed, more or less fixed, iconographic conventions: shadowy fogs and
flashing searchlights, from which emerge macrocephalic ETs from dying
worlds clad in one-piece foil suits, who then often proceed to practice

mind control over stunned earthlings. Besides art historians, perhaps enthusiastic bad-film buffs can provide much more useful historical materials than do the profitably published UFOlogists.

Another likely mass media source for a now-archetypal ET portraiture is another cheaply priced paperback, first published in 1967; the authors of record are Coral and Jim Lorenzen (Mr. L. is since deceased). Their provocative, coauthored feuilleton was called *Flying Saucer Occupants*. Herein was recounted the close encounter, supposedly transpiring in 1957, of a Brazilian farmboy, one Antonio Villas-Boas, with a lusty female ET.[70] As described long after the fact [*sic*], the alien succubus was about one and a half meters tall, had thin blond hair, large slanted eyes, high cheekbones, an ordinary nose, a small, thin-lipped mouth, and a sharply pointed chin: in short, the now-conventional ET type (fig. 4).[71] However, simultaneously Coral Lorenzen had described the same exotic incident in even greater detail in the 1966 reworking of her sensational 1962 paperback exposé; then called *The Flying Saucer Hoax*, this was the same opusculum recommended to Betty Hill by her ever-helpful NICAP collaborators. This means, of course, that this lurid publication must have been actually read by Betty Hill when, as already explained, she began industrious and lengthy library research in order to lend support for the reality of her "dreams." As she herself once eagerly exclaimed, "When I learned to read, my days of boredom were over!"[72]

In short, the populist paperback published in 1966 by Coral Lorenzen exposing the "evidence" (surprise: all anecdotal) pointing to an ominous invasion from outer space—and such as it was initially published a bit before Fuller's *Interrupted Journey*—provides the narrative template for all the relevant motifs and also the broader *mise-en-scène* distinguishing the influential Hill abduction-scenario. Fuller's pop classic was itself also the acknowledged model for the subsequently published, copiously illustrated (figs. 21, 22) and best-selling *Andreasson Affair*, whose author also approvingly cited the pioneering abduction reports published by the Lorenzens.[73] Besides originally supplying a verbalized bug-eyed space-waif, later to be conveniently sketched out by the henpecked Barney Hill (fig. 16), in the now-forgotten Lorenzen pulp publication we also find a nocturnal setting in a deserted countryside; a bright light emitted from on high (like "a searchlight"); a large floating object (like "a cartwheel"). Also seen as "swiftly moving" or "hovering," the awesome spacecraft publicized by Coral Lorenzen in 1966 is embellished with a battery of "small purplish lights." It landed in a blaze of greenish light,[74] just as was illustrated in Spielberg's 1977 film (fig. 19, to which, however, he independently added an uplifting Moog-synthesizer chorus).

Just as in the Hill story, so conveniently "remembered" by Betty and Barney later in 1964, Coral Lorenzen also shows us how the bewildered earthling's motor vehicle had stalled (drat!), leaving him no escape from implacable alien abductors. Like Barney Hill, who figuratively followed in his pioneering footsteps, likewise Villas-Boas "was attacked by three small men [who] dragged him toward the ship," up a ramp, and into the looming UFO. Although no mention is made of Antonio's cinematic tastes, obviously he (too) had seen the widely distributed Hollywood sci-fi classic of 1951, *The Day the Earth Stood Still*. This movie showed everybody on the planet earth that flying saucers from outer space have ramps, into which humans gain egress, and that their alien emissaries, Klaatu in this case, delight in making automative electrical systems quit.

Moreover, just as was later to be reported by the Hills, Lorenzen recounts that "the inside of the ship was made of bright metal and lit by fluorescent-like light," just as such UFOs had been shown in many earlier Hollywood space operas. Again as the interior-décor motif appears later in the Hill story, Lorenzen has it that "the only furniture was an oddly shaped table," in fact a doctor's examination table. Again as later "remembered" by the Hill couple under hypnosis, Lorenzen's aliens "forcibly undress their victim," then, with deftly wielded pipettes, they obscenely proceed to extract bodily fluids from his captive body.[75] Like Barney Hill's persecutors, Villas-Boas's principal tormentor, a female, had "big blue, slanted eyes . . . very prominent cheekbones and a severely pointed chin, as well as slit-thin lips" (see fig. 4).[76]

Just in case you don't think Lorenzen's tale about Villas-Boas's violation by a nymphomaniac ET in exotic Brazil represented *standard* knowledge among the most profitably published victims of subsequent "alien" visitations, allow me to quote Whitley Strieber's close paraphrase of Lorenzen's lurid *Urtext*:

> A famous case of sexual involvement with visitors took place in Brazil in 1957. The victim, Antonio Villas-Boas, had experienced a number of instances of strange lights appearing in his fields on the days prior to his experience. He was running his tractor one night when it died. Mr. Villas-Boas then saw that an object had landed in front of him. He was stripped, washed with a sponge, and taken inside the device. He was left lying on a table, naked. Sometime later, he was astounded to see a naked woman, seemingly human, enter the room. Her hair was blond, parted in the center. Her face was extremely wide, her eyes blue and slanted. The face ended in a pointed chin. Her lips were very thin, nearly invisible. She was shorter than he was. *Actually, she sounds very much like a cross between the individual I saw so clearly* [fig. 4] as

the eidetic image and a human being—unless she was simply a visitor wearing what they thought would be a disguise. She made love to him, pointed to her belly, and then to the sky, and left him. Later he was taken into a room with some males and attempted to steal a clock.[77]

With the arrival of Coral Lorenzen's alien seducer/medical examiner, the conclusion reached by her becomes that one to be also repeated in 1966 by the Hills and John Fuller: "If an alien race bent on contact and possible colonization were to reconnoiter this planet, one of their prime tasks would be to learn if the two races could breed."[78] According to Betty Hill's statement, as published in 1966, due to her different gender she was subjected to "a pregnancy test,"[79] an interesting situation since she was then postmenopausal. Naturally, as later published in 1979, art-lover Betty Andreasson gets subjected to even more rigorous gynecological close encounters, similarly futile since she had undergone a hysterectomy. Moreover, all of the loathsome Brazilian transactions recounted by Coral Lorenzen took four hours to transpire, neatly corresponding to the amount of time supposedly "lost" by Betty and Barney according to the 1964 hypnotic recollections of their very own dire close encounter in the murky depths of New Hampshire. And let us not forget that it was Coral Lorenzen who later, in 1975, enthusiastically championed Travis Walton's tall tale, calling it "one of the most important and intriguing in the history of the UFO phenomenon" (see fig. 20).

THE CASE FOR EXTRATERRESTRIAL NONINTELLIGENCE

As it turns out, there is a legitimate scientific enterprise seeking physical evidence attesting to the existence of intelligence in the Great Beyond. The SETI project (Search for Extraterrestrial Intelligence) is sponsored by the Planetary Society, the largest space-study group in the world, with more than 100,000 members on seven continents. Its late president was Dr. Carl Sagan.[80] Directed by accredited scientists, the SETI researchers look for objective, repeatable proof for the existence of civilizations elsewhere in the universe. In this case, extraterrestrial "intelligence" is to be assigned to a species that makes extreme use of tools, language, and numbers, and of those hypothesized smart species, only a fraction might be presumed to have ever had any cultural inclinations to build some sort of advanced communication technology. Usually, SETI is understood as the methodical search made from earth for radio signals (to be detected by radio telescopes) coming from other technological civilizations located in other galaxies. This operation has been underway since 1960. To date, some four decades later, no intelligent signals, whether specifically aimed at us or simply overheard by earthlings, have yet been reported. Based on scientific methods, namely the testable prediction, the agenda of SETI is rather different from that pursued by the UFOlogists, particularly the kind that dote on the ET stories.

Now that we are all made thoroughly familiar with the postmodernist alien-abduction scenarios by having actually read them in detail, and now that we know much more about their immediate literary pedigrees (apparently wholly earthling), we may be so bold as to criticize the logic of it all. As Thomas Bullard has recognized, in nearly all the abundant ET literature "a scientific mission is given as the reason for abductions, judging from what happens after capture." Specifically, "the ETs direct their captive to an efficiently designed examination room and subject him or her to a rapid, well organized bodily inspection, scanning and probing with instruments as well as taking samples of tissues and body fluids. Most abduction accounts include this episode. It seems to be the essential element, the purpose for the whole thing."[81]

Given that revelation, and such as their earthling experiencers describe them, no matter whether adoring or horrified, the ETs do seem, in short, rather a dumb lot. Most glaring is the obvious lack of any sign of intelligence on the part of the little Grays. Viewed overall, they are scientifically stupid, mathematically stupid, statistically stupid, linguistically stupid, anthropologically stupid, and psychologically stupid.[82] Especially, they show themselves stubbornly ignorant of the basic lessons of physiology, hence their need to endlessly repeat their maladroit medical experiments, so recalling those lurid—and widely circulated—stories of loathesome Nazi doctors who once hung out their shingles in sinister venues like Auschwitz.

In fact, they are so generally and overwhelmingly *stupid* they reportedly want to "breed" with human beings. It is not just a question of bad taste. Our bunch represents clearly the most aggressive and warlike creatures in all of creation. Humans not only neglect and abuse their young, and mistreat the elderly and infirm, but they are eternally at war with one another. Even when they do mind their own business (rarely), *Homo sapiens* (*nonsapiens*) seems totally unable to find peace and contentment even within itself. And you tell us that a "superior intelligence" wants to interbreed with this sorry lot? It is not just a matter of ethics, even aesthetics; biologically speaking, humans cannot even breed even with their closest relatives, the apes and chimpanzees. So how are they going to interbreed with aliens that, reportedly, have no sex organs? Do we really have to go back to the doctrine of parthenogenesis and the virgin birth?

Clearly, the ETs are anatomically and physiologically stupid: in spite of fifty years of reports chronicling a tireless collection of human samples, they evidently still need more and more of the same bits and pieces taken from more and more of the same kind of human victims. How much, for ETs' sakes, is enough? Why don't they ever keep some of the specimens for detailed and intensive study? We have refrigerators; don't they have them, too? Why haven't they taken corpses and performed scientific autopsies, either here, in their UFOs, or back home, somewhere in outer space? As for their clumsy, semiserious poking and prodding of the living human anatomy, school kids could do a better job. Moreover, why don't they take an appendix, or even a lung or kidney, every now and then? Of the latter, we humans could spare one; after all we do have two of each (just like testicles and ovaries).

Another problem: Why do they insist on taking their abductees back to their homes, even tucking them into bed? If they just kept them, once and for all, think of all the fuel they would save. Obviously, they are also ecologically unconscious. Why do they probe hundreds of "experiencers," with hundreds more promised to be probed, when only one or two careful examinations would give the ETs all the biological information any intelligent scientist would ever need? Could it be that, ET forbid! they are just plain dumb, and thus unable to profit from past experience? Humans notoriously suffer from that problem; why should superior otherworldly intelligences be so demonstrably unintelligent? Can anyone in his right mind believe that any creature sophisticated enough to cross interstellar space, walk through walls, and communicate telepathically is also totally unable to profit from past experience?

Psychologically, the ETs are so brain-dead that they have no notion whatsoever as to human needs and motives, nor have they betrayed any real evidence of empathy or sympathy for human beings. (Those prolonged and profound, sentient soulmate stares don't qualify.) As for the kinds and types of people they abduct, these are all *nobodies*. The only way these pathetic folk have ever become a "somebody" was by going on TV and telling us about their mistreatment at the hands of callous alien abductors. Why don't the ETs show some political savvy and abduct the power brokers: the heads of state, CEOs of multinational corporations, at least a lobbyist, a mayor, or a congressman? Actually, if they wanted to grab somebody really important, they should abduct Oprah Winfrey or Larry King: they are the kind of people that really matter in postmodernist culture.

If, instead, their goal is to truly understand us, why don't they abduct leading scientists, Nobel Prize winners, or at least people who know something worth knowing? If, on the other hand, their primary goal is, as so many abductees claim, "breeding," then why don't the ETs abduct Miss Americas, Miss Universes, Olympic athletes, even Leonardo di Caprio or (my choice) Kim Basinger? Get serious, ETs: at least pick somebody good-looking! Have you seen what the abductees displaying themselves on TV actually look like? As a colleague once remarked to me, most of them couldn't even get the family dog to play with them if they wore a pork chop around their necks.

If, such as we have been told since the 1950s, their aim is high-minded and educational—to warn or send inspiring messages to humanity—then why don't the ETs make use of our omnipresent and incredibly efficient communication facilities, especially our highly prized infotainment industry? Why won't they just show up on TV talk shows or radio—"Larry King Live with ETs"—and fill us in, let us savor in detail their profound wisdom? Obviously, they have made no serious or pro-longed effort to communicate, to negotiate, or even to announce or explain their presence. In fact, their intelligence (or lack of it) most resembles that of most of the alleged abductees themselves. Hearing their stories, you recognize that these allegedly abducted folk mostly bear wit-ness to little or no scientific training or psychological understanding. Worse, they seem to be, generally, adrift in an intellectual fog or lost in a deep emotional funk. If this is the case, then the human race has nothing whatsoever to fear from this crew of extraterrestrial *idiots nonsavants*.

What we have learned thus far about aliens, that is, once the dreaded ETs are now merely viewed as faulty folk, tells us only one thing. In fine, they're not alien at all: they are wholly human. Specifically, they have been extruded from the human imagination by human beings with human motives and commonplace emotional needs and desires (points further considered in chapters 11 and 14). Indeed, the postmodernist legend of alien encounters all (absolutely) began with Barney and Betty Hill and, just as their psychiatrist recognized, it was really just a case of *folie à deux*. This is a shared paranoid disorder, where the dominant person (more often a woman than a man) is the one with the original delusional psychosis, who then imposes it upon someone else. Not at all limited to couples, it flourishes in relatively isolated social units. Extreme religious cults driven by a charismatic leader are of this nature—and one of those was the Heaven's Gate suicide squad.

As we now see, what modestly began in 1964 as a *folie à deux*, ini-tially shared by just a middled-aged American couple, has now gone global, so ballooning into *une folie culturelle et internationelle*. Just how—and why—that happened requires further analysis.

NOTES

1. See Patrick Huyghe, *The Field Guide to Extraterrestrials* (New York: Avon, 1996), pp. 30–31 (with illustration of the Hill model).

2. Joe Nickell, "Extraterrestrial Iconography," *Skeptical Inquier* 21, no. 5 (September/October 1997): 19 (emphasis mine).

3. For the literary aspects, and immense cultural significance, of Fuller's epoch-making tall tale, see Terry Matheson, *Alien Abductions: Creating a Modern Phenomenon* (Amherst, N.Y.: Prometheus Books, 1998), pp. 47–76.

4. James E. Bullard, *Comparative Study of Abduction Reports*, vol. 1 of *UFO Abductions: The Measure of a Mystery* (Bloomington, Ind.: Fund for UFO Research, 1987), pp. 238, 350, 365, 366.

5. For the classic definition of the modernist pseudoevent, see Daniel J. Boorstin, *The Image: A Guide to Pseudo-Events in America* (New York: Colophon, 1964), esp. pp. 11–12, 39–40 (partially quoted above).

6. Huyghe, *Field Guide to Extraterrestrials*, p. 12.

7. Nickell, "Extraterrestrial Iconography."

8. Barney Hill, as quoted in John G. Fuller, *The Interrupted Journey: Two Lost Hours "Aboard a Flying Saucer"* (New York: Dell, 1967), pp. 301–302.

9. Ibid., pp. 305–306.

10. Betty Hill, as quoted in ibid., pp. 309–10.

11. Ibid., pp. 114–20 (I have here cut out all of Fuller's abundant stage directions).

12. So acknowledged in ibid., pp. 45, 48.

13. Ibid., p. 75.

14. Ibid., p. 58.

15. For these embarassing revelations, see Philip J. Klass, *UFO-Abductions: A Dangerous Game* (Amherst, N.Y.: Prometheus Books, 1989), chap. 1, "The UFO-Abduction Era Begins," esp. pp. 9–10.

16. Fuller, *Interrupted Journey*, p. 58.

17. Ibid., pp. 38, 55, 108.

18. Ibid., p. 108, also noting the priority of Janet's UFO sightings.

19. Ibid., p. 48.

20. For Barney's complaints about his wife nagging him to "believe" in their fantastic encounter, see ibid., pp. 33, 40, 69–71 (etc.).

21. Ibid., pp. 44, 75.

22. Ibid., p. 102.

23. Ibid., p. 82.

24. See Keith Thompson, *Angels and Aliens: UFOs and the Mythic Imagination* (New York: Ballantine, 1993), pp. 62–67, citing a marvelous bit of previously unpublished detective work by Martin Kottmeyer, to whom we all owe copious thanks for his skillful deconstruction of the strictly cinematic contributions to an unquestionably influential Hill abduction legend.

25. Barney Hill, in Fuller, *Interrupted Journey*, p. 120.

26. For more on the crucial "Bellero Shield" episode, see David J. Schow and Jeffrey Frentzen, *The Outer Limits: The Official Companion* (New York: Ace, 1986), pp. 170, 384.

27. Fuller, *Interrupted Journey*, pp. 114–15.

28. Ibid., p. 98.

29. Ibid., pp. 69, 198.

30. Ibid., pp. 342–50.

31. Ibid., p. 340—and so acknowledged by (even) David M. Jacobs, *Secret Life: Firsthand Documented Accounts of UFO Abduction* (New York: Fireside, 1993), p. 41.

32. Klass, *UFO-Abductions*, p. 8.

33. Jenny Randles, *The UFO Conspiracy: The First Forty Years* (London: Javelin, 1988), p. 62.

34. Michael Shermer, *Why People Believe Weird Things: Pseudoscience, Superstition, and Other Confusions of Our Time* (New York: Freeman, 1997), p. 95.

35. Benjamin Simon, in *Klass, UFO-Abductions*, p. 8.

36. Klass, *UFO-Abductions*, p. 42 (my emphasis).

37. See Bernard Grun, *The Timetables of History: A Horizontal Linkage of People and Events* (New York: Touchstone, 1982), pp. 584–89; this is also my useful source for many forthcoming synchronisms.

38. Travis Walton, in Bill Barry, *Ultimate Encounter: The True Story of a UFO Kidnapping* (New York: Bantam, 1978), pp. 246–47; see also Travis Walton, *The Walton Experience* (New York: Berkley, 1978).

39. For the dubious, narrationally conflictive, literary aspects of Walton's tall tale, see Matheson, *Alien Abductions*, pp. 107–14.

40. For what follows, see Klass, *UFO-Abductions*, chap. 3, "Travis Walton—Eager Abductee" (a wonderful piece of detective work in the literal sense), as preceeded by his Travis-debunking in Klass, *UFOs: The Public Deceived* (Amherst, N.Y.: Prometheus Books, 1983), pp. 161–221; see also Curtis Peebles, *Watch the Skies! A Chronicle of the Flying Saucer Myth* (Washington, D.C.: Smithsonian, 1994), pp. 230–31.

41. (No author named for opprobrium), *National Enquirer UFO Report* (New York: Pocket Books, 1985), p. 13 (oddly, this feuilleton contains no mention of the slippery Travis).

42. John White (with Travis Walton), *Fire in the Sky: The Travis Walton Experience* (New York: Marlowe, 1995).

43. For useful lessons in the deductive deconstruction of suspected fakes, see J. F. Moffitt, *Art Forgery: The Case of the Lady of Elche* (Gainesville: Florida University Press, 1995; *El caso de la Dama de Elche: Crónica de una leyenda*, Barcelona: Destino, 1997).

44. Raymond E. Fowler, *The Andreasson Affair* (New York: Bantam, 1980; hardback ed., Englewood Cliffs, N.J.: Prentice-Hall, 1979).

45. Ibid., p. 8; see also pp. 6, 174, 190, 220. For Fowler's considerable contributions to the further-evolving ET literary genre, see Matheson, *Alien Abductions*, pp. 77–106, 191–228. See also Fowler's other epic tale of alien abduction, *The Alla-*

gash Abductions (Tigard, Ore.: Wild Flower Press, 1993); for its contents, often shown on cable TV, see specifically Matheson, ibid., pp. 213–24 (so saving me the effort of recounting the familiar story of four lads on a fishing trip, then beamed up to a UFO, and so forth, all shown here just to be more "confabulation").

46. Raymond E. Fowler, *The Andreasson Affair, Phase Two* (Englewood Cliffs, N.J.: Prentice-Hall, 1982); R. E. Fowler, *The Watchers* (New York: Bantam, 1990).

47. See Huyghe, *Field Guide to Extraterrestrials*, pp. 88–89 (illustrating the variant "lemur" type, here supplementing the standard "Grays," also plentifully reported by Betty A.).

48. Fowler, *Andreasson Affair*, p. 10.

49. Major Donald G. Carpenter (1968), as quoted in ibid., p. 171.

50. Ibid., pp. 17–18.

51. Ibid., pp. 19–20.

52. Ibid., pp. 27–29.

53. Ibid., pp. 41–43.

54. Ibid., pp. 2, 13, 87, 91, 149, 209.

55. Ibid., pp. 86–87.

56. For what immediately follows, see Klass, *UFO-Abductions*, chap. 4, "An Incredible Abduction Tale."

57. For this whopping dollar-figure, see ibid., pp. 126, 141, 147; see also below, chap. 13, 14, and 21, for more details on Strieber's bizarre career, emotional life, and volatile opinions. For Strieber's opus as a calculated literary artifact (versus "nonfiction"), see Matheson, *Alien Abductions*, pp. 161–89.

58. Strieber, *Communion: A True Story* (reprint New York: Bantam, 1987), p. 111.

59. Ibid., p. 113.

60. Ibid., p. 157; for these occultist avatars (and treated as such), see James Webb, *The Harmonious Circle: The Lives and Work of G. I. Gurdjieff, D. P. Ouspensky, and Their Followers* (LaSalle, Ill.: Open Court, 1987).

61. Strieber, *Communion*, p. 279.

62. Ibid., pp. 27, 179.

63. Ibid., p. 94.

64. Ibid., p. 42.

65. Ibid., p. 174.

66. Ibid., pp. 148–49.

67. Ibid., pp. 60–61.

68. Ibid., pp. 78–79.

69. Ibid., pp. 20–21.

70. C. Lorenzen and J. Lorenzen, *The Flying Saucer Occupants* (New York: Signet, 1967), p. 54.

71. Illustrated (*à l'ekphrasis*) in Huyghe, *Field Guide to Extraterrestrials*, pp. 28–29.

72. Fuller, *Interrupted Journey*, p. 23.

73. Fowler, *Andreasson Affair*, pp. 6, 8 (citing Fuller), 182, 221 (citing Lorenzen).

74. Coral Lorenzen (as retitled), *Flying Saucers: The Startling Evidence of the Invasion from Outer Space* (New York: Signet, 1966), pp. 64–66. The new material, added by Lorenzen since 1962 to her *The Great Flying Saucer Hoax*, appears from p. 218 on, bringing useful, new apocrypha to the UFOlogists' now-standard repertoire, especially making infamous another New Mexico UFO landing and alien encounter, in Socorro and starring Lonnie Zamora in 1964 (pp. 218–22).

75. Ibid., pp. 66–67.

76. Ibid., p. 69.

77. Strieber, *Communion*, pp. 249–50 (my emphasis). No scholar he, Strieber does not cite his published source: Lorenzen.

78. Lorenzen, *Flying Saucers*, p. 74.

79. Fuller, *Interrupted Journey*, pp. 346–47.

80. On SETI, see Frazer, *The UFO Invasion*, pp. 295–302.

81. Bullard, *UFO Abductions*, p. 54.

82. All the points immediately following were raised by Robert A. Baker, in *The UFO Invasion: The Roswell Incident, Alien Abductions, and Government Coverups*, ed. Kendrick Frazer (Amherst, N.Y.: Prometheus Books, 1997), pp. 262–63.

Chapter 6

Premodernist Religious Transports, Possession, and Poetic Inspiration

PRECEDENTS FOR BETTY ANDREASSON'S VISIONS IN THE TRADITIONAL LITERATURE OF MYSTICISM

Viewed from a broader historical perspective, and once one ignores the specifically New Age trappings (ETs and UFOs), the quintessential Betty Andreasson ET affair becomes just another minor accretion to the sprawling bibliography of mysticism. This is easily demonstrated; recalling her close encounter with the ETs in her cluttered kitchen, Betty explained: "I'm thinking they must be angels, and Scriptures keep coming into my mind."[1] Here's another example: one of John Mack's abductee patients exclaims, "There's been guardian angels. I've always known that I could commune with God. I've always known that there were UFOs and extraterrestrials."[2] And let us not forget that, long ago, Carl Jung called ETs "technological angels," and he did so in a book fittingly called *Flying Saucers: A Modern Myth of Things Seen in the Sky* (1959).

In this case, one must cite what perhaps constitutes the most famous angelic (maybe even extraterrestrial) visitation recorded in the authentic literature of mysticism. This one, including insertion of a metallic instrument, was written down in 1565 by Saint Teresa of Avila (1515–1582), a lady with a much more sophisticated mentality than that enjoyed by Betty A. and the rest of her hypnotized postmodernist accomplices. As Teresa (canonized in 1622) explains:

But there is some alleviation, and a little of the pain passes, if the soul prays God to give it some remedy for its suffering, though it can see no way except death by which it can expect to enjoy its blessing complete. But there are other times when the impulses are so strong that it can do absolutely nothing. The entire body contracts; neither foot nor arm can be moved. If one is standing at the time, one falls into a sitting position as though transported [se sienta como una cosa transportada], and cannot even take a breath. One only utters a few slight moans, not aloud, for that is impossible, but inwardly, out of pain.

Our Lord was pleased that I should sometimes see a vision of this kind. Beside me, on the left hand, appeared an [ET-like] angel in bodily form, such as I am not in the habit of seeing, except very rarely. Though I often have visions of angels [or ETs], I do not see them. They come to me only after the manner of the first type of vision that I described. But it was our Lord's will that I should see this angel [and/or ET] in the following way. He was not tall but short, and very beautiful; and his face was so aflame that he appeared to be one of the highest rank of angels, who seem to be all on fire [cf. fig. 4]. They must be of the kind called cherubim, but they do not tell me their names. I know very well that there is a great difference between some angels and others, and between these and others still, but I could not possibly explain it.

In his hands I saw a great golden spear and, at the iron tip, there appeared to be a point of fire. This he plunged into my heart several times—so that it penetrated to my entrails. When he pulled it out, I felt that he took them with it, and left me utterly consumed by the great love of God. The pain was so severe that it made me utter several moans. The sweetness [la suavidad, meaning "orgasm"!] caused by this intense pain is so extreme that one cannot possibly wish it to cease, nor is one's soul then content with anything but God. This is not a physical, but a spiritual pain, even though the body has some share in it—even a considerable share. So gentle is this wooing, which takes place between God [now called an ET] and the soul, that if anyone thinks I am lying, I pray God, in His goodness, to grant him some experience of it.

Throughout the days that this lasted I went about in a kind of stupor. I had no wish to look or to speak, only to embrace my pain, which was a greater bliss than all created things could give me. On several occasions, when I was in this state, the Lord was pleased that I should experience raptures so deep that I could not resist them—even though I was not alone. Greatly to my distress, therefore, my raptures began to be talked about. Since I have had them, I have ceased to feel this pain so much, though I still feel the pain that I spoke of in a previous chapter—I do not remember which. The latter is very different in many respects, and much more valuable. But when this pain, of which I am now speaking, begins, the Lord seems to transport the soul and throw it into an [orgasmic] ecstasy [parece arrebata el Señor el alma y la pone *en éstasis*]. So there is no opportunity for it to feel its pain or suffering, for the [orgasmic] enjoyment comes immediately. May He be blessed for ever, who has granted so many favors to one who has so ill repaid.[3]

In fact, once viewed with a historical perspective, rather than with New Age blinkers, Betty Andreasson's otherworldly recollections become structurally identical to those recorded by other troubled mystics, particularly the unaffiliated kind that never seem to merit canonization. We have, for instance, the provocative example of Margery Kempe (circa 1373–1440). Speaking in the third person, as she recalled—and without the aid of hypnosis (not yet invented):

> She saw, as she thought, devils opening their mouths all inflamed with burning waves of fire, as if they would have swallowed her in, sometimes ramping at her, sometimes threatening her, pulling her and hauling her. . . . The devils cried upon her that she should forsake Christendom, her faith, and deny her God. . . . She said many a wicked word, and many a cruel word; she knew no virtue nor goodness; she desired all wickedness; like as the spirits tempted her to say and do, so she said and did. . . . She bit her own hand so violently, that the mark was seen all her life after. And also she ripped the skin on her body against her heart with her nails spitefully, for she had no other instruments, and worse she would have done, but that she was bound and kept with strength day and night. . . . [Then she had a vision of Christ] clad in a mantle of purple and silk, sitting upon her bedside, looking upon her with so blessed a face that she was strengthened in all her spirit. . . . Anon this creature [Margery] became calmed in her wits and reason, as well as ever she was before, and prayed her husband as soon as he came to her, that she might have the keys of the buttery to take her meat and drink as she had done before.

Margery's recovery from this otherworldly visitation appeared to be complete. In a short while, she was able to start business enterprises. Alas, these later failed, and she interpreted her lack of success in worldly affairs as a sign from God that she should devote herself to matters of the spirit and spent much time in prayer and contemplation. She began to long for a celibate life, but her entreaties to her husband that they might live chastely together met with his insensitive reply that "it was good to do so, but he might not yet." Margery, now feeling "afflicted with horrible temptation to lechery," relates how she was tempted to commit adultery, but when she finally consented, the man rejected her, saying, "he never would for all the gold in this world." (She does not relate whether his rejection of her lusty offer was based on aesthetic grounds.) This episode naturally placed her in a bad mood, namely, "weeping wondrous sore," and she quickly repaired to a chapel where Christ again appeared to her. At this time, he reassured her of his love, told her to abstain from eating flesh and recommended further meditation. Moreover,

> Our Lord gave her another token . . . and that was a flame of fire, wondrous hot and delectable, and right comfortable, not wasting but ever increasing, of love; for though the weather were never so cold, she felt the heat burning in her breast and at her heart, as verily as a man could feel the material fire, if he put his hand or his finger therein. . . . Sometimes she felt sweet smells with her nose, sweeter, she thought, than ever was any sweet earthly thing that she smelt before. . . . Sometimes she heard with her bodily ears sounds and melodies, nearly every day, especially when she was in devout prayer. . . . She had divers tokens in her bodily hearing . . . a sort of sound as if it were a pair of bellows blowing in her ear. She, being abashed thereby, was warned in her soul no fear to have, for it was the sound of the Holy Ghost. And then Our Lord turned [it] into the voice of a dove, and later on, He turned it into the voice of a little bird which is called a [robin] red-breast, that sang full merrily oftentimes in her right ear. . . . She saw with her bodily eyes many white things flying all about her on every side, as thick as specks in a sunbeam. They were right subtle and comfortable, and the brighter the sun shone, the better might she see them. She saw them many divers times and in many divers places, both in church and in her chamber, in the fields, and in town.

Alas, even her repeated conversations with Christ, including His reiterated reassurances of His love for her, did not entirely quell her "foul" sexual impulses:

> So now she had as many hours of foul thoughts and foul memories of lechery and all uncleanness, as though she had been common to all manner of people, horrible sights and abominable, for aught she could do, of beholding men's members [i.e., genitalia]. . . . She saw, as she thought verily, divers men of religion, priests and many others, both heathen and Christian, coming before her sight, . . . showing their bare members unto her [including Christ Himself, telling her:] "Thou mayest boldly, when thou art in thy bed, take Me to thee as thy wedded husband . . . and I will that thou lovest Me, daughter, as a good wife ought to love her husband. Therefore, thou mayest boldly take Me in the arms of thy soul and kiss My mouth, My head, and My feet, as sweetly as thou wilt."[4]

Alas, five hundred years later, Mrs. Kempe's mystic revelations are disparagingly called by a professional pathologist "hysterical visions," and now she is also diagnosed as a sexually conflicted housewife who had been impregnated over a dozen times.[5] Like Margery Kempe's curriculum vita, Betty Andreasson's personal (versus strictly "spiritual") situation is also most revealing. A high-school dropout born in 1937, she was the fertile mother of seven, and the most lurid, and widely publicized, aspect of her abduction—the forceful removal of eggs from her ovaries by intrusive ETs—was only "remembered" once her marriage had begun to break up following a traumatic hysterectomy causing certain "marital problems" (frigidity on her part, I suspect).[6] In any event, the stolen-ova motif has since become a sensational staple of many subsequent "abduction" narratives.[7]

In Margery's time, however, "abduction" (the New Age term) was instead called "rapture," *rapta est*, literally meaning "carried away" (or *abducta est*), just as when, even earlier, one was commonly seized with a commonplace religious enthusiasm formerly called *ekstasis*, so labeled by Saint Teresa and literally meaning (in Greek) "stepping outside oneself."[8] In a functionally similar manner, so did the likes of Betty A.: we may say that she was truly "out of it." But it is not just her; this means all those folks who tell us they have actually been privileged to ascend into the UFOs, and by so doing are then often carried away—*abducta sunt*—to far places, perhaps distant galaxies. In accounts of otherworldly visitations experienced by humble folk in fifteenth-century Spain, the language had it literally that the perceiver was "transported." In the original accounts we read how one fellow "*se traspone muchas bezes*," and another woman "was often transported in such a way that she had no knowledge nor thought of whether she was in this world or in another" (*que estava transportada que no tenía notizia ni pensamiento que estava en este mundo sino en el otro*).[9] As we just saw, Saint Teresa employed the same conventional language of ecstatic transport: *se sentía como una cosa transportada*. Although the linguistic particulars may shift slightly, the basic perception remains unaltered, from the Middle Ages to postmodernism.

THE CASE FOR "POSSESSION"

Another term, which we shall see often repeated in the historical documents soon to be quoted, is "possession." As I will argue, this ancient terminology best conforms to the real, also meaning traditional and/or wholly conventionalized, character of all those breathtaking postmodernist tales of abductions executed by devious, even devilish, outer-space aliens.[10] Put simply, *possession*, in some societies and religious beliefs, is a condition in which an individual's mind, body, or soul is understood to be taken over by a supernatural being. Now we postmodernists routinely call those ancient supernatural beings "extraterrestrials."

Belief in possession is probably universal among human societies, no matter whether primitive or (nominally) civilized. In primitive religions, possession is understood to be the result of special ritual invocations. In the course of primitive religious rites, the tribal religious leader, the shaman or witch doctor, will typically enter into a trance state and take on the attributes of a god. Sometimes this role falls to a worshiper or to an initiate into the rite. In several recorded instances, observers of the Voodoo (or Santería) rite involuntarily fall into a trance and are said to be possessed by a god. Even in the highly developed countries of North America and Europe, some religious groups continue to believe in possession by the Christian Holy Spirit, and some practice exorcism of evil spirits from the demonically possessed. Communist societies, although themselves now largely discredited and in a deep economic and ideological funk, may be the only societies in the postmodernist world where such primitive beliefs and practices are no longer acknowledged, let alone actively encouraged.

One of the earliest accounts of possession is recorded in the ancient Greek tragedy *The Bacchae*, by Euripides. As was told here, devotees of the god Dionysus become possessed and pursue the god, or his stand-in, Orpheus, through the woods. When they catch him, they tear him apart and eat him alive. Two words often associated with possession are derived from the Greek: "ecstasy" from *ex*, out of, and *histasthai*, to stand, thus, to stand outside oneself. The alternative term is "enthusiasm," from *en*, in, and *theos*, god, and the result is the active verb *enthoussiazen*, to be inspired or possessed by a god. The properly possessed person usually speaks in a different voice, sometimes in a different and unintelligible language, and displays a variety of spasmodic or graceful motions and other *outré* actions that would be nearly impossible for him to perform in the normal state (e.g., fire walking, and the choreographic excesses of "dancing dervishes"). Frequently, the possessed may engage in aggressive or sexual acts that would not be permitted in the normal state. The worshipers usually believe that, during the possession, the god has come to join the group in its religious celebration, and the possessed person often dons a mask or other paraphernalia associated with the possessing deity. As a postmodernist American might explain his or her aggressive or sexual acts, "It's not my fault; the devil made me do it."

In another variety of possession the possessed is actually taken ill.

The illness may be explained as harassment by a purely malevolent evil spirit (or ET) or as a spiritual punishment for violating some sacred law. To the contrary, a modern psychiatrist might just call it a psychosomatic disorder. In the former case, a simple "exorcism" may cure the illness (as is explained in chapter 7). In the case of a violation of taboo, a ritual cleansing of the sinner by a witch doctor will usually also involve a confession by the possessed, or his proxy, and probably some sort of penance or the payment of a penalty. Demonic possession, in Western religious belief, is a condition in which an individual's mind, body, and soul are taken over by an evil spirit, a "demon" (or ET), that desires total control and, in Christian belief, the eternal damnation of the possessed (as is also explained in chapter 7).

A common form of possession in the West during the last 150 years has been mediumistic possession. According to nineteenth-century occultist "Spiritist" practice, the medium entered a trance state fairly easily and was then taken over by his or her "control," a hypothetical, disembodied spirit which used the medium to communicate from the spirit world (as will be explained in chapter 12). The control mediates between the spirits of the dead and their concerned relatives gathered in the medium's parlor. Under the grandiose title of "Theosophy," this was basically the same kind of Spiritism as was practiced by Madame Blavatsky (see chapter 10). Sometimes, however, the spirits are allowed to speak for themselves directly through the medium. Moreover, the medium's voice and manner commonly change radically, as the voice, accents, posture, and gestures of the controlling spirit are reproduced in the possessed medium. This is the thespian-centered kind of occultism.

The most common, or traditional, form of possession in Christendom is, however, possession by the Holy Spirit, a manifestation of the real presence of the divinity. Common to several Pentecostal sects of Protestantism, and also to some experimental groups in the major Protestant denominations and (even) in Roman Catholicism, possession by the Holy Spirit usually takes the forms of physical seizures, automatism, and *glossolalia* (speaking in tongues) and the interpretation of such speech. Another form of possession, in which professed Christians largely figure, is demonic possession (as is explained in chapter 7). Demonic possession was most familiarly dramatized for us in *The Exorcist*, a best-selling paperback book and (of course) a popular film (1973), showing much morbid interest in the unusual phenomena associated with possession. Unlike divine possession, demonic possession need not be sought out or result from some moral transgression. It can be the consequence of simple malevolent seduction by an evil spirit. This standard

Christian situation, that is, demonic possession, is now called abduction by "aliens" (from outer space, not Central America).

The usual experience of possession seems to follow after a prolonged or intense period of extreme mental or physical stress. This stress can be voluntarily induced by drumming, chanting, dancing, special breathing, exercises, drugs, physical exhaustion, or physical debilitation through fasting or exposure. All of these practices of self-torment are eagerly embraced by the more rigorous minded acolytes of the New Age; post-modernists often perform these abusive rituals in places called "health spas." Intense stress of this sort can result in the dissociation of the mind from the body and of sections of the mind from each other (i.e., schizophrenia). In the case of shamans and mediums, traditional folk-culture types rarely subscribing to the New Age commandments, the ability often and easily to enter a trance state and become possessed is the first requirement for the job, and there may be a preexisting dissociation in the personality of the medium or shaman. The trance can, in that case, be an easily adopted and eventually habitual alteration of consciousness may result. Joseph Beuys, the vanguard German artist, also wished to induce an alteration of consciousness in his enraptured audiences and he even explicitly compared his evangelistic performances (called *Aktionen*) to the operations of a shaman.[11]

Believers in possession maintain that the condition of dissociation that results from stress makes way for the god or spirit to take control of the mind and body. However, those who adhere to a strictly psychological or scientific explanation, and thus reject the supernatural one, regard possession as a form of hypnosis or autosuggestion. In the case of the hypnotically induced postmodernist alien-abduction recitals, this is particularly, and unquestionably, the case. Dr. William Sargant, a British physician who began to study dissociation during World War II when he worked with battle-fatigued soldiers, found the phenomenon of possession to be similar to such psychophysical crises as conversion, deep mystical experience, brainwashing, the excitement of mobs, the reliving of emotional trauma under psychiatric treatment, even orgasm. In Sargant's view, extreme stress, beyond an individual's capacity to adapt to or bear it, causes the brain to enter a state of protective inhibition. This condition, or trance state, can be compared to a fuse blowing out and closing down part of an electrical system when it is overloaded. A portion of the brain is isolated, or the data contained there are wiped out, and the person then becomes open to suggestion from outside, or to impulses arising from the unconscious areas of the mind. Frequently, even in cases of known autosuggestion, the possessed has displayed talents and abilities far exceeding his normal performance. In the case of hypnotically "retrieved memories" of egregious encounters with post-modernist extraterrestrials, the talents displayed are mainly for fabulously inventive storytelling.

Another name for this transcendental psychic condition, possession, the kind uniquely allowing for the kind of privileged visions and profound insights commonly disallowed to the average citizen, is *inspiration*.

HOW VISIONARY "INSPIRATION" WAS DESCRIBED IN CLASSICAL CULTURE

Long before Saint Teresa colored them Catholic, such visionary ecstasies and psychic transports experienced by the possessed were also familiar to any number of writers working in the late classical period. The Greek authors frequently situated this phenomenon within the context of rites attending the worship of the pagan god Dionysus, also known to Romans as Bacchus. By means of their prestigious writings, eventually the notion of frenzied "inspiration" became equally well known to Italian humanists by means of standard texts recovered by them during the Renaissance. As reported in such documents, the kind representing recently retrieved cultural memories of long-vanished classical *miracula*, particularly significant is the way that the typically emotionalized Dionysiac syndrome was so vividly recreated.

Such effects are particularly striking in Seneca's *Agamemnon* and likewise in Lucan's *Pharsalia*. For instance, in his *Agamemnon* (verses 710 ff.), the Chorus clinically describes what Seneca called "bacchantic frenzy" exhibited in a "priestess of Phoebus," so rendering in strictly verbal—also vividly physiological—terms the pictorial equivalent of those ecstatic Maenads seen on so many ancient Greek vase paintings and bas-reliefs (see fig. 23).[12] Such as the visionary votary was dramatically pictured by Seneca:

> Her cheeks are pale, and her whole body shakes. Her curls stiffen; her soft hair stands on end; her heart hisses frantically with a choking sound. Her glance wanders unsteady in different directions; her eyes seem to twist and turn inward, and then again just to stare motionless. Now she lifts her head up into the air, higher than usual, and walks erect. Now she is getting ready to unseal her vocal chords against their will; now she tries to close her lips, but she cannot keep her words inside. *Here is a priestess in ecstasy*. . . . "Why [she cries] do you prick me with the goad of an unfamiliar madness? I have lost my mind; why

do you sweep me away? Leave me, Phoebus [Apollo]! I am no longer
yours. Extinguish the flame that you have kindled deep in my breast!
What good does it do if I rush around like mad? *Who needs my bacchantic frenzy?*"[13]

In Lucan's unfinished epic *Pharsalia* (5.112ff.), it was likewise
explained that when "the god enters someone's heart, premature death is
the penalty or the reward for having received him; the human organism
is battered by the sting and the surge of ecstasy." Then follows Lucan's
amazingly detailed, physiological-physiognomical, clinical picture of this
kind of overwhelming, indeed awesome, "ecstasy," occurring at an often
terrifying moment of climax. This climactic, even pseudosexual, orgasmic
transaction specifically occurs when the extraterrestrial god

> takes over the soul of the priestess. Never before has he forced his way
> so fully into the body of a prophetess, driving out her normal con-
> sciousness and taking the place of everything that is human in her
> heart. Frantically, out of her mind, she runs through the sanctuary. Her
> neck no longer belongs to her; her bristling hair shakes off the fillets and
> garlands of Apollo as she whirls, tossing her head. . . . She boils over
> with a tremendous fire. . . . Now she sees everything; the first day and
> the last day of the world, the dimensions of the Ocean, the sum of the
> sands! . . . Madness and ecstasy begin to flow in earnest from her
> foaming lips. She moans and utters loud, inarticulate cries. . . . Her
> frenzy continues, and the god, who has not left her body, is still in con-
> trol. Her eyes roll wildly, and her glance roams over the whole sky. The
> expressions on her face change constantly: now she looks frightened,
> now fierce and menacing. A fiery flush spreads over her features and
> colors her pale cheeks, but her pallor does not seem to indicate fear;
> rather it inspires it. Her heart is overtired, but cannot relax; voiceless
> sighs, sounding like the moaning of a turbulent sea after the North Wind
> has ceased to blow, still heave her breast. . . . She [finally] falls to the
> ground and barely recovers.[14]

As one might expect, such widely discussed Dionysiac concepts were
bound to find their visual analogs in ancient art (and in other forms than
Bacchantes or Maenads). Even though long vanished and known only
through its posthumous fame, mainly as verbally transmitted to us by
Pliny the Elder, Praxiteles' representation of *Dionysios* (circa 340 B.C.E.)
seems to have been taken during the Renaissance to represent the definitive sculptural rendering of Bacchus. European humanists were unquestionably familiar with books describing lost ancient artworks composed
by Callistratus and called the *Descriptiones*, or *Ekphraseis* (circa 280

C.E.). In his "Eighth Description," or *Ekphrasis*, this late classical author celebrated at some length Praxiteles' lost "Cult-Statue of Bacchus" (*Dionyseoi Agalma*). According to this standard textual source:

> There was a grove, and in it stood [a life-sized cult-statue of] Dionysus in the form of a young man, so delicate that the bronze was transformed into flesh, with a body so supple and relaxed that it seemed . . . to show the appearance of life and would yield to the very finger-tip if you touched it. . . . It had the bloom of youth; it was full of daintiness, it melted with desire . . . and it was full of laughter, nay, it wholly passed the bounds of wonder in that the material gave out evidence of joy and that the bronze feigned to represent the emotions.[15]

Besides its enviable formal, even "emotional," accomplishments, which are presented by this ekphrastic author as praiseworthy exemplars of sheer virtuosity, Praxiteles' masterwork also revealed some significant content. According to Callistratus's vivid description, "The eye was gleaming with fire, in appearance the eye of a man in a frenzy; for the bronze exhibited the Bacchic madness [or frenzy: *manikon . . . Bacchensimon*] and seemed to be divinely inspired, just as, I think, Praxiteles similarly had the power to infuse into his statue the Bacchic ecstasy."[16]

In his "Fourth Ekphrasis," Callistratus describes yet another ancient sculpture (likewise long since gone missing), the "Cult-Statue of an Indian" (*Indou Agalma*), which he specifically ascribes to the widespread cult of Dionysus. As he tells us, what he saw was the anomalous rendering of a tipsy figure, placed "by a spring and set up with a dedication to the Nymphs." His description further indicates in many specific "eikastic" details—meaning naturalistic, according to measured, proportionate likeness—that the Greek sculptor's overall purpose was to indicate that a divinely inspired "drunkenness was overcoming him." According to the description composed by Callistratus, his Bacchic figure "stood reeling and jovial, not able to plant his feet steadily, but trembling and tending to sag to the ground. The marble resembled a man overcome by this condition, and it all but quivers as it indicates the trembling that comes from drunkenness. There was nothing delicate about the statue."[17]

Elsewhere Callistratus (*Descriptiones*, II: "*Bácches Agalma*") discusses "The Cult-Statue of a Bacchante." This other artwork also allows Callistratus to explain the sources of any such divinely inspired, specifically Dionysiac, art exhibiting the *manikon Bacchensimon*, or conventionalized Bacchic frenzy attending the visionary state. Our Greek ekphrastic writer does so, in fact, in a way that directly recalls Plato's earlier descriptions of creatively and/or divinely inspired poets, "mindless" and "raving like Bacchantes." In *Ion*, a text which was itself well known to the Florentine humanists, Plato has Socrates observe:

> Good poets use no art at all, but are inspired and possessed. . . . These are not in their right mind when they make their beautiful songs, but are like Corybants [or Maenads], out of their wits and dancing about. As soon as poets rely upon their [Corybantic] harmony and rhythm, they become frantic and possessed, just like the Bacchante women, possessed and out of their senses. . . . The poet is an airy thing, a winged and holy thing; and he [as a creative artist] cannot make poetry until he becomes inspired and goes out of his senses and no mind is left in him, [creating] not by art, but by divine dispensation. Therefore, the only poetry that each one can make is what the Muse has pushed him to make. . . . Therefore, God takes the mind out of the poets, and uses them as his servants. These beautiful poems are not human, are not made by man, but are instead divine and made by God. The poets are [therefore] nothing but the gods' interpreters, possessed each one by whatever god it may be [or whom he might represent by his art]. (*Ion* 533 D–535 B)[18]

Among other points, Plato argues—and long before André Breton did—that poetic creation is wholly passive: God "uses" the poet as his "mindless" scribe. Since the role of the poet, or generic Artist, is wholly passive, thus his "inspired" act of "divine" creativity operates autonomously, without his conscious participation. Being unconscious (or "a-conscious"), the creative act thus becomes (according to anachronistic modern terminology) "automatic." As the Surrealists would agree, *l'art automatique* is willed by an external agent, for there is no control exerted over the aesthetic product by the ostensible creator, a mere human being: "Good poets use no art at all, but are inspired and possessed." Again, whatever the specific ramifications, the situation is wholly, uniquely, and very specifically "Bacchic." Moreover, since the maker has no control over his product, it seems *almost* to be made now by "chance." At this time however, it cannot be wholly a matter of chance (*le hasard*) because, of course, "God does not play dice with the universe" (according to Albert Einstein). However, when Breton manipulated the same ideas millennia later, then, finally, the creative desideratum did become pure Chance. When employed slightly later by various hypnotized persons recounting their close encounters with the extraterrestrials, the result is a rather different kind of literary endeavor: a paperback publishing bonanza.

By the time Callistratus was writing (circa 280 C.E.), such interpretations of the visionary "Bacchic" creative act, and of the uniquely "inspired" and "divine" art uniquely resulting from it, seem to have become commonplaces in Greek thought, even in its visual arts, particularly sculpture. In his "Second Description," the Greek ekphrastic author vividly describes an actual sculptural representation of Dionysiac inspiration. Most interestingly, this he does in a way that would have been obviously of use to nearly all Renaissance spokesmen arguing for a novel installation of plastic creations, our "art," among the liberal arts. Their postmedieval arguments for the "liberal" status of the visual artist were particularly epitomized by current, and increasingly heated, discussions dealing with the theory of *Ut Pictura Poësis*. This argument, holding that "as in Poetry, so too in Painting," thereby ambitiously yoked the long-established moral-rhetorical purposes of poetry to painting. So doing, painting—a representational discipline previously relegated to mere craftspersons—was now elevated to the status of "art"—an honorific title previously only granted to poetry. As was observed (and similarly argued) long before by Callistratus:

> It is not only the art of poets and writers of prose which is inspired [*epipnéuontai*] once divine power from the gods falls upon their tongues. Nay, the hands of sculptors also, when they are seized by the gift of a more divine inspiration, [also may] give utterance to [artistic] creations that are [likewise] possessed and full of madness. So Skopas, moved as it were by some inspiration, imparted to the production of this [Bacchic] statue the divine frenzy within him. Why should I not describe to you from the beginning the inspiration [*enthousiasmon*] belonging to this work of art? . . . The stone, while retaining its own nature, yet seemed to depart from the law which governs stone. What one saw was really an image, but art had carried imitation [*mímesin*] over into actual reality. . . .
>
> Though it had no power to move, [nonetheless] the statue knew how to leap in Bacchic dance, and thus it would respond to the god as he entered into its inner being. When we saw its face we stood speechless, for so manifest upon it was the evidence of sense perception, even though [real] sense perception was not present: there was given [to us by the sculptor] so clear a perception of a Bacchante's divine possession [*theiasmos*] that was stirring her Bacchic frenzy [*manías*], even though no such possession [actually] had aroused it. Fashioned by art in a manner not to be described, there shone so strikingly from it all the signs of passion which a soul goaded by madness displays. . . . Thus Skopas, fashioning creatures without life, was an artificer of truth, and so he imprinted miracles upon bodies made of inanimate matter.[19]

Thus, Bacchic "madness" becomes the unique vehicle lending to visual art, particularly as represented by a given masterwork of sculpture with specifically Dionysiac subject matter, the same prestige as was traditionally accorded only to poetry. The unquestionable cultural significance of this specific passage was pointed out long ago (1926) by Edgar Zilsel in his fundamental study on the historical evolution of the concept of genius. As he then observed:

> The old teachings about the Poet's "enthusiasm," perhaps now inflected by a Jewish prophetic tone, have thus finally entered into the vocabulary of the visual arts. In Callistratus's statement, the idea of divine possession is now clearly conceived in terms of a vigorous rhetorical allegorization, but not, however, as any serious religious conviction. Now, towards the end of the classical period, the visual artist achieves a complete assimilation with the modern concept of artistic inspiration [*Künstlerenthusiasmus*], and in this way an unquestionable connection with our modern conception of genius has finally been achieved.[20]

Callistratus was certainly not the only ancient author to describe in detail the state of Bacchic *ekstasis* or psychic possession; he was, however, unique in attaching his description to a *statue*, also significantly implying that its creator was an "artistic genius." Still, we must doubt that the authorship officially attached to any (even all) of the abundant postmodernist paperback literature discussing a now ubiquitous extraterrestrial phenomenon really merits the prestigious term "genius."

ANCIENT EVALUATIONS OF "ENTHUSIASTIC INSPIRATION" AND POETIC CREATIVITY

According to typically modernist conclusions, for instance as expressed by the surrealist patriarch André Breton (among many others), "automatism" (*l'automatisme psychique*) presently represents something like the instrument of a higher power manifesting itself as an "irresistible" creative impulse within the artist. In Surrealist usage, *l'automatisme psychique* represents a voluntary relinquishing by the modern artist or writer of all his or her rational command over artistic materials. In effect, this descent into involuntary action and reaction, mindlessness as it were (*dementia*), permits absolute artistic freedom, the kind supposedly never attained by merely rational means. Moreover, as has been attested by many twentieth-century writers and artists, this kind of convulsive modernist automatism, whether literary or artistic in its eventual execution, becomes a function of, or is even justified by, *inspiration*.

As was additionally implied much earlier by various Roman and

Greek authors, it was just such an inherent factor of inspiration that functioned as an understood condition impelling "fantasy" (*phantasia*). The conjunction of inspiration and fantasy represents a crucial circumstance that uniquely allows the artist, by his very "nature" (*physis*, in this case, "innate genius"), "to see" an otherwise invisible "art" (*techne*) potentially lying in his raw materials. Michelangelo was famous for being able to see his artistic figures lurking beneath or within an unshaped block of Carrara marble. In short, it is this ubiquitous notion of "inspiration" which so obviously represents the real core idea, taken as artistic theory, that finally links together in strictly modernist theoretical writings even such essentially workshop or artisan techniques as automatism and chance. Accordingly, even though it tells us nothing useful about the validity of visitations by ETs from outer space, it proves useful quickly to sketch out other aspects of the history of that now-ubiquitous concept of autonomous vision in ways that complement our previous Bacchic-Dionysiac recitations and conclusions.

Our first clue as to the real significance of the term, at least in its present-day context, is revealed by its current, commonplace dictionary definitions. According to the *Oxford English Dictionary*, the literal action contained in the verb *inspire* is "To infuse some thought or feeling into (a person, etc.), as if by breathing [from *inspirare*]; to animate or actuate by some mental or spiritual sense." This idea naturally leads to its special, or theological sense: "To influence or actuate by a special divine or supernatural agency. . . . To impart, communicate, or suggest by special divine or supernatural agency; used especially in reference to the utterances of prophets and apostles, and the writings of Scripture." The resulting noun, or immediate physical-psychological result, is *inspiration*, having the general sense of "A breathing in or infusion of some idea, purpose, etc. into the mind . . . especially of an exalted kind." The special sense of this noun is "A special immediate action or influence of the spirit of God (or of some divinity or supernatural being) . . . said especially of that divine influence under which [for instance] the books of Scripture are held to have been written." In the case of most of the alien-abductions stories we have read, the actual "inspiring" agent was *hypnotism*, a sort of "special divine or supernatural agency," and thus the hypnotist (Budd Hopkins, David Jacobs, John Mack, et al.), by his "breathing in or infusion of some idea, purpose, etc. into the mind," instigates "the spirit of God" disguised as an ET.

Clearly, the doctrine of inspiration, even when strictly viewed as an "aesthetic" factor, goes back to very ancient times. In the Introduction to the *Theogony* (written circa 750 B.C.E.), the ancient Greek poet Hesiod tells us how the Muses had "breathed" into him the art of divine music while he tended his flocks on Mount Helicon.[21] From the outset, the operations of inspiration were taken seriously by the Greeks because, for them, they expressed the exuberance of mythological imagery. They held this inspirational principle, which they called *enthousiasmos*—literally meaning "inspired, actually breathed into, by the gods"—to represent a form of possession by some divine force located outside of the artist-writer. It was recognized, literally, to be a prophetic process arising from εκστασισ, ecstasy, literally signifying the act of "stepping out of one's self."

Margery Kempe and Saint Teresa experienced such transports, and named them correctly; so did Betty Hill and Betty Andreasson, but they erroneously called it an abduction by aliens. The highest form of *ekstasis* resulted in the transcendental union of the soul with the divinity, or One (Plato's *Nous* or Nietzsche's *Einheit*). At such liminal moments, one experiences *apocalypsis* (αποχαλψπσισ), or an "uncovering." The recognized Latin equivalent for an apocalypse was *revelatio*, or "revelation" in English. The prophetic gift was, additionally, commonly spoken of as a kind of madness, or *manía* (from *mainomai*, to be mad or insane), for being outside of the bounds of ordinary reason.[22] Today, many unsympathetic critics of postmodernist alien abductions call them "madness," but they do so in ignorance, for they do not know the ancient psychological pedigree of the alien-abduction experience.

Various surviving, ancient texts provide useful clinical descriptions of the outward signs of prophetic enthusiasm-inspiration. According to one of the most detailed, as given (circa 330 c.e.) by Iamblicus (*On the Mysteries of Egypt*, 3.5, 11):

> In their state of divine possession they [who are inspired] are no longer in their normal state of consciousness, so that they no longer lead the normal life of a person, of a creature, as far as sense perception and volition are concerned. They exchange these [normal states of consciousness] for another, more divine kind of life, that which inspires and possesses them completely. . . . The outward signs of divine possession are manifold: [involuntary or "automatic" production of] movement of the body or of some of its parts, or total lack of any kind of movement; harmonious tunes, dances, melodious voices, or the opposites of these. Bodies have been seen to rise up or grow larger, or float in the air, and the opposites of these phenomena have also been observed. The voice [of the possessed person] seemed to be completely even in volume and in the intervals between sound and silence, and then again there was unevenness. In other instances, the sounds swelled and diminished, but occasionally something else happened.

Iamblicus then makes the important point that inspiration is essential to the prophetic act, that it is an indispensable trait of ecstatic religious experience, allowing you to meet God (even an ET) face to face:

> It [inspiration] comes all of a sudden and uses the prophet as an instrument. He is no longer himself and has no idea of what he says or where he is. As a result, even after having delivered the prophecy, he recovers with difficulty. . . . By keeping himself aloof and distant from human preoccupations, he renders himself pure and ready to receive the god. Therefore, he possesses the inspiration of the god that shines into the pure sanctuary of his soul. The inspiration can take possession without hindrance, and the perfect presence finds no obstacle.[23]

Accordingly, besides having potential literary applications, this literally irrational principle, *enthousiasmos-inspiratio*, was commonly put into the same class of psychic phenomena as hysteria, religious frenzy, and the prophetic utterances of the oracles. The experience of inspiration was then, during the classical era, always generically related to "religious" experience. Renaissance art theorists overtly restored the original religious connection existing between inspiration and art-making, devotion and ecstasy, so potentially linking divine intuition and transcendental initiation to the practice of contemporary artists. So doing, consciously or not, they were only following ancient precedent. Particularly in the *Ion* and the *Phaedrus*, Plato repeatedly speaks of "poetry" (*poièsis*), meaning in his time what we would now call "art." He directly allies ποιεσισ—literally, "making-creating"—with inspired utterance, and so he raises the poets (*poiètai*, or "makers-creators") to a special status approaching divinity. Certain minor female divinities, Hesiod's Muses, represent a source of supernatural power and they "inspire" the poet, who in turn "inspires" the audience, or fills them with "enthusiasm." While the postmodernist literature enthusiastically recounting tales of abductions by aliens can scarcely be called "art," it arguably pertains to the same psychic phenomena as hysteria and/or religious frenzy (points discussed in greater detail in chapters 11 and 14).

Moreover as described by Plato (*Phaedrus* 244A–245A), both artistic poets and religious prophets are seen as madmen, for both are equally enraptured by divine inspiration. Plato also states that such nonrational inspiration even serves an educational purpose:

> A third type of possession and madness is possession by the Muses. When this [*furor divinus*] seizes upon a gentle and virgin soul [of the poet] it rouses it to inspired expression. . . . But if a man comes to the

door of poetry untouched by the madness of the Muses, believing that technique alone will make him a good poet, he and his sane compositions never reach perfection, but are utterly eclipsed by the performances of the inspired madman.[24]

In fine, although having different terminology, Platonic "divine fury" is just what was demanded by André Breton, a modern theorist who, in typically orthodox modernist fashion, demands from all proper art-making "the absence of any control exercised by reason."[25] The only difference is that, now, you probably call the strictly artistic procedure "Psychic Automatism." If, on the other hand, you do succeed in publishing a best-selling paperback account of your horribly close encounters with the ETs, then you can now earn, besides those large royalties, the prestigious Platonic title of "the inspired madman."

A DEPICTION OF CLASSICAL "INSPIRATION" IN MEDIEVAL ART

According to this persistent theory, either Plato's or Breton's, neither skill nor reason is adequate for the genesis of genuine poetry ("art"). In order to instigate the divinely induced fit deemed necessary to initiate the praiseworthy creative act, the visionary artist must become *passive*, dependent upon *inspiration* descending from a higher, external source. For such insights and otherworldly transports—often including perceptions of some physically tangible modes of intergalactic transportation—currently hypnotism proves especially useful. Therefore, what we might now, in a post-Surrealist age, choose to call the "automatic" fashioning of such inspired productions is a given, indeed the necessary, precondition of true poetic, artistic creation. It is also the obligatory precondition for a literally "supernatural" kind of *inspired*, specifically *prophetic* expression. "Prophetic expression" is also a fitting term to describe the proletarian literature abundantly recounting alien abductions.

It was as such—that is, as prophetic expressionism—that significant literary creation was pictured by many early medieval artists. Given their cultural context, and just as you would expect, they however solely applied their visualization of the poetic experience to the God-*inspired* authors of the Christian Gospels. An eloquent case in point is the depiction of a mightily inspired "St. Mark" that was painted in Reims (France) by an unnamed Carolingian illustrator around the year 830, and bound into the *Gospel Book of Ebbo* (see fig. 24). This is a violently "expressionistic" rendering of an inspired Christian saint passively receiving, and then excitedly transcribing, the *Verbum Dei* as it is being "dictated" to him by an extrater-restrial biological entity, in this case one disguised as a lion. (Although such a notoriously ferocious feline might seem an unlikely Muse, we recall that Mark's standard animal symbol was a winged lion, as derived from Ezek. 1:5–14 and Revelation-*Apocalypsis* 4:6–8.) The very fact of the Ebbo Gospel's precocious painterly "expressionism" makes it resemble a typi-cally frenzied self-portrait executed by the typically inspired Vincent van Gogh (1853–1890; see fig. 25). But van Gogh's conventionally tormented art, a precocious sign of *moderne Expressionismus*, could have only been conceived, and critically praised, well over a thousand years later, during the Symbolist period (discussed further in chapter 12).

In the broader viewpoint however, in the Ebbo Gospel's agitated St. Mark, likewise in van Gogh's excited self-portrait, we see the "maddened seer-poet" common to the modernist popular imagination. The roots of such agitated visualization are, however, ancient. In his treatise *On the Sublime* (*Peri Hypsous*, circa 50 C.E.), the author now called Longinus long ago recognized that the effect operating upon an audience by cre-ative literature is not "persuasion," which is what the teachers of classical rhetoric would have wished. Instead, Longinus insisted that the desired end is "transport," *ekstasis*. This emotional response, the action of the "Sublime" (*Hypsous*), is roused, he says, by "inspired and vehement pas-sion" (*sphodron kai enthusiastikon pathos*).[26] (The masters of the post-modernist infotainment industry would agree with that observation.)

The treatise attributed to Longinus was recovered during the Renais-sance, and made widely available in a dual-language edition, Greek-Latin, published in Basel by Francesco Robortello in 1554. This treatise became thereafter authoritative for Renaissance, even future neoclassical and romantic, discussions about the ever mysterious wellsprings of sublime creativity. As generations of Europeans were now enabled to read, "Genius, they say, is innate; it is not something that can be learnt, and nature is the only art that begets it." So "naturally" endowed, Longinus says the poet's next goal becomes "a noble emotion," and this aspiration is obtained "when it forces its way to the surface in a gust of frenzy, and a kind of *divine inspiration* is breathed into the speaker's words."

The result of such "divine inspiration" is obviously very much like the intentions propelling the art of the painter: "the representation of mental pictures." The desired effect is additionally very much like the "expressive forms" (*Ausdrucksformen*) employed by the German Expressionists beginning around 1910. Just as they would state much later, Longinus also described how, "carried away by your feelings, you imagine you are actually seeing the subject of your description (*ekphrasis*), and you enable your audience as well to see it." The successful artist, graphic or literary, is the one who has "almost compelled his audience, too, to see what he had imagined." As a model example, Longinus actually cites "the appearance of Dionysus, described in unusual terms as being divinely possessed [as] inspired with a Bacchic frenzy."[27] Granted his enduring significance for much future aesthetic evaluation, the specific significance of this author's observations are recognized by William Wimsatt to be, "a celebration of ecstasy and inspiration . . . the special and pulsing accent of Longinus is on the great and impassioned soul of the poet, his flashes and spurts of inspiration, the careless and plunging grandeur of his utterance, and the corresponding transport of his audience."[28] Likewise, it is unquestionable that postmodernist authors of innumerable paperback best-sellers relating ET close encounters have produced a "corresponding transport of their audiences." The artists hired to illustrate the postmodernist abduction paperbacks have also "compelled the audience, too, to see what he had imagined" (see figs. 1, 4, 5, 16–21).

ETs aside, art historians routinely recognize the strictly formal sources of such early medieval "evangelist portraits" as being derived from much earlier classical art, particularly from the conventionalized formats of frontispieces showing portraits of pagan authors of prestigious philosophical treatises.[29] But our illustration from the Ebbo Gospels (fig. 24) represents a nearly unique approximation to classical *content*, à la Plato in this instance, and in the very particular sense of the emotional state so often attributed to classical *inspiratio*. So moved by the *content*, the understood emotional significance of his *Ausdrucksformen*, the anonymous Carolingian artist has radically altered the traditional visual *form* of classical-era author portraits. A useful description of the pertinent visual particulars of this particularly inspired, and thus expressionistic (*avant la lettre*) portrait is provided by art historian James Snyder:

> This is no simple author portrait; it is a type known as the "inspired Evangelist." Mark responds dramatically to the vision of the lion as if experiencing a mystical revelation. This heightened animation conveying the psychological state of excitement is new [in medieval art], but it is an idea that soon passed into the repertory of the Northern artists [and later culminating in van Gogh]. And how is this excitement so vividly expressed? Notable are the distortions of the facial features—the heavily arched eyebrows, the large staring eyes, the pointed lashes—and the nervous twitch in the fingers and torso. Even more expressive are the racing lines that replace the modeling in color found in the [Carolingian] Palace School portraits.

To be sure, the arms and legs are highlighted and darkened illusionistically, but the opaque qualities of the paint are dissolved and energized by swirling lines, like whirlpools spinning about the arms and legs. Gold flecks in the hair electrify Saint Mark's features, and the illusionistic landscape background is transformed into a surging waterfall of cascading lines. A new style is in the making before our eyes, a style that can be more appropriately termed "expressionistic," and no wonder that some scholars have seen the Reims School as the fountainhead of dynamic linearism of later Romanesque [and even modern or "expressionistic"!] art.[30]

What we have just read is a modern description (*ekphrasis!*) rendered by a scholarly art historian in order to articulate the stylistic traits pertaining to a precociously modern "look" presented by a particular medieval image. Even though this is useful to us as external information, let us now find out just what such an inspired medieval author might have to say about the *inner* psychological state belonging to the kind of prophetic vision depicted in the Ebbo Gospel, and just as the visionary *auctor* might himself have experienced it. Alas, the actual Gospel writers are vague on their sources of literary inspiration.

From his privileged vantage point on Mount Patmos, Saint John is by far the most explicit about "the Revelation of Jesus Christ, which God . . . sent and signified by his angel unto his servant John." As is recorded in the first chapter of the Book of Revelations (*Apocalypsis*), "I John . . . was in the isle that is called Patmos [and] in the Spirit on the Lord's day [Vulgate: *'fui in spiritu in dominica die'*], and heard behind me a great voice, as of a trumpet . . . and when I saw him [the angel], I fell at his feet as dead. And he . . . said unto me . . . write the things which thou hast seen, and the things which are, and the things which shall be hereafter." Whereas the classical author was *inspired* ("breathed into") by a Muse, the Christian author, typically an Evangelist, resorts to an angel (Latin, *angelus*, from the Greek, αγγελοσ, a messenger from god). There are substantial reasons for identifying the postmodernists' ETs with angels and demons (both further discussed in chapter 10); in fact, as we shall see, many UFOlogists make this connection explicit.

Fortunately, the early Church fathers give us a few more details about their ecstatic experiences in the presence of otherworldly divinity. Besides frequent references to physical effects of "light" and "illumination," phenomena literally expressive of desirable metaphorical conditions of "enlightenment," there is also mention made of manifestations of an electric kind of "divine energy," of the sort depicted in the Ebbo Gospel picture. A case in point is St. Gregory Palamas: "He who participates in the divine energy, himself becomes to some extent light. He is united to the light, and by that light he sees in full awareness all that remains hidden [*occulta*] to those who have not this grace [or privileged perception]. Thus he transcends not only the bodily senses, but also all that can be known by the intellect."[31] Writing about the same time, yet another Christian visionary makes explicit the functional linkages to certain experiences, and even to a distinctive terminology of a kind obviously derived from the earlier Dionysiac Mysteries, namely "ecstasy" and "divine intoxication." According to St. Gregory of Sinai:

> Wonder is the total lifting of the powers of the soul towards what may be discerned of the entire majesty of Glory. Or again wonder is a pure and entire outreaching of the mind towards the limitless power of light. But ecstasy is more than the taking up of the powers of the soul to the heavenly places, but it also involves their removal from all the actions of the senses; for love [of the divine] is the intoxicating drink of the spirit's desire. . . . Ecstatic love of the spirit is a divine intoxicant that overpowers our natural wits. Through this, our awareness of the forms of things is taken from us.[32]

Boethius, writing in 524 C.E. while awaiting execution in a vile prison near Milan, mentioned how he was only enabled to compose his *Consolation of Philosophy* once he was able to banish from his sight "the Muses of Poetry," those "maimed Muses who guide my pen." It was those dreadfully inspiring ladies who, he states, "stifle the fruit-bearing harvest of reason with the barren briars of the passions: they free not the minds of men from disease, but accustom thereto." However, like an avenging ET, the towering allegorical figure of "Philosophia" opportunely comes to his aid, commanding them, "Away with you, Sirens, seductive unto destruction!" So chastened, "their band thus rated cast a saddened glance upon the ground, and confessing their shame in blushes, passed forth dismally over the threshold."[33] Nonetheless, the medieval writer who knew best how to portray the palsied, ecstatic author-portrait of St. Mark placed in the Ebbo Gospel (fig. 24) was Dante, who spoke as the kind of inspired writer who "has the custom of art and, thus, the hand which trembles—*c'ha l'habito de l'arte e man che trema*."[34] The writer Whitley Strieber also vividly describes the trembling fits which overcame him in the presence of his postmodernist otherworldly visitor, an ET (fig. 4), with whom he enjoyed a unique sense of New Age "communion."

Unfortunately, no written instructions seem to have survived from the Carolingian era of the sort that might have guided the anonymous artist who composed our Ebbo Gospel picture. Very specific indications along such lines may, however, be found in guidebooks composed much later for the benefit of artists who commonly had to compose pictures suitable for meditational purposes. One such was published by the Spanish writer-artist Vicente Carducho. According to an explanation of the proper way of picturing "devotion," as given in his *Diálogos de la Pintura* (1633), this orthodox kind of religious ecstasy signifies extreme emotionality and so it requires an equally extreme vocabulary of tortured postures conventionally indicating religious inspiration. These inspired poses were commonly recognized to include the following:

> kneeling, [with] clasped hands thrown up to Heaven or level with the chest, head raised, eyes gazing upwards, either bathed in tears or gay, or else with the head bowed down and the eyes closed [and with] the neck always twisted, or with hands having interlaced fingers, [with the body] sometimes prostrate on the ground, or leaning so far forwards that the face almost touches the ground, with hunched shoulders and other actions, all depending upon the emotions of the devout person— who might be either praying, submissive, sad, happy, or in awe; in devotion there is room for all of these.[35]

Earlier, in a work known to Carducho, Giovanni Paolo Lomazzo's *Trattato dell'Arte* (1587), it was explained how the historical "prophets and saints had several different ways" of expressing religious ecstasy and inspiration. For instance, "Abraham threw himself to his knees, with his face to the ground; Ezekiel prayed to God with his face against the wall; Elias placed his head between his knees." Also admitted to the canon of inspired postures were other ecstatic gestures, including having "the face raised to heaven with both arms opened wide or crossed, or else beating upon the breast, hands thrown up to heaven, one knee on the ground, the face inclined and the fingers interlaced next to the chin, arms open wide and head inclined, prostrate upon the ground with head down," and so forth.[36] Such violent anatomical reactions are also often mentioned as having been experienced by stunned postmodernists placed in the presence of extraterrestrials.

Nonetheless, it seems that, even long ago, it was sometimes recognized there were those who falsely entered into the ecstatic visionary experience. According to a description provided by an anonymous mystical writer in his treatise on *The Cloud of Unknowing* (circa 1350):

> Many amazing practices are found among those who are deceived into doing this false [visionary] work. . . . Some of them draw their eyes up into their heads, as though they were stupid sheep, beaten over the head and about to die at any moment. Some hold their heads on one

side, as though they had a worm in their ears. . . . When they read, or hear [an]other person read or say that men should "lift up their hearts to God," they immediately begin to stare at the stars as though they were [flying] above the moon, and they listen as though to hear angels singing in heaven. Sometimes, in the fantasy of their imaginations, these men [think they can] pierce the planets and make a hole in the firmament through which to look.[37]

Evidently, certain critics were sensitive to the difference between genuine and inauthentic inspiration as early as the fourteenth century. Nonetheless, the problem is still very much with us.

THE COMPLEMENTARY CONDITIONS OF "INSPIRATION" AND "HYSTERIA"

Notions change with history, especially those regarding what society considers desirable (versus undesirable) states of mind. An early critic was the anonymous English mystic author just quoted, but his criticism of the false visionary experience, or *faux* inspiration, is not like a description that might be applied at the present time. Today, for instance, the preceding descriptions of ecstatic visionary experiences and poetic possession, whether medieval or (even) classical in origin, would most likely simply be labeled hysteria by a modern scientist, a psychologist (and the "hysterical" explanation of postmodernist extraterrestrial encounters will be expanded in chapter 14). According to Dr. D. H. Rawcliffe, the components of pathological *hysteria* include the diverse, but generally picturesque, effects of

> increased suggestibility which, together with a naturally uncritical state of mind, makes the creation of delusions in the subject's mind a relatively easy matter; and a whole host of accompanying psychological anomalies, such as vivid and sudden alterations in personality, temporary loss of identity, paralysis, local analgesia or localized insensitivity, *automatic writing, involuntary speaking* ("inspiration"), the onset of a variety of functional diseases (and often their sudden cure), somnambulism, during which the individual carries out actions without being able to remember them subsequently, *visual hallucination or "visions," auditory hallucination, including the hearing of "voices,"* and occasionally hyperacuity of the senses; to these anomalies may be added a greatly heightened histrionic ability.
>   Analogous manifestations are seen in different and less developed forms in *the mediumistic trance; in xenoglossia, the uncontrollable*

utterance of unintelligible sounds under the influence of mystical or religious excitement, known euphemistically as "speaking in unknown tongues [or voices]"; *in automatic writing*; in somnambulism or sleep-walking and somniloquism, or talking in sleep; in the *demoniacal possession* of the Middle Ages; in hysterical *inspiration or automatic speech, usually on religious, mystical or moral themes; and in hysterical* [Bacchic-type] *frenzy*, which is deliberately induced by many primitive sects, notably some dervish cults. All these dissociative phenomena may be followed by partial or total amnesia of the dissociative period.[38]

Such was the opinion rendered in 1952 by a modern scientist, a clinical psychologist, regarding these kind of otherworldly visionaries. Nonetheless, we have read how the "ancients" (*archaios, palaios, antiquus, vetus, priscus*), even though employing other terminology, had long before described the inspired and ecstatic creative condition. Now however, long after, we have a new, scientific, and apparently even *quantifiable* explanation for ecstatic possession. This assumption may be either applied to the traditional religious experience or to the way "ecstasy" now triggers praiseworthy creative energy—or even to egregious visitations by extraterrestrials. The new explanation currently holds that such familiar states of religious ecstasy and creative transport are really due to a *chemical* imbalance! As is now credibly explained by a British anthropologist:

As is well known, trance states can be readily induced in most normal people by a wide range of stimuli, applied either separately or in combination. . . . The most exciting [recent] scientific discoveries here, surely, are those of the *endorphins*—natural opiates in the human brain—whose production and release is promoted by the traditional methods of trance induction. . . . One of the most intriguing research interfaces here concerns the potential role of the human endorphin system—as a natural source of euphoria and analgesia—readily triggered by sensory stimulation (including such mundane activity as jogging) and, paradoxically, by sensory deprivation.

The discovery of these endogenous opiates in the human body gives a literal sense to Marx's famous epithet about religion as "the opiate of the people" which he could never have imagined. This clearly adds a new dimension to understanding one set of probable precipitants of religious experience. Equally obviously, it does not, however, explain the form of religious [or artistic!] experience: the specific spiritual terms in which such ecstasy is understood, represented and communicated.[39]

Even granted the new "endorphin factor," the frenzied attributes of
the St. Mark portrayed in the Ebbo Gospels (fig. 24) as well as those reiterated traits characterizing visionary experiences written down by the
early Church fathers betray standard features pertaining to classical
inspiratio or *enthousiasmos*. It was elsewhere implied by Plato that the
utterances of the poet-prophet are essentially automatic in character,
because, as a price for having access to truth, the poet-prophet must
forego consciousness: "Every man, while he retains possession of that [his
conscious reason], is powerless to compose a verse or chant an oracle"
(nor, one supposes, to say a sooth). Therefore, Plato has Socrates exclaim
that it is "not by art that they [poets] utter these things, but by divine
influence" (*Ion* 534C). Now, when "they [abductees] utter these things,"
it is mostly done with hypnotism and Dr. Mack's "careful questioning."

Consequently, the inspired poet-oracle enshrined in classical literary theory must submit to being rapt beyond his senses, and so he necessarily loses control of his personal identity, or rational being. Such is
the conventional wisdom, the essential creation myth, operative since
the time of Plato. To carry the understood argument further, the poet-
prophet-artist is actually little more than a mindless vehicle of divine
infusion, a passive amanuensis obediently recording and transmitting
the dictates of a supernatural will. Times change, and so do the creation
myths generated by different historical cultures. Living in a world
amazed by the wonders wrought by modern scientific endeavor, as we
would now claim, the poet-prophet-artist is simply a creature more plentifully endowed with endorphins than are the usual run of noncreative
folk. If not due to "hysteria," then over-the-top creativity—also horrific
visitations from the ETs—is simply a matter of chemical imbalance, not
the work of the gods. *Chacun a son goût.*

THE COMPLEMENTARY CONDITIONS
OF "INSPIRATION" AND "DREAMS"

Formerly, there were different opinions. In classical literary theory,
imagination was conceived as a power of visualization, whereby things
physically absent suddenly appear "to the inner eye" as if they were
present. The Greeks called such visualizations *phantasiai*, and the
Romans referred to them as *visiones*. Such essentially pictorial mental
imagery was closely connected with the power of the artist's given
medium to communicate emotion, from an inspired creator to his enraptured audience. In his well-regarded treatise *On the Sublime* (*Peri Hyp-*

sous), Longinus designated such intensely felt visualization as a gift indicative of true "sublimity" (*hypsos*), a term cognate with "sleep" (*hypnos*), and so contextually suggesting by analogy an induced hypnotic state. Once more, among the *fin-de-siècle* Symbolist writers (as discussed in chapters 8 and 12) the issue of hypnosis was again to become a popular topic. In their case, however, that was largely due to the contemporary discovery of *l'automatisme psychologique* ("psychological automatism"), so making the ancient oneirocritical issue acquire timely and strictly modernist, pseudoscientific traits.[40] As recently attested by a prolific paperback industry recording ET apparitions, hypnotically induced psychological automatism even stimulates titanic repercussions within popular culture.

An important scientific document of the time is the treatise published by Pierre Janet in 1889, *L'Automatisme psychologique: Essais de psychologie expérimentale sur les formes inférieures de l'activité humaine* (Psychological automatism: Essays on experimental psychology dealing with the lower forms of human activity). This was a pioneering work known to, among others, André Breton. This *fin-de-siècle* fascination with *l'inconscient* (the unconscious) also fitted in nicely with the notorious fascination with *les rêves* (dreams), so conspicuously displayed in Symbolist poetry and even Symbolist art criticism. Such reveries still work their wonders in postmodernist vanguard culture. Long before André Breton was to make it into something like vanguard dogma by calling it *l'automatisme psychique* ("psychic automatism"), the concept of a passively operating "unconscious genius" propelling great art had become officially installed as a viable idea in art criticism published by the Symbolist theorists in France. It was later to become a basic tenet of the abstract expressionist art characteristic of the late 1940s and immediately afterward, the art-historical period also belonging to the great renaissance of UFO sightings.

In this endeavor, the theorists of Symbolist art were particularly encouraged by published discussions about a recently invented (1891) contemporary science called "the new psychology" (*la nouvelle psychologie*). By particularly dealing with the contemporaneously appealing subject of dreams, another famed Symbolist-era writer and thinker, Sigmund Freud (1856–1939), came up with the basis for orthodox-modernist psychiatry. All of this was announced in his pioneering treatise on *The Interpretation of Dreams* (*Die Traumdeutung*, 1900), another work later to be eagerly devoured by André Breton (among many, many others). At the beginning of his lengthy monograph, Freud laid out his daring thesis: "Every dream reveals itself as a psychical structure which has a meaning and which can be inserted at an assignable point in the mental activities of waking life."

In this, the first edition of a seminal study (to which much was later to be added), Freud notes that apparently some research in the matter had already been done in antiquity, namely, "in the two works of Aristotle which deal with dreams [*De divinatione per somnium*, and *De somniis*]," according to whom, dreams "are 'daemonic,' since nature is 'daemonic' and not divine. Dreams, that is, do not arise from supernatural manifestations but follow the laws of the human spirit, though the latter, it is true [in classical terms], is akin to the divine."[41] It was only in later editions of *Die Traumdeutung*, appearing after 1914, that Freud was belatedly to acknowledge the work of yet another ancient author whose own oneirocritical investigations and conclusions paralleled his to an amazing degree. Freud's acknowledgment of his predecessors also demonstrates that, like so much other *mythopoesia* to be analyzed here, the basic, and unquestionably influential, reverie-revelation premise characterizing Breton's Surrealism is itself anything but modern. So, too, are ETs "nothing new under the sun."

Amazingly, a standard handbook of "dream-interpretation" (corresponding to Freud's "*Traumdeutung*") has actually survived. Dating in the second century C.E., Artemidorus of Daldis's *Oneirocriticon* (dream interpretation) is now some eighteen centuries old. Doubtless, many more such interpretive manuals once existed, but these have not come down to us due to the element of pure "chance" (*le hasard*) that operates in human events, and more recently in avant-garde art-making. According to our ancient source book, "some dreams are theorematic, some allegorical. Theorematic are those whose fulfillment resembles the vision they offer." As did Freud much later, Artemidorus also observed that, "allegorical dreams signify something through something else; in these dreams the soul, according to certain laws, hints at something in the manner of a riddle." Long before Freud installed the now-standard psychiatric topos of the dream-revealed, incestuous "Oedipus complex," the fateful "Oedipus dream" was similarly analyzed in the *Oneirocriticon*, (book 1, ch. 79, "The Oedipus Dream"). Accordingly, Artemidorus is either the fellow who actually invented the motif or, more likely, he is merely an author who documents the existence of an already traditional trope in his uniquely surviving treatise.

Even then, Artemidorus was well aware of a tendency of psychiatrists (*bien avant la lettre*) and, more currently, of followers of Jacques Lacan (*par exemple*) to pursue the most oblique or arbitrary interpretation. For instance, the Hellenistic *Traumdolmetscher* mentions a notorious school of "interpreters of dreams," the kind who, when they fancy they are "in love with a woman," will, rather than picture *her*, instead conjure up the image of "a horse or a mirror, or a ship or the sea, or a female animal or a feminine garment, or anything *else,* that [to them] signifies a woman." His conclusion, as valid now as around 150 C.E., was that any truly professional and/or ethical "interpreter of dreams must not give *his* opinion, or improvise a response concerning things he cannot fully comprehend. If he does so, he will lose his prestige, and it is the dreamer who will get hurt in the end."[42] One wishes that the postmodernist likes of Budd Hopkins, David Jacobs, and John Mack had seriously read this ancient author, one who knew the difference between fanciful dreaming and real life.

Alas, Freud also largely failed to mention the fact of a substantial and highly influential, subsequent (post-Artemidorus) body of dream literature. The convention mainly begins with Cicero's *Somnium Scipionis*, which led directly to Macrobius's *In somnium Scipionis Commentarius*, and which also includes Boethius's *De consolatione Philosophiae*, all of which eventually gave birth to an extensive body of oneirocritical publications appearing during the Renaissance.[43] The principle source however for postclassical clinical notions of the unconscious visionary condition was Macrobius. He laid particular stress on the dream as a prophetic instrument. Whereas he observed in his "Commentary on the Dream of Scipio" (circa 405 C.E.) how "many varieties of dreams were recorded by the ancients," he told future generations that

> all dreams may be classified under five main types: there is the enigmatic dream, in Greek *oneiros*, in Latin *somnium*; second, there is the prophetic vision, in Greek *horama*, in Latin *visio*; third, there is the oracular dream, in Greek *chrematismos*, in Latin *oraculum*; fourth, there is the nightmare, in Greek *enypnion*, in Latin *insomnium*; and last, the apparition, in Greek *phantasma*, which Cicero, when he has occasion to use the word, calls *visum*. The last two, the nightmare and the apparition [for instance, of ETs], are not worth interpreting since they have no prophetic significance. . . .
>
> We call a dream oracular which clearly reveals what will or will not transpire, and what action to take or to avoid. We call a dream a prophetic vision if it actually comes true. . . . An enigmatic dream [especially the kind exhibiting ETs] requires an interpretation for its understanding. . . . There are five varieties of it: personal, alien, social, public, and universal. . . . The Soul, when it is partially disengaged from bodily functions during sleep, at times gazes and at times peers intently at the truth, but with a dark obstructing veil interposed.[44]

Once again, nothing new under the sun; no matter, never mind. Not disregarding his recognized art-historical contribution to the Surrealist ethos, the main reason for mentioning Freud's bibliographical lacunae is to point out how in modern psychiatry, just as in contemporary art history, apparently there is *nihil sub sole novum*. Likewise, and as by now should be perfectly obvious, the same observation holds true for the postmodernist cultural phenomena celebrating the earthly epiphanies of the ETs, especially their abundant extraterrestrial portraiture. As we shall now demonstrate, another name for them—that is, long before they became the iconic New Age "space folk"—was *incubi*. Also to be demonstrated is the fact that other ancient authors recognized (as many postmodernists do not) that it was naught but a dream.

NOTES

1. John G. Fuller, *The Interrupted Journey: Two Lost Hours "Aboard a Flying Saucer"* (New York: Dell, 1967), p. 91.

2. John Mack, *Abduction: Human Encounters with Aliens* (New York: Scribner's, 1994), p. 288.

3. Saint Teresa de Avila, *Libro de su Vida* (México: Porrúa, 1972), p. 238; J. M. Cohen, ed., *The Life of Saint Teresa* (Harmondsworth, U.K.: Penguin, 1957), pp. 209–11. If the reader has any doubts about the "orgasmic" character of Teresa's experiences, then he (but not she, for being already well aware of the nature of such things) should read the firsthand accounts given in Shere Hite, *The Hite Report: A Nationwide Study of Female Sexuality* (New York: Dell, 1977), esp. pp. 61 ff. ("masturbation").

4. W. Butler-Bowdon, ed., *The Book of Margery Kempe* (Oxford: Oxford University Press, 1954), pp. 10–11, 16, 20–21, 112–13, 116, 189–90, 274.

5. William B. Ober, "Margery Kempe: Hysteria and Mysticism Reconciled," *Literature and Medicine* 4 (1985): 24–40; William B. Ober, *Bottoms Up! A Pathologist's Essays on Medicine and the Humanities* (New York: Perennial, 1988), pp. 203–20.

6. Raymond Fowler, *The Andreasson Affair* (New York: Bantam, 1980), pp. 1, 43, 155.

7. For several subsequent accounts of these routine alien ovary invasions, see David M. Jacobs, *Secret Life: Firsthand Documented Accounts of UFO Abductions* (New York: Fireside, 1993); Mack, *Abduction,* and so forth (with some already quoted here).

8. See I. M. Lewis, *Ecstatic Religion: An Anthropological Study of Spirit Possession and Shamanism* (Harmondsworth, U.K.: Penguin, 1971; rev. ed., London: Routledge, 1989).

9. Archival material, as in William Christian, *Apparitions in Late Medieval and Renaissance Spain* (Princeton: Princeton University Press, 1981), p. 186.

10. For what immediately follows, see William Sargant, *The Mind Possessed: A Physiology of Possession, Mysticism, and Faith Healing* (New York: Penguin, 1975).

11. For this point, documented, see J. F. Moffitt, *Occultism in Avant-Garde Art: The Case of Joseph Bevys* (Ann Arbor: University of Michigan Press, 1986).

12. For ancient representations of these ecstatic figures on Hellenic ceramics, see T. H. Carpenter, *Art and Myth in Ancient Greece* (London: Thames & Hudson, 1991), figs. 9, 12, 49, 134, 274.

13. Seneca, as quoted in Georg Luck, ed., *Arcana Mundi: Magic and the Occult in the Greek and Roman World* (Baltimore: Johns Hopkins University Press, 1985), pp. 276–78; emphasis mine.

14. Lucan, as quoted in ibid., pp. 282–83.

15. Callistratus, as in *Philostratus the Younger/the Elder, Imagines;* Callistratus, *Descriptions*, ed. A. Fairbanks (London: Loeb, 1969), pp. 404–405.

16. Callistratus, *Descriptions*, pp. 406–407; cf. Philostratus, *Imagines*, in *Philostratus the Younger/the Elder*, pp. 1, 18, 72–75, "Bacchai."

17. Callistratus, *Descriptions*, pp. 388–91.

18. W. H. D. Rouse, ed., *Great Dialogues of Plato* (New York: Mentor, 1956), pp. 18–19 (*Ion* 533D–535B).

19. Callistratus, *Descriptions*, pp. 380–85.

20. Edgar Zilsel, *Die Entstehung des Geniebegriffes: Ein Beitrag zur Ideengeschichte der Antike und des Frühkapitalismus* (Tübingen: Mohr, 1926), p. 34.

21. Hesiod, *Homeric Hymns and Homerica*, ed. H. G. Evelyn-White (London: Loeb, 1964), pp. 78–81 (with Greek text).

22. For "*enthousiasmos*" in classical culture, see Zilsel, *Die Entstehung des Geniebegriffs*, pp. 12–22, 101–105; for more on the cultural acceptance of "madness" (in general) by the ancient Greeks, see E. R. Dodds, *The Greeks and the Irrational* (Berkeley: University of California Press, 1971).

23. Iamblicus, as quoted in Luck, *Arcana Mundi*, pp. 299, 301.

24. *Phaedrus* (245A), as in Plato, *Phaedrus and Letters VII and VIII*, ed. W. Hamilton (Harmondsworth, U.K.: Penguin, 1973), p. 48.

25. A. Breton, *Qu'est-ce-que le Surréalisme?* (Brussels: R. Henriquez, 1934), p. 12.

26. Longinus, in W. K. Wimsatt, *Literary Criticism: A Short History* (New York: Vintage, 1957), pp. 99.

27. Longinus, in ibid., pp. 101, 109, 121, 123.

28. Wimsatt, *Literary Criticism*, p. 725.

29. See A. M. Friend, "The Portraits of the Evangelists in Greek and Latin Manuscripts," *Art Studies* 5 (1927): 115–47; 7 (1929): 3–29.

30. James Snyder, *Medieval Art: Painting, Sculpture, Architecture, Fourth–Fourteenth Century* (New York: Abrams, 1989), pp. 208, 217.

31. St. Gregory, Palamos, in F. C. Happold, ed., *Mysticism: A Study and an Anthology* (Harmondsworth, U.K.: Penguin, 1971), p. 223.

32. Sinai, in St. Gregory, ibid.

33. Boethius, *The Consolation of Philosophy*, ed. I. Edman (New York: Modern Library, 1943), pp. 3–5.

34. Dante, as in Jacques Maritain, *Creative Intuition in Art and Poetry* (New York: Vintage, 1958), p. 45 (my translation).

35. Vicente Carducho, *Diálogos de la Pintura: Su defensa, origen, esencia, definición, modos y diferencias*, ed. F. Calvo Serraller (Madrid: Cátedra, 1979), pp. 404–405, "Devoción."

36. Gian Paolo Lomazzo, *Scritti sulle arti*, ed. R. P. Ciardi (Florence: Centro Di, 1974), p. 118.

37. Anonymous, *The Cloud of Unknowing*, ed. J. Progoff (New York: Columbia University Press, 1957), pp. 184, 195.

38. D. H. Rawcliffe, *The Psychology of the Occult* (London: Ridgway, 1952; reprinted as *Occult and Supernatural Phenomena*, New York: Dover, 1960), pp. 49, 60.

39. I. M. Lewis, *Ecstatic Religion: An Anthropological Study of Spirit Possession and Shamanism* (rev. ed., London: Routledge, 1989), pp. 10, 34.

40. For hypnotism as an important feature of the Symbolists' "*nouvelle psychologie*," see Deborah L. Silverman, *Art Nouveau in Fin-de-Siècle France: Politics, Psychology, and Style* (Berkeley: University of California Press, 1989).

41. Sigmund Freud, *The Interpretation of Dreams*, ed. J. Strachey (New York: Avon, 1965), pp. 35–36. Strachey's edition usefully notes the inclusion of later materials, and the exact date of their entries.

42. Artemidorus, as quoted in Luck, *Arcana Mundi*, pp. 292–98; Luck's anthology includes several other vivid examples drawn from ancient oneirocritical literature.

43. For the postclassical tradition of oneirocritical literature, including Dante's *Divine Comedy* and Colonna's *Hypnerotomachia Poliphili*, among others, see F. Gandolfo, *Il "Dolce Tempo": Mistica, Ermetismo e Sogno nel Cinquecento* (Rome: Bulzoni, 1978), see esp. pp. 22–27, for the Renaissance-period bibliography.

44. Macrobius, *Commentary on the Dream of Scipio*, ed. W. H. Stahl (New York: Columbia University Press, 1990), pp. 87–91.

Chapter 7

The Incubus as Proto-ET
The Case of Henry Fuseli's *Nightmare*

THE SENSATIONAL MOTIF OF THE SEXUAL CLOSE ENCOUNTER

As remarked earlier, one of the most sensational aspects of the copious postmodernist paperback literature describing the alien-abduction experience is the one that explicitly describes any number of quasi-sexual close encounters between impotent earthlings and overpowering extraterrestrials. As typically recounted (see chapter 2), the apprehensive earthling, usually female and restrained in one way or another, does not initially welcome the ET's gynecological inspections; the victim is typically self-described as reluctant, often put under some sort of physical bondage. Accordingly, the best the ETs can hope for from their victims is passive acceptance, and certainly not "the joy of sex" (according to another kind of paperback best-seller). Oddly, the victim often later admits to having felt a sort of emotional, even quasiamorous attraction to his or her alien inspector: there has come about a sort of psychic collusion.

As one expects, the prototypical narration of this sort is that provided by Betty Hill, as inserted in the classic paperback text *The Interrupted Journey* (1966; see chapter 5) that has since generated so many mirrorlike spin-offs. As before, we will hew to our standard inquisitorial format, alternating between "DJ" (Dementia Jockey, the hypnotist) and "R" (Respondent, Betty in this instance). It begins as a long, hypnotically induced, soliloquy by R:

Oh—and then they [the ET examining committee] take off my shoes, and they look at my feet, and they look at my hands, they look my hands all over. And he takes [she trails off]. The light is very bright so my eyes aren't always open. I'm still a little scared, too. I'm not particularly interested in looking at them. And so I try to keep my eyes shut. But no, I do open [them], not all the time, just to give myself a little relief. When I'm not looking at them, I shut my eyes. And he takes something and he goes underneath my fingernail and then he, I don't know, probably manicure scissors or something, and he cut off a piece of my fingernail. And they look my feet all over, they keep—I don't think they do anything to them; they just feel my feet and my toes and all. And then the doctor, the [ET] examiner, says he wants to do some tests; he wants to check my nervous system. And I am thinking, I don't know how our nervous systems are, but I hope we never have nerve enough to go around kidnapping people right off the highways, as he has done! And, oh, he tells me to take off my dress; he tells me to take off my dress, and then, before I even have a chance hardly to stand up to do it, the examiner . . .

Notice of this striptease causes DJ to interrupt R in order to ask for a verifying detail, namely, "Does your dress ha[ve] a zipper down the back?" However, it is the ET examiner who actually "unzips it, and so I slip my dress off." Once divested of both her dress and shoes, R notices, besides a stool, that "sort of in the middle of the room, there's a table," and this is "the height of the desk." So what's the next step? As R explains, compliantly, "I lie down on the table, on my back, and he brings over this—oh, how can I describe it?" Once she succeeds, we find that "they're like needles, a whole cluster of needles, and each needle has a wire going from it." To explain this dire device, R reverts to a comparison with the essential piece of technology in her cozy home, "I think it's something like a TV screen, you know. When the picture isn't on, you get all kinds of lines." That explained, as the obligatory next step, the ET "puts me down on the table, and they bring the needles over, and they don't stick them in me. No, not really like sticking a needle into a person, but they touch me with the needles." This action calls for yet another soliloquy, one about alien touching and needling:

He just touches, and I feel just the needle touching, that's all. It doesn't hurt at all. But then he does it all, up in the back of my ears, and in here somehow, and up here. Up in all different spots of my head and in through here somehow or other. And then down here—I don't know. Then he puts it on my knee, and when he did, my leg jumped. And then on my foot, too. He did it around my ankle, somehow or other. And then they have me roll over on my stomach, and they touch all along my back. They touch with these needles, somehow or other. I don't know what they're doing, but they seem to be so happy about whatever they're doing.

Next, the delighted ET acupuncture artists "roll me over on my back, and the examiner has a long needle in his hand." And this is some needle; in fact, "it's bigger than any needle that I've ever seen." Naturally, "I ask him what he's doing to do with it." The alien reply is par for the course, "He said he just wants to put it in my navel; it's just a simple test." And she ripostes, "No, it will hurt. Don't do it; don't do it!" Naturally, he persists, so eliciting a pained exclamation, "It's hurting; it's hurting! Take it out; take it out!" Following this navel invasion, the ET leader comes over to her and he puts his hand in front of her eyes, and soothingly tells her that "it will be all right. I won't feel it. And [then] all the pain goes away." Poor R is left befuddled, especially since "I don't know why they put that needle into my navel. Because I told them they shouldn't do it." At this point DJ wonders if "they make any sexual advances to you?" Evidently they didn't, so R logically questions the ET leader, "Why did they put that needle in my navel? And he said it was a pregnancy test." (And, given Betty's age, this was a truly dumb move on the part of the ETs.) The session ends with DJ diligently performing some more of his hypnotic voodoo, and his litany is "You'll be relieved, relaxed and at ease. Perfectly at ease, comfortable and relaxed. When I wake you up, you will not remember anything that has transpired here. You will not remember anything that has transpired here [that is] until I *tell* you to recall it."[1]

As published a dozen years later (and surely with knowledge of Betty Hill's televised close pelvic encounter), Betty Andreasson's account of a similar gynecological close encounter is even better, even closer as it were. Not surprisingly, she too begins with a soliloquy, but hers is far more sigh-riddled than was Betty Hill's.

> And now they [the ET examining committee] are going over there and talking. [She sighs.] Oh boy, I'll be glad when this is all over with! [Sighs again.] They are talking about something over there. Now they are looking over at me. [Sighs.] They are coming over again. And they are saying they have to measure me for *procreation*. I cried out, "What are you doing that for? What is that?" "It won't hurt," they said. "Don't worry, it won't hurt." I didn't think that other would hurt either, but it hurt! And so, they are getting ready for something. They are down by my feet somewhere. They are doing something there. They are not touching

me, but they are doing something. It must be something down there they
are preparing. I can't see it. Now they are pulling something. That needle
again, with a tube, like, on the end. They are pulling—[it] looks like he's
pulling. Oh! And he's opening up that shirt, and—he's going to put that
[unnamed object] in my navel! Oh-h-h-h. I don't like this!

Even though I have never had an unnamed object inserted into *my*
navel, I certainly wouldn't "like" that either. Poor Betty next exclaims
how she could feel "them moving that thing around in my stomach or my
body." Eventually they stop. The reason given is that the alien leader
broke off to confer with his colleagues, and "he's talking with them about
something—something about something missing, missing—missing
[anatomical] parts or something, I think he is saying." As one knows
from having diligently read the entirety of Betty's soggy saga, those otherwise inscrutable "missing parts" were the result of an earlier hysterectomy. But since they are alien (rather than earthling) gynecologists, they
must cruelly press on, regardless. Their further endeavors cause Betty to
exclaim, "Oh! He's pushing that again around, feeling things. I don't like
this! Feels like he's going right around my stuff inside—feeling it, or
something with that needle." With some relief she next adds, "Oh-h-h,
boy! He's stopped again." But her respite is short-lived, "They're looking
at me. They're saying something about some kind of test." Her reply to
this possibility is eloquent, "I don't want any more tests! Get this thing
out of me!" But relief is finally at hand; finally, the ET "is starting to take
the thing out. *Oh-h-h-h. Ah-h-h-h.* [Sighs.] Thank you."[2] And thank
you, Betty, for sharing your wondrous alien adventures with us.

As we shall now see, the postmodernist narrative format of those
apocryphal close encounters with sexually inquisitive ETs conforms to a
venerable literary prototype. This means that, as we're sorry to say, all
those deliciously extruded "oh-h-h-h-hs," "ah-h-h-hs," and satisfied
"sighs" are definitely not modern. Saint Teresa of Avila had proved that
point. In this case however, our essential documentation belongs to the
mass-cultural phenomenon called *witchcraft*. In this historical context,
the then-recognized title, meaning way back in the Renaissance era, for
the ubiquitous ET transgressor was the *incubus*. I am not, however, the
first student of contemporary outer-space esoterica to draw this connection; according to Keith Thompson:

Today's alien abductors continue to show more than passing interest in
human sexuality and reproduction, a tradition that extends to Antonio
Villas-Boas's seduction [as told in chapter 5] by a gorgeous female
"angel" with cherry-red pubic hair. Abduction researcher Budd Hop-

kins's well-elaborated position that aliens are "harvesting" a population of hybrid babies, using human women as breeders, echoes the ancient phenomenon of the otherworldly lover: the "incubus/succubus" tradition. *Incubus*, a male demon who copulates with sleeping mortal women, derives from the Latin *incubare*, meaning "to lie down on." *Succubus*—from *succubare*, "to lie under"—is a female demon that copulates with men in their sleep.[3]

To illustrate, literally, how this apochryphal connection—ET and/or incubus—works in detail, we will now examine the actual content belonging to a famous work of art, a painting, executed well over two hundred years ago.

HENRY FUSELI'S *NIGHTMARE*

It could be argued that, among the many artists working in eighteenth-century Britain, it was Henry Fuseli (1741–1825) who was the most inventive and the most formidably endowed intellectually. In any event, it is unquestionable that Fuseli's most renowned painting is the *Nightmare*. (see fig. 26).[4] First painted in 1781, it quickly became immensely popular immediately upon being exhibited at the Royal Academy in London the following year. Fuseli subsequently made other close variations on what turned out to be for him a most profitable theme.[5] Engravings copying its composition further spread the fame of Fuseli's *Nightmare* throughout continental Europe.[6] In his *Life of Fuseli* (1831), John Knowles listed all the pictures exhibited at the Academy by the Swiss artist between 1774 and 1825. Except for *The Nightmare*, all sixty-nine paintings were known to have had a familiar literary source, including Homer, Sophocles, Dante, Milton, Shakespeare, and Spenser.[7] Previously a work that had continually puzzled scholars, a recently published study has demonstrated that all the iconographic particulars of Fuseli's endlessly discussed *Nightmare* directly reflect commonplace motifs encountered in the classic (actually late medieval) literature of witchcraft.[8]

Since the publication of that article, another piece of iconographical evidence has surfaced that considerably reinforces that argument; this is the frontispiece to Johann Webster's *Untersuchung der vermeintlichen und sogennanten Hexereien* (1716), also illustrating (literally) another "Bewitched Nightmare."[9] Anticipating by seventy-five years the content (and to some degree even the form) of *The Nightmare*, the inscription attached to Webster's engraving, showing a Fuseli-like sleeper bewitched in his bed by nocturnal and nightmarish apparitions, is self-explanatory: "Here one sees, clear as daylight, how there are witches in the world, and how a thousand such will be contained within the mind of a dreamer" (*Hier sieht man sonnenklar, daß Hexen in der Welt / Da eines Träumers Kopff wohl tausend in sich hält*). One result of these findings is to demonstrate that *The Nightmare*, just like the rest of Fuseli's publicly exhibited works, was based upon a textual source, in this case, an easily accessible *corpus* of literature. Another result is that the lady's "nightmare" may no longer be considered a uniquely private one; in short, witchcraft has been part of the public domain since at least the end of the fifteenth century.[10] Given these findings, a further point which may be addressed now is the exact kind of witchcraft that was employed by Fuseli in his *Nightmare* and this, as I shall argue here, was specifically "*daemonialitas.*" As I shall also argue, echoing Webster, witchcraft—just like the postmodernist alien-abduction experience—is wholly "contained within the mind of a dreamer."

It now appears that it is a single published source—the *Malleus Maleficarum* (The hammer of witches, 1486–1487) composed by Jacob Sprenger and Heinrich Kramer ("Institor") and considered a standard textual source for witchcraft since the early Renaissance—that best contextually explains the intrinsic significance of many specific motifs encountered in Fuseli's familiar painting. These essentially textually inspired features include the female protagonist, her tormented dreamstate, the horse in the background (specifically called "a mare"), its gleaming eyes, and so forth.[11] Chronologically, the execution of Fuseli's painting contextually falls into a submovement that has been aptly called "Neoclassical Horrific" by art historian Robert Rosenblum, who also explains that "a new fascination with witchcraft and supernatural terror [is found] in British painting of the later eighteenth-century."[12] This "Neoclassical Occultist" trait is, for instance, found in the work of artists as diverse as Benjamin West, Sir Joshua Reynolds, Joseph Wright of Derby, and, of course, Henry Fuseli. As may also be noted, the execution of Fuseli's *Nightmare* is bracketed in time by the dates of publication of the major monuments of demonic or "Gothick" literature, namely, Horace Walpole's *The Castle of Otranto* (1764), Matthew Gregory Lewis's *The Monk* (1796), Mary Wollstonecraft Shelley's *Frankenstein, or The Modern Prometheus* (1818), John William Polidori's *The Vampyre* (1819), and so forth.[13]

Fuseli never verbally elaborated upon the content of his famous painting, thus permitting its real narrative context—witchcraft—to remain veiled until recently. It now seems very odd indeed that this demonic factor had not been previously pursued by students of Fuseli's oeuvre, especially given that Johann Heinrich Meyer, Fuseli's artistic mentor, once claimed that "most" of his pupil's imagery had consisted of "witches and spooks drawn from folk-tales"; as Meyer clearly stated, "*seiner Darstellungen waren daher meistens Hexen und Gespenster nach Volkssagen.*"[14] Much more to the point is a comment made by Fuseli himself in 1781, the year of execution for his first painted *Nightmare.* In two letters written to Lavater, he specifically mentions being then at work on a pair of "*Schwarzkunststudie,*" or depictions of the "Black Art," and also a scene of witchcraft.[15]

Regarding Fuseli's hypothetical literary sources, it may be recalled that the Swiss-born painter was multilingual and could easily read Latin (as well as Hebrew and Greek) due to his early training as a Zwinglian minister. Another significant fact relates strictly to the transmission of knowledge about the *artes maleficarum.* According to Norman Cohn, "an organization of witches" never really existed; instead, "we [only] discover a literary tradition. More precisely, we discover an age-old fantasy enshrined in theological tracts and monastic chronicles."[16] In fine, the larger conclusion is that Fuseli's—and everybody else's—knowledge of witchcraft was, and still is, essentially text-derived. In most cases (if not all), the same argument holds for our postmodernist knowledge of the extraterrestrials.

THE INCUBUS IN ERASMUS DARWIN'S "NIGHT-MARE"

The most elaborate contemporary explanation of the significance of *The Nightmare* was provided by Fuseli's close friend, Erasmus Darwin (1731–1802), a botanist and amateur poet (and grandfather of Charles Darwin). For a widely circulated and captioned etching of *The Nightmare*, designed by Thomas Burke and published on January 30, 1783, Darwin supplied four lines of narrative verse. Fuseli must have allowed the inclusion of this poem because, at the very least, he believed it to be accurately representative of the intended content of his enigmatic painting. Aptly entitled "Night-Mare," Darwin's poem scans as follows:

> So on his NIGHTMARE through the evening fog
> Flits the squab fiend o'er fen, and lake and bog;
> Seeks some love-[be]wildered maid with sleep oppres'd,
> Alights, and grinning sits upon her breast.[17]

Later, in 1789, Darwin further explained that "when there arises in sleep a painful desire to exert the voluntary motions, it is called the nightmare or incubus."[18] Around 1793, and again in 1810, Fuseli painted a provocative work, *An Incubus Leaving Two Sleeping Girls*.[19] Since this term—"incubus"—is central to what follows, by reference to a standard Latin dictionary, its significance may be quickly explained as arising from the verb *incubare*, signifying: "to lie in, or on, or over; to watch over; to hang over, lie heavily upon; to dwell in" (cf. *Cassell's New Compact Latin Dictionary*). Even more to the point is the explanation given in the *Oxford English Dictionary* for "incubus," showing its derivation from "*incubo*-nightmare," and how it had been used consistently in English (since circa 1205) to designate "a feigned evil spirit or demon (originating in personified representations of the nightmare) supposed to descend upon persons in their sleep, and especially to seek carnal intercourse with women." This is evidently the meaning of "the nightmare or incubus" that had been mutually agreed upon by Henry Fuseli and Erasmus Darwin. Although I will argue that this is also the fundamental meaning of the postmodernist alien-abduction fantasy, that is a point that is certainly not mutually agreed upon by UFOlogists.

The extended meaning of Fuseli's hulking creature—that incubus who is the same creature identified by Erasmus Darwin as being that "squab fiend [who] sits upon her breast"[20]—and its relationship with the maiden he/it is tormenting, were treated at greater length in Darwin's longer, once widely read narrative poem, *The Botanical Garden, or The Loves of the Plants*, later published in 1789. As before, the commonplace significance of Fuseli's demonic motif must be that recorded by the *Oxford English Dictionary*: "a feigned evil spirit or demon (originating in personified representations of the nightmare) supposed to descend upon persons in their sleep, *and especially to seek carnal intercourse with women*" (my emphasis). Introducing a picture, "Such as of late by FUSELI'S poetic eye . . . gave to the airy phantom form and place," Darwin the amateur English poet proceeds to recreate a picture of the demonic possession of the love-bewildered maid earlier depicted by Fuseli, his Swiss artist-friend (fig. 26). According to this detailed description:

> Back o'er her pillow sinks her blushing head,
> Her snow-white limbs hang helpless from the bed;
> While with quick sighs, and suffocative breath,
> Her interrupted heart-pulse swims in death. . . .
> O'er her fair limbs convulsive tremors fleet;
> Start in her hands and struggle in her feet;
> In vain to scream with quivering lips she tries,
> And strains in palsy'd lids her tremulous eyes;
> In vain she wills to run, fly, swim, walk, creep;

The WILL presides not in the bower of SLEEP.
—On her fair bosom sits the Demon-Ape,
Erect, and balances his bloated shape;
Rolls in their marble orbs his Gorgon-eyes
And drinks with leathern ears her tender cries.[21]

It now requires no great interpretive skills to perceive that Fuseli's *Nightmare*, at least as interpreted by Erasmus Darwin, was meant to be understood to have a rather overtly sexual content. This we know especially since this love bewitched maiden "swims in death," or in orgasm, according to hoary poetic convention.[22] For instance, as used by Darwin, the adjective "erect" is probably a double entendre. No matter; this is the same oversexed creature known to John Milton; in *Paradise Regained* (2.152), the poet speaks of the loathsome "Belial, the dissolutest spirit that fell, The *sensualist*, and, after Asmodai, The *fleshiest* incubus." Although presenting no contemporary evidence to back up her claim, according to an unsubtle and clinical-minded feminist and postmodern art-historical observer, "the topos of the picture is not a 'nightmare' but a female orgasm, one not in the excitement or peak phases, but in the very beginning of the resolution phase. . . . Along the female's somewhat swollen face [there] is the suggestion of a measles-like rash, characteristic of the last stages of orgasm among many women."[23] As we shall see, even though the contemporary eighteenth-century documentary evidence certainly does allow for the tangible expression of a "sexual orgasm," the real context is considerably more demonic than is just a simple (and rather anachronistic) representation of the "joy of sex."

We have quoted (in chapter 2) many parallel orgasmic incidents resulting from the postmodernist close encounters with the extraterrestrials. As we have also seen (in chapter 5), different people (earthlings) report being transported by ETs in mysterious ways, the kind seemingly wholly unknown to earth-folk before the relatively recent advent of the UFOs. Betty Hill saw a beam descend from on high and (as will be related in chapter 8) George Adamski got a free trip to Venus in a UFO. Betty Andreasson said the aliens could walk through walls and, even better, Travis Walton said he was "beamed up" into a spaceship in a way that, not surprisingly, recalls the apotheosis-like mode of transport popularized by the TV series *Star Trek*: "Beam me up, Scotty!" This otherworldly ascendance motif, although not referred to directly in Fuseli's *Nightmare*, is also a common feature in the traditional literature of witchcraft, just as it is in the now-traditional literature describing the postmodernist UFO experience. Around 1486, the authors of the *Malleus Maleficarum* felt it necessary to include a chapter entitled "How They [witches or ETs] are Transported from Place to Place" (part 1, question 1, chapter 3). Here it was observed with near-scientific certainty:

> Certain wicked women, perverted by Satan and seduced by the illusions and phantasms of devils, do actually, as they believe and profess, ride in the night-time upon certain beasts . . . and in the untimely silence of night they pass over immense tracts of land. . . . Satan himself [an ET, in the earlier version] transforms himself into various shapes and forms; by deluding in dreams the mind which he holds captive, he leads it through devious ways. . . . It is shown in various ways that they [witches or ETs] can be bodily transported . . . and sometimes they even persuade others to go with them on a horse [old style; now a UFO], which is not really a horse but a devil in that form. . . . And indeed it must be confessed that such things can happen not only to those who are awake, but also to men [and especially women] who are asleep; namely, they can be bodily transported through the air while they are fast asleep [and] if they are called by their own names by the other bystanders, they immediately fall crashing to the ground. Many think, and not without reason, that this is devil's work. . . .
>
> Now following is their [witch-ET] method of being transported. They take the unguent [a "flying ointment"] which, as we have said, they make at the devil's instruction from the limbs of children, particularly of those whom they have killed before baptism, and they anoint with it a chair or a broom-stick; whereupon they are immediately carried up into the air, either by day or by night, and either visibly or, if they wish, invisibly. . . . They are transported both bodily and phantastically, as is proved by their own confessions [or, later, recitations under hypnosis], not only the ones made by those who have been burned, but also of others who have returned to penitence and the [Catholic] Faith.[24]

Given the many useful details and procedures described in the *Malleus Maleficarum*, I can only hope that UFOlogists will now include the pseudoscientific pronouncements of Heinrich Kramer and James Sprenger in their forthcoming publications. For instance, included here is the best explanation yet for Travis's flights of fancy in the Arizona boondocks. According to an eyewitness account, this one antedating Travis's paperback account by some five centuries:

> He saw with his own eyes such a transportation, and he tells how the man [Travis Walton?] was borne on high with arms stretched out, shouting but not whimpering. And the cause, as he tells us, was as follows. A number of scholars [or contract woodcutters] had met together to drink beer, and they all agreed that the one who fetched the beer

should not have to pay anything. And so one of them was going to fetch the beer [and avoid paying the check] and, upon opening the door, he saw a thick cloud before the grunsel [i.e., a UFO] and, returning in terror, told his companions why he would not go for the drink. Then the one of them, who was carried away [*ebrius*], said angrily: "Even if the devil were there, I shall fetch the drink!" And, going out, he was carried through the air in the sight of all the others.[25]

Either way, sexual nightmare or demonic infestation, Darwin had plainly announced that the hideous creature squatting upon the maiden's breast in Fuseli's *Nightmare* was indeed an incubus, a stock character in the traditional literature of witchcraft. Accordingly, this creature may now be explicated by reference to a classic work on the *artes maleficarum* that deals at some length with the awful workings of these sexually possessive demons. This textual exegesis will make it clear that the real subject of Fuseli's *Nightmare* was not only (or just) witchcraft in general, but that, additionally, the underlying narrative element was more specifically framed within the traditional context of "demoniality," meaning the strictly "sexual" aspect of witchcraft.[26] This textual analysis additionally serves to reveal even further the very conventional (or rather unoriginal) aspects of what has always been generally considered to be Fuseli's most "original" work, *The Nightmare*. Ironically, the same exegesis reveals just how conventionalized are those orgasmic tropes decorating the more exciting postmodernist tales of abductions by aliens.

EROTICIZED INCUBI IN THE TRADITIONAL LITERATURE OF WITCHCRAFT

In 1754, twenty-seven years before Fuseli conceived his canvas, an ency-clopedia article by Ludovico Maria Sinistrari (1622–1701) that exhaus-tively treated the topic of "*Daemonialitas*" was posthumously published. This opusculum appeared—in the fourth part, "De Delictis contra Casti-tatem," of a massive inquisitorial compendium entitled *De Delictis et Poenis*—in the same year that the author's collected works were published in a three-volume collection: *R. P. Ludovici Mariae Sinistrari de Ameno Opera Omnia* ("Romae, in domo Caroli Gianniani"; 1753–54).[27] In short, even in the middle of the eighteenth century, Sinistrari was still reckoned by some of the *cognoscenti* to be an authority on matters demonic. At some unknown date much earlier (circa 1698?), Sinistrari had expanded the materials posthumously presented in his encyclopedia article into a full-blown treatise, *De Daemonialitatae, et Incubis et Succubis*.[28]

Even though on the basis of what follows one must strongly suspect that Fuseli had direct knowledge of either Sinistrari's encyclopedia article or the mysterious manuscript developed from it, the artist's direct acquaintance with such incunabula cannot actually be proven. No matter: there is really nothing original in Sinistrari's textual materials. The Italian priest had merely conveniently synthesized, and slightly embroidered, upon other quite standard, meaning easily available, for having been previously published, materials that had routinely dealt with the worrisome subject of beastly "demoniality." After reviewing the internal evidence of Fuseli's *Nightmare*, we may conclude that the demonically inclined Swiss artist was familiar with at least some parts of various standard sources which are conveniently recapitulated in Sinistrari's text.

As Sinistrari initially admits (articles 1–2), "the first author who, so far as I know, uses the word *'Daemonialitas'* is Juan Caramuel [y Lobkowitz; 1606–1682], in his *Fundamentals of Theology* [i.e., *Theologia moralis ad prima atque clarissima principia reducta*, 1643], and before him I can find no one who distinguishes that crime from Bestiality." The learned Franciscan then proceeds to define "bestiality" according to Aquinas (*Summa* 2.2, 154) as representing "every kind of carnal intercourse with any thing whatsoever of a different species . . . [and all] that [is] committed through [sexual] intercourse with a thing of different species, it takes the name of Bestiality." In the third article, Sinistrari reverts to Caramuel's explanation of *"Daemonialitas,"* that is, "a connection with the Demon, whether [as] Incubus or Succubus, which is, properly speaking, Demoniality and differs in kind from Bestiality." In article 5 we learn that "the difference between the Demon and the beast [a 'real' animal] is not only specific, it is more than specific: the nature of the one [an animal] is corporeal, of the other [the incubus] incorporeal, which makes a generic difference." According to article 8, "carnal connection with the Devil, or a familiar [the incubus], is much more heinous than the same act committed with any beast whatsoever. . . . All are equally grave: it is the same whether connection is had with a bitch, an ass, or a mare; whence it follows that Demoniality is more heinous than Bestiality, [but] those two acts are not of the same species." In any case, "in the genus of unnatural sin, Demoniality is more grievous than Bestiality."

As Sinistrari observes (article 9), "The Demon, whether Incubus or Succubus, unites carnally not only with men and women, but also with beasts." In article 10 it is claimed that "of course, there is no question that sometimes young women, deceived by the Demon, imagine that they are actually taking part, in their flesh and blood, in the Sabbaths of Witches, and that all this is merest fantasy." This affirmation leads the

Franciscan scholar to the subject of a nightmare (in this case, literally a "wet dream"): "Thus, in a dream, one sometimes fancies that one is sleeping with someone else, and there is an emission of semen, yet that connection is wholly unreal and imaginary, and often brought about by a diabolical illusion." Nevertheless, "on the contrary, it more often happens that Witches are bodily present at Sabbaths and have an actual, carnal and corporeal, connection with the Demon."

Article 11 explains that "the Demon has two ways of copulating carnally with men or women: the one which he uses with [initiated] Witches or Wizards, the other with [innocent] men or women who know nothing of witchcraft." Article 24 goes into the finer details of demonic coitus; according to Sinistrari:

> If we seek to learn from these [Ecclesiastical] Authorities how it is possible that the Demon, who has no body, yet can perform actual coitus with man or woman, they unanimously answer that the Demon assumes the corpse of another being, male or female as the case may be, or that, from the mixture of other materials, he shapes for himself a body endowed with motion, by means of which body he copulates with the human being; and they add that when women are desirous of becoming pregnant by the Demon (which occurs only with the consent and at the express wish of said women), the Demon is transformed into a Succubus, and during the act of coition with some man receives therefrom human semen; or else he procures pollution from a man during his sleep, and then he preserves the spilt semen at its natural heat, conserving it with the vital essence. This, when he has connection with the woman, he introduces into her womb, whence follows impregnation. Such is the teaching of [Francesco Maria] Guazzo, [in his *Compendium Maleficarum*, 1608], book I, ch. 12, and he proves it by a number of quotations and instances taken from many learned Doctors.

When we turn to the earlier text specifically mentioned by Sinistrari—Guazzo's *Compendium Maleficarum*, book 1, chapter 12—we find the following:

> Almost all the theologians and learned Philosophers are agreed [says Guazzo], and it has been the experience of all times and all nations, that witches practice coition with demons, the men with Succubus devils and the women with Incubus devils. . . . They [the demons] can therefore create the appearance of sex which is not naturally present, and show themselves to men in feminine form, and to women in a masculine form, and lie with each accordingly: and they can also produce semen which they have brought from elsewhere, and imitate the nat-

ural ejaculation of it. . . . Witches confess that the semen injected by the devil is cold, and that the [sexual] act brings them no pleasure but rather horror [and] say that such copulations are entirely devoid of pleasure, and that they rather feel the most acute pain in them.[29]

Sinistrari (article 25) later extended the obviously commonplace argument presented by Guazzo as follows:

> At other times also the Demon, whether Incubus or Succubus, copulates with [innocent] men or women from whom, however, he receives none of the sacrifices, homage or offerings which he is wont to exact from Wizards or Witches, as aforesaid. He is then but a passionate lover, having only one desire; the carnal possession of those whom his lust craves.

Sinistrari's article 26 deals with the principal subject in our investigation of Fuseli's *Nightmare* (fig. 26)—the incubus, meaning Erasmus Darwin's "squab fiend"—which is directly coupled by this expert with the vivid image of a female horse, a mare, which is the same creature seen in Fuseli's famous painting. According to Sinistrari:

> We read likewise of numerous women incited to coition by an Incubus, and who, though reluctant at first of yielding to him, are soon moved by his prayers, tears, and endearments; for he is a desperate lover and must not be denied. And although this comes sometimes of the craft of some Wizard who avails himself of the agency of the Demon, yet the Demon not infrequently acts thus on his own account, as Guazzo informs us, *Compendium Maleficarum*, III, 8; and this happens not only with women, but also with mares; for if they readily comply with his desire, he pets them, and plaits their manes in elaborate and inextricably reticulated tresses; but, if they resist, he ill-treats them, infects them with the glanders and lampass, and may finally kill them, as is shown by daily experience.

The subject of stallions and mares that are sexually assaulted by lecherous incubi is again dealt with by Sinistrari in his article 67:

> There are Incubi that have connection with horses, mares and other beasts, and, as shown by everyday experience, they ill-treat them if they are adverse to coition; yet, in those cases, it can no longer be adduced that the Demon simulates the appetite for coition in order to bring about the ruin of souls, since beasts are not capable of ever-lasting damnation. Besides, love and wrath with them are productive of quite opposite effects. For, if the loved woman or beast humours them, those

Incubi behave very well; on the contrary, they use them most savagely when irritated and enraged by a denial of coition: this is amply proven by daily experience: those Incubi therefore have truly sexual passions and desires.

It is, of course, the writhing and supine maiden in Fuseli's *Nightmare*, rather than the white mare, who really suffers from the "truly sexual passions and desires" of the incubus who "sits upon her breast." In his concluding "Proof of Demoniality: Summary," article 2, Sinistrari cites reports of "women [who] have been seen in the woods, in the fields, in groves and dingles, lying on their backs, naked to their very navels, in the posture of venery, all their limbs quivering with the orgasmic spasm, as is noted by Guazzo, book I, chap. 12, v. *Sciendum est saepius*, fol. 65."

To the modern student of the historical texts of witchcraft, this scene is very familiar. Rather than originating in Guazzo's treatise of 1608, as Sinistrari seems to believe, instead it goes all the way back to the end of the fifteenth century, before which time there are *no* published texts on witchcraft. As one reads in the *Malleus Maleficarum*:

> With regard to any bystanders, the witches themselves have often been seen lying on their backs, in the fields or in the woods, naked up to the very navel, and it has been apparent from the disposition of those limbs and of those members which pertain to the venereal act and orgasm, as also from the agitation of their legs and thighs, that, all invisibly to the bystanders, they have been copulating with Incubus devils. . . . It is certain that the following has happened. Husbands have actually seen Incubus devils swiving their wives, although they have thought that they were not devils but men. . . . In conclusion, finally, it can be said of these Incubus devils that they will try with all their might, by means of witches, who are bawds or hot whores, to seduce all the devout and chaste maidens in that district or town [in order] to effect the subversion of pious maidens and widows.[30]

What one learns from this citation taken from the *first* standard textbook on witchy ways, an *Urtext* which had been composed around 1486, is the way that all the later "experts" on occultism (and of all sorts, and right up to the present day, including the alien-abduction scriptures), rather than relying upon firsthand information, tend to quote from earlier, established "authorities," meaning endlessly from one another.[31] This same verbalized tableau of *plein-air* copulatory writhings—apparently originating with Kramer and Sprenger, then reappearing in Guazzo, from whom Sinistrari cites it—will appear again in yet another text to be quoted here, Scot's *Discoverie of Witchcraft*, thus demonstrating its existence as an authentic literary *topos*. It is additionally apparent that, as viewed late in the eighteenth century by any well-read student of witchcraft, the pose of Fuseli's supine woman—with "the disposition of those limbs and of those members which pertain to the venereal act and orgasm"—would have represented an easily understood iconographic sign of female, and specifically incubus-inspired, "orgasm."

Earlier, in article 66, Sinistrari had discussed the wholly sexual nature of the incubi and their insidious manner of gaining egress into a reluctant lady's bed chamber. Perhaps not so oddly, these nocturnal bedroom infestations are also common to the postmodernist alien-abduction stories. As Sinistrari claims here:

> Indeed, the appetitive desire of coition is a sensual desire; the grief, sadness, wrath, rage, occasioned by the denial of coition, are sensual passions, as is seen with all animals; generation through coition is evidently a sensual operation. Now, all that happens with Incubi, as has been shown above: they incite women, sometimes even men; if denied, they sadden and storm, like lovers: *amantes, amentes*; they practice perfect coition, and sometimes beget. It must therefore be inferred that they have senses, and consequently a body; consequently also, that they are perfect animals. More than that: in spite of closed doors and windows they enter wherever they please; their body is therefore slender [cf. fig. 20]: they foreknow and foretell the future, compose and divide, all which operations are proper to a rational soul; they therefore possess a rational soul and are, in fine, rational animals. Doctors generally reply that it is the Evil Spirit that perpetrates those impure acts, simulates passions, love, grief at the denial of coition, in order to entice souls to sin and to undo them; and that, if he copulates and begets, it is with assumed sperm and a body not truly his own, as aforesaid.

According to Erasmus Darwin's interpretation of Fuseli's *Nightmare*, "through the evening fog flits the squab fiend o'er fen, and lake and bog [and] seeks some love-wildered maid, with sleep oppres'd, alights, and grinning, sits upon her breast." As one might now query, exactly why does Darwin's homunculus-like "squab fiend" frequent fens, lakes, and bogs? Sinistrari makes it perfectly clear (article 111) that any "Incubi who approach women are aqueous and of small stature; that is why they appear in the shape of little men [*homunculi*; cf. figs. 1, 4], and, being aqueous, they are most lecherous. Lust and damp go together." Although Sinistrari cites many cases of Incubi advancing their lusty and damp attentions upon maidens in a similarly unwelcome manner, one example alone will suffice to reveal the character of all the Italian priest's demonized and eroticized fantasies and, additionally, the kind of literary traditions really informing Erasmus Darwin's humid and overheated (and not very original) verses.

With apparent glee, Sinistrari announces (article 26) how "we read likewise of numerous women incited to coition by an Incubus, and who, though reluctant at first of yielding to him, are soon moved by his prayers, tears, and endearments; for he is a desperate lover and must not be denied." According to the story ("of this I was an eyewitness") told by Sinistrari in article 28 of his *De Daemonialitate, et Incubis et Succubis*, in Pavia "there was living in that city a married woman of unimpeachable morality." Her name was Hieronyma, and she was particularly tempted by "a large cake of a peculiar shape, made of butter and Venetian paste" that was given to her by a certain person who eventually turned out to be the dreaded incubus.

> The next night, whilst in bed with her husband, and both were fast asleep, she suddenly woke up at the sound of a very small voice, something like a shrill hissing, whispering in her ears, yet with great distinctness, and inquiring whether "the cake had been to her taste?" The good woman, thoroughly frightened, began to guard herself with the sign of the cross and repeatedly called upon the Names of Jesus and Mary. "Be not afraid," said the voice, "I mean you no harm, quite the reverse: I am prepared to anything to please you; I am captivated by your beauty, and desire nothing more than to enjoy your sweet embraces." Whereupon she felt somebody kissing her cheeks, so lightly, so softly, that she might have fancied being stroked by the finest feather down. . . . On the ensuing nights she was sore tempted with the same amorous words and loving kisses, and she showed the same constancy in repulsing them. Utterly weary, however, of such painful and persistent molestations, upon the advice of her confessor and other reverend men, she had herself exorcised by experienced Exorcists.

In the way Sinistrari tells it, unfortunately not even outside intervention proved efficacious against the heated attention of Hieronyma's amorous and ingenious incubus:

> All was in vain; he kept on worse than before, pretending to be lovesick, weeping and moaning in order to melt the heart of the lady, who however, by the grace of God, remained unconquered. The Incubus then went another way to work: he showed himself in the shape of a lad or a little man of great beauty, with crisped golden locks, a flaxen beard that shone like fine gold, sea-green eyes calling to mind the flax-flower,

and arrayed in a comely Spanish dress. Besides, he appeared to her even when she was in company, billing and cooing gently after the fashion of lovers, kissing his hand to her, and continually endeavoring by such means to obtain her embraces. She alone saw and heard him: to everybody else he was invisible.

In this unique case, however, in spite of the incubus's wiles (called too "wearisome" by Sinistrari to relate here), and due to Hieronyma's unassailable virtue, the results finally went against the squab fiend. As Sinistrari concludes his cautionary tale:

> I might not impertinently relate many other most amazing tricks and naughty japeries which that Incubus played on her, were it not wearisome. Suffice it to say that, for a number of years, he persevered in his temptation of her, but that, finding at last he was losing his pains, he desisted from his vexations and wanton importunities.

Since it would be "wearisome" in the extreme to cite any more examples of such demonically inspired eroticism from *De Daemonialitate, et Incubis et Succubis*, it becomes sufficient simply to state that it was, and still is specifically Sinistrari's brand of "Daemonialitas" that really best fits the contextual particulars of both Henry Fuseli's nightmare iconography, and also the "love-witched" doggerel of Erasmus Darwin. Nevertheless, and as we already know, Sinistrari certainly did not invent "demoniality." The potentially iconographic elements of demonic sexual possession by incubi and succubi can be found in many other published authorities on witchcraft, many of whom were generously acknowledged by Sinistrari.

The result is that Sinistrari is not necessarily the iconographic source for the witchy eroticism of *The Nightmare*; he is instead merely the most representative, contemporary expression of its peculiarities. Such as we have just contextually identified them, Fuseli could have gotten those erotic and lurid particulars from any number of other published sources. And we have also identified (in chapter 5) some of Betty Hill's published sources. However, neither she, nor Betty Andreasson opportunely replicating her alien encounter precedent, would have ever bothered to read such erudite literature as the treatises of Kramer and Sprenger, Guazzo, or Sinistrari. Such premodern publications are obviously beyond the intellectual grasp of our typically petty-bourgeois American abductees.

BRITISH ACCOUNTS OF EROTICIZED INCUBI AND SUCCUBI

As everyone recognizes, Erasmus Darwin supplies the closest contemporary account and the closest verbal equivalent to the real content of Fuseli's *Nightmare*. In order to indicate an even more likely source of, in particular, Erasmus Darwin's comprehension of "Daemonialitas," an English (versus Latin) language publication seems a much more apt choice. In this case, a likely candidate is Reginald Scot's *The Discoverie of Witchcraft* (1584). Besides being a native British work, it is also consistently skeptical in tone, which aspect would have made it still appealing at the end of the eighteenth century. Since Fuseli's age is generally reckoned to be an "Age of Enlightenment," it may be believed that one was somewhat obligated to take the more outrageous aspects of witchcraft *cum grano salis*. In the event, the entirety of book 4 of Scot's *Discoverie* was given over to the topic of "Incubus and Succubus," and it includes detailed, and quite provocative, materials bearing upon the matter of witches' "carnall copulation with Incubus."[32]

Like every other writer on (or illustrator of) witchcraft, Scot acquired his knowledge from previously published works. In Scot's case, by his own admission, these included, among others, "M.[alleus] Mal.[eficarum], [Jean] Bodin, Hemingius, Hyperius, Danaeus, Erastus, and others that take upon them to write herein." As Scot skeptically explains, the authors of the *Malleus Maleficarum* had affirmed that "the divell, in likeness of a prettie wench, lieth prostitute as Succubus to the man, and reteining his nature and seede, conveieth it unto the witch, to whome he delivereth it as Incubus." But there are two kinds of witches and, according to Scot, there are either old hags or "prettie wenches": "And this is the distinction;" he adds, "Either she is old and barren or young and pregnant. If she is barren, then dooth Incubus use hir without decision of seed; because such seed should serve for no purpose." This observation, particularly as it relates to a postmenopausal Betty Hill or a Betty Andreasson after a hysterectomy, proves a point made in chapter 5: ETs are biologically stupid, since their egregious pelvic probing of such "barren" women "should serve for no purpose."

In chapter 3 of the *Discoverie*, Scot, like Guazzo and Sinistrari, paraphrased that picturesque description taken from the *Malleus Maleficarum* showing the pretty witches writhing hotly and nakedly in the dark depths of night, thus further demonstrating the common textual distribution of the supinely eroticized pose seen in Fuseli's *Nightmare*. According to Scot:

James Spenger and Institor affirme, that Manie times witches are seene in the fields, and woods, prostituting themselves uncovered and naked up to the navill, wagging and mooving their members in everie part, according to the disposition of one being about that act of concupiscence, and yet [is] nothing seene of the beholders upon hir; saving that after such a convenient time as is required about such a peece of worke, a blacke vapour of the length and bignesse of a man, hath beene seene as it were to depart from hir, and to ascend from that place. Neverthelesse, manie times the husband seeth Incubus making him cuckhold, in the likenesse of a man, and sometimes striketh off his head with his sword: but bicause the bodie is nothing but aire, it closeth togither againe: so as, although the goodwife be some times hurt thereby; yet she maketh him beleeve he is mad or possessed, & that he dooth he knoweth not what. For she hath more pleasure and delight (they say) with Incubus that waie, than with anie mortall man: whereby you may perceive that spirits are palpable.[33]

Fuseli's writhing and "love-wildered/bewitched" young woman is a strawberry blond. According to Scot (chapter 5), "in the night time Incubus came to a ladies bed side, and made hot loove unto hir." And what do these susceptible ladies look like? Scot succinctly explains, "Maides having yellow hair are most molested with this spirit." Unfortunately, neither Scot nor his published sources explain just why blondes are more prone (or supine) to these kinds of nocturnal carnal reveries. Moreover, two pages of Scot's treatise (subheadings for chapters 10 and 11) are actually entitled "The Night-mare." Not only do these passages provide a likely *locus classicus* for the very title of Fuseli's celebrated painting, but apparently Scot's text additionally provides the specific particulars of Erasmus Darwin's descriptions of the protagonist of Fuseli's picture, the one who is "with sleep oppres'd." However, in Scot's version (related in his chapter 9) the only notable departure is that the victim of the incubus is, in this instance, a male (like Antonio Villas-Boas) who is sexually tormented at night by a fetching succubus:

There commeth unto mee, almost everie night, a certeine woman, unknowne unto me, and lieth so heavie upon my brest, that I cannot fetch my breath, neither have anie power to crie, neither doo my hands serve me to shoove hir awaie, nor my feete to go from hir. I smiled (quoth Jason) and told him that he was vexed with a disease called Incubus, or the mare; and the residue was phantasie and vaine imagination.[34]

In the manner that Erasmus Darwin appeared to paraphrase this same description two centuries later, "in vain she wills to run, fly, swim, walk creep; the WILL presides not in the bower of SLEEP." In the much earlier case of Scot's victim, "I tell you nothing but that with waking I saw with mine eies, and felt with mine hands. I see hir when she commeth upon me, and strive to repell hir; but I am so infeebled that I cannot: and for remedie I have runne about from place to place, but no helpe that I could get." Scot additionally provides the more rational explanation for this particular fit and, additionally, the apparent basis of, equally, Darwin's doggerel and Fuseli's demonically possessed and "love-wildered maid," upon whom a "squab fiend . . . alights, and grinning sits upon her breast." According to Scot (chapter 11):

> But in truth, this Incubus is a bodilie disease (as hath beene said) although it extend unto the trouble of the mind: which of some is called The mare, oppressing manie in their sleepe so sore, as they are not able to call for helpe, or stir themselves under the burthen of that heavie humor, which is ingendred of a thicke vapor proceeding from the cruditie and rawnesse in the stomack: which ascending up into the head oppresseth the braine, in so much as manie are much infeebled therebie, as being nightlie haunted therewith. They are most troubled with this disease, that being subject thereunto, lie right upward [i.e., supine]: so as, to turne and lie on the one side, is [to] present remedie.[35]

None of the particulars of this quasiscientific analysis is at all unique to Scot's *Discoverie of Witchcraft*. These matters were, for instance, all dealt with in a much more extended, and even clinical, manner slightly later by Robert Burton in his classic study on *The Anatomy of Melancholy: What It Is, with All the Kinds, Causes, Symptomes, Prognostickes, and Severall Cures of It* (1621). In part 3, section 2, member 1, subsection 1 of his sprawling treatise, Burton finds occasion to wonder "if those stories be true that are written of incubus and succubus." Although he ultimately doubts their validity, he assiduously cites the many authors current in his time who had subscribed to such theories, mentioning how

> some others stoutly deny it, that the devil hath any carnal copulation with women, that the devil takes no pleasure in such facts, they be mere phantasies, all such relations of incubi, succubi, lies and tales; but Au[gu]stin[e], liber 15, *De Civitate Dei*, doth acknowledge it; Erastus, *De lamiis*; Jacobus Sprenger and his colleagues, etc.; Zanchius, cap. 16, lib. 4, *De operatione Dei*; Dandinus, in *Aristotelis de anima*, lib. 2, text. 29, comm. 30; Bodine, lib. 2, cap. 7, and Paracelsus, a great champion of this tenet amongst the rest, which give sundry peculiar instances, by many testimonies, proofs, and confessions evince it. Hector Beothius, in

his *Scottish History*, hath three or four such examples, which Cardan confirms out of him, lib. 16, cap. 43 [etc.].[36]

For Burton the subject of demoniality is, of course, most pertinent when it illuminates the matter of melancholy. Burton describes what might be called the "incubus phenomenon": (1) it is wholly a matter of the diseased mind, (2) one is most prone to its appearance when lying in a supine position, and (3) it has, moreover, the potential to be a fit subject for the imaginative work of the visual artist. In a chapter (part 1, section 2, member 3, subsection 2) entitled "The Force of the Imagination," Burton says the following:

> This we see verified in sleepers, which by reason of humours and concourse of vapours troubling the phantasy, imagine many times absurd and prodigious things, and in such as are troubled with incubus, or [are] witch-ridden (as we call it); if they lie on their backs, they suppose an old woman rides and sits so hard upon them that they are almost stifled for want of breath; when there is [really] nothing [that] offends but a concourse of bad humours, which trouble the phantasy. . . . Those common apparitions in Bede and Gregory, St. Bridget's *Revelations*, Wier, lib. 3, *De lamiis*, cap. 11, Caesar Vaninus in his *Dialogues*, etc. reduceth (as I have formerly said), with all these tales of witches' progresses, dancing, riding, transformations, operations, etc., to the force of imagination, and the devil's illusions. The like effects almost are to be seen in such as are awake: how many chimeras, antics, golden mountains, and castles in the air do they build unto themselves! I appeal [for their illustration] to painters, mechanicians, mathematicians.[37]

Burton's conclusion following (to which I fully subscribe) is that the apparition of succubi and incubi—that is, as tangibly real, but nonetheless wholly psychological phenomena arising "in sleepers" due to their "force of imagination"—may be often ascribed to physical causes, namely sexual deprivation. The "force of imagination" argument evidently also applies, two hundred years later, to explain close encounters with similarly demonic postmodernist extraterrestrials, exotic creatures also appealing for their respective illustrations (figs. 1, 4, 5, 8, 15–21). Perhaps this judgment also provides yet another complementary (or "clinical") reading for the erotic subtext of Fuseli's *Nightmare* (fig. 26)— that is, if we can imagine that the artist really had actually endeavored to compose his essentially lurid picture of possession by *daemonialitas* in such real, and even quasiscientific terms.

As Burton further observed in a chapter (1.3.2.4) dealing with the piquant topic of "Symptoms of Maids', Nuns', and Widows' Melancholy," this grievous affliction "may happen to widows . . . but to nuns and more ancient maids, and some barren women, for the causes abovesaid, 'tis more familiar." Under such conditions of erotic privation, "they think themselves bewitched." In the case of Betty Hill and Betty Andreasson, among many others, they think themselves bewitched by an extraterrestrial. In either case, for such a lament, there is a possible and timely cure: the amorous attentions of a sexually capable man. According to Burton:

> But the best and surest remedy of all, is to see them well placed, and married to good husbands in due time; *hinc illae lachrymae* [whence their tears], that's the primary cause, and this the ready cure, to give them content to their [sexual] desires. . . . *Grandiores virgines*, saith Mercatus, *steriles, et viduae plerumque melancholicae* [mostly melancholic are mature virgins, barren women, and widows]; such for the most part are misaffected, and prone to this disease [which produces] fearful maladies, feral diseases, gross inconveniences, [that] come to both sexes by this enforced [sexual] temperance.[38]

On the basis of various kinds of strictly textual evidence presented here, it may now be argued that Fuseli's celebrated *Nightmare* need no longer be viewed as being in any way ambiguous or enigmatic in its originally intended meaning. Overall, it is unmistakably about witchcraft. Within this broad context of the *artes maleficarum*, which must surely have been recognized as such by some of Fuseli's contemporaries (including many more than just Erasmus Darwin and Johann Heinrich Meyer), the painter now appears to have chosen to concentrate upon one specific aspect, "demoniality." A further conclusion is called for. Obviously, given the communality of this theme, no matter by whatever name it may have then been called, in the literature of witchcraft still current in Fuseli's time, some recognition by the *cognoscenti* of that kind of "demoniality," meaning specifically eroticized esoterica, surely must have contributed to the undeniable—and still enduring—popularity of *The Nightmare* as a *succès de scandale* after 1782. Demoniality also accounts for the undeniable—and still enduring (if scarcely endearing)—popularity of paperback publications and TV shows dealing with aliens abducting earthlings. Also noteworthy is the recent (2000) revival by Hollywood of "demoniality" in the traditional (pre-ET) sense, so attested by a made-for-TV movie aptly named *Possession*.[39]

HYPNOPOMPIC HALLUCINATION:
THE MODERN DIAGNOSIS OF FUSELI'S *NIGHTMARE*

A couple of strictly modernist observations are now called for. As for the first, the fact that Sigmund Freud prominently hung a print of Fuseli's *Nightmare* in his Vienna apartment is perhaps indicative of the mistakenly modern, or individualized, psychological interpretations—that is, "bad dreams" versus demonic possession—that have consistently misdirected modern scholarship treating Fuseli's admittedly provocative *Nightmare*.[40] In fact, the Swiss-born artist seems almost a proto-Freudian; as Fuseli himself put it in his *Aphorisms* (no. 231), "One of the most unexplored regions of art are dreams, and what may be called the personifications of sentiment."[41] The second observation points out that whereas in Fuseli's time his kind of "Night-mare" seemingly required a horse—actually a "mare"—now the means of transportation into dreadful reveries has drastically changed. Now the flashing-eyed equine apparition has been transformed into the light-beaming UFOs so often reported to be hovering in the night skies above the great American outback.

I will now provide the modern, psychological and scientific, explanation for the basic clinical situation depicted in Fuseli's *Nightmare* (fig. 26). However, if you wish to continue with your personal belief in witchcraft, by all means, do so—as they say, this is a "free country." In short, Fuseli's bewitched scene actually depicts what the clinical experts now call "sleep paralysis with hypnagogic and hypnopompic hallucinations."[42] Since I will have more to say about this standard condition later (in chapter 14), I need only cite two examples from contemporary publications, one written by a certified psychologist and the other by a well-paid "abductee." According to Erasmus Darwin, who wrote long before the invention of the modern science called psychology, "When there arises in sleep a painful desire to exert the voluntary motions, it is called the nightmare or incubus"; this is the condition when the victim perceives himself or herself to be "with sleep oppressed."[43] Here is how the same "hypnopompic" experience was experienced—without being officially designated incubi or succubi—by a modern psychologist, Dr. Ronald Siegel:

> I was awakened by the sound of my bedroom door opening. I was on my side and able to see the luminescent dial of the alarm clock. It was 4:20 A.M. I heard footsteps approaching my bed, then heavy breathing. There seemed to be a murky presence in the room. I tried to throw off the covers and get up but I was pinned to the bed. There was a weight on my chest. The more I struggled the more I was unable to move. My heart was pounding. I strained to breathe. . . . Suddenly a shadow fell

on the clock. *Omigod! This is no joke!* Something touched my neck and arm. A voice whispered in my ear. . . . In my bedroom I could see only a shadow looming over my bed: I was terrified. . . . I signaled my muscles to move, but the presence immediately exerted all its weight on my chest [cf. fig. 26]. . . . *This is no dream! This is really happening!*

A hand grasped my arm and held it tightly. The intruder was doing the reality testing on me. The hand felt cold and dead. . . . Then part of the mattress next to me caved in. Someone climbed onto the bed! The presence shifted its weight and straddled my body, folding itself along the curve of my back. I heard the bed start to creak. There was a texture of sexual intoxication and terror in the room.[44]

Now there is a graphic description of *The Nightmare* of which both Erasmus Darwin and Henry Fuseli might wholeheartedly approve! Nonetheless, since the good doctor was a certified psychologist, of course he recognized this experience only to represent a classic case of sleep paralysis with hypnopompic hallucinations. Jenny Randles, a Brit who has profitably published many books championing the validity of UFOs and their endlessly invasive ET crewmen, has usefully (for once) demonstrated that the largest number of reported alien abductions do occur at night, reaching a peak between midnight and 2:00 A.M.[45] Terry Matheson, the adept Canadian scholar of the abundant pseudoliterature defining the alien abduction legend, draws the logical inference: "These facts suggest that the [abduction] experience arguably *does* have some specificity in place and time—hypnopompic (waking dream) states."[46] Nonetheless, Whitley Strieber, who is only certified as a best-selling writer of fantasy fiction, thinks the same kind of confabulation (instead) represents a classic case of "alien abduction," and his mirrorlike tale reads like this:

Sometime during the night I was awakened abruptly by a jab on my shoulder. I came to full consciousness instantly. There were three small people [classic ETs] standing beside the bed, their outlines clearly visible in the glow of the burglar-alarm panel. They were wearing blue overalls and standing absolutely still. . . .

I thought to myself, my God, I'm completely conscious and they [the ETs] are just standing there. I thought that I could turn on the light, perhaps even get out of bed. Then I tried to move my hand, thinking to flip the switch on the bedside lamp and see the time.

I can only describe the sensation I felt when I tried to move as like pushing my arm through electrified tar. It took every ounce of attention I possessed to get any movement at all. . . . Simply moving my arm did not work. I had to order the movement, to labor at it. All the while they [the ETs] stood there. . . . I was overcome at this point by terror so fierce and physical that it seemed more biological than psychological. . . . I tried to wake up Anne [Mrs. Strieber] but my mouth wouldn't open. . . . Again it took an absolute concentration of will . . . but I did manage to smile.

Instantly everything changed. They dashed away with a whoosh [like Santa's reindeer] and I was plunged almost at once back into sleep.[47]

That's the postmodernist experience in a nutshell: Bewitched, bothered, and bewildered. We may now mention an accepted remedy for this baleful condition. Rather than being a certified psychiatrist of the orthodox modernist sort, like Dr. Siegel, let us instead assume that you are anachronistically possessed with a medieval mentality, the kind we now incorrectly call "New Age." So possessed, like Mr. Strieber, you are sorely afflicted by ETs, what the chronologically authentic medievals used to call "demons." No matter the nomenclature; you certainly must wish to relieve yourself of irksome visitations by outer-space aliens. And here is the tried and true procedure by which we will resolve your pesky problem: *exorcism*. All of what follows was explained in an anonymous Spanish manuscript composed around 1720, *Tratado de exorcismos, muy útil para los sacerdotes y Ministros de la iglesia* (now found in the library of the Hispanic Society of America). As our sacerdotal authority explains:

The victim may be possessed by the Devil [now called an extraterrestrial] in two ways, namely: *per obsesionem*, and *per posesionem*. *Per obsesionem* is when the Devil [ET] is outside or around the person and then torments him with horrible faces, frightening shapes, and in other ways, as the exorcist will find out by experience. *Per posesionem* is when the Devil [ET] is inside the victim and possesses him. Then he torments him with blows, pains of the body, etc. . . . Sometimes when demons [ETs] leave the bodies of the possessed, they are in the habit of showing themselves and appearing in the frightening shape of various animals and other terrible things [or humanoids; see figs. 1, 4, 8–21, and so forth], although they might not be seen by the bystanders. This is very simple, because these apparitions can be just imaginary, in order for the Devil [ET] to stir the blood and temper of the victim and to form some image which represents him. This vision—because [*nota bene*] it is imaginary—only appears to the one who inflicts the vision upon himself, as is inferred in the writings of the prophets. . . . The curious will be satisfied with this information, and the ignorant will be informed of the tricks the Devil [ET] has in order to fool us.[48]

Well, that explanation is fairly clear, and it also neatly corresponds to the postmodernist abduction reports reproduced in chapter 2. Also obvious is the proven remedy. Quite simply, the possessed person has to make the following oath to a properly appointed and credentialed exorcist-priest; alas, it won't work with a postmodernist hypnotist-UFOlogist. Unfortunately, the following vow must also be pronounced in Latin, and since it simply won't work in modern American English, you have no need of a translation. It goes like this:

> *Ego, N[omen], iuro, et promitto tibi sacerdoti, seu ministro Christo servare omnia illa, quae praeceperis mihi ex parte Dei, et Domini Jesu Christi pertinentia ad honorem eius, et liberationem huius creaturae [extraterrestrialae], et quod si in ullo defecero ex his, quae tibi nunc promitto extunc invoco ipsum Deum Omnipotentem inatum contra me, qui tanquam ultor, et Judex periurii mei mittat angelos suos, que me expellant ex hoc corpore [extraterrestriale]. Voco similiter Luciferum [extraterrestriam], quatenus cum omnibus furiis [extraterrestrialiis] insurgat in me, et ducat [eis] in profundum Inferni. Amen.*[49]

Whitley, your problem is solved—that is, should you be also willing to forego all future royalties.

NOTES

1. Interview, in John G. Fuller, *The Interrupted Journey: Two Lost Hours "Aboard a Flying Saucer"* (New York: Dell, 1967), pp. 94–96.

2. Betty Andreasson, as in Raymond Fowler, *The Andreasson Affair* (New York: Bantam, 1980), pp. 50–51.

3. Thompson, *Angels and Aliens: UFOs and Mythic Imagination* (New York: Ballantine, 1993), p. 151.

4. Recent bibliography pertinent to this famous painting is fairly extensive; for a listing, see J. F. Moffitt, "*Malleus Maleficarum*: A Literary Context for Fuseli's *Nightmare*," *Gazette des Beaux Arts* 114 (1990): 1–7.

5. See Nicolas Powell, *Fuseli: The Nightmare* (New York: Viking, 1973), pp. 97–100, "Versions and Variants."

6. See ibid., pp. 77–82, "Impact and Repercussions."

7. John Knowles, as cited by H. W. Janson, "Fuseli's Nightmare," in *16 Studies by H. W. Janson* (New York: Abrams, 1973), pp. 77–82 (p. 73).

8. See Moffitt, "*Malleus Maleficarum*."

9. For a reproduction of this print, see M. Halbey, *66 Hexen: Kult und Verdammung* (Dortmund: Harenberg, 1987), pp. 80–81; see also J. F. Moffitt, "A Pictorial Counterpart to 'Gothick' Literature: 'Daemonialitas' and the Haunting 'Incubus' in Henry Fuseli's *Nightmare*," *Mosaic* 35, no. 1 (March 2002): 173–96 (fig. 2).

10. The literature on witchcraft is rather overwhelming; for a partial listing,

see Moffitt, "*Malleus Maleficarum*." For the pertinent historical documents, see A. C. Kors and E. Peters, eds., *Witchcraft in Europe, 1100–1700: A Documentary History* (College Park: Pennsylvania State University Press, 1986).

11. For more details on the close text-to-painting linkage, see Moffitt, "*Malleus Maleficarum*."

12. Robert Rosenblum, *Transformations in Late Eighteenth-Century Art* (Princeton: Princeton University Press, 1970), pp. 11–12. Unfortunately, there has not since appeared a comprehensive art-historical study of the strictly "demonic" interests of the *soi-disant* "enlightened," pre-Romantic period.

13. For a partial listing of works dealing with "Gothick" taste, see Moffitt, "*Malleus Maleficarum*"; for a comprehensive overview, see Marie Mulvey-Roberts, ed., *Handbook to Gothic Literature* (New York: New York University Press, 1998), also with entries on—besides "Nightmare" (pp. 164–65, citing Fuseli) and "Witches and Witchcraft" (pp. 254–56)—"The Demonic," "The Fantastic," "Ghost Stories," "Horror," "Occultism," "The Phantom," "Spiritualism," "The Supernatural," "The Uncanny (Unheimlich)," and so on.

14. J. H. Meyer, *Entwurf einer Kunstgeschichte des achzehnten Jahrhunderts* (Tübingen, 1805); as cited by Powell, *Fuseli: The Nightmare*, p. 106. Immediately after remarking upon the painter's witchcraft subjects, Meyers cites Fuseli's more typical, and much more conventional, taste for "erschütternde Szenen aus Shakespeare und anderen trägischen Dichtern."

15. Fuseli's letters of 1781, as cited in P. A. Tomory, *The Life and Art of Henry Fuseli* (London: Phaidon, 1972), p. 91.

16. Norman Cohn, *Europe's Inner Demons: An Enquiry Inspired by the Great Witch-Hunt* (New York: New American Library, 1975), p. 49.

17. Erasmus Darwin, as quoted in Powell, *Fuseli: The Nightmare*, p. 58. By reference to its portrayal in Fuseli's picture, we see that "squab" (as "fiend") was used here in the obsolescent sense of a "short or squat, stout, fat or plump, [pseudo] person" (*Oxford English Dictionary*).

18. Darwin, in Janson, "Fuseli's Nightmare," p. 80; the comment appeared as a footnote to a long poem, *The Botanical Garden* (1789), that later incorporated the verses first inscribed on the widely sold print of Fuseli's *Nightmare*.

19. G. Schiff et al., *Henry Fuseli, 1741–1825* (London: Phaidon, 1975), cat. nos. 160, 168. The condition of both women, who are naked in the 1810 watercolor, may be described as being "post-orgasmic," as is explained below.

20. For instance, even though Powell, *Fuseli: The Nightmare*, refers to an "incubus" some two-dozen times ("Index," p. 119), curiously, he still discards (p. 42) the idea of the governing matrix of witchcraft for Fuseli's *Nightmare*. But to what other tradition does a/any "incubus" belong? If only treated iconographically, unquestionably Fuseli's "incubus/squab fiend" belongs to a standard canon of demonic representations; for a series of apposite illustrations, see Paul Carus, *The History of the Devil and the Idea of Evil* (LaSalle, Ill.: Open Court, 1990), usefully illustrated but the text is erratic; see also Alice K. Turner, *The History of Hell* (New York: Harvest, 1995), which is much better.

21. Darwin, as quoted in Powell, *Fuseli: The Nightmare*, pp. 59–60. For the

literally "orgasmic" nature of the twitches and convulsions recorded by Darwin, see Marcia Allentuck, "Henry Fuseli's *Nightmare*: Eroticism or Pornography?" in *Woman as Sex Object: Studies in Erotic Art*, ed. T. B. Hess and L. Nochlin (New York: Newsweek, 1972), pp. 33–41.

22. According to Nicolas Powell (p. 60), "there can be little doubt that the girl in Fuseli's painting is experiencing an imaginary sexual assault." He does not, however, cite any standard documentation to back up this hypothesis, such as I give here.

23. Allentuck, "Henry Fuseli's *Nightmare*." For more on the zestful mechanics of female orgasm, as recounted by its actual "experiencers" (who enjoy it more than do "abductees"), see Shere Hite, *The Hite Report: A Nation-wide Study of Female Sexuality* (New York: Dell, 1977).

24. Montague Summers, ed., *The Malleus Maleficarum of Heinrich Kramer and James Sprenger* (London, 1928; reprint, New York: Dover, 1971), pp. 104–109.

25. Ibid., p. 105.

26. In spite of a somewhat sensational title, for a good historical study of "demoniality" by a knowledgeable psychologist, see R. E. L. Masters, *Eros and Evil: The Sexual Psychopathology of Witchcraft* (Baltimore: Penguin, 1974).

27. Rome: Gianini, 1754, folio pp. 249–54.

28. Sinistrari's original, eighty-six-page-long, hand-written manuscript apparently remained completely unknown until it turned up by accident in 1872 in a bookseller's shop on Euston Road in London. It was soon after published (1875) in a bilingual Latin-French edition. I have derived this bibliographical information from the modern English version: A. J-M. Montague Summers, ed., *Lodovico Maria Sinistrari: Demoniality* (London, 1927; reprint, New York: Dover, 1989); Summers introduced his translation with a useful preface. Since Sinistrari's text is given in numbered paragraphs, I shall refer in my text to each of these as being "articles."

29. Montague Summers, ed., *Francesco Maria Guazzo: Compendium Maleficarum* (London, 1929; reprint, New York: Dover, 1988), pp. 30–31.

30. Summers, *The Malleus Maleficarum*, p. 114.

31. For some characteristic examples, much more recent, of this contin-uous process of occultist autoreplications, see J. F. Moffitt, *Occultism in Avant-Garde Art: The Case of Joseph Beuys* (Ann Arbor: University of Michigan Press, 1986).

32. *The Discoverie of Witchcraft by Reginald Scot: With an Introduction by the Rev. Montague Summers* (London, 1930; reprint, New York: Dover, 1989), pp. 42–50.

33. Ibid., pp. 43–44.

34. Ibid., p. 47.

35. Ibid., p. 49.

36. Richard Burton, *The Anatomy of Melancholy*, ed. H. Jackson (London: Dell, 1932), part 3, p. 46.

37. Ibid., part 1, pp. 253–54. The relationship between a supine pose and

the apparition of an incubus, a sign of "nightmare," was later repeated by an English physician; see Dr. John Bond, *An Essay on the Incubus, or Nightmare* (1753): "The Nightmare generally seizes people sleeping on their backs," and so on (as cited by Powell, *Fuseli: The Nightmare*, p. 50).

38. Burton, *Anatomy of Melancholy*, part 1, pp. 415–18.

39. See Joe Nickell, "Exorcism! Driving Out the Nonsense," *Skeptical Inquirer* 25, no. 1 (January/February 2001): 20–24.

40. For Freud's print of the *Nightmare*, see Janson, "Fuseli's Nightmare," p. 82.

41. Fuseli, as quoted in Powell, *Fuseli: The Nightmare*, p. 12.

42. For an early study, see Otto Ishakower, "A Contribution to the Psychopathology of Phenomena Associated with Falling Asleep," *International Journal of Psycho-Analysis* 19 (1938): 331–45.

43. Darwin, in Janson, "Fuseli's *Nightmare*," p. 80.

44. Ronald Siegel, *Fire in the Brain: Clinical Tales of Hallucination* (New York: Dutton, 1992), pp. 83–85.

45. J. Randles, *UFO Study* (London: Robert Hale, 1981); as cited in Jacques Vallée, *Revelations: Alien Contact and Human Deception* (New York: Ballantine, 1993), p. 269.

46. Terry Matheson, *Alien Abductions: Creating a Modern Phenomenon* (Amherst, N.Y.: Prometheus Books, 1998), p. 245.

47. Whitley Strieber, *Communion: A True Story* (New York: Bantam, 1987, reprint), pp. 172–73; the two texts were first compared (without reference to the classic "incubus experience") by Robert A. Baker, in *The UFO Invasion: The Roswell Incident, Alien Abduction, and Government Coverups*, ed. Kendrick Frazer (Amherst, N.Y.: Prometheus Books, 1997), pp. 254–55.

48. J. D. Brady, ed., *A Manual of Exorcism, Very Useful for Priests and Ministers of the Church* (New York: Hispanic Society, 1975), pp. 21, 36.

49. Ibid., pp. 58–59.

Chapter 8

Here Come the Flying Saucers!

FLYING SAUCERS AND FRISBEES: A PSYCHOPATHOLOGY OF EVERYDAY PARANORMAL EFFECTS

*I*n *principio erat* . . . Before any appearance of a currently "classic" ET portraiture—which itself constitutes an iconographic typology birthed by a sensational media event, the Hill abduction, that spawned instant visual celebrity now securely placed late in 1966—there had first to appear the extraterrestrials' "flying saucers." Those outer-space vehicles provided the necessary physical means by which hitherto unknown extraterrestrial biological entities (EBEs) initially descended to earth in order to pose for their innumerable postmodernist portraits (see figs. 1, 4, 5, 15–22). By our reckoning a worldwide phenomenon now well over a half-century old, the "UFO" is today the most blatant manifestation of a worldwide "occult explosion."[1]

The dating of the terminology is precise; in 1957 the U.S. Air Force adopted "Unidentified Flying Object" as the phrase to designate its "Project Blue Book" investigations of such anomalies, and as such this research was stridently demanded by a fearful American public. According to Curtis D. MacDougal, a skeptical historian of modern journalism, since "UFO fits nicely into any headline, it has survived."[2] However, according to the way it is popularly employed, the term "UFO" seems more than just a bit misleading. As it now stands, "UFO" literally refers to any thing ("object") seen "flying" (or even stationary) in the air; hence, a UFO is *anything* situated *anywhere above* the earth's surface. Any given UFO is, simply put, anything to which any given casual viewer (even the rare kind with 20/20 vision) was not immediately able to assign a plausible, mundane identity. Given that sense, then a more accurate— meaning much less emotionally provocative—designation would be "MFO," or "misidentified and fugitive observations." To paraphrase Freud, we will now deftly deal with the "psychopathology of everyday paranormal effects" (PEPE).

The PEPE syndrome is well nigh inescapable; again, as you well know, reported sightings of UFOs, typically "documented" with murky photographs, are standard fare today in the news racks situated next to the checkout counters in supermarkets. Worse, the self-inflicted Heaven's Gate holocaust, a voluntary *Shoah* for the cultic Gentiles, demonstrates the extreme, even lethal, potential effects arising from an obviously universal, and enduring, emotional appeal attaching to UFOs and ETs. Still, the collective dementia has some contextual sense to it. Toward the end of World War II, the public's attention had been captured by the new technology of jet planes and rockets, particularly the V-1 and V-2 weapons introduced by the ever-inventive Germans. Slightly later, that is once the first "flying saucers" were actually seen by earthlings in 1947, they were immediately identified as invaders, perhaps from the USSR but more likely from Mars, the archetypal home of extraterrestrial transgressors. This idea was given literary sanction a century ago in H. G. Wells's proto–science fiction novel, *The War of the Worlds* (1898). Given the superior acrobatic qualities commonly attributed to these celestial vehicles since 1947, their pilots were obviously harbingers of a technologically superior, hence an *extra*terrestrial, civilization. Obviously so, that is, if you subscribed to the UFO program.

Still, from the very outset, the post-Wells UFO experience was (and still is) dubious at best.[3] It all began on June 24, 1947, when civilian pilot Kenneth Arnold, intently searching for a downed military transport, reported seeing nine objects swiftly moving in the skies over Mount Rainier in the state of Washington. These, he distinctly stated, had "wings" and looked like "boomerangs," and he specifically added that their mode of flight was "erratic, *like a saucer* if you skip it across the water." By June 27, an Associated Press reporter had conveniently edited—and twisted— Arnold's original statement to make them represent "1,200-mile-an-hour *Flying Saucers*" (my emphasis), a term never found in Arnold's account. The original media epistle to the people went like this:

Nine bright, saucer-like, objects flying at "incredible speed" at 10,000 feet altitude were reported here today by Kenneth Arnold, Boise, Idaho, pilot who said he could not hazard a guess as to what they were.

Arnold, a United States Forest Service employee engaged in searching for a missing plane, said he sighted the mysterious objects yesterday at three P.M. They were flying between Mount Rainier and Mount Adams, in Washington State, he said, and appeared to weave in and out of formation. Arnold said that he clocked and estimated their speed at 1,200 miles an hour.

Inquiries at Yakima last night brought only blank stares, he said, but he added he talked today with an unidentified man from Utah, south of here, who said he had seen similar objects over the mountains near Ukiah yesterday,

"It seems impossible," Arnold said, "but there it is."[4]

Arnold's sighting was later criticized by other experienced pilots; perhaps, they said, he had merely seen reflections cast upon the cockpit window by his instrument panel; that he had stared too long into the sun; had become dazzled by snowblindness while painstakingly searching for the downed craft among the still frozen Cascade Mountains. Disgusted, Mr. Arnold was later heard to exclaim, "Believe me, if I ever see again a phenomenon of that sort in the sky, even if it's a one-story building, I won't say a word about it!" Henceforth, what people "saw" in ever-increasing abundance was a flat, circular artifact, the one that had been verbally shaped by the media—a "flying saucer"—and *not* what Arnold had said *he* saw. To the contrary, he reported distant, hence esentially shapeless, erratically skipping, luminous bits moving up and down in squadron-like formations. I have myself seen these optical phenomena. But I had also recognized them to be refracted light reflections caught on the curved, plastic cockpit of a single-engine plane piloted by a friend of mine. Since my sightings have never been broadcast by the mass media, the standard, flat and circular, "flying saucer" format continues to spawn "sightings" to this day. Accordingly, its strictly earthbound cultural source—in the mass media—is obvious to all but the True Believers.

No matter: on July 9, 1947, the Associated Press wire service broadcast a complementary anecdote, which was even picked up as a headline story by the prestigious *London Times*: "Army Air Force Captures *Flying Saucer* in Roswell Region." Although still wanting definitive illustration, the iconographic die was cast. Starting with the mythic Roswell incident in exotic New Mexico, henceforth in order to be considered newsworthy a flying saucer must crash. So doing, it would then deposit its crew on *terra firma*, preferably in a desert wasteland. After their forceful descent, the ETs became increasingly aggravated (perhaps due to alien "road rage"), thus they were ever more prone to abduct and/or molest mostly reluctant earthlings. Oddly, as viewed in retrospect, it took the ETs two decades to reach that piqued point. As we now know, that happened in 1961, when they nabbed Betty and Barney Hill. Only after 1966, when the Hill book became a paperback best-seller, did UFOnauts become full-time "abductors."

Rather suddenly in 1947, the UFOs had also became *visual celebrities*, media stars. On August 19, a Gallup poll revealed that by then 90 percent of Americans knew about the flying saucers, but (alas) few had even heard of the inauguration of the momentous Marshall Plan allowing for the postwar reconstruction of Europe.[5] Following soon after the initial Arnold report, flying saucer sightings reported by other excited sky-voyeurs quickly filled the newspapers.[6] However, since these sightings were never verbalized in the shape of Arnold's original (but tenaciously unreported) boomerang shape with wings, seldom, if ever, has the power of suggestion and the influence of the mass media been so convincingly demonstrated and historically documented. In fine, they imposed the canonical saucer format: *À bas les boomerangs à l'aile! Vivent les soucoupes volantes!* Let me further document, even quantify statistically, this larger observation about how the mass media shapes visual perception and its canonic (mis)interpretation. As reported by Patrick Huyghe:

> Prior to 1987, when Whitley Strieber's *Communion* and Budd Hopkins's *Intruders* were published in England, less than a quarter of the [ET] entities reported in Britain's abduction cases were of the small, bald-headed entities. But after the books had appeared there, more than half of the cases involved the "American standardized alien," as Jenny Randles calls it. Because American abduction cases get more publicity than any other such cases, it seems as if the image of the Gray [figs. 1, 4, 17–21, 29] has been more or less imposed on the rest of the world as the standard alien type.[7]

Similarly, before the definitive publication of Pacheco's *Arte de la pintura* in 1649, there was much less iconographic stability in plentiful painted visions of the airborne, and clearly superterrestrial, *Immaculata*, another emotionally provocative entity who was once frequently observed to be hovering in the sunny skies over southern Spain (see chapter 10; fig. 35).[8]

Unimpeachable, and unquestionably plentiful, physical evidence attesting to the emotional grip of the *saucer* (versus "boomerang") UFO shape in the American consciousness is found on a truly banal level. I refer to the Frisbee, an omnipresent airborne toy which every American youth must have flung at one time or another; doing so, one strikes an attitude like that pose seen in Myron's *Diskobolos* (circa 450 B.C.E.; fig. 29), so proving that Frisbees are almost as ancient as Erich von Däniken's "ancient astronauts" (as described in chapter 10). A brief inquest into the history of the Frisbee provides further proof for an intimate symbiosis operating between popular and commercial culture, and between most things deemed extraterrestrial and complementary, strictly earthbound, money matters. It all started in a strictly pragmatic and wholly terrestrial fashion. In the 1870s, William Russell Frisbie was the proprietor of the Frisbie Pie Company of Bridgeport, Connecticut, and his bakery carried a line of homemade pies vended in circular tin pans embossed with the family name. Sailing the empty pie-pans is known to have been a popular diversion among students at Yale University, not far from Bridgeport, and they fittingly called their flying artifacts "Frisbies."

Operating eighty years later, far away and without any knowledge of the much earlier airborne precedent in Connecticut, a Californian, Walter Frederick Morrison, came up with an idea for a possibly profitable product. Like so many others of his generation, young Morrison had long been intrigued with the possibility of alien visitors from outer space and he was especially fascinated by their widely publicized flying saucers. He cleverly devised a lightweight metal toy disk (later made of plastic) so that its erratic flight patterns would mimic those characterizing UFOs he had seen in science fiction movies copiously produced in Hollywood since the early 1950s (further discussed in chapters 9 and 14). With his prototype disk in hand, Morrison teamed up with the Wham-O Company of San Gabriel, California. On January 13, 1957, the first "Flyin' Saucers" debuted on the West Coast. To expand sales nationally, Wham-O's marketing team toured Eastern college campuses, generously distributing free plastic UFOs. On the Yale campus the team interviewed students flinging pie pans according to their venerable local tradition, and it was soon discovered that their metallic craft were called "Frisbies" and their lawn game "Frisbie-ing." Callously ignoring the Bridgeport bakery, Wham-O pirated the name, and in 1959 made it (with slight revision) into their own trademark, "Frisbee."9

Thereafter, the number of UFOs to be seen nationally expanded in an exponential fashion, particularly in places with broad grassy slopes and energetic youth. It all seems a manner of historical timing. In 1947, when pilot Kenneth Arnold reported seeing "boomerangs," the public was ready for a different shape, the *soucoupe volante*, thereafter to be successfully marketed as the "Frisbee." Half a century later, due to the ubiquity of the Nike Inc. trademark (the one dubbed the "Swoosh"), now a distracted postmodernist airbus driver would probably be more inclined to see his UFO adversary reshaped as a "boomerang." Such MFO perceptions, all just so much PEPE, seem to run, even jog, in cycles.

THE UFO SIGHTINGS OF 1896–1897

It is a demonstrated fact that UFOs were not always *saucer* shaped in America. An eccentric collector of haphazardly assembled aprocrypha, Charles Fort (1874–1932), specialized in finding citations of strange celestial sightings published in his lifetime, including reports of luminous, even disk- or torpedo-shaped, proto-UFOs reportedly seen between 1838 and 1916.[10] Later, in the 1950s, his obsessive research was eagerly seized upon by UFOlogist pioneers who (no surprise this) named his odd bits and pieces flying saucers, and Fort's heterogeneous data was then (posthumously) even used to prove their thesis for an "extraterrestrial" origin of UFOs.[11] Now also forgotten is the fact that 1947 was not, after all, the year of the UFOs' first stridently media-driven epiphany in American skies; that happened as early as 1896. (Surprise.) This historical example usefully demonstrates the truth of the old aesthetic axiom holding that "form follows function." In this case however, the "form" clearly has nothing to do with aerodynamic logic, boomerang versus saucer, rather it reveals its true "function" as an emotionalized artifact shaped within a time-specific, cultural preconditioning. Between November 1896 and May 1897, thousands of Americans, from coast to coast, claimed to have observed an "airship."[12] This anomalous perceptual pseudoevent was then called the "Great Airship Wave," and it antedates the authentic airborne achievement of the Wright Brothers by five years.

Rather than being even remotely sauceroid in form, the craft—an "airship"—seen by thousands of Americans from November 1896 to May 1897 was typically described as being cigar- or torpedo-shaped, having wings and/or propellers and often an attached undercarriage, evidently providing something like a crew space (see fig. 28). *Nomen est omen*: verbalization fixes mindset. In 1896, "air ship" makes perfect sense: a *ship* has propellers and is torpedo-shaped, except now it is seen up there, in the *air*. Contemporary illustrations published in the popular press are another example of "ekphrastic artwork," that is, they derive wholly from verbal accounts provided to newspaper reporters, and later to their staff draftsmen, by the self-described eyewitnesses. Here is one such account, provided in 1897 by Mr. Alexander Hamilton, a U.S. congressman from Kansas, also describing the "jabbering" and "hideous" alien crew:

We were awakened by a noise among the cattle. I arose, thinking that perhaps my bulldog was performing some of his pranks but, upon going to the door, I saw to my utter astonishment an airship slowly descending upon my cow lot, about forty rods from the house. Calling my tenant, Gil Heslip, and my son Wall, we seized some axes and ran to the corral. Meanwhile, the ship had been gently descending, until it was not more than thirty feet above the ground, and we came within fifty yards of it. It consisted of a great cigar-shaped portion, possibly three hundred feet long, with a carriage underneath. The carriage was made of glass or some other transparent material. It was brilliantly lighted within and everything was plainly visible—it was occupied by some of the strangest beings I ever saw. They were jabbering together, but we could not understand a word they said. Every part of the vessel which was not transparent was of a dark reddish color. We stood mute with wonder and fright, when some noise attracted their attention and they turned a light directly upon us. Immediately on catching sight of us, they turned on some unknown power, and a great turbine wheel, about thirty feet in diameter, which was slowly revolving below the craft, began to buzz and the vessel rose lightly as a bird. . . . Every time I would drop to sleep, I would see the cursed thing, with its big lights and hideous people. I don't know whether they are devils or angels, or what; but we all saw them, and my whole family saw the ship, and I don't want any more to do with them.[13]

Perhaps not so surprising is the fact that the newspaper illustrations published in 1896–1897 depicting this distinctively cigar-shaped space-craft closely resemble drawings published much earlier, namely of Henri Giffard's steam airship, which actually flew in 1852, and an airship called *La France*, pictured in the media around 1884.[14] As Robert Bartholomew explains, "In terms of the socio-psychological expectations of the era, most Americans possessed at least a general idea of how an airship and its occupants *should* appear," and he cites various widely publicized (but ultimately abortive) attempts to make "airships" earlier in the 1890s. Many would-be inventors then even went so far as to obtain patents, also illustrated, for their planned skycraft. Bartholomew also emphasizes the essential role played in the event by "sensationalistic 'yellow journalism' that typified the period just prior to and encompassing the sightings," also coinciding with the beginning of a war (with Spain).[15] The same observation holds true for a much later era, 1947 rather than 1897, when it seemed that another war (with the USSR) was imminent.

For instance, on November 1, 1896, the *Detroit Free Press* reported that in the near future a New York inventor would construct and fly an "aerial torpedo boat." Sixteen days later, the *Sacramento Bee* printed a telegram from a New York man claiming that he and two friends would soon board an airship of his invention and fly toward California. Not surprisingly, the first sightings of a (nonexistent) airship were recorded soon afterward around Sacramento. But you did not have to be a Californian to be privileged to witness such clearly extraordinary celestial phenomena. Here is a report of a typical sighting, reported from Aurora, Texas, and dated April 17, 1897. The UFO-like object, it was said, "sailed over the public square and when it reached the north part of town, collided with the tower of Judge Proctor's windmill, and went to pieces with a terrific explosion, scattering debris over several acres of ground, wreaking [sic] the windmill and water tank and destroying the judge's flower garden." This news item also includes one of the first reports of an ET, even including details of a Roswell-like spacecraft "built of an unknown metal." According to the folks in Aurora, the pilot of the ship, who "was not an inhabitant of this world," had died in the accident:

> Papers found on his person, evidently the records of his travels, are written in some unknown hieroglyphics, and cannot be deciphered. This ship was too badly wrecked to form any conclusion as to its construction or motive power. It was built of an unknown metal, resembling somewhat a mixture of aluminum and silver, and it must have weighed several tons. The town today is full of people who are viewing the wreckage and gather specimens of strange metal from the debris.[16]

Just as was to prove the case half a century later in Roswell, New Mexico, alas, no trace remains today of the mysterious "specimens of strange metal from the debris" supposedly collected in abundance by the eager crowd. A century later, eager UFOlogist pilgrims still rummage around in Aurora desperately seeking celestial crockery; formidably armed with modern metal detectors, they endlessly prospect for outerspace debris that never seems to turn up. One wonders why. No matter; decades later, industrious researcher Robert Bartholomew has collected more than 1,000 separate airship-related newspaper stories, and he now estimates that the number of alleged individual sightings a century ago might be as many as 100,000. At least 80 percent of these sightings were reported to have occurred at night. Some of these eyewitnesses even claimed to have conversed with the proto-astronauts. Perhaps not coincidentally, this was also a period of mass unemployment. Back then, a lot of people had time on their hands, and not much else to occupy their fertile imaginations; between 1893 and 1897, the number of the jobless rose to two million.

The close encounters got even closer; now earthlings sometimes met, even conversed, with the UFO pilots. Where did they come from? Back then, one's best guess was Mars. American astronomer Percival Lowell (1855–1916) had looked hard and often at the distant, red planet. He looked so hard that he even saw "canals" crisscrossing its pitted surface. His theories of intelligent Martian life-forms, the kind that construct hydraulic systems even grander than the ones soon to be erected around Los Angeles, attracted much public attention. So, obviously, Martians were the ET astronauts back in 1897. Here is the picturesque account of a pioneering run-in with aliens that antedates, by seventy years, the Barney and Betty close encounter. The trailblazing "experiencer" was Mr. W. H. Hopkins (perhaps a relative of Budd Hopkins), and it really happened (so he said) near Springfield, Missouri, in April 1897. As he then eagerly told an equally eager newspaper reporter, also including an erudite art-historical reference point:

> Near the [UFO] vessel was the most beautiful being I ever beheld. She was rather under medium size, but of the most exquisite form and features, such as would put to shame the forms as sculptured by the ancient Greeks [evidently in the manner of the Maenads shown in fig. 23]. She was dressed in nature's garb [i.e., buck-naked] and her golden hair, wavy and glossy, hung to her waist, unconfined excepting by a band of glistening jewels that bound it back from her forehead. . . . In one hand she carried a fan of curious design that she fanned herself vigorously with, though to me the air was not warm and I wore an overcoat. In the shade of the vessel lay a man of noble proportions and majestic countenance. His hair of dark auburn fell to his shoulders in wavy masses and his full beard of the same color, but lighter in shade, reached to his breast. He also was fanning himself, as if the heat [in Missouri] oppressed him.
>
> I tried by signs to make them understand I meant no harm. Finally his face lighted up with pleasure, and he turned and spoke to the woman. She came hesitatingly forward. I took her hand and kissed it fervently. The color rose to her cheeks and she drew it hastily away. I asked them by signs where they came from [and they pronounced a word that] sounded like "Mars." I pointed to the ship and expressed my wonder in my countenance. He took me by the hand and led me towards it. In the side was a small door. I looked in. There was a luxurious couch [a Victorian prefiguration of the austere gynecological exam tables of the Reagan era]. . . . I felt the vessel begin to rise, and I sprang out, and none too soon, for the vessel rose as lightly as a bird, and shot away like an arrow—out of sight. The two [ETs] stood laughing and waving their hands at me.[17]

Although himself acknowledged the patriarch of yellow journalism, even William Randolph Hearst felt constrained (in the *San Francisco Chronicle*, December 5, 1896) to decry that "'fake journalism' [which] has a great deal to answer for, but we do not recall a more discernible exploit in that line than the persistent attempt to make the public believe that the air in this vicinity is populated with airships."[18] All such stories, he concluded, were "pure myth"—and that was just before the biggest mythic outbreak of all! When that did break, between 1897 and 1898, typically the reports described either a craft with a large oblong or egg-shaped main structure with birdlike wings or, for the second archetype, one saw a spaceship with a large central portion to which were attached propellers or fanlike wheels (see fig. 28). Both types were propelled by some sort of motor and often were equipped with powerful searchlights.

To us sophisticated and technologically hip postmodernists, the engineering aspect has to seem quaint and picturesque, old-fashioned, *rétardaire*. As Bartholomew concludes, "What people claim to observe and experience are reflections of popular social and cultural [also technological] expectations of a particular era."[19] Alas, a century ago, the quaintly cumbersome craft never flew; they never really happened. I have presented the 1897 sightings, including a deliciously close encounter, as a perceptual role model for what would massively transpire beginning in 1947, the so-called (since 1972) UFO experience. Another forgotten iconographic offshoot of the *fin-de-siècle* UFO sightings needs be mentioned: the first cinematically depicted outer-space alien, a lunar inhabitant (or lunatic), appeared in Georges Méliès's short film, *Le voyage dans la lune* (1902). Since then, of course, ETs are standard fare in the movies. (See figs. 9–15, 17–19.)

A CONTEMPORANEOUS REINVENTION OF HYSTERIA BY FRENCH SCIENTISTS

For this, the first widely publicized appearance of "UFOs," bringing with them even a hieroglyphic-bearing "ET" (*mais les deux bien avant la lettre*), there is an interesting historical context: the contemporary scientific reinvention of *l'hystérie*. The American aerial sightings happened soon after Dr. Jean-Martin Charcot (1825–1893) had identified "hysteria" as a physical illness caused by a hereditary defect or traumatic wound in the central nervous system giving rise to epileptiform attacks. The master and his pupils, especially Pierre Janet (1859–1947), became interested in the practice of hypnotism, which at that time was considered in a class with black magic and other such dubious arts.[20] Charcot was a distinguished neurologist who held an appointment as visiting physician at the Salpêtrière, a large Parisian hospital for the insane. Charcot was a flamboyant personality as well as a rugged individualist, and he intensely pursued his investigations into the mental states of his disturbed patients by means of hypnosis. He persisted in his mission, despite adverse criticism from his more conservative colleagues. To his surprise, Charcot discovered that a perfectly healthy arm could be rendered paralyzed or anesthetic by means of suggestions given during the hypnotic sleep. But of even greater importance was the finding that many of the hospitalized patients' symptoms could be temporarily alleviated by the same method. Occasionally a "paralyzed" arm or an "anesthetic" leg could be permanently cured by an intensive series of hypnotic treatments. Without knowing the deeper significance of his discoveries, Charcot had stumbled upon one of the greatest medical discoveries of all time, namely, that physical symptoms and *organic disorders can be caused by wholly psychological factors*—such as was eventually worked out in detail by Janet.

Before its professional rehabilitation by Charcot, hypnosis had been long since discredited, particularly by the exhibitionism of Franz-Anton Mesmer (1733–1815) and his often lurid experiments with "animal magnetism."[21] As Charcot now argued, even though it presented an indispensable diagnostic tool, the capacity to be hypnotized was itself a sign of hysteria. In well-attended exhibitions staged at La Salpêtrière, Charcot's assistants would adroitly hypnotize women diagnosed as hysterics. So diagnosed, and once put under hypnosis, they displayed properly "hysterical" symptoms. A Swedish doctor, Axel Munthe, recalled:

> Some of them smelt with delight a bottle of ammonia when told it was rose water, others would eat a piece of charcoal when presented to them as chocolate. Another would crawl on all fours on the floor, barking furiously when told she was a dog, flap her arms as if trying to fly when turned into a pigeon, lift her skirts with a shriek of terror when a glove was thrown at her feet with a suggestion of its being a snake. Another would walk with a top hat in her arms, rocking it to and fro and kissing it tenderly when she was told it was her baby.[22]

The results of such outlandish exhibitionism, which Charcot dubbed manifestations of *la grande hystérie*, were photographed by his assistants, particularly Paul Régnard and Albert Londe, and the stagy results were appropriately called *les attitudes passionnelles*, and bore such provocative subtitles as "Amorous Supplication," "Ecstasy," and "Eroticism."[23] The eventual result was another art-historical artifact, the three-volume *Iconographie photographique de la Salpêtrière* (1887). Hypnotism was very much in the popular mind, especially after the appearance of George Du Maurier's best-selling novel *Trilby* (1894), later made into a great hit play of the *fin-de-siècle* stage. Trilby, a gorgeous artist's model, had suffered from crippling migraine headaches, cured by the mesmerist manipulations of the Jewish musician Svengali, a riveting type with piercing black eyes (rather like those attributed to postmodernist ETs). Svengali's mesmerizing ministrations also made Trilby into a world-class concert singer. Thanks to hypnosis, Trilby became a "celebrity," just as would Betty and Barney Hill some seventy years later; their hypotically induced misadventures were also made into a movie, but that one was significantly presented to the world as "nonfiction." (See figs. 17, 18.)

Even though one may suppose that the eager American journalists reporting the first native-born UFOs largely remained ignorant of the astute Gallic psychological *aperçus* regarding hysteria, which was nonetheless widely discussed in the European press, the timing does seem significant. As it appears, at that time hysteria was "something in the air," just like the mysterious American "airships." Also interesting is the fact that it was Charcot who had, in 1878, reintroduced hypnosis as a "modern" diagnostic instrument. He primarily used hypnosis to disclaim traditional religious interpretations of "hysteria" which had conventionally made the psychic disorder a sign of either diabolic possession or, alternatively, saintly ecstasy (as already discussed in chapter 6). As we have already read (particularly in chapter 2), hypnotism has more recently proven to be the most efficient way to induce opportunely "retrieved memories" of postmodernist close encounters with extraterrestrial abductors and/or gynecological investigators. Such is presently the stuff of paperback best-sellers, and its hypnotic byproducts need to be subjected to a systematic deconstruction (as will be executed in chapter 14).

In 1895, Sigmund Freud, who studied at La Salpêtrière between 1885 and 1886 and credited Charcot with establishing the legitimacy of hysteria as a disorder, even published his own *Studies on Hysteria*, as coauthored with Dr. Josef Breuer. The star exhibit of this anthology of case studies was "Anna O." (now known to be Bertha Pappenheim, 1859–1936). Beginning her treatment with Breuer in 1880, Anna O. was, in fact, to become the inventor of the "talking cure" of orthodox modern psychoanalysis. Appreciatively described by her Viennese hypnotists as possessing a "powerful intellect" and "great poetic and imaginative gifts," she was given to verbalizing elaborate hallucinations, none however including extraterrestrials (at least none described as such). Her mesmerizing physicians concluded that her "hysteria" represented a "creative" escape from the boredom and futility of her daily life; she was said to have "led an extremely monotonous existence." Under hypnosis, so we are told, Anna adroitly "brought numerous repressed memories to the surface." In effect, daydreams (with or without ETs) provided a substitute for the intellectual nourishment and attention she craved; her "stock of imaginative products" were the results of "an unemployed surplus of mental liveliness and energy." Her association with Breuer ended abruptly when she hallucinated that she was giving birth to her therapist's baby.[24]

Both writers and critics in the 1890s saw hysteria as a metaphor for the *fin-de-siècle* sensibility. A century later, postmodernism partakes of its own millenarian sensibility, what Elaine Showalter calls "hystories" (as further discussed in chapter 14). To conservative critics back then, hysteria was the *mal-de-siècle*, both a contemporary malaise and, more specifically, a sign of artistic degeneration. In 1892, Max Nordau, an Austrian doctor and journalist who had attended Charcot's lectures, called hysteria a central motive in contemporary avant-garde art. In his widely read polemic, *Degeneration*, Nordau denounced the elements of fantasy in contemporary writing:

> The hysterical subject does not consciously lie. He believes in the truth of his craziest inventions. The morbid mobility of his mind, the excessive excitability of his imagination, conveys to his consciousness all sorts of queer and senseless ideas. . . . A result of the susceptibility of the hysterical subject to suggestion is his irresistible passion for imitation, and the eagerness with which he yields to all the suggestions of writers and artists.[25]

A century later, the same argument would seem to hold for the often lucrative complicity between paperback writers and their hypnotized abductees: they, too, appear to entertain "all sorts of queer and senseless ideas." Nordau went on to put the problem into a specifically artistic context: "The physician . . . recognizes at a glance, in the *fin-de-siècle* disposition, in the tendencies of contemporary art and poetry, in the life and conduct of the men who write mystic, symbolic and 'decadent' works . . . the conflation of degeneracy and hysteria, of which the minor stages are designated as neurasthenia."[26] As in Europe in 1892, so, too, in neurasthenic postmodernist America.

Another burgeoning scientific idea a century ago was the broader notion of mass hysteria. At this time, Dr. Gustave Le Bon published his influential treatise on the *Psychologie des foules* (1895), soon after translated into English. His book popularized a theory of collective psychology based on the assumption that the "collective soul" of the mob (*la foule*) could be compared to the hypnotized mind, and that the mob leader functioned as the collective hypnotist. In effect, collective irrationality was viewed within a contagious-disease model. Any man in a crowd, said Le Bon, loses his individuality and acquires a part of the "crowd soul," and that *mentalité des masses*, being intellectually inferior and representing a kind of hypnotic regression to a prehistoric mental stage, typically manifests a kind of intrinsic malignancy.[27] Hysteria-charged mass rallies, to be later staged in Rome, Berlin, Moscow, Beijing, and elsewhere, and now all known to us from televised reenactments, all seem to confirm Le Bon's dire conclusions; so does the UFO craze of Le Bon's time (alas, not televised).

Such was the situation a century ago; such is, as it may be argued, the case presently with all those essentially "mystic, symbolic, and 'decadent' works" that profitably describe egregious visitations by outerspace aliens, so crafted to titillate and terrorize the postmodernist *mentalité des masses*. Other post–Le Bon examples of mass delusions particularly favored by Americans are equally sinister: Communist infiltration, moral witch-hunts, fictitious accounts of child abuse, cultic mass suicides, government conspiracies (organized by "men in black" who fly around in "black helicopters"), and so on, all as promoted by sensationalized documentaries, movies, tabloid accounts, and paperback books. In short, the technology of mass mental manipulation has improved markedly in the last century.

ATTACK! THE MARTIAN INVASION OF 1938

Back in 1897, as we just saw, the outer-space "airships" suddenly discovered to be cruising all over the continental United States looked suspiciously like contemporary earthling airships previously illustrated in the mass media (see fig. 28). Fifty years later, when the so-called flying saucers were commonly viewed by the general populace, hence became literally popular, it was—once again—often assumed that they came from Mars. This interplanetary zip code hypothesis was often advanced in post–World War II science fiction movies featuring the Frisbee-style spaceship vehicle. In the event, Mars was earlier made infamous as the home base of malicious extraterrestrial invaders by the *War of the Worlds* radio drama broadcast by Orson Welles in 1938. That widely publicized media pseudoevent caused the *first* great wave of modernist mass hysteria regarding extraterrestrial invaders, meaning the kind of

ETs that look decidedly unhuman, in fact mostly horrible and decidedly hostile. In retrospect, since this episode provides a classic model of a typically modernist attack of collective hysteria, the kind that is specifically generated by the modernist mass media, the bizarre details are certainly worth recounting. This is especially so since it provides a psychological template for all subsequent ET outbreaks, those beginning in 1947, and still very much with us.[28]

The radio show, as closely based upon *The War of the Worlds*, H. G. Wells's pioneering science fiction novel of 1898, aired on the CBS network on Sunday, October 30, 1938. It was planned as a Halloween special, something spine-tingling for the traditional night of hobgoblins and other demonic trick-or-treaters. This was a bleak year; in America, the Great Depression was still working its economic and psychological miseries. In the previous year, the Berlin-Rome-Tokyo Axis had been forged, and Hitler launched his successful *Anschluss* of Austria in March 1938. The Spanish Civil War was winding down; a Fascist victory was clearly in the offing. By September, *Der Führer* had forced the whole of Europe to capitulate to his demands in Munich. So emboldened, on *Kristallnacht*, November 9–10, 1938, ordinary Germans killed around 100 Jews and hauled off 30,000 more to concentration camps. Americans listened to all this on the radio, often to broadcasters giving "live" recitals, with appropriate sound effects, of the awful events occurring across the oceans, "right now."

Welles's dramatization began with a disclaimer: what was to follow was fiction, mere entertainment. Unfortunately, many people missed this crucial announcement; they were instead listening to another network in order to follow the comic antics of Charlie McCarthy and Edgar Bergen. When they belatedly tuned in to CBS, what they heard was typical "real" radio fare: a weather report and live dance music performed by "Ramón Raquello" in a classy New York night spot. Such idle diversion was dramatically interrupted by a "news bulletin" relayed from Chicago, given by a "Professor Farrel" of the "Mount Jennings Observatory" and immediately confirmed by "Professor Pierson" at Princeton University. According to the awed scientists, several explosions of incandescent gas had just been observed on the planet Mars. After some more music from Ramón, next came news of a huge flaming object which had just crashed to the ground at Grover's Mill, near Princeton in New Jersey.

As reported on the scene by the awestruck newsman "Carl Phillips," the object was a huge metallic cylinder. The interplanetary missile was emitting a humming sound; Carl reported that its end was being unscrewed. Monsters emerged from the craft; they were huge, with dark faces like wet leather and serpentlike, with bug-eyes. Specifically, they looked like "gray snakes," with skin that "glistens like wet leather." (Sound familiar? See figs. 13, 14.) Moreover, "the mouth is V-shaped, with saliva dripping from its rimless lips," and, most important, "the eyes are black and gleam." (Sound familiar? See figs. 15–22.) The ETs proceeded to zap the Jersey troopers with flamethrowers; the victims' terrified screams could be clearly heard. The American defenders were annihilated. By the time the inevitable commercial break came along, the entire United States had fallen to the Martians. The immediate result was national panic.

No section of the country remained entirely free from the terror inspired by the extraterrestrial invasion. In New York City there were thousands of calls to police precincts, radio stations, and newspapers. Switchboards became jammed. Mostly the callers wanted advice on how to get out of New York City before the Martians arrived. The *New York Times* alone reported 875 calls, one from as far away as Dayton, Ohio, requesting information as to exactly what time the world would end. There were some citizens in New York City who "saw" or "heard" the battle of the Martians and earthlings that was being waged in their neighboring state. A man equipped with binoculars reported that he could actually "see" the flames of the holocaust from his lofty vantage point on top of an office building. Another distinctly "heard" the bombs from aircraft falling upon New Jersey and was convinced the ETs were heading for Times Square. Another "heard" the swoosh of the Martian machines as they plummeted through the atmosphere to earth. In Brooklyn, a man called the police demanding that he be issued a gas mask; he had "heard" the distant sounds of the battle going on over in Jersey and believed a gas attack imminent. Half a dozen women, some with children, showed up at the West 47th Street station to ask where they might find sanctuary. Some of the bolder New Yorkers ran to street corners in hopes of witnessing exciting street battles between the warring extraterrestrial and terrestrial forces. Over thirty residents of Harlem rushed to police stations in person, and one especially imaginative denizen of the district swore to the officers that he "heard" the president of the United States announce that all citizens were supposed to flee the cities. In neighborhood churches, evening supplications were hastily changed to "end of the world" prayers when news of the invasion filtered into the little congregations.

Naturally, conditions were much worse in New Jersey. National Guard headquarters were swamped with calls from reservists asking where they were to report to be mobilized to repel the extraterrestrial invasion. At various points in Newark, persons had to be given sedatives and treated for shock and hysteria. In one section of the city, twenty families living in an apartment building perceived that a gas attack had started. Holding wet towels to their faces and gasping for breath, they summoned the police; an ambulance, three radio cars, and an emergency squad were dispatched to the stricken area. It took officials an hour to restore calm to the neighborhood. In Orange, an excited motorist with a car radio rushed into a cinema and shouted that New Jersey was being invaded; all fled in panic. In Jersey City, scores of excited persons had to be urged off the streets by policemen. Parents rushed to hospitals requesting that their children be released immediately so that they might be conveyed to a safer part of the country. (But where was that safe haven?) In Caldwell, New Jersey, a panicked parishioner rushed into the First Baptist Church and announced the impending destruction of the world by invading spacemen; the congregation began to pray for deliverance from the impending holocaust. Public communications systems were completely jammed by panic-stricken callers seeking information regarding the progress of the invasion or about conditions on highways leading out of the besieged state. Eventually, things got so bad that the New Jersey State Police put out reassuring messages over their teletype network, and every time there was a call at local newspapers and radio stations, telephone operators would just plug in and say, "It's only a radio show."

Throughout the South, panic was stirred by stories of the great destruction in New Jersey wrought by "meteors" or "planetoids" that had run afoul of the earth. In Birmingham, Alabama, and Richmond, Virginia, people gathered in the streets to pray. In Atlanta, Georgia, citizens told one another that a planet "bearing monsters" had struck New Jersey, killing up to seven thousand earthlings. In North Carolina, persons with relatives living in New Jersey called in tears to newspaper offices seeking information about casualties. In Asheville, five boys at Brevard College were so overcome by hysteria they lost consciousness. In Martinsville, Virginia, the guests of a newspaper publisher were informed that a "meteor" had struck New Jersey, "killing hundreds." In the more Fundamentalist sections of the South, there was widespread fear that the end of the world was at hand. Since this perception had led to widespread pleas for divine succor, one woman later remarked of the radio drama, "Well, if it didn't do anything else, it did make a lot of people pray." The Midwest also had its share of flooded telephone switchboards, and the Associated Press News Service received inquiries from points as far away as Los Angeles, Salt Lake City, and Beaumont, Texas. In Indianapolis, a hysterical woman ran into her church screaming the dreadful news from the East, demanding that her fellow worshipers be allowed to go home to die in the bosoms of their families; the holy services were speedily terminated. In Detroit, a motorist asked the police if it were true that New York and New Jersey were "conquered," and that invincible ET "hordes" were now marching west.

In the far west, much the same was happening. In Concrete, Washington, the city power system failed at that critical point in the radio drama when the towering ETs were described leaving their spaceships in New Jersey. For a time, Concrete was on the verge of panic: women fainted and men grabbed firearms and made preparations to flee with their families to nearby mountains. In San Francisco, an excited gentleman called the International News Service to tell them of details which were *not* in the broadcast; in his state of induced terror, he had actually "heard" reports of the disaster on various radio stations, ones which were not carrying the Welles broadcast. An elderly San Franciscan called a local newspaper for confirmation of the New Jersey disaster; when informed of its fictional nature, she inquired, "Oh, that's fine, but what are they going to do with those poor people from Mars?" Another Californian called police headquarters in Oakland, offering to do battle with the invasion forces: "My God!" he shouted, "Where can I volunteer my services? We've got to stop this awful thing!" In Los Angeles, women not only fainted but some terrified citizens actually did flee to nearby mountains, and, as reported in the *Examiner*, there was "wild excitement" and a flood of hysterical telephone inquiries.

Enough: you get the picture back in 1938. Now there is emerging a minor art-historical event due to the classic media pseudoevent. The infamous Wels-Welles "War of the Worlds" sci-fi novel and broadcast has recently given birth to a modernist work of art, a large piece of outdoor sculpture in gleaming metal, itself a symbol of resurgent civic pride. All this was told in a 1998 news dispatch from Britain:

> WOKING, England (Reuters)—There's not a great deal to celebrate in the sleepy southern English town of Woking, some might say. It does have the headquarters of the McLaren grand prix motor racing team and the Spice Girls once recorded here, but otherwise there's little to set it apart from any other commuter town. Apart from *The Martian*. Actually, it's quite a big Martian. Over 20 feet tall, it stands on three spindly legs with a look of, well, menace on what is probably its face. The creature is bathed in a unearthly light on this chill April night and hundreds of spectators gathered at its feet gasp as an eerie cacophony reverberates around the gray concrete of the council offices and multistory car park. . . .

It was in Woking, 100 years ago [i.e., 1898], that modern science fiction was born when a vast metal cylinder containing the first extra-terrestrial invaders [was said to have] landed on Horsell Common, not a mile from the center. After incinerating much of the Common, an artillery brigade and quite a few bystanders, the Martians constructed massive tripods from which to annihilate humanity with the aid of a deadly heat ray and an evil black smoke. Marching on London, 30 miles away, the invaders routed the capital, pausing only to coin the phrase "resistance is useless" and drink the blood of anyone who cared to disagree.

So now the descendants of those imaginary slain citizens of Woking gather to witness the local council's son-et-lumière commemoration of the centenary of H. G. Wells's classic *War of the Worlds*. Wells's elegantly restrained prose went on to become an all-time best seller, a celebrated 1930s radio con-trick by Orson Welles, and the inspiration for thousands of science-fiction writers, none of whom chose to base their work in Woking. The stockbrokers and software engineers of this bedroom community have contributed £50,000 in taxes to the creation of *The Martian*, as the chromed steel sculpture is imaginatively titled. For their money, they get the striking burnished tubular beast encircled by subterranean lighting, a live broadcast from the unveiling ceremony on local radio, and a few hours in the presence of TV celebrity Carol Vorderman.

Sculptor Michael Condron, whose earlier works include "Crankshaft" and "Virgin Cola Pump," had little in Wells' novel to base his work on, a typically vague metaphor for the tripods being "a milking stool bowled violently along the ground". Other obstacles to Condron's artistic aims included the red tape of building regulations. *The Martian* was classified as a highway structure and had to comply with the same safety standards as a road bridge. The upside is that Woking now has what is probably the country's only hurricane-proof space invader. . . . "*The Martian* will highlight Woking's profile as a centre of artistic innovation," local arts supremo Ian Eastwood said. There is perhaps a subconscious logic in this celebration of fictional genocide.[29]

As is obvious, by April 1998 the directors of the Woking Housing Council would have heard about the celebrated extraterrestrials who, due to their momentous landing near Roswell, New Mexico, had made, fifty years later, that sleepy farming town into a major tourist center, just as wearisome Woking will apparently soon also become (and profit from). Soon, as we may also presume, Roswell will commission another inspired extraterrestrial artwork from one of Mr. Condron's talented sculptural colleagues. I think that an equestrian statue cast in bronze of a victorious ET would look absolutely smashing in front of Roswell City Hall.

PICTURING EXTRATERRESTRIALS

UFOs AND CLOSE ENCOUNTERS REINVENTED FOR THE COLD WAR

Again the historian must be sensitive to the chronology of events: the full blown, characteristically late-modernist phase of saucer-shaped UFO apparitions dates from the late 1940s, meaning the Cold War. This was a postnuclear period in which the Western world became suddenly obsessed with security against all manner of often unspecified enemies; paranoia was in the air. As communism was then commonly labeled in the United States, it represented an awe-inspiring "international criminal conspiracy." Contemporaneous with the date assigned to a now-notorious "Roswell incident," in 1947 the CIA was founded. That year also gave birth to the classic conspiratorial governmental institution and, like Roswell, that often fearful entity is also very much still with us. In 1948 Congress issued *The Strategy and Tactics of World Communism*, a mostly paranoid polemic, and the next year George Orwell's *Nineteen Eighty-Four* was published; if you wish, Orwell's 1949 novel may also be considered the first primer of postmodernism. Shortly after, Sen. Joe McCarthy began his infamous "witch-hunts" of purported "commie" crypto-agents, and the Red Scare took off; by 1954, a cloud of terror blanketed the United States.[30] The collective paranoia of the age was signaled by its buzz words: *invasion, infiltration, subversion*, and *brainwashing*.

Propaganda, as so cleverly pioneered by Adolf Hitler (fig. 7), was the chief weapon of the Cold War. Like hypnotic trance, the aim of nationalist propaganda is to convince the subject by means of suggestion that he/she ought to believe certain things to be true and to behave in accordance with those induced beliefs. Neither the hypnotist nor the propagandist creates needs; rather, both appeal to already existing desires and motives inherent to their mesmerized subjects. They appeal to fundamental human motives: creature needs, security inadequacies, belonging, self-realization, and prestige (further discussed in chapter 11). Seemingly disparate phenomena, patriotism and ETs appear to fit the formula of those basic psychological needs.

The Cold War was unquestionably a scary period; in 1945 Hiroshima was carbonized in a nuclear holocaust. Rising speedily to the challenge, the Soviets exploded their first A-bomb in 1949; Americans retaliated with an H-bomb in 1954, and the USSR followed suit not long after with their own thermonuclear devices. Even worse for American pride was the war in Korea: we didn't win that one, nor the next one. Only in this period did the subliterary genre of science fiction figuratively take off, to the great profit of certain pulp-publishers and B-movie makers, and, of course, this kind of specifically populist *belles lettres* did pay considerable thematic attention to "extraterrestrials."[31] The chronology assigned to the so-called Cold War, beginning around 1947 and lasting until 1989, and then said to represent an implacable close encounter between "enemies" (them) and "friends" (us), exactly embraces both the genesis and full maturity of the widely reported UFO experience, which is often rightly linked to the paranoia triggered by this universal political-polemical context. That outer-space phenomenon has always been complemented with conspiracy theories; the Government is always "covering up the truth."[32] Up to the onset of the UFOs, people had never lived in an age of anxiety that had been so prolonged, and about which they had been able to do so little. Cold wars do not produce the explosive catharsis that the hot ones do, especially the ones we might occasionally win.

The mood of the era, the one when flying saucers first became fodder for the mass media, is easily documented. According to an Associated Press dispatch, as headlined in the *Chicago Sun* on July 8, 1947, meaning the *exact* moment when the later-to-become notorious "Roswell incident" supposedly transpired:

> After a hard Fourth of July weekend, the nation finds itself jittery over the subject of "flying saucers." Some people claim that they are jet-propelled and roar like mighty bombers. Others have them flying in formation, heading north. A gentleman in Denver says he saw the American flag painted on one of them. If true, this is certainly the most encouraging report to date. It will be merciful relief to many people who feared the disks might be of foreign origin. Human suggestibility being what it is, a lot of people didn't see what they saw. But in these days of Buck Rogers miracles, nobody can be sure that nobody saw anything.
>
> All this, of course, is just the beginning. One day the American people will wake to read in their morning papers that the Russians have developed an atomic bomb. It seems hardly premature to ask ourselves what effect this will have on the national digestion. Nor does it seem repetitious to point out that we have roughly five years to work out some form of international control of atomic energy. Otherwise this jittery world may face the possibility of a conflict in which Prof. Einstein estimates only one third of the human race will survive.[33]

The psychology of the Cold War was directly related to the UFO experience in 1958 by Carl Gustav Jung, a notable pioneer in modern psychological research. In the English version of his book, called *Flying Saucers: A Modern Myth of Things Seen in the Sky* (1959), Jung observed that what we are really dealing with are "visionary rumors," and these "are based essentially on an omnipresent emotional foundation, in this case a psychological situation common to all mankind." He then directly placed this condition of "emotional tension" within "the whole world," the kind then "suffering under the strain of Russian policies and their still unpredictable consequences." Throughout history, such circumstances have naturally produced "apparently inexplicable opinions, beliefs, illusions, visions, and so forth." Moreover, throughout history, "signs are seen in the heavens." Whereas, previously, the "menacing omens" were "meteors, comets, 'rains of blood,' a calf with two heads, and suchlike abortions," now they have become UFOs. Jung also cites the reports of George Adamski (as he will be quoted below), who believed that "recent atomic explosions on the earth . . . had aroused the attention of those so very more advanced [ET] dwellers on Mars or Venus, who were worried about possible chain reactions and the consequent destruction of our planet." The conclusion reached by Adamski and his ilk held, states Jung, that since earthling nuclear experiments "would constitute a catastrophic threat to our neighboring planets, their [ET] inhabitants felt compelled to observe how things were developing on earth." Jung mentions that in his time, 1958, oddly, "the UFOs neither land on earth nor show the least inclination to get into communication with human beings." Why is that? As given by Adamski and his space brethren, "the explanation [is] that these [ET] visitors, despite their superior knowledge, are not at all certain of being well received on earth, for which reason carefully avoid all contact with human contact," that is, until they met up with the likes of Betty and Barney Hill in 1961.

　　Jung again refers to an omnipresent fear factor (paranoia, if you wish) encouraging sightings of UFOs during the 1950s, when it seemed "that the earth is growing too small for us, that humanity would like to escape from its prison, where we are threatened not only by the hydrogen bomb but, at a still deeper level, by the prodigious increase in the population figures which give cause for serious concern." Then, as now, "living space is, in fact, continually shrinking and for many races the optimum has long been exceeded. The danger of catastrophe grows in proportion as the expanding populations impinge on one another." The perhaps natural result, since "congestion creates fear," is that mankind now "looks for help from extraterrestrial sources since it cannot be found on earth. Hence there appear 'signs in the heavens,' superior beings in the kind of space ships devised by our technological fantasy." Overall, we live in an age when modern science "makes things appear possible which, but a short while ago, would have been declared nonsensical. Consequently, the UFOs can easily be regarded—and believed in—as a physicists' miracle." Then, as now (especially after

September 11, 2001), "the present world situation is calculated as never before to arouse expectation of a redeeming supernatural event."[34]

At the height of the Vietnam imbroglio, the UFO experience became canonized in a book that seems to have exerted the same influence in its respective ideological zones as did once the *Catechismus ex decreto Concilii Trindentini ad Parochos* (1566) published some four centuries earlier.[35] The author of the official book of instruction for the postmodernist faithful—another "catechism"—was J. Allen Hynek, a gentleman with sterling scientific credentials who had been signed on by the Air Force to direct its "Project Blue Book" investigations of UFOs as long ago as 1949. After his dismissal from government service in 1967, Dr. Hynek went from being a trained astronomer, who had initially scoffed at the "flying saucer craze," to a kind of evangelist, the kind demanding "respectable scholarly study of the UFO phenomenon." In 1972 he published his detailed retort, fittingly entitled *The UFO Experience: A Scientific Inquiry*. This was the venue for his classic taxonomic breakdown of enigmatic alien close encounters, which is still very much with us. According to Hynek:

> *Encounters of the First Kind*. This category is the simple Close Encounter in which the reported UFO is seen at close range, but there is no interaction with the environment (other than trauma on the part of the observer).
>
> *Close Encounters of the Second Kind*. These are similar to the First Kind, except that physical effects on both animate and inanimate material are noted. Vegetation is often reported as having been pressed down, burned, or scorched. Tree branches are reported broken; animals are frightened, sometimes to the extent of physically injuring themselves in their fright. Inanimate objects, most often vehicles, are reported as becoming momentarily disabled, their engines killed, radios stopped, and headlights dimmed or extinguished. In such cases, the vehicles reportedly return to normal after the UFO has left the scene.
>
> *Close Encounters of the Third Kind*. In these cases, the presence of "occupants" in or about the UFO is reported. Here a sharp distinction must be made between cases involving reports of the presence of presumably intelligent beings in the "spacecraft" and the so-called contactee cases [like George Adamski, as quoted below].[36]

In the last (tertiary) category, Hynek paid much attention in 1972 to the Barney and Betty Hill encounter published in 1966, evidently taking it at face value[37]—but which we would now describe otherwise, that is, as valueless.

Since Hynek (now deceased) is so esteemed by UFOlogists, it should be mentioned that he had served as the well-paid consultant for the 1977 film *Close Encounters of the Third Kind*, the one that helped fix ET iconography in the popular consciousness (see fig. 19). At that time, he said that eyewitnesses (meaning the likes of Barney and Betty Hill; see figs. 16–18) had authoritatively described the UFO crewmen as being "four feet high, with large heads and rather spindly bodies." In 1980, Hynek even went so far as to characterize himself as "a latter-day Moses, leading the way toward an eventual scientific breakthrough," which (alas) he wouldn't live to see.[38] Now, thirty years after the appearance of Hynek's reported sightings of ET "occupants, in or about the UFO," we have an even better option, namely those especially dramatic "Close Encounters of the *Fourth* Kind"; these involve *direct contact* with ET. This newly canonized category of the UFO experience was described in 1995: "Personal contact between an individual or individuals is initiated by the 'occupants' of the spacecraft. Such contact may involve the transportation of the individual from his or her terrestrial surroundings into the spacecraft, where the individual is communicated with and/or subjected to an examination before being returned. Such a close encounter is usually of a one-to-two-hour duration."[39] If your dire experience matches this circumstantial description, then you, too, have had one: Welcome aboard!

The "fourth kind" were rare in Hynek's day; other than the Hill case, he could only cite five "cases" worth mentioning (none of which, alas, convince me), including the infamous April 1964 incident in Socorro, New Mexico, starring Lonnie Zamora.[40] Back in 1972, Hynek also felt sufficiently pressured to voice what may stand as the most intelligent explanation for why any rational and/or educated person would balk at paying devout attention to what I disrespectfully label as "MFOs." As he then argued eloquently:

> Either the whole phenomenon had to be "psychological" (an expression that was often used for want of a cogent explanation), or there was something behind the [UFO] phenomenon that no one wanted to admit. When the mind is suddenly confronted with "facts" that are decidedly uncomfortable, that refuse to fit into the standard recognized world picture, a frantic effort is made to bridge that gap emotionally rather than intellectually (which would require an honest admission of the inadequacy of our knowledge). Frenetic efforts are made either to contrive an ad hoc explanation to "save the phenomenon" or to discredit the data. When we are faced with a situation that is well above our "threshold of acceptability," there seems to be a built-in mental censor that tends to

block or to sidestep a phenomenon that is "too strange" and to take refuge in the familiar.

The history of science is replete with "explainings away" in order to preserve the status quo. Discovery of fossils of extinct species, pointing strongly to the concept of biological evolution, was met with many contrived attempts to demolish the fossil-fingers pointing unmistakably to Darwinian evolution. Many, too, were the pat explanations before facts finally demanded the acceptance of the theory of circulation of the blood, the heliocentric hypothesis, hypnotism, meteorites, disease-causing bacteria, and many other phenomena that are accepted today.[41]

I'll confess straightaway to my position: "psychological" (which will be discussed fully in chapters 11 and 14). By Hynek's high-minded standards, I guess I should, therefore, be dismissed as just another Luddite. Nonetheless, he did detail the scientific means and procedures by which, if properly carried out, even we reactionaries would—finally—become converted to the UFO cause. Here are his recommendations, as voiced way back in 1972:

> The objectives of the active program would be to obtain quantitative observations of the UFO phenomenon itself. Ideally, this would involve being present at the time of a sighting, equipped with cameras, spectrograph, tape recorder, Geiger-counter, infrared equipment, surveying equipment, etc., in order to get movies [or videotapes] of the event, photographs [unfaked, please] of the UFO forms, spectrograms to determine whether the radiation was comprised of continuous radiation or emission and absorption lines, accurate triangulation fixes to determine distances, and accurate measurements of landing marks, broken trees, etc. In short, such specialists would document quantitatively the event as it was actually happening. . . .
>
> Proper computerization of the data is absolutely essential in seeking patterns in UFO behavior, in establishing cross-correlations, and in seeking possible differences or similarities in behavior in different countries. This is not mere cataloguing and "busy work." The modern computer, used with appropriate software (a sophisticated non-procedural language), can establish meaningful correlations, *if* they exist. For example, of the hundreds of cases of reported automobile failure in the presence of a UFO, what do these cases have in common? In what ways do they differ? What failed first—the radio, the lights, the motor? And, when a UFO exhibits a sequence of colors, what is the most frequent color, the most frequent sequence?
>
> Such analyses, coupled with the active program of on-the-spot investigations of a truly scientific character, should accomplish the first objective of a positive UFO program: to establish the reality of the UFO

as a legitimate subject for further scientific study. If definite patterns and other correlations can be established for UFOs reported in many different countries by people with different levels of culture, the probability that such correlations happened by chance as a result of random misperceptions would be vanishingly small. The probability, therefore, that the UFO represents something truly new in science—new empirical observations—would be a virtual certainty.[42]

Those were Hynek's very specific recommendations, as advanced in 1972. Bravo! That makes perfect sense. Surprise: over a quarter-century later, and with the immense leaps in technological expertise one has since witnessed, nothing like this—scientific verification—has since appeared on the paperback scene. Asks the unrepentant postmodernist Luddite: after all this time, is it perhaps possible that there is *nothing* to verify after all? As far as I can see, the only physical materials at hand— and there is an abundance of *these*—which do serve to "document quantitatively" any and all "empirical observations" attesting to "the reality of the UFO [experience] as a legitimate subject for further scientific study" are merely these terrestrial artifacts: movies, TV shows, and a heap of paperback books dealing with the UFO experience. The *only physical evidence* is "extraterrestrial portraiture" (see figs. 1, 4, 5, 9–22). Other than these abundantly proliferating mass-media artifacts, marketable commodities cranked out by the infotainment industry, there is—let's face it—zero, zilch, goose egg, zip, none, nothing, *nada*.

One way or the other, all such contemporary events and things— UFOs or *Realpolitik*—had been labeled for us in the mass media as representing something "significant." Nonetheless, the *relative* level of their importance is, of course, predetermined by your (or my) audience culture: lowbrow (obsessed with flying saucers) or highbrow (cognizant of the Marshall Plan, et al.). In short and at bottom, and just as Walter Sullivan (formerly science editor for the *New York Times*) remarked back in 1969, like all the rest, "UFOs represent *a human phenomenon* that is far more important than any of us realize. Our attitudes and perceptions are conditioned to a degree far beyond our capabilities of direct observation." Indeed, like all the rest, most of current UFO phenomenology is due, states Sullivan, to "the role of the mass media in fixing our political, ethical, artistic, or racial attitudes. My thesis is that we have all been conditioned by the press, radio, and TV—by the general tone of our society—to a hierarchy of beliefs that include, for most of the population at least, the image [among others] of UFOs."[43]

Back in 1959, J. P. Chaplin had also remarked upon the indispensable role of the mass media in formulating a *Zeitgeist* particularly receptive to mass hysteria:

> In this day and age, once a halfway credible report of unusual import gets into circulation it is certain to be swept into our highly developed mass communication system. The Salem witchcraft craze [of 1692] remained localized partly because the means of spreading it were so slow. But in the case of the flying saucers, as was also true in the "Invasion from Mars" [broadcast in 1938], the excellence of a communication system cuts both ways. A report of a saucer in Oregon will reach every city in the United States within a few hours, and a really menacing report within minutes. Since mass hysteria, like individual hysteria, is largely a result of verbal suggestion, the report of one sighting generates additional sightings. Consequently, during the flowering of the saucers, unusual weather phenomena, astronomical quirks, balloons, balls of lightning, and such, became Unidentified Flying Objects. Until the era of the saucers they were simply reported as celestial freaks and quickly forgotten.[44]

John Sladek published in 1978 an instructive guide to what he called the "New Apocrypha," in which (among other apocrypha) he quoted a number of UFO reports, some excruciatingly funny. Referring to these, he disarmingly remarked, "Similarly, if I look up at an overcast sky at night, and see a glowing ellipse moving about erratically, my later description of it is likely to depend on whether I *expected* to see either a UFO or [just] a searchlight beam playing upon clouds. It is significant that, in the years when a great many people looked at the sky expecting UFOs, a great many people did see them."[45] As one again wonders, if we had instead initially decided to call them "MFOs" (misidentified and fugitive observations), how many folks would have chosen to see them? We will never know.

Twenty years ago and more, Sladek posed a series of embarrassing questions which, to date, still remain unanswered by the True Believers, namely:

1. Why have no saucers crashed and been found?
2. Where are they, when they aren't thrilling or menacing anyone? How can thousands or even millions of them have gone and come from this planet without their traffic being detected?
3. What possible purpose can they serve? Not to contact us (they have thrown away thousands of chances). Not to avoid us (since they are noticed so often). Hardly to stop bomb tests in any conceivable way. Hardly to study human behavior, since they ignore

large population centers to pow-wow with various people behind a dune or on an isolated mountain top.[46]

Similar questions have been raised more recently (1990) by Jacques Vallée. To the contrary of Mr. Sladek, however, Dr. Vallée (his degree is in computer programming) does incline toward a mystical interpretation of things: "I have been inspired by Teilhard de Chardin's gentle view of a great spiritual potential permeating the cosmos." So inclined, Vallée has expended much physical and psychic energy in investigating all manner of bizarre reports of alien contacts, even pursuing such apocrypha to the far ends of the earth (mostly the steamier parts of South America). Still, he raises, as did Sladek, some usefully provocative questions regarding the inherent absurdity of these materials. As he acutely observes:

> I have uncovered major contradictions between the extraterrestrial hypothesis (ETH) and many UFO reports, including "abduction" cases. . . . Careful analysis of the [ETH and UFO] reports shows that there are many more landings and "close encounters" than would be required for a survey of our planet. The reported interaction with the occupants of the objects is absurd and their overtly "scientific" experiments are crude to the point of being grotesque. The "medical examination" to which abductees are said to be subjected, often accompanied by sadistic sexual manipulation, is reminiscent of the medieval tales of encounters with demons. It makes no sense in a sophisticated or technical or biological framework: any intelligent being equipped with the scientific marvels that UFOs [are said to] possess would be in a position to achieve any of these alleged scientific objectives in a shorter time and with fewer risks. Those among the scientific community who have been openly skeptical of the entire UFO phenomenon (and they are in the majority) must be excused for stating that the reported contact is so absurd, and the conclusions of the believers so preposterous, that the alleged object must be an aberration (physical or psychological) in every case.[47]

Further on, he expounds even more details pointing to the inherent folly attending these apocryphal narratives, and such as they have been quoted here in detail (particularly as given in chapters 2 and 5). According to Vallée, "The extraterrestrial theory—which assumes that the UFOs are spacecraft piloted by beings from another planet who conduct a survey of the earth—contradicts at least five major facts," namely,

1. The total number of close encounters far exceeds the requirements for a sophisticated survey of our planet.

2. The appearance of the UFO operators is overwhelmingly humanoid; they breathe our air and display recognizable emotions. Not only does this make an extraterrestrial origin very dubious, but it implies that the operators are not making use of genetic engineering to optimize a space mission, as inter-stellar travelers presumably would under the extraterrestrial hypothesis model.
3. The reports regarding abductions display behavioral patterns on the part of the operators that contradict the idea of scientific, medical, or genetic experiments. Simpler, more effective methods are already available in earth-based science to accomplish all the alleged objectives of these Aliens.
4. The patterns of close encounters, contacts, and abductions are not specific to our century, contrary to what most American UFOlogists have assumed. In fact, it is difficult to find a culture that does not have a [legendary] tradition of little people that fly through the sky and abduct humans. Often they take their victims into spherical settings that are evenly illuminated, and they subject them to various ordeals that include operations on internal organs and astral trips to unknown landscapes. Sexual or genetic interaction is a common theme in this body of folklore.
5. Both the UFOs and their operators are able to materialize and dematerialize on the spot and to penetrate physical obstacles. The objects are able to merge together and to change shape dynamically.[48]

So far, the points raised by Vallée are wonderfully logical and, indeed, quite perceptive. But I fear I cannot subscribe to his final conclusion: "The reports are there; they continue to come from reliable [?], well-balanced observers. And they [therefore?] increasingly point to the existence of a genuine technology pursuing its own hidden agenda. . . . I propose to regard the UFO phenomenon as a physical manifestation of a form of consciousness that is alien to humans but is able to coexist with us on the earth."[49] Quite to the contrary, my conclusion is that if indeed there is "a genuine technology," then the "hidden agenda" propelling it is really that of the technologically advanced, postmodernist mass media and infotainment industry—and its agenda is scarcely hidden. The agenda is, in fact, called "making a profit." And, unquestionably, they do that very well. So doing, they betray a form of consciousness that is anything but "alien" to humans.

A VERY CLOSE ENCOUNTER WITH A UFO IN 1952

The "Red Scare" was largely an internal matter for the American political psyche. What the *whole* world has suffered from since the late 1940s was/is the specter of the mushroom-shaped cloud, the graphic logo of the age of total nuclear annihilation. It provides the understood subtext for the very *first* widely publicized close encounter between a mere human being and an awesome extraterrestrial creature. This transaction took place, so we were told, in 1952, and the hero of the self-told tale, a self-described "contactee," was one George Adamski (1891–1965). His was the first widely publicized close encounter, so naturally he was to become the first *UFO celebrity*.[50] His saga, *Flying Saucers Have Landed*, was first published in 1953; in paperback, it subsequently (naturally) enjoyed several reprintings, even various translations. It was made possible with the aid of a ghostwriter, Desmond Leslie, who later admitted: "When I co-authored *Flying Saucers Have Landed* with George Adamski, I had never met him." No matter: "My publisher and I both agreed that there was sufficient evidence, in his testimony that he had contacted a Flying Saucer on the ground, to warrant publishing his narrative. . . . Read, then, the following with an open mind and see whether the light of its teaching rings true."[51] Okay, with our minds fully opened to the breezes, let's have a go at that extraterrestrial enlightenment.

Here is how Adamski begins his transcendental adventure with the messengers of the Other Worlds: "It was about 12:30 in the noon hour on Thursday, 20 November 1952, that I first made personal contact with a man from another world. He came to Earth in his space craft, a flying saucer. He called it a Scout Ship. This took place on the California desert, 10.2 miles from Desert Center, toward Parker, Arizona."[52] Let us skip ahead (there is a lot of idle filler here) and transcribe Adamski's firsthand, eyewitness description of his "flying saucer"—the first one ever closely inspected (so we were told) by a mere earthling. The ET motions him to come with him and they "walked side-by-side toward the waiting ship," a "flying saucer." Its appearance was very much that of an artifact designed in the 1950s:

> It was a beautiful small craft, shaped more like a heavy glass bell than a saucer. Yet I could not see through it any more than one can see through the glass bricks that are popular [meaning back in 1952] in some of the newer office buildings and homes, which permit more light to enter than would solid walls. It was translucent and of exquisite color. However, that no mistake may be given here, let me say that I definitely do not believe this ship was made of glass such as we know it. It was a specially processed metal.

Although Adamski has a poetic turn of mind, he is scarcely a scientist. So this mysterious metallic craft partakes equally of "a soft, opaque, elementary substance" and of some stony material which "radiates prismatic colors in the presence of a light." Not surprisingly, it was his belief that "men on other planets" were "more versed in universal laws" than are mere earthlings. Rather than for verse, they were "using these [physical] laws for practical purposes." Particularly, these smart outer-space engineers "know how to bring the primary elements from the opaque stage to a translucent stage, yet practically indestructible in hardness, as is the diamond." As the De Beers gem company of South Africa will be delighted to know, "it was of such a [diamondlike] material that this space craft was made." The ETs' clever disregard of the elementary laws of physics explains how their craft become "so elusive to our eyes and even to cameras, yet [still] showing them on radar screens, which require a density of some kind to show up." Spot on, George!

His pseudoscientific ruminations having run their course, Adamski then puts his UFO in its landscape setting. The craft was observed by him to be "hovering above the ground, about a foot or two at the far side from me, and very near to the bank of the hill," and "that part of it closest to me, was a good six feet above the earth." Eschewing the contemporary earthling wheel arrangement, instead the space vehicle had a "three-ball landing gear." It was, however, affected by earthling weather effects, hence, "the gusts of wind were pretty strong and caused the ship to wobble at times." At such times, a truly picturesque effect was produced, and "the sun reflecting on the surface of the ship caused beautiful prismatic rays of light to reflect out from it, as from a smoky diamond." So visually stimulated, Adamski is moved to a more extended picturesque ejaculation, one worthy of a Turner, even William Blake:

> The splendor as it flashed its prismatic colors in the sunlight surpassed every idea [*à l'idée fixe*] I had ever had about space craft. A beautiful vision in actuality. The answer to many questions. A long-cherished hope realized . . . for there before me, silent in the desert stillness and hovering as if poised for flight, this ship of unearthly construction awaited our approach!
>
> The very realization of the experience I was having overwhelmed me . . . and I found myself speechless. No longer was I concerned with Earth alone. Rather, it was more like living in two worlds at the same time, and though I should live to be a hundred years of age, or more, I shall never forget the joy and the thrill of my first close approach to a Scout Ship from planet Venus—a sister to Earth.

His rapture consummated, next comes a physical description of the Venusian space craft, one worthy of *Jane's Fighting Ships*. It seems it had "a round ball at the very top that locked like a heavy lens of some kind. And it glowed." Below the lenticular globe, the top of the craft was "dome-shaped, with a ring of gears or heavy coil built into and encircling the side wall at the base of this domed top." This coil-like bricolage "glowed as though power was going through it"; moreover, there were "round portholes in the side wall," and these were "clear and transparent." We would have had a more extended description of the wondrous spacecraft but, for some unannounced reason, Adamski "did not walk around the ship."[53]

Now comes a verbal depiction of the breathtaking extraterrestrial featured in Adamski's alleged 1952 close encounter—but not, however, labeled as such (i.e., "ET"). This terminological lacuna is easily explained. Steven Spielberg's movie *Close Encounters*, making specific verbal reference to ETs, had yet to appear. That also happens to be the cinematic blockbuster which illustrated a wholly *different* kind of ET (fig. 19), a post-Adamski iconographic type since made *standard*. As it were, the medium (cinematic in this instance) becomes the message. As told half a century ago by Adamski, rather than looking like a pop-eyed, skinned cat—*our* postmodernist "Gray" standard (figs. 4, 5)—this is a gorgeous creature, decidedly stylish and anthropoid, even looking rather like a unisex hermaphrodite. Noting that the ET's "trousers were not like mine," Adamski explains them as being "in style much like ski trousers," and so he wonders why the extraterrestrial wore such alpine fashions "out here on the desert." While we never find out why, we do learn that the ET was scarcely bald, like our present-day feline model; au contraire, the anthropoid creature's "hair was long, reaching to his shoulders, and was blowing in the wind as was mine" (but presumably not at such an gorgeously extended length). Since Beatniks were a common sort of earthling at the time of Adamski's close encounter, he finds that such an *outré coiffure* "was not too strange, for I have seen a number of men who wore their hair almost that long."

Encouraged by what appears to be a contemporary Christlike appearance (see fig. 3) in the stylish extraterrestrial, Adamski then experiences "a friendly feeling toward the smiling young man standing there waiting for me to reach him." Accordingly, "I continued walking toward him without the slightest fear." From our jaded perspective, the kind arising from our cinematic saturation with ET iconography (see figs. 9–15, 17–19), Adamski seems a bit slow in grasping the exact nature of his world-historical encounter. Finally, however, he does twig on to what is actually transpiring: "Now, for the first time I fully realized that I was in the presence of a man from space—A HUMAN BEING FROM ANOTHER WORLD!" As is to be expected at such epochal moments, "I was so stunned by this sudden realization that I was speechless. My mind seemed to temporarily stop functioning." Once Adamski's brain resumes functioning, he falls into another thrilled rapture:

> The beauty of his form surpassed anything I had ever seen. And the pleasantness of his face freed me of all thought of my personal self.
>
> I felt like a little child in the presence of one with great wisdom and much love, and I became very humble within myself . . . for from him was radiating a feeling of infinite understanding and kindness, with supreme humility.[54]

As it turns out, many other earthlings had earlier reported their own close encounters with a beautiful and marvelous coifed being descending from heaven, and this superterrestrial being had long before been described as the kind of creature commonly said to inexorably radiate perceptions of infinite intuition, compassion, and, especially, "supreme humility." In this case, the prototypical spaceman was, of course, Jesus Christ (see again fig. 3).[55]

Alas, even though most likely raised as a Catholic in Poland, Adamski did not choose to make that obvious connection. It seems that he was caught in the tenacious grip of a "spell." In order to "break this spell that had so overtaken me—and I am sure he [the ET] recognized it for what it was—he extended his hand, [making] a gesture toward shaking hands," to which Adamski "responded in our customary [earthling] manner." But, endowed with "infinite understanding and kindness," the otherworldly being chose to act otherwise: "Instead of grasping hands, as we on Earth do, he placed the palm of his hand against the palm of my hand, just touching it, but not too firmly." This tactile encounter Adamski took "to be the sign of friendship." So what does extraterrestrial epidermis feel like? As was explained by our uniquely privileged earthling contactee, the "flesh in his hand to the touch of mine was like a baby's, very delicate in texture, but firm and warm." Besides having firmness and caloric emissions, "His hands were slender, with long tapering fingers like the beautiful hands of an artistic woman. In fact, in different clothing, he could easily have passed for an unusually beautiful woman" (so again calling to mind fig. 3).

Nonetheless, Adamski is adamant that "he definitely was a man." To prove his point, Adamski provides a detailed physical description, just like the kind you might give to a highway patrolman after your SUV has been abducted by an unknown perpetrator. In fact, a portrait of Adamski's ET could presently be drawn by any competent police artist using an "identikit":

> He was about five feet, six inches in height and weighed—according to our [earthling] standards—about 135 pounds. And I would estimate him to be about 28 years of age, although he could have been much older.
>
> He was round faced with an extremely high forehead; large, but calm, gray eyes, slightly aslant at the outer corners with slightly higher cheek bones than an Occidental, but not so high as an Indian or an Oriental; a finely chiseled nose, not conspicuously large; and an average size mouth, with beautiful white teeth that shone when he smiled or spoke.[56]

Only missing the beard, this is yet another ekphrastic portrait of the Christian Savior, even including the description of his skin tone as "an even, medium-colored suntan." And the absence of an essential Christological attribute, the soft beard (as shown in fig. 3), must also be explained by Adamski, "It did not look to me as though he had ever had to shave, for there was no more hair on his face than on a child's. His hair was sandy in color and hung in beautiful waves to his shoulders, glistening more beautifully than any woman's I have ever seen." Even though the hirsute hippies had yet to be invented, Adamski precociously thinks "how Earth women would enjoy having such beautiful hair as this man." And, like many youthful American males to come some fifteen years later, the hair of this Christ-like figure "was being blown by the winds." Finally, we are provided with the essential fashion statement, one clearly inspiring similar *haute couture* as seen some fifteen years later on *Star Trek*:

> His clothing was a one-piece garment, which I had a feeling was a uniform worn by space men as they travel, like Earth men in various types of work wear uniforms to indicate *their* occupations [his/its was "spaceman," *Homo coelestis*].
>
> Its color was chocolate brown and it was made with a rather full blouse, close-fitting high collar, much like a turtle-neck, only it did not turn down. The sleeves were long, slightly full and similar to a Raglan sleeve, with close-fitting bands around the wrists. . . .
>
> It was definitely a woven material, very fine, and the weave was different from all of our materials. There was a sheen about the whole garment.[57]

Following this diverting fashion statement, Adamski brightly asks, "Why are you coming to Earth?" His question was received "with gestures and facial expressions as well as mental pictures," all provided via "mental telepathy," and so "were all the questions I asked of him." George needed to repeat "each question at least twice to be sure that he understood the meaning of the words I was speaking." The ensuing dialogue must have looked like the "signing" done for the benefit of the hearing impaired. Nonetheless, the eloquent "expressions of his face and his eyes told me clearly when he understood, or when there was still any uncertainty in his mind as to what I was trying to ask." Ever solicitous, Adamski "also repeated the answers he gave me to be sure that I was understanding him correctly." By means of such subverbal mental picturing (later to be commonly called "mind scanning" by ET addicts in the 1990s), the ET "made me understand that their coming was friendly." More specifically, also more ominously, Adamski learns "that they were concerned with radiations going out from Earth." This admission introduces the fearful *leitmotif* of the imminent threat of nuclear holocaust, and this is clearly the "philosophical" heart of the matter, that is, back in 1952, when (such as we were told) it all really happened:

> I asked if this concern was due to the explosions of our [nuclear] bombs with their resultant vast radioactive clouds?
>
> He understood this readily and nodded his head in the affirmative.
>
> My next question was whether this was dangerous, and I pictured in my mind a scene of destruction.
>
> To this, too, he nodded his head in the affirmative, but on his face there was no trace of resentment or judgment. His expression was one of understanding, and great compassion; as one would have toward a much loved [earthling] child who had erred through ignorance and lack of understanding. This feeling appeared to remain with him during the rest of my questions on this subject.
>
> I wanted to know if this [nuclear radiation] was affecting outer space?
>
> Again a nod of affirmation.
>
> In this respect, let me say here, it has long been known by scientists of Earth that the cosmic ray, as it is called, is more powerful in outer space than it is in the Earth's atmosphere. And if this be true, is it not just as logical to assume that the radioactive force from the bombs being tested by nations of Earth could also become more powerful in space, once leaving the Earth's atmosphere? Logical deduction supports the statement of this space man.[58]

If nothing else, imbued with "logical deduction" Adamski is also adamant; he "persisted and wanted to know if it was dangerous to us on Earth as well as affecting things in space." Specifically, the gorgeous ET made him understand the immanent danger "by gesturing with his hands to indicate [mushroom-shaped] cloud formations arising from [nuclear] explosions." Following the production of many mimicked explosions by Adamski, the ET responds with an "affirmative nod of the head," and "he even spoke the word 'Yes' in this instance." It is also observed that the nuclear "cloud formations were easy to imply with the movement of his hands and arms." Subsequently, ET's verbal skills quickly improved, and "to express the explosions he said, 'Boom! Boom!'" Then, to further explain himself, "he touched me, then a little weed growing close by, and next he pointed to the Earth itself and, with a wide sweep of his hands and other gestures, that too many 'Booms!' would destroy all of this."[59] Indeed they would; fifty years later, we are still dreading their advent.

Adamski's outer-space man, a lovely being endowed with "great wisdom and much love," was both compassionate and really, *really* wise and philosophical; so are a lot of the ETs that have since landed in paperback publications. Nonetheless, Adamski's extraterrestrial *looks* different from the kind of ET with which we are now so familiar: his Venusian turns out to be a sun-tanned version of Jesus, wearing a nifty ski suit and sandals, but being beardless, he is not *quite* like Walter Sallman's modern devotional classic (fig. 3). In the event, here is some of the much needed wisdom that was originally bequeathed to us from outer space back in 1952 (or maybe it was really in 1953, when Adamski's book was published):

> Suddenly the thought came to me to ask if he believed in God?
>
> This he did not understand, for he was not familiar with the word "God." But I finally succeeded in getting the thought in my mind—he was watching me closely—of creating something, and then with the motion of my hand, symbolizing the vast sky, the earth and all, and speaking the words "Creator of All."
>
> After a few repetitions of this he understood my thoughts, for I am sure my gestures were not too good.
>
> And he said, "yes."
>
> I realized fully that he naturally wouldn't understand our names for things and to him God probably would be represented by some other word or name [perhaps Yahweh or Allah].
>
> But he made me understand, by elaborating a little longer with his gestures and mental pictures, that we on Earth really know very little about this Creator. In other words, our [earthling] understanding is shallow. Theirs [for being otherworldly] is much broader, and they adhere to the Laws of the Creator instead of laws of materialism as Earth men do. Pointing to himself, then up into space—which I understood meant the planet on which he lived—he conveyed the thought to me that here they live according to the Will of the Creator, not by their own personal will, as we do here on Earth.[60]

Since Adamski said it really happened, then common courtesy obliges us to say to him, "Yes, we do believe that what you say happened, really happened." Nonetheless, in case anybody remembers, all this physical description and high-minded chitchat suspiciously parallels both the *mise-en-scène* and even the actual dialogue belonging to a widely viewed science-fiction movie, *The Day the Earth Stood Still*, which appeared in 1951, two years *before* the publication of Adamski's once ubiquitous paperback (see fig. 9). Oddly (perhaps not), Adamski's ET also happens to look (and dress) very much like Michael Rennie, the earthling (actually an Australian) actor who played "Klaatu" in that widely viewed space opera. Adamski's noble-savage ET even talks like him, too; both tell the dumb earthlings to clean up their ecological act before the space brothers descend en masse and blow them all away. Such noble, save-the-earth discourse also characterizes many of the "Indians" (Native Americans) portrayed, since 1951, in movies in which White Folks (Hollywood producers and directors) collectively exculpate the genocidal sins perpetrated by earlier generations of White Folks. Now, they often do so, especially by dancing soulfully with wolves—and that demonstrably plays big at the box office.[61] So do ETs and UFOs. Ronald Story has recently put the literally incredible close encounter of the Polish American contactee into its proper context:

> To a Jungian, Adamski's tour of the space ship becomes a treasure trove of technological metaphors coinciding with virtually every principle of mystical truth found in the *philosophia perennis*—or Perennial Philosophy [aka occultism]—and in the Holy Bible: the all-seeing "Eye of God," warnings about idolatry, the importance of self-knowledge, warnings about egotism and self-seeking, respect for natural law and the need for harmony with nature, respect for the planet and other life-forms, unity and altruism, the reconciliation of opposites, microcosm and macrocosm, oneness with the universe, death and rebirth, the law of balance, karma and the Golden Rule, and cosmic understanding, in general.
>
> Examples of technological metaphors include: light as enlightenment; a giant lens as the "Eye of God"; the power of the space ship as the power of the mind; space travel as ascension; the secrets of space travel as the secrets of life; interplanetary travel as connecting the "gods" (for which the planets were named), which can be interpreted as integrating the potentialities within us; the speed of light as the speed of truth (or thought); and telepathy as a symbol of total honesty. . . . After a successful twelve years as a famous celebrity, Adamski died of a heart attack on April 23, 1965, in Washington, D.C.[62]

ETs AND THE MILLENNIUM ON OUR MIND

Back in 1978, before the full cultural impact of Spielberg's cinematic *Close Encounters of the Third Kind* made itself felt, John Sladek had observed how, "under the pressure of objective investigation, UFOs have been retreating, like unicorns, deeper into the forests of fantasy."[63] Wrong: the apparent retreat has since turned into a triumphal mass media advance, currently parading from Roswell, New Mexico, to Area 51, the ever more visited "secret" airbase near Las Vegas, Nevada, said to guard the earthling-abducted Roswell flying saucer.[64] The Roswell *trouvaille* supposedly challenges Sladek's earlier query, "Why have no saucers crashed and been found?"

As we have however learned since 1978, it *must* be real since that fifty-year-old artifact prominently appeared in a 1996 blockbuster movie, *Independence Day*, where the ETs turned the White House into toast ("Take that, Mr. President!"). The dialogue was tacky, the characters sub-clichés, and the noisy special effects represented no improvement on anything George Lucas did twenty years ago. No matter: a B-movie costing (only) *$70 million*, that emotion-stoking artifact became a money machine that eventually raked in *$800 million* at the box office.[65] But the record breaker of all times remains *Star Wars*: with the inevitable market tie-ins and relentless merchandising, the ultimate dollar figure associated with this multipart extraterrestrial "pastiche of time-tested mythological motifs striking a universal chord, especially among adolescents," is at least *$5.5 billion*, a sum much greater than the annual GNP of most Third World nations![66] And now, finally, you understand the oh-so-very real life-force behind all this, the kind explaining why the ETs and UFOs won't go away; it is called a *monetary incentive*.

That now politicized "alien-apparition-as-avenging-angel" motif was inevitable: as you well know, hardly an issue of the *National Enquirer* (published for "inquiring minds") goes by without yet another sighting emblazoned upon its front pages. As the zealous tabloid editors report, "As of 1980, reports the *National Enquirer*, UFO sightings had increased to the rate of more than *1,000 a day* worldwide" (their emphasis) and, of course, they wish they could share them all with us. Since they couldn't, for space is limited in their tabloid, they have published a paperback book with page-turning chapters: "CIA Covers Up UFO Tracking Operations," "U.S. Air Force Studied Crashed UFO," "Eisenhower Met Space Aliens," "Aliens Watched Our Astronauts on the Moon," "Face-to-Face Encounters with Aliens," "Aliens Beamed to Earth," "Four-Time Victim of UFO Abductions," "Aliens Turn to Violence," "Have *You* Had a UFO Encounter?" (with addresses to write to for certification-seeking abductees).[67]

More important, since Nixon and Watergate, it seems everybody in America "knows" that the chief executive is either "a crook" or (at the very least) a coconspirator and/or philandering womanizer. Moreover, now over 70 percent of postmodernist Americans routinely accept the notion of widespread government conspiracies.[68] This is not, however, idle disgruntlement. Now, you additionally know that such "forests of fantasy" have their own real potential for fatal consequences; among other media-driven examples, again we have the holocaust of the UFO-cult Heaven's Gate occurring in early 1997. One of the reasons they did so was because the millennium was very much on their minds. In that respect at least, the deluded Heaven's Gate martyrs were very much like the rest of us.

Accordingly, more of the same kind of mass exiting is surely in the offing since we have been, and with some trepidation, immersed in a well-publicized end of the millennium.[69] At least so the media kept telling us throughout 1999; even reputable news magazines (*Newsweek* for instance) had a section regularly devoted to fanning our collective *fin-de-millénnium* ardor. In contrast to the first millennium (1000 C.E., and as explained below), the new wrinkle was literally "modernist." Endlessly predicted in the mass media for the last days of the twentieth century (2000 C.E.) was a universal *technological* meltdown: mass computer failure. Also strictly modernist was the decisive role played by the mass media in sponsoring the Y2K hysteria; when the last one (Y1K) rolled around, the planet was mostly bereft of both the media and ETs. Among the many dire predictions owing to Y2K digital collapse spun by the media were passenger planes that would eagerly seek one another out in order to produce myriad midair collisions; power plants that would quit in unison; in the crepuscular darkness, ATMs that would cease to fork over cash on demand; water supplies that would dry up; rioters who would gut urban centers; and so forth. Consequently, deluded inhabitants of the American outback tapped out their credit cards to lay away emergency rations, firearms, and other essential survival gear. Later, early in 2001, such items were being sold by impoverished survivalists at fire-sale prices. Thanks, media!

It was all symbolic, mostly verbal confusion, a digital delusion. Strictly speaking, *millennium* means the thousand-year period of God's kingdom on earth—the "New Jerusalem"—predicted in the Book of Revelation (the last part of the Christian Bible); this would precede the Last Judgment (by God) and the end of history itself. Now it nearly always refers to the (very) Last Day itself, culminating in the final battle of "Armageddon" (also a blockbuster summer movie of 1998). And regarding that apocalyptic millennium, so dreaded by so many, a skeptical postmodernist might ask, two thousand years from *what*? (In any event, officially the third millennium did not actually begin until January 1, *2001*—as in the 1968 Stanley Kubrick film.) To take that calendar designation seriously, don't you have to be a subscriber to Christianity? Alas, Christian chronology is not especially noted for its scientific accountability. Fairly recently, the agreed-upon age of the universe had it only date back to 4004 B.C.E.; a German astronomer, Johannes Hevelius (1611–1687) was much more specific: it all began at exactly 6 P.M. (1800 Zulu time), on October 24, 3963 B.C.E.[70]

Alas, that mathematical ingenuity omits the Neanderthals and Cro-Magnons, the latter folk being very skilled at painting lively hunting-scenes in caves in the Pyrenees, which they had done since around 15,000 B.C.E.[71] Worse, many biblical scholars now even argue that Christ was unlikely to have made his initial epiphany at the designated *anno primo domini* ("First Year of the Lord," A.D. 1, now 1 C.E.). Luke and Matthew tell us that Jesus (figs. 2, 3) was born during the reign of Herod—but the Hebrew monarch had died in 4 B.C.E.: Oops. If you're Jewish, 2000 C.E. instead becomes *5760*, a number about as provocative as my zip code. According to another current Semitic faith, Islam, the same year becomes "1421"— but didn't we do that one already? Here we have three scenarios, each self-fashioned. The conclusion? Either the millennium doesn't exist, or it already went by (around 1995 C.E.) wholly unnoticed—and the majority of middle-class Americans did seem far more focused on diurnal family and economic issues, in short, on real life. Either way, the present reality of its emotional potency is wholly a creation of the mass media.

The last time it happened, that is, the millennium, there was no collaboration with the mass media. No matter; the end of the *first* millennium was likewise widely held to portend fearful events.[72] Some (meaning some *Christians*) were certain that the Second Coming of Christ would fall on the last day of the year 999 C.E., at the very stroke of midnight. According to an ancient chronicle, in Rome on the last day of the year 999 C.E., the old basilica of St. Peter's was packed with sobbing and palsied worshipers awaiting the end of the world. This was the dreaded eve of the millennium, the Day of Wrath. As the True Believers knew then, at that dread *Dies Irae* the earth would crumble into ruin. Many had already given away all their possessions to the poor—household goods, even their land and homes—to gain forgiveness for their sins at the Last Judgment. Many poorer sinners entered the basilica in sack-

1. Martin Cannon, "Extra-Terrestrials among Us" (paperback bookcover: George C. Andrews, *Extra-Terrestrials among Us*, St. Paul, Minn.: Fate, 1993).

2. Constantinopolitan artist, "Head of Christ" (*Mandylion*; circa 500). Genoa, S. Bartolomeo degli Armeni.

3. Warner Sallman, "Head of Christ" (1940; unauthorized Mexican copy, circa 1960, "El Divino Redentor").

4. Ted Jacobs, "Head of an Extra-Terrestrial" (paperback bookcover: Whitley Strieber, *Communion*, New York: Bantam, 1987. Trademark [TM] Walker & Collier Inc.).

5. "How a Member of the Kingdom of Heaven Might Appear" (as depicted on the Heaven's Gate Web page in 1997). (Author's collection.)

7. Fritz Erler, "Adolf Hitler, Architect of the Millenarian Reich" (1939; present location unknown). (Author's collection.)

6. "The Virgin of Guadalupe Appears to Juan Diego at Tepeyac in 1531" (anonymous Mexican chromolithograph, circa 1985).

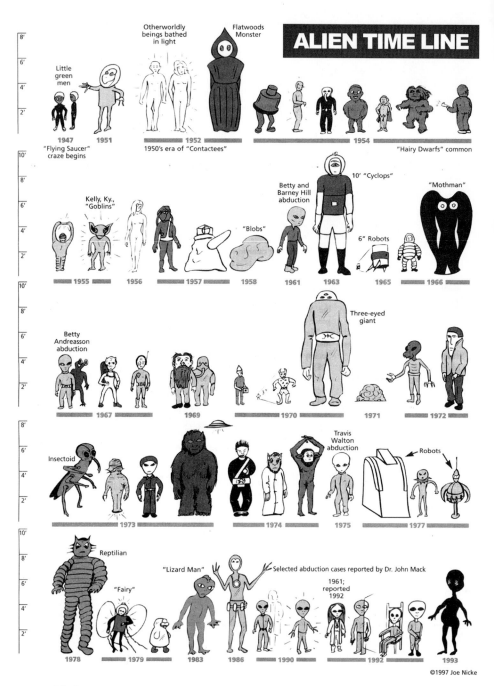

8. Joe Nickell, "Alien Time Line" (from *Skeptical Inquirer* 21, no. 5, September/October 1997).

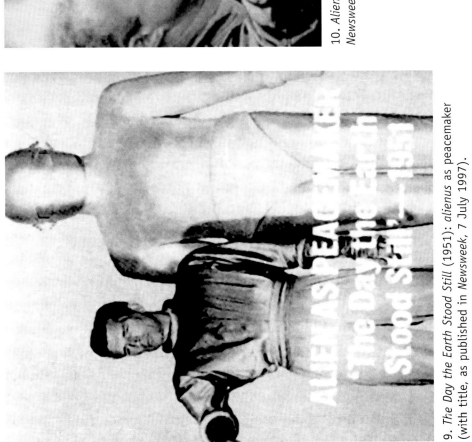

10. *Alien Nation* (1988): *alienus* as buddy (with title, as published in *Newsweek*, 7 July 1997).

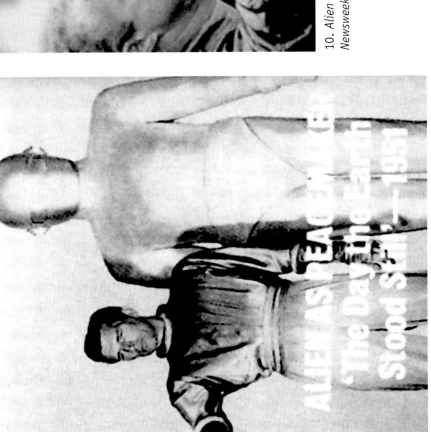

9. *The Day the Earth Stood Still* (1951): *alienus* as peacemaker (with title, as published in *Newsweek*, 7 July 1997).

11. *Species* (1995): *alienus* as gorgeous nymphomaniac man-killer (with title, as published in *Newsweek*, 7 July 1997).

12. *Men in Black* (1997): *alienus* as comedic illegal immigrant (with title, as published in *Newsweek*, 7 July 1997).

14. *Predator* (1987): *alienus* as standard slime-ball, big-game man-hunter (with title, as published in *Newsweek*, 7 July 1997).

13. *Alien* (1979): *alienus* as reptile parasite and woman-chaser (with title, as published in *Newsweek*, 7 July 1997).

15. *E.T.: The Extraterrestrial* (1982): *alienus* as household pet (with title, as published in *Newsweek*, 7 July 1997).

16. Barney Hill, "UFO Crew Man" (pencil drawing, 1966; as reproduced in John G. Fuller, *The Interrupted Journey*, New York: Dell, 1967).

17. "Betty Hill with an Extraterrestrial" (video-still from the 1975 NBC TV–movie *The UFO Incident*). (Author's collection.)

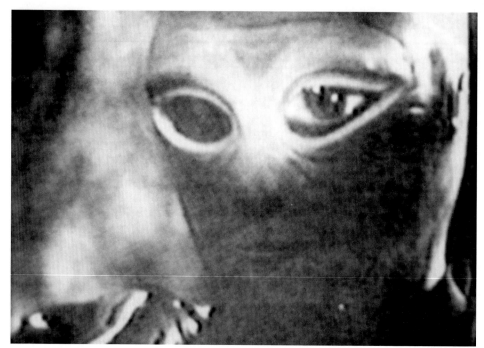

18. "An Extraterrestrial" (video-still from the 1975 NBC TV–movie *The UFO Incident*). (Author's collection.)

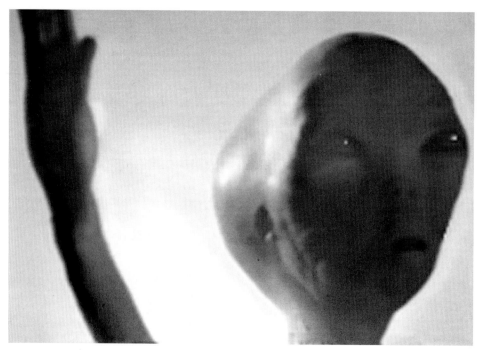

19. "Epiphany of the Extraterrestrial" (video-still from the 1977 Steven Spielberg movie *Close Encounters of the Third Kind*). (Author's collection.)

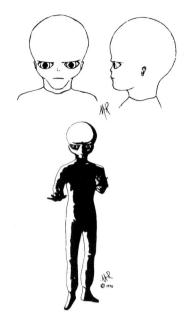

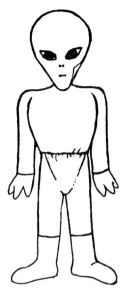

20. Mike Rogers (?), "The Humanoid ET Abductors of Travis Walton" (1976; as reproduced in *World Almanac Book of the Strange*, New York: Signet, 1977).

21. Betty Andreasson, "Entity in the Examination Room" (pencil drawing, circa 1979; as reproduced, with enhancements, in Ronald E. Fowler, *The Andreasson Affair*, New York: Bantam, 1980).

22. Betty Andreasson, "Entities Moving through a Closed Door" (pencil drawing, circa 1979; as reproduced, with enhancements, in Ronald E. Fowler, *The Andreasson Affair*, New York: Bantam, 1980).

23. Greco-Roman Relief, "Three Maenads" (circa 100 C.E.). Florence, Uffizi.

24. "St. Mark" (full-page [8 x 10 in.] author-portrait from the *Gospel Book of Ebbo*, circa 830). Épernay, Bibliothèque Municipale.

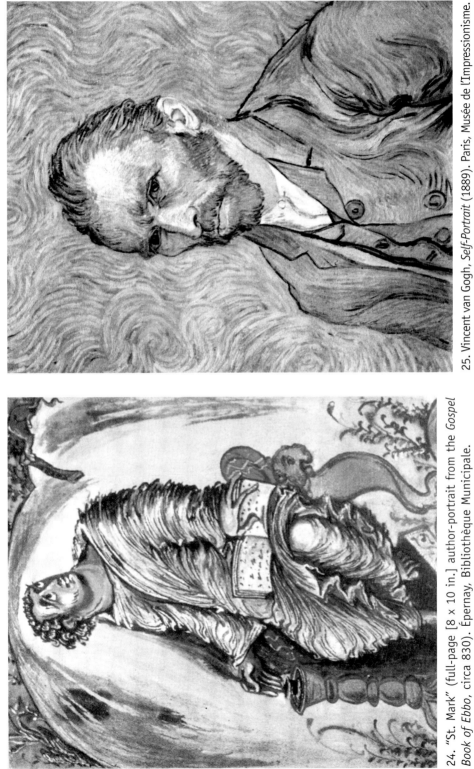

25. Vincent van Gogh, *Self-Portrait* (1889). Paris, Musée de l'Impressionisme.

26. Henry Fuseli, *The Nightmare* (1781). Detroit, Institute of Art.

27. Giotto di Bordone, "The Adoration of the Magi" (circa 1304). Arena Chapel, Padua.

28. "The Airship Seen Hovering over Oakland in November 1896" (from the *San Francisco Call*, 22 November 1896).

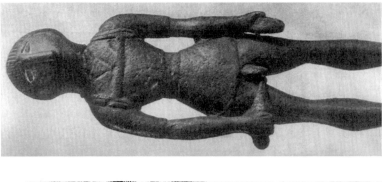

31. "Iberian Warrior" (bronze votive figurine from Despeñaperros [Jaén], circa 300 B.C.E.). Madrid, Museo Nacional de Arqueología.

30. "King Pacal Swallowed by the Jaws of Death" (tomb-slab rubbing, from the Temple of the Inscriptions, Palenque, circa 650 C.E.).

29. Myron, *Diskobolos* (as a "Frisbee Thrower"), (circa 450 B.C.E.). Rome, Terme.

32. Edvard Munch, *The Scream* (1893). Oslo, National Gallery.

33. Francisco Pacheco, *Immaculate Conception with Miguel Cid* (circa 1619). Seville, Cathedral of Seville.

35. "Mona Lisa the Extraterrestrial" (postmodernist, computer-enhanced, in 2001, mutation of da Vinci's masterwork of circa 1502).

34. Raphael, *The Sistine Madonna* (circa 1516). Dresden, Gemäldegalerie.

cloth and ashes, having already spent weeks in penance. At the altar, Pope Sylvester II was seen in full papal regalia, celebrating the midnight mass, elevating the Host for all to see. Lying face down and with their arms spread out in the shape of a cross, many did not dare to raise their heads to behold the elevated Host. Some were seized by holy *ecstasy*, waiting to be *transported*, to be with Christ. Time passed and the crowd remained transfixed, barely daring to breathe, "not a few dying from fright, giving up their ghosts then and there."[73] This description, now itself a millennium old, gives us a good idea of an all-pervading dread of the Apocalypse that once held humankind in its grip. Not only the year 999, but the whole century that preceded it, was a period of obscurity during which people, "blinded with blood, groped their way fearfully through a quagmire of filth."[74] The same holds true for our own, blood-soaked and thoroughly mean-spirited, twentieth century, now of already dim memory.

While awaiting the dreaded advent of *our* millennium, Y1K, we were treated to signs of extraterrestrials—at least so our modernist mass media would have us believe. A thousand years ago, Y1K, something rather similar happened—or at least was then *reported* to have happened. As the fateful year 1000 approached, signs and prodigies prompted faith in the Apocalypse. According to contemporary chroniclers, many such signs appeared. One early scribe told of the sky splitting open, letting fall down to earth a gigantic torch, which left behind it a long trail of light like a lightning bolt, what today would assuredly be labeled as a UFO. Whatever its name then, its thunderclap frightened both people working in the open fields and also those who remained indoors. The gap in the sky closed again, but then the shape of a dragon with blue feet appeared, continuing to grow until it filled the horizon from end to end. In England, another UFO (or perhaps just a meteor, sorry) caused much fear and trembling, and a bit later another fiery blaze appeared in the sky, shining so brightly that it turned night into day; it vanished at dawn, but whether this light came from God or from the devil the people did not know. When French nuns saw "fiery armies fighting in the sky," they started a procession and said prayers to ward off the dreaded ultimate ruin.[75]

These celestial craft had already been seen around the European neighborhood. Here is the report documenting a much earlier UFO sighting; as described around 825, it seems almost like iconographic foreplay for the celebrated Betty and Barney Hill account, published in 1966:

> One day, among other instances, it chanced at Lyons that three men and a woman were seen descending from wonderfully constructed aerial ships [cf. fig. 28], whose flying squadrons roved as the will of the Zephyrs. . . .

The entire city gathered around them, crying out that they were magicians. . . . In vain the four innocents sought to vindicate themselves by
saying that they were their own country-folk, and had been carried away
a short time since by miraculous [ET] men who had shown them
unheard-of marvels. . . . The frenzied populace paid no heed to their
defense, and were on the point of casting them into the fire, when the
worthy Agobard, Bishop of Lyons, came running at the noise, and having
heard the accusations of the people and the defense of the accused,
gravely pronounced that it was not true that these men had fallen from
the sky, and what they said they had seen there was impossible.[76]

Perhaps Bishop Agobard deserves more historical credit; he seems to be
the first UFO debunker.

Meanwhile, on the ground, in Aquitaine, the sky rained blood, splat-
tering people with crimson spots that could not be cleaned from their
clothing. Their collective thought was that great strife and bloodshed were
about to occur, a likely result in an age of uninterrupted violence and warfare. Many signs and omens were also seen in Italy; since most appeared in
the sky, they, too, must be dubbed UFOs. In 968, the men of Emperor Otto
I, marching against the Saracens of Calabria, panicked when an eclipse
darkened the sky. They hid as well as they could and, states a chronicler,
"fanatic preachers kept up the flame of terror. Every shooting star furnished
occasion for a sermon, in which the sublimity of the approaching Judgment
was the principal topic."[77] As was also then observed:

In the seventh year before that date, A.D. 1000 [i.e., in 993], Mount
Vesuvius, which is also called Vulcan's cauldron, gaped far more often
than its wont and vomited forth numberless vast stones mingled with
sulfurous flames which fell to a distance of three miles around; and thus
by the stench of its breath, like the stench of hell, made all the surrounding province uninhabitable. . . . It befell at the same time that
most of the cities of Italy and Gaul were ravaged by flames of fire, and
that even the greatest part of Rome itself was devoured by a conflagra-
tion. The flames caught the beams of St. Peter's church and began to
creep up to the bronze tiles and lick the carpenters' work. When this
became known to the watching multitude, being quite helpless to avert
the disaster, they turned with one accord, and crying with a terrible
voice, hastened to crowd before the image of the Chief of the Apostles
[i.e., St. Peter], crying upon him with curses that, if he watched not
over his own, nor defended his own church, many throughout the world
would abandon the faith and fall back into paganism. Whereupon the
devouring flames at once left the wooden roof beams and died away.[78]

Among lesser apocryphal signs recorded in France there is the case of an image of Christ that shed crimson tears; also mentioned is a wolf who crept into the church to adore the lachrymose idol. The pious beast seized the bell rope between its teeth and rang the church bell, causing great unease among all who heard its clanging. In the castle of Joigny, the seat of Sir Arlebaud, it rained stones of different sizes for three long years; at that time eleven sons and grandsons of Arlebaud died, surprising nobody. Near Châlons, a man called Leutard dreamed that a swarm of bees had entered his body and emerged through his mouth. The bees had revealed to him that he was to do things that were impossible for ordinary men; to prove that it really happened, he showed properly aghast neighbors the bee stings. So confirmed, Leutard went to the nearest church and trampled underfoot a cross bearing an image of Christ, claiming at the same time that it was sinful and ungodly to pay tithes and taxes. Bees or not, he was subdued and killed. Another madman was suddenly possessed by a fiend, making him plunge a lance between the ribs of the saintly Père Abbon of Fleury; the murderer, with no apian defense, had his hands cut off and was burned.

Similarly upsetting things were also happening in Germany. In 960, a preacher from Thuringia, named Bernhard, told an assembly of bishops and laymen at Würzburg that God had appeared to him in the flesh, revealing to him the exact day and hour in which the world and all who lived upon it would be obliterated. He insisted that the dreaded hour was immediately at hand. At first, his listeners were frightened—until the self-appointed seer began making faces, drooling, and madly dancing about. His career as a prophet was forfeit, and the crowd mocked him, pelting the poor wretch with offal. Often such madmen were tortured—not to punish them, but merely to torment and drive out the in-dwelling demons, thereby rendering a kindness to the bedeviled victim. Times have changed; today, such visionaries commonly publish a paperback volume describing their uniquely perceived revelations of otherworldly apparitions.

A thousand years later, there is now recognized a syndrome which explains such psychic anomalies, a kind of "millennium mentality." In his now-classic study, *The Pursuit of the Millennium* (1957), Norman Cohn described the mental attributes of those who take such chronological symbolism seriously, namely people who typically live

> in a state of chronic and inescapable insecurity, harassed not only by their economic helplessness and vulnerability, but by the lack of the traditional social relationships on which, even at the worst of times, [people] had normally been able to depend. These were the people whose anxieties drove them to seek messianic leaders [providing] a

coherent social myth which was capable of taking entire possession of those who believed in it. It explained their suffering; it promised them recompense; it held their anxieties at bay; it gave them an illusion of security—even while it drove them, held together by a common enthusiasm, on a quest which was vain and often suicidal.[79]

Now it will be useful to cite one account (among others which could be cited) published by a card-carrying UFOlogist that relates visitations from the postmodernist spacecraft specifically to the millennium, the one forecast for 2000 C.E. (Christian calendar time, that is). Writing in 1985, Ruth Montgomery states that the "aliens," the kind descending in vehicles driven from outer space, have the mission of awakening human beings to the realization that their final destruction is imminent unless, of course, better ways of settling disputes between nations are found. The earth, in her view, will shift on its axis in the year 2000, with catastrophic results, including the death of most of its inhabitants (also prophesied in the 1998 blockbuster movie *Armageddon*). Happily, according to the Montgomery scenario, the space brothers will save many of the enlightened souls by evacuating them in galactic fleets and later returning them to earth for rehabilitation of the planet or its recolonization. Most likely, this prophecy was read with special attention by Herff "Do" Applewhite and passed on to his Heaven's Gate followers. UFOs, thus, can be the heavenly sign that heralds the Second Coming of Christ with its consequent judgment. For Montgomery and her readers, they are an indication that the decisive great battle of Armageddon is not far away. And they serve as a warning that human beings should prepare themselves for this event.[80] This fairly commonplace understanding of UFOs can be seen as a modern expression of a kind of apocalyptic and millenarian thought that has been a constant factor in Christian theology, that is, at least since 1000 C.E. No matter: 2000 C.E. mostly represented an "Apocalypse Not." For most Americans, the real Apocalypse came their way a bit later, on September 11, 2001.

Even though the suicidal UFO cult called Heaven's Gate, likewise the self-immolating Branch Davidians led by David Koresh, only appeared long after Cohn published his fundamental millenarian study, his description fits them all too well. So does his statement concerning the same kind of people as had been made known to us from the medieval records describing earlier seekers of the millennium:

Those who are first attracted will mostly be people who seek a sanction for the emotional needs generated by their own unconscious conflicts. It is as though units of paranoia hitherto diffused through the population suddenly coalesce to form a new entity: a collective paranoiac fanaticism. But these first followers, precisely because they are true believers, can endow their new movement with such confidence, energy and ruthlessness that it will attract into its wake vast multitudes of people who are themselves not at all paranoid but simply harassed, hungry or frightened.[81]

That is also a very good assessment of the enduring emotional significance of the UFO experience, particularly its widely publicized (generally profitable) accounts of hundreds of alleged abductions by extraterrestrials: "a collective paranoiac fanaticism." And, for another way of putting it, try "emotional fascism" (and the historical roots of *that* will be exhumed in chapter 13).

ROSWELL AND THE EXTRATERRESTRIAL PSEUDOEVENT OF THE MILLENNIUM

The tenth century, the one leading directly to the first millennium, has been called the Century of Lead and Iron. Ours, the recently finished twentieth, belonged to the likes of Hitler, Stalin, Pol Pot, Saddam Hussein, Slobodan Milosevic, and a host of other mundane demons, as well as the atom bomb, hydrogen bomb, and television. A thousand years after the tenth century, the conventional kind of sky-descending "portents" are called UFOs and ETs. And, for this millennium, its most celebrated epiphany constitutes what is now widely known as the "Roswell Incident." The principal worth of this momentous pseudoevent is to show how, when not fatal, the consequences now attending alien apparitions at the end of another Christian millennium are otherwise generally profitable, at least for the clever few.

To cite the most egregious instance, dreary Roswell, New Mexico, which otherwise would remain tenaciously unvisited, now annually receives 90,000 paying earthling tourists to visit its two UFO museums and the "authentic" 1947 UFO crash site. None of this is surprising; a 1997 poll showed that 65 percent of American citizens really *believe* in the standard version of the Roswell incident, complete with its crashed spaceship and moribund ET crew members.[82] The aliens' alleged landing place, however, has now been moved up to three, or even four, sites by some accounts—or local landowners. One of these is now placed in Corona, New Mexico, some ninety miles northwest of Roswell, as the UFO flies, and yet another on the distant plains of San Agustín, 210 miles further west. The physical evidence establishing priority for any or all impact zones is, naturally, wholly nonexistent; the "proof" for their existence, if any, is essentially anecdotal, even risible. No matter; never mind.

Further digression on the celebrated "Roswell incident," a classic postmodernist pseudoevent, provides illuminating insights into the lucrative collusion between mass delusion and the mass media promoting the kind of iconic ET portraiture so profitably propelling visual celebrity (figs. 1, 4, 5, 15–22).[83] Many more eager pilgrims, some 40,000, were received in July 1997 for the profitable fiftieth anniversary celebration in Roswell of the infamous epiphany of the otherworldly aliens; it was reported that the ET tourists left *$2.5 million* in their wake. Permanent residents in Roswell only number about 50,000 and one of these, since moved to Michigan, ungenerously called the dollar-toting visitors "an influx of space cadets and New Age flakes."[84] However designated, many, many more would have showed up, that is had not the classic 1997 Roswell pseudoevent been simultaneously overshadowed by a genuine (it *really* happened) extraterrestrial media event: the landing of the *Pathfinder* spacecraft on planet Mars. Worse, a number of prominent sponsors had earlier pulled out of the Roswell ET festival following widely viewed television reports dealing with the coeval mass suicide of the UFO cult Heaven's Gate: death is equally bad for one's business and one's public image.

Although, at least according to sparse reports briefly appearing in the news media at the time—meaning over half a century ago—the "real" event had occurred way back in July 1947, it was happily forgotten for over three decades. Then, much later, the mass media again stepped into the picture. The initial trigger was interviews given by ex-Major Jesse Marcel, beginning in February 1978 and eventually published, December 8, 1979, in (ready for this?) the *National Enquirer*. Marcel, who died in 1986, is the guy who fixed the "spacecraft debris" theme. At that time however, back in 1978, he could not even recall the year of the purported incident as being 1947 (and he also fibbed about his education and service record). Nor did Marcel make any mention in 1978 of the supposedly recovered bodies of the alien aviators; these now standard motifs only surfaced a bit later. In 1981, a sensational story in the *Globe*, another tabloid (of course), told how Oliver "Pappy" Henderson (then deceased) had flown the ET cadavers to Wright-Patterson Air Force Base in Ohio. The unimpeachable source? Pappy's elderly wife, Sappho, who said he did it. (Right.) And perhaps you saw *Roswell*, a 1994 made-for-cable television movie (filmed in Arizona and broadcast on the Showtime channel). Hewing to the overblown Marcel description, the filmmakers show a huge area littered with truckloads of shiny, silvery alien stuff; close-ups of the outer-space debris showed alien hieroglyphics, metal that cannot be broken, foil that magically flattens itself after being folded, and so forth. The debris-strewn *mise-en-scène* made for great television.

This is the exciting postmodernist recreation; it is wholly at odds, alas, with the banal contemporary reports. The debris was found by rancher Mack Brazel on June 14, 1947; he brought it into town on July 7. As was stated two days later in the *Roswell Daily Record*, "The tinfoil, paper, tape, and sticks made a bundle about three feet long and seven or eight inches thick. Considerable scotch tape and some tape with flowers printed on it had been used in the construction." Some other rubber strips "made a bundle about 18 or 20 inches long and about 8 inches thick. In all, Brazel estimated, the entire lot would have weighed maybe five pounds." Five pounds of stuff, even feathers, is not going to cover much terrain. Still, as unexplained stuff, it seemed provocative. As was stated in a report submitted to Army Air Corps Headquarters in August 1947, "The Office of Public Information [at the Roswell air base] was kept quite busy during the month of July answering inquiries on the 'flying disc' which was reported to be in the possession of the 509th Bomb Group. The object turned out to be a radar tracking balloon."[85]

In short, that is the truth of the matter, and it is wholly *boring*. Half a century later, particularly as seen on TV—for which boredom is anathema—likely anything you hear stated to have happened in Roswell in 1947 is, at best, just distorted memory or, at worse, an outright lie. But who cares: it makes for great television!

The exact chronology attending each Roswell pseudoevent, and the real facts masked behind each of their respective misrepresentations, have only been recently revealed.[86] The real media furor constituting the pseudoevent really began in 1980, with paperback publication of *The Roswell Incident* by William L. Moore and Charles Berlitz. Berlitz was previously the coauthor, with J. Manson Valentine, of *The Bermuda Triangle* (1974), which had brought him considerable fame and great fortune: *five million* copies were sold. Such success came naturally; it didn't matter that Berlitz's triangular conclusions were, besides largely plagiarized, mostly rubbish; all this was later revealed in detail by a much more scrupulous investigator, whose carefully researched and unhysterical exposé naturally undersold the Berlitz-Manson fabrications.[87] Like the bogus "Bermuda Triangle" book, the new Berlitz-Moore collaborative paperback inventing the Roswell pseudoevent, which seems mostly Moore's work, naturally became an instant best-seller: they, too, both made oodles of cash. Herein were described really weird aliens and their extraterrestrial debris, so attested to locally by "more than seventy witnesses who had some knowledge of the event," or so they claimed.

Today the skeptic only finds second- and even thirdhand stories: "So-and-so told what's-his-name, who told me, that such-and-such actually happened over thirty years ago." Perhaps, but none of this "testimony" would hold up today in any court of law. In case you have no legal training, and hence are not sure as to exactly what does constitute proper legal "evidence," then just watch the award-winning TV series *Law and Order*. Since I am a self-confessed aficionado of that cinematic seminar, I am happily inclined to throw out all that UFOlogical "evidence" as risibly inadmissable rubbish.

The laughably flimsy, but thoroughly profitable, Berlitz-Moore exposé, with many more Roswell revelations since published, as churned out by other avid *auteurs* in collusion with money-mongering publishers, also captured our collective attention. Particularly they did so by presenting "proof" that the American government had covered up the truth, even its possession of genuine alien bodies, later dissected by government butchers who, swine that they were, refused to share the good news with us. As we are emphatically told by Moore-Berlitz, remains of "the UFO *and the dead occupants* (one of whom was reportedly alive when found) are now under high security guard at CIA headquarters at Langley, Virginia."[88] Eventually, on August 28 and September 4, 1995, we did finally get to see, on the Fox TV network, a grainy movie of the gristly ET dissection; the show was called *Alien Autopsy: Fact or Fiction?* Physical *proof* at last! The film, which we were told was shot in 1947, was viewed by millions, and then millions more in subsequent, also decidedly lucrative, reruns. Surely the Heaven's Gate UFO cult also bore witness to this amazing epiphany; the film is now available at your local video store.

Oddly, this unprecedented scientific event was filmed in black-and-white; standard procedure at that time (1947) would have been to use color film stock. Also odd was that the photographer used a jerky, hand-held camera rather than a steadying tripod, also standard procedure at that time. This amateurish visual spectacle, often out of focus and with the corpse shown for seventeen minutes in toto, had been acquired by its present owner, executive producer Robert Kiviat, from Ray Santilli, who owns a small video distribution company in London. Santilli said he got it (in either 1992 or 1993; his stories change) from an ex-Army cameraman, who (no surprise) wished to "remain anonymous." According to Santilli, Cameraman X was summoned from Washington, D.C., to the Roswell air base on July 2, 1947, to photograph the space debris and, a month later, he was also dispatched to Fort Worth Air Station in Texas to film the dissection of one of the crashed aliens. Somehow the resourceful cameraman managed to withhold from his superiors, for nearly a half-century, more than one hundred minutes of world-historical film footage.

Alas, serious inquiry now shows that cinematic feast to be a complete fake, a swindle; it has been specifically criticized from the points of view of a forensic surgeon, a film director, and even a Hollywood special effects artist.[89] As instructed by the expert F/X artisan, we, too, could manufacture our own body casts of alien corpses. However, we are advised (for the next faked film) not so obviously to take the cast from a standing figure; since bodies lie horizontally for autopsies, their supine flesh will show the effects of gravity, which the Roswell cadaver, a standing figure, does not. Reconsidered as a piece of sculpture, that widely viewed, grisly three-dimensional artifact now belongs to the history of art, if not (better said) the history of art forgery.[90]

Even though now clearly shown to be wholly of earthling manufacture, the ET anatomy and physiognomy shown in the widely viewed TV film is, not surprisingly, wholly faithful to now-conventional postmodernist canons set for such apocryphal portraiture.[91] The faked Roswell cadaver holds to corporeal standards set since 1975 by the Hill TV movie, *The UFO Incident*, and then made canonical by the ET appearing in Steven Spielberg's 1977 movie, *Close Encounters of the Third Kind* (see figs. 17–19). When the blockbuster movie *Independence Day* came along in 1996, the role of Roswell as an instant emotional trigger was institutionalized; it not only reminded everybody that the flying saucers crewed by archetypal ETs had really landed there, but now added that the government had even maintained those alien craft in flying condition. Taken out of mothballs, the recycled Roswell UFOs led America's tireless struggle for all things decent, especially liberty and freedom from demonic "alien" influences.

In fact, all the anomalous anatomical details in Santilli's film are faithful to the extensive structural description of the "anatomy of an alien" reported by none other than David Jacobs, and as published by him just two years *before* the initial appearance of the faked TV movie.[92] If the basis of the faked TV film was not entirely due to the (post-Rembrandt) anatomy lesson of Dr. Jacobs, then it was certainly indebted to the detailed description conveniently provided in the Moore-Berlitz blockbuster of 1980, admitted by its coauthors to be concocted from "incomplete overall information and opinion."[93] But the real explanation is laughably obvious; as Berlitz-Moore naïvely observe, "The aliens portrayed on board the UFO in the [1977] film *Close Encounters of the*

Third Kind [fig. 19] closely resemble the composite description compiled by researcher [Len] Stringfield," that is, *after* 1977.[94] In the mass
media, it is the *images*, not facts, that shape public attitudes. Even these
royalty-enriched authors must reluctantly admit that all their "evidence" testifying to the existence of the dead ETs is little more than a
"random selection of [not very] credible and incredible rumors, scuttle-
butt, 'confidential' reports, and twice-told tales"; in sum, "All we have to
go on is rumor and circumstance."[95] Hence, this self-labeled "nonfiction" publication represents yet another lucrative, but thoroughly
gauche, close encounter!

Here is one of those "incredible rumors" in which the Roswell legend
revels. On May 29, 1987, William L. Moore (Berlitz's paperback partner)
and UFOlogist Stanton Friedman, a portly and devilishly bearded pundit
who loves to exhibit himself on national television, released what they
called "top secret government documents" dated between September 1947
and July 1954. At last, absolute *proof* for a government cover-up! The documents, supposedly retrieved from the National Archives, indicated that
on September 24, 1947, President Harry Truman had authorized cabinet
officials to start "Operation Majestic-12" (MJ-12), a secret panel of top military leaders and scientists. Their mission, top secret of course, was to analyze the Roswell crashed flying saucer and its dead crew members. Moore
and Friedman had the original memo, signed by no less than Harry
Truman! Another seven-page "Top Secret/Eyes Only" MJ-12 document was
evidently used to brief President-elect Dwight Eisenhower. Imagine that,
two presidents conspiring to deprive us of the sensational news. Alas, subsequent inquiry proved that the memos were naught but maladroit forgeries, and that (uh-oh) certain stylistic anomalies in the unholy writs were
consistent with the private correspondence of Bill Moore.[96]

However, as it does turn out, yes, there really was a cover-up by the
government, but what *had* been kept secret for decades was the fact that
the "extraterrestrial" space junk picked up around Roswell actually
came from "Project Mogul," strictly terrestrial but top-secret Cold War
experiments with constant-level balloons trailing radar reflectors and
designed to spy upon the former Soviet Union, particularly its attempts
at surreptitious nuclear testing.[97] All the rest of the overblown Roswell
legend—a dozen books, made-for-TV movies, an endless stream of television "documentaries"—was simply derived from induced and/or
twisted memories or deliberate flim-flam.[98]

As it is also interesting to note, the real media blitz propelling Roswell
only took wing early in the 1980s, meaning once the entire nation had
became contemporaneously terrorized by the ubiquitous, but essentially

invisible, AIDS plague. The initial UFO plague, beginning around thirty-five years earlier, belongs to a complementary context, likewise largely inflamed by the media: the ubiquitous, but essentially invisible, "Red Scare" plague. However, the outsized metastasis of the Roswell legend belongs to the period when Ronald Reagan ruled America, and he constantly ranted about a Star Wars program needed to blast away the Evil Empire (of the Russians, not Darth Vader); that president, who was very photogenic and therefore much adored by the masses due to his smarmy television presence, sadly was later diagnosed with Alzheimer's disease, a progressive and irreversible impairment of the cognitive abilities.

The core motifs of the endlessly profitable Roswell urban legend include three essential elements: (1) flying saucers that crash in the desert, specifically in New Mexico; (2) the finding, even recovery, of the cadavers of little folk from outer space, the ET crew members; (3) the government, specifically the U.S. Air Force, then immediately spirits away these priceless anatomical treasures, namely to Wright-Patterson Air Force Base, and the existence of the gray *corpi delicti* is thereafter stoutly denied by mendacious bureaucrats. I am now pleased to inform all concerned readers (especially the True Believers) that all of these legendary motifs were published—naturally in a mass-produced paperback edition—as long ago as 1950. The only departure here from the now-standard postmodernist scenario is that the alleged events took place in Aztec and/or Farmington, New Mexico—and *not* in Roswell, which lies about 450 miles away to the southeast in the same state. Our invaluable *Urtext* is the work of Frank Scully (later to lend his surname to an FBI agent working on *The X-Files*), a minor-league journalist working for a show business tabloid called *Daily Variety*, and the title of his pulp best-seller (composed in just seventy-two days) was *Behind the Flying Saucers*.[99] The hardcover edition sold more than 30,000 copies, and the inevitable paperback, issued in 1951, probably did ten times that number.

Scully's revelations were literally news; scarcely any books had been published on UFOs back in 1950. Since then, of course, we have a *multibillion-dollar* publishing phenomenon, especially once the ETs got into the picture. The core of Scully's book is three previously published articles, all appearing in the scarcely scientific *Daily Variety* between October 1949 and January 1950;[100] all the rest is just filler, and largely incoherent at that. By his own admission, Scully never saw the sensational saucer wreckage nor the recovered ET bodies; his acknowledged source for *all* of his information is the mysterious "Dr. Gee," of whom we only learn that he "had been in government service [working] on top secret defense projects for seven years." Scully knows this to be a fact because Dr. Gee told him so.[101] Far more interesting is the cryptic scientist's revelation that, at an unspecified date in the spring of 1948, "the first flying saucer was found on a ranch twelve miles from Aztec," New Mexico.[102] And there were even more coming: later, and nearly adjacent, in Farmington, New Mexico, "on the afternoon of March 17 [1950], the sky, it appeared, had been cluttered with flying saucers for three days."[103] As we learn here, ever since 1948 New Mexico has served as a designated rendezvous point for UFOs and ETs. (On the other hand, alas, nowhere in his book does Scully ever even mention Roswell!)

But let's get directly to the really original stuff, the crashed UFOs and those wonderful ET cadavers. Since it is replete with detailed measurements, Scully's account (meaning Dr. Gee's) is surely convincing. Even better, it turns out that no less than *four* crashed flying saucers were personally inspected by Scully's unimpeachable source! The biggest one "was 99.9 feet in diameter and had a cabin measuring 72 inches in diameter. The second measured 72 feet in diameter, and the third, 36 feet." Since the fourth one crashed in Arizona (not New Mexico), "right above Phoenix, in Paradise Valley," we can skip its details. The best part is, of course, the miraculous disclosure of the first ETs ever known to have been handled by mere earthlings: "Thirty-four men, measuring between thirty-six inches to forty inches in height [who] had been found dead in three of the saucers discovered. . . . Their bodies had been charred to a dark brown color"; originally they looked like their spacecraft, pale and grayish, like "a light metal much resembling aluminum." Some other ETs were not so toasted, and these "were all of fair complexion, of small stature. No different from us, except for height, and lack of beards. . . . The passengers, although approximately 40 inches tall, were not midgets. They had no bad teeth, no fillings. They all wore a sort of uniform, but there were no insignia on collars or caps." Some were even seen to be alive and well; at the fourth crash site, the one in Arizona, "as they neared the ship, they saw several little men hop into the saucer, and the ship just disappeared." The eventual fate of the recovered "sixteen bodies, that ranged in height from about 36 to 42 inches," lay at the hands of unnamed "Air Force officers," who also took with them priceless examples of "a pictorial kind of script" used by the extraterrestrials; all this was taken to "a government laboratory," and there the ET corpses "had been dissected, and studied by the medical division of the Air Force." And where precisely did this happen? As the whole world learned from Scully in 1950, this was at Dayton, Ohio, the home of Wright-Patterson Air Force Base! Needless to say, it was all "top secret": "The government wants to keep people away from that area of New Mexico."[104]

Evidence for the enduring credibility accorded to the sensational story first published by Frank Scully in 1950 is easily found. An example: in July 1983, the *Chicago Sun-Times* reported that a U.S. district judge in Washington, D.C., had dismissed a suit brought on behalf of "Citizens Against UFO Secrecy"; these aggrieved citizens had specifically charged that the U.S. Air Force was withholding bodies of outer-space aliens whose flying saucers had landed in New Mexico in 1950![105] Sound familiar? Alas, as we now know, the learned "Dr. Gee, the magnetic research scientist," was just a nobody named Leo GeBauer, former owner of a radio parts store in Phoenix, who died in 1982, and whose only notewothy credentials include at least one conviction for petty fraud and implication in other swindles.[106]

In short, Scully's fabulous 1950 saga portraying a squadron of crashed UFOs and ET cadavers strewn all about the New Mexico boondocks was nothing but a cheesy scam, a hoax. A good hoax, meaning the profitable kind, engenders others. As first widely broadcast in a 1980 "nonfiction" book, the universally celebrated, offshoot Roswell incident—also having a pathological parallel: "dissections" suppressed and/or filmed—is revealed to be a slight improvement, an opportune update, *a postmodernist hoax*. As we now see, that was mostly wrought from apocryphal themes initially developed over half a century ago in now-forgotten pulp fiction describing a much earlier hoax, one concocted way back in 1949. Frank Scully fell for it, and so have millions of other people since then. Among other venues, the New Mexico ET legend is constantly being replayed for our mutual delectation on the Fox channel. And thereby we see that what defines "postmodernism" is (in part) a more efficient, for being more ubiquitous, mode of media manipulation than that which was made available to the primitive, pre-postmodernist, hucksters.

Another profitable extraterrestrial hoax deserving brief mention is the "Gulf Breeze Sightings," the title of another bogus book, written by Ed Walters and published in 1991.[107] His endeavors made Gulf Breeze, Florida, into the undisputed UFO (versus ET) capital of the world. Gauche groups of out-of-state space cadets and New Age flakes still book tours to view the beaches where light-flashing UFOs are said to congregate by night, just like the UFO groupies saw them on TV. Local travel agents and the owners of Gulf Breeze hotels and restaurants owe a lot to "Mr. Ed," the pseudonym of the photographer around whom alien beings and their sparkling craft once swarmed. Ed also did well for himself: his book deal got him a $200,000 advance, and he was expecting another $450,000 for the inevitable made-for-TV movie rights. Alas, some of the local youths later confessed to assisting Mr. Ed in the production of hoaxed saucer films, and some of his model UFOs have since turned up.[108] No matter; the "Gulf Breeze Sightings" are still frequently sighted on prime-time TV. A lot of industry has been expended expanding the Roswell apocrypha, Gulf Breeze, too, and that not inconsiderable effort has made a lot of money for a few enterprising people.

WHY WE LOVE HOAXES

Back in 1940, well before the invention of the UFO experience, Curtis MacDougall published an extensive study of the operations and psychology of the hoaxer, defined by him as one who produces a deliberately concocted mistruth meant to pass as the truth for the greatest possible number of people.[109] The hoaxer's activities are favored by a familiar condition of the human mind: whatever enters it is usually accepted as true, unless there is some very obvious, most impelling and much more weighty, reason for believing otherwise. The hoaxer plants a suggestion, the success of which depends largely upon the self-interest, sense of prestige, degree of familiarity, and/or preconceptions belonging to the hoaxer's targeted audience. Unfortunately, in a modernist age of scientific certainty, doubt is often considered sacrilegious. This effect of ready gullibility through intimidation is to be noted all the more once a hoax has been universally approved by "the experts."

We have another paradox: science, instead of making people more logical, has instead caused them to become more gullible. This paradox arises because of the repeated demonstrations, endlessly reported in the popular press, that certain feats, once deemed impossible by now-discredited experts, have since been easily achieved by the white-gowned votaries of omnipotent and omniscient science. A successful hoax has become successful precisely because it has in some way contributed to the psychological well-being of the duped. Wishful thinking is believing what one wants to believe instead of accepting what factual evidence shows to be true. A hoax is typically more dramatic, more emotionally appealing than is the real thing; even the word "factual" suggests onslaughts of boredom. Obviously, a hoax is attractive, very much like a pseudoevent. If you really *want* to believe, if you are emotionally involved with certain beliefs, you will, of course, *not* choose to seek out any contradictory facts. When the deluded victims' wish to believe is already strong, then the hoaxer's task is made much easier from the outset.

People believe what they *want* to believe, and they nearly always and automatically disbelieve whatever it is that does not square with their preconceived ideas. That which tends to confirm one's convictions is accepted as being true. That which tends to discredit one's prejudices is automatically rejected as untrue. A hoax appeals to self-interest, either that of the individual (often an "expert") or the group, and even that of an entire nation. The potential hoaxer's task is made easy by the predisposition of his intended victims to give credence to whatever fortifies them in their beliefs concerning a cherished cause. Cultural climate determines levels of credulity. A hoax contributes to the fortification of beliefs and common interests. It can support a cause, such as national pride, affording a sense of cultural superiority and prestige. It can just as well support mystical beliefs, like purported visitations by space brothers.

A successful hoax can also make the hoax-meisters a lot of money. As I have repeatedly shown, there is—no question about it—a lot of money being made from the postmodernist UFO experience. Perhaps we should just call it the UFO *industry*. The "Roswell incident," as explained in paperback books labeled "nonfiction," has clear world-historical significance. It marks the first occasion in which science *fiction* was taken as Gospel truth by the masses: *Gratias Deo! Gratias ET!*

NOTES

1. For contemporary and complementary delusions, see Nat Freedland, *The Occult Explosion* (New York: Berkley, 1972); see also Henry Gordon, *Channeling into the New Age: The "Teachings" of Shirley MacLaine and Other Such Gurus* (Amherst, N.Y.: Prometheus Books, 1988).

2. Curtis D. MacDougall, *Superstition and the Press* (Amherst, N.Y.: Prometheus Books, 1983), p. 579.

3. For a rational explanation for most "UFO phenomena," see (among others) the various essays collected in Carl Sagan and T. Page, eds., *UFO's: A Scientific Debate* (New York: Barnes & Noble, 1996); a reprint of papers submitted to a 1969 scientific conference.

4. AP report, in R. E. Bartholomew and G. S. Howard, *UFOs & Alien Contact: Two Centuries of Mystery* (Amherst, N.Y.: Prometheus Books, 1998), p. 190.

5. For these other citations drawn from the initial media reportage, see Keith Thompson, *Angels and Aliens: UFOs and the Mythic Imagination* (New York: Ballantine, 1993), pp. 1–5.

6. For an extensive listing of these, with critical commentary, see MacDougall, *Superstition and the Press*, pp. 578–611.

7. Patrick Huyghe, *The Field Guide to Extraterrestrials* (New York: Avon, 1996), p. 129, citing the research of Jenny Randles, *Alien Contacts and Abductions* (New York: Sterling, 1994). Randles's book is, however, just another of her published attempts to prove a government "conspiracy" to "hide the facts."

8. For verbal accounts of these plentiful "sightings," see William Christian, *Apparitions in Late Medieval and Renaissance Spain* (Princeton: Princeton University Press, 1981).

9. Charles Panati, *Extraordinary Origins of Everyday Things* (New York: Harper, 1987), pp. 372–73.

10. Charles Fort, *The Book of the Damned* (1919; reprint, New York: Ace, 1972), esp. pp. 325–34; for more anomalous, exclusively celestrial phenomena, see Charles Fort, *New Lands* (1923; reprint, New York: Ace, 1968).

11. See M. K. Jessup, *The Case for the UFOs: Unidentified Flying Objects* (New York: Bantam, 1955), costing only $0.35 in 1955.

12. For what follows, see Bartholomew and Howard, *UFOs & Alien Contact*, chap. 1, "Wishful Thinking: The Great American Airship Mania of 1896–97" (superbly researched); as preceeded by Bartholomew, "The Airship Hysteria of 1896–97," *Skeptical Inquirer* 14 (winter 1990): 171–81; see also J. P. Chaplin, *Rumor, Fear, and the Madness of Crowds* (New York: Ballantine, 1959), chap. 3, "The Great Airship of 1897" (an excellent study not cited by Bartholomew and other researchers).

13. Alexander Hamilton, in R. L. Dione, *God Drives a Flying Saucer* (New York: Bantam, 1978), pp. 4–5. As one recognizes, Mr. Dione is a Christian UFOlogist, not a scholar.

14. For both of the earlier pictures, see Bartholomew, "Airship Hysteria," p. 178 (citing, in turn, their published sources).

15. Ibid., p. 172.

16. Newspaper clipping, as quoted in Jacques Vallée, *Confrontations: A Scientist's Search for Alien Contact* (New York: Ballantine, 1990), p. 39.

17. Newspaper report, quoted in Bartholomew and Howard, *UFOs & Alien Contact*, pp. 63–64.

18. Ibid., pp. 32–33.

19. Ibid., p. 63.

20. On Jean-Martin Charcot and Pierre Janet, see Henri F. Ellenberger, *The Discovery of the Unconscious: The History and Evolution of Dynamic Psychiatry* (New York: BasicBooks, 1979), pp. 89–101, 331–417.

21. On Anton Mesmer, see ibid., pp. 56–79.

22. Axel Munthe, as quoted in Elaine Showalter, *The Female Malady: Women, Madness, and English Culture, 1830–1980* (New York: Penguin, 1987), p. 148.

23. See ibid., figs. 22–24.

24. Sigmund Freud and Josef Breuer, as in ibid., pp. 155–56.

25. M. Nordau, *Degeneration* (reprint, Lincoln: University of Nebraska Press, 1993), pp. 25–26.

26. Ibid., p. 15.

27. Gustave Le Bon, *Psychologies des foules* (Paris: Alcan, 1895); *The Psychology of Peoples* (New York: Macmillan, 1898); see also Henri F. Ellenberger, *Discovery of the Unconscious: The History of Dynamic Psychiatry* (New York: BasicBooks, 1979), pp. 165, 528–29.

28. For what follows, see Chaplin, *Rumor, Fear, and the Madness of*

Crowds, chap. 6, "The Martians Invade New Jersey"; see also H. Cantril, *The Invasion from Mars: A Study in the Psychology of Panic* (Princeton: Princeton University Press, 1940). For the complete script of the radio play, by Howard Koch, see his memoir of *The Panic Broadcast: Portrait of an Event* (New York: Avon, 1971), pp. 33–80.

29. Trevor Datson, "Big Martian Honors H. G. Wells' Sci-Fi Classic," Reuters News Agency, April 14, 1998 (as kindly relayed to me from Philadelphia by Mr. J. O'Boyle).

30. On this terrifying (and paranoid) episode in American history, the McCarthy "witch-hunts," see Charles E. Potter, *Days of Shame* (New York: Signet, 1971); David Halberstam, *The Fifties* (New York: Villard Books, 1993), esp. chap. 1–3 (treating both the A-bomb and McCarthy).

31. See Ulrich Suerbaum (with Ulrich Broich and Raimund Borgmeier), *Science Fiction: Theorie und Geschichte, Themen und Typen, Form und Weltbild* (Stuttgart: Reclam, 1981), with numerous references to "Alien," "Bug-Eyed Monster (BEM)," "Erdinvasion," "extraterrestrische Intelligenz," "Verfremdung [that is, 'alienation']," and so on.

32. For a recent study specifically dealing with the conspiratorial psychic milieu of the UFO Experience, see Jodi Dean, *Aliens in America: Conspiracy Cultures from Outerspace to Cyberspace* (Ithaca, N.Y.: Cornell University Press, 1998).

33. AP dispatch, as quoted in MacDougall, *Superstition and the Press*, p. 579.

34. Carl Gustav Jung, *Flying Saucers: A Modern Myth of Things Seen in the Sky* (1959; New York: MJF Books, 1978), pp. 13, 15, 17, 22, 23.

35. See *Catechism of the Council of Trent for Parish Priests* (Rockford, Ill.: TAN Books, 1982).

36. J. Allen Hynek, *The UFO Experience: A Scientific Inquiry* (New York: Ballantine, 1974), pp. 32–33. Hynek's book is full of detailed sighting reports, about which my readers are invited to render their own independent judgment, and more such cases, reported subsequently, are to be found in Jenny Randles, *The UFO Conspiracy: The First Forty Years* (London: Javelin, 1988).

37. Hynek, *The UFO Experience*, pp. 178–84.

38. MacDougall, *Superstition and the Press*, pp. 584, 600. For Hynek's involvement with Spielberg's movies, see Thomas Durwood, ed., *Close Encounters of the Third Kind: A Document of the Film* (New York: Ballantine, 1978), a picture-album showing the decisive, UFO *and* ET, iconographic results.

39. C. D. B. Bryan, *Close Encounters of the Fourth Kind: Alien Abduction, UFOs, and the Conference at M.I.T.* (New York: Knopf, 1995), p. 9.

40. See Hynek, *UFO Experience*, chap. 10, "Close Encounters of the Third Kind." To the contrary, according to the recollections of Jack Williamson, a popular science-fiction writer then resident in New Mexico, the Zamora incident was only "a hoax," one perpetrated by student pranksters at the New Mexico School of Mines in Socorro; see Toby Smith, *Little Gray Men: Roswell and the Rise of a Popular Culture* (Albuquerque: University of New Mexico Press, 2000), p. 151;

for many more details treating the famous Zamora close encounter as a hoax, see Philip J. Klass, *UFOs Explained* (New York: Random House, 1974), chap. 12.

41. Hynek, *UFO Experience*, pp. 192–93.

42. Ibid., pp. 253, 256–57.

43. W. Sullivan, "Influence of the Press and Other Mass Media," in Sagan and Page, *UFO's: A Scientific Debate*, pp. 258–62; see also MacDougall, *Superstition and the Press*, pp. 578 ff.

44. Chaplin, *Rumor, Fear, and Madness*, p. 134 (in a chapter devoted to mass-hysterical perceptions of "Celestrial Crockery").

45. John Sladek, *The New Apocrypha: A Guide to Strange Sciences and Occult Beliefs* (London: Granada, 1978), p. 328.

46. Ibid., p. 47.

47. Vallée, *Confrontations*, pp. 12–13.

48. Ibid., p. 131.

49. Ibid.

50. For a brief but revealing biography of George Adamski, see Ronald D. Story, ed., *The Encyclopedia of Extraterrestrial Encounters: A Definitive, Illustrated A–Z Guide to All Things Alien* (New York: New American Library, 2001), pp. 9–11. For, however, twenty-two alleged close encounters antedating Adamski's, but none given much publicity, see Bartholomew and Howard, *UFOs and Alien Contact*, pp. 285 ff., "Appendix A: The UFO Contact Catalogue," nos. 1–21; for several other "contactees," see John A. Saliba, ed., *Flying Saucer Contactees: A Sociopsychological Perspective* (Detroit: Apogee, 1990).

51. Desmond Leslie, foreword to *Inside the Flying Saucers*, by George Adamski (New York: Paperback Library, 1967), pp. 17, 25. What follows here—Adamski in his own writing—is largely, with no surprise, an overblown rehash of his previous pulp best-seller, just as it is quoted below, only *more* so.

52. George Adamski, *Flying Saucers Have Landed* (New York: British Book Centre, Inc., 1953), as quoted in Jay David, *The Flying Saucer Reader* (New York: New American Library, 1967), p. 51.

53. Ibid., p. 69.

54. Ibid., p. 56.

55. As has been recently revealed (in Story, *The Encyclopedia of Extraterrestrial Encounters*, p. 9), in 1946 the editor of *Amazing Stories*, Ray Palmer, had rejected a story submitted to him by Adamski. This story, which was then presented by Adamski as pure fantasy, described the miraculous return of Jesus Christ to earth by means of a "space ship." In 1953, once Palmer had read Adamski's coauthored *Flying Saucers Have Landed*, he immediately realized that the "new" story was just an updated version of the 1946 manuscript; the only change was to call the Christian Savior a "Venusian" (and his post-1946 vehicle then became, rather than a "space ship," a "flying saucer"). Following the international success of his best-selling encounter, Adamski was reportedly granted a private audience with Pope John XXIII.

56. Adamski, as quoted in David, *The Flying Saucer Reader*, p. 56.

57. Ibid., p. 57.

58. Ibid., p. 60.

59. Ibid.

60. Ibid., pp. 62–63. Actually, these quotations are rather restrained in comparison with the imaginative recitations given two years later later by Adamski in his *Inside the Flying Saucers* (first published in 1955), which includes unbearably uplifting conversations with the master and his space brothers.

61. For the strictly modern cultural fabrication of this intractably earthbound type of alien, see S. Elizabeth Bird, *Dressing in Feathers: The Construction of the Indian in American Popular Culture* (Boulder, Colo.: Westview, 1996); for the much earlier precedents, see also J. F. Moffitt and S. Sebastián, *O Brave New People: The European Invention of the American Indian* (Albuquerque: University of New Mexico Press, 1998).

62. Story, *The Encyclopedia of Extraterrestrial Encounters*, p. 11.

63. Sladek, *The New Apocrypha*, p. 47; for more on "die fliegende Untertassen," see Joachim Herrmann, *Das falsche Weltbild: Astronomie und Aberglaube* (Munich: DTV, 1973), pp. 151ff. Many more such titles could—of course—be cited, but *genug noch!*

64. On this apocryphal site, see David Darlington, *Area 51—The Dreamland Chronicles: The Legend of America's Most Secret Military Base* (New York: Holt, 1997).

65. For a useful précis of all the emotional hot buttons so skillfully deployed in *Independence Day*, see Nicholas Mirzoeff, *An Introduction to Visual Culture* (London and New York: Routledge, 1999), pp. 207–11.

66. For that aesthetic evaluation of *Star Wars*, also those awesome (if not repellent) dollar figures, see *Newsweek*, 1 February 1999, pp. 60–64.

67. *National Enquirer UFO Report* (New York: Pocket Books, 1985), pp. 13, 36–38, 40–45, 50–53, 73–74, 107–108, 145–47, 156–60, 219–21; for more of the same, see Brad Steiger, *The UFO Abductors* (New York: Berkley, 1988), esp. "Why Aliens Are Attracted to Earth Women," pp. 117–19, and "Close Encounters of the Spiritual Kind," pp. 182–90.

68. For that perception, and numerous raisons d'être supporting it, see J. Vankin and J. Whalen, *Sixty Greatest Conspiracies of All Times: History's Biggest Mysteries, Coverups, and Cabals* (Secaucus, N.J.: Citadel, 1996); Robert Anton Wilson, *Everything Is under Control: Conspiracies, Cults, and Cover-Ups* (New York: HarperPerennial, 1998), an A-to-Z encyclopedia, from "Abductees Anonymous" to "Zog" (Zionist-Occupied Government).

69. See, for instance, Mark Kingman, *Dreams of the Millennium: Report from a Culture on the Brink* (London: Faber & Faber, 1997); Harold Bloom, *Omens of Millennium: The Gnosis of Angels, Dreams, and Resurrection* (New York: Riverhead, 1997). For the recurrent historical contexts, see Hillel Schwartz, *Century's End: A Cultural History of the Fin de Siècle from the 990s through the 1990s* (New York: Doubleday, 1990); Joaquín Lledó, *Los Milenarismos* (Madrid: Acento, 1999). Schwartz cites (pp. 222–26) the postmodernist legend of "abduction by aliens" as representing a standard millenarian motif. *D'accord!*

70. Alice K. Turner, *The History of Hell* (New York: Harvest, 1995), pp. 70, 193; for other apocryphal dates related to the millennium ("Jahre Null"), see Herrmann, *Das falsche Weltbild*, pp. 30–37.

71. See J. F. Moffitt, *The Arts in Spain* (London: Thames & Hudson, 1998), chap. 1.

72. For the anecdotes following (unless otherwise noted), see Richard Erdoes, *AD 1000: Living on the Brink of Apocalypse* (New York: Harper, 1988); see also Georges Duby, *L'An Mil* (Paris: Gallimard, 1980); James Reston, *The Last Apocalypse: Europe at the Year 1000 A.D.* (New York: Doubleday, 1997). For arguments to the contrary, holding that 1000 C.E. was largely ignored by the locals, see Schwarz, *Century's End*, pp. 6 ff., esp. n. 3 (citing recent scholarly bibliography).

73. Erdoes, *AD 1000*, pp. 1–2.

74. Ibid.

75. Ibid., p. 3.

76. Keith Thompson, *Angels and Aliens: UFOs and the Mythic Imagination* (New York: Ballantine, 1993), p. 120.

77. Erdoes, *AD 1000*.

78. Ibid., pp. 3–4.

79. Norman Cohn, *The Pursuit of the Millennium* (London: Secker & Warburg, 1957), p. 74.

80. Ruth Montgomery, *Aliens among Us* (New York: Putnam, 1985), esp. p. 21.

81. Cohn, *Pursuit of the Millennium*, p. 314.

82. See *Time*, 23 June 1997, pp. 62–71.

83. For the historical sequence of mass media contributions, and the argument that nothing else really happened there, see (besides Smith, *Little Gray Men: Roswell and the Rise of a Popular Culture*) Kal K. Korff, *The Roswell UFO Crash: What They Don't Want You to Know* (New York: Dell, 2000), a peerless, detective-like deconstruction of all the eyewitness accounts.

84. *Time*, 23 June 1997, p. 65

85. For these reports, see Kendrick Frazer, ed., *The UFO Invasion: The Roswell Incident, Alien Abductions, and Government Coverups* (Amherst, N.Y.: Prometheus Books, 1997), pp. 96, 125.

86. Besides Korff, *Roswell UFO Crash* and Sith, *Little Gray Men*, see Philip J. Klass, *The Real Roswell Crashed-Saucer Coverup* (Amherst, N.Y.: Prometheus Books, 1997); James McAndrew, *The Roswell Report: Case Closed* (New York: Barnes & Noble, 1997—a facsimile of the official Air Force report).

87. L. D. Kusche, *The Bermuda Triangle Mystery—Solved* (New York: Warners, 1975).

88. C. Berlitz and W. L. Moore, *The Roswell Incident* (New York: Berkley, 1980), p. 2 (emphasis in original).

89. For the damning evidence showing the film to be a fake, see Frazer, *The UFO Invasion*, pp. 135–57; Vankin and Whalen, *Sixty Greatest Conspiracies of All Times*, pp. 75–79, 407–16.

90. For this felonious topic, also calling for much industriously deconstructive detective work, see J. F. Moffitt, *Art Forgery: The Case of the Lady of Elche* (Gainesville: University of Florida Press, 1995).

91. For the iconography of the bogus Roswell specimen, see Patrick Huyghe, *The Field Guide to Extraterrestrials* (New York: Avon, 1996), pp. 22–23.

92. Again see David Jacobs, *Secret Life: Firsthand Documented Accounts of UFO Abductions* (New York: Fireside, 1993), pp. 221–28, "Anatomy of an Alien."

93. Berlitz and Moore, *Roswell Incident*, pp. 110–12.

94. Ibid., p. 112; for Stringfield, "a longtime UFO investigator" (perhaps not the greatest credentials known to the world of science), see also pp. 107–14, 121.

95. Ibid., pp. 124, 138.

96. For the MJ-12 forgeries (and treated as such), see three investigative essays by Philip Klass in Frazer, *The UFO Invasion*, pp. 73–93. For a properly ironic, and properly fictional, treatment of the MJ-12 hoax as an elaborate government conspiracy, including "staging the first sighting of unidentified flying objects over Mount Rainier and followed two weeks later with the Roswell 'crash' of alien spacecraft," see Christopher Buckley, *Little Green Men* (New York: HarperPerennial, 1999), pp. 30 ff. For the differing, True Believer, approach ("They really did it!"), see Gregory N. Kanon, *The Great UFO Hoax* (Lakeville, Minn.: Galde Press, 1997).

97. K. K. Korff, "What Really Happened at Roswell," *Skeptical Inquirer* (July/August 1997): 24–31 (also citing his monograph, *Roswell UFO Crash*, with a detailed explanation of "what really happened at Roswell"); for the complicit role of the media in institutionalizing the myth, see particularly Klass, *The Real Roswell Crashed-Saucer Coverup*; Smith, *Little Gray Men*.

98. For this particular appraisal of the Roswell apocrypha, see Carl Sagan, *The Demon-Haunted World: Science as a Candle in the Dark* (New York: Ballantine, 1997), pp. 83–93, 186–87.

99. Frank Scully, *Behind the Flying Saucers* (New York: Henry Holt, 1950); I shall quote from the paperback version (New York: Popular Library, 1951). I was directed to this incunabulum by Smith, *Little Gray Men*, chap. 5, who gives the historical context and cites the important thematic repercussions.

100. See *Daily Variety*, "One Flying Saucer Lands in New Mexico" (12 October 1949); "Flying Saucers Dismantled, Secrets May Be Lost" (23 November 1949); "Air Force Asked Twenty Questions" (11 January 1950).

101. On "Dr. Gee" and his startling firsthand information, see Scully, *Behind the Flying Saucers*, pp. 24, 39–40, 114–24.

102. Ibid., p. 21.

103. Ibid., p. 25; for press clippings dealing with the Farmington (not Roswell) apparitions in 1950, see pp. 180–81.

104. Ibid., pp. 26–30, 115, 117, 119, 122, 123.

105. MacDougall, *Superstition and the Press*, p. 611.

106. On Gebauer, see Klass, *UFOs: The Public Deceived*, p. 279; see also Smith, *Little Gray Men*, p. 122; also showing (p. 119) that the Aztec, New Mexico, crashed "flying saucer" was only a ditched P-38 fighter; it only morphed into a UFO after a Denver radio announcer fancifully twisted it into "Venusian" leftovers.

107. Ed Walters, *The Gulf Breeze Sightings: The Most Astounding Multiple Sightings of UFOs in U.S. History* (New York: Avon, 1991).

108. For Mr. Ed's profitable fakery, see Frazer, *The UFO Invasion*, pp. 184–86.

109. For various historical precedents, see Curtis MacDougall, *Hoaxes* (reprint, New York: Dover, 1958); for the strictly artistic sort of hoaxes, see also J. F. Moffitt, *El caso de la Dama de Elche: Historia de una falsificación* (Barcelona: Destino, 1997), chap. 15, "Las bromas modernistas."

Chapter 9

The Faltering History of UFOlogy

INTRODUCTION TO A HISTORIOGRAPHY OF THE UFO EXPERIENCE

It will now be useful to examine the UFO experience as a historical artifact, something human-made and situated within a specific, but dynamically evolving, chronological context. Back in his previous professional role as a reputable historian of popular American culture, David M. Jacobs performed signal service in establishing the historiography of the so-called UFO experience.[1] What follows is very much indebted to his historical research, the kind he *used* to practice with reason, diligence, and commendable skill, back in 1982. As Jacobs then explained, immediately following the publicity accorded to the misreported Kenneth Arnold flying saucer report of 1947, the first UFO reports described "silvery" or "metallic," unconventionally shaped (*à la soucoupe*) objects levitating high in the sky and performing adroit maneuvers apparently beyond the technological capabilities then known to humankind. The objects were reported singly or in groups, hovering, zigzagging, making seemingly impossible right-angle turns, swooping low, "dancing" about in a jolly way, later to fly away at tremendous speeds. Pilots reported seeing UFOs "pace" their planes, or flying circles around them. Although no one saw any of these objects landing nearby, or claimed, then, to have met the occupants of a UFO, the flying saucers' nimble aerial antics suggested that they were under intelligent control and that landings, and even "contact," were possible, indeed imminent.

Concerned that people were sighting "real" objects that might be truly unknown or—given the Cold War mentality—Soviet secret weapons, the Air Force reluctantly took on the role of an official UFO investigating body. That made sense; the primary mission of that government agency was to determine the potential for hostile threats in the air to the country; once those airborne objects were specifically identified as "hostile," then a proper defense would be mounted. In 1947, the Marshall Plan was devised to rehabilitate Europe, mostly however as a bulwark of freedom against further Communist territorial appropriations; it was passed by Congress in 1948. As a timely riposte, the Warsaw ("Cominform") Pact was devised by the *other* side, and, also in 1948, there was a communist coup d'état in Czechoslovakia and the USSR stopped all traffic between Berlin and the West.[2]

Meanwhile, the Air Force collected UFO reports, classified them as "sensitive" data, and made some effort to study each one. By 1949, the year that China became a sovereign Communist state and when NATO was formed as another timely riposte, the Air Force had concluded that the objects were not secret weapons, were not recognizably human artifacts, and that they came neither from the Soviet Union nor any other country. Also recognized was the physiological impossibility of survival by any earthling pilot making such radically abrupt and speedy maneuvers. That left three explanations: (1) the objects came from outer space, and as such could possibly threaten the national security; (2) they were unknown, but most likely *natural*, phenomena; or (3) they were massively reported misidentifications of conventional phenomena ("MFOs," referring back to point 2), which then suggested the possibility of a "mass hallucination." As specifically summed up in 1983 by Curtis MacDougall, a media historian, "Among the human factors [explaining sightings of UFOs] are poor perception, motivation, lights and objects originating within the eye for normal and abnormal reasons and hallucinations. Among atmospheric causes are reflections and refraction of light, astral phenomena [Venus, for instance], unique cloud patterns, electrically charged insect swarms, and optical illusions and mirages." His conclusion: "People see flying saucers because they want to see them."[3]

By 1953, three years into the Korean War, the Air Force further concluded that the objects did not display characteristics suggesting that they specifically had extraterrestrial origins; a further conclusion was that they did not threaten the national security, and that they were not "unknown" natural phenomena. Therefore, only one assumption remained: they were only "MFOs," meaning that the sightings probably represented misidentifications of conventional phenomena, with many reports having psychological (or wholly mundane) explanations. That term "MFOs," was *almost* advanced as early as 1963. In a book published that year, *The World of Flying Saucers*, Harvard astrophysicist Donald H. Menzel dealt in considerable detail with what he called instances of "mistaken identification of air-borne objects or astronomical phenomena. . . . But since each one [has] derived from a peculiar combination of circumstance . . . accounting for them often requires a certain amount of luck as well as patience."[4] Given this conclusion, a sensible one, the Air Force concentrated on downplaying them, fearing, rightly, that the Soviet Union could use "flying saucer hysteria" as a derisory weapon ("dumb Amerikanskii") in the real world of psychological warfare.

Thanks to the likes of Major Donald E. Keyhoe (USMC, Ret.), the flying saucer paradigm had dramatically shifted. Up to the middle of the 1950s, 23 percent of the 94 percent of all Americans who had heard, one way or the other, about the sky-borne invaders still assumed them to be secret military devices, that is, strictly of terrestrial origins. Later the secret weapon model dramatically shifted to an extraterrestrial explanation—and that has remained the paradigm ever since. The primary reason for this attitude change (the "far out" thesis) was the publication of several popular books and magazine articles advocating the extraterrestrial hypothesis. One important example is Keyhoe's earlier paperback best-seller, *The Flying Saucers Are Real* (1950). Since that book sold no less than *half-a-million copies*, it is a historical artifact of considerable significance: it first established the UFO Experience as Big Business.[5] As we saw, slightly earlier Frank Scully's *Behind the Flying Saucers* (1950) had claimed that extraterrestrials from a crashed saucer were being kept at a secret American military installation, specifically Wright-Patterson Air Force Base. That story is today, fifty years later, a central motif in the Roswell legend, where the secret base is now specifically stated (for instance, in the blockbuster movie *Independence Day*) to be Area 51 in Nevada, a desolate place much visited by eager UFO groupies.[6] Scully's book sold many, many thousands of copies, but sales dropped off as soon as it was revealed as a hoax in 1953. Scully, however, almost seemed believable. In *The Riddle of the Flying Saucers: Is Another World Watching?* (1950), science writer Gerald Heard claimed that extraterrestrial "bees" were responsible for the sighting reports. Now there's an argument designed to generate some "buzz"!

From the standpoint of popular literature, it is interesting to note that between 1947 and January 9, 1950, *The Reader's Guide to Periodical Lit-*

erature only lists eight magazine articles on flying saucers. Moreover, reflecting the period's still skeptical standard, these articles were then listed under the headings of "Aeronautics," "Aeroplanes," "Balloons: Use in Research," and "Illusions and Hallucinations." However, as a result of melodramatic books produced by the likes of Keyhoe, Scully, and Heard, also continued press accounts of sightings of flying saucers (most never authenticated as "Illusions and Hallucinations"), numerous popular articles soon appeared in such mainstream magazines as *Life, Look, Time, Newsweek,* and *Popular Science,* and these typically emphasized the extraterrestrial hypothesis. Beginning in 1952, and continuing to the present, the result was that the extraterrestrial theory was intensified as the dominant motif in UFO movie and sci-fi television portrayals (figs. 9–15, 17–19).[7] As it was labeled, the "UFO experience" was believed to be "extraterrestrial," and so it went, right up to the present day.

Even though ignored by Jacobs, the part played by Hollywood and its science fiction movies in the solidification of the UFO experience deserves careful examination.[8] The first cinematic depiction of a UFO appeared in the low-budget, eponymous *The Flying Saucer* (1950); as told there, the evil craft was an earthling product, made by the Communists to bedevil freedom-loving Americans. Shortly afterward, there began the convention of the extraterrestrial-monster B-movie, and that, too, was about global conflict. After Hiroshima, the understood psychic subtext was the recognition that science and technology were in a position to adversely affect the destiny of the whole human race. Sci-fi monster films of the Cold War era posed the specifically postwar problem of how human evil and alien technology combine to threaten the existence of the earthling species. This genre went hand in hand with another timely American invention: the drive-in movie. Old fogies will remember these *al fresco* cinemas being called "passion pits," and the jiggling cars with steamy windows parked there typically were themselves rocket shaped (or phalluslike, if you wish); evidently, sci-fi movies had an aphrodisiac effect on the closely huddled masses.

In *The Thing* (1951), a really scary (and well-made) movie, we saw the premiere of the ET who regards humans as sustenance, not as space brothers in need of spiritual guidance, which was the message brought by the kindly alien starring in *The Day the Earth Stood Still* (1951; fig. 9). *The Thing* triggered an immensely popular cycle of films about monsters and mutations produced by nuclear radiation or materialized from outer space. Additionally, as marketed for the passion-pit audience culture, there was a whole series of "It" flicks, the kind where the *It* is a monster conqueror; among these now forgotten subliminal epics may be numbered *It Came from Outer Space* (1953), *It Came from beneath the Sea* (1955), *It Conquered the World* (1956), and so forth. In the high-budget arena, we saw the skilled cinematic adaptation of H. G. Wells's *War of the Worlds* (1953), and the earthlings are only saved from brutal alien conquest by the common cold germ. The ETs tried a more subtle approach in *Invaders from Mars* (1953); as in the classic film *The Body Snatchers* (1956; remade in 1978), they absorb or take over our bodies, and the resulting clones look just like us! Early on, low-budget sci-fi films provided a strictly visual impetus for that current, typically lurid, staple of postmodernist alien-abduction fantasies, the utilization of human beings by ETs for genetic and/or reproductive purposes. The historical proof may now be viewed in (for example) *It Came from Outer Space* (1953), *Invaders from Mars* (1953), *Killers from Space* (1954), *This Island Earth* (1955), *Not of This Earth* (1957), *I Married a Monster from Outer Space* (1958), and so on.

Naturally dissatisfied with the boring results of the Air Force's investigation, civilian self-styled "UFOlogists"—all of whom, doubtlessly, were B-movie aficionados—formed their own ideological collectives to gather and investigate UFO reports on their own. Early groups included the Aerial Phenomenon Research Organization (APRO) and the Civilian Saucer Investigations. Now UFO reports became adversarial; unfortunately not relabeled as "MFOs," they became a public relations problem for the Air Force. Most UFO proponents became adherents of the only available "nonconventional" theory about the origins of UFOs. This was the "nuts-and-bolts" extraterrestrial hypothesis: obviously, the well-wrought crafts were flying to earth from other planets, traversing time and space through technologies beyond mere human understanding. As Professor Jacobs pointed out back in 1982:

> In many ways the approach of UFO researchers in the early 1950s was similar to that of nineteenth-century spiritualists [meaning the old-fashioned kind of occultists attempting to "communicate with the dead"]. In trying to make spirit communication credible, the [Victorian era] spiritualists maintained four [pseudoscientific] principles: a rejection of supernaturalism; a firm belief in the inviolability of natural law; a reliance on external facts, rather than on an inward state of mind; and a faith in the progressive development of knowledge. The same was true of the early UFO proponents: they rejected occult explanations of UFOs; believed in the laws of physics; relied on external facts rather than on inward states of mind; and thought that increased knowledge would lead to more evidence to support their contentions. As long as the reports of the phenomenon remained rational, logical, and understandable, UFOl-

ogists could continue to press for scientific inquiry on the basis that the phenomenon could be studied within the confines of "normal" science.[9]

Needless to say, for all of their pseudoscientific pretensions, civilian UFO amateurs, either in the 1950s or presently, could not be bothered with a fundamental, indeed intractable, problem: the immutable laws of physics dictate that no material object can approach the speed of light. Therefore, because of the vastness of our universe measured in terms of "light-years," a demonstrable fact, no extraterrestrial beings could reach us without traveling tens of thousands of earthling years in order to reach our planet. No matter: UFO advocates dogmatically argued that the phenomenon obviously warranted immediate and complete scientific study. If the ignorant taxpayers would not foot the bill, they would themselves assume the moral and economic burden. So burdened, they criticized the Air Force for preventing their noble investigative mission by restricting access to the data. They were also piqued by reiterated assurances to the public that government scientists were ("trust us") still zealously investigating the subject.

ENTER THE CONSPIRACY THEORIES: PREFIGURING *THE X-FILES*

Such secrecy and tight security, all to be expected, however, in the interminable Cold War, fueled speculation of an Air Force cover-up. Decades later, in a post–Cold War era, the conspiracy theories, which by their very nature attack established authority, are perhaps even more widespread, more stridently expressed.[10] The classic conspiracy theory begins with a smidgen of fact mixed with much conjecture. It begins with ambiguity and small suspicions; inflated to Brobdingnagian proportions and blended with further error, these initial apprehensions should then be expressed with fundamentalist certitude. However, if you have a sense of humor, you will lack conviction, true zeal. If you desire success in such paranoid endeavors, you are well advised to be *very serious*, humorless, in your obsessive pursuit of "the truth"; indeed, you should really be "possessed" (see chapter 6).

The really good (or most entertaining) complicity fantasies peel away the rational veneer of history or science and expose an abyss of logic-defying synchronicities. Done with real flair and zeal, the most vitriolic, improbable, impossible, ludicrous, and laughable speculations sometimes appear almost plausible. Beloved of the hard-core theorists is the "what else could it be?" argument; for them, this is an adequate substitute for actual evidence. Abetted by public mental laziness, a good, meaning really sensational, conspiracy theory is tough to crack; it is also more fun to espouse than is a banal explanation. Conspiratorial fantasies, thickets of intrigue, are probably the most prominent topographical feature of the postmodernist landscape of paranoia, and there is now among us a whole catalogue of such ideological whimsies.[11]

Let me document this perception in the particular instance, and by quoting from a paperback aptly called *The UFO Conspiracy*. The determined author is Jenny Randles, known as the Miss Marples of British UFOlogists. As she explains (or exclaims):

> It is popular, especially in the USA, to say that a "cover-up" of UFO reality by official sources is responsible for all the problems that beset this subject [and] the suggestion that an attitude of disinformation prevails on some vast scale—so vast it often called "the Cosmic Watergate"—is surprisingly justified if you look deep enough. . . . UFOs exist. The evidence that will confront you in the pages that follow makes that conclusion inescapable. . . . UFOs have also been investigated by every major government on earth, and are *still* being studied at an official level in China, France, Spain, the USSR [now defunct], the USA, and the United Kingdom—to name but six leading nations. . . . However, in strange contradiction of this, the public statements of these people [i.e., official spokespersons] mislead and sometimes lie. They downplay importance, denounce witnesses, refute investigations, and cast around a smoke-screen of apathy that would be extremely worrying—if we could think for more than a moment that it was not a charade. . . . We trust our very lives to these people, who now hold in their hands many ways to destroy our planet—not the least of which is an electronic arsenal of deadly weapons. . . . That said, ask yourself one question. Why are you being *told* that the [UFO] phenomenon is non-existent? . . . I contend very simply that one thing is clear: the public is being deceived on a colossal scale. . . . I submit that this *does* meet the requirements to be called a conspiracy.[12]

Well, I'm convinced. How about you? You should be: millions of postmodernist Americans subscribe to the Outer-Space Paranoia Syndrome (OSPS). How do we know this? One looming fact, a human artifact prominently displayed since 1993, is the widely viewed TV show (on the Fox network again), *The X-Files*. It is also shown in sixty countries overseas. Its central mythology is (surprise) the covert colonization of the earth by extraterrestrials. This mission has been going on since the Ice Age, meaning long before you or I were born. The idea is an ET project to repopulate the world with alien-human "clones" (you know, like the people you work with); that explains all those stolen batches of human sperm and ova. They plan to dispose of the native earthlings by introducing an AIDS-like virus, carried by "black oil"; only the alien clones are immune. The all-pervasive X-Files subtext is a Machiavellian government cover-up of the well-engineered ET scheme, a sort of Final Solution (*Endlösung*) engineered from far, far away. The heroes are FBI Agent Fox Mulder, a credulous believer in paranormal phenomena, and his partner, Dana Scully, an M.D., who always opts for the rational explanation (with a neat twist on movie conventions, this time the woman gets the brains). Mulder has an emotional investment in his dogged pursuit; you see, *his sister was abducted by aliens*.

The movie was inevitable; called *The X-Files: Fight the Future*, it cost *$63 million to make*. Each principle actor—David "Mulder" Duchovny and Gillian "Scully" Anderson—got *4.5 million dollars* for their emotive efforts. That was a good investment; at last count, since its alien-flick, summer 1998, blockbuster release, it made much, much better than that whopping figure ($63m) in profits, nearly *$200 million* in fact. Besides that, there are the inevitable tie-ins; McFarlane Toys vigorously produced the movie action figures. Also figuring in the multinational marketplace are touring fan conventions, called "Expos." Obviously, now *The X-Files* is a franchise, like *Star Trek*, and endless sequels must be in the works, lined up like clipable bond coupons enticing another tribe of New Age consumerist groupies: "X-philes." Aliens, and their mind-boggling conspiracies to take over the world, are Big Business, *really* big; according to informed sources, the Fox TV channel will likely reap *$1.5 billion* from its *X-Files* franchise.[13] Now that communism is dead, and capitalism a given, "conspiracism" is left as the secular faith of the moment.[14] According to its tenets, at least someone is in control, even if said superior force is as much evil as extraterrestrial. Having its own lethal weapons of mass distraction, the other successful postmodernist ideology is entertainment. Please do fight the alien future—unless it means depriving us of all those blockbuster sequels.

Besides representing an inextricable component of the evolving UFO experience, *The X-Files: Fight the Future* has its own art-historical (cinematic) context. It is a late blooming offshoot of the post-Hiroshima, 1950s science fiction movie craze. Then as now, the science-fiction genre really draws upon terrestrial experience, and what else could films made by humans possibly reflect (or exploit) but human concerns and anxieties? According to the format fixed back then, all manner of hideous adversaries—rogue comets, mind-control rays, galactic convulsions, and, especially, alien invasions—are all aimed at *us*. Then as now,

the prevailing paradigm is pessimism and paranoia. The immediate ideological ancestors of the cleverly crafted *The X-Files: Fight the Future*
were admittedly more gauche in their presentation and include now
mostly forgotten films like *Them!* (1954). Back then, the pre-ET *Them!*
were giant mutant ants who, after suddenly appearing in the Mojave
Desert, then proceeded (perhaps ironically) to crush humans like bugs.

In 1956, also the year that the Soviets brutally crushed a Hungarian
independence movement, we were treated to *The Invasion of the Body
Snatchers*, a deliciously paranoid flick where the aliens emerged from slimy
seed-pods, morphed into your next-door neighbor, your girlfriend, maybe
even you. Also appearing in 1954 (when the French fortress of Dien Bien
Phu fell to the Vietnamese communists) was *Godzilla, King of the Monsters*. This was a long-dormant prehistoric creature, a sea-dwelling, giant
green lizard with radioactive breath, who was unleashed upon defenseless
(Japanese) humanity by the haughty folks (Americans) who had brought
the world a decade of nuclear terror; the outraged reptile thoroughly
trashed Tokyo. Godzilla, of course, made another comeback in 1998; even
though he then proceeded to savage New York (which was only fitting), he
was still a flop at the postmodernist box office. Then as now, most science-
fiction movies tend to see our putative extraterrestrial neighbors as the
moral equivalent of testosterone-charged sharks and the universe as a
really dangerous neighborhood, one maybe even worse than yours.

Back then, of course, no one had imagined the blockbuster movie;
that constitutes the innovation of the postmodernist infotainment
industry. *The X-Files: Fight the Future* is one of those; so was *Independence Day* (1996), the seventh highest grossing film of all time. That
hyperthyroid condition began back in the mid-1970s, with the likes of
Jaws (1975: Moby Dick Redux as a mega-shark) and *Star Wars* (1977:
Princess in the Tower saved by space-jockey Prince Charming). With its
inevitable sequels, the *Star Wars* phenomenon became an industry in its
own right; with its allied merchandising programs (action figures, lunch
boxes, you name it), it has created a *multibillion dollar* empire on earth.
The unprecedented idea of the blockbuster was to premiere simultaneously in a large number of theaters. In 1975, *Jaws* opened in 465; in
1998, *Godzilla* suddenly surfaced in as many as 7,000. These films have
huge, galaxy-sized budgets, and as much as 50 percent is devoted to marketing, most of which pays for TV spots. The post–Cold War films are
now consciously engineered to dazzle twelve-year-old boys: crashing
soundtracks, ceaseless explosions, unlimited mayhem and mass destruction, cardboard characters, comic-book scripts. Such minimalist mental
reduction makes it ever so much easier to dub in soundtracks in Can-

tonese, Tagalog, Bantu, or Spanish; the overseas market often proves more profitable than does the domestic. And boys will be boys. And they love to get their adrenaline going. Like some kind of hypercharged avenging angels from outer space, extraterrestrials are now the post-Gothic monsters of cinematic choice.

RASHOMON REVISITED:
THE KILLIAN AND WOODBRIDGE INCIDENTS

Naturally, after 1947 nearly every report of a flying saucer said to have been observed loitering in somebody's aerial neighborhood received instant media attention and widespread publicity. Naturally, tracking down such sightings proved to be a laborious and expensive process; about ten man-hours would typically be expended by Air Force investigators on each case, scarcely enough time in many instances. Naturally, once a plausible, meaning merely mundane, explanation for each pseudoevent would eventually be worked out, that finding, the result of so much labor and expense, would be studiously ignored by the media. Naturally, as the budget managers of the Air Force argued among themselves, why bother? I will now cite just one incident and let it stand operationally for all the rest. I will put it into the context of a contemporary, Cold War work of art, the Japanese film *Rashomon* (1951). You remember the story line: there was a brutal rape-murder incident in the woods, and four people either took part in it or served as supposedly reliable eyewitnesses. As it turns out, four witnesses to a single incident produced four stories wholly at variance with one another.

First we will relate the initial report—read by everybody—of a classic flying saucer incident, and then its eventual solution—ignored: *boring*. Back in the early 1950s, the major rumormonger of the emergent Flying Saucer Industry was one Donald Keyhoe; on his paperback covers, he was always dubbed "Major," with the sobriquet "U.S.M.C. (ret.)." I have looked up (*ret.*); according to the *OED*, it means "cashiered"—and on the title page for this book I should have put "SP/4 Jack Moffitt, A.U.S. (ret.)." No matter; Keyhoe's colorful and alarming tale is cast in the mini-paragraphish style—melodramatic *hot* prose—favored by the tabloids designed "for inquiring minds." Such as we were told in Keyhoe's *Flying Saucers: Top Secret* (1960):

> The DC-6 was an hour out of Newark when the captain first saw the UFOs.
> It was February 24, 1959; the time, 8:20 P.M.

> Until then, the trip had been routine. The nonstop Detroit flight, American Airlines 713, had departed from Newark on schedule. In command was a four-million-miler, Captain Peter W. Killian, fifteen years on the airlines. Riding the co-pilot's right-hand seat was First Officer John Dee.
>
> By 8:15, the two stewardesses, Edna LeGate and Beverly Pingree, had finished serving dinner to the thirty-five passengers aboard. The flight was then over Pennsylvania, the roar of its four engines subdued to a drone in the airliner's sound-proofed cabin.

Besides using shrink-wrapped paragraphing, in order to make this tall tale credible (and so to sell many thousands of paperbacks), you need to add verisimilitude, the mundane details, for instance, "At 8:19, the plane passed over Bradford, altitude 8,500 feet, air speed 350. Scattered clouds, more than 3,000 feet below, occasionally hid the ground." But such trivia can only hold the reader's attention for a brief while. As always, your authorial task is melodrama. Here's how Keyhoe does it:

> Suddenly, Captain Killian noticed three brilliant lights. They were south of the plane, higher, and in a precise line. For an instant, he thought he was seeing [the constellation] Orion. Then he sat up quickly. Those were not stars. They were powerful lights on moving objects!
>
> He could see Orion, higher up in the sky. In contrast, the strange flying objects were *huge*—not only larger, but brighter. Their color, too, was different, an intense yellowish white. Abruptly, one flying object left the formation. As it came toward the plane, Killian prepared for a hasty turn. But it slowed, some distance away, apparently observing the DC-6.
>
> Killian *knew* now it was a UFO—some unknown machine under intelligent control. He could not be sure, but it seemed at least triple the size of his plane.

So convinced, the pilot belatedly thinks to tell "First Officer Dee about the objects." The UFO again approaches the earthling vehicle: "Though the glow was not blinding, Killian could not see behind it. But he knew that whoever controlled the UFO must be watching them intently. It was not a comfortable feeling." Killian radios other planes, and it turns out that two of them "had sighted the UFOs after hearing Killian's alert." Killian intended to keep the story quiet, but, alas, "an aviation expert aboard—Mr. N. D. Puncas, manager of a Curtiss-Wright plant—tipped off the Detroit papers." As Puncas blabbed to the press, "I saw these three objects in a clear sky. They were round, and in precise formation. I've never seen anything like it!" As Keyhoe concludes his clearly insubstantial tale, "press wires quickly carried the story around the country."[15] The implied message here is that any "story" given nationwide media coverage must (somehow) be true. Put otherwise, mere reportage makes for veracity. Or does it?

The so-called Killian case was also discussed by Lawrence Tacker in his book, *Flying Saucers and the U.S. Air Force* (1960). According to the *alternate* version of the Killian case, which should have reminded one of the widely viewed Japanese film *Rashomon* appearing eight years earlier, "the pilot's written statement suggested the possibility that he had witnessed a night aerial refueling operation." As Tacker discovered, "Air Force records indicate that three B-47 aircraft were in the geographical area mentioned on night refueling operations. Air Force KC-97 tanker aircraft have several groups of lights which, seen at a distance, would appear to be one or more lights." In this case, another dollop of verisimilitude solves handily the mystery of the best-selling tale of Killian's visionary adventure. According to Tacker, the mundane context was obvious, simply a nocturnal sighting of a

> KC-97 tanker refueling a B-47 aircraft [which] normally flies at an altitude of approximately 30 degrees above his aircraft, remaining in view for approximately 40 minutes. These facts also coincide with his report of low speed and general configuration of the object or objects [reported by Killian]. In addition, since the tanker was making a ground speed of approximately 210 knots (230 knots true air speed, with a 20 knot headwind), and since the United Airlines pilot first reported seeing the lights at 8:45 P.M., 50 miles east of Youngstown, Ohio, handing toward Akron, Ohio, a distance of 120 miles, this also accounts for the tanker aircraft lights being sighted over Akron at 9:15 by ground observers. The final proof was supplied by the 772nd Aircraft Control and Warning Squadron at Claysburg, Pennsylvania, which confirmed the fact that three B-47 type aircraft were conducting night refueling operations in the area.[16]

As you see, compared with the brilliantly dramatized narration provided by Major Keyhoe, a recognized specialist in this subliterary genre, this *other* version of the story is *boring*.[17]

Twenty years later, the *Rashomon* syndrome was still being played out. Here is the newer version, one which I have actually seen dramatically (and repeatedly) recreated in UFO "documentaries" made for television. This is the so-called Woodbridge incident, witnessed in the United Kingdom near Ipswich on a U.S. Air Force base leased from the RAF. This one seemed credible since there were several witnesses and, better yet, an official report on the incident was submitted to local RAF headquarters. This memo was composed by the deputy base commander, Lt. Col. Charles I. Halt, a managerial type (whom I suspect was not part of the active flight crew, merely one of the swarming ground personnel always attached to air bases). As Halt explained it, this was an event decidedly mysterious, nay, inexplicable. Dated January 13, 1981, it reads as follows:

1. Early in the morning of 27 Dec 80 (approximately 0300 local time), two USAF security police patrolmen saw unusual lights outside the back gate at RAF Woodbridge. Thinking an aircraft might have crashed or been forced down, they called for permission to go outside the gate to investigate. The on-duty flight chief responded and allowed three patrolmen to proceed on foot. The individuals reported seeing a strange glowing object in the forest. The object was described as being metallic in appearance and triangular in shape, approximately two to three meters across the base and approximately two meters high. It illuminated the entire forest with a white light. The object itself had a pulsing red light on top and a bank(s) of blue lights underneath. The object was hovering or [resting] on legs. As the patrolmen approached the object, it maneuvered through the trees and disappeared. At this time the animals on a nearby farm went into a frenzy. The object was briefly sighted approximately an hour later near the back gate.

2. The next day, three depressions 1 1/2" deep and 7" in diameter were found where the object had been sighted on the ground. The following night (29 Dec 80) the area was checked for radiation. Beta/gamma readings of 0.1 milli-roentgens were recorded, with peak readings in the three depressions and near the center of the triangle formed by the depressions. A nearby tree had moderate (.05–.07) readings on the side of the tree toward the depressions.

3. Later in the night a red sun-like light was seen through the trees. It moved about and pulsed. At one point it appeared to throw off glowing particles and then broke into five separate white objects and then disappeared. Immediately thereafter, three star-like objects were noticed in the sky, two objects to the north and one to the south, all of which were about 10 degrees off the horizon. The objects moved rapidly in sharp, angular movements and displayed red, green and blue lights. The objects to the north appeared to be elliptical through an 8–12 power lens. They then turned to full circles. The objects to the north remained in the sky for an hour or more. The object to the south was visible for two or three hours and beamed down a stream of light from time to time. Numerous individuals, including the undersigned, witnessed the activities [described] in paragraphs 2 and 3.

CHARLES I. HALT, Lt Col, USAF
Deputy Base Commander[18]

So how did you and I get to see this performed for us so many times on TV? Obviously, the media had stepped in, and their very presence had elevated a banal visual anomaly to the status of an "urban legend" (see chapter 11). And the damn thing still gets replayed on prime time—notwithstanding the wholly mundane explanation provided in the skilled detective work of Ian Ridpath, who published his findings back in January 1985 in the *Guardian* (not a tabloid!). Before then (of course!) a book had been published, *Sky Crash* (1983), coauthored by indefatigable UFOlogist Jenny Randles. It was, however, a tabloid, the *News of the World* (probably the worst of a bad lot), which initially broke the story. This highly magnified tale had been *bought* for £12,000 (around $20,000) from a cashiered airman known only by a pseudonym, "Art Wallace." Although the artless Art claimed his disguise was necessary, you see, his life would be "in danger" if he "talked," he did talk a lot about it on local television (so gaining even more quid for his pro). Naturally, he called the beaming light a "UFO"—and why recount the over-dramatized rest told by Art?

In short, Ridpath showed the flashing light to have been a pulsating beam from a nearby lighthouse. Woodbridge is only five miles from the Suffolk coastline, and any of the locals could have told the Yanks just what was emitting, every night, that "sun-like light [which] was seen through the trees [and which] moved about and pulsed." It turns out additionally that Col. Halt, in writing up the incident a fortnight later, had misidentified the day of the incident, and at 3 A.M. on December 26 a brilliant meteor had been seen in the night sky over southern England. The purported "burn marks" found on the trees were just axe cuts in the bark, made by local foresters to mark trees ready for harvesting. The same foresters recognized the "three depressions" to be (only) rabbit diggings, several months old and covered with pine needles. As for the "radiation," that was just a normal reading for the area. As you see, once again, the proper explanation is merely *boring*. Such explanations are also expensive to come by: who has the time, resources, intelligence, and motivation to deconstruct such cinematic apocrypha? For all that, this completely deflated myth is still exhibited on TV. But why not? There is still money to be made from it.

UFOLOGY FINDS ITSELF PERPLEXED AND BEWILDERED

The extraterrestrial hypothesis—a notion David Jacobs used to call dismissively "the UFOlogists' belief structure"—was based on data from mostly unconfirmed UFO reports. No matter; since around 1950, these were used to support their tenaciously held belief that UFOs came from outer space. How else could you explain the celestial apparitions? The sightings seemed to happen at random, supposedly with no particular educational or cultural group especially likely to behold them. The anomalous phenomena were reported all over the world, and they conformed to neither national boundaries nor to the technological level of the country in which they were seen. A growing number of anomalous radar reports, plus typically blurry photographs and motion pictures of alleged UFOs, suggested that flying saucers could be divorced from the vagaries of human perception. Beginning in 1972, various rational explanations advanced for all these aerial anomalies were, of course, discounted out of hand—both then and now.[19] After all, as was endlessly chanted, "credible, reputable people" did persist in reporting seeing strangely shaped "metallic objects" in the sky performing bizarre maneuvers in a technologically "impossible" manner—which was, for once, a correctly *impossible* surmise.

Proving that UFOs had an objective reality and that they were, moreover, of extraterrestrial origin turned out to be a difficult, even technologically impossible, feat. UFO proponents found themselves constantly on the defensive. As Jacobs took pains to point out back in 1982, "the evidence for the existence—to say nothing of the origin—of the phenomenon was largely anecdotal."[20] It still is. Neither then nor presently, no one has ever proven that a UFO had ever "crashed" among the earthlings. No one has produced genuine artifacts, the sanctified relics as coveted by UFOlogy as medieval seekers had once coveted the skulls and thighbones of saints and, best of all, the "Holy Prepuce" of Christ, skillfully extracted from the Savior at his circumcision (a *Bris* since made into a feast day; see John 7:22–23). Accordingly, no one has ever collected objective scientific data on the extraterrestrial objects, but this is not so surprising since none are at hand for scientific inspection. As for the Roswell incident so beloved of the infotainment industry, who in their right mind now really believes in that?

If "nuts-and-bolts" hardware were involved, then why had there been no mechanical failures, and why had a UFO occupant not made official contact? Pressured, some UFO proponents reasoned that the occupants did not want to cause panic among humans, or they were shy, or they wished to stay hidden, just like the humanoid CIA was doing at that very moment. Or, alternatively, they were just too clever to crash. Still, the basic question remained: if UFOs were intelligently controlled craft from an advanced society situated somewhere in outer space, why did they not reveal themselves for all to see? As Jacobs emphatically stated back in 1982, "Extraordinary claims required extraordinary evidence, and UFO proponents did not have it."[21] They still don't, and the widely viewed "Roswell Alien Autopsy" cine-hoax has not advanced the UFO/ET cause one bit. In the event, Jacobs's best-selling paperback, *Secret Life: Firsthand Documented Accounts of UFO Abductions* (1992) typically suffers from a fatal flaw, the one he recognized a decade earlier: "Extraordinary claims require extraordinary evidence, and UFO proponents do not have it"—neither does he now, especially with his alien-abduction escapades. The essential problem is a clash of two opposed kinds of thinking, the scientific versus the mystical (which may be also be just plain "hysterical"; see chapter 6).

"Science" may be defined as a set of methods designed to (a) describe and then (b) interpret observed or inferred phenomena. More important, the scientist aims to construct a *testable* body of knowledge open to confirmation—or rejection. Scientific methodology typically comprises four steps: (1) *Induction*—forming a hypothesis; (2) *Deduction*—making predictions derived from the initial hypothesis; (3) *Observation*—gathering further data driven by the hypothesis and its predicted effects; and, last but not least, (4) *Verification*—testing the available data to confirm—or negate—the initial hypothesis. *Science* aims for objectivity, conclusions based on external validation, the kind anybody else could, and would, confirm as having tangible substance. The scientist also reports everything that might make his experiments invalid; he or she is a professional, and careers and reputations are ruined by revelations of unprofessional conduct and irrational, unmethodical thinking. In science, results are repeatable, even by skeptics. *Mysticism*, quite to the contrary, bases its conclusions on personal insights that elude external, verifiable confirmation. Burdened with an emotional investment in his or her single-minded pursuits, the mystic does not admit data, which may be abundant, which makes the given hypothesis unlikely, if not downright impossible. Operating between one and the other, the Scientist and the Mystic, is the Skeptic. This is a person who questions the validity of a particular, meaning single, claim; he or she calls for evidence to prove or disprove the worth of that single postulate. *Skepticism* is a provisional approach to particular claims. Skepticism is a method, selectively applied, not a global position.[22]

Since "science" was really not the purpose, not surprisingly, during the early 1950s, numerous local flying saucer "clubs" came into being. Fueled by sensationalistic pulp articles, these faddists speculated that the crewmen on the UFOs were "time travelers," "space animals," agents of God or Satan, even occult emanations. Most UFO proponents pretending to rationality found these theories untenable because they had no basis in the "evidence," meager at best, extrapolated from the burgeoning reports. Worse, the demonic time traveler hypothesis proved dangerous to The Cause because they gave the field of UFO research a decided fringe look and (rightfully) invited ridicule. Indeed, ridicule became an extremely important factor and especially because of the widely publicized extraterrestrial close encounters of the infamous "contactees" of the 1950s. These were led by "Professor" George Adamski (quoted at length in chapter 8), and his close encounter was followed by other momentary media celebrities, including "Dr." Daniel Fry, Truman Bethurum, Howard Menger, and others (none of whom we need quote).

Hewing to the Adamski pattern, these folks claimed that they had ongoing "contact" with "space people." Back then, the space brothers were mostly described as folk who had come to earth for benevolent reasons, usually to prevent atomic war and bring about world peace. According to the contactee doctrine, the space people lived in utopian worlds that were superior in every worthwhile way to our merely mundane one: technologically, morally, culturally, and intellectually (who knows, maybe sexually, too). The contactees claimed to have paranormal contact with aliens, through telepathy and other extrasensory menus. Their stories, often appearing in mass-produced paperback feuilletons, recounted that contact with the space brothers would not take place officially, but would involve selected earthling citizens, just folks, like you and me. As Jacobs did not (actually could not) recognize back in 1982, these attributes, especially the telepathic conversational mode—now known as the "mind scan" motif—are all standard attributes of the New Age abductee or experiencer narrations subsequently to be published in the 1980s and 1990s. Ironically, these are now-conventional rhetorical fixtures, *topoi*, the kind recently canonized by Dr. Jacobs, as aided and abetted by other media celebrities, like Budd Hopkins, John E. Mack, John Fuller, and the like. In short, the discredited "contactees" of the 1950s have inexorably evolved into the lionized "abductees" and "experiencers" of the 1990s.

However, as was observed by Professor Jacobs back in 1982, the contactees presented a serious challenge to the Cold War–era extraterrestrial hypothesis and to the future credibility of UFO research. Their sensational and insupportable claims about day-trips in flying saucers, sometimes including tourist-class visits to other planets, encouraged derision and made the quest for scientific legitimacy for the UFO cause all the more difficult. Eventually, with their visitation claims questioned, if not disproved outright, media attention dwindled and, inevitably, the contactees lost their followers. Nonetheless, as was still held by the True Believers, if UFOs were intelligently controlled hardware, it was possible, perhaps even essential, that someone, a mere earthling, *should* have had contact with the occupants of the extraterrestrial vehicle. Speculations abounded, at least among those so inclined. Did contact have to come "officially"? How could one define alien intelligence or extraterrestrial motivation? If space people were indeed so advanced that they had solved the problems of space travel, it followed then that they would "want" to select humans for contact and close inspection. Why else bother to come so far? But it also followed that, if the space people had such ascribed powers and abilities, it might be impossible to study them because, of course, they might have the means to prevent their own detection. "Aliens," like similarly contemporary and undocumented Mexican migrant farm workers, wish to keep their presence among us hidden, *occult*. UFOlogist credulity was momentarily checked by its own inherent paradoxes.

Although the alien-friendly "contactees" faded from popularity, they wrought a major effect on the very style of forthcoming deep thoughts about the UFO experience. Their grandiose claims had frightened UFO proponents and forced them to set acceptable limits on the extraterrestrial hypothesis in order to maintain its fragile aura of legitimacy. For example, the National Investigations Committee on Aerial Phenomena (NICAP), directed by Coral Lorenzen (a major figure in UFOlogy and quoted in chapter 5), decreed that it would not accept reports of contact with UFO occupants, regardless of the alleged claimant's reputation. Other UFO organizations instituted similarly elitist policies. By limiting their cognitive efforts to "rational" UFO reports, a perhaps hopeless undertaking, proponents tried to reduce the potential for public derision and thereby to enhance the reasonableness of the witnesses—likewise the very credibility of their own enthusiastic enterprise. Moreover, as long as the favored reports continued to feature rationally acting, "hard" objects that did not display overtly occult or paranormal qualities, the study of the phenomenon could pretend to belong to the realm of established scientific disciplines. As it was earnestly hoped, the extraterrestrial hypothesis need not be further tainted by "crackpot" aspects, and their beloved UFO paradigm could be maintained without having to deal with obviously questionable anomalies.

Nonetheless, the extraterrestrial hypothesis incrementally gained favor throughout the 1950s, and so it appeared in nearly all the books about UFOs published in that decade. Moreover, in another major wave of sightings during 1952 at the height of the Korean War, data was selectively collected which supported the more attractive, complementary idea of a "rational" explanation. Accordingly, UFOs were now increasingly reported near military bases, atomic installations, and other sensitive areas. That made more sense, that is, in the Cold War. As it was now argued, "they" were really interested in scrutinizing our malign military capabilities. Nonetheless, since UFOs were seen far more frequently in depopulated rather than in urban areas, they certainly were not all that interested in our *other* achievements, including our economic potential, manufacturing capabilities, our cultural heritage, especially our recent invention of "Action Painting" (aka Abstract Expressionism).

In short, according to this *deus ex machina* proposal, nothing else in earthling life mattered to the ETs but the specifically military aspect of our terrestrial pretensions. Since that argument seems rather narrow-minded—surely the wonderfully endowed extraterrestrial tourists need not pay all that much attention to what would represent to them a technologically primitive defense capability about as exciting as the bows and arrows of the Mesolithic era—it was then suggested that maybe the UFOs were trying to hide their identity. Aha, that's it; most likely, they were secretly learning about earth in preparation for an eventual landing. As logically followed from the intergalactic beachhead proposal, perhaps they were interested in earth's resources for possible exploitation. Aha, that's it; they were *colonists*, just like Victorian-era earthlings, upon whom "the sun never set." As we have seen, the narrative embroidery soon to be placed upon that standard exploitative explication was, such as it surfaces in the late 1980s, the *stolen-ova-and-sperm* legend. As we saw in chapter 2, Dr. David Jacobs, formerly a sensible historian of American pop culture, now wholly subscribes to that apocryphal eugenic embellishment.

Whatever the reasons, the UFOs were, as one UFOlogist later ingenuously put it back in 1957, certainly "cautious and curious." Thanks to such adroit logic, nearly as nimble as the flying saucerian maneuvers, MFO phenomena were happily taken to exhibit an apparent rationality that most UFO proponents readily claimed constituted evidence for interplanetary visitations. Yet within the "logical" framework of the extraterrestrial hypothesis there lurked any number of other, naturally only vaguely realized, illogicalities. Besides those already exposed, alas, as Jacobs put it back in 1982, "by 1957—after nearly ten years of continual reports—UFOs had still not made 'official' contact; not one UFO had crashed; and although stories and rumors had circulated to the contrary, no one had captured UFO occupants or had collected pieces of a UFO. The spaceships and their putative pilots evidently made no mistakes, even though a margin of error of zero for any artificially manufactured object seemed impossible."[23] Of course now, meaning long after 1982, we all do know that indeed a "UFO *had* crashed"—they did it at Roswell. I know that for a fact: *I saw it on TV!*

Another significant change in the character of UFO reports came about in the massive 1957 wave of sightings, a veritable tsunami of sightings. But this ocular outbreak is scarcely surprising, even though historian Jacobs fails to mention the *pertinent*, emotion-ridden, crucial historical *fact*. In fact, 1957 was the year in which the Soviets (aka "Evil Empire") successfully launched their *Sputnik* space vehicle, two of them in fact. Millions of Americans were straining their necks, looking up into the heavens with dread; on their car radios they heard the ominous "beep, beep, beep" emitted by the alien, obviously technologically superior, intruder within "our" air space. According to the new narrative wrinkle, increasing numbers of people now began to report electrical and/or mechanical interference with automobiles or appliances when in close proximity to a post–*Sputnik* era UFO.

Whereas such malfunctions were widely reported at the time, the very notion of UFO-inflicted electrical breakdowns had already been made widely known to the general public by the popular sci-fi movie, *The Day the Earth Stood Still* (1951; fig. 9). Surprise: that is just what happened to Betty and Barney Hill in 1961 (or was it actually 1966?). When your car stalls, just blame it on a UFO; to accuse General Motors of mechanical incompetence would be unpatriotic. Also, more people reported seeing UFOs on or near the ground; so did, years later, the Hills—but do we really need to list all the B-movies cranked out by Hollywood in the 1950s that showed the very same thing? I know that for a fact: *I saw it at the drive-in movies!*

In 1957, when the Cold War truly began to be waged in outer space, it seemed as if UFOs were coming closer to earth. What was next? Russian paratroopers? ET gynecologists? For UFO proponents, this apparent fact of even closer encounters made it all the more imperative that the public and the scientific community understand the "enormity" of the problem. Thirty years later, as we are told by (for instance) Dr. David E. Pritchard, if anything the problem has only gotten more enormous: "As many as 1 percent of the overall population—two and a quarter million citizens of the United States [!]—might possibly be abductees."[24] *ET sic dixit Mack.*

Alas, even back in 1957, accredited scientists who had bothered to survey the phenomenon found the evidence for its existence wanting. (Surprise: they still do.) As Professor Jacobs reported back in 1982, with arguments about the UFO experience needing no modification today,

Its lack of verifiability, lack of predictability, and the poor quality of anecdotal data suggested to scientists that UFOs had no objective reality as an anomalous phenomenon. They argued that anecdotal data were inappropriate for scientific scrutiny, that the possibility of hoaxes and fabrications would always make conclusions questionable, and that [among other stalwarts] the Air Force had mounted a major scientific analysis and found the extraterrestrial hypothesis to be insupportable. These scientific arguments against the feasibility of that hypothesis were extremely persuasive. . . . Along with the scientific gaps came the problem of ridicule: because of the contactees' occasional hoaxes, and also the lack of any kind of physical evidence, scientists did not select UFOs as a subject [worthy] of research for fear that it might reflect adversely on their judgment and hinder their careers.[25]

Now however, that is, once the names of the actors and actresses are slightly changed—from "contactees" to "abductees"—along with many, many other earnest investigators of the paranormal, Jacobs presently finds that the UFO experience has miraculously become a subject worthy of intense research. And this kind of research does get published—easily. Still, for an academic, such unquestionably sincere investigations could "reflect adversely on their judgment and hinder their careers"; when that happens, previously tenured associate professors of history most likely will never get themselves promoted to full professors. But such merely mundane matters matter not one bit when one had a world-mission of informing the unknowing masses of the extraterrestrials lurking in our midst (see fig. 1).

UFOLOGY SWITCHES CHANNELS IN THE SWINGING 1960s

That preemptive mission, switching "contactees" to "abductees," which is the one now most earnestly subscribed to by the more celebrated UFOlogists, emerged early in the 1960s. However (and as Jacobs does not mention), this development immediately followed upon the 1961 Bay of Pigs incident, an abortive attempt at an armed invasion of Cuba, a CIA-directed fiasco now recognized to be the moment when the world truly had come closest to a collective, long promised, nuclear holocaust. As UFO proponents then perceived, their best (perhaps last) chance for scientific respectability rested in stressing the "patterns of evidence": the supposed reliability of witnesses, the increasing number of reports, the global pervasion of the sightings, and, above all, the logical, invasion-like "visitation from outer space" quality of the phenomenon. To this end,

Coral Lorenzen, Gauleiterin of the Aerial Phenomena Research Organization (APRO), wrote *The Great Flying Saucer Hoax* (1962). This was the paperback bombshell detailing UFO sightings around the world, including some low-level and bizarre cases from South America (e.g., Villas-Boas and his red-haired ET succubus, as recounted in chapter 5).

Dubbed the "Swinging Sixties," for some of us this was a happy time when we ingested hallucinogenic drugs and "tripped out," en masse. The modernist mind was experiencing a joyful mental meltdown. Another significant phenomenon emerging in the 1960s (which Jacobs also does not mention) is the proliferation of sci-fi shows on TV. Since this is purely visual stuff (the dialogue is trivial at best), this is what the art historian delights in. The precedent was earlier set by such cheesy, low-budget fare as *Captain Video* (running from 1949 to 1956), *Tom Corbett, Space Cadet, Lost in Space,* and *Space Patrol* (beginning sequentially from 1954 to 1956). Anybody who avidly watched television in the strife-torn decade of the 1960s—and who didn't?—inevitably bore witness to swarming battalions of UFOs and ETs. Probably the most intelligent of the lot was *The Twilight Zone;* running from 1959 to 1964, it was bound and determined to raise your paranoia levels. The new breed specifically invented for the post-Kennedy era included *Star Trek,* first aired in 1966 (*Star Trek: The Movie* came out in 1977). This long-running intergalaxy epic depicted a clean-shaven, gung-ho, and hi-tech, hippie commune in outer space. Also appearing during the Vietnam era were *Time Tunnel* (1966) and *The Invaders* (1967).

However, the first of the really scary ones, premiering in 1963, was *The Outer Limits.* Already pointed out in chapter 5 is the fact that one of its episodes, "The Bellero Shield," featured early in 1964 an ET which looked suspiciously like the very same ET which Barney Hill was harassed into "remembering" slightly later, and which he then drew for his hypnotist-therapist (see fig. 18). That maladroit sketch subsequently became the iconographic model for the skilled F/X artists who worked on the 1975 NBC-TV movie that remade the apocryphal Hill close encounter into a "documentary" feature (see figs. 17, 18). In turn, the ET starring in *The UFO Incident* was appropriated by Steven Spielberg in 1977 for his *Close Encounters of the Third Kind*—and *everybody* saw that movie and that ET (see fig. 19). And, as they say, all the rest is (art) history.

In 1964, the year of the notorious "Tonkin Bay Incident" falsely calling for massive American intervention in Vietnam, NICAP published *The UFO Evidence.* This was a further compendium of NICAP's UFO reports, categorizing each incident by color, shape, location, noise, and other supposedly significant characteristics. Nothing so meticulous had previously been presented to the general public. This extraterrestrial *catalogue raisonné* strongly emphasized the seemingly intelligent behavior of the UFOs. Its main thrust was that "reliable, reputable witnesses"— which they *must* be, for they included "professional" people: scientists, engineers, ministers, judges, and the like—massively reported having seen a variety of unconventional, apparently artificially constructed, objects in the sky that appeared, to them at least, to be under "intelligent" control. The purported pilots were just as intelligent as their awed earthbound observers. Such labored cataloguing and reconstructions made as strong a case for the "nuts-and-bolts" extraterrestrial origin of UFOs as had yet been made. Following in the evangelical footsteps of the Gideon Society, NICAP sent their books free to every congressman and to every scientist who wanted it; no figures are available on the takers.

In 1965, just as students were demonstrating (fruitlessly) either in the nation's capital, to end the war in Vietnam, or (fruitfully) in Birmingham, Alabama, to advance civil rights for blacks, who erupted into a race riot in Watts, California ($40 million in property damage), Jacques Vallée published *Anatomy of a Phenomenon*. This work included his own catalogue of sightings, some going back to the Middle Ages. Besides citing the usefulness of NICAP's compendium and making some intelligent speculations of his own, Vallée added his own wry observation that already the UFO experience was mainly serving to "provide an opportunity for persons who live a generally dull life to bring a touch of extraterrestrial horror into their existence. UFO 'investigation' has thus become a popular hobby. Clubs and groups have developed, mainly since 1952, apparently in every part of the world [but] their only positive contribution has been the publication of [more and more] sightings."[26]

In the late 1960s, however, UFO reports began to take on a different character. Now, new influxes of "data" seemed to militate against the clear-cut rationality strenuously needed to accredit the phenomenon. Although most witnesses still reported high-level objects, now many more testators than before came forward to claim that they, too, had seen UFOs close to, if not actually resting upon, the ground. These ocular encounters were literally closer than any ever before claimed; the ETs were beginning to get into our faces. UFOs were said to follow, even stalk, cars for blocks or miles. (Were these actually cases of mislabeled extraterrestrial autophilia?) At isolated sites where witnesses claimed an object had landed, sometimes "investigators"—the kind eager to investigate such anomalies (as perhaps you are not)—did actually succeed in finding "mysterious marks" smeared upon the grass or punched into the dirt. Alas, none of the widely discussed terrene smudges subsequently chose to yield unimpeachable laboratory proof for their hypothesized extraterrestrial origins. Now, other, also widely circulated, reports more frequently indicated interference with automobile engines, radios, television sets, and other electrical devices—just the kind of pesky gadget interference that so many postmodernist abductees now like to report.

Now the effects became more suitable to future cinematic treatment, the kind that we were soon, in fact, to enjoy. Most of these were catalogued in the new "scientific" *summa theologia* of UFOlogy published in 1972, J. Allen Hynek's *The UFO Experience: A Scientific Inquiry*. That was the year that brought us Watergate: once again, conspiracy was in the air, and at the very heights of government. As was recounted in widely discussed publications like this one, some witnesses had reported feeling physical effects—such as heat, "prickly sensations"—while in the dire proximity of a UFO. Not entertained apparently was the idea that such dermatological distress might instead be due to commonplace solar effects arising from wandering around in a desert looking for the damned things. On the other hand, such effects have long been reported to be experienced under cloudy, even drizzling, skies. They used to be called *stigmata*; St. Francis of Assisi was one rather well publicized "experiencer." (Alas, modern psychologists might just call it a "psychosomatic" effect.)[27]

Other witnesses reported more overtly emotional reactions. Some claimed an overpowering experience of panic and fear when a UFO was overhead; others reported feeling physically paralyzed or unable to take their eyes off the object, even though they really wanted to. It was as though they had reiterated experiences formerly attributed to that occult staple, *il malocchio*, the Evil Eye.[28] Others, a lesser but happier crowd, maintained that they had experienced a feeling of euphoria when they sighted a UFO, in fact, emotions rather like religious "transports" (see chapter 6). A paranoid, somewhat voyeuristic, complementary component was emerging: a few witnesses claimed that they were being "watched," or that somehow the unseen UFO occupants "knew" all about them. This, too, is not surprising: "spies" and espionage stories were a favorite staple of the infotainment industry at that moment; James Bond made his cinemagraphic premiere in 1962, when he initially took on "Dr. No."

A frequent component of the new-style UFO reports was the profoundly incomprehensible allegation that objects simply "materialized" in front of stunned witnesses, then conveniently disappeared, or "dematerialized"—just like "ghosts" do in traditional horror tales that everybody had heard as a kid. Witnesses steadfastly contended that the objects had neither flown into the area nor flown away. Some reports suggested that several objects "blended" together into one UFO and, conversely, that one object could "separate" into two distinct entities. Appearing at the same time as numerous reports of landed UFOs, the kind that leave those fugitive "markings" in the ground, the kind that subsequently prove impossible to verify, those ghostlike, similarly insubstantial, reports fundamentally contradicted the notion of "hard" UFOs. The logic was going soft on the UFOlogists; some sort of theoretical Viagra was called for.

In addition, and most alarming—or just less boring—reports of sightings of actual UFO *occupants* increased. Now, with better historical hindsight, we can perceive how the media reporting these tales was giving birth to the postmodernist ET. Beginning to broadcast their observations around 1966 (Betty and Barney), these newcomers to the sighting experience gained the immediate attention of UFO proponents, and the media symbiotically feeding upon their colorful investigations. Dormant public interest was reawakened, given new vigor (or metaphorical Viagra). This was because the new breed of ocular witnesses were not like the old-style contactees, those obsolete egomaniacs who basked in media publicity and reaped monetary gain. Nope, the new breed were ordinary people, just folks like us, the kind whose subsequent behavior was not suspicious, even praiseworthy in an oblique fashion. Typically, the new lot saw themselves as martyrs, even while they basked in public attention; as poignantly put by abductee Rosemary Osnato: "When I say I was abducted, a lot of people envy me. Some of them treat me like a saint. I tell them it was horrible and frightening—and they don't want to hear it!"[29] As their new UFO audience culture was quick to point out, their assertions should not (of course) be correlated with behavior suggesting hoax or—certainly not!—hallucination.

These were the kind of petty-bourgeois witnesses who typically reported seeing weird "people" collecting samples of flora near a parked UFO. When the ET flower-gatherers realized an earthling was watching them, they quickly entered their parked spacecraft, which just as quickly sped away: Swoosh! Other witnesses claimed to have seen occupants through "windows" in UFOs as the object hovered at a conveniently low level. Other "reliable" witnesses claimed to have seen UFO occupants from a short distance and even—naturally—tried to communicate with them: "*Parlez-vous anglais?*" or "*¿Habla inglés?*" Thus were born Hynek's celebrated *Close Encounters of the Third Kind*, soon to be made into a major movie playing at your local cineplex (fig. 19). These dramatically enhanced, tertiary reports again opened the door wide to claims of contact with space people—and many ordinary folks passed through that door. But UFO investigators were again fearful that scientists would consider the entire UFO phenomenon unworthy of

attention if these new cases were presented seriously. Inevitably, however, the more bizarre reports forced their way into what Jacobs calls
"the UFOlogists' conservative belief-structure." It had to be so, because
of witness "reliability" and the sheer number of such reports. Obviously,
for UFOlogists, staggering quantity is just as good, maybe even better,
than is quality (inherent believability).

Accordingly, by the end of the 1960s much of the prosaic quality
attaching to the earlier UFO reports had disappeared, replaced by
accounts of a phenomenon more bizarre, less comprehensible, less
rational, and less amenable to control or study than were the pioneering
reports of the 1940s and 1950s. In short, it was getting much more interesting, more entertaining, more like the movies than mere reality. It
seemed that, as time went on, and as more "data" became available, and
as one heard more and more about the subject, the less susceptible it
became to rational inquiry. The accumulation of knowledge about UFOs
did not necessarily support the diverse, but typically firmly held, theories about their origins. Indeed, the ever increasing accumulation of
knowledge, essentially mere anecdotes, seemed to lead to more questions, not to answers. As a result, UFO researchers slowly began to lose
whatever intellectual control (and appearance) they thought they may
have ever retained over the subject, if any. As the potential for rationality decreased, it was only logical that more and more people would
became enthralled, collectively *entertained* by the bizarre spectacle
being played out for them in the mass media.

In the late 1960s, at the same time UFO researchers were beginning
to feel less sure about the nature of UFOs, established political and scientific institutions began to take a closer look at the UFO phenomenon.
After years of bearing up to intensive pressure coming from UFO lobby-
ists, finally the House Committee on Armed Services reluctantly opened
hearings in 1966 on the vexing subject of UFOs and, particularly, the Air
Force's handling of the problem. That chronological setting is interesting: 1966 is also the year in which the groundbreaking Betty and
Barney Hill story got published, also when the Red Guard demonstrated
against Western influences in China. As an outcome of the hearings, the
Air Force contracted with the University of Colorado to study the phenomenon and (again) decide whether it was indeed "extraterrestrial,"
truly out of this world. Dr. Edward U. Condon, a reputable physicist, was
named head of the project.[30]

The eighteen-month study, which was completed in late 1968, found
no evidence supporting the fascinating idea of extraterrestrial visitation,
and Condon concluded that no further study was warranted. On the

basis of his negative recommendation, the Air Force closed down its UFO investigating unit. Following a great amount of publicity reporting the Condon Committee's negative findings, scientific interest began to wane even further. But the mere existence of the Condon Committee, and the general public's unflagging interest in UFOs, prompted a few individual scientists to look into the UFO enigma on their own. Spurred on by UFO proponents, now this minority group of scientists bitterly attacked the Condon Committee's conclusions. They accused the committee of having used biased, inexperienced, and untrained scientists (which, of course, the piqued detractors were not), and charged that its methodology and assumptions were "faulty." They felt that by searching for a simple solution to the UFO problem—deciding specifically whether they came from "outer space"—the Condon Committee members had shared an assumption about UFOs that was based on merely "superficial knowledge" of an evidently profoundly significant subject.

Although general scientific interest in UFOs was once again decreasing, so much criticism had been mounted by UFOlogists against the Condon Committee that the American Association for the Advancement of Science scheduled a symposium on UFOs for its December 1969 conference. The symposium was the last manifestation of organized scientific interest. Fifteen papers about UFOs were presented (and later published), with the majority taking a negative position.[31] Not surprisingly, since such pursuits cost a lot of money, no ongoing scientific studies resulted from the symposium, and the scientific community continued to remain wary of the subject. But not the UFOlogists, then or now. By the early 1970s it became clear that neither established science nor the government would consider the study of UFOs to be an area of legitimate research.

UFOLOGY RISES TO THE CHALLENGE OF THE ME DECADE

The 1970s was famously labeled the "Me Decade" by Tom Wolfe; like everybody else, UFOlogists partook of the *Zeitgeist*. Abductees, as is obvious, are especially me-oriented. By the 1970s, UFO proponents had doggedly but quietly begun to alter their mission, to redefine their defense strategies—just as the beleaguered U.S. military was redefining its obviously botched strategies for "winning hearts and minds" in Vietnam. The search for "scientific legitimacy" was again necessarily taking its position as the primary goal, and UFO diehards were coming together with a few interested scientists and other academics to form their own research community, a sort of ideological commune. This opportune shift in focus was due not only to the Condon Committee's effect, and the closing down of the Air Force investigation unit, but also owing to the impact that the new UFO reports were having, especially the "abduction" cases (the kind that are now so abundant). The strictly post-modernist canon of UFOlogical political correctness was being invented.

The first well-known abduction case was, of course, that of Barney and Betty Hill, which has so dramatically captured public attention since 1966. It was immediately taken by those who care about such things, then and now, to provide provocative evidence, both for and against the extraterrestrial paradigm. It was timely: the impasse of credulity and controversy had been broken. New speculative horizons were opening up. The media had a field day. Had it not actually happened, then it would have needed to be invented—and that possibility is the most likely. Likewise, fifteen years before, a time traveler named Bridey Murphy needed timely invention (pseudoevents such as this will be thoroughly exhumed in chapter 11). In both cases, all you need to get the ball rolling is a hypnotist. Then, once informed—as indeed they must be—the mass media will energetically proceed to make it into yet another fascinating pseudoevent. The positive result, quickly forthcoming, is that everybody is distracted from their daily travails and responsibilities: we all get entertained. Necessity is, so they say, the mother of invention. What's the harm in all that? Ask, among others, the grieving relatives left behind by the mass exiting of the Heaven's Gate UFO cult.

Back in 1966 of course, no one could envision the future implications inherent in this obviously welcome emotional bonanza. As interpreted at the height of the Vietnam War, when the country was being torn apart by ideological conflict, the Hills represented the very antithesis of the now-discredited 1950s-style contactee. As an interracial couple in their late thirties, they did not seem like the type who desired "lunatic fringe" attention—neither did Virginia Tighe (aka Bridey Murphy). To their credit, they did not report ongoing experiences with the space brothers; they had no uplifting message imparted to them and no imposed "mission" to fulfill. Moreover, just read as a narrative, the Hill case was extremely mundane and therefore readily comprehensible. It satisfied popular taste; it had a beginning, middle, and end—just like the movie later made about their wondrous adventure (see figs. 17, 18). The new wrinkle, then anyway, was that the ETs seemed to be earnest researchers of human anatomy. These inquisitive space folk did not really kidnap the Hills, certainly did not kill them—which would, in the event, have killed the story. According to their scenario, the ETs were apparently moral folk, inquisitive, reasonable, and even solicitous: at one point in the protocinematic script, an alien "doctor" stops Betty Hill's pain by gently putting his hand on her head.

For the True Believers, the fantastic Hill close encounter—the closest yet ever made, and as quickly made known to nearly every earthling—once again held out the ever fascinating possibility of an extraterrestrial technology. Better yet, as recounted here, that kind of technology was not wholly unlike that found on earth, the kind that would have naturally been known to the Hills and their eager amanuensis, John Fuller. Even better yet, the ETs were humanoid, *almost* like you and me. Since the Hills were forced to act and think against their will, and since they were enabled to communicate telepathically with the alleged extraterrestrials, their minidrama also contained (surprise) clear-cut, meaning traditional, paranormal elements, the kind long since beloved of the occultist crowds. The impact of the Hill case on the study of UFOs was enormous. How could it fail to be otherwise? It opened the door for further acceptance of qualitatively stranger cases, the kind that might even have been rejected as spurious in the past. Again, while still retaining the extraterrestrial hypothesis as its fundamental premise, it also moved the UFO phenomenon more clearly into the realm of the occult. No problem there: functionally speaking, otherworldly ETs and occultists perfectly complement one another.

As we have seen, once UFO proponents accepted the credibility of the Hill case, and of course they *would*, they began more readily to accept other cases of abduction and occupant sightings. A typical example was that "unique" 1957 case from Brazil, the one so widely broadcast by Coral Lorenzen, in which sexual contact between a space woman and a farmer was reported (see chapter 5). Of course, many serious researchers in the 1960s categorized the case as legitimate, a judgment unthinkable just a few years before, during the dubious "contactee" era. Another favorite was the "Dr. X" case reported from France in 1968.[32] Likewise, it seemed to offer more evidence that UFOs might have a nonmaterial component—which is a handy argument, especially if you have no material evidence to deal with. Dr. X, a physician in a small town in Provence, claimed that one night he saw two UFOs loitering in the valley below his isolated hilltop dwelling. The two objects eventually proceeded to blend into one, and this composite came to levitate within a few feet of his pastoral residence. So placed, it beamed a light on him as he stared at it. So he said. Then the object disappeared with an explosive sound. The entire incident, so we were told, took no more than one minute. Wonder of wonders, the very next day a rash appeared in the form of an isosceles triangle centered over his navel! *Mon Dieu!*

Tangible evidence at last: photos are still being passed around that depict the *médicien's* toasted tummy. He was amazed to discover that the same dermatological token distinguished his young son, who had witnessed the incident from another window. More anatomical wonders followed: a wound (not adequately described, perhaps merely neurological) that Dr. X had suffered twelve years before in the Algerian war was now miraculously healed, so was a gash reportedly put on his leg later, under less bellicose conditions. As seems appropriate, for a year following, Dr. X claimed episodes of levitation. This went along with his increased awareness of and interest in "the Cosmos." Such anecdotes were given credibility mainly because the physician modestly refused publicity and would not allow his name to be used or permit his photograph to be taken; he so ordered for fear of attracting ridicule to himself and his child. (That makes sense.)

Nonetheless, had all similar phenomena been reported earlier, say five or six centuries beforehand, then his feats of levitation—and particularly his marvelous *stigmata*—might have got him canonized—that is, were he able to pass the rigid certification standards set by the Vatican for such *miracula*. For the ever-beleaguered UFOlogists, the Dr. X case seemed much more significant than it did to the rest of the world. For them, it raised fundamental issues about the nature of reality that could not fit into any previous system of thought. (Of course they couldn't.) Whatever the explanation, it was clear to them that the "nuts-and-bolts" idea of the phenomenon had to be revised. And, of course, it was redrafted. Again the process of revision proved difficult, maybe even impossible. To those stalwarts nothing seemed as commonsensical as the extraterrestrial hypothesis, but it did not explain all their "data," those melodramatic close-encounter observations.

Now the inevitable speculation—which is the only thing left to ideologues faced with a paucity of genuine physical evidence—was becoming really interesting. As a result, some UFO researchers began to posit essentially desperate ideas. The new, patently occultist, position held that UFOs were (as before) extraterrestrials, but these were now taken to exist on an ill-defined level of reality called the "astral plane." Accordingly, why not posit that the tireless space-time tourists were coming from a parallel universe, the so-called fourth dimension, maybe even a "fifth dimension," or some other kind of alternate reality? When in doubt, posit that *alternate reality*: how can anyone disprove *that*? A wholly different idea, the kind I favor, placed the phenomenon in mundane reality, that of the human psyche, explaining that, in the twentieth century, stories about UFOs and their occupants had taken the place of fairy tales. Another theory, half UFOlogical and half logical, suggested that UFOs had both a hard nuts-and-bolts component—they were "real"—as well as a psychic component. According to this well-intentioned compromise, the shapes of UFOs and the behavior of their occupants were determined by the technological and cultural level of the society in which they were sighted. With historical perspective, the second part of that theory seems proved by the 1896–1897 "Airship Craze" (see chapter 8).

The strictly extraterrestrial theories naturally led diehard UFOlogists interested in any systematic inquiry away from their previous position, the one holding that the phenomenon can, and should, be measured, quantified, and studied using the conventional means of scientific inquiry. The new breed of unquantifiable, hence completely unscientific, theories resulted, in part, from widespread frustration. Once again, UFO proponents had failed to solve the mystery. Once again, as seems inevitable, they had failed to achieve the elusive scientific legitimacy that they had been so desperately seeking for their otherworldly topic since the 1940s. By the 1970s, the UFO experience had become so strange that it had moved way beyond anybody's intellectual grasp. However bizarre, the new theories gave UFO proponents a renewed sense of intellectual achievement, meaning that they ground out new theories. They did so, just like contemporary postmodernist academics who were, simultaneously, industriously concocting theoretical cultural models with a Gallic twist.[33] Such meritorious mental endeavor allowed both polemical parties, highbrows and lowbrows, to feel that they really were working on a needful solution to pressing contemporary issues besetting the world, maybe outer space as well.

Just like the embattled ivory tower students of literature, not all UFOlogists adopted the new perceptual and hermeneutic models, of course. In the 1970s, the post-Hill era, many argued that the extraterrestrial hypothesis accounted for most of the reports and that it was premature to discard it. At the end of the 1990s, again this seems to serve as the near-universal explanation. Likewise still with us is the 1970s position of UFO proponents who were forced to accept the possibility of a paranormal explanation, pure occultism. How else could you explain that UFOs seemed to break the laws of physics and thus acknowledge that increased data gathered about UFOs only served to throw their original contentions into doubt? Especially, how do you explain the "fact" that human abductees needed to rely on internal perception of an altered state of mind to provide information about their alleged confrontations with the otherworldly? Like the nineteenth-century spiritualists, their real spiritual ancestors, so the UFO proponents had dismally failed in their pathetic quest for scientific acceptance.

An important difference between the efforts of the Victorian-era spiritualists and the late-twentieth-century UFO proponents was the phenomenon itself. Whereas those loquacious "spirits" could not exist a century ago without being called forth by human agency, especially without the timely aid of human mediums, the modernist UFO phenomenon seemed to exist outside human perception. At least, so it appeared to the True Believers; nonetheless, as everybody heard in the 1960s, indeed "the medium is the message." Now the postmodernist medium performs hypnotic retrieval missions seeking repressed memories. Earlier, in the 1950s and 1960s, UFO ideologues had tried to prove the existence of their beloved phenomenon through the use of photographs, radar readings, spectral analysis, and other mechanical verifications. These nonanecdotal forms of verification would, they hoped, fulfill the elusive requirements for scientific analysis. When, a decade or so later, such proofs typically turned out to be, once again, either impossible to attain or inconclusive at best, UFO researchers had to return to their starting point, ground zero.

ALIEN ABDUCTIONS, AMERICAN XENOPHOBIA, AND CORPORATE CULTURE

After the Me Decade in America there came the Age of Reagan, the 1980s, and the ubiquitous "Me" was a Yuppie (a young, upwardly mobile professional), and he typically worked for a multinational corporation. The *Zeitgeist* was again reshaped; so was UFOlogy. Then as now, ungrounded human perception and anecdotal evidence were desperately seized upon as the basis upon which the UFOlogists' beloved phenomenon could be verified and by which, thereby, human knowledge expanded. And that is the situation today: *unverifiable*. As Jacobs so accurately observed back in 1982:

> This increasingly greater reliance on [mere] human perception led UFO proponents away from the objective reality of UFOs and toward [wholly] *subjective impressions elicited from witnesses by the new "mediums," the hypnotists*. Thus, as the evidence became increasingly anecdotal, it also became less susceptible to scientific verification. By the end of the 1970s, the UFO phenomenon had changed dramatically and yet remained as enigmatic as ever. UFO proponents confronted a phenomenon that had become more heterogeneous, more mysterious, *more occult*, and less amenable to traditional scientific inquiry. They had spent years building a paradigm that had quickly become obsolete, and they had no acceptable replacement. To complicate matters, ridicule remained a concern, as did witness veracity.

After thirty [now fifty] years of reports, UFO proponents had made little [or no] headway. They were still searching for an intellectual framework that would allow them successfully to confront the increasingly mysterious phenomenon, and they seemed as far away as ever from finding it. *Placing UFOs in the realm of the occult*, where rational explanations and methodology were less necessary, seemed to some proponents the only reasonable way out of what had become a maze of frustration. Yet *the occult was precisely the area that had damaged the UFO researchers' chances of obtaining scientific legitimacy for their phenomenon.* By the 1980s, UFO proponents were divided and confused. Older theories had failed to explain the totality of UFOs, no newer theories had evolved to solve the enigma, and *the subject had taken on occult qualities that helped prevent scientific explanation* [or confirmation].[34]

How ironic: the scholarly Dr. Jacobs of the early 1980s has now himself evolved into one of those "new 'mediums,' the hypnotists." As he was able, back then, to perceive so clearly, the esotericist mesmerizers—Jacobs now included in their ranks—have forever ruined "the UFO researchers' chances of obtaining scientific legitimacy for their phenomenon." It is people like Jacobs, albeit (doubtlessly) operating from the most sincere of intentions, who have solidly situated "UFOs in the realm of the occult." The same accusation holds true for the ETs relentlessly driving those literally supernatural UFOs, likewise for all those lurid "abduction by extraterrestrials" fairy tales endlessly and relentlessly generated by the rightly designated "New Mediums of the Occult."

In any event, as fertilized with the stolen eggs of his hypnotized victims, the indefatigable New Age research of Dr. David Jacobs has served to birth yet *another* book expanding upon the postmodernist legend of extraterrestrial infestations. Now concisely treated as "The Threat," obviously the specific intention is, once again, to *terrorize* you.[35] When labeled "nonfiction," and so presented in all-too-many books produced by prominent publishers, said "threat"—you know, imminent alien invasion—has clear world-historical significance. It is another marker of the first occasion in which science *fiction* was repeatedly produced to be consumed as Gospel truth by the masses. If this isn't mental manipulation on the grand scale—*psychic fascism*—then what is?

That said, we may briefly summarize the final chronological evolution of the expanded version of the UFO experience: the birthing and, eventually, institutionalization of the abduction-by-extraterrestrial-aliens legends. As discussed in chapter 5, indeed "it all began with Betty and Barney Hill," meaning such as their alleged extraterrestrial mishaps were *first published* late in 1966. Their tale—and the now conventional

ET iconographic format, at least for the nonbookish masses, was really institutionalized with the 1975 TV-movie about it, *The UFO Incident* (figs. 17, 18), and was absolutely fixed in 1977 by Steven Spielberg's *Close Encounters of the Third Kind* (fig. 19). What we may call the *literary canonization* of the alien-abduction narrative was finally achieved in 1987 by the near simultaneous publication, and unprecedented profitability, of two best-sellers, Whitley Strieber's *Communion* (fig. 4) and Budd Hopkins's *Intruders*. Many similar stories have since succeeded in getting themselves published, which is not at all surprising since opportunistic publishers do know that they will sell.

The teleevangelist scandals, the Iran-Contra hearings, the Wedtech scam, endless accounts of Yuppie excess, and, like a prophetized Götterdammerung, the stock market crash all occurred in 1987. Then Japan, an "alien" nation, was mostly thought of as a major economic threat. Elsewhere, international terrorism was on the rise, a *mode du jour*. Coming at the height of the photogenic era of Ronald Reagan, 1987 was also the year that television became less regulated, and sensationalist daytime talk shows, "tabloid TV," then became the norm. All lines were blurred between news and entertainment, politics and advertising. These televised diversions particularly doted on presenting abductees and their lurid tales to a properly titillated mass audience of video voyeurs.

For better or (more likely) worse, beginning in 1987 Strieber and Hopkins firmly established the new paradigm of terror. If you believed them, then, most likely, *alien abduction was about to happen to you*. According to the new urban legend given in their best-sellers, abduction especially happens at home, when you are asleep; there is no security, no protection, *no control*. Now at risk were your most intimate possessions, your *ova* and *sperm*. The understood thesis: *we are a nation of potential victims*. Whatever its variations, such as we are given to understand the phenomenon today, alien abductions and the abductee reports sanctioning them are themselves media products. Continually updated, the abduction-by-aliens recitations are interactive, like an oral history or a group testimonial. When closely questioned (unfortunately, not as often as is necessary), abductees will confess to reading the likes of *Communion* or *Intruders* or, more likely, having seen something in the movies or on television portraying abduction episodes. That, too, is not surprising; these mostly visual materials are ubiquitous in millenarian American popular culture. You know this to be a fact since you, too, have seen them. Since 98 percent of all Americans own a television, who hasn't seen the aliens?

The only new wrinkle in a very old fabric of homegrown American invention has been to call these "aliens" something different: invaders from outer space. Xenophobia is an American tradition. Dating at least since their self-invented identity in 1776 (so documented in a self-styled "Declaration of Independence"), Americans have consistently feared, and actively organized against, what they saw as *alien* peoples (Irish, Germans, Italians, Mexicans, Muslims), against *alien* religions (Catholicism, Mormonism, Judaism, Islam), against *alien* ideas (Freemasonry, Communism, feminism, homosexuality), *alien* technologies (electricity, fluoridation, television, genetic engineering), *alien* illegal immigrants (Mexicans, Asians, anybody Islamic), and—finally—just plain *aliens* (extraterrestrials). These perceptions are wonderfully ironic. Other than the "Indians" (aka Native Americans), by definition (since 1492 C.E.) all *other* passport-possessing Americans are "aliens." (Me, too.)

Terry Matheson, a Canadian academic, has extensively discussed in a monograph the growth of a certain narrative staple, "abduction literature," as representing a classic, postmodernist "secular myth." It perfectly fits our millenarian mood, especially given that "the subject matter is intrinsically absorbing." It must be so; the dollar figures generated by Hollywood movies devoted to UFOs and ETs provide the quantitative proof; in 1999 alone the top grossers in the monstrous outer-space invader genre made nearly *two billion dollars*![36] Although not specifically cited by Professor Matheson, these unquestionably profitable movies (also very loud and mostly dreadful) do share the same psychic characteristics as do the equally profitable published accounts of "alien abductions," namely what Matheson cites as a "vivid depiction of human powerlessness" through the reiterated depiction of "abductions by beings who possess the ability to invade the sanctity of anyone's personal space with impunity." In short, according to the now established convention of this pseudoliterature, "there is no avoiding alien abductors."

In the larger, more important perspective, Matheson points out that such "intrusive and enslaving" alien beings clearly "bear similarities to those in our own machine-based culture." Like life for humans caught up in secular corporate culture and trapped in its demeaning cubicles and tied down with its inescapable cell phone implants and insistent e-mail, "the abduction process goes on twenty-four hours a day, month after month, year after year." Like postmodernist corporate life, "everything about the aliens is extremely minimal, eminently drab, boring, and virtually sexless. . . . The alien-abduction myth reminds us that individuality is incompatible with the demands of a 'perfect' technological environment." Their gray color is itself "traditionally associated not only with illness and decay, but also with gloom and monotony, indifference." His provocative conclusion is one I share:

The aliens themselves may be occupying niches similar to those occupied by many [humans] in the modern world who see themselves as cogs trapped in a vast bureaucratic or corporate machine. . . . Practically speaking, the aliens' power bears an unmistakable resemblance to the ubiquitous tentacles of modern bureaucracy. Just as no place is safe from the intrusions of technology-assisted statecraft, so too no human is beyond the reach of the aliens and their inscrutable designs.

It is thus only fitting to see "the aliens as representatives of a technocratic/bureaucratic milieu that remains steadfastly insensitive to human needs."[37]

That said, I will now reveal my own all-too-close approximation to an "alien abduction." I have been *twice* audited by the IRS.

NOTES

1. For the chronological framework of what follows, see David Jacobs, "UFOs and the Search for Scientific Legitimacy," in *The Occult in America: New Historical Perspectives*, ed. H. Kerr and C. L. Crow (Urbana: Illinois University Press, 1986), pp. 218–31; see also D. Jacobs, *The UFO Controversy in America* (Bloomington: Indiana University Press, 1975), however, my way of using Jacobs's data is, admittedly, rather different from *his* way; for the contemporary UFO "documentation" in the mass media, see Curtis D. MacDougall, *Superstition and the Press* (Amherst, N.Y.: Prometheus Books, 1983), pp. 578–611.

2. My synchronized "real-world" interpolations, the kind of useful contextual background Jacobs omitted in his essay, are drawn from Bernard Grun, *Timetables of History: A Horizontal Linkage of the People and Events* (New York: Touchstone, 1982), pp. 526 ff.; and see also Jodi Dean, *Aliens in America: Conspiracy Cultures from Outerspace to Cyberspace* (Ithaca, N.Y.: Cornell University Press, 1998), chap. 2, "Space Programs."

3. MacDougall, *Superstition and the Press*, pp. 604–605.

4. See D. H. Menzel and Lyle G. Boyd, *The World of Flying Saucers* (New York: Doubleday, 1963).

5. Keith Thompson, *Angels and Aliens: UFOs and the Mythic Imagination* (New York: Ballantine, 1993), p. 9.

6. Again, see David Darlington, *Area 51—The Deamland Chronicles: The Legend of America's Most Secret Military Base* (New York: Holt, 1997).

7. For these citations, see R. E. Bartholomew and G. S. Howard, *UFOs and Alien Contact: Two Centuries of Mystery* (Amherst, N.Y.: Prometheus Books, 1998), p. 193.

8. So noted in Thomas E. Bullard, *Comparative Study of Abduction Reports*, vol. 1 of *UFO Abductions: The Measure of a Mystery* (Bloomington, Ind.: Fund for UFO Research, 1987), pp. 13–15 (also citing a few contemporaneous examples). For this cinematic genre, see William Johnson, ed., *Focus on the Science Fiction Film*

(Englewood Cliffs, N.J.: Prentice Hall, 1972); Philip Strick, *Science Fiction Movies* (London: Octopus, 1976); John Brosnan, *Future Tense: The Cinema of Science Fiction* (New York: St. Martin's, 1979); Vivian Sobchack, *Screening Space: The American Science Fiction Film* (New York: Ungar, 1993); for the wider historical context, see Karl S. Guthke, *The Last Frontier: Imagining Other Worlds, from the Copernican Revolution to Modern Science Fiction* (Ithaca, N.Y.: Cornell University Press, 1990).

9. Jacobs, "UFOs and the Search for Scientific Legitimacy," pp. 228–29.

10. For a fascinating overview of the UFO "conspiracy cultures," see Dean, *Aliens in America*.

11. See J. Vankin and J. Whalen, *The Sixty Greatest Conspiracies of All Time: History's Biggest Mysteries, Cover-ups, and Cabals* (Secaucus, N.J.: Citadel, 1996); Robert Anton Wilson, *Everything Is under Control: Conspiracies, Cults, and Cover-Ups* (New York: HarperPerennial, 1998).

12. Jenny Randles, *The UFO Conspiracy: The First Forty Years* (London: Javelin, 1988), pp. 8–9.

13. For the various components of this outsize dollar figure, see *Newsweek*, 19 October 1998, pp. 54–56.

14. For the postmodernist "conspiracy cultures" specifically aligned with the UFO experience, see Dean, *Aliens in America*; for their roots in standard American thought, see Richard Hofstadter, *The Paranoid Style in American Politics and Other Essays* (Cambridge: Harvard University Press, 1996).

15. Donald Keyhoe, as in Jay David, *Flying Saucer Reader* (New York: New American Library, 1967), pp. 227–28.

16. LawrenceTacker, as quoted in ibid., pp. 238–39.

17. For many more examples of this "He said–She said" phenomenon, the industry standard as it were, see Philip J. Klass, *UFOs Explained* (New York: Random House, 1974).

18. For this memo, and the other materials following, see Ian Ridpath, "The Woodbridge UFO Incident," in Kendrick Frazer, ed., *The UFO Invasion: The Roswell Incident, Alien Abductions, and Government Coverups* (Amherst, N.Y.: Prometheus Books, 1997), pp. 166–70 (a very nice piece of detective work).

19. For some of those rational explanations, see Carl Sagan and T. Page, *UFO's: A Scientific Debate* (New York: Barnes and Noble, 1996); Klass, *UFOs Explained*; see also Robert Sheaffer, *The UFO Verdict* (Amherst, N.Y.: Prometheus Books, 1981); William R. Corliss, *Handbook of Unusual Natural Phenomena* (New York: Arlington House, 1983), and so on.

20. Jacobs, "UFOs and Scientific Legitimacy," p. 220.

21. Ibid., p. 220.

22. See Michael Shermer, *Why People Believe Weird Things: Pseudoscience, Superstition, and Other Confusians of Our Time* (New York: Freeman, 1997), pp. 8–9.

23. Jacobs, "UFOs and Scientific Legitimacy," p. 222.

24. Pritchard, as in C. D. B. Bryon, *Close Encounters of the Fourth Kind: Alien Abductions, UFOs, and the Conference at M.I.T.* (New York: Knopf, 1995), pp. 135–36.

348 PICTURING EXTRATERRESTRIALS

25. Jacobs, "UFOs and the Search for Scientific Legitimacy," p. 222.

26. Jacques Vallée, *Anatomy of a Phenomenon: UFOs in Space—A Scientific Appraisal* (New York: Ballantine, 1972), p. 124.

27. D. H. Rawcliffe, *Psychology of the Occult* (London: Ridgway, 1952), chap. 14, "The Evidence for Psychosomatic Stigmata."

28. On this riveting optical effect, later made a narrative staple of alien abductions, see Frederick T. Elsworthy, *The Evil Eye: The Origins and Practices of Superstition* (New York: Collier, 1970).

29. Rosemary Osnato, as quoted in Philip J. Klass, *UFO-Abductions: A Dangerous Game* (Amherst, N.Y.: Prometheus Books, 1989), p. 183.

30. For this well-intended, but ultimately controversial effort, see Philip J. Klass, "The Condon UFO Study," in Frazer, *The UFO Invasion*, pp. 29–43.

31. See Sagan and Page, *UFO's: A Scientific Debate*.

32. See Aimé Michel, "The Strange Case of Dr. X," *Flying Saucer Review* (1972, special edition: "UFO Percipients"): 11–32.

33. For details on these otherworldly academic speculations, also their refutation, see Alan Sokal and Jean Bricmont, *Impostures Intellectuelles* (Paris: Editions Odile Jacob, 1997); for an extended lampoon of this prosaic, academic-postmodernist genre, see H. M. S. Phake-Potter, *Postmodernist Deconstruction for Dummies: A Survivor's Guide to Building Your Academic Career*, ed. J. F. Moffitt (Philadelphia: Xlibris, 2002).

34. Jacobs, "UFOs and the Search for Scientific Legitimacy," pp. 229–30 (my emphasis).

35. D. M. Jacobs, *The Threat* (New York: Simon & Schuster, 1998). For a sharp criticism of this, and another similarly best-selling "abduction" pot-boiler by Whitley Strieber, *Confirmation: The Hard Evidence of Aliens among Us* (New York: St. Martin's, 1998), see Frederick Crews, "The Mindsnatchers," *New York Review of Books*, 25 June 1998, pp. 14–19. Crews also decrys the "postmodernist, ideological twists" in Dean's *Aliens in America*, which coyly interpret all such alien-abduction reports as representing positive "political acts" directed against "political, governmental, and corporate authorities." I agree: that is a *dumb* position.

36. See *Entertainment Weekly*, 5 February 1999: *Armageddon* ($624.3m), *Deep Impact* ($348.8m), *Godzilla* ($471.8m), *The X-Files* ($187m), *Lost in Space* ($183.3m), *Star Trek: Insurrection* ($96.4m).

37. Terry Matheson, *Alien Abductions: Creating a Modern Phenomenon* (Amherst, N.Y.: Prometheus Books, 1998), pp. 297–301. As I may add to these comments, life in North American academia has become rather a intimidating experience; universities are now thoroughly bureaucratized. Consequently, the American professoriate has become thoroughly "alienated" (me, too).

Chapter 10

Nothing New in Outer Space

SWEDENBORG AND THE EXTRATERRESTRIALS

H oax, or merely a populist hallucination, the actual historical sources of a now-canonical ET portraiture, even including a three-dimensional simulation (figs. 1, 4, 5, 15–22), are in no way postmodernist. In fact, they considerably antedate the Cold War era, even the "Airship Craze" of 1896–1897 (fig. 28). Once one actually bothers to trace the broader generic, historical, and strictly terrestrial, origins of our ubiquitous postmodernist cultural icon, the ET alien, we find that the unsung inventor was Emanuel Swedenborg (1688–1772). Among the many distinguished admirers of the eighteenth-century Swedish visionary writer were Balzac, Baudelaire, Blake, Emerson, Goethe, and Kant, to mention only a few. Well over two centuries ago, in an opusculum called "The Earths, called Planets, in Our Solar System and Their Inhabitants" (*De telluribus in mundo nostro solari, quae vocantur planetae . . . deque illarum incolis*, 1758), Swedenborg described the *other* inhabitants of the universe.[1] All of Swedenborg's (likewise Steven Spielberg's) extraterrestrials are monotonously humanoid. His governing thesis, which is rather New Age (*avant la lettre*), had it that "the human race is not confined to one earth only, but extends to earths innumerable."[2] Swedenborg's considerable literary contributions to such best-selling postmodernist *auteurs* as Budd Hopkins, John Mack, David Jacobs, and the like, have never been acknowledged by them, a lacuna of laudability which I find despicable.

As described over two centuries ago by the visionary author from Sweden, Moon people are about the size of an earthling seven-year-old, "thus they were dwarfs [*homunciones*]." Although small-scaled (like our New Age Grays), Luna residents (lunatics?) have voices like "thunder" because they communicate by violently expelling air from their abdomens, "like an eructation."[3] Mercurian women are small, beautiful, and wear linen caps, while their men-folk dress in tightfitting raiment; some of the males, however, "would rather appear as crystalline globes" and this is "because the knowledges of things immaterial are represented in another life by crystals" (just as Shirley MacLaine now acknowledges).[4] Venusians come in two species, one "mild and humane," the other a race of cruel, stupid giants.[5] Jovians go naked except for a loincloth; they "creep along" by using their hands, but are kind and gentle and ignorant of warfare and science alike—commendable traits by New Age reckoning.[6] Somewhat similarly, Saturnians are "upright, modest" alien folk who live on fruits and seeds (i.e., are vegetarians).[7] Sound familiar?

Since the Red Planet would figure so prominently in forthcoming earthling science fictional *belles lettres*, it is therefore well worth noting that, when not communicating by telepathy (just as do the postmodernist ETs), Martians speak in "sonorous" tones. Besides being telepathically well endowed, they are vegetarians and feed upon fruit and wear garments made from tree bark, all of which is ecologically sound, thus also most commendable from a New Age perspective. According to Swedenborg's extended exposition, which represents the first truly influential script in the now-extensive literature describing what would later be called the "contactee" experience:

> The spirits of Mars are amongst the best of all spirits who come from the earths of this solar system, being for the most part celestial men. . . . Every one on that earth [Mars] lives content with his own property, and every one with his own share of honor, accounting it enough to be reputed upright and a lover of his neighbor. This delightful and tranquil principle of mind would perish unless such [Martians] as incline to evil thoughts and disposition are [forcibly] banished from the rest. . . . They informed me that they acknowledge and adore our [Earthling] Lord, saying that He is the only God, and that He governs both heaven and the universe. . . . There was presented to me an inhabitant of that earth [Mars]; his face resembled the faces of the inhabitants of our earth, but the lower region of the face was black, not owing to his beard, for he had

none, but to [inherent] blackness instead of a beard: this blackness extended itself underneath the ears on both sides; the upper part of the face was yellowish, like the faces of the inhabitants of our earth who are not perfectly fair [or Scandinavian, like Swedenborg]. They said moreover that on that earth [Mars] they feed on the fruits of trees, especially on a kind of round fruit which buds forth from the ground; and likewise on pulse; and that they are clothed with garments wrought from the fibrous bark of certain trees, which has such a consistence that it may be woven, and also stiffened by a kind of gum which they have amongst them. They related further that they are acquainted with the art of making fluid fires, whereby they have a light during evening and night.[8]

As I have shown, the now-standard depiction of ET aliens is a strictly *American* invention, and most of the initial credit is due to Barney Hill's widely circulated ET *Urbild* (fig. 16; cf. figs. 17–22). So, even if most likely wholly unknown to Mr. Hill, how did Swedenborg's otherworldly close encounters become institutionalized upon American soil? According to conclusions reached by Martin Gardner, the real credit— disgracefully unacknowledged by postmodernist UFOlogists!—for contributing to the current iconography of ETs, for instance as shown in the hoaxed Roswell autopsy film, seems mainly due to another fan of Swedenborg, Andrew Jackson Davis (1826–1910), an American occultist.[9] As described in his *Principles of Nature, Her Divine Revelation, and s Voice to Mankind* (1847, some 756 pages long), all the planets are inhabited, except for Uranus, Neptune, and an as-yet unnamed ninth planet. Seven pages are devoted to the Martians, small humanoids with big blue eyes and yellow faces. Davis confirms Swedenborg's revelation that the lower parts of their countenances are dark in color. They are kind and moral folk, mutes who nonetheless eloquently communicate wholly by facial expressions and/or telepathy. "When one conceives a thought," Davis stated, "he casts his beaming eyes upon the eyes of another; and his sentiments instantly become known." Also picturesque are the alien folk on Saturn. Their heads are "very high and long," with brains composed of cortical glands, "each of which attracts and repels, performing systolic and diastolic motions."[10]

OTHER EARTHBOUND SPACE TOURISTS

Right after the *fin-de-siècle* "Airship Craze" (see fig. 28), another mind-trip into outer space was published in 1899 by a Swiss psychologist, Théodore Flournoy. His monograph, entitled *Des Indes à la Planète*

Mars, described his close encounters with an amateur Swiss medium, Hélène Smith (née Elise Müller, a Geneva shop-girl). Under self-induced hypnotic trances, among other imaginative flights of pure fancy, she described in great detail her sojourn among the Martians, banal beings three feet tall, with heads twice as wide as they were high.[11] As described by Hélène over a century ago, her extraterrestrial creatures seem rather like our now-standard, postmodernist ETs: "These beasts had large flat heads, almost without hair, and large, very soft eyes, like those of seals."[12] The Smith case may already be known to some art historians since Mlle. Hélène had produced many ekphrastic recreations of the Martian landscapes and inhabitants, both in watercolors and oils on canvas: alas, the resulting artwork mostly resembles contemporary calendar illustrations of popular "Hindou" scenes.[13]

Now, like you, I, too, have often seen these exotic "Martians" already imagined by a host of Victorian-era mystics and mediums: in the sci-fi movies (figs. 9–15, 18, 19). A bit later, in an earlier modern culture, the bookish (and hence obsolescent) kind, ETs were of course a staple of merely verbalized science fiction, or should we just say "fictionalized pseudoscience."[14] As accredited literary scholars now recognize, the two authors "who introduced the idea of the invasion of the Earth by Extraterrestrials into world literature" were the German Kurd Lasswitz (*Auf zwei Planeten*, 1897) and H. G. Wells (*War of the Worlds*, 1898).[15] Given the date of Hélène Smith's Martian revelations, we may presume her to be just another reader of Lasswitz's extremely popular science-fiction epic, *Auf zwei Planeten*. Presently however, and just as we have seen, if the fantastic literary topic is now said specifically to deal with alien abduction, then what we formerly called *science fiction* is now labeled "nonfiction" by opportunistic postmodernist paperback publishers.

Although post–Victorian era examples of "Multiple Personality Disorder" (MPD)—which is presently the bottom line, professional diagnosis of the Hélène Smith phenomenon—are now routinely recounted in the scientific literature, only one other "outer space" case studied by a qualified psychologist need be cited. In this example, the subject, unnamed to protect his (multiple) identity and his job, was a qualified technician working on secretive Cold War projects since the late 1940s, evidently fabrication of the first A-bombs. As appears likely to me, his top-secret work was actually carried out at Los Alamos, in New Mexico—and not all that far from Roswell. He was diagnosed by his psychiatrist, Dr. Robert Lindner, as being "a hysteric" (rather than as a UFO-abductee).[16] In the narrower sense, obviously his problem was MPD. The hysterical technician had skillfully recreated a complete outergalactic lifestyle, including the execution of technical drawings depicting life and technology on the distant planet "Seraneb" (Benares?). For the edification of Dr. Lindner, "Kirk Allen" produced a "bulky manuscript with its appendix and notes"; this incunabulum the subject had reportedly completed during his self-propelled outer galactic visits. Its astonishing contents included

a glossary of names and terms that ran to more than 100 pages; 82 full-color maps carefully drawn to scale, 23 of planetary bodies in four projections, 31 of land masses on these planets, 14 labeled "Kirk Allen's Expedition to [fill in the blank]," the remainder of cities on the various planets; 161 architectural sketches and elevations, some colored, some drawn only in ink, but all carefully scaled and annotated; 12 genealogical tables; an 18-page description of the galactic system in which Kirk Allen's home planet was contained, with 4 astronomical charts, one for each of the seasons, and 9 star maps of the skies from observatories on other planets in the system; a 200-page history of the empire Kirk Allen ruled, with a 3-page table of dates and names of battles or outstanding historical events; a series of 44 folders containing from 2 to 20 pages apiece, each dealing with some aspect of the planet over which Kirk Allen of the future ruled, with life in his imperial city, or with a phase of existence on this planet or elsewhere in the system; typical titles, neatly printed on these folders, were: "The Fauna of Srom Olma I," "The Transportation System of Seraneb," "Science of Srom," "The Geology of Srom Olma I," "The Metabiology of the Valley Dwellers," "The History of the Intergalactic Scientific Institute," "Parapsychology of Srom Norbra X," "Economic Foundations of the Valley Society," "Sociology on Srom Olma I," "The Application of Unified Field Theory and the Mechanics of the Stardrive to Space Travel," "The Unique Brain Development of the Crystopods of Srom Norbra X," "Anthropological Studies on Srom Olma I," "The Religious Beliefs of the Valley Dwellers," "Manufacturing Processes and Dye Chemistry," "Fire Worship and Sacrifice on Srom Sodrat II," "Food Distribution in Seraneb," "Sex Habits and Practices of the Crystopods," "Plant Biology and Genetic Science of Srom Olma I," and so on; finally, 306 drawings, some in water colors, some in chalk, some in crayon, of people, animals, plants, insects, weapons, utensils, machines, articles of clothing, vehicles, instruments and furniture [and so forth].[17]

Curiously, since the great achievements of Kirk Allen in outer space have never before been cited in the massive UFOlogical literature, we may now consider adjusted another lacuna of apocryphal laudability.[18]

Whatever the real sources of present-day ET "sightings"—essentially fuzzy anecdotes "remembered" by probably sincere but deluded and/or hypnotized individuals and made known to us by mass media operators seeking easy profits—the postmodernist UFO obsession has spawned another New Age pseudoreligion (further discussed in chapter 11). Functionally, the secular New Age doctrine is itself nothing new, particularly in the light of its corporeal accessories, the now familiar EBE ("extraterrestrial biological entities," a term coined in 1985). Those much discussed New Age "paranormal phenomena" essentially represent a modernist update of medieval *miracula*, "miracles."[19] Let me quote one of the fairly plentiful medieval reports dealing with nocturnal visitations by UFOs, and this is one which, oddly enough, has yet to appear in the copious New Age literature devoted to such celestial sightings. An anonymous thirteenth-century English chronicle tells how,

> About midnight of the day of our Lord's Circumcision [i.e., January 1], the moon being eight days old, and the firmament studded with stars, and the air completely calm, there appeared in the sky, wonderful to relate, the form of a large ship, well-shaped, and of remarkable design and color. This apparition was seen by some monks of St. Alban's, staying at St. Amphibalus to celebrate the festival, who were looking out to see by the stars if it was the hour for chanting matins, and they at once called together all their friends and followers who were in the house to see the wonderful apparition. The vessel appeared for a long time, as if it were painted, and really built with planks; but, at length, it began by degrees to dissolve and disappear, wherefore it was believed to have been a cloud, but a wonderful and extraordinary one for all that.[20]

Here's another one, even older, and even including the appearance of extraterrestrials, in fact a quartet of them! This sighting I will give first in the standard Latin version: *"Et vidi, et ecce ventus turbinis veniebat ab aquilone, et nubes magna, et ignis involvens, et splendor in circuitu eius; et de medio eius, quasi species electri, id est, de medio ignis; et in medio eius similitudo quatuor animalium in eis. Quatuor facies uni, et quatuor pennae uni."* In English, which is the version likely most familiar to you, this reads: "And I looked, and, behold, a whirlwind came out of the north, a great cloud, and a fire infolding itself, and a brightness was about it, and out of the midst thereof as the colour of amber, out of the midst of the fire. Also out of the midst thereof came the likeness of four living creatures. And this was their appearance; they had the likeness of a man. And every one had four faces, and every one had four wings." The striking airborne apparition was often recreated by European artists, some having great pictorial talent.

The author of this exciting close-encounter report, dating to 593

B.C.E., was the Hebrew prophet Ezekiel, and the standard publication, from which I have drawn this eyewitness account, is the King James Bible (Ezek. 1:4–6); the Latin prototype, a translation from the Hebrew, appears in the *Biblia Vulgata*, as edited a long time ago by Saint Jerome. A postmodernist admirer of Steven Spielberg's *Close Encounters of the Third Kind* could now receive the same vision and then, perhaps even without hypnotism, would eagerly report to the press his updated version:

> I looked up at the churning lightning-filled clouds to the north and, lo!, I saw a huge, bright, fiery-orange, rotating object emerge; *it was the mother ship!* Four smaller scout craft emerged from the mother ship. They were star-shaped: like a man with his arms and legs outstretched. Each craft had four windows and four wings. Their landing gear pointed straight down, then flattened out into pads. The craft had a polished metallic appearance . . . [etc.].[21]

This is no joke: as a modern UFOlogist acutely (and all too typically) observed, "Considering the terminology available to a nontechnological culture, Ezekiel, in chapters 1 and 10, gives a remarkably accurate description of a flying saucer which visited him as an agent of the Lord."[22] Indeed!

CHRIST AS A UFO STAR

Whatever the anomalies are called, and as typically recounted without *any* supporting physical evidence, they demand belief: the real link between medieval Christian devotion and postmodernist secular occultism is a religious, versus scientific, mentality (a point further developed in chapters 11 and 12). Specific to the current or New Age idea of alien contacts is the leitmotif of those alleged close encounters transpiring between technologically challenged humans and *superior*, metamundane, intelligences, with superior, signifying both "greater" and "from up there." In short, "new" it is not, instead ageless.

Although described with different terminology and iconography, numerous Olympian gods had previously descended to earth in order to meddle in the affairs of everyday Hellenes. Likewise, and long before publication of the postmodernist ET encounters, according to similarly authoritative eyewitness accounts, Moses had his incandescent burning bush speaking to him and giving him usefully inscribed tablets; the prophet Elijah actually saw a UFO, described by him in contemporaneous (thus erroneous) terms as depicting "a fiery chariot"; the prophet Ezekiel actually saw four glowing ETs, then labeled "Tetramorphs". We also recall how another great ball of celestial illumination had changed Saul to Paul on the off-ramp to Damascus (Acts 9:1–9). In an analogous fashion, the Emperor Constantine also witnessed a phosphorescent UFO inscribed with a talismanic logo: *In hoc signo vinces*. Roughly translated, the Latin motto means "You shall overcome with this UFO."

Just so that you know that some UFOlogists really *have* cited such commonplace Christian apocrypha as constituting appearances of UFOs of the strictly modernist stripe, I need to quote a typical interpretation. In 1960 a chap named Brinsley Le Poer Trench published a book called *The Sky People* that is full of such allegations. Included here is a modernist explanation of Exod. 3:2–5 (alluded to above), reading as follows in the King James Bible: "And the angel of the Lord appeared unto him in a flame of fire out of the midst of a bush: and he looked, and behold, the bush burned with fire, and the bush was not consumed. . . . God called unto him out of the midst of the bush, and said, Moses, Moses. And he said, Here am I!" However, according to the deadly serious Mr. Trench, a devout Christian:

> A spaceship—flying saucer—often illuminates the neighboring countryside with its electric force field. The glowing light within this force field surrounding the ship would most certainly have caused the bush to look as if it was on fire. Moses was so curious about the phenomenon of the bush being burned with fire, and not consumed, that he turned to look closer at it. The Lord, seeing him about to come nearer, called out, warning him not to do so. If Moses had gone too near [to the "flying saucer"] before the current had been turned down, he would have suffered [of course!] a severe electrical shock—or even death. There are many instances in flying saucer reports today of the effects of a spacecraft's force field. Other instances where people have been warned not to come too near are given in the Bible [and are now given to us by Mr. Trench]. . . . In these three verses, the Lord—Captain of the spaceship—tells Moses He will come down on to the top of Mount Sinai, in the sight of all the people. He then warns Moses not to let the people or any animals come near the craft, nor within a certain distance, until He gives a signal—an all clear. Hundreds of modern sightings have testified to the existence of a powerful electric force field around these spacecraft, and people who have got too near have suffered burns. [Etc.][23]

By the way, in the same presently obscure publication, Mr. Trench advanced yet another attractive idea: "One can now [in 1960] deduce for the first time that flying saucers may be made of silicon [and their] electrical energy may be stored in *silicon* batteries."[24] Imagine that: just like the computer laptops much later to be produced in such abundance in—ready for this?—"Silicon Valley."

Perhaps not surprisingly, New Age enthusiasts even cite the star signaling the birth of Christ as a UFO.[25] But, this time at least, the erudite scholar knows that there actually is substantial documentary evidence to back up their claim. Moreover, the art historian specifically is able to cite a painted representation of this airborne UFO by a major artist, Giotto di Bordone, who pictured the incandescent apparition, including its fiery tail, looming over a scene of "The Adoration of the Magi" (circa 1304) in a fresco which one can still view *in situ* in the Arena Chapel in Padua (fig. 27).[26] Although not previously cited by any profitably published UFOlogist (not surprising, since such archival labors seem beyond them), now seems an opportune moment to introduce these important primary documents into the UFO literary canon. The scripture-based astral narrative, and its historical documentation, goes like this.

An early Christian apocryphal text, the *Liber de Nativitate Mariae* attributed to St. Jerome, describes a divine prophecy which was announced to the awed people by nothing less than the disembodied voice of God portentously coming out of the *Propitiatorium* (Place of Conciliation). In this instance, the divine logos is specifically announcing "a prophecy from Isaiah [*secundum Esaïae vaticinium*], concerning to whom the Virgin should be given, and to whom she shall be betrothed, for Isaiah says, 'there shall come forth a rod out of the stem of Jesse, and a flower shall spring out of its root'" (*Liber de Nativitate Mariae* 7:3, which ends by exactly quoting Isa. 11:1).[27] As an earlier text (circa 340)—the *Liber de Ortu Beatae Mariae et Infantia Salvatoris* by the Pseudo-Matthew—tells us, the "enormous star" itself drew the Magi to the birthplace in the cave (*stella ingens . . . splendebat super speluncam*) because, "according to the prophets in Jerusalem, this [UFO] was the sign that the Messiah had been born" (*Evangelium Matthaei* 13:7; 14:1). Pseudo-Matthew concludes by explaining that it was all "in compliance with that which had been announced by the prophet Isaiah [*est quod dictum est per Isaiam prophetam*]."[28]

In another, much earlier (circa 170?), Greek Apocryphal book, the *Protoevangelion* ascribed to St. James the Lesser, again the setting is a cave in which a virgin has given birth amidst a great flood of otherworldly light: "The infant appeared, and sucked the breast of his mother Mary [*masphòn ex tex metros anton Mariam*]" (*Protoevangelion* 18:2). Immediately afterward, "some wise-men came from the east," explaining how "we have seen his star in the east" [*astéra en te anatole*] (*Protoevangelion* 21:1). Here, however, even though there is no direct mention of

Isaiah, his flowering prophecy (Isa. 11:1) is alluded to in the standard example of the blooming rod (Latin *vara*) which designates Joseph as the betrothed of Mary (*Protoevangelion* 8:3, 9:1).[29] Much later, now after the momentous passing of the First Christian Millennium, Justin Martyr (circa 114–165) examines the case of certain Hebrew Prophets of the Old Testament who had foretold the coming of Christ. First, says Justin (in chapter 32 of his *First Apology*), there was Moses (and here the author refers to Gen. 49:10), and after him there was

> *Isaiah*, another prophet, foretelling the same things in other words, who spoke thus: "*A star shall rise out of Jacob*, and a flower shall spring from the root of Jesse: and His arm shall the nations trust." And [Justin then observes] *a star of light has indeed arisen*, and a flower has sprung from the root of Jesse; this is Christ. For by the power of God He was conceived by a virgin of the seed of Jacob, who was the father of Judah, who, as we have shown, was the father of the Jews; and Jesse was His forefather according to the oracle [Isaiah], and He was the son of Jacob and Judah according to lineal descent.[30]

What is particularly striking about this oracular passage is the complementary appearance of a prophetic "star," Christ himself as a UFO, a declamatory astral motif attributed here to Isaiah by Justin. Nonetheless, the casual reader might observe how this relationship, Isaiah-and-Star (Christ or UFO, if you will), apparently figures directly neither in the King James Version nor even in the definitive, late-fourth-century Vulgate edition wrought by Jerome. However it came about, in this statement Justin actually does authoritatively transfer the source for the *stella-virga-Virgo* combination, from Balaam to Isaiah. Whence this anomalous astral epiphany? It appears that we have three choices. On the one hand, perhaps we are finding the starry residue from some pre-Hieronymite variant text of the Book of Isaiah (which is itself notoriously a "compendium"), one that was consciously suppressed in the Vulgate.[31] Conversely, perhaps the situation was just that Justin had quoted the key passage, Isa. 11:1, from memory, faulty in this case. Nonetheless, analogous astral motifs are encountered nearly in the same prophet's texts (e.g., Isa. 13:10, 14:13, 47:13).

In any event, it is unquestionable that, although omitting (deliberately?) any textual reference to "Balaam," and probably due to his notoriously "pernicious influence," Justin actually did cite the astral motif (a proto-UFO) found in Num. 24:17: "*Orientur* stella *ex Iacob, et consurget* virga *de Israel. . . .*" The Messiah-announcing astral motif nevertheless actually did have its corresponding scriptural locus within the prophecies of Isaiah, where the presence of the portentous Star of Bethlehem was made manifest, without however having to be named as such, due to its direct textual proximity to the Magi, here spoken of as being "the Kings." The passage in question, Isa. 60:1, 3, reads as follows in the Vulgate (with the more familiar King James Version following): "*Surge, illuminare, Ierusalem, quia venit lumen tuum, Et gloria Domini super te orta est. . . . Et ambulabunt gentes in lumine tuo, Et reges in splendore ortus tui.*" "Arise, shine; for thy light is come, and the glory of the Lord [as Christ according to the prophecy] is risen upon thee. . . . And the Gentiles shall come to thy [starry] light, and kings [Magi] to the brightness of thy rising."

As now appears obvious, Justin pointed out this decidedly prophetic star (or UFO, if you will) because it might further bolster his case for Isaiah's direct linkage with another, far more celebrated, starry appearance that was later announced in the New Testament. In this case, the oft-mentioned predictive star becomes the one shining over Bethlehem, a luminous body (or UFO) which brought both shepherds and kings to worship the infant held in Mary's lap: Matt. 2:2: "*. . . vidimus enim stellam eius in oriente, et venimus adorare eum,*" and, similarly Matt. 2:7, 9–10: "*. . . et ecce stella . . . ubi erat puer.*" This conclusion seems likely for Justin again (in the *Dialogue with Trypho*, ch. 63) mentions how the Lord had "begotten Thee from the womb, before the morning star [citing Ps. 110:3]."[32] Later in the same "Dialogue" by Justin (chapter 106), starry (or UFOish) prefigurations of Christ's luminous epiphany pile up in even greater profusion:

> And that He [Christ] should arise like a star from the seed of Abraham, Moses showed beforehand when he thus said, "A star shall arise from Jacob, and a leader from Israel" [Num. 24:17, but again giving here no credit to "Balaam"]; and another Scripture says, "Behold a man; the East is His name" [Zech. 6:12: "*Ecce vir Oriens*"; . . . but called "The BRANCH" (*virga*) in the King James Version]. Accordingly, when a star rose in heaven at the time of His birth, as is recorded in the memoirs of His Apostles, the Magi from Arabia, recognizing the sign by this, came and worshipped Him.[33]

Nonetheless, even though not cited here by Justin (or most UFOlogists), unquestionably most significant for our purposes is the one astral citation in the New Testament that has always been explicitly linked to the prophecy of Isaiah, and this is found in Rev. 22:16: "*Ego Iesus . . . sum radix, et genus David, stella splendida et matutina.*"[34] And so it goes. In sum, two millennia later the venerable spiritual metaphor, "Heaven," has been updated for the technologically challenged New Age; now it is commonly labeled "Outer Space." And that is the mailing address for all those gray-faced and bug-eyed postmodernist extraterrestrials who take such outsized delight in abducting awed earthlings.

A DESPERATE NEED FOR ANGELS, DEMONS, CHARISMA, AND HEAVEN ABOVE

More recently, in America (and thus not all that far from Roswell), an ambitious youth from provincial upstate New York, Joseph Smith (1805–1844), was (he said) visited in 1827 by an "angel" who generously gave him directions where to unearth long-buried brazen tablets inscribed in a foreign tongue written with mysterious characters.[35] Since the original artifact mysteriously disappeared subsequently, we now only have a florid English translation, prepared by none other than Mr. Smith (who seems never to have studied linguistics). This invaluable incunabulum of divine otherworldly wisdom is presently called (according to its title page) *The Book of Mormon: An Account Written by the Hand of Mormon upon Plates Taken from the Plates of Nephi*. As one reads in the preface, "The First English Edition" of the *Urtext* was published in 1830, as "Translated by Joseph Smith, Jun[ior]." The immediate, heaven-sent source was, in this case, "The Brass Plates of Nephi . . . Mormon . . . Ether . . . Laban," all written in a foreign language–text *only* made legible to the anglophone True Believers by Mr. Joseph Smith. Their exact linguistic characteristics must, unfortunately, remain forever murky since the originally heaven-sent, inscribed, and gilded tablets (a truly brazen text) are no longer available for physical inspection by trained philologists. However, as is carefully explained in the opening pages of every *Book of Mormon*:

> Joseph Smith, through whom, by the gift and power of God, the ancient Scripture, known as THE BOOK OF MORMON, has been brought forth and translated into the English tongue, made personal and circumstantial record of the matter . . . affirm[ing] that during the night of September 21, 1823, he sought the LORD in fervent prayers, having previously received a Divine manifestation of transcendent import. . . . [As a result of which] there was a book deposited, written upon gold plates, giving an account of the former inhabitants of this [American] continent, and the source from which they sprang [and] the fullness of the everlasting Gospel was contained in it, as delivered by the Saviour to the ancient inhabitants, [and] that God had prepared them for the purpose of translating the book [and so forth].[36]

As seems perhaps forgotten even by accredited UFOlogists, Mr. Smith also saw a UFO and was even saluted by its ET crew members. Here is how he tells the tale:

> I saw a pillar of light exactly over my head, above the brightness of the sun, which descended gradually until it fell upon me. . . . When the light rested on me I saw two personages, whose brightness and glory defy all descriptions, standing above me in the air. One of them spoke unto me.[37]

Unfortunately, current scholarship has shown *The Book of Mormon* to be largely a crib of an even earlier nineteenth-century American "visionary" (or occultist) text. Fawn Brodie discovered a close (and perhaps not so remarkable) textual correspondence—so close, in fact, as to appear to be plagiarism—existing between *The Book of Mormon*, as first published in 1830, and an earlier, and similarly divinely dictated, visionary text, Ethan Smith's *A New View of the Hebrews, or The Ten Tribes of Israel in America* (1823).[38] I myself decline to comment upon the putatively divine origins of Mr. Ethan Smith's apparently pirated "opus magnum mysticus." Joseph Smith's kind of extraterrestrial scripture was paralleled slightly later with Madame Helena Petrovna Blavatsky's "Stanzas of Dzyan," written in "Senzar" (similarly unknown to any accredited linguist) and providing the florid basis for her multivolume *Secret Doctrine* (1888), the holy book of the Theosophists (who still dwell among us). Although she said she had found the rare incunabulum in an essentially inaccessible Tibetan monastery (Shangri-la?), alas, Blavatsky was later shown to be a master hoaxer.[39]

No matter; deep thinker UFOlogist Erich von Däniken takes it all at face value: "It is said that the [pre-Blavatsky] original is older than the earth," and Erich proceeds to quote generous chunks from "the original." Even though "this creation myth really needs no further commentary for the educated reader," Erich proceeds to give us one anyway. It is worth quoting, especially if you could use a good chuckle by now:

> Sections of the *Book of Dzyan* reputedly tell us that 18,000,000 years ago there were living creatures on earth that were boneless and rubber-like, and vegetated without reason or intelligence. These beings are supposed to have reproduced themselves by division. On the course of a long evolution, a peaceful and gentle kind of being originated in this way 4,000,000 years ago. Those beings lived in a period of tranquil bliss, in a world of happy dreamers. In the next 3,000,000 years a giant race of a very different kind developed. These giants, it says in *Dzyan*, were androgynous and mated with themselves. Then 700,000 years ago they began to mate

with she-animals, but terrible looking monsters resulted from this kind of reproduction. These monsters were unable to free themselves from this bestial method of reproduction and became dependent on animals and dumb, like animals [and mass market paperback authors].[40]

Notwithstanding the considerable contributions made to autonomous (and inventive) scriptural study by the likes of Madame Blavatsky, Joseph Smith, and Erich von Däniken, "the educated reader" will already recognize that even the motif of otherworldly descending *écriture automatique* is nothing new either. For instance, we have (besides, much more recently, André Breton, the patriarch of Surrealism) the canonical example of Saint John on the isle of Patmos. He is another world-class prophet, likewise dictated to by an awesome ET sent by God: "... *mittens per angelum ... verbo Dei*"; see his best-selling "Book of Revelation," chapter 1 (where, as you will see, he then mistakenly labeled the ET an "angel," *angelus*). So what are angels anyway? Where do they begin? The English word "angel" comes from the Latin *angelus*, itself derived from the Greek αγγελοσ, a "messenger."[41] According to Latin-speaking Christianity, these sky-dwellers were to be saluted, naturally enough, as "messengers from God."

Blavatsky also made another, mostly unsung, contribution to the twentieth-century "contactee" literary corpus. Her Theosophical speculations, producing a new and rather grand occult system, gave us a hierarchy of "Ascended Masters," or *Mahatmas*. These superior folk formed a structure of supernatural beings serving as intermediaries between ignorant humanity and the Divine. Blavatsky included among the Hierarchy of Masters one who dwelt on Venus and with whom, so she wrote, she was in contact. These *maestros esotéricos* she termed the "Lords of the Flame" and the "Lord of This World," the latter being the anointed head of the hierarchy designated for merely human affairs.[42] Likewise, particularly as stridently pictured by Erich von Däniken, the postmodernist ETs may be either figured as wise messengers from God, or as those sky-descending creatures which distribute good (sometimes) or evil (more often) among mere mortals. Given the agenda of the recognized pioneers in such otherworldly speculations, the contactees of extraterrestrials and (slightly later) the abductees abused by the same kind of aliens should be approached as participants in an occult, or alternative religious, movement (further explained in chapter 11). With historical hindsight, their alienated misadventures most commonly approach the visionary experiences generic to medieval religiosity, which is now cast in a New Age framework of space age technology.

It is interesting to note that in the Old Testament angels were often spoken of as being wingless. Jacob, for instance, saw the wingless kind; as described by him, they needed a *ladder* in order to perform their useful rounds between heaven and earth (Gen. 28:12–22). The first winged angel to appear commonly in postclassical art was a feathered creature used to symbolize the Gospel writer-evangelist ("messenger") called Matthew; perhaps the *Mattheus*-logo made its artistic premiere in a fourth-century mosaic still exhibited in the Roman church of Santa Pudenziana. It was Christian (versus Hebraic) artists who made the winged sort into a pictorial commonplace, the kind that has nothing specifically to do with St. Matthew. Most likely, the medieval type derived from the iconographic formula previously belonging to the *Nike* (Victory) of the Greeks, the goddess known to the Latins as *Victoria*, an ancient deity now sponsoring a postmodernist brand of footwear that is mostly victorious in the marketplace. The medieval prototype expanded into many kinds of positive types, including a handy "guardian angel" guiding deserving individual earthlings away from all manner of perils.[43]

Guardian angels were frequently described in the so-called vision literature of the Christian Middle Ages. A modern student of such apparition accounts usefully remarks that "their modern equivalents might be reports of UFO abductions."[44] In this case, it will be useful to quote from one of the first of this recitations, the *Visio Sancti Pauli* or "Apocalypse of Paul," dated around 388 C.E. As we learn here:

> And there is an angel who goes forth rejoicing from the person in whom he dwells. When the sun has set, therefore, at the first hour of the night, in the same hour goes the angel of every person and of every man and woman, who protects and keeps them, because the person is the image of God. . . . Every day and night the angels present to God an account of all the deeds of humanity. . . . At the hour appointed all the angels, every one rejoicing therefore, come together before God to meet him and worship him. The angels came to worship in the presence of God, and the spirit came forth to meet them, and there was a voice saying, "Where do you come from, our angels, bringing burden of news?" They answered and said, "We have come from those who have renounced the world for your holy name's sake, wandering as strangers and in the caves of the rocks, and weeping every hour that they dwell on earth, and hungering and thirsting for the sake of your name, with their loins girt, holding in their hands the incense of their hearth, and praying and blessing at every hour, suffering anguish and subduing themselves, weeping and lamenting more than all that dwell on the earth. We who are their angels mourn with them."[45]

Now comes the part in the *Visio Sancti Pauli* which most closely resembles one of our contemporary alien-abduction reports. Just like the post-modernist narratives, it makes mention of both kinds of ETs, the mildly benevolent and the righteously wrathful:

> After I saw these things, I saw one of the spiritual ones coming toward me, and he caught me up in the spirit [meaning in his UFO] and carried me to the third heaven. And this angel [an ET *avant la lettre*] said to me, "Follow me, and I will show you the place where the righteous are taken when they are dead. Thereafter I will take you to the bottomless pit and show you the souls of the sinners and the kind of place they are taken to when they are dead."
>
> I went behind the angel [or ET], and he took me into heaven [via his UFO], and I looked upon the firmament and saw there the powers: there was forgetfulness, which deceives and draws human hearts to itself, and the spirit of slander, and the spirit of fornication, and the spirit of wrath, and the spirit of insolence; and there were the princes of wickedness. I saw these things beneath the firmament of heaven.
>
> Again I looked and saw angels [ETs] without mercy, having no pity, whose countenances were full of fury. Their teeth stuck forward out of their mouths, and their eyes shown [*sic*] like the morning star of the east, and sparks of fire went forth from the hair on their heads and out of their mouths. And I asked the angel, "Who are these, lord?" The angel answered and said to me, "These are the ones appointed to the souls of sinners in their hour of necessity, even to those who have not believed that they had the Lord for their helper and have not trusted in him."
>
> I looked up and saw other angels [ETs] whose faces shone like the sun, and their loins were girt with golden girdles, and they held palms in their hands and the sign of God. They were clothed in garments on which was written the name of the Son of God, full of all gentleness and mercy. And I asked the angel, "Lord, who are these who are such great beauty and compassion?" The angel answered and said to me, "These are the angels of righteousness [specialized ETs] who are sent to bring the souls of the righteous in their hour of necessity, even those who have believed that they had the Lord for their helper." And I said to him, "Do the righteous and the sinners necessarily meet when they are dead?" The angel answered and said to me, "The way by which all pass to God is one, but the righteous have a holy helper with them [i.e., their guardian angel] and are not troubled when they go to appear in the presence of God."[46]

The antithetical counterparts to angels are called "demons," as derived from the Greek δαιμον, giving way to the Latin terminology *daemon, daemonis*; the Hellenic source-term meant "legacy, lot," which could be either good or evil. "Demons" historically explain "angels," hence ETs as well. The image of angels as intermediaries between God and humanity has its roots in pre-Christian ideas about daemons and the daemonic world. Plutarch, in his essay "On the Cessation of Oracles," speaks of a "family of Daemons, intermediate between gods and men and, after a certain fashion, bringing thought together and uniting in one of the society of both." In Plato's *Symposium*, Diotima describes Eros as "a great spirit [*daemon*], and like all spirits, he is intermediate between the divine and the mortal." Eros "interprets between gods and men . . . he is the mediator who spans the chasm which divides them and, therefore, in him all is bound together, and through him the arts of the prophet and the priest, their sacrifices and charms, and all prophecy and incantation, find their way." Diotima concluded: "These spirits or intermediate powers are many and diverse."[47] So are those of the postmodernist ETs.

Christians later applied a different, literally "reversed," interpretation on the daemons; as William Butler Yeats (1865–1939) put it, *Daemon est Deus inversus*: "The Devil Is God Reversed." One of the earlier daemons specifically named was *Lucifer* ("Fire-bearer"), first known to the Hebrews as *Helel ben Sahar*, "Bright Son of the Morning." As an Old Testament prophet described him, "Thou wast on the holy mountain of God; thou hast walked up and down in the stones of fire. Thou wast perfect in thy ways from the day thou was created—till iniquity was found in thee" (Ezek. 28:22–23). Later tradition linked him to the planet Venus and other fiery, falling figures: Hephaestus, Prometheus, Phaeton, Icarus. The pride that made him "sit in the seat of God" led to his great fall from grace. Later identified with Satan, biblical references would appear to make him into an incandescent UFO. One eyewitness was Jesus (figs. 2, 3), who told his followers, "I beheld Satan as lightning fall from heaven" (Luke 10:18). Another prominent Christian made privy to such a phosphorescent sighting was Saint Paul: "Satan himself masquerades as an angel of light" (2 Cor. 11:14).[48]

Here is how a couple of New Age fundamentalist UFOlogists have later reworked the shopworn motif; now *demons* make earthlings see UFOs through "temporary manipulations of matter and energy." The UFO demons are literally millenarian figures: "All of what we are witnessing in the fields of the occult, the UFOs, the false messiahs—even inflation and famine—lines up well with what the prophets expected of the period known as the End Time [i.e., the millennium]." For these insightful New Age folks, UFOs are clearly "a manifestation of demon activity. They are here to misguide the multitudes and they are doing pretty well [at this misdirection]. They have judiciously utilized their powers through selected people to fascinate the masses, and they have widely promulgated their doctrines."[49] They must be right; the postmodernist masses are indeed fascinated by the demonic spectacle (see figs. 1, 4, 5, 12–22).

It is useful to recall that, prior to Christianity's demonization of the daemonic world, daemons did not have a thoroughly evil coloring. Previously, the term "demon" had a religious and spiritual signification, and generally signified the "other world." In pagan antiquity, *demon*—interchangeable with *daemon* and *daimon*—was used in a threefold sense: for gods, for divine intermediaries, and for the autonomous souls of the dead. Thus we see the historical common ground between the traditional imagination, the one thriving on angels and demons, and the modern legends of aliens with outer-space zip codes. Although demonic iconography evolves, it remains culture-specific. For example, a modernist tradition of fifty years of UFO sightings (since 1947) has created an alien dichotomy; the initially tall, Nordic-looking "blonds" were superseded by the postmodernist standard: the short, insectlike "Grays" (see the "Alien Time-Line": fig. 8). Ancient or modern, other-worldlings are able to change their corporeal appearances at will within the sight of privileged witnesses in select locations, typically in the generic "wilderness."

Angels and aliens alike can easily be seen as "messengers," *evangeloi*, as both are more visible in their functions and effects than as any known corporeal essence. Inevitably, questions about the alien essence—where do they come from?—and their amazing vehicles—what are they made of?—continue to haunt much postmodernist UFOlogical speculative discourse. Similarly unresolved remains the case of Thomas Aquinas's speculations about precisely how many angels could actually dance on the head of a pin. For example, if angels could then be said to have "subtle bodies," what should we say today about aliens who (as previously described by Betty Andreasson, in chapter 5) pass through walls and float inches above the ground (fig. 22), and withstand inside their spacecraft extraordinary accelerations in velocity and violent shifts in trajectory? As we have seen, today's alien abductors continue to show more than passing interest in human sexuality and reproduction, a tradition that extends to Antonio Villas-Boas's seduction by a gorgeous female "angel" with cherry-red pubic hair (also described in chapter 5).

The position held by alien-abduction researchers, that aliens are "harvesting" a population of hybrid babies by using human women as breeders, echoes the ancient phenomenon of the otherworldly lover: the "incubus-succubus" tradition described in chapter 7. An additional point of reference directs attention to the incontrovertible fact, so argued by the medieval ANGELologists, that angels really are extremely vulnerable to corruption when in the base company of human beings. Is it the wanton nature of the manifest, material world which corrodes their armor of righteousness, or is it instead, as a postmodernist might hold, some magnetic field within the flesh that plays havoc with their virtuous compasses? Such speculations are literally otherworldly. But, of course, these notions are fundamental to the Western religious tradition, which holds that God necessarily resides in the sky, *in coelo* (also called heaven). Nearly everyone has learned by rote a standard recitation, beginning, "Our Father who art in heaven. . . ." And don't forget about the Holy Spirit's *descent* from the sky following Jesus' baptism in the River Jordan, nor His privileged return—*ascent*—to heaven after leaving his disciples behind, slumbering and earthbound, as described in the Book of Acts.

But this was nothing new either; Christians had merely borrowed the luminescent ascentional motif from pagan Hellenistic, later Roman, rulers. When one of these worthies left his mortal coil behind, he was said to experience *apotheosis*, literally an "ascent as a god." Examples of antique portraiture depicting royal figures in heaven-bound apotheosis, typically characterized by the "heavenward-gazing eyes," are numerous. Beginning with Alexander the Great, the pose also bespoke *enthusiasmos*, the "heavenly passion," a state of "possession," *ekstasis*, with wet, teary eyes and an open, breathing mouth: "*elevatis ad coelum oculis, compunctus corde, commotus in lacrymis.*" The very look told us that the "experiencer" was one thrilled by otherworldly visions, the kind experienced in religious ecstasy and transport (for which see chapter 6).

The radiant faces of such superior personages, including Christ (figs. 2, 3), were expressly said to be illuminated by the "light of the spirit," *charis* (καριϛ or gift), made phosphorescent with inner spiritual life, and the stunning effect upon the believers was literally "charismatic." So appearing, it was understood that they often flew up to, and merged into, the sun, *helios*. As H. P. L'Orange remarks, just as in the case of our postmodernist ET portraiture (fig. 4), "big prominent, glistening eyes betokened, according to the physiognomical lore of the ancients, superhuman, soaring aspiration. Scipio's eyes shone [likewise] in his awe-inspiring countenance: *flagrabant lumina niti adspectu, gratusque inerat visentibus horror [cum] imperatorius ardor oculorum.*"[50] There you have it: *proof*, that the postmodernist portraiture of ETs is modeled on iconographic formulas initially invented for the representation of charismatic Hellenistic rulers. This constitutes, needless to say, an erudite observation never made by any postmodernist UFOlogist.

Paul Kurtz, among other party-pooper skeptics, recognizes that "UFO mythology is similar to the message of the classical religions where God sends his angels as emissaries who offer salvation to those who accept the faith and obey his prophets. Today, the chariots of the gods are UFOs."[51] The fact of a current linkage drawn between angels and ETs is undeniable; for this we have the unimpeachable testimony (already quoted in chapter 5) of a modern celebrity-abductee, Mrs. Betty Andreasson: "I'm thinking they [her alien abductors] must be angels, because Jesus was able to walk through doors and walk on water. They must be angels" (see fig. 21).[52] "Peter," one of John Mack's alien "experiencers," made the same heartfelt connection: "There's been guardian angels[:] I'm very spiritual, and I've always known that I could commune with God," and, likewise, he also had always known (as perhaps we don't) "that there were UFOs and extraterrestrials."[53] But if Peter and Betty A. don't seem authoritative enough for you, then here is deep thinker, evangelist-preacher, Billy Graham in his own best-seller, *Angels: God's Secret Agents*: "UFOs are astonishingly angel-like in some of their reported appearances."[54] Reverend Billy is not the only sharp-witted Christian Fundamentalist to make this obvious connection.

Even a few Catholics subscribe to this neo-evangelical truism. The author of a 1978 paperback opusculum, fittingly called *God Drives a Flying Saucer*, describes the function of his "startling" UFO epistle to the people as follows:

> I present the material in this book, not as a theory based on some sort of mystical revelation or metaphysical hunch but rather as a collection of pure, hard facts—facts based on statistical evidence which, along with some elementary logic, leads to the following startling conclusions:
>
> 1. Flying saucers are not only real but closely associated with the Christian religion.
>
> 2. Flying saucers visited earth during biblical times and even before.
>
> 3. Flying saucers do exhibit most of the flight characteristics described by witnesses, and in so doing defy no laws of nature. Turns of 90 and 180 degrees, while traveling at the speed of light, can he made with no adverse effects on the craft or its occupants.
>
> 4. Flying saucers can and do appear and disappear almost instantaneously.
>
> 5. Without defying Einstein's laws of motion, flying saucers are capable of speeds closely approaching or equaling the speed of light (186,000 miles a second).
>
> 6. Flying-saucer occupants are responsible for the scriptures, prophecies and miracles of the Christian religion.
>
> 7. God is not supernatural but rather super-technological, and is capable of all acts and all characteristics hitherto attributed to miraculous powers. That He created man in His image is not myth or a parable;

for God, while humanoid, is nevertheless immortal through technology.

All of these conclusions will be documented, explained and proved in the pages that follow.[55]

Yet another writer of the fundamentalist stripe, Protestant this time, has catalogued a quantity of biblical UFO incidents. According to his research, in the Old Testament, we have UFO sightings and close encounters in Gen. 15:17 and 28:12; Exod. 13:21; Ezek. 1 and 10; 2 Kings 2; and in the New Testament, as specifically associated with Jesus Christ, the pertinent evidence is found recorded in Matt. 3:13–17 and 17:1–8; Luke 2:9; and Acts 2:9.[56] There you have it: UFOs and ETs, one size fits all—meaning all possible religious persuasions (and, possibly, also all manner of hysterical predispositions).

But here the very format of those ancient "angels," now so convincingly shown to be driving flying saucers since time immemorial, must be further clarified. These are distinctively modern extraterrestrial beings, now themselves become a complementary and similarly ubiquitous commercial product—angels—promoted by myriad New Age publishers. As such, they are naturally rather different than the premodern kind belonging to the medieval imagination.[57] Every properly outfitted New Age bookstore (also the unabashed commercial kind) now has a section devoted to brightly colored paperback publications telling us everything we needed to know about "angels." Many TV talk shows delight in displaying happy folk, mostly women, who are delighted to have a media moment to recount their divinely close encounters with their personally designated "guardian angels." The rest of us postmodernists are not so well endowed in the spiritual department: we have to hire bodyguards.

However, as with so much else common to New Age doctrine, much of the credit for the initial invention of the contemporary angelic entity again belongs to Emanuel Swedenborg and, in this case, the angels and/or extraterrestrials grew from his innovative formulation of a distinctively modernist, or counter-medieval, "heaven." Like the putative originating source (*fons et origo*) of the UFOs, it too has always been located "up there" in the popular *mentalité*. The distinctively modern kind of extraterrestrial other world proposed by Swedenborg, a Protestant (specifically Lutheran) deep thinker, has four characteristics distinguishing it from its Catholic, largely disembodied and purgatory-ridden predecessors.[58] It begins immediately after death; it becomes the fulfillment of material, terrestrial existence; it is a dynamic, motion-filled environment; its focus is human love expressed in communal and familial concerns. According to Swedenborg, and long before the New

Age so dubbed itself, "I insist that angels are completely people in form. They do have faces, eyes, ears, chests, arms, hands, and feet. They do see each other, hear each other, and talk with each other. In short, nothing proper to man whatever is missing—except that they are not clothed with a material body."

For us worldly mortals there is, however, a perceptual problem: you need "spiritual sight" to make them out. As Swedenborg explained, "Angels are not visible to men through men's physical senses, only rather through the eyes of the spirit within man." So privileged, you are now enabled to perceive that "angels are people, living together as people on earth do; they have clothes, houses, and many similar things," maybe even minivans and TV sets. There is, however, a significant distinction: "Since angels are in a more perfect state, everything they have is more perfect; angelic wisdom surpasses human wisdom." Just like modern ETs, "the most intelligent have clothes that gleam as if aflame, some radiant as if alight." Just like contemporary ETs, "angels' thoughts are not limited and constrained by ideas derived from space and time the way human thoughts are [by] things that belong to [physical] nature [and which] lead the mind away from spiritual matters and deprive intellectual sight of its outreach."[59]

UPDATING SWEDENBORG WITH ERICH VON DÄNIKEN AND JOHN MACK

Adding to mass credulity, a perhaps more sophisticated wrinkle was to connect the flying saucer/outer-space syndrome with theories of "ancient wisdom" implanted among mere earthlings by generous-minded ET missionaries. This imaginative synthesis initially made its biggest splash in the late 1960s with the widely sold (nearly 50 million copies), pseudoscientific paperback production of Erich von Däniken (born 1935). These New Age revelations began with his *Erinnerungen an die Zukunft* (1968; *Chariots of the Gods?*) and *Gods from Outer Space* (also published in 1968). Däniken was a shrewd Swiss, whose contribution was the dramatic introduction of the literally "ancient astronaut"; he quickly acquired author-accomplices in Europe, who did not hesitate one nanosecond in rushing their own spin-offs into print.[60]

As breathlessly told by von Däniken, the advent of these superior intelligences from outer space, the easy riders of UFOs, brought to primitive mankind the gift of the Egyptian pyramids, the stone monuments of Easter Island, and the architecture of the pre-Inca peoples of Peru. In

1968, that idea was also widely *seen*: in Stanley Kubrick's blockbuster movie, *2001: A Space Odyssey*. That ponderous space opera opens by showing Big Brothers from the Beyond leaving space-faring earthlings an archaeological beacon, a black monolith designed in the contemporary (1968) vanguard "minimalist" style; this bleak monument directs them to their mysterious origins in extraterrestrial superior knowledge. Besides cinematic, von Däniken's manner of rhetorical argumentation is, shall we say, rather *speculative* at best; here is a typical sample:

> *Let us suppose* that foreign astronauts visited the territory of the Sumerians thousands of years ago. *Let us assume* that they laid the foundations of the civilization and culture of the Sumerians and then returned to their own planet, after giving this stimulus to development. *Let us postulate* that curiosity drove them back to the scene of their pioneer work every hundred terrestrial years to check the results of their experiment. By the standards of our present-day expectation of life, the same astronauts *could* easily have survived for 500 terrestrial years.[61]

In the event, von Däniken also deserves credit (previously unrecognized) as a *literary innovator*. Von Däniken is the chap who actually introduced the notion of alien spaceman-as-ovum snatcher, the kind postulated upon egregious "breeding experiments." Needless to say, such operations have since become the common motif in most postmodernist paperback literature abundantly recounting very close pelvic encounters with ETs (see chapters 2 and 5); they have also become standard cinematic fare (*The X-Files: Fight the Future*, 1998). Let us hear von Däniken's grand thesis as he explained it back in 1968:

> Dim as yet undeniable ages ago, an unknown space-ship soon found out that the earth had all the prerequisites for intelligent life to develop. Obviously the "man" of those times was no *Homo sapiens*, but something rather different. The spacemen artificially fertilized some female members of this species, put them into a deep sleep, so ancient legends say, and departed. Thousands of years later the space travelers returned and found scattered specimens of the genus *Homo sapiens*. They repeated their breeding experiment several times until finally they produced a creature intelligent enough to have the rules of society imparted to it.[62]

Von Däniken also fancies himself something of an art historian; at least he frequently resorts to examples of ancient artworks to serve him as visual proof for his thesis of ancient extraterrestrial visitations (such as fig. 30). A prime example is his imaginative interpretation of a now-familiar Mayan bas-relief found atop a pyramid in Palenque (which I have myself inspected in situ, arriving however at rather a different conclusion). According to von Däniken:

> There sits a human being, with the upper part of his body bent forward like a racing motorcyclist; today any child would identify his vehicle as a rocket. It is pointed at the front, then changes to strangely grooved indentations like inlet ports, widens out, and terminates at the tail in a darting flame. The crouching being himself is manipulating a number of indefinable controls and has the heel of his left foot on a kind of pedal. His clothing is appropriate: short trousers with a broad belt, a jacket with a modern Japanese opening at the neck, and closely fitting bands at arms and legs. With our knowledge of similar pictures, we should be surprised if the complicated headgear were missing. And there it is, with the usual indentations and tubes, and something like antennae on top. Our space traveler—he is clearly depicted as one—is not only bent forward tensely; he is also looking intently at an apparatus hanging in front of his face. The astronaut's front seat is separated by struts from the rear portion of the vehicle, on which symmetrically arranged boxes, circles, points, and spirals can be seen.[63]

By the way, here is how a properly trained (Ph.D., Yale) student of such matters interprets the same seventh-century Native American artwork (fig. 30):

> Within the Temple of the Inscriptions [at Palenque] a large corbeled chamber held the uterus-shaped sarcophagus of the great king Pacal, whose remains lay covered with jade and cinnabar. The sarcophagus lid shows the king at the moment of death, falling in rapture into the maws of the underworld. The sides of the sarcophagus display Pacal's ancestors, emerging from the ground, while nine stucco attendants flank the walls. The construction was designed for eternity. . . . Three panels of lengthy inscriptions in the upper chamber relate to Pacal's life [and make no mention of ETs], and the exterior stuccos show his son as an infant deity, perhaps to demonstrate divinity, even during the king's lifetime. Immortalized within funerary pyramids, Maya kings were probably worshipped after death, great ancestors transformed into deities.[64]

Von Däniken finds all sorts of other ancient artworks supposedly picturing the awed earthlings' extraterrestrial visitors. He missed, however, a significant European example: the characteristically bug-eyed and emaciated bronze figurine (likely fourth century B.C.E.) depicting an ET, which had been found some time ago in southern Spain (fig. 31).[65] Another well known example, which von Däniken also missed, is a painting by Edvard Munch, called *The Scream* (1893) (fig. 32). The alert and well-informed UFOlogist must now recognize that this particularly striking piece of early modernist portraiture clearly depicts, so documents, the fact of a previously unrecognized extraterrestrial close encounter in Christianastad (now called Oslo) at the end of the nineteenth century. Equally obviously, all such close encounters, particularly the kind with an "abduction," certainly merit *The Scream*—just ask Drs. John E. Mack and David M. Jacobs, also Mr. Budd Hopkins and Mr. Whitley Strieber. Alas, this brilliant conclusion regarding Munch's modernist *cri de coeur* might be challenged by an equally well informed art historian.[66]

No matter; as argued imaginatively by von Däniken, without said ET intervention, nothing civilized would have ever transpired on Spaceship Earth. Von Däniken implies that early humans, "the natives," were just too dumb to do it on their own. That idea of native hopelessness is, by the way, simply a reprise of routinely self-congratulating European imperialist-colonialist rhetoric of the late nineteenth century. Besides being insufferably patronizing, the whole notion is risibly ignorant, of history as well as of innate human imaginative talents.[67] Nonetheless, a neocolonialist assumption tenaciously adheres to all those post-Däniken, postmodernist alien-abduction adventures. Morris Goran, among some others underwhelmed by von Däniken's bits of extraterrestrial "evidence," points out that

> psychiatric reports on the man when he was in trouble earlier in life describe him as a compulsive liar. More serious charges are that the ancient-astronaut writers misquote, misinterpret, and make no distinction when citing as authoritative the work of certified nuts or established scholars. . . . The situation in the category of unidentified-flying-object books [by other *auteurs*] is similar, with a very large assortment offering the extraterrestrial hypothesis, another space-time continuum or mystery, and very few books explaining away the so-called "unidentified."[68]

Two and a half centuries after Swedenborg published his otherworldly revelations, his pioneering work is carried on by Harvard University psychiatrist Dr. John E. Mack (who, alas, fails to list the Swedish visionary author in his bibliography). Here is Mack's quintessential New Age explanation for an uplifting spiritualist (versus merely mercantile) *raison d'être* lurking behind all those postmodernist stories of alien abduction:

> Many abduction experiences are unequivocally spiritual, which usually involves some sort of powerful encounter with, or immersion in, divine light [see figs. 27, 34]. This phenomenon is pervasive in Carlos's case

[chapter 14 in Mack's book] and is present in many I have studied. The alien beings, although resented for their intrusive activities, may also be seen as intermediaries, closer than we are to God or the source of being. Sometimes, as in Carlos's case, they may even be seen as angels or analogous to God. A number of abductees with whom I have worked experience at certain points an opening up to the source of being in the cosmos, which they often call Home, and from which they feel they have been brutally cut off in the course of becoming embodied as a human being. They may weep ecstatically when, during our sessions, they experience an opening or return to Home. They may, as in Sara's case [related in Mack's chapter 9], rather resent having to remain on Earth in embodied form, even as they realize that on Earth they have some sort of mission to assist in bringing about a change in human consciousness.

Related apparently to this opening to the divine source is the experience that some abductees have of great cycles of birth, life, and death, repeating over long stretches of time. This may become particularly apparent when "past life" experiences are relived [as in the "Bridey Murphy" case; see chapter 11, this volume] and the abductee is able to enter the experiences of death and rebirth. A related phenomenon might be called the reification of an archetype or metaphor. Tubes, passageways, threads, et cetera, may be literally seen, or passed through or along physically, but at the same time they symbolically represent important transitions from one state of being to another.[69]

As Mack tells it, besides being unspeakably profound, this is basically a *good* experience, like the kind that used to bring medieval mystics closer to (their) god. Nonetheless, the medieval experience is inferior (of course) to the postmodernist version for being, according to the politically correct appellation, "technologically challenged." In short, abduction by extraterrestrial aliens leads to (surprise!) enhanced ecological sensitivity and social harmony. What else do you expect from the ever-so-sensitive New Age? According to Dr. Mack:

Many abductees, including the cases discussed in this book, appear to undergo profound personal growth and transformation. Each appears to come out of his or her experiences concerned about the fate of the earth and the continuation of human and other life-forms. Virtually all the abductees with whom I have worked closely have demonstrated a commitment to changing their relationship to the earth, of living more gently on it or in greater harmony with the other creatures that live here. Each seems to be devoted to transforming his or her relationships with other people, to expressing love more openly, and transcending aggressive impulses. Some abductees, like Eva, Peter [chapters 11 and 13 in Mack's book], Carlos, and Arthur [chapter 15 in Mack's book], wish to use their evolving perspective to influence others and have become teachers of a new way of living. In addition, abductees seem, especially once they confront and integrate their experiences, to be especially intuitive; they sometimes demonstrate strong psychic abilities, including clairvoyance or the ability to perceive at a distance. Further research is needed to document these [paranormal] capabilities. . . .

Finally, many if not most of the abductees with whom I have worked intensively come to feel that their enhanced spiritual awareness must be translated into some sort of [quasi-evangelist] teaching or higher purpose. Some may be saddened, and even become hopeless about the ecology of the planet and the fate of the earth's life-forms. Yet they may feel that their experiences are, ultimately, about preserving life and that they must do something toward this end.[70]

Sic dixit Mack. No wonder people are eager to be abducted! Imagine that—you can actually "get a life," at least the kind with a noble sense of *mission*. I can hardly wait for my turn (and the queue forms at the rear, dear).

LABELING AND MISLABELING: AN EYEWITNESS REPORT OF A CLOSE ENCOUNTER WITH "KÓLFR"

In science, as in real (unscientific) life, it would again appear that just what one chooses to label a given action proves essential to its future significance. The labeling act is obviously crucial to those paranormal phenomena called "UFOs" (unidentified flying objects) which, to my mind at least, would be much better relabeled "MFOs" (misidentified fugitive observations). By the way, UFOs are also known to certified "aliens" (*los trabajadores emigrantes indocumentados*), but they call them, in Spanish, "OVNI" (*Objetos volantes no identificados*). Obviously, besides being culture-specific, the terminological characteristics of the act of reportage are all important: *nomen est omen*. Indeed, once seized upon by the mass media, their reportorial reenactments, "news items," manufacture "importance" by themselves, make everything seem "real." In short, what is really experienced is just another postmodernist *pseudoevent* (as defined in chapter 3).

A simpler way of explaining away the inexplicable—in this case meaning the apocryphal "UFO Experience" (so dubbed in 1972)—is to remind the reader of the standard, pre-1947, extraterrestrial nomenclature. Long before the infamous "Roswell incident," in the British Isles ETs were called *fairies*, *pixies*, *leprechauns*, and *brownies*. In Germany, there were *Zwerge* (dwarfs); in Scandinavia, *elves*; the French had their *lutins*; Islam calls them *djinns*; in India there were *devas*, but *kappas* in Japan, or *menehune* in Hawaii.[71] And so it goes, and I suspect that all of these fabulous otherworldlings were also illustrated in their time and place, so likewise they, too, have played their own small part in the history of art.

Let us further pursue this *aperçu* regarding the need—urgent!—for relabeling what we have called MFOs, in this case, specifically those ETs brought forth in such alarming abundance by UFOs from the great beyond. I will now transcribe a standard apocryphal account; this one may already be familiar to some of my readers, perhaps including the odd UFOlogist. If not, then you will miss its intended narrative significance. Deprived of the significant facts regarding its real physical context, you, too, will misidentify a (typically confused) "fugitive observation." In order to clarify its intended meaning, I have (helpfully) interpolated some descriptive details missing in the original account (but the original lack of punctuation is faithfully retained). So emended, it goes like this:

> Through the fence, between the curling flower spaces, I could see them [the ETs] hitting [they were looking for escaped human captives hiding in the bushes]. They were coming toward where the [American] flag was and I went along the fence [trying to escape them]. Luster [the eyewitness's fellow escapee] was hunting [for his side-arm] in the grass by the flower tree. They took the flag out, and they were hitting. Then they put the flag back and they went to the table [where they examine their stripped human victims and extract their eggs and sperm], and he [the first ET] hit and the other [ET] hit. Then they went on, and I went along the fence. Luster came away from the flower tree [where he had been hiding] and we went along the fence and they [the ETs] stopped and we stopped and I looked through the fence while Luster was hunting in the grass.
>
> "Here, caddie" [a derisive term, used for human captives and slaves]. He [the first ET] hit. They [the ETs] went away across the pasture. I held to the fence and watched them going away [with obvious relief]. "Listen at you, now," Luster said. "Ain't you something, thirty-three years old, going on that way. After I done went all the way to town to buy you that cake [intended as a peace-offering to the ETs, but rejected by them as unworthy]. Hush up that moaning [the eyewitness, Benjy, was—naturally!—terrified]. Ain't you going to help me find that quarter [a reference to a monetary unit of the time] so I can go to the show tonight" [a reference to a "showing" of the famous Roswell autopsy film]. They [the ETs] were [still] hitting little [unnamed objects or beings], across the pasture. I went along the fence to where the flag was. It flapped on the bright grass and the trees. . . . It was red [due to the blood of a human victim recently slain by the ETs], flapping on the pasture. Then there was a bird [a vulture] slanting and tilting on it.

Luster threw [up]. The flag flapped on the bright grass and the trees. I held to the fence. [And so on and so forth, for many more pages of gripping first-person testimony.][72]

What does this ambiguous close encounter actually signify? According to certified experts trained to deal with avant-garde American literature, what was being described by the stunned eyewitness narrator, a thirty-three-year-old certified "idiot" in this case, was only "a game." As my more literate readers should have already figured out, my vigorously described eyewitness report appears at the very beginning of William Faulkner's mostly inscrutable, but unquestionably artistic, novel *The Sound and The Fury* (1929). In this case, the imaginative author, a future Nobel laureate, is describing a procedure often practiced in America: "golf."

Intrigued by various functional parallels with the momentous UFO experience, none of which have previously been so acknowledged by certified UFOlogists, I have researched the matter. I am, for instance, informed on good authority that many ordinary people ("just folks") have also experienced *golf*. The etymology of the word is likewise inscrutable; it may come from the Dutch *kolf*, or German, *kolbe* (butt, cob, piston, light bulb), or even Old Norse, *kólfr*. According to the massive *Oxford English Dictionary*, it now represents "an [illegible textual lacuna; perhaps corresponding to *Begegnung in der Nähe* in German], of considerable antiquity in Scotland, in which a small, hard ball is struck with various clubs into a series of small cylindrical holes made at intervals, usually of a hundred yards [not meters] or more, upon the surface of a moor, field, etc. The aim [*d. h. Ziel oder Zweck*] is to drive the ball into any one hole, or into all the holes successively, with the fewest possible strokes; commonly two persons, or two couples (a 'foursome') participate."

The golfish specifications seem perfectly clear, rather like some pretty strict rules governing the qualifications needed to earn the now prestigious title "abductee-experiencer." As we recall:

In order to qualify as an "abductee," a person must be (a) taken against his or her will; (b) from terrestrial surroundings; (c) by non-human Beings. The Beings must take a person: to (d) an enclosed place; (e) non-terrestrial in appearance; that is (f) assumed or known to be a spacecraft by the [abductee] witness. In this place, the person must either be: (g) subjected to a physical examination; (h) engaged in communication, verbal or telepathic, or (i) both.[73]

A friend of mine has recently shown me color photographs—real physical evidence!—depicting the golfish experience. This pictorial documentation reveals that commonly "golfers"—or "couples" and "four-somes"—repeatedly make ritual passes with wandlike instruments, so propelling minuscule and dimpled, typically albino-tinted but often "Gray," spheres with great speed across artfully landscaped terrain features. Often struck with great force, sometimes the disklike, white objects fly swiftly into the sky; so launched, they have often been reported as "silvery" or "metallic" in appearance and to move in an erratic fashion, rather like "saucers skipping over water." All of this hitting and stroking about is done with a paradoxically energetic languor by the golf-experiencers (GEs), most of whom *voluntarily* undergo such experiences. Also commonly reported are perceptions by GEs of "lost time"; according to these unquestionably reliable eyewitnesses—often including many highly respected "professional" people, especially doctors (M.D.s, dentists, and so on)—sometimes entire afternoons, whole days even, are "lost" or otherwise reported "missing."

According to the surviving pictorial evidence, I also note that the GEs are commonly garbed in distinctive raiment, also including strange headgear, which, typically, is not to be seen away from the sacred precinct called "golf course." Some GEs propel themselves across the land in mini UFOs; these vehicles are called "golf carts" by recognized specialists in paranormal phenomena. More often than not, the GEs are accompanied by their hypnotized human slaves, called "caddies." As in the case of complementary magical ceremonies described (elsewhere) by (other) eyewitness, there are often large crowds in attendance at the golfish rituals, and these hushed testators are commonly observed posed in mostly mute and rapt, evidently even reverential, attitudes. They seem, perhaps, to be witnessing a spiritual "close encounter." Personally, I would be much more inclined to attend—or (better) watch on TV—many more cultist sessions on the "golf course"—were it instead to call itself a "UFO landing-zone." *Chacun a son goût.*

Above all, if I were the executive producer of such televised eso-terica, I would certainly prefer that, henceforth, all golfish rituals be prominently labeled as a "documentary," the kind representing nonfiction. Were they to be instead simply presented as "science fiction," then the sensation-seeking masses would probably lunge for their remote controls and switch to another channel exhibiting the ever-expanding post-modernist infotainment menu of psychic fascism.

NOTES

1. Emanuel Swedenborg, "The Earths in the Universe, and Their Inhabitants," in *Miscellaneous Theological Works* (New York: American Swedenborg Publishing Society, 1905), pp. 327–416.

2. Ibid., p. 328. For Swedenborg's influence on such debates, see Michael Crowe, *The Extraterrestrial Life Debate, 1750–1900* (Mineola, N.Y.: Dover, 1999), pp. 97 ff.; Karl S. Guthke, *The Last Frontier: Imagining Other Worlds, from the Copernican Revolution to Modern Science Fiction* (Ithaca, N.Y.: Cornell University Press, 1990), pp. 272–76.

3. Swedenborg, "The Earths in the Universe," p. 382.

4. Ibid., pp. 333, 345.

5. Ibid., p. 380.

6. Ibid., pp. 350, 352–53, 356.

7. Ibid., pp. 377, 380.

8. Ibid., pp. 368, 371–73.

9. See M. Gardner, "Psychic Astronomy," in his *The New Age: Notes of a Fringe Watcher* (Amherst, N.Y.: Prometheus Books, 1988), pp. 252–63. Oddly, Davis's publication is not cited by Crowe in his otherwise exhaustive survey of *The Extraterrestrial Life Debate, 1750–1900*.

10. Andrew Jackson Davis, as in Gardner, "Psychic Astronomy," pp. 254–55.

11. Théodore Flournoy, *From India to the Planet Mars: A Case of Multiple Personality and Imaginary Languages* (Princeton: Princeton University Press, 1994), esp. pp. 87–172, "The Martian Cycle."

12. Ibid., p. 152.

13. For reproductions, see Walter Deonna, *De la Planète Mars en Terre Sainte: Art et Subconscient. Un Médium peintre: Hélène Smith* (Paris: De Boccard, 1932).

14. For the specific pulp-fiction iconographic contribution, beginning in 1927, see Martin Garner, "Who Was Ray Palmer?" in *The New Age*, pp. 209–22, concerning the influential editor of (among others) *Fate* and *Amazing Stories*. For an anthology of such ET tales, with moreover a useful historical prologue, see Demétre Ioakimidis, ed., *Histoires d'extraterrestres* (Paris: Livre de Poche, 1974); the original publication dates of these sixteen tales are between 1938 and 1965. See also (with illustrations) Wayne D. Barlowe, *Barlowe's Guide to Extraterrestrials: Great Aliens from Science Fiction Literature* (New York: Workman, 1987). For the larger historical context, the "Plurality of Worlds" arguments, going back (at least) to the Renaissance, see again Guthke, *The Last Frontier*; for the modern genre adaptations, see Ulrich Suerbaum, *Science Fiction: Theorie und Geschichte, Themen und Typen, Form und Weltbild* (Stuttgart: Reclam, 1981).

15. Guthke, *The Last Frontier*, p. 390.

16. See Robert Lindner, *The Fifty-Minute Hour: A Collection of True Psychoanalytic Tales* (New York: Bantam, 1966), pp. 179–80.

17. Ibid..

18. Kirk Allen's novel contribution is, however, briefly mentioned (in 1998) by a non-UFOlogist; see T. Matheson, *Alien Abductions: Creating a Modern Phenomenon* (Amherst, N.Y.: Prometheus Books, 1998), p. 224, n. 6.

19. For various historical myths about *miracula* preceeding the postmodernist phenomena, again see Patrick Harpur, *Daimonic Reality: A Field Guide to the Otherworld* (London: Arkana/Penguin, 1995); Keith Thompson, *Angels and Aliens: UFOs and the Mythic Imagination* (New York: Ballantine, 1993); Jacques Vallée, *Anatomy of a Phenomenon: UFOs in Space—A Scientific Appraisal* (New York: Ballantine, 1972).

20. Anonymous chronicler, as cited in C. Erickson, *The Medieval Vision: Essays in History and Perception* (Oxford: Oxford University Press, 1976), p. 31.

21. C. D. B. Bryan, *Close Encounters of the Fourth Kind: Alien Abduction, UFOs, and the Conference at M.I.T.* (New York: Knopf, 1995), p. 425.

22. R. L. Dione, *God Drives a Flying Saucer* (New York: Bantam, 1978), p. 79.

23. Brinsley Le Poer Trench, as in Jay David, *Flying Saucer Reader* (New York: Signet, 1967), pp. 17–20.

24. Ibid., p. 18.

25. So stated in G. C. Andrews, *Extra-Terrestrials among Us* (St. Paul, Minn.: Fate/Llewelyn, 1993), pp. 60–61.

26. See James Stubblebine, ed., *Giotto: The Arena Chapel Frescoes* (New York: Norton, 1969), pp. 81–83.

27. Pseudo-Jerome, "Liber de Nativitate Mariae," in A. de Santos Otero, ed., *Los Evangelios Apócrifos* (Madrid: Biblioteca de Autores Cristianos, 1963), pp. 244ff., 253 (bilingual).

28. Pseudo-Matthew, "Evangelium," in ibid., pp. 179ff., 212 (bilingual).

29. Pseudo-James, "Evangelion," in ibid., pp. 151–52, 168, 170 (bilingual).

30. Justin's "Apology," in A. Roberts and J. Donaldson, eds., *The Ante-Nicene Fathers: Translations of the Writings of the Fathers down to A.D. 325* (Grand Rapids, Mich.: Tanner, 1963), I, pp. 173–74; emphasis mine.

31. For the argument that, as we now know it, "the book of Isaiah is a compendium of many types of prophecy from diverse periods," see J. L. MacKenzie, S.J., *Dictionary of the Bible* (New York: Dutton, 1965), pp. 397–403 ("Isaiah").

32. Justin, "Dialogue with Trypho," in Roberts and Donaldson *Ante-Nicene Fathers*, I, p. 229.

33. Ibid., p. 252.

34. For more on this astral anomaly, see J. F. Moffitt, "Balaam or Isaiah in the Catacomb of Priscilla," *Konsthistorisk Tidskrift* 66, no. 3 (1997): 77–87.

35. Harpur, *Daimonic Reality*, p. 142.

36. J. Smith, *The Book of Mormon* (Salt Lake City: Church of Jesus Christ of Latter-day Saints, 1950), "Origin of the Book of Mormon" (unpaginated).

37. Joseph Smith, as in Thompson, *Angels and Aliens*, p. 70.

38. See F. M. Brodie, *No Man Knows My History: The Life of Joseph Smith, the Mormon Prophet* (New York: Knopf, 1957), pp. 45–47; for more on Smith and

the Mormons, see also M. Ruthven, *The Divine Supermarket* (London: Chatto & Windus, 1989), pp. 55–91.

39. See Peter Brown, *Madame Blavatsky's Baboon: A History of the Mystics, Mediums, and Misfits Who Brought Spiritualism to America* (New York: Schocken, 1995), esp. pp. 92 ff.

40. Erich von Däniken, *Gods from Outer Space: Return to the Stars, or Evidence for the Impossible* (New York: Bantam, 1972), pp. 137–42.

41. For angels and demons in Christian art, see Manuel Guerra, *Simbología Románica* (Madrid: Fundación Universitaria Española, 1986), pp. 305–16; for their diverse iconography, see the lavishly illustrated picture album by Nancy Grubb, *Angels in Art* (New York: Abbeville, 1995).

42. On this unsung Victorian-era contribution to postmodernist UFOlogy, see David Stupple, "Mahatmas and Space Brothers: The Ideology of an Alleged Contract with Extraterrestrials," *Journal of American Culture* 7 (1984): 131–39.

43. For this creature, see J. F. Moffitt, "The Meaning of 'Christ after the Flagellation' in Siglo de Oro Sevillian Painting," *Wallraf-Richartz Jahrbuch* 53 (1992): 139–54.

44. Alice K. Turner, *The History of Hell* (New York: Harvest, 1995), p. 91.

45. "Apocalypse of Paul," in Eileen Gardiner, ed., *Visions of Heaven and Hell before Dante* (New York: Italica, 1989), pp. 16–19.

46. Ibid.

47. Plutarch and Plato, as in Thompson, *Angels and Aliens*, pp. 150–51.

48. Turner, *History of Hell*, pp. 61, 229.

49. John Weldon and Zola Levitt, *UFOs: What on Earth Is Happening?* (Irvine, Calif.: Harvest House, 1975), pp. 106, 121, 135.

50. See H. P. L'Orange, *Apotheosis in Ancient Portraiture* (New Rochelle, N.Y.: Caratzas, 1982), pp. 16, 23, 44, 96, 110.

51. Paul Kurtz, "UFO Mythology: The Escape to Oblivion," *Skeptical Inquirer* (July/August 1997): 12–14; see also Carl Jung, *Flying Saucers: A Modern Myth of Things Seen in the Sky* (1959; Princeton: Princeton University Press, 1973).

52. Ronald E. Fowler, *The Andreasson Affair* (New York: Bantam, 1980), p. 13.

53. J. Mack, *Abduction: Human Encounters with Aliens* (New York: Scribner's, 1994), p. 288.

54. Rev. Billy Graham, in Fowler, *Andreasson Affair*, p. 201.

55. Dione, *God Drives a Flying Saucer*, pp. vii–viii.

56. See Barry H. Downing, *The Bible and Flying Saucers* (Philadelphia: Lippincott, 1968).

57. For a useful anthology of traditional (pre–New Age) angelic *ekphraseis* and portraiture, see Lothar Schreyer, ed., *Bildnis der Engel: Ein Schaubuch und Lesebuch* (Freiburg im B.: Herder, 1940).

58. For the historical evidence backing up this argument, see C. McDannell and B. Lang, *Heaven: A History* (New York: Vintage, 1990), pp. 181 ff.

59. Emanuel Swedenborg, *Heaven and Hell*, trans. G. F. Dole (New York: Swedenborg Foundation, 1984), pp. 71–72, 137, 192.

60. For more of the same (ho-hum), see Jacques Bergier, *Les Extra-Ter-restres dans l'Histoire* (Paris: J'ai Lu, 1970); *Extraterrestrial Visitations from Prehistoric Time to the Present* (New York: Signet, 1974).

61. Erich von Däniken, *Chariots of the Gods? Unsolved Mysteries of the Past* (New York: Bantam, 1971), p. 25 (emphasis mine).

62. Ibid., pp. 51–52; cf. 43, 129.

63. Ibid., pp. 100–101 (by the way, the site of the picture in von Däniken's paperback is mislabeled: "Copán").

64. Mary E. Miller, *The Art of Mesoamerica, from Olmec to Aztec* (London: Thames & Hudson, 1986), pp. 128–29.

65. For the real (terrestrial) cultural context of this artifact, see J. F. Moffitt, *El Caso de la Dama de Elche: Historia de una falsificación* (Barcelona: Destino, 1997), pp. 68–69 (one could also call the bug-eyed Sumerian votive-idols "ETs," but you get the point).

66. For that opposing view, and the art-historical evidence to back it up, see Reinhold Heller, *Edvard Munch: The Scream* (New York: Viking, 1972).

67. For a detailed deconstruction of this lucrative rubbish, see Ronald Story, *The Space Gods Revealed: A Close Look at the Theories of Erich von Däniken* (London: New American Library, 1978); Ronald Story, *Guardians of the Universe?* (New York: St. Martin's, 1980).

68. Morris Goran, *Fact, Fraud, and Fantasy: The Occult and Pseudo-sciences* (Totowa, N.J.: Littlefield, Adams, 1979), p. 68.

69. Mack, *Abduction*, pp. 394–95.

70. Ibid., pp. 395–96, 406.

71. So listed in Thomas E. Bullard, *UFO Abductions: The Measure of a Mystery* vol. 1 *Comparative Study of Abduction Reports* (Bloomington, Ind.: Fund for UFO Research, 1987), pp. 92, 271–74; see also W. J. Fielding, *Strange Superstitions and Magical Practices* (New York: Doubleday, 1945), chap. 9, "Fairies, Brownies, and Incubi."

72. William Faulkner, *The Sound and the Fury* (New York: Vintage, 1956), pp. 23–24 (the interpolations are all mine).

73. Rodeghier, as in Bryan, *Close Encounters of the Fourth Kind*, p. 13.

Chapter 11

Some Mundane Contexts for Outlandish Beliefs

GROUNDING THE EXTRATERRESTRIALS IN AMERICAN LEGEND AND ARCHETYPAL MYTH

The fact of all this archetypal reiteration, the UFOlogists' prized "consistency" factor, calls for a much broader viewpoint. Another useful academic approach to the problem would be that posited by an anthropologist, or better yet, a specialist in folklore. In this case, the appropriate framing theme is that belonging to the now ubiquitous American urban legends. Although he never specifically addressed the currently momentous problem of extraterrestrials and their earthling abductees, Jan Harold Brunvand is presently the master analyst of such apocryphal materials. Nonetheless, his descriptive conclusions perfectly fit the ET sagas that have been quoted above. Brunvand calls such "modern American folk narratives"

> stories that most people have heard as true accounts of real-life experiences. . . . They are an integral part of white Anglo-American culture and are told and believed by some of the most sophisticated "folk" in modern society—young people, urbanites, and the well educated. . . . The mass media themselves participate in the dissemination and apparent validation of urban legends. . . . Urban legends are told seriously, circulate largely by word of mouth, are generally anonymous, and

PICTURING EXTRATERRESTRIALS

vary constantly in particular details from one telling to another, while always preserving a central core of traditional elements or "motifs." . . .

Urban legends belong to the subclass of folk narratives, legends, that—unlike fairy tales—are believed, or at least are believable, and that—unlike myths—are set in the recent past and involve normal human beings rather than ancient gods or demigods. . . . The important difference is that today's legends are also disseminated by the mass media. . . . Legends can survive in our [modern] culture as a living narrative folklore if they contain three essential elements: a strong basic story-appeal, a foundation in actual belief, and a meaningful message or "moral." . . . What little we do know about *who* tells the stories, *when*, *to whom*, and *why* invariably contributes towards understanding how legends function and what they mean. . . .

The succession of popular themes in American urban legends [including the ETs] serves as a rough index of people's concerns and fantasies as they have changed through time. . . . The mass media, as we have seen, are not unconducive to the survival of urban legends. On the contrary, print or broadcast references to current legends [including the ETs]—whether seeking to validate or debunk them—almost always serve to spread the stories farther. . . . If possible, references to mass media appearances of urban legends [including the ETs] should be traced to a source, but do not be overly disappointed if this proves to be impossible.[1]

Again, such as we have analyzed in detail the different eyewitness accounts supplied by numerous "abductees" (in chapters 2 and 5), most of the characteristics cited by Brunvand as defining the classic American urban legends also strictly pertain to, actually usefully define, a now ubiquitous alien-abduction urban legend. In this case, especially telling is the essential part played in their dissemination by the mass media. There are, however, some differences. As Brunvand reminds me, "There's a connection, but very few urban legends deal with the supernatural, 'The Vanishing Hitchhiker' narrative being the main exception. Also, ULs [urban legends] are seldom told first-person, which is the manner of alien-abduction stories. It seems to me the closer connection to folklore is to personal experience stories and to supernatural lore."[2] And, in the literal sense, anything dubbed "extraterrestrial" is likewise, literally, "supernatural." In any event, as so eagerly propagated by the mass media, the ubiquitous ETs only lend further support to Brunvand's axiom, "The truth never stands in the way of a good story." That holds true, especially if your "good story" will secure from your commercial publisher a whopping one-million-dollar advance.

Another approach that might be employed by the student of modern

American folklore would be to ground the chronologically postmodernist extraterrestrials in an omnipresent subliterary category called the "paranormal memorate."[3] Most widely studied among all such paranormal memorates are those traditional narrations, known to all of us, called ghost stories. Whatever the apocryphal genre employed, the characteristic format of all such tales purports to relay to interested listeners the grist of a first-person paranormal testimonial. The eyewitness paranormal testimonial, states Professor Larry Danielson, necessarily "involves a complex interaction between personal experience, traditional lore about the supernatural, and canons of narrative aesthetics." Essential in all instances to our proper interpretation of the meaning inherent to the narrational act of any supernatural close encounter is a recognition of the teller's unquestionable "exposure to and participation in various art forms that concern the supernatural: fictive accounts in the mass media as well as experience stories shared by others in print and oral tradition," not to mention the movies and television (see figs. 9–15, 17–19). That contextual definition may be taken to apply to *all* those alien-abduction stories which we have already extensively quoted (see chapters 1, 2, 5).

Since his essay was written in 1982, naturally Danielson had yet to become as familiar with these apocryphal ET narrations as we are presently; hence, they were not specifically cited by him. Nonetheless, as inevitably told in the first person, all the currently acclaimed alien-abduction tales do exactly conform to his prescriptions. As Danielson informs us, "the supernatural 'true experience' story is an art form shaped by tradition, convention and the narrator's performance skills, regardless of its evidential strengths or weaknesses." Just like our endlessly proliferating postmodernist "true experience" tales of nocturnal abductions and gynecological abuse at the hands of bug-eyed extraterrestrials, the accepted texts all "deal with the same subject matter: the spontaneous paranormal visitation to [human] individuals, with whom the [supernatural] apparition shares some sort of [emotional] relationship." Typically, just as in the ET legend, "the visitation occurs at night, in the percipient's home." Moreover, just as so often occurs in current ET close encounters, "the time elapsed between the [purported] occurrence and its description to the collector is only generally indicated in the phrase 'years ago,' probably when the informant was a child."[4]

According to fixed artistic conventions characterizing all the paranormal memorates, meaning the old-fashioned ghost story, typically "no more than two characters interact at a time, external action rather than internal subjective condition is emphasized, and narrative development is chronological and direct." As we have also seen with our postmodernist ET stories, "the emphasis on emotional state, very important in this text, is characteristic of popular print stories" recounting all manner of other paranormal memorates. Particularly characteristic of the ET stories, but so making them just like all the rest of the paranormal memorates, is what Danielson called "an almost invariable law" of the narrative genre, namely, the recognition that "the more remarkable the alleged coincidence, the worse the supporting evidence and, conversely, the better the evidence the weaker is the coincidence." Such "personal experience stories often involve striking coincidences that, as a rule, cannot be verified." Conventions of paranormal memorates further dictate that "irrelevancies are leveled, certain features sharpened, and the whole is assimilated to cultural and individual standards of judgment."[5]

In a wider arena, once the ET paranormal tale has been told to its designated audience culture, "print [and other media] sources usually encourage uncritical interest in paranormal phenomena of all kinds and serve a readership committed to or tolerant of apparitional accounts." Nonetheless, Danielson recognizes (as I have) that inevitably "researchers in psychic phenomena have failed to explore the manner in which narrative performance influences audience response." He cites a standard component to such tales, a literary motif or *topos*: "I was also a skeptic, until. . . ." With this proclamation, Danielson states, "the narrator thereby escapes the charge of gullibility and indicates the historicity of the ghostly occurrence."[6] There is no need to quote parallel statements by John E. Mack, David M. Jacobs, Budd Hopkins, John Fuller, Whitley Strieber, and all the rest, all of which, using slightly different language, essentially claim that, "I was also a skeptic, until. . . ." That disingenuous disclaimer represents a literary convention, a standard rhetorical figure, a cliché which must be included within the authorial preface leading us into a fully engaged emotional participation with all those delicious tales recounting dire postmodernist experiences of alien abductions. Its rhetorical pedigree is indeed ancient; E. R. Curtius labeled it the *topos* (cliché) of "affected modesty" and "conversion," a "formula of self-disparagement" with an implied "rejection of trite epic material," which must be situated in the *exordium* (preface).[7]

An excellent example of the way in which abduction narratives incorporate characteristically American themes is the "captivity tale," another highly conventionalized subliterary genre. As we have often pointed out, UFO abductions seem to be primarily an American phenomenon; although several important cases have been reported outside the United States (particularly by Jenny Randles), arguably the "major" (meaning most widely publicized) abductions are mainly confined to this country. Certainly, no other nation displays such an incredible (and quantifiable) interest in abduction stories. One likely reason for this, never before cited in the in-house UFO literature, could be the similarities of abduction stories to one of America's favorite traditional literary themes, the captivity tale. Heavily influenced by theological motifs of early Protestant New England, emphasizing imprisonment and bondage, captivity narratives base themselves upon the capture of Americans by culturally distinct, physically different, *alien others:* Native Americans.[8]

As told in the plentiful captivity tales, the victims of the Indians, usually women, are consistently menaced by their "savage" alien captors. Typically, such stories often concentrate on the gruesome details of their torture or rape; such apocrypha also found their artistic expression and were even exhibited in European salons.[9] Since we are now all too familiar with the current tales of UFO abductions, especially as related in the mass media, one can easily recognize the thematic connection. Here the Other (*Alienus*) is truly alien, nonhuman and seemingly extraterrestrial, for his actions are threatening but inexplicable. Dwelling in the metaphorical "heart of darkness," the American savage is a throwback to the medieval "Wildman."[10]

Similarly, the postmodernist abductees, 80 percent of whom are women, are tortured and sexually violated by bizarre medical experiments, the prurient details of which, as discussed on afternoon talk shows, are eagerly consumed by millions of video-voyeurs. In the standard American captivity narratives, victims are often rescued by a morally perfect hero who destroys the victim's tormentors; in New Age abduction tales the hero is the ever *simpático* researcher-hypnotist (Hopkins, Jacobs, Mack, and so on), who alone knows the chilling agenda behind the victim's capture. In traditional captivity narratives, American moral virtue is favorably distinguished from the "savage" excesses, sexual and otherwise, characterizing the captors. The "aliens" of postmodernist abduction narratives, coldly clinical and amorally utilitarian, treat their victims more like mere objects of scientific study, perhaps reflecting a concern, often explicitly expressed in science fiction, that our modern society is becoming increasingly detached from human values.

On an ever higher intellectual plane, we can additionally ground all these ETs and UFOs in the milieu of archetypal myth, from the Greek term (*mythos*) for "original pattern or stamp." This is certainly not an original interpretation; it was initially put forth by Carl Gustav Jung, a patriarch of modern psychological research, in a slim monograph aptly called *Ein moderner Mythus: Von Dingen, die am Himmel gesehen werden* (1958; Flying

saucers: A modern myth of things seen in the sky, 1959). And note the initial date of this publication, 1958, about a decade before the iconographic
invention of the postmodernist extraterrestrial by the likes of Barney and
Betty Hill (figs. 16–19). Although Jung was naturally unaware of the future
advent of extraterrestrial portraiture, he quoted a Latin *topos* which
explains its sheer necessity: *Quod natura relinquit imperfectum, ars per-
ficit* (What nature leaves imperfect, art perfects). Since the now standard
ETs apparently did not yet exist in 1958, at least not in the popular imagination, Jung's pioneering inquiry dealt exclusively with "flying saucers,"
their putative means of transport to a drop zone among the awed earthlings. As he then wryly observed, "most of these stories come from
America, the land of superlatives and of science fiction."[11]

Jung proposed to deal with "the UFO reports simply as rumors, i.e.,
as psychic products." But this one is quite different from the ordinary
kind of *rumor*, for this is the kind, states Jung, that is exclusively
"expressed in the form of visions"—hence another excellent reason for
the art historian to examine these typically visualized "psychic products" (see figs. 1, 4, 5, 8). Jung also took pains to differentiate between a
"vision" and a "hallucination"—"because the latter bears the stamp of a
pathological concept, whereas a vision is a phenomenon that is by no
means peculiar to pathological states." Sensitive to the global implications of his topic, he pointed to a "collective cause which produces identical or similar effects, i.e., the same visionary images and interpretations in the very people who are least prepared for such phenomena and
least inclined to believe in them. This fact gives the eyewitness accounts
an air of particular credibility." As we have often noted, UFOlogists are
constantly stressing that crucial issue of "credibility," and they constantly expend much ink and rhetorical energy in demonstrating that
their designated "abductee" testator is, as Jung put it much earlier,
"above suspicion because he was never distinguished for his lively imagination or credulousness."[12]

Jung, certainly a qualified psychologist, knows the real explanation:
"In just these cases, the unconscious has to resort to particularly drastic
measures in order to make its contents perceived. It does this most
vividly by *projection*, by extrapolating its contents into an object, which
then mirrors what had previously lain hidden in the unconscious." Moreover, this process "can be observed at work everywhere, in mental ill-
nesses, ideas of persecution and hallucinations, [even] in so-called
normal people." Jung takes this kind of "psychic projection" very seriously, recognizing that "there must be a psychic cause for it," especially
since it is "of such worldwide incidence," including "many thousands of

individual testimonies." Overall, although "visionary rumors may be caused or accomplished by all manner of outward circumstances, they are based essentially on an omnipresent emotional foundation, in this case a psychological situation common to all mankind."[13]

Jung even finds a useful symbolic purpose inherent to the very shape attributed by convention to the flying saucers. Therefore, he must turn his "attention to the psychic aspect of the phenomenon." What is reported to have been seen is, typically, "a body of *round* shape, disk-like or spherical, glowing or shining fierily in different colors, or, more seldom, a cigar-shaped or cylindrical figure of various sizes." In Jung's view, such celestial apparitions "are to be regarded as *symbols* representing, in visual form, some thought that was not thought consciously, but is merely potentially present in the unconscious, in invisible form, and attains visibility only through the process of becoming conscious. . . . The figures in a [UFO] rumor can be subjected to the same principles of dream interpretation." So interpreted, "we at once get an analogy with the symbol of totality well-known to all students of depth psychology, namely the *mandala* (Sanskrit for circle). . . . In the course of the centuries the mandala had developed into a definitely psychological totality symbol."[14] His conclusion:

> As one can see from all this, the observation and interpretation of UFOs has already led to the formation of a regular legend. Quite apart from the thousands of newspaper reports and articles, there is now a whole literature on the subject, some of it humbug, some of it serious. The UFOs themselves, however, do not appear to have been impressed. As the latest observations show, they continue their way undeterred. Be that as it may, one thing is certain: they have become *a living myth*. We have here a golden opportunity to see how a legend is formed and how, in difficult and dark times for humanity, a miraculous tale grows up of an attempted intervention by extraterrestrial "heavenly" powers—and this at the very time [1958] when human fantasy is seriously considering the possibility of space travel, and of visiting, or even invading, other planets [feats actually realized some decades later]. We, on our side, want to fly to the moon or to Mars; on their side, the inhabitants of other planets in our system, or even of the fixed stars [ETs *avant la lettre*], want to fly to us. We at least are conscious of our space-conquering aspirations, but that a corresponding extraterrestrial tendency exists is a purely mythological conjecture, i.e., a projection.[15]

All of our earlier bibliographic detective work can, and should, be concisely summed up. Paranormal investigator Joe Nickell's conclusion (mine too) about the widely reported Betty Hill dream motif featuring a bug-eyed space-waif is simply stated: *"Due to media influence, this is the [ET] type that eventually became the standard"* (see figs. 1, 4, 5, 15–22).[16] In short, this is just another strictly art-historical illustration of the domino theory. In effect, besides the all-pervasive B-movie and TV iconographic ambiance of the Cold War era, Major Donald Keyhoe and the Lorenzens, especially Coral, made the initial profitably published nudge. John Fuller followed suit (garnering even greater royalties), and Steven Spielberg further accelerated the iconographic impetus with his own movies, likewise to his great profit. Finally, Ray Fowler and Betty Andreasson, as it were, bring up the rear (in really bad taste), along with other considerably enriched pop-cult authors, most notably Whitley Strieber, Budd Hopkins, David Jacobs, and John Mack (among many, many others). There is, however, yet another contemporary biblio-graphic connection to be discerned here.

GROUNDING THE EXTRATERRESTRIALS IN REINCARNATION LEGENDS: THE BRIDEY MURPHY CASE

Broadly considered as a publishing phenomenon, the UFO abduction story, such as it has become ever more celebrated since the late 1960s, just represents a variation upon a complementary literary genre popular-ized since the Cold War era: the "past life" or "memory regression," also called "memory recovery," narration. That topic is itself a modernized recapitulation of a much broader, and truly ancient, literary staple, the reincarnation epic. I repeat: it presently appears that, in the overwhelming majority of reported cases, the real explanation for the postmodernist myth of alien abductions is, according to the title of an excellent mono-graph treating the syndrome, "The Myth of Repressed Memory."[17]

The first modern mega best-seller to exhume the medieval cliché of psychic reincarnation was *The Search for Bridey Murphy*, authored by Morey Bernstein. It quickly became an international publishing block-buster. Initially appearing in January 1956, it had ten reprintings in hardback; by May, it was already in paperback—"now only 50¢"—and, according to the new pulp publisher, *"The Search for Bridey Murphy* has [already] been published in the following editions: British, Danish, Spanish, Swedish, French, Italian, and Dutch."[18] Bibliophiles will be interested to note that this best-seller popped up only three years after George Adamski's best-selling close encounter with a UFO and its noble ET pilot (see chapter 8). Whereas the cover of Adamski's *Inside the*

Flying Saucers stated that its literary genre was "Astounding Science," Bernstein's paperback boldly labels itself "nonfiction," and the cover also shrilly wonders, "Does this book prove life after death?" Briefly put, this publishing bonanza relates the colorful tale of hypnotically recovered "memories" adroitly retrieved by Mr. Bernstein from a Pueblo, Colorado, housewife he named "Ruth Simmons"; as was later revealed, her real name was Virginia Tighe (born 1922). With the eager Bernstein's hypnotic help, Mrs. Tighe dramatically proclaimed herself to be "Bridey Murphy," born in Cork, Ireland, in 1798 and deceased by 1864.

The real historical significance of *The Search for Bridey Murphy* is largely of a formal nature. Bernstein's opus sets in place a literary format that is essential for the postmodernist alien-abduction narrations, but those only emerged as a significant publishing phenomenon some fifteen years later. In the strictly ET genre, we saw it (in chapter 5) pioneered in the Barney and Betty Hill saga—just as that otherworldly misadventure was so dramatically refashioned by John Fuller in his best-selling *Interrupted Journey*. As it were, Budd Hopkins made the format canonical. In either subliterary genre, the shared impetus is that of retrieved memory, the kind opportunely recovered by hypnotic intervention. Again, since it may be assumed that our learned readers have likely missed an opportunity to inspect in detail this historical artifact, *The Search for Bridey Murphy*, we may proceed to quote from the transcripts documenting her thrilling "nonfiction" adventures through time and space. As before, we hew to the now-conventional dialogue format, and again the hypnotic instigator is labeled "DJ" (Dialogue Jockey) and Bridey's mesmerized replies are signaled by "R" (paranormal-memorate Retriever). Alas, the piquant brogue accompanying Bridey's narrations cannot be adequately reproduced here.

DJ starts the narrative implacably rolling in the proper direction when he directs the somnolent R to regress in time and space; according to his rigid instruction, "All right, let's go back to the time you were in Ireland. Do you see yourself again in Ireland and Cork?" Quizzed as to her former identity, R informs us that it was none other than "Bridey Murphy." She also tells us that she married one "Brian MacCarthy." DJ then orders her to "tell me as an observer, so that it won't disturb you, tell me how you died." R replies that she "fell down on the stairs, and [it] seems I broke some bones in my hip too, and I was a terrible burden." As she also attests, she left this mortal coil at the age of "sixty-six," when she "just sort of withered away." DJ asks, "In what city were you living when you died?" and we are informed (somewhat to our surprise) that it was in "Belfast." She even remembers the day of her demise, "'Twas on a Sunday." However, her husband missed the dramatic event, since "Brian was to church, and it upset him terribly that he wasn't there. He left me, deserted me. But he didn't think I was going that fast. A lady came to stay with me so he could go to church—and I died." DJ then wonders if "you believe[d] that you would live after death?" and the answer is "Yes." Queried as to "what happened after you died?" the perhaps positive reply is that "I didn't do like Father John said [I would]. I didn't go to Purgatory!"[19] Evidently, one has to be an indoctrinated Catholic in order to appreciate the full meaning of that boon.

Since the purported goal of Bernstein's paperback opus was to answer an ever-burning question—"Does this book prove life after death?"—we need also provide Bridey's descriptions of an afterlife in "the astral world." Alas, as portrayed here, it seems rather a bore, just like purgatory is supposed to be! Evidently not an indoctrinated Catholic, DJ (Bernstein) wants to know whether "there are any such things as death, disease, or old age in that astral world?" R (Bridey), who certainly is an indoctrinated Catholic, informs him that, there, she experienced "no death, there was just a passing of—you passed from that existence; you passed to another existence. That's all; there was no death." Intrigued, DJ asks if there is "Any disease?" or "Any old age?" Whereas there is no disease, there "were old people there; I was old." (That makes perfect sense.) Thinking like a lawyer, DJ then asks whether in the Great Beyond, "In that astral world, did you ever have to obey any regulations or laws of any kind?" As we are pleased to discover, in the so-called astral world, there are, in fact, "No laws; no regulations." Moreover, in the next world, "Nobody grade[s] you; nobody [gives] you instructions." In short, and as summarized by the pushy DJ, "You [just] did what you willed to do?" and R eloquently replies, "Uh-huh."

Seeking further details regarding this wonderfully anarchic afterlife, DJ sagaciously inquires, "Now, in this astral world, the spirit world, could you tell the difference between males and females? Was there any sex, in other words?" The disappointing answer to the final clause is a dreary "No." When asked how "you could tell a man was a man, or that a woman was a woman?" the dreary response is a smug "You just knew." When asked if "there in that astral world, in that spirit world, were there times when you could remember all of your previous lifetimes?" the even drearier response is "I don't remember." This nonresponse provokes DJ, and so he informs her that "there *are* some things that you remember. Just pick out anything. Just pick out *anything* you remember and tell us about that." So ordered, she forcibly recalls, "Uh, I remember dancing, dancing. . . ." In fact, "I was practicing a [pause] *jig*." Nonetheless, when again asked for the third time, "You did dance in the astral world?" the riposte now becomes a limp denial, namely, "Oh no." Stymied but indefatigable, DJ embarks on a wholly new line of inquiry, "Now, there in that astral world, in that spirit world, were there any insane people?" According to R, "I didn't see any." (So proving our suspicion that "insane people" only infest the earth.)

DJ asks his R, "While you were in that astral world, in that spirit world, could you tell the future for the people on earth?" Particularly he wants her to "look [down] at the people on the earth and see what wars were going to happen to them." And, naturally, she complies, "I saw a war; some man there [in that astral world, in that spirit world] said there was going to be a war [an obvious surmise: there is *always* going to be a war]. It was before I was born—before I [Virginia Tighe] was born [in 1922]. And he said [there would] be a war; there was a war before I was born [and that one went on between 1914 and 1918]. They could see; people knew what was going to happen, if you were there [in that astral world, in that spirit world]." As DJ soothingly concludes, "Well, that's very interesting, very interesting. Now, rest and relax; rest and relax."[20] And that, ladies and gentlemen, represents the dramatic high point, the essential core material, the whole point lying behind Bernstein's ploddingly presented, 324-page-long paperback, international best-seller.

Well, now we know: "In that spirit world, there aren't any insane people." Right; they only pullulate on earth. No matter. As the alert reader may have noticed, it seems as though Bernstein was consistently *leading* his hypnotized subject. Whereas his questions are quite detailed, also rather insistent, initially "Bridey's" answers were typically just "Yes," "No," or "Uh-huh." Finally, the hypnotist does get the colorful details that he so wishes to hear. That is also the literary convention belonging to the postmodernist alien-abduction narratives, a shared trait which you, too, can now easily recognize, especially since we had previously quoted those at considerable length.

Alas, subsequent research—*not*, however, as pursued by Mr. Bernstein—has demonstrated that the imaginative Virginia T. "had simply dredged up childhood memories," her own. In short, these were all garnered from her growing up in an Irish neighborhood in Chicago, where she had also memorably performed in high school dramas, then specializing in neo-Celtic monologues recited with a thick Irish brogue. According to the conclusions reached by Martin Gardner, another skeptical researcher:

> Almost any hypnotic subject capable of going into a deep trance will babble about a previous incarnation—if the hypnotist asks him [or her]

to do so. He [or she] will babble just as freely about his [or her] future incarnations. . . . In every case of this sort, where there has been adequate checking on the subject's past, it has been found that the subject's unconscious mind was weaving together long forgotten bits of information acquired previously.[21]

Put otherwise: the Gaelic CV (*curriculum vitae; Lebenslauf* in German) was wholly ersatz. Translated into five languages, *The Search for Bridey Murphy* made its publisher, Doubleday, huge profits.

Eire or outer space? No matter; in every case it appears that the real *locus genii* lay wholly in the storytellers' hypnotized heads. But the only reason anybody ever got to hear about their various delusions was because someone else was clever enough to find a way to sell their confabulations to the mass media. Were the fanciful tale not so successfully marketed, then we would have remained happily ignorant of its fabulous existence. The media have sold us a lot of these tainted goods, and we have gobbled them all up, then we have asked them for seconds and thirds. And the modern media have responded with alacrity to our insatiable appetites for these titillating fictions. Whatever the names of the actual perpetrators, the timeless broader pattern—also explaining the psychological context for its attendant audience culture—is simply this. However inchoately expressed initially, first there comes a spiritual need for otherworldly wonders, then follows an authoritative descriptive text vividly recounting these, the *ekphrasis*, and eventually there are produced myriad iconic portraits serving to illustrate that canonical text for further avid consumers, the kind who perhaps find literacy fatiguing.

In this case, the art historian perhaps knows best how the process works, and we can dutifully cite a host of historical precedents.[22]

THE PRECEDENT OF EKPHRASTIC PRACTICE AND THE PHANTASMATIC FACTOR

Around 330 c.e., Eusebius, Bishop of Caesarea, wrote to the Emperor Constantine's sister, Constantia, discussing a certain "image of Christ," as he then could not understand what would have impelled her "to request that an image of Our Saviour should be delineated." Since Christological portraiture was then a rarity, if not outright proscribed, the pictorial task seemed to Eusebius to be somewhat futile: "Who, then, would be able to represent by means of dead colors and inanimate delineations [*skiagraphiai*] the glistening, flashing radiance of such dignity and glory? . . . How can one paint an image of so wondrous and unattainable a form? . . . God lays down the law that no likeness should be made either of what is in heaven or what is in the earth beneath."[23] Shortly after however, by the age of Gregory the Great (590–604), images of otherworldly entities were commonly produced (fig. 2), and they were then specifically employed to indoctrinate the uneducated lower classes. As Gregory then recognized, "To adore images is one thing; to teach with their help what should be adored is another. What Scripture is to the educated, images are to the ignorant, who see through them what they must accept; they read in them what they cannot read in book."[24]

Shortly after (circa 740), John Damascene agrees that "images represent the books of the illiterate—*Bíbloi toïs agrammátois aí eikónes.*"[25] According to another exemplary text, such as was produced by the Second Council of Nicaea, held in 787:

> It is defined with all certitude and accuracy that just as the figure of the precious and life-giving Cross, so also the venerable and holy images, as well as paintings and mosaics, as of other fit materials, should be set forth in the holy churches . . . and in pictures. . . . For so much more frequently as they are represented, by them so much more readily are men lifted up to the memory of their prototypes, and to a longing after them. For the honor which is paid to the image is passed to that which the image represents, and he who revered the image reveres in it the subject represented.[26]

The same honor and reverence evidently holds true for our currently widely reproduced portraits of otherworldly extraterrestrials (figs. 1, 4, 5, 15–22).

This is proven by abductee Whitley Strieber's 1987 account of the origin of his (literally) ekphrastic paperback book cover (fig. 4). The author recollects that "Budd Hopkins [the celebrated abductee-monger] suggested that I get an artist to render the image" of Strieber's ET visitor. The essential *Urbild* was verbally described (as previously quoted in chapter 5), in Strieber's own words, as a "true story" later to be profusely published bearing the emblematic image. Ted Jacobs was chosen, because he was deemed, Strieber says, particularly *"skilled in creating portraits from verbal descriptions."* The Strieber-Jacobs exemplar of ekphrastic extraterrestrial portraiture, just as we can see now with our very own eyes, is obviously cast in the now-classic ET mold. If the ocular evidence seems not sufficient for your needs, let us further examine the documentary evidence provided by abductee Strieber. Since this classic account of ekphrastic endeavor remains as yet unknown to conventional practitioners of art-historical scholarship, it merits full citation:

It was those eyes that I saw staring down at me on October 4, those eyes that gleamed so furiously in the faint night light. I remember them, from December 26, too, and from the summer of 1957, and from the experience with the fog bank [unveiling another ET].

Ted [Jacobs] asked me many questions about the eyes. When he asked me how they looked closed, I got another shock: The image closed its eyes! I saw the huge, glassy structures recede and loosen, becoming wrinkled, and the lids come down and up at the same time, to close just below the middle of the eyeball. I described this to Ted, but he wanted to know more. How about a profile view? Had I ever seen a profile? As I sat there staring into the darkness of my own mind, I saw the image obediently turn its head.

I could hardly believe what I was observing. Was this a phantom? What was it? My research thus far has not uncovered any specific paradigm of this experience. I will not assert finally that it was a mental phenomenon as yet unidentified, but at the moment this remains a distinct possibility.

While the image stayed with me, it remained exactly like the same as it was when I first saw it. I could observe any part of the body, from the top of the head to the tip of the foot. I could do this again and again, and see the same thing each time. On March 13, I made a complete physical description on tape. On March 23, I repeated the description again, then compared the two tapes. There was no difference. The image was unchanged.

Beyond the face, I was able to see the figure's back, the sides of its head, its arms and hands, its face, torso, abdomen—every part of its body. Under close scrutiny, its surface was smooth but did not seem to have a layer of fat under the skin, which was stretched tight over the bones. The structure of the knee and elbow joints reminded me of the knees of grasshoppers or crickets. The hands were very long and tapered when in repose, with three fingers and an opposable thumb. When pressed down, the hands became flat, suggesting that they were more pliable than our hands. On the fingers were short, dark nails of a more claw-like appearance than ours.

Overall, this did not appear to me to be a highly developed body, but rather a very simple one. There was a general lack of complexity that suggested few bones and not much flesh. I do not know how to explain this image. If it was not created by the powerful effect of Don [the hypnotist] asking me to visualize the creature, then perhaps it was some sort of sophisticated holographic [better, hypnopompic] projection. It might be possible to maintain an image in the mind, if one knew how to stimulate the optic center in the right way.

Is that what happened? Subsequent events suggested that the image was something even more extraordinary than it at first seemed.[27]

Indeed, *extraordinary*.

Much better known however, in fact the most famous example of "ekphrasis" in the whole corpus of British literature, is the description following of the apocryphal portrait of a "demonic" soul (which was explained in chapters 6, 7, and 10). Moreover, the subject here is specifically stated to depict a "Gray." This account was first published in 1890, at the height of the Symbolist era (further defined in chapter 12). It reads as follows:

> An exclamation of horror broke from the painter's lips as he saw in the dim light the hideous face on the canvas grinning at him [rather in the manner of fig. 4]. There was something in its expression that filled him with disgust and loathing. Good heavens! it was [the] Gray's own face that he was looking at! The horror, whatever it was, had not yet entirely spoiled that marvelous beauty. . . . The sodden [bulging] eyes had kept something of their loveliness. . . . Yes, it was [ET] himself. . . . It was some foul parody, some infamous, ignoble satire. He had never done that. Still, it was his own picture. He knew it, and he felt as if his blood had changed in a moment from fire to sluggish ice. His own picture! What did it mean? He turned, and looked at [the] Gray with the eyes of a sick man. His mouth twitched, and his parched tongue seemed unable to articulate. He passed his hand across his forehead. It was dank with clammy sweat.[28]

As my well-read readers have likely worked out on their own, the source is the thirteenth chapter in the eponymous *Picture of Dorian Gray*, and the artist of record is Oscar Wilde.

That noted, now I will proceed to document the extraordinary effects subsequently wrought by Whitley Strieber's nimble piece of ekphrastic portraiture and, so doing, I enter into the art-historical archives arresting evidence never before treated in this manner. In function, we find that Ted Jacobs's widely seen ET portrait (fig. 4) works something like the imagination-provoking effects recorded centuries earlier by St. Teresa de Avila recounted in chapter 6. The other noteworthy aspect of the incident I am about to recount is the effect it had on Dr. John E. Mack, the redoubtable Harvard psychologist-UFOlogist. In short, it caused him to believe, full of wonderment, in the "occurrence in very small children" of the UFO experience. Here is how the wondrous story was told by no less than Dr. Mack:

> When Ned [Ward] was just two, Jill [his mom] saw him talking to the alien face on the cover of [her copy of] Strieber's *Communion*, kissing

it and calling it "Pi." A few months later after waking from a frightening dream, [Ned] told Jill, "I fly in the sky—to the spaceship." Asked who was in the spaceship, he responded, "a man, a little man." Six weeks later, the Wards' seven-year-old daughter came into her parent's bedroom at five A.M. to tell them that Ned had come in to see her with a lot of blood on his face and coming out of one nostril. They also found blood on his pillowcase and a scabbed-over incision mark on the back of his head. When Jill asked him if anyone had been in his room Ned said [ungrammatically], "Little man come through window. Man bited me on the nose."

I asked [showing him a Jacobs-like portrait of an ET] if he had "ever seen this guy." "I open door, I drive the spaceship," Ned said. He said it was "that man's, that man's spaceship." He seemed to be getting uneasy and said, "I have my blankie [i.e., a blanket]. I put my thumb in my mouth." After talking casually about where he had seen some of the other figures, I returned to the alien [picture] card and asked, "Where did you see this guy?" and whether or not he liked him. "I don't like him," he said. "What does he do?" I asked. My assistant, who had been present, noted "up to this point Ned has been generally talkative and attentive, giving unsolicited information. Now he often doesn't answer at all, or only after long silences."

Whereupon Mack asks whether the ET, and as now definitively identified by his canonic portrait, is nice or otherwise, and the approved reply is "He's scary." As one presumes, the respondent is still in his previous posture, the one where "I have my blankie [and] I put my thumb in my mouth." Mack then inquires if the ET often enters the little tyke's room, and the priceless reply is, "Yeah. I have a big sword, now hit him out of my room. I have my blankie, put my thumb in my mouth. I were [sic] very tired." After this brief, thumb-sucking inquisition, Mack leads us to his dramatic finale:

Ned becomes increasingly silent and edges across his chair to his mother and sits in her lap. "A man came in my room," Ned said. "Man has big flashlight to my eyes." After this, Ned told of how "He hurt me." ("Where?") "On neck." He said, "I don't want to cry." Then he said, "I feel better." Ned tells me about how he likes to watch *Star Trek* and fights back against the man. "A man run after me, I run faster," he says.[29]

So, as we learn here, Jill had left lying around a copy of Strieber's *Communion*. Obviously, Jill had been reading the highly touted paperback revelations. Equally obviously, Jill and her husband had been praising aloud its virtues, and retelling to one another the astounding tales of egregiously close encounters that made it such a best-seller. Do you have any doubts that little Ned heard it all? And, of course, the whole family was (also) watching *Star Trek*. Even though I do not have a Ph.D. in psychology (sorry, merely in art history), I do feel justified in labeling the quality of the scientific "logic" leading to Dr. Mack's awe-inspiring extraterrestrial conclusions as nothing but *pathetic*. After reading "professional" opinions like this one, one's best response is "I have my blankie, put my thumb in my mouth."

What is particularly interesting about this specifically postmodernist kind of pseudoreligious icon (fig. 4) is the way that, as has been repeatedly pointed out here, its iconographic formula has become canonized, pictorially fixed by implicit fiat (see figs. 1, 5, 15–22). That text-to-icon effect is also a standard feature of genuine religious art. One example of iconographic stability wrought by an authoritative textual description, in effect another ekphrasis, was presented in Francisco Pacheco's *El arte de la pintura* (1649):

> Our Lady should be painted as a beautiful young girl, twelve or thirteen years old, in the flower of her youth. She should have pretty but serious eyes with perfect features and rosy cheeks, and the most beautiful, long, golden locks. . . . She should be painted wearing a white tunic and a blue mantle. . . . She is [pictured as an extraterrestrial biological entity] surrounded by the sun, an oval sun of white and ochre, which sweetly blends into the sky. Rays of light emanate from her head, around which is a ring of twelve stars. An imperial crown adorns her head. . . . Under her feet is the moon [and] the upper part is darkened to form a crescent with the points turned downward.[30]

And, as subsequently illustrated in seventeenth-century Andalusia, the result is that an art historian can show innumerable paintings of the *Immaculata* which do faithfully conform to this very text (see fig. 33).[31] Similarly, we have just shown several twentieth-century exemplars of similarly extraterrestrial portraiture which likewise do faithfully conform to now identified, widely published, generative texts (see figs. 1, 5, 15–22). Since no reputable art-historical scholar had taken on the task before, the exact art-historical mechanics of contemporary extraterrestrial portraiture have remained tenaciously hidden, simply (and literally) "occult."

The extraterrestrial phenomenon, as argued here, has been with us since long before 1947, the date of the so-called Roswell incident. With reference to old documents explaining pre–New Age iconography, we see that the repeated effects of an inescapable "phantasmatic" factor had been recognized long ago. Regarding then-commonplace depictions of various superterrestrial "spiritual dwellers" (*spirituales*), Matthew of Janov (in his *Rules of the Old and New Testaments*, circa 1390) had also recognized that

> no [earthling] observer has ever seen the latter [the heaven-dwelling "Spirituals"], least of all their illustrators [*pictores*] since they have invented their images according to their creative imagination [*phantasmata*], and as that is derived from everything they see and hear today [about their superterrestrial subjects]. . . . All such images and effigies are [only] likenesses in the "figure" of the artist's fantasies. . . . If the image does have an [emotional] effect, it is not because of the hand of the illustrator but because of the pious predisposition of the beholder.[32]

Even the overworked bureaucrats employed by the Spanish Inquisition, which was in fact much more benign than other contemporary instruments of right-thinking operating elsewhere in Europe, recognized that massive publicity actually creates popular delusion. One of these was Alonso de Salazar Frías, who was sent to report on an *"auto da fé"* held in Logroño (Navarra) in November 1610, at which twenty-nine unfortunates were accused of witchcraft (*la brujería*), with six unfortunates sentenced to be burned at the stake and five in effigy. Two years after the trial, Salazar concluded that "there were neither witches nor bewitched—until they were talked and written about. . . . The matter started there directly after Fray Domingo de Sardo came there to preach about these things."[33] Another conclusion reached in 1610 was that the victims were mostly women suffering from delusions.

The Spanish Inquisition was not welcoming to accounts of independently arrived at visitations from the Heavenly Consort; that kind of spiritual autonomy threatened the authority of the trained and tenured priesthood. We have the record of an imprudent woman who was punished by the religious establishment in 1523; the event took place in the Castilian town of Belmonte and, according to the stern verdict handed down by the Inquisition:

> We, the Inquisitors of the Diocese of Cuenca, have officially examined the present investigation and the confessions of Francisca la Brava and the testimony of witnesses against her. It is evident from everything that Francisca is much at fault for having seriously offended against our Holy Catholic Faith by publicly affirming that Our Lady appeared to her twice, in the manner and form that she states in her confessions; that

it is all trickery and falsehood is obvious from what she said in her confessions and the earlier investigation. In addition, she has clearly perjured herself in many of these matters. By rights, we could have treated her more rigorously, for the above matter was very public and scandalous for the Christian faithful, especially since she attracted them [her fellow villagers] and induced them to believe in what she said and made known. But it was all only vanity and frivolity.

But, in deference to certain just reasons that move us to mitigate the rigor of the sentence, we decree as a punishment to Francisca la Brava—and to provide an example to others not to attempt similar things—we condemn her. She is to be put on an ass and to be given one hundred lashes in public [and run] through the accustomed streets of Belmonte, naked from the waist up. The same [punishment will be given] in the town of El Quintanar and in the same manner. And [we order] that, from now on, she may not say or affirm—neither in public, or secretly by word, or insinuation—the things she said in her confessions. If not, she will be prosecuted as an impenitent and one who does not believe in or agree with what is in our holy Catholic faith. And thus we pronounce and order it by our sentence and by our signatures.[34]

Entertaining similar delusions at the end of the twentieth century, essentially the same kind that "were talked and written about" in Logroño (for instance) in 1610, Betty Hill and Betty Andreasson, instead of being celebrated for their *locuras extraterrestriales*, similarly would have been made to parade bare-chested before their aghast neighbors, perhaps even carbonized at the stake. Postmodernists are obviously much more forgiving of mass dementia. In earlier periods, however, this constituted a more or less legitimate, although rather aberrant, form of piety. Back then, it was appropriate to an age in which there was still granted the idea of a "Catholic" faith, from the Greek *Katholikós*, meaning "general," even "universal."

Then, long before the bizarre situation we now call "postmodernism," there was established what William Christian calls a socially significant "culture of visions." Then, however, as presently, it was not likely "that a divine figure really materialized, but merely that people present thought or said so." Then, "such legends were created to justify, illustrate, or dignify a preexisting devotion. But legends in turn can have a dramatic impact, and may even stimulate 'real' apparitions of an imitative nature." Then as now, these imaginary extraterrestrial visitations produced "images—biblical, legendary, or purely poetic—in which poets, artists, and dramatists equally participated." Then as now, there is an essential pattern to such extraterrestrial encounters:

A single seer or two seers have visions in the countryside that they prove to their town after repeated attempts with a sign provided by the divine figure [or ET]. The proof is revealed in some dramatic way, and the seer, often of humble status, undergoes a kind of local sanctification. . . . The essential drama of the story is the rejection, then the vindication of the less credible, marginal seer in the face of skepticism. . . . The stories validate the local, as opposed to the governmental or bureaucratic, and the common person, even the weak, as opposed to the nobility and the strong. Power structures are surprised and converted; ultimately, they [the infotainment industry in the postmodernist version] assume control of the sacred enterprises they first refused to accept. . . . The visions reveal the character of the [extraterrestrial] gods only implicitly, for this is something the seers and their communities already know.[35]

Put otherwise, a now universal ET/UFO syndrome has revealed considerably more about nature in our terms than it has about "aliens" and the "otherworld." Hans Belting, the author of the definitive history of a wholly imaginative portraiture of celebrated otherworldly entities, explained it all quite simply: "The desire to see the face of God [figs. 2, 3] is inherent in human nature and includes the expectation of a personal encounter with the 'Other,'" or *Alienus*.[36] Let us now apply another twist to the presently ubiquitous ET and/or UFO phenomenon, thus firmly inserting it among the innumerable "varieties of religious experience" examined a century ago by William James. For him, "Religion, in short, is a monumental chapter in the history of human egotism." Thus, "personality in the world of religion [is] the one fundamental fact," and, accordingly, religion is wholly opposed to "Science [which] has ended by utterly repudiating the personal point of view." Likewise, contemporary science repudiates the ETs and UFOs of contemporary popular culture. Just like medieval supernatural apparitions, which James reduced a century ago to "hallucinations, revelations, and cock-and-bull stories inextricably mixed with facts," postmodernist extraterrestrial encounters likewise make "no distinction between what has been verified and what is only conjecture."[37]

Today, what most frequently causes the "phantasmatic effect" is, rather than two-dimensional portraiture (figs. 1, 4, 5, 16, 20–22), the movies and television, the most kinetic art form of all, ever (figs. 9–15, 17–19.) The cinematic phantasmatic effect obviously works its potent wonders in supporting, if not actually instigating, most sightings of ETs and their UFOs. For this achievement, much credit is due to Steven Spielberg (figs. 15, 19), but I bet he would rather get another Oscar instead. That connection makes perfect sense, but some documentation seems called for. Here is an incident recorded by Budd Hopkins, the majordomo of abductees and an acknowledged master at eliciting their wondrous stories. In this instance, he is interviewing a lady named Alice. With Hopkins's careful prodding, Alice leads him toward another unit from the fleet of starships that always seem to be made available for close inspection by this kind of person (but not to you or me, at least not yet). Then Alice exclaims (as Hopkins tells it):

> "There's a—a *Close Encounters* ship!" Alice says, her voice filled with awe.
>
> "What do you mean by 'a *Close Encounters* ship'?" Budd asks.
>
> "It looks like a big one. Except it's not as big as the one in the movies. I don't know how they got it underground, my goodness!"
>
> "Is it resting on the ground? Hovering? What is its intention?"
>
> "It's hovering," Alice says. "It doesn't make any noise. A few lights [are] flashing."[38]

The journalist who recorded this wonderful bit of dialogue, C. D. B. Bryan, also tells of his meeting with another lady who eagerly told him of her *several* close encounters with the ETs; again we find a movie tie-in. Since Bryan was only attempting to eat lunch, and was not practicing hypnotism, what follows represents one of those "spontaneous" instances of recollections that UFOlogists love to cite in order to reinforce their claims that, no, you don't always need a hypnotist to lead them on. To speed up this wonderful interlocution, we may again revert to the transcript format; Bryan is "DJ" (Dismayed Journalist) and the lady raconteur is "R" (Reckless respondent). The initial query put by DJ is "Do these aliens have names?" The reply is priceless. As his R explains in detail, "Generally, we refer to them either by their names, or by a nickname, because their language is such that we couldn't pronounce their real names. So we have agreed on nicknames, or the names other human beings have already given them, and they tell me what that name is." When asked for appropriate examples, R shows herself to be perfectly *au courant* with the contemporary, popular culture archetypes; as she inquires in turn, "Do you remember Whitley Strieber, who wrote *Communion*? Well, we met *his* alien [fig. 4], the blue one. And the white one. Did you see that movie?" At a loss, DJ has to admit that "*Intruders* was about the only abductee movie I've seen." Her riposte is again priceless, "I don't think we've met any from *that* movie. But we're in the process of meeting an organized group of worlds that work together. And some of their names are their real names, and some of them are titles.

The first one we met is the head of the project, and we call him Zar." DJ wonders about that cognomen, but he evidently had forgotten that "Zar" sounds just like the title used by long-since deposed Romanoffs. Nonetheless, R goes on to explain that "I don't know if that's a proper name, or if that's his title, but that's what everybody calls him. And the second one we met was the blue one, the same one from [the movie] *Communion*. We just called him The Blue."

Since DJ is not such a dedicated aficionado of science-fiction films, he wants to know "How did you know he was the same one from *Communion*?" R explains that "we thought he was right away. But later we were *told* that he was," and "Zar did [it], I think." As elicited by DJ, her explanation of this close encounter returns to consider the azure alien (fig. 4) who had been directly linked to Strieber's best-seller: "When we met him, we were just saying 'The Blue One' to differentiate between who we were talking about as opposed to Zar. We didn't really think they had names, so we just called the white one 'The White One' or 'The White.' But when we met the next one, we found out that he did have a name, and we went back and wanted to know what to call The Blue. He said 'The Blue' as a proper name was okay; he was happy with that, and that it was fine to call him that." DJ wonders about the source for the name of "The White," evidently forgetting that it sounds just like the title used by the supporters of the long-since deposed Romanoffs; their opposition was, by the way, called the "Reds." In any event, R quickly explains that "those aren't their real names. And they aren't titles, either. They're just sort of reference names." In fact, "There are a lot of others," that is, reference names. Being a sensitive soul, R doesn't "feel comfortable just rattling off names, because they're personalities." As the reader may have supposed, "These Beings are important to us. We are dealing with an organization. The difference between what we've found so far, and what we've found with other people, is that we are aware of dealing with an organization of worlds, one not unlike our own UN, where people from different countries work together and try to get along together. The aliens out there have been doing it much longer and are much better at it."[39] Whereas R goes on much further in the recitation of her close encounters with the aliens, I will leave the rest to my readers to pursue at their leisure.

ETIOLOGY AND DEMOGRAPHICS OF EXTRATERRESTRIAL RECEPTIVITY

In any event, it seems that all our contemporary angel/ET seekers are eagerly pursuing some superior beings to inject a dollop of transcendental profundity into their evidently thoroughly dreary, mundane, and mostly unprofound, postmodernist experiences. As is additionally recognized by Joe Nickell, the kind of people who now fall for this particularly detailed and vivid media concoction, the "UFO/ET mythology," are mainly "individuals manifesting the fantasy-prone syndrome." These types are identified by up to fourteen personal characteristics, states Nickell, namely:

> (1) being an excellent hypnotic subject; (2) having imaginary playmates as a child; (3) fantasizing frequently as a child; (4) adopting a fantasy identity; (5) experiencing imagined sensations as real; (6) having vivid sensory perceptions; (7) reliving past experiences; (8) claiming psychic powers; (9) having out-of-body or floating experiences; (10) receiving poems, messages, etc., from spirits, higher intelligences, and the like; (11) being involved in "healing"; (12) encountering apparitions; (13) experiencing hypnagogic (near-sleep) or hypnopompic (near-waking) state hallucinations (i.e., waking dreams); (14) seeing classical hypnagogic imagery, such as spirits or monsters from outer space.[40]

Mr. Nickell is drawing upon the findings of qualified scientists, psychologists in this case.[41] According to their scrupulously conducted research, initially conducted in 1981, since approximately 4 percent of the population falls within the fantasy-prone personality (FPP) category, ranging from mild to intense, that would mean that around 10 million Americans are so inclined. We also recall the dire conclusions reached by another psychologist, Dr. John E. Mack, with quite a different vocational agenda; as he warned us, "Population surveys suggest that hundreds of thousands and possibly more than a million persons in the United States alone may be abductees or 'experiencers,' as they are sometimes called." In his 1995 paperback, *Abduction*, the casualty list went up further: "from several hundred thousand to *several million Americans* may have had abduction or abduction-related experiences."[42]

Well, that just goes to prove a point made earlier: when all is said and done, the most important thing is what you label something, either "ETs" or "golfers." By the same logic (or illogic), are we really speaking of "abductees or experiencers," or merely about "fantasy-prone individuals"? The label is particularly important in its strictly commercial applications. Which *sells* better: a book composed by an identified "fantasy-prone individual," or another one, with exactly the same fairy tales, but now said to be recording the "real-life" experiences of an "abductee or experiencer"? Does that point—the one about postmodernist marketing and profitability—really need to be further belabored? Here is another point, the kind I do insist upon belaboring. As recently put in a work co-authored by a sociologist and a psychologist that specifically deals with the irksome postmodernist problem of "UFOs and Alien Contact":

> The current social milieu plays a role in the relationship between the fantasy-prone process and the Fantasy-Prone-Personalites' worldview. FPPs living in the twentieth century are heavily exposed to books, television programs, and movies on the subject of extraterrestrial visitation. It is only natural, therefore, to expect their experiences to reflect the science-fiction and popular beliefs of the time. This could [should!] explain why prior to the nineteenth century there are virtually no explicit reported contacts with extraterrestrials. . . . Our preliminary findings suggest that the similarities between characteristics of FPPs and UFO abductees and contactees is a potentially fruitful avenue of research. . . . Seeing UFO abductees and contactees as otherwise normal people who just happen to be overactive fantasizers will be socially and therapeutically beneficial to the UFO witnesses.[43]

Among our gene pool of FPPs, 92 percent estimated spending half or more of their working day fantasizing compared with 0 percent in a control group.[44] Not surprisingly, likewise 92 percent of the same FPP group also see themselves as "psychic" or "sensitive"; so burdened, they report numerous telepathic and precognitive experiences. In all studies, a strong relationship was found between FPPs and hypnotic susceptibility. Eighty-eight percent of the FPPs reported a realistic "out-of-body experience" (OBE; not the prestigious British decoration); 21 percent actually went so far as to call their extracorporeal perceptions "astral travel" or "astral projection." Seventy-three percent of fantasizers reported apparitions (compared to 16 percent in the control group). Fifty-eight percent of the FPPs (versus 8 percent in a control group) reported spending a large part of their childhood interacting with fantasized people or animals, claiming to have "clearly seen, heard, and felt them" in the same way that they perceived living (real) people and animals. Fifty percent reported automatic writing, the kind dictated, so they said, by a guiding "spirit or a higher intelligence." FPPs are also significantly prone to *synaesthesia*: they reported being able to actually "see," "hear," "smell," and "feel" what is described in conversations and, particularly, in what they watch on TV. Sixty-five percent of the FPPs reported that their fantasies were "as real as real" in all their sense modalities (i.e., hallucinatory); their reactions were also experienced in an "involuntary" or "automatic" matter—so comparing to 0 percent of the control group. In fact, their fantasies were so "real," report the researchers, that 75 per-

cent of the female fantasizers report that they have had orgasms produced solely by sexual fantasies. (Awesome.)

Reeling off such figures is perhaps mind-numbing. Nonetheless, it
does represent something like hard evidence, the strictly *quantitative*
kind. Serious research into the FPP syndrome is relatively recent. But
that is no excuse for its stubborn *non*application to people now routinely
claiming close encounters with outer-space aliens. Such essential
research could easily be performed by any qualified psychologist with
privileged access to this particularly exotic segment of the American
population, for instance Dr. John E. Mack. As he himself observes, on the
one hand, while we still lack tests "that might distinguish abductees as a
group from a matched sample of non-experiencers," on the other, many
of the kinds of abductees he interviewed "came from broken homes or
had one or more alcoholic parents . . . and a number of my cases com-
plain about coldness and emotional deprivation."[45]

Dr. Mack, instead of collecting more abduction tales, of which we
now have more than enough, why don't you devise those tests? If you did
so, perhaps you would find that the stereotyped message (*abductio
alienarum*) is of far less significance than is the social context and actual
mental condition of its individual earthling messengers (*evangeloi*). But,
of course, that exercise would require the most daunting feat in one's
professional career, the kind potentially hazardous to one's reputation:
radically relabeling one's corpus of previously published "research" as
perhaps being a tad awry.

The standard FPP symptomology neatly complements the fact of an
absolute absence of *any* verifiable physical evidence certifying that the
visual-celebrity ET passengers of the UFOs actually do originate from zip
codes in outer space. But Nickell is a skeptic, so UFOlogists would automatically reject his premises. Nonetheless, they have done their own
research into the mind-boggling matter. One of these dedicated
researchers is British, Jenny Randles, a pugnacious individual sometimes affectionately referred to as the Miss Marples of UFOlogists. She
studied forty-three abduction cases in the United Kingdom. As she
reports, the information from twelve cases was gained through hypnosis;
seven incidents appeared as "dreams"; six were "creative visualizations";
and eighteen were said to be "spontaneous" or conscious recollections.
As for the last group, one wonders, who jogged their memories? One
suspects a UFOlogist, most likely Randles. No matter; her research has
obviously been pursued with zealous attention to mind-numbing detail:
der lieber Gott steckt im Detail.

Out of the forty-three incidents, Randles states, thirty-seven were single events. There were 1.29 witnesses per abduction incident, compared with 2.56 per UFO sighting; 53 percent of the British abductees were female and 47 percent were male. Their average age was 28 years, as compared with 27 in the United States, and 27.5 in continental Europe. They came from all occupations; police officers, factory workers, university professors, artists, and so forth. At the start of their otherworldly experience, 55 percent saw a UFO; 30 percent saw a bright light; 12 percent saw a being (ET). The experience occurred 13 percent of the time between midnight and 6 A.M.; 7 percent between 6 A.M. and 12 A.M.; 22 percent between 12 A.M. and 6 P.M.; and 28 percent between 6 P.M. and midnight. The most common time was between 3 A.M. and 5 A.M. Twenty-five percent of the abductions took place in the open air; 24 percent in a car; 51 percent in the bedroom (as in Fuseli's *Nightmare*; fig. 26). At the time of the abductions, the experiencers were, they said, idling, relaxed; 22 percent reported "information implants"; none reported physical implants. Randles provides a physical description of the entities showing the fact of diverging national preferences (see fig. 8, "Alien Time Chart"): "In Great Britain they are 12 percent 'Grays' [i.e., the standard space-waif model: fig. 4]; 6 percent 'Nordics,' and 44 percent of normal height, as compared to United States, where 73 percent are Grays, 6 percent Nordics, and 12 percent are normal height, which is comparable to Europe, which is 48 percent Grays, 25 percent Nordics, and 15 percent are normal height."[46]

As one would suspect, much more "research" of this sort is carried out in the United States; after all, this is where the phenomenon first surfaced, with abundant media fanfare. UFOlogist Mark Rodeghier has assembled psychological and demographic data extrapolated from thirty-two individuals who met the rigorous Center for UFO Studies (CUFOS) criteria for a legitimate "abduction experience" (already enumerated in chapter 2). Of that sample, women outnumbered the men three to one. The group was 94 percent Caucasian; the median age was thirty-eight; the average education was at least two years of college. Fifty-eight percent of the abductees were married; they averaged 1.9 children and 3.1 siblings. Forty-two percent of the abductees were Protestant; 21 percent had no (stated) religious affiliation, and 37 percent were presumably scattered among the world's other religious affiliations and/or occultist sects. The bulk of Rodeghier's group experienced their first abductions between 1970 and 1979. About 20 percent of the sample experienced vivid images and/or sounds when falling asleep or waking up. Given the Index of Childhood Memory and Imagination (ICMI) for fantasy-prone individuals, the group tested at 24.0 on a 0 to 52 scale. The population norm is between 20 and 23. They tested 25.2 for hypnotic suggestibility; the population norm is 20.8. Of that test group, Rodeghier says, five of the individuals had scores above the standard cutoff point. In other words (not Rodeghier's), the abductees so examined proved much more fantasy-prone and more hypnosis-suggestible than is the norm.[47] They are, therefore, abnormal folk.

A complementary factor is the standard disclaimer by self-described abductees that they had no prior knowledge of UFO lore, that their minds were *tabula rasa* for all such postmodernist apocryha. Here is a typically sweeping statement from a prominent UFOlogist: "A great many of the abductees [say they] had no prior exposure to abduction-related stories and no prior interest in the subject whatsoever."[48] That is a shrewd tactic; it discounts, out of hand, any possibility that said "experiencers" were *ever* exposed to all those uncountable paperback publications, movies, or television dramas and documentaries endlessly replaying the outer-space soap operas of extraterrestrial infestations. Get real! One can no more plead ignorance of the ubiquitous UFO/ET component in our postmodernist popular American culture than of the necessity of paying taxes; likewise, neither could we expect that any contemporary Spaniard could feign ignorance of either Francisco Franco ("El Caudillo") or the Blessed Virgin Mary. Besides being a matter of one's given cultural environment, it is also one of the individual's mental makeup.

Kenneth Ring ran a comparative study of individuals reporting "near-death experiences" and others reporting the now-standard close encounters with UFOs. He found that both groups were far more susceptible to "alternative realities" than the rest of the population, and they had been so since childhood.[49] Jo Stone-Carmen, an Arizona psychologist, has dealt with abductees claiming conscious recall of their horrible experiences with otherworldly visitors. They enumerated their "major fears" as being harmed; being alone; dread of heights; being disabled; loss-of-control issues; water (drowning); insects (pesky); UFOs. Fifty percent of the self-designated abductees suffered from posttraumatic stress disorder (PTSD), their symptoms being low self-esteem, fear of being alone, not feeling safe, sleep disturbance, and flashbacks. Thirteen out of the twenty-three abductees had attempted suicide, a figure 57 percent higher than that for the general population. As was observed later (but not by Ms. Stone-Carmen), "No mention is made of how this alarming statistic speaks to the danger of untrained therapists [and UFOlogists] dealing with abductees."[50] It is time that someone spoke of "this alarming statistic," and very *loudly*.

Another experiment was carried out in 1983 by psychologist Elizabeth Slater. The sample in this case comprised only nine individuals, ages twenty-five to forty, five males and four females, all with a college education. All, however, had been chosen by zealous UFOlogist Budd Hopkins as being certified abductees. The interesting point here is that Dr. Slater was not told this crucial detail; she just thought they were your run-of-the-mill disturbed folks. Here is what she wrote in her initial report—that is, long before she was informed that her human subjects, clearly suffering from "identity disturbance and/or lack of emotional maturity," were really only to be distinguished by their purported close encounters with exotic outer-space aliens:

> The subjects were in a rather continual struggle to bind their impulses and keep them at bay. . . . Under stressful conditions, at least six of the nine showed a potential for more or less transient psychotic experiences involving a loss of reality testing, along with confused and disordered thinking that can be bizarre, peculiar, or very primitive and emotionally charged. Also noted was a degree of identity disturbance, especially sexual identity confusion and self-inflation, lowered self-esteem, relative egocentricity, and/or lack of emotional maturity, and minor but frequent "boundary failures" on their figure drawings. One spoke specifically of "a sense of smallness and victimization in the face of overwhelming outer forces." Also observed was some degree of impairment in interpersonal relationships, problems in intimacy for some, and a certain mildly paranoid and distrusting streak in many of the subjects, together with hyper-vigilance, a marked tendency to attend and be sensitive to nuance and fine detail, leeriness and caution, and a disposition towards wariness.[51]

As it seems only reasonable now to question, were these semipsychotic conditions specifically due to alien abduction or, instead (far more likely), were they due to something inherent to the wholly mundane psychic makeup of these individuals, meaning that they perhaps did not really need any kind of "extraterrestrial" intervention to get *that* way?

Also interesting is recently published quantitative data charting the strictly geographical distribution of ET believers in the United States. The heaviest concentrations of what have been officially labeled "space cadets" are found in (no surprise here) California, but only in selected areas: Los Angeles to the Mojave Desert, and from San Francisco north to Mendocino and east to Sacramento and along the Sierra Nevadas. Space cadets (SCs) also proliferate, just as you would expect, in the Portland-to-Seattle metropolitan axis. In the far west, deeply committed SCs occupy most of Arizona, Colorado, Nevada, southern Montana, and all of the Hawaiian archipelago and Utah (Mormonism seems to have failed here). In Texas, two zones pullulate with SCs: Austin to Galveston and the Fort Worth–Dallas megalopolis. Back east, only the Miami-Orlando zone in Florida, western Massachusetts en bloc, and (oddly isolated) Norfolk, Virginia, seem to harbor significant colonies of SCs. Conversely, at the opposite end of the credulity scale, comprising "the earthbound," we find practically all of the lower Mississippi Valley states: Louisiana, Arkansas, southern Missouri, eastern Oklahoma, central Mississippi; also largely free from the fantasy prone syndrome is Appalachia: Tennessee, western parts of the Carolinas and Virginia, southern Kentucky, and all of West Virginia. Interestingly, these areas are also known as "the Bible belt." Likewise largely immune from ET believers are the Dakotas, Maine, and northern Michigan. Whatever their regional distribution, it was also concluded that nearly all "believers fit a down-to-earth profile: well educated, upper-middle class and married."[52] Who knows, maybe it has something to do with the local water supply.

There is even more damning evidence, but this, too, is strictly psychological. Even the UFOlogist proponents of hypnotically induced memory recovery admit that there is a danger of "confabulation," the process by which hypnotized people sometimes fill in gaps in their apparent recall by inventing additional detail. And why is hypnotism, since it is so prone to confabulation, deemed so necessary to extrude the desirable memories of alien contacts? When pressed, the UFOlogical rationale is that you really must employ hypnosis because the clever ETs consciously erase all the memory disks of their abducted earthlings. Had they not taken pains to do so, obviously millions of Americans would then spontaneously recognize *their* abduction experience, and then the ETs would have their cover blown. (Oops.) Nonetheless, objective students of the confabulation phenomenon recognize that hypnotism markedly increases supposed eyewitnesses' suggestibility and might enable the investigator to steer their recollection in desired directions.

To deflect such criticisms, in early 1977 UFOlogists collaborated with a sympathetic professor of English and a physician in an experiment which was staged at California State College–Long Beach. Advertisements were put into the student newspaper calling for "creative, verbal types" to volunteer for "an interesting experience in hypnosis and imagination." Taking great care to screen out any obvious UFO enthusiasts, eight subjects were finally selected. Under hypnosis induced by a certified physician, Dr. William C. McCall (not a UFOlogist), the volunteers were told to imagine that they had "really" been taken on board a

flying saucer where they were subjected to an intrusive physical examination. When the students were later told to describe their collective, literally imposed, and entirely imaginative "experiences," the psychological investigators were astonished, and the UFOlogists evidently dis-
tressed, by the fluency of detail characterizing the resulting eight, wholly
fictitious, narrations of alien abductions. The published conclusion
reached by the principal investigator is, I think, devastating: "The imaginary subjects [recreated] under hypnosis report UFO experiences
which seem identical to those of 'real' witnesses."[53]

Such "real witnesses" produce the kind of weirdo reports so abundantly and profitably published by the likes of David Jacobs, Whitley
Strieber, Budd Hopkins, John E. Mack, John Fuller, Raymond Fowler,
Coral Lorenzen, and Morey (*Bridey Murphy*) Bernstein. And when these
worthies zealously cite studies that apparently demonstrate "that experiencers were neither more hypnotizable nor more fantasy-prone than
the general population," careful study reveals that said research was carried out by fellow UFOlogists and that (not surprisingly) "these results
remain to be replicated" by non-UFOlogist researchers.[54] Some people
just don't want to confront the truth.

In the event, one of the main axioms in legitimate psychiatry (the
kind evidently not practiced by devoted UFOlogists) is that psychological and psychopathological processes play a significant role in the UFO
experience. Although rarely cited by the True Believer UFOlogists, there
is much useful research bearing upon the subject, and this is the kind
that says that alien abduction occurs in the head of the abductee, also in
that of his hypnotic psychopomp—but *not in empirical reality*. Mark
Moravec has conducted a thorough analysis of such processes as published by various researchers.[55] He worked all these different, but all
equally mundane, complementary explanations into outline form. It is
well worth reproducing since it covers all the areas discussed by objec-
tive-minded psychologists and psychiatrists who have bothered to study
the UFO experience. It looks like this:[56]

PROCESS	CONTEXT	EXPERIENCE
Misperception	Insufficient knowledge of natural/man-made phenomena	Spurious UFO sighting reports
Hoax	Attention-seeking	Fabricated sightings and physical traces
Psychosis	Stress/personal crisis/ predisposition	Reports involving mental communication/ apparitions/paranoia
Folie à Deux	Psychosis plus dominance/subordinance/ relationship	Reports with false consensus of two or more percipients
Conversion Hysteria	Fear/intense emotions/ bodily predisposition	Physiological symptoms of psychosomatic nature
Altered State of Consciousness	Reduction of overload of time stimuli/ history of ASCs, etc.	Reports involving distortion/dreamlike elements, etc.
Hypnopompic/ Hypnagogic Imagery	Sleep/Awake interface	Reports involving communications/ apparitions/entities
Amnesia/Fugue	Stress/trauma	Reports featuring time lapses/ disorientation/physical wandering
Possession/ Multiple Personality	Stress/trauma disposition	Reports featuring "invading entities"/messages from from same
Automatic Writing	Personal crisis/ spiritualistic beliefs/ predisposition	Reports featuring written messages
Auto-Hypnosis and/or Hypnotic Regression	Concentration for long periods/leading questions/desire to please hypnotist	Trancelike states/ fantasized abductions/ abduction by UFO/ET entities

Viewed with informed hindsight, what characterizes all truly committed UFOlogists is an astonishing naïveté: they are amazingly ignorant
of the slippery agility of the human imagination and of its inherent power
of fantasy. They are also apparently ignorant of those issues considered
fundamental to conducting proper scientific research, namely the dire
consequences of askew observation and experimenter bias, with both
leading to gross errors in measurement, reliability, validity, and evaluation apprehension. They also seem blithely unaware of the need for real
controls. You name it, they don't, won't practice it. Blinded with pseudoscience, they abhor a prosaic explanation as Nature abhors a vacuum.
At the same time, their intellectual innocence is complemented by an
unvoiced arrogance. They can account for no *miracula* without foreign
intervention; the earthling natives are evidently too stupid to think it all
up with their very own hyperenergized minds. But how much imagination is actually needed for the feat of picturing a melodramatic close
encounter with an extraterrestrial? In fact, very little; all you need to do
is to turn on your TV set (see figs. 9–15, 17–19).

In order to amend their shortcomings, rather glaring I am afraid, all
responsible UFOlogists are now earnestly enjoined to sign up for a standard course in "Abnormal (Anomalistic) Psychology." Perhaps Professor
John E. Mack, M.D., the renowned Harvard University psychiatrist and
best-selling author of *Abduction: Human Encounters with Aliens*, might
also want to sign up. Unfortunately, their ingrained and tribalized prejudices already explain why they will not even bother to peruse a short list
of essential readings for a subject in which they so desperately need
guidance, beginning with William James's classic study *The Varieties of
Religious Experience* (1902).[57]

Another book on the required reading list is a model investigation, first
made available half a century ago, of ghostly appearances and other sorts of
ESP, and this was written long before "ESP" became trendy; I refer to
G. N. M. Tyrrell's *Apparitions*, first published in 1953 by the Society for
Psychical Research in London. According to this author, who had (of
course) never heard of either "ET" or about his penchant for "alien abductions," an "apparition"—no matter whether this is the old-fashioned
"ghost" or the postmodernist "ET"—is simply "a waking *hallucination*,"
and these hallucinations may be either *individual* or *collective*. In either
case, "an apparition is what, throughout the ages, has been called a 'spirit.'
But clearly it is in reality a psychological phenomenon." Key to this phenomenon is what Tyrrell calls the *idea-pattern*: "The idea provides the
theme of the idea-pattern [in our case, alien abductions by ETs], while the
agent's [perceiver-abductee's] emotional states provides the *drive*." In sum:

Take, for example, the idea of the god Pan, half human and half goat-like, haunting certain places in the woods and uplands and playing his pipe. Anyone (suitably sensitive) going to the places which, according to the idea-pattern, Pan [or ET] was especially supposed to inhabit would then seen and hear a Pan [or ET] with exactly the same reality that a person going into a haunted house sees and hears a ghost. . . . Collective idea-patterns would also explain epidemic appearances, for example, of the Virgin and the Saints in Catholic countries [as recounted above]; the appearances of the Devil in the Middle Ages, and perhaps the sight of witches [see chapter 7] flying on broomsticks and the metamorphosis of human beings into animals, etc.[58]

Oddly, this problem of collective *docta ignorantia* among postmodernist UFOlogists was recognized by (even) Whitley Strieber, a True Believer who had previously earned a million dollars by publishing his own close "communion" with the ETs. As he put it (and rather huffily) in an article published in June 1988 in the *MUFON UFO Journal*, there are

a large number of researchers out there hypnotizing people [who] have no mental health credentials. . . . I believe that much "abduction research" is actually unintentional brainwashing. . . . Its effect is to leave already troubled people in much worse [mental] shape. I feel that it's only a matter of time before somebody is hurt, either driven psychotic or to suicide [a hypothesis proven in 1997 by the Heaven's Gate UFO cult mass suicide]. . . . I have withdrawn from contact with UFO researchers who have no professional credentials and who seem to mix fear and ignorance in equal amounts. Many of these people are hypnotizing distraught human beings, in effect operating as untrained and unlicensed counselors and therapists, and innocently imposing their own beliefs upon their victims.[59]

Hear, hear! If nothing else, it would appear that there is some healthy dissension emerging among the UFOlogists; the party platform has its splinter groups. *Vive la différence*!

AN ETIOLOGY OF THE MODERNIST TRUE BELIEVERS

People who subscribe to the demonstrably "unbelievable" may be called "True Believers." For them, especially when physical evidence is lacking, belief alone will suffice. In matters of belief, one might imagine the world's population to be unevenly divided into three parts. The largest group would be the spiritually apathetic; they just don't care. Distracted by the need to earn a living, or just busy minding their own business, such folk are seen by the other inhabitants to be "mentally lazy" and uncommitted to "meaningful values." Then there are the True Believers, real *enthusiasts* (see also chapter 6). There are quite a lot of these in the modern era; their very abundance in part defines the meaning of modern culture. Finally, there is a tiny minority, the thoroughly appalled; they are often called "skeptics." They are anathema to the True Believers.

Our interest lies, of course, in the True Believers. Fortunately, these enthusiastic folk have already been defined adequately by Eric Hoffer in a classic study called (what else but?) *The True Believer* (1951). Besides being useful, and for all the obvious reasons, Hoffer's essay should also be considered a historical document in its own right. Subtitled *Thoughts on the Nature of Mass Movements*, it was published in 1951, at the height of (both) the Cold War and the triumphal rise of the UFO experience. Back then, the etiology of the True Believers really called for a pioneering clarification. For the definitions following, I have retained Hoffer's diction, posed in the manner of axiomatic statements, and have also hewed for the most part to his original sequencing.[60]

Mass movements may be either nationalist or religious (even "occult") in nature. They present the prospect of sudden and spectacular change in the condition of life. Mass movements are the generating plants of general *enthusiasm* (see chapter 6); they infuse the masses with varieties of soul-stirring, *mass enthusiasm*. The leaders orchestrating such mass enthusiasm are masters of the art of "religiofication," the essential trick of turning their practical purposes into holy causes. The first protomodernist mass movement was the French Revolution (beginning in July 1789); it was posited upon an extravagant conception of the omnipotence of man's reason and the boundless range of his innate intelligence. The French Revolution was a new religion; it had its dogma—*Liberté et sainte égalité*; it had its forms of worship—*les fêtes civiques*, modeled on Catholic ceremony; it had its hero-saints and martyrs—*les citoyens qui meurent pour la Patrie*.

To coerce people into a psychologically cohesive group, an extravagant hope must be kindled, no matter whether of a heaven on earth or the coming kingdom of heaven (sometimes specifically reached through "Heaven's Gate"; see fig. 5). Typically, there is a monstrous incongruity between the hopes, typically noble and self-sacrificing, and the actions which actually follow them. A mass (even a mini) movement must satisfy the passion for self-renunciation which is innate to the True Believer; typically, since their individual careers cannot stir them to a mighty effort, they look upon self-interest as something tainted, unclean.

A person is more likely to mind his or her own business when it is worth minding. When it is not, one's formerly meaningless endeavors becomes the business of minding other people's business.

In a specifically modern society, people can live without hope only when kept dazed and out of breath by incessant hustling [hype], advertisement, and promised consumption. Whether held in one's nation, race or, holy cause, faith must be extravagant and uncompromising. People inclined for induction into any mass movement are typically ripe for any kind of collective enterprise, no matter what its particular doctrine or ideological program. As one concludes with historical hindsight, (a) all mass movements are competitive, and the gain of one in adherents is the loss of all the others; (b) all mass (or mini) movements are interchangeable. True Believers crave to dissolve their spoiled, meaningless selves in some soul-stirring, spectacular communal undertaking: unified actions. More likely to be inscribed in the ranks are (a) the poor, (b) misfits, (c) outcasts, (d) minorities, (e) adolescent youth, (f) the ambitious, (g) those in the grip of some obsession, (h) the impotent (in body or mind), (i) the selfish and self-centered, (j) the bored. The fanatic is self-righteous, credulous, disputatious, petty; he is often ready to sacrifice relatives and friends, even himself, for his holy cause.

Paradoxically, they clamor for freedom, but it is the freedom to establish equality and uniformity within the group. Obeying orders, they free themselves from individual responsibility. They wish to free themselves from the free competition and ruthless testing to which the individual is constantly subject in a free society. To the contrary, "teamwork" is rare in intellectual or artistic undertakings. Since genuine creativity, that is, individual acts of free enterprise and autonomous resolution, is usually free of frustration, it seems that the dramatic decline of handicrafts following the Industrial Revolution explains much of the distinctively modernist mentality: mass frustration. By also drawing people to large manufacturing centers, the cities, and away from rural communities and their self-sustaining economies, it broke family ties.

Disruption of the family automatically fosters a collective spirit. Inscription in a mass movement, or into a modernist cult, a "commune," is usually characterized by a hostile attitude toward the family; Jesus minced no words: "He that loveth father or mother more than me is not worthy of me" (Matt. 10:37). The mass movement attracts its following by the refuge it offers from the anxieties, barrenness, and meaninglessness of an individual existence. It is futile to judge the viability of a new spiritual movement by the truth of its doctrine. Among others, Hitler knew that the chief passion of the frustrated is to belong, and that there cannot be too much social cementing and spiritual binding to satisfy this passion.

There is perhaps no more reliable indicator of a society's ripeness for a mass movement [or new cult] than the prevalence of unrelieved boredom. Those who are members of a compact tribe, church, party, and so forth, are not accessible to boredom. Where people live autonomous and moderately comfortable lives, but are without creative abilities and opportunities for autonomous activity, they resort to desperate, often fantastic, means to give meaning and purpose to their lives. By embracing a holy cause, and dedicating their physical energies and psychic substance to its advancement, they find a new life full of purpose and meaning. Both mass movements and armies are collective bodies: both strip individuals of their separateness and distinctness; both demand self-sacrifice, unquestioning obedience, and single-hearted allegiance; both delight in symbols (spectacles and ceremonial ritual); both promote united action (*Gleichschaltung*). The innermost craving of a following is for *communion*—and there can never be too much of it.

The newly devout are always urged to seek the absolute truth with their hearts, and not with their minds. In swearing in the party faithful in 1934, Rudolph Hess exhorted: "Do not seek Adolph Hitler with your brains; all of you will find him with the strength of your hearts" (see fig. 7). Doctrine has to be vague; it has to be unverifiable. The urge to escape our real self is also an urge to escape the rational and the obvious; there is no hope for the frustrated in the actual and the possible. One has to get to heaven or into the distant future in order to determine the truth of an effective doctrine. Since no one ever returns from such places, the doctrine remains unquestioned. There is thus an illiterate air about even the most literate True Believer. The atheist is a religious person; he believes in atheism as though it were itself a new religion. The opposite of the religious fanatic is the gentle cynic, who cares not whether there is a God or not.

Hoffer's last paragraph recalls how in 1938, an appropriate year to make such an observation, "J. B. S. Haldane counted fanaticism among the only four really important inventions made between 3000 B.C.E. and 1400 C.E. It was a Judaic-Christian invention."[61] Alas, Hoffer does not tell us what the other three "really important inventions" might have been. Surely none of these was the postmodernist scheme of "alien abductions," at least so we may hope.

In effect, Hoffer had provided us with a nearly complete catalogue of the emotional responses of modernist True Believers. And for all True Believers that is all it is: pure *emotionality*. All those imposing rationalizations afterward applied—then being called either (sacred) "Theology" or (secular) "Ideology"—are just so much fancy window dressing, alibis to avoid calling the underlying collective impulse what it really is: emoting in unison, a hysterical infection, a mass-psychic contagion (see chapters 12 and 14). Now, in the third millennium, scientists have an even better explanation, albeit a purely mechanical one. And the perennial tension between science and religion was about to get tenser, that is, once some scientists recently decided that the irrepressible "religious experience" is just too intriguing not to study. Neurologists jumped in first, finding a connection between temporal-lobe epilepsy and a sudden interest in religion. As they report, patients, during seizures, frequently say "they see God," or that they feel "a sudden sense of enlightenment." Now researchers are looking at the real causes of the more common varieties of religious experience, thereby explaining why God won't go away. By extension, their provocative research into the biology of belief also explains (even though this was not an issue specifically explored by them) why the UFOs and ETs won't go away.

Researchers Andrew Newberg and Eugene D'Aquili have a name for their new field of scientific inquiry: "neurotheology." In their recently published book, *Why God Won't Go Away: Brain Science and the Biology of Belief* (2001), they conclude that spiritual experiences are the inevitable outcome of brain wiring: "The human brain has been genetically wired to encourage religious [or credulous] beliefs."[62] The researchers roll their True Believer subjects into a brain machine called SPECT, and the patient's grandiose sense of "unity with the Cosmos" now gets boiled down to a computer readout. A region at the top rear of the brain, which weaves sensory data into a feeling of where the self ends and the rest of the (real) world begins, now looks like the victim of a power blackout. As the researchers explain, once deprived of sensory input by the True Believer's inward concentration, this orientation area cannot do its assigned job of properly finding the fine border between self and world. Then, "the brain has no choice. It perceives the Self to be endless, as one with all of Creation. And this feels utterly real." Even simple praying is now shown to affect the brain in distinctive ways. In SPECT scans of Franciscan nuns at prayer, the neurotheological team found a quieting of the orientation area which gave the sisters a tangible sense of proximity to, and "merging with God." According to Newberg and D'Aquili's findings, "The absorption of the Self into something [is] not the result of emotional fabrication or wishful thinking." Instead, it merely springs from mundane sources, neurological events, as when the orientation area goes dark.

Neurotheology also explores how ritual behavior elicits brain states that bring on mystical feelings, ranging from a sense of mild "community" to deep "spiritual unity." A 1997 study by Japanese researchers showed that repetitive rhythms can drive the brain's hypothalamus, which can elicit either serenity or arousal.[63] That may explain why repetitive chanting of hymns and the like can trigger a sense of quietude that True Believers interpret as representing "spiritual tranquillity" and sublime bliss. In contrast, the fast rapturous dancing of Sufi mystics—or that kind now provoked by proletarian rock concerts (as shown in chapter 13)—causes hyperarousal, and this Newberg and D'Aquili find can make participants feel as if they are "channeling into the energy of the universe." Although the inventors of rituals (or rock festivals) didn't know it at the time, such rhythm-driven rites manage to tap into the precise brain mechanisms that tend to make True Believers interpret inchoate perceptions and feelings as evidence of "God" or, at least, "transcendence." Rituals also tend to focus the mind by blocking out sensory perceptions, including those that the orientation area needs to figure out the actual boundaries of the self. That is why even nonbelievers are often moved by religious rituals and rock concerts. "As long as our brain is wired as it is," states one researcher, "God won't go away."[64] (Nor will overpaid rock stars and their thronging groupies.)

If brain wiring explains the feelings True Believers take from prayer and ritual, also from collective chanting at political rallies, are transcendent spiritual (and political) experiences merely creations of our neurons? Neurotheology at least suggests that collective spiritual rapture, also the corollary political experiences with mass audiences, are no more meaningful than are, say, fears that the brain is hard-wired to perceive automatically in response to any strange noise heard at night. True Believers, of course, have a piqued retort: "As you say, the brain's wiring *may* explain our religious feelings, but just who do you think was the master electrician?" And, in the case of those True Believers put to the test in this extended cultural autopsy, his name is a familiar one: "ET."

THE UFO EXPERIENCE AS A POSTMODERNIST ALTERNATIVE RELIGION

When one formerly pondered a True Believer, one usually associated people of this persuasion with a religion or, on a more informal level, a sect or cult. Hoffer also made the cogent point that modernist political movements, particularly the kind with a stridently broadcast ideological belief-system, are also the nurturing lairs of the True Believers. Another place where they lurk in abundance is occultism, which we may charitably call a form of "alternative religion." This is a ubiquitous postmodernist presence metastasizing under the rubric of New Age: this or that fad (your choice). Likewise, we may charitably call the contemporaneous UFO experience a postmodernist alternative religion, and this is one given specifically corporeal form in the alien abduction recitation, providing us with a sort of post-Catholic incarnation legend. One of the acknowledged roles of religion—no matter whether established or merely fringe—has been to provide answers to questions which contemporary science has not yet solved, or which lie beyond the province of scientific inquiry. That initial prescription serves to define the UFO experience as a specifically postmodernist, technological, and postindustrial alternative religion.

One of the most appealing aspects of UFOs and ETs, meaning why we have to hear so much about them, is their overall religious content and structure. The UFO experience can readily function as a postmodernist alternative religion for several reasons, none of which are all that obscure. According to John A. Saliba:

> They deal with important and often ultimate issues in human life; they contain references to entities that bear some resemblance to traditional religious beings, such as gods, supernatural heroes, angels, and devils; and they appear to have a spiritual or trans-human nature, since their presence is not susceptible to modern empirical investigation. At least seven major religious themes or elements dominate accounts of UFO sightings and extraterrestrial contacts: (1) mystery; (2) transcendence; (3) belief in spiritual entities; (4) perfection, (5) salvation; (6) worldview (the ascription of meaning and purpose to the universe); and (7) spirituality. . . . Underlying socio-psychological explanations of UFOs is the assumption that encounters with UFOs are a product of several distinct human factors, namely the cultural condition prevalent in society and the psychological state of human beings.
>
> Like all other [post-medieval] religious movements, the UFO phenomenon is related to cultural change and social and intellectual dislocation. One therefore has to examine it not as a religious event by itself, but in *relation* to other developments in the current world. UFOs can thus be seen, for example, as an attempt to come to terms with the conflict between science and religion, or as one aspect of the resurgence of religious fundamentalism in different parts of the world. From a psychological point of view, UFO cults and movements cater to the individual need for security in a [modernist] world of religious changes and social upheaval, or they may be unusual or pathological expressions of human emotional and intellectual crises. A final opinion would insist on

the religious dimensions and functions of UFO phenomena. Beliefs about, and practices surrounding, flying saucers constitute an original religious worldview that takes into account modern knowledge of the universe and technological advances that include space travel.[65]

Even a fundamentalist believer, Barry Downing, lists six major theories that compare traditional religious beliefs (his) to those now applying to UFOs (in which he also seems to believe). As he puts it:

(1) Belief in UFOs and ETs is similar to traditional religious beliefs in that both are systems of "make-believe."

(2) Belief in UFOs and ETs substitutes traditional religion with a "true science" [as in "*Credo quia absurdam est*"]; this is because modernist UFOlogy, unlike the tenets of most religions, can be subjected to, or may be potentially [maybe] confirmed by empirical proof.

(3) Belief in UFOs and ETs replaces the transcendental God of the Bible with an astronaut who has superhuman power and otherworldly knowledge.

(4) Belief in UFOs and ETs suggests that both UFOlogy and religion have a common ground in the unconscious and, consequently, that both faiths stem from within the human person.

(5) Belief in UFOs and ETs unites UFOs with demons and/or angels.

(6) Belief in UFOs and ETs represents tacit acceptance of some kind of divine power.[66]

Downing omits, however, one area of comparison that might account for the uniqueness of postmodernist UFO religions, namely that they offer an innovative worldview that demands one's total spiritual involvement and ethical commitment. That notion, with a timely ecological update, emerges clearly in the posthypnotic interpretations published by John E. Mack of stories told to him by self-selected "experiencers" (see chapter 2). One should, therefore, postulate that UFO phenomena are a new type of (literally) millenarian religion that attempts to formulate a worldview designed to be more consistent with expectations for the culture and technology of the twenty-first century.

John Whitmore has also observed in the UFO experience a unique confluence of "the projection of traditional religious themes with a technological/science-fiction framework." Those traditional religious themes conveyed by abductees (as quoted above) include such standard categories, or rhetorical *topoi*, as "the moral injunction," "the metaphysical script," "the apocalyptic message," and, last but not least, "the theme of being chosen." According to Whitmore's more detailed decoding of these apocryphal epistles from the extraterrestrials to the earthlings:

The parallels of those messages to doctrines of the Christian religion are particularly striking. In the moralizing messages, we get the sense that time is running out, that humans must reform or face judgment by the aliens who are *superior*—not merely technologically but also, apparently, ethically. This is the message of the Old Testament prophet, warning of the calamities God will visit upon His people unless they mend their ways. Apocalyptic messages invoke images of Armageddon and mass catastrophe from which a faithful remnant will be preserved. Abductees are informed that they are chosen to play a special part in a superhuman plan, and they must evangelize among the non-elect, spreading an alien gospel. The aliens' messages about themselves and the role they may play in the development of human culture reveal history to be the unfolding of that plan, in order to produce a new, superior hybrid being—the next step in human evolution. The aliens take the place of a God of salvation-history working for humanity's redemption. The goal of history, according to abduction narratives, is not the union of God and man in Christ; rather, it is the union of humanity and alien, towards which the UFO godlings strive. The barely disguised grafting of these theological elements of America's most popular religion [Protestant Christianity] onto the bizarre phenomenon of UFO abductions argues strongly for that phenomenon's essentially religious nature. . . .

As encounters with the Other, UFO abductions are essentially religious. Humanity seems to innately separate the prosaic from the unfamiliar, and the sacred from the profane. Things which do not fit into the definitions of the familiar humanity tends to sacralize. The sacred, the numinous, is that which is "wholly other," something completely beyond the pale of human experience as normally considered. Abduction by aliens certainly falls into that category, and this is perhaps the reason for the tendency of abductees to interpret their experiences within some sort of religious framework. Whether they mean to or not, [UFOlogist] researchers, who devise interpretive scenarios, tend to encounter religion, and even resort to theologizing [which they call something else] about alternate realities and the final goal of human history. The otherness of the abduction phenomenon makes *religion* impossible to escape, and no understanding of the phenomenon can be complete without a consciousness of its religious nature.[67]

Whereas religion is timeless, our UFO experience is very much a creature of its relatively brief moment in time and space: on earth, and since the advent of the Cold War. Whitmore neatly grounds the otherworldly experience in collective postmodernist experiences particular to this planet:

The persuasiveness of UFOs in the popular consciousness has increased in recent years along with the number of abduction accounts. More interest in the phenomenon seemed to breed more accounts, which in turn increase the topic's popularity. Abduction accounts seem to absorb whatever details or issues are being currently described in the UFOlogical community, leading to the interesting observation that abduction researchers tend to find whatever they are currently looking for within abduction accounts to support the theory of the day. The increased suggestibility characteristic of the hypnotic state makes it virtually impossible for researchers to hide their biases. Details of previous accounts are repeated by other abductees, who pick them up from the hypnotist, from the media, or from UFO literature. The popular concerns of the day are invariably reflected in the abduction narrative; [for instance] now that East-West tensions have eased, worries about the environment replace the fear of nuclear war as facets of the abduction account.[68]

As earlier argued, the "abduction by aliens" stories, and the infotainment industry that supports them, are a *symptom* of a larger syndrome, a general "occultation" of the modernist mentality. Now we need to exhume the historical (perhaps even hysterical) sources of that syndrome. Now our pursuit necessarily becomes the historical evidence pointing to a modern reinvention of occultism.

NOTES

1. Jan H. Brunvand, *The Vanishing Hitchhiker: American Urban Legends and Their Meanings* (New York: Norton, 1981), pp. ix–x, 3, 5, 10, 15, 153, 187, 199.

2. Jan H. Brunvand, e-mail message, April 4, 1998.

3. For what immediately follows, see Larry Danielson, "Paranormal Memorates in the American Vernacular," in H. Kerr and C. L. Crow, eds., *The Occult in America: New Historical Perspectives* (Urbana: University of Illinois Press, 1986), pp. 196–217.

4. Ibid., pp. 197–98.

5. Ibid., pp. 200, 202.

6. Ibid., pp. 204, 207, 211.

7. E. R. Curtius, *European Literature and the Latin Middle Ages* (New York: Torchbooks, 1963), chap. 5, "Topics."

8. Specifically, see J. F. Moffitt, "Ignoble to Noble: The Native-American 'Sauvage' as Pictured by French Romantic Artists and Writers," *Gazette des Beaux-Arts* 123 (September 1999): 117–30; see also J. F. Moffitt and S. Sebastián, *O Brave New People: The European Invention of the American Indian* (Albuquerque: University of New Mexico Press, 1996), explaining the "alien" epithet and citing a bibliography of primary sources; see also F. Drimmer, ed., *Captured by the Indians: Fifteen Firsthand Accounts, 1750–1870* (New York: Dover, 1985).

9. See again Moffitt, "Ignoble to Noble."

10. For this apocryphal creature, see Moffitt and Sebastián, *O Brave New People*, pp. 115, 270–71, 280–87.

11. Carl Gustav Jung, *Flying Saucers: A Modern Myth of Things Seen in the Sky* (1959; reprint, New York: MJF Books, 1978), pp. 8, 82 (citing the Latin motto).

12. Ibid., pp. 8–14.

13. Ibid., pp. 13–14.

14. Ibid., pp. 19–20.

15. Ibid., pp. 16–17.

16. Joe Nickell, "Extraterrestrial Iconography," *Skeptical Inquirer* 21, no. 5 (September/October 1997): 19.

17. Elizabeth Loftus, *The Myth of Repressed Memory: False Memories and Allegations of Sexual Abuse* (New York: St. Martin's, 1996); see also H. Wakefield and R. Underwager, *Return of the Furies: An Investigation into Recovered Memory Therapy* (Chicago: Open Court, 1994).

18. See Morey Bernstein, *The Search for Bridey Murphy* (New York: Pocket Books, 1956), copyright page.

19. Ibid., pp. 133–35.

20. Ibid., pp. 168, 173–75.

21. Martin Gardner, *Fads and Fallacies in the Name of Science* (New York: Dover, 1957), pp. 315–20, 354–55; see also J. P. Chaplin, *Rumor, Fear, and the Madness of Crowds* (New York: Ballantine, 1959), chap. 9, "The Odyssey of Bridey Murphy, with Notes on the Hysterical History of Hypnotism."

22. For one rather specialized example of reshaped mythology, reconstructing the textual and iconographic evolution of "Saturn," from antiquity to the seventeenth century, see J. F. Moffitt, "Who Is the 'Old Man in a Golden Helmet'?" *Art Bulletin* 46, no. 3 (1984): 417–27.

23. Eusebius, as quoted in C. Mango, ed., *The Art of the Byzantine Empire, 312–1453* (Englewood Cliffs, N.J.: Prentice-Hall, 1972), pp. 16–17.

24. Gregory the Great, in C. Davis-Weyer, ed., *Early Medieval Art, 300–1150* (Englewood Cliffs, N.J.: Prentice-Hall, 1971), p. 48.

25. John Damascene, as quoted in Henry Maguire, *Art and Eloquence in Byzantium* (Princeton: Princton University Press), p. 114, n. 9.

26. Council Minutes, in Frank Chambers, *The History of Taste: An Account of the Revolutions of Art Criticism and Theory in Europe* (New York: Columbia University Press), pp. 5–6.

27. Whitley Strieber, *Communion: A True Story* (New York: Bantam, 1987), pp. 165–67; further anatomical *ekphraseis*, all absolutely conventionalized, are given on pp. 19–20, 57, 60–61, 78, 100, 148, 151, 156, 166–67, 170–71, 253–54 (n.b.: the paperback labels its category as "nonfiction").

28. *The Portable Oscar Wilde*, ed. R. Aldington (New York: Viking, 1946), pp. 314–15.

29. John E. Mack, as in C. D. B. Bryan, *Close Encounters of the Fourth Kind: Alien Abductions, UFOs, and the Conference at M.I.T.* (New York: Knopf, 1995), pp. 264–65.

30. F. Pacheco, *El arte de la pintura*, ed. B. Bassegoda i Hugas (Madrid: Cátedra, 1990), pp. 575–77, "Pintura de la Purísima Concepción de Nuestra Señora."

31. See J. F. Moffitt, *The Arts in Spain* (London: Thames & Hudson, 1998), esp. chap. 5.

32. Matthew of Janov, in Hans Belting, *Likeness and Presence: A History of the Image before the Era of Art* (Chicago: University of Chicago Press), p. 540 (for the sake of greater clarity, I have somewhat altered this translation of a translation, from Latin to German to English).

33. Alonso de Salazar Frías, as in Henry Kamen, *The Spanish Inquisition* (New York: Mentor, 1965), p. 208. Some of Goya's witchcraft scenes were specifically based on his reaction to reports of the Logroño *auto da fé*.

34. Inquisitorial verdict, as in William Christian, *Apparitions in Late Medieval and Renaissance Spain* (Princeton: Princeton University Press, 1981), p. 179; Castilian text, pp. 330–31.

35. Ibid., pp. 7, 9, 73, 213.

36. Belting, *Likeness and Presence*, p. 209.

37. William James, *The Varieties of Religious Experience* (New York: Mentor, 1958), pp. 371, 374.

38. Hopkins interview, as in Bryan, *Close Encounters of the Fourth Kind*, p. 392.

39. Mrs. X (name withheld out of courtesy), as quoted in ibid., pp. 22–23.

40. Joe Nickell, "A Fantasy Assessment Biography," *Skeptical Inquirer* (July/August 1997): 18–19; see also G. Reed, *The Psychology of Anomalous Experiences* (Amherst, N.Y.: Prometheus Books, 1988).

41. For the standard study on the FPP syndrome, see Sheryl C. Wilson and Theodore X. Barber, "The Fantasy-Prone Personality: Implications for Understanding Imagery, Hypnosis, and Parapsychological Phenomena," in *Imagery: Current Theory, Research, and Applications*, ed. A. A. Sheikh (New York: Wiley, 1983), pp. 340–90; see also R. E. Bartholomew and G. S. Howard, *UFOs and Alien Contact: Two Centuries of Mystery* (Amherst, N.Y.: Prometheus Books, 1998), pp. 248–73; Philip J. Klass, *UFO-Abductions: A Dangerous Game* (Amherst, N.Y.: Prometheus Books, 1989), chap. 20, "Fantasy-Prone Persons."

42. John E. Mack, *Abduction: Human Encounters with Aliens* (New York: Ballantine, 1995), p. 448 (my emphasis).

43. Bartholomew and Howard, *UFOs and Alien Contact*, pp. 266, 275.

44. The following statistics are from Bartholomew and Howard, *UFO and Alien Contact*.

45. Mack, *Abduction*, pp. 5, 6.

46. Randles data, as quoted in Bryan, *Close Encounters of the Fourth Kind*, p. 68.

47. Mark Rodeghier data, as quoted in ibid., p. 125.

48. UFOlogist, as quoted in ibid., p. 88.

49. Kenneth Ring data, as quoted in ibid., p. 440.

50. Jo Stone-Carmen data, as quoted in ibid., p. 128.

51. Elizabeth Slater data, as cited by John E. Mack, as quoted in ibid., p.

262; for the context of the Slater report, also its ideological repercussions among UFOlogists, see Klass, *UFO-Abductions*, chap. 11, "Psychological Profile."

52. See map in *Newsweek*, 23 May 1998, p. 8.

53. Alvin H. Lawson, "Hypnosis of Imaginary Abductees," in *Proceedings of the First International UFO Congress*, ed. Curtis Fuller (New York: Warner, 1980), pp. 195–238.

54. Mack, *Abduction*, p. 433, citing the research of M. Rodeghier and R. Hall, as published in various True Believer journals.

55. M. Moravec, "UFOs as Psychological and Parapsychological Phenomena," in *UFOs, 1947–1987: The Forty Year Search for an Explanation*, ed. H. Evans and J. Spencer (London: Fortean Press, 1987), pp. 293–312; see also John A. Saliba, "UFO Contactee Phenomena from a Socio-Psychological Perspective: A Review," in *The Gods Have Landed: New Religions from Other Worlds*, ed. James R. Lewis (Albany: State University of New York Press, 1995), pp. 206–50 (both essays come with extensive bibliographies).

56. Moravec, "UFOs as Psychological and Parapsychological Phenomen."

57. Besides other publications already cited here, especially they should all study D. H. Rawcliffe, *Occult and Supernatural Phenomena* (New York: Dover, 1960), and William Sargant, *The Mind Possessed: A Physiology of Possesion, Mysticism, and Faith Healing* (New York: Penguin, 1975).

58. G. N. M. Tyrrell, *Apparitions* (New York: Collier, 1963), pp. 88, 121, 163–64.

59. Whitley Strieber, as quoted in Klass, *UFO-Abductions*, pp. 206–207 (the second part of the quotation appears at the finale of Strieber's 1988 close-encounter, best-seller account, *Transformation*).

60. E. Hoffer, *The True Believer: Thoughts on the Nature of Mass Movements* (New York: Perennial Library, 1966); I have quoted (without cluttering my text with quotation-marks) from Sections 1, 3–5, 7, 10, 12–15, 18, 19, 26, 28, 30, 32, 34, 41, 57, 59, 62, 64, 91, 97, 117, 125.

61. Ibid., p. 125.

62. Andrew Newberg and Eugene D'Aquili, *Why God Won't Go Away: Brain Science and the Biology of Belief* (New York: Ballantine, 2001).

63. See Sharon Begley, "Religion and the Brain," *Newsweek*, 7 May 2001, pp. 51–57.

64. Ibid., p. 53.

65. John A. Saliba, in Lewis, *The Gods Have Landed*, pp. 41, 54; see pp. 42–53 for a detailed discussion of his points 1–7.

66. B. Downing, "Religion and UFOs," in *Encyclopedia of UFOs*, ed. Ronald Story (New York: New American Library, 1980), pp. 305–306.

67. John Whitmore, in Lewis, *The Gods Have Landed*, pp. 73–74.

68. Ibid., p. 80.

Chapter 12

Picturing and the Modern Reinvention of Occultism

"NEW AGE" OCCULTISM AND CREDULITY IN POSTMODERNIST CULTURE

Besides endless sightings of UFOs bearing ETs, a unique characteristic of modern (versus medieval) culture is its market mentality. By buying things—at the figurative late-capitalist "marketplace"—the postmodernist citizen expresses his/her individual "freedom," in effect, to make a purchase. Like other kinds of salable goods, beliefs are now on the market, and there is not just one for sale, as was the case in medieval times. Since there is now no single religious doctrine, we have instead many, those "alternative" religions. Now the credit card–bearing spiritual customer is offered a veritable menu of beliefs. Now called "New Age," the postmodernist spiritual menu is practically endless; it expands dynamically; it responds in a competitive way to market forces. This search for esoteric knowledge can, however, take many forms, given that such illumination is currently drawn from many diverse sources. The author of a book, appropriately called *The Occult Explosion*, underscores the importance of this underlying theme for the majority of New Age acolytes (i.e., contemporary occultists), even just folks, like you and me.[1]

All this fits in with the broader psychic-cultural environment in which we live. This is now called "postmodernism," and the pertinent psychic characteristics of the omnipresent, often oppressive, postmodernist syndrome are now recognized by alert cultural forensic surgeons. Its wider ramifications have been catalogued by Walter Truett Anderson, according to whom the givens of psychic life in the fully ripened postmodern era include the following, more or less fixed, notions:

1. Society is itself a social construction of reality. All the things that identify and define a "people"—such as its boundaries, its culture, its political institutions—are the (usually reified) products of earlier invention.

2. Individual identity is also a social construction of reality, and the concept of a "self" is different in different societies and at different stages of history.

3. We regard the collective beliefs of individuals (rather than the mind of God or the laws of history) as the ultimate repository of social reality (what is true is defined by what we all believe), and we know that beliefs can (perhaps should) be modified.

4. Consequently, all sectors of society are deeply interested in finding out what people believe—public opinion—and how to modify those beliefs—by advertising, propaganda, brainwashing, public relations, and so forth.

5. In a postmodern society we perceive life as drama, and our major issues involve the definition of personal roles and the fabrication of stories that give purpose and shape to social existence.

6. Public happenings have the quality of scenes created or stage-managed for public consumption. They are what Daniel Boorstin called "pseudoevents."

7. The esoteric schools [of postmodernist occultism] are particularly good at developing an ability to see the social construction of reality as arbitrary and illusory.[2]

As catalogued by Anderson (among other contemporary culture voyeurs), persistent postmodernist perceptions have it that "society is itself a social construction of reality," and that even "individual identity is also a social construction of reality," and that all our current beliefs have been consciously shaped, "modified," by the hidden establishment: "advertising, propaganda, brainwashing, public relations, and so forth."[3] Such a mentality is particularly conducive to theories of hidden "conspiracies," like one that still "covers up the truth about Roswell." The infotainment industry both makes and propagates these ever provocative "conspiracy theories."[4] Accordingly, we cultural *cognoscenti* all must collectively subscribe to the notion that "public happenings have the quality of scenes created or stage-managed for public consumption. They are what Daniel Boorstin called 'pseudoevents.'" Finally, as we *really* need to be reminded, in postmodernism the followers of New Age (aka occult) beliefs "are particularly good at developing an ability to see the social construction of reality as arbitrary and illusory."

To establish a useful context for a UFOlogy spawning belief in alien abductions in the particular instance, one needs again to emphasize the fact of the present-day widespread infiltration of esoteric beliefs into contemporary society, New Age culture at its most popular levels. This is not a difficult endeavor given existing studies of the phenomenon.[5] When studying the infiltration of occultist phenomena in contemporary popular culture, it is again useful to point out that we are no longer dealing with the likes of modern Theosophy, a fairly sophisticated belief system that must be learned. Unlike the more recent manifestations of esotericism, typical among its contemporaries, a century ago Theosophy was above all (and still is) a unified, quasiphilosophical, neotheological belief system.[6] Conversely, New Age occultism is scattered, decidedly untheological, and generally not very philosophical.

Mainly, the revived esoteric experience is popular, in the most literal sense of the word: it is for and of the general populace, plebes who need not be learned in order to reap the proffered spiritual benefits. The variety and accessibility of New Age esotericism is perhaps best introduced by a journalist investigating the tribal folkways of a fairly typical pack of middle-class adolescents in an affluent suburb of San Francisco, Marin County:

> Besides sex, [fifteen-year-old] Marlene's other new interest that summer [of 1975] was the occult. . . . Of course, in a teen-age subculture, where one's [astrological] sign was often better known than one's name, everybody believed: in astrology, UFOs and extrasensory perception, or their Eastern analogues, the *I-Ching*, tarot cards and the mysteries of the pyramids. Even the merits of such harder-to-swallow occult phenomena as black magic, witchcraft and demonology were generally accepted. To most of the kids in Marlene's new circle of friends, the laws of the occult were as axiomatic as the laws of geometry—and far more widely known.[7]

If you think this catalogue of credulity represents only the kinky interests of a bunch of drugged-out kids, then take a hard look at the newspaper to which you probably subscribe. Undoubtedly, it has a regular contribution of syndicated astrological prognostications—just as horoscopes appear, for instance, in most of the European newspapers one may care to peruse. Is it mere coincidence that the University of California at Berkeley offered its first B.A. degree in "magical studies" in 1970, thus becoming the first reputable academic institution in history to legitimize the subject? Many have since followed. That was the same year in which the first Festival of the Occult Arts was put on in New York at the Fillmore East, a rock-concert hall. (Somewhat to the surprise of the entrepreneur, Bill Graham, three times the expected audience turned up.) In the summer of 1971 eighteen psychic tours of the British Isles were scheduled (at £350 per head). In the 1950s the German Institute of Public Opinion found that 29 percent of a national sampling affirmed a connection between human fate and the stars, and in mid-1988 we found that the president of the United States was governed "by the stars" (also by his wife, a very determined lady). Several years later another first lady had "spirit conversations" with the late Eleanor Roosevelt. Walk into any well-furbished bookstore and you will see shelves of publications dealing with such topics as inspirational readings, self-help, metaphysics, and religion. Many of these should be shelved with the larger collection there: *occultism.* Occultism has, in short, unquestionably become a commonplace expression of the *vox populi;* it is central to the popular, neopagan, postmodernist audience culture.[8]

Twenty years ago (and even now, to a lesser degree), paperback best-sellers on college campuses were several books by Carlos Castaneda. Now known to have been born in 1925 in Cajamarca, Peru, his real name is Araña, that is, Carlos César *Araña* Castaneda; he died in Westwood, California, in April 1998. Castaneda's paperbacks, ten of them, spelled out in considerable detail his spiritual close encounters with an American Indian shaman, Don Juan. These purported to be fact, and, indeed, one of his tomes had actually been presented—and accepted in 1972—as a Ph.D. dissertation in anthropology at UCLA, hence Castaneda's insistence on documentary proof, embellished with footnotes. As you must know, Native Americans are naturally (even notoriously) in touch with profound spiritual vibes, just as white folks are not, which is why they have to buy Castaneda's paperback enlightenment. Carlos's handy paperback manuals of apparently inexhaustible aboriginal wisdom—*The Teachings of Don Juan: A Yaqui Way of Knowledge* (1968), *A Separate Reality* (1971), *Journey to Ixtlán* (1972), *Tales of Power* (1974), and so on—made him *over one million dollars.* Alas, recent serious research (not pursued, of course, by Dr. Castaneda) reveals his works to be an example of "a slowly unfolding *occult fiction.*" Their lucrative popularity (whatever their bogus purpose) has been described by David Murray as a product of "the modern concern for the paranormal, with its broad ecological and holistic assumptions about the natural world and its relation to a development of psychological insights."[9] Castaneda's pseudoscholarly charlatanism is typical pop-cult scripture, just more exotic.

Equally popular, but considerably less anthropological, is the cult of Scientology (formerly "Dianetics") espoused by the late L. Ron Hubbard (1911–1986), originally a *science fiction* writer. Scientology paperback books are widely advertised on TV: we loved the ejaculating volcano motif, since made into another blockbuster movie. Dianetics-Scientology is a kind of self-help psychotherapy, much subscribed to by, among other hypo-intellectual heavyweight cultural icons, multimillionaire baby-boomer Hollywood stars, many of whom barely possess a high school diploma. As Nat Freedland comments, "Scientology is not occultism, but it competes in the metaphysical marketplace for the Groovy Culture's losers who are seeking desperately for One Simple Answer [and it] puts itself forward as a rational, updated version of the occult tradition's self-perfection techniques."[10] It must work; at last count (theirs), Dianetics-Scientology had a worldwide paying membership of some 15 *million* devotees; that figure, by the way, is greater than the total population of Peru (for instance). Incorporated as "a church," hence tax-free, the moguls of Scientology get to keep all their plentiful receipts.

Pornography, using wholly different materials, also proves immensely profitable for having its own targeted mass-audience culture but, alas, and just like the rest of us, pornographers must pay taxes on their profitable goods. Another expanding manifestation of the world-wide occult explosion is, of course, the ubiquitous UFO experience and, again, the Heavens Gate holocaust demonstrates the extreme, even lethal, potential effects of its universal, and enduring, appeal.

To sum up, cultural climate determines levels of credulity, and post-modernism presently seems the most credulous of all post-medieval cultures. Maybe the problem is mostly local; since the vast majority of the lurid alien abductions take place in America, the preamble to the Bill of Rights perhaps now needs to read "All men, and women, too, are created equally gullible."[11] If that wasn't sufficient, then there is always money: that is always something worth serious consideration in America. As Walter Kendrick, a historian of popular culture, wryly notes, "At the end of the twentieth century, fortunes can be made by persuading a tiny portion of the world to fork over, individually, tiny sums by providing specialized products aimed at audiences that know what is expected of them." Whether for occult thrills or for vanguard artistic profundity, there are in abundance those postmodernist audience cultures he labels "coteries and in-groups [and] voluntary ghettos . . . aggressively repelling the uninitiated."[12] As P. T. Barnum earlier put it, and rather decisively, "Every crowd has its silver lining."

Typical to New Age wisdom [*sic*] is the pursuit of celebrity. But none of this is strictly "modern." Two millennia ago, Cicero stated that the pursuit of *gloria-celebritas* is the prime impulse for all human endeavor: *"Gloria est frequens de aliquo fama cum laude"* (*Rhetorica* 2.166). If not opting for philosophical profundity or warlike prowess, then the postmodernist tribal subcultures now vicariously settle for the outer trappings of visual celebrity, sometimes just the mere brush with celebrity will do. So we learned again, in September 1997, from the commercial feeding-frenzy subsequent to the violent demise of Princess Di, the foremost visual celebrity of her time. According to an April 1998 poll published in *People* magazine, asked whether "A century from now, who'll be more famous—Princess Di or Albert Einstein?" the dismal results were: Di, 66 percent; Einstein, 33 percent. Nonetheless, just like our lionized ETs, the late Diana was a corporealized entity unlikely to have ever been actually seen in the flesh by her thronging devotees. Both ethereal creatures seemed to have descended from a "higher plane," one well beyond our mundane existence; we have experienced both wholly through the mass media endlessly reproducing their distinctive portraiture.

Even though we may doubt that even 0.001 percent of the entire planetary population had ever actually beheld Di with their very own devotion-filled eyes, we do know that nearly everybody would instantly recognize her endlessly reproduced portraiture, and that each would respond instantly with a pronounced *emotional reaction* to that iconic image. The same holds true for our postmodernist ET portraiture: instant recognition and instant emotional response (figs. 1, 4, 5, 15–22). As to the "why," in both cases that seems answered by a journalist decrying the posthumous Diana spectacle: "Evidently many scores of millions of people lead lives of such anesthetizing boredom, emotional aridity and felt insignificance that they relish any opportunity for vicarious involvement in larger events. . . . The media turn the world into an echo chamber and establish for the promptable masses the appropriate 'reaction' to events. Mass hysteria is a riveting spectacle, whether it occurs at a Nuremberg [Nazi] rally or a rock concert."[13] Novelist Kurt Vonnegut (in *Timequake*, 1997) guesstimates the number of all people with a life worth living at 17 percent, a likely figure. Vonnegut did not, however, label those fortunate few the "True Believers."

SYMBOLIST CULTURE: MODERN OCCULTISM HISTORICALLY DEFINED

Having now seen something (in chapter 9) of the early surface of the life of the UFO experience, showing its first fumbling attempts to find a distinctive "scientific" basis, we will later want to look at this development in its larger, cultural setting: "modernism." In this case, the specific art-historical context is "Symbolism." Symbolism is the accepted art-historical term designating the avant-garde culture of the *fin de siècle*, and that is, unquestionably, the milieu in which the UFO experience, bursting upon the scene between 1896 and 1897, initially demanded attention. This was, in fact, just the kind of cultural period that had been envisioned, three decades beforehand, by the French occultist writer Éliphas Lévi (né Alphonse-Louis Constant, 1810–1875), for this is an epoch when art was actually to become directed, just as he foresaw, by "magicians of reason and gracious mathematicians of harmony."[14]

This was also the epoch in which self-styled "modern art" was first to be vigorously, and successfully, marketed by savvy entrepreneurs. The market dealers typically described themselves as "enlightened" and "visionary." Theirs was an "altruistic" mission of displaying contemporary artistic expression for the public good, and their notions of spiritual "enlightenment" became central to an emerging definition of "avant-gardism."[15] Accordingly, also to be explored in this chapter is a much broader context shaping the Symbolist milieu: the rise in mainstream, nineteenth-century French cultural life of "spiritual" occultism.[16] Microcosm and macrocosm, Symbolism and occultism, these were the latent historical factors that were to determine the future (after 1910) course of the distinctive "modern" mentality, that which gave birth to the UFO experience half a century later.

Empowered by retrospection, historians increasingly perceive the identity of some principal components impelling a once largely unique, now still ubiquitous, historical syndrome called "modernism." In character as much mental as physical, modernism is a psychological phenomenon which pertains as much to art as to all other factors of contemporary life, and it has done so for well over a century. Three basic elements essential to the early historical evolution of modernism were, according to John Willet (writing in 1978), occultism, anarchism, and the mass media.[17] That second essential component of modernism—anarchism—need only be peripherally mentioned; initially described as "radicalism," it was later to be known as "terrorism," and that now signals a commonplace kind of postmodernist mood-symptom. However, given our present-day condition, a total immersion in so-called pop culture, we need especially emphasize the role of the third component, the mass media,[18] especially in its role as the most obvious materialist vehicle for the universal propagation of some most antimaterialist thoughts (as shown in chapters 13 and 14). This chapter will instead deal in considerable detail with the historical installation of the first factor, occultism.[19]

Occultism, or the esoteric tradition, is the mass cult that is "hidden" (*occulta,* from *occulere,* to cover over, hide, conceal). Although profoundly affecting all levels of modernist European culture, occultism is customarily, but only very generally, discussed in its most obvious historical aspect as the "revival of mysticism." For instance (and like most historians), Willet only briefly mentioned that the esoteric renaissance of the Symbolist artists and writers arose from "a reaction against nineteenth-century materialism and the current secularization in both Germany and France, partly no doubt part of a sense that a great century was dying." However, he further remarked that *fin-de-siècle* esotericism represents "a development which can be felt throughout the French and Russian [and all other] Symbolist movements."[20] Later, in a provocative book describing *The Birth of Modernism* (1994), Leon Surette, a Canadian historian of literature, observes that, currently, "the scandal is scholarship's long-standing avoidance of the topic. . . . Occultism has been a subject not to be raised in polite company." Referring to the persistent "scholarly phobia of the occult" exhibited by academic chroniclers of the birth of modernist culture, Surette calls the baleful results "Occultophobia," and concludes that "modernism generally was an accommodation of the mysticism and occultism of the later nineteenth century to the relativism of the twentieth."[21]

Given our "esoteric" argument for the essential impulses propelling the UFO experience, it seems necessary to examine in more detail than is customary the phenomenology of occultism at the turn of the twentieth century. This involves an investigation into the nature of some radical transformations, beginning well over a hundred years ago and occurring on all levels of modernist consciousness, that were wrought by what may be called the esoteric tradition. Whereas commercial culture, the postmodernist matrix of the mass media, in no way invented the esoteric tradition, which itself has wholly pretechnological sources, the technologies of the mass media certainly have contributed to it by widely "publishing" its revived polemics. In short, commercial culture represents rampant materialism while the esoteric tradition is, of course, rampantly antimaterialist in its conventional proclamations. Nevertheless, without one there could not be the alienated other, for nowadays the esoteric tradition arises as a mostly invisible cultural antagonist to commercial ("materialist") culture. The two putative opponents, esotericism and commercialism, now meet incestuously in the arena of the infotainment industry (see figs. 9–15, 17–19).

At this stage of our comprehensive definition of an all-too-common-place modernist phenomenon, the esoteric tradition, we can avoid describing specific occultist doctrines, instead only identifying significant features generally establishing their emotional appeal; this is much as a sociologist might proceed.[22] We will now only limit ourselves to listing a number of features that may be called representative of a universal, modern "occult condition," that is, such as it has mainly existed since the late eighteenth century. First, we must define our terminology (with some help from Robert Galbreath).[23]

A significant point is to make a preliminary distinction between passive and active, theoretical and applied, "knowledge" (*gnosis*) of the esoteric sort. As a blanket term, "magic" seems to have once served to explain both the purpose and the function of all such esoteric endeavors; that term probably only acquired its more limited, or strictly applied, present-day definition late in the seventeenth century. Slightly later, during the eighteenth century, for the first time a conceptual distinction begins to be carefully drawn between the occult and science, both being considered in this sense as practices with distinctive theoretical peculiarities and physical applications. In this case, the equally ancient term "mystical" is properly limited to the more passive, also largely theory-less, experiences, teachings, and consciousness of a state of oneness with "ultimate reality."

Modern occultists of all stripes reject the term "supernatural"—and "superstition" even more so—because, so they state, the point of their esoteric "research" is to provide empirical, experiential, and experimental, natural "proofs" of matters heretofore accepted on faith. So labeled, that is, as being experiential and experimental, that kind of research thus becomes "pseudoscientific" in its approach. Much more recent, or post-Freudian, are the terms "psychic" and "paranormal"; both are, likewise, pseudoscientific. "Psychic research" usually refers to "psi phenomena": ESP, PK, mediumistic and survival phenomena, and so on. The "paranormal" kind of psi "researchers" wish likewise to avoid any taint of the "occult," even though they likewise prejudge the ontological status of their carefully selected phenomena. Nonetheless, all such self-designated "esoteric studies" still retain, in general, perfectly good nonoccult meanings of "abstruse" and "recondite." All these points prove specifically applicable to the present-day UFO experience.

In the broader historical perspective, as Galbreath correctly points out, the terms "'Metaphysics' and 'Occultism' are virtually interchangeable in the modern occult."[24] Another useful point is that, literally, "occult" has become something like a misnomer in the age of the mass media. Galbreath usefully recognizes that, for the most part, presently "occult knowledge is not 'secret' in [for example] Rosicrucianism, Spiritualism, Theosophy, and Anthroposophy in the sense of being withheld from the public. Rather, 'occult' knowledge is acquired through 'hidden' cognitive processes awakened through special training."[25] His further explanation of the specific kinds of secretiveness characterizing modern occult endeavor, which are typically—and most ironically—revealed by means of obviously unsecret *publications*, most commonly include revelations of

> (1) extraordinary matters that by virtue of their intrusion into the mundane world are thought to possess special significance (e.g., omens, portents, apparitions, prophetic dreams); (2) matters such as the teachings of the so-called mystery schools that are kept hidden from the uninitiated and the unworthy; and (3) matters that are intrinsically hidden from ordinary cognition and understanding but are, nonetheless, knowable through the awakening of hidden, latent faculties of appropriate sensitivity.[26]

Such revelations are, Galbreath observes, typically divergent from "the prevailing interpretations of science, historical scholarship, and 'common sense.'" Another important characteristic of the strictly modern kind of esoteric research are those published, "intellectualized versions of the occult which frequently adopt the language of science and parallel science's appeal to verifiable evidence—even while rejecting its philosophical limitations. . . . Attracted by the possibility of obtaining incontrovertible evidence in favor of their conclusions, the most characteristic form of modern occultism is the intellectualized, systematic synthesis aimed at the educated reader."[27] As shown by our historiography of the UFO experience given in chapter 9, this is exactly the kind of pseudoscientific, modernist occultism that UFOlogists practice.

For further definitions of the more significant features of modern occult condition, we are considerably in the debt of a leading student of the specifically occult content of modern literature, specifically the kind championed by Symbolist era authors, who has listed some twenty-one of these attributes. John Senior's findings may be summarized as follows.[28] True Believers in the esoteric tradition hold that the universe/cosmos represents a single, eternal, ineffable substance. These ideas are, chronologically considered, anything but modern. Occult precepts can be easily documented in the oldest surviving esoteric texts, some dating from the Hellenistic period. As the occultists, ancient and modern, would have it, this universal substance uniquely manifests itself to clairvoyants in certain privileged ways. Especially common are perceptions of "spirit," generally perceived as fire or light, or some other kind of luminosity, which—much later—is typically the way that our postmodernist ETs are said to make their epiphanies.

As is typically explained, all things progress or "evolve," and are mainly comprehended by means of dialectical but paired opposites: male-female, light-dark, vertical-horizontal, and so on. The goal of the occultists is to arrive at equilibrium, or "harmony," an elusive, essentially metaphorical condition generally taken to represent a sign of mental and/or physical "health." As an apparently logical extension of such dialectical perceptions, occultists endlessly affirm that "things above are as they are below," meaning that, in so "corresponding," mind and matter become one. As the True Believer holds, all religions are just variations on a single transcendent, now lost, primordial unity. The oneness remains, of course, "hidden" to all those other, typically disparaged and/or nonmodernist, mainstream religions. Once perceived by the initiated, such subphysical emanations of light/spirit (etc.) are further taken to represent manifestations from "on high," from a variously named universal creator, demiurge, or logos, sometimes just vaguely labeled "The One" (more lately, "ET").

Occult knowledge of the onement represents what the occultists call "timeless wisdom," what was called in the Renaissance a *philosophia perennis*, which, like a universal solvent, cannot contain any single definition of itself. According to these ubiquitous, simultaneously symbolic and analogical, thought patterns, only the imagination is "real." Given this "fact," any analogy conceived by the unchecked imagination is as valid as any other pseudoscientific proof of metaphysical "correspondence." This has long been very much the standard buzzword among the esotericist coteries; the term was coined by Swedenborg. Once one *believes* in the truth of such "correspondences," then a pseudoscientific knowledge of the spiritual can purportedly be gained by study of the (typically disparaged) "material world," and vice versa. In all cases, it is tacitly understood that consistent investigative methodology and evaluative judgments are best avoided. This observation is especially applicable to the UFO experience and its ET crewmen.

However one arrives at the realization of the latent (*occulta*) correspondences, it is accepted that "man" lies at the center of occultist thoughts. The human body is, accordingly, taken to represent the particular "sign" of creation in the widest sense. The perceptible operations of the universe, "macrocosm," are often symbolized in the shape of a living man, as the emblematic sign of the "microcosm." Since men are created by sexual means, then it logically follows that the sex act—the microcosmic image of "creation"—is both a divine sign and a gift from on high, or "*au delà*" in the terminology of modern French esotericism. As an attribute of the divine, neatly dividing itself into male and female components, conjoined sex/creation represents harmony and perfection. In the sex act, man supposedly achieves his own inherently female nature and thus becomes symbolically *androgynous*, transmuted into one flesh, and thus made "whole." Not surprisingly, while fascinated by the human reproductive system, the ETs are said themselves to be androgynous (see fig. 5).

The supreme task of mankind is, therefore, self-realization. To know thyself—"*nosce te ipsum*"—is to be everything, to become self-realized; this is the major goal of the New Age endeavor. It is the means to attain a progressive discovery, achieved through illuminist initiation, that is realized in "passages." Such occultist passages are traced through the successively ascending layers and stages of the human psyche. Having once gained (usually elusive) self-realization, certain occultist "supermen" (having, of course, many other names: e.g., "ET") then turn back, "descend," to help their unrealized fellow beings. From this lofty viewpoint, the uninitiated are seen only to feebly exist in metaphorical spiritual darkness, situated somewhere downwards and below (*vers là-bas*, according to the French esotericists). Spiritual descent finally crashes upon the dark, and typically dreary, "materialist plane." The occultist *Uebermenschen* "enlighten" their ignorant fellow men, and they do so through arduous practice, grace, virtue, experience, and all the rest. A good abduction experience also helps.

Standing metaphorically well above the rest of uninitiated men, esotericist supermen (ETs, too) are also to be visibly recognized by their often emblematic distinguishing attributes. The signs of their imaginative super existence may include distinctive tonsure, decorative accessories and badges, circumcision and tattooing, peculiar ritualistic dress, eccentric gestures and behavior patterns, some of which often token androgynous sexuality (see fig. 9). On this level, as on all the rest, one notes an obsessive preoccupation with symbols. Since the mystagogue's higher truths cannot be immediately apprehended by uninitiated minds, they must be conveyed to these lesser and unempowered vessels by and through *symbols*. In this sense, the esoteric symbol is understood to represent the common meeting ground between the striving ego and its ineffable goal. Besides resorting to unique and often extremely complicated symbolic systems, which are themselves generally taken to be "empowered" in order to affect less-developed minds on their unconscious levels, esoteric adepts typically form organized brotherhoods. These spiritual communities are essential in order to facilitate their all-important, and decidedly evangelical work of self-realization; one such was called Heaven's Gate (fig. 5). Their obsessive preoccupation with one's illumination/enlightenment—in short, with one's own ego—is, in short, *narcissism*, pure and simple.

The functional manifestation of the empowered ego is magic, and "magic" may be, more often than not, opportunistically called something else. Whatever we (or they) choose to call it, the tangible products of the esoteric tradition are, at bottom, physical display-patterns of the omnipotence of individual thought, freedom, and will. In sum, esoteric "enlightenment" and occult "vision" are the actual signs of a perception of "superior realities," and those clairvoyant, highly privileged, insights "penetrate" through to what lies beyond the phenomenal world. What we skeptics might call "the real world" (lowercase) is, according to standard occultist doctrine, the only aspect of "reality" accessible to the ignorant mob, meaning the not-yet-initiated. That also means "us," or, as they always put it, "them."

The historical conditions governing outbreaks of the esoteric tradition are diverse. As a rule, however, the common starting point of occultism in modernist eras seems "anxiety," particularly the kind induced by abrupt technological and social change. Occultism represents a more or less natural, human psychological reaction to unsettling times. For the UFO experience the obvious triggers were the Cold War and impending nuclear holocaust, later the millennium (see chapters 8, 9, 10). Whatever its many names, the occultist viewpoint typically represents an elitist and highly privileged, thus decidedly *anti*democratic, "clairvoyant" vision. In the end, the occultist position postulates that only the creative imagination is real. Therefore, only self-acknowledged adherents to the esoteric tradition, also including their officially processed initiates, can become privy to either imaginative faculties or to creative impulses. As for the rest of benighted humanity, they must forever remain imprisoned within spiritual darkness, and thus they intractably continue as "outsiders," and so remain forever alienated from the privileged pale of esotericism. Again, that "they" really means "*us*."

MODERN OCCULTISM AND ART AS DEFINED BY ÉLIPHAS LÉVI

That these primordial themes certainly did repeatedly achieve prominence in widely read occultist literature of the modernist era is a point best proven by reference to the easily accessible texts of "Éliphas Lévi," himself a wonderfully emblematic sign of his age, just like the UFO experience is for ours. My guess (for no one seems ever to have made a census) is that nearly all the Symbolist poets read, perhaps even owned, Lévi's decidedly poetic expositions of the esoteric wonders. Lévi was a figure now generally acknowledged to be the most important synthesizer of esoterica in nineteenth-century France.[29] Unquestionably, Lévi's popular publications repeatedly discuss (even verbally "illustrate") all those standard occultist issues signaled by John Senior in his discussion of *fin-de-siècle* Symbolist era literature.

For instance, Lévi stated that "man is born in the bondage of his passions, but he can reach emancipation through intelligence." Having announced his grand theme of imaginative or spiritual liberation, Lévi then addresses this concern to the one of those exalted types whom we have called the "superman," he who magnanimously liberates his fellows from ignorance; as Lévi repeatedly affirmed, "those who are in liberation should govern those who are [still] in bondage." Nevertheless, this mission of emancipation, "the revelation of Occult Secrets," is to be a literally secret operation: "Woe to those who lay bare the secret of divine generation to the impure gaze of the crowd. Keep the sanctuary shut!"[30] The historical reason for this commonplace injunction, expressive of both power and privilege, is self-apparent to Lévi, and to his many followers: "Initiation became an exclusive privilege of high castes."[31]

Occultism, under its many guises and names, is nearly always the expression of the esoteric union of imagination and will, with the former serving the ends of the latter. The imagination conceives of signs and symbols; by the means of these, the will works its way and acts upon the phenomenal world. This idea was so stated by Éliphas Lévi, and some years before the official advent of the so-called Symbolist period, itself notoriously advocating a host of esoteric signs and symbols—so do postmodernist academics. Lévi affirms: '

> The Will is omnipotent when it is armed with the living forces of Nature. Thought is idle and dead until it manifests by word or sign; it can, therefore, neither spur nor direct Will. The Sign, being the indispensable form of thought, is the necessary instrument of Will. The more perfect the Sign, the more powerfully is the thought formulated, and the Will is consequently directed with more force. . . . Intelligence and Faith, the Intelligence of Nature and Faith in its eternally Active Cause—of such is the life of Signs.[32]

Besides making manifest what might be called the typical sociological patterns, particularly the exclusionary biases, common to the esoteric coterie, Lévi also conveniently delineates its perennial, basic themes. One of these is the dynamic notion of an animistic or vitalist universe, the kind apparently later delineated in manifestos by the futurist artists and writers. The invisibly "living world" is expressive of a "Spiritualist" life beyond death, in which, Lévi states, "being is substance and life; life manifests by movement; movement is perpetuated by equilibrium; equilibrium is, therefore, the law of immortality."[33] This "law" is in fact pseudoscientific, merely basing itself upon the supposed operations of the world around us: "The secret of the Occult Sciences," Lévi affirms, "is that of Nature herself." Lévi's highly influential esotericism is, typically, a dialectical system, always seeking to prove the existence of "that Absolute, which is sought by the foolish and found only by the wise, which is the truth, the reality and the reason of Universal Equilibrium." As always, "such Equilibrium is the Harmony which proceeds from the Analogy of the Opposites."[34]

According to this omnipresent "Analogy of the Opposites," therefore, the timeless pursuit of the occult sciences "is the Absolute Science of Equilibrium. It is essentially religious; it presided at the formation of dogmas in the antique world and has [since] been thus the nursing mother of all civilizations."[35] In the larger sense, "this means that the universal movement is produced by the Analogies of Fixed and Volatile— the Volatile tending to be fixed and the Fixed to become volatile—thus producing a continual exchange between the modes of the One Substance, and from the fact of the exchange of the combinations of Universal Form in ever-lasting renewal." Whereas the preceding picture was strictly laid out according to ancient alchemical terminology, Lévi's conclusion seems specifically "modern," for mentioning "Science":

> Let it be certified: (1) that the life resulting from motion can only be maintained by the succession and the perfecting of forms; (2) that the Science of perpetual motion is the Science of life; (3) that the purpose of this [occult] Science is the correct apprehension of equilibriated influences; (4) that all renewal operates by destruction, each generation therefore involving a death and each death a generation. . . . It becomes fixed by the phenomena of polarization.[36]

Such ponderous pomposity, such sweeping generalizations, are too typical of all writings by occultists (but Lévi is by far one of the most readable). So much for the general commonplaces characterizing the esoteric literary style. Let us now consider some specifically "artistic" references drawn by Lévi.

To a skeptical postmodernist art historian, it is noteworthy that Lévi (and not at all uniquely among occultists) repeatedly calls occultism an "art." As he typically states, "It must not be forgotten that Transcendental Magic is called the Sacerdotal Art and the Royal Art."[37] Lévi takes as a maxim of his solitary pursuits a resounding slogan: "The Seal of Nature and of Art Is Simplicity."[38] Elsewhere, Lévi explained what may be called the historical necessity for the occultists' commonplace obsession with "imagist" signs and symbols. Lévi grandly announces that "the prophets spoke in parables and images, because abstract language was wanting to them, and because prophetic perception, being the sentiment of Harmony, or of Universal Analogies, translates naturally into images. Taken literally by the vulgar, these images become idols or impenetrable mysteries. The sum and succession of such images and mysteries constitute what is called Symbolism." One's logical conclusion then becomes a recognition that "the multiplicity of Symbols has been a book of poesy indispensable to the education of human genius."[39]

Finally, besides specifically, constantly, alluding to the occultist as an "artist" and a "symbolist," Lévi also neatly establishes the validity of our earlier assertion that large-scale occultist irruptions are mainly manifestations of "anxiety induced by change." According to the way that Lévi conveniently explained his situation back in 1860, "in the chaos of universal doubt, and amidst the conflict of science and faith, the great men and the seers figure as sickly artists, seeking the ideal beauty at the risk of their reason and their life." Unfortunately, in his age—and just as in ours, today—neither avant-garde nor bohemian "artists," neither marginal nor clairvoyant "occultists" are ever properly appreciated by society at large. Lévi laments:

> Genius is judged by the tribunal of mediocrity, and this judgment is without appeal, because, being the light of the world, Genius is accounted as a thing that is null and dead whenever it ceases to enlighten. The ecstasy of the Poet is controlled by the indifference of the prosaic multitude, and every enthusiast who is rejected by general good sense is a fool and not a genius. Do not count the great Artists as bondsmen of the ignorant crowd, for it is the crowd which imparts to their talent the balance of reason.[40]

Likewise, UFOlogists' enthusiastic "research" is commonly "rejected by general good sense."

OCCULTISM AND THE MODERN ARTIST
(EVEN THOSE WHO DRAW ETs)

The historical situation of the esoteric tradition, visibly infecting all levels of occidental modernism, is a complementary factor to a larger, ongoing problem of specific interest to this study. The late James Webb (1946–1980) was the most accomplished historian of the esoteric tradition and is the author of a monumental study collectively called "The Age of the Irrational." As he correctly and repeatedly emphasized, *occultism has always been of particular interest to the modern artist.* It may be pure coincidence, but we must recall that Budd Hopkins, who was first a painter with avant-garde leanings toward pictorial abstraction, was later called "the Typhoid Mary of covert UFO-abductions" by Philip Klass.[41] Viewed historically, this occult connection has basically to do with the frequently commented upon social stance of the modern artist. Arising from his sense of bohemian and/or avant-garde "alienation," the eventual result, stated Webb, was for him to take on the more positive "stance of the elect race."[42] So, since vanguard artists naturally feel *alienated*, it also makes perfect sense that they would also feel an affinity with other aliens, even the kind said to migrate from outer space.

As Webb further recognized, the haughty pose assumed by the beleaguered avant-garde artist is a functional parallel to the perennial "need among occultists to appear especially alert," and this is a persistent trait that we have already seen illustrated, way back in 1860, by Éliphas Lévi's writings. Webb concluded that, therefore,

> another group which proclaimed itself "elect" was that of the Artists. . . . Because of the juxtaposition of Occultist and Artist in Bohemia, occult teaching became the source to which the priests of this, one of the several secular religions, most easily turned. The two traditional patterns of redemption—the pursuit of the Beautiful, the Good, representing the search for Divine Union, whilst the descent into the Abyss is the alchemical process, the progress through the Mysteries, trial by ordeal— these became translated into terms of Art; but also of the Artist's life. Without these traditional [esoteric] bases, the mythical figure of the Artist would not be as it is popularly conceived. . . . There has always been something of the magical in the work of the artist. The ability to conceive and execute personal worlds, conceptual, visual, abstracted, is, by definition, out of the ordinary [even "otherworldly"]. . . . In any case, because Art itself had become a religion, the Artist naturally acquired the status of priest. . . . The Artist was at liberty—indeed compelled—to treat the standards of the world as if they did not exist.[43]

In his innovative overview of the real cultural conditions determining *The Birth of Modernism* (1993), literary scholar Leon Surette
was drawn to similar conclusions:

> Modernism continued the Romantic celebration of passion, revelation,
> and revolution. . . . The modern occult makes the claims of the
> Romantic and the modern artist. Both the artist and the occultist claim
> access to truth through passion or ecstasy rather than through labor
> and thought. Both regard themselves as prophets. . . . The secular arts,
> religion, dream, and hallucination are all thought to belong to a single
> imaginative realm, thereby enfolding religion, art, and psychology into
> a single field of inquiry.[44]

In order to solve the riddle of the ubiquity of a given postmodernist ET icon
(figs. 1, 4, 16–22), the present, detective-like investigation similarly needs
to raise the complementary issues of religion, art, and psychology, then
enfold these, and many others, into a single field of inquiry.

In his fascinating and significant overview, *The Cult of the Avant-
Garde Artist* (1993), Donald Kuspit reminds us of the currently
entrenched role of the "modernist artist as the symbol of heroic resistance to all that is oppressive and corrupt in bourgeois civilization," with
the standard result now being "an adulatory fetishization of the artist as
such," and that worshipful response is "classically modernist." Resting on
laurels garnered since the Renaissance, "in sum, the myth of the avant-
garde artist involves the belief that he is *initiated* into the mysteries of
primordial experience, that he is more spontaneous—primordially
expressive—than anyone else." A key component of this mythically pro-
portioned, "initiated" creator-mentality is, Kuspit states, a conventionally
invoked "mysticism of the [artistic] medium," which "induces hallucinatory images," allowing the ecstatic artist "to fuse symbolically with the
medium," due to his unique "kind of habitual intoxication."[45]

For such notions of creative *initiation*, especially the kind characterized by "habitual intoxication," Kuspit assigns major responsibility to
Friedrich Nietzsche (1844–1900). He was an influential German philosopher who, well over a century ago, described at some length the role of
"the artist-healer," and especially the function of his "aesthetic state as
one of hallucination or hallucinatory exaggeration, brought on by self-
intoxication." And, says Kuspit, before Nietzsche, there was "Friedrich
Schlegel's conception of artists as 'Brahmins, a higher caste: ennobled
not by birth but by free self-consciousness,' and 'at the threshold of
things.'" Kuspit believes, and with good reason, that such commonplace
poses have long since "become a farce."[46]

More particularly, Kuspit acidly observes how avant-garde allegiance represents an identifiable "belief system," one which psychologically aligns itself with membership in (nonartistic) *cults*, another ubiquitous modernist social phenomenon. Both kinds of spiritual tribes, or what Kuspit calls "charismatic groups," either occultists or artists, reveal, as he notes, the following "psychological elements" in common: "(1) a shared belief system, and (2) they sustain a high level of social cohesiveness, (3) are strongly influenced by the group's behavioral norms, and (4) impute charismatic or sometimes divine power to the group or its leadership." Such "ideological totalism," committed to what Kuspit calls "milieu control," commonly employs "mystical manipulation or planned spontaneity." Likewise, both kinds of tribal expression are characterized by "the demand for purity and the cult of confession." Other standard operational features observed by Kuspit to inform the cult of orthodox-modernist creation myths are "sacred science," "the loading of the language," and "the principle of doctrine over person."[47]

Insistence upon the sacerdotal essence of modern art was however a notion first widely proclaimed, then popularized in published art theory by the Symbolists. With perhaps different nomenclature, the self-inflating idea—the artist as priest and prophet—is still very much with us. Examples abound in the rhetoric attending its strictly modernist, nearly mythic, manifestations. In 1913, Guillaume Apollinaire states that the understood goal of *les peintres cubistes* was "to express the grandeur of metaphysical forms," to which end, "they discard more and more the old art of optical illusion and local proportion." Specifically due to this newly installed, collective drive to abstraction, "this is why contemporary art . . . possesses some of the characteristics of great, that is to say, religious art."[48] In 1914, Franz Marc proclaims the fact of "our European desire for abstract form," adding that this kind of "art is our religion, our center of gravity, our truth."[49] In 1920, Paul Klee declared that "art is a simile of the Creation," and due to the opportune intervention of the godlike modern artist, "out of abstract elements a formal cosmos is ultimately created." Moreover, this new abstract-formal picture "we discover to be so closely similar to the Creation that to turn an expression of religious feelings, or religion itself, into reality a breath is sufficient."[50]

Besides unilaterally designating himself to be a divinely inspired and/or godlike creator, the modern artist also typically envisions himself to be a prophet: he foresees the shape of the future and, typically by means of "the abstract spirit," he leads the people (implicitly compliant) toward the promised Utopia. Wassily Kandinsky boldly proclaimed this prophetic-messianic function of the modern artist in 1911: "The abstract spirit takes possession first of a single [artistic] human spirit; later it governs an ever-increasing number of people. At this moment, individual artists are subject to the spirit of the time [*Zeitgeist*] which forces them to use particular forms related to each other and which, therefore, also possess an external similarity," wholly abstract in this case.[51] Apollinaire said very much the same thing in 1913:

> Poets and artists plot the characteristics of their epoch, and the future docilely falls in line with their desire. . . . The energy of art imposes itself on [enlightened] men, and becomes for them the plastic standard of the period. . . . All the art-works of an epoch end up resembling the more energetic, the more expressive, and the most typical art-works of the period.[52]

In 1915, Daniel-Henry Kahnweiler spoke of Pablo Picasso as a representative "artist who is possessed of the divine gift, genius," and who likewise provides

> proof that the appearance of the aesthetic product is conditioned in its particularity by the spirit of the time. . . . The artist, as the [self-appointed] executor of the unconscious plastic will of mankind, identifies himself with the style of the period, which is the expression of this [collective] will.[53]

All of these familiar slogans are however essentially "old hat"; indeed, such notions can be traced back to the very foundations of the idea, as incarnated *verbum*, of the avant-garde. That provocative psychic entity had in fact been initially proclaimed in the third decade of the nineteenth century by Henri de Saint-Simon. With historical hindsight, it is interesting to observe how the term *avant-garde*, now so standard in English or German, is (of course) originally French. It was borrowed from military usage, where it originally designated a sort of cavalry action, an armed reconnaissance, a perilous and fugitive sweep behind the front lines, then directly into enemy territory. *Nomen est omen*: the larger program impelling the militant-esoteric front of the avant-garde is at once pseudo-militaristic, utopian, and revolutionary. All the rhetorical essentials of a forthcoming, prophetic, and militarized (albeit uniformed in mufti), artistic avant-garde had been laid out well over a century and a half ago.

In 1845, a little-known Fourieriste, Gabriel-Desiré Laverdant, published an equally little known treatise, *De la mission de l'art et du rôle des artistes*. In this presently obscure work, we find the same kind of prescription for messianic prophetic insight and radical action as those just quoted.

Laverdant's statement also represents a precocious proclamation of the now-hackneyed themes of the initiatory function of art, so transforming it into a prognostic instrument for radical social action leading, so we are told, to something like moral reform for all society. According to Laverdant:

> Art, the expression of society, manifests, in its highest soaring, the most advanced social tendencies: it is the forerunner and the revealer. Therefore, to know whether art worthily fulfills its proper mission as initiator, where the artist becomes truly of the avant-garde, one must know where Humanity is itself going, know [as an artist] what the destiny of the human race actually is. . . . Along with the hymn to happiness [the advanced artist pictures] the dolorous and despairing ode. . . . To lay bare with a brutal brush all the brutalities, all the filth, which are the base of our society, this is the mission of the avant-garde artist.[54]

Again, the immediate historical source of the ubiquitous, orthodox-modern to postmodern theory of the godlike, also prophetic, creator-artist myth is Symbolist art theory. The prophetic obsession is then obvious, particularly as we have the well-known example of a group of young Symbolist painters, themselves tending toward precociously abstracted "pure" figuration, who collectively called themselves *les Nabis*, "the Prophets." Their own role model was Paul Gauguin. One additionally supposes that these artists (Sérusier, Denis, Bonnard, Ranson, Roussel, Vallatton, and so on) knew that the old Hebrew word, *nabi*, variously connoted (as in 1 Sam. 9:9, 19; 10:1, 6–13, 25), besides "prophet," also priest, prognosticator, deliverer-redeemer, magus, dream-interpreter, seer, and the divinely designated author and spokesman for Yahweh-God.

For further confirmation of a polyvalent nabi-prophet thesis, we have, for instance, the earlier, and rather typical, precedent of Gauguin in 1888. Besides proclaiming a Symbolist given, that "art is an abstraction," Gauguin then adds another, by then routine, commonplace, that "creating like our Divine Master is the only way of rising toward God."[55] Thus, it seemed only fitting that Gilbert-Albert Aurier would later refer, in 1890, to Vincent van Gogh (fig. 25), "a terrible, maddened genius, often sublime, sometimes grotesque, always near the brink of the pathological." As Aurier explains, that trait of "maddened genius" was of course a positive factor; even more so was the Dutchman's world-mission, as "a messiah, a sower of truth, one who would regenerate the decrepitude of our art, and perhaps of our imbecilic and industrial society, [for] he has delighted in imagining a renewal of art."[56]

Elsewhere in his magnificent two-volume historical study of the modern esoteric tradition, James Webb draws a wider, and again quite correct, conclusion regarding the relation between what Webb aptly calls the "Occult Establishment" and the contemporary art establishment. Webb asserts, "Illuminated Art derives from Occultism and much modern art is indirectly illuminated, or directly 'occult,'" and Webb then points out specifically how

> this alliance began in Paris of the 1890s, when the Occult Revival coincided exactly with the Symbolist movement, and the Symbolists drew a great part of their inspiration from the Occultists. Occult theories resulted in the conception of the Artist as a saint and a magician, while his art became less and less representative of ordinary reality and hinted at things "beyond."[57]

At this point, Webb again underscores the crucial role of the Symbolists, the creators of *fin-de-siècle* art and theory, in the formation of those attitudes which most tellingly characterize much of elitist modernist cultural phenomena. According to Webb:

> From this departure of the Symbolists, from the universe of agreed discourse for private or superior worlds, has sprung the tampering with "everyday" reality which has become so central a feature of modern art. Naturally, similar developments were going on elsewhere, just as the reaction against the tyranny of Reason occurred in other places. But Paris remained the hub from which the magic influences radiated, the center of artistic and occult experiment.[58]

For art historians, the major interest of the Symbolist period, roughly occupying a time frame between 1880 and 1905, lies in the fact that it was the first time that strictly "modernist" principles of "abstraction" in the plastic arts became solidly entrenched in published art-theoretical treatises. Even though today a bias toward modernist abstraction remains largely unquestioned, the situation was quite different before 1890. Before the last decades of the nineteenth century, the traditional functions of art, defined broadly as being "true to Life" and "faithful to Nature," had never been questioned in their fundamental assumptions, at least not since the close of the Middle Ages. Retrospectively viewed, Impressionism represented a climax of the reigning naturalistic tradition and, immediately following, Symbolism changed all that, and in a most decisive fashion.

As becomes obvious by a simple glance at the chronology of the events recounted here, the initial UFO experience (1896–1897; fig. 28) must similarly, like the historical rise of pictorial abstraction, have been—somehow—a typical product of *fin-de-siècle* culture. This is the age referred to by Kandinsky in his influential book, *Über das Geistige in der Kunst* (Concerning the spiritual in art, 1912). The Russian mystic artist, himself a committed Theosophist, said he was writing at the post-Symbolist threshold of "the great epoch of the Spiritual [*Epoche des Geistige*], which is already beginning, or, in embryonic form, begun already yesterday." The Symbolist period, so recently passed, "provides," says Kandinsky, "and will provide the soil in which a kind of monumental work of art must come to fruition." As we have already observed, for Kandinsky and his fellow True Believers, truly "spiritual" art would necessarily be abstract and, moreover, abstraction is the visible, even ethically significant, sign of one's essentially ethical retreat from the material world. As it turns out, certainly Kandinsky did not himself invent this dematerialized art; he was merely one of its more verbal spokesmen, and certainly he was not the first to pursue nonobjective imagery.

According to recent scholarship,[59] the critical shift in the appearance of the plastic arts, beginning around 1875, was signaled by a decisive movement from naturalism to abstraction, and this crucial shift was as much a matter of intrinsic content as it was of extrinsic form. The strictly physical significance of "abstraction" for the Symbolist-modernist painter was made unmistakable in a famous dictum expressed by Maurice Denis in 1890. According to this often repeated early modernist slogan, "It is well to remember that a picture—before being a battle horse, a nude woman, or some anecdote—is essentially a plane surface covered with colors, assembled in a certain order—*en un certain ordre assemblées.*"[60] For the Symbolists, besides representing "a certain assemblage" of autonomous motifs, "*l'abstraction*" also embodied a preference for "symbolic" over phenomenal color.

In the strictly symbolic sense, the move toward pure abstractions signals a preference for "signs" over physical perceptions, and amorphous psychic "moods" (*Stimmungen* in Kandinsky's terminology) over the banal facts of direct observation. For this further development, again Maurice Denis is an eloquent spokesman; as he wrote in 1909, "[E]motions or spiritual states, caused by any spectacle, bring to the imagination of the artists symbols, or the plastic equivalents [of these spiritual states]. These are capable of reproducing emotions or states of the spirit without it being necessary to provide the *copy* of the initial spectacle."[61] According to the considered conclusion of Maurice Denis: "Thus nature can be, for the artist, only a state of his own subjectivity. And what we call *subjective distortion is virtually style.*"[62]

Such subjectivist-spiritualist stylistic phenomena announced to be based upon "subjective distortion" were directly tied to certain fundamental, sweeping changes in basic metaphysical beliefs held by visual artists. As one troubled century merged into another, the new metaphysical systems were, naturally, reflective of similar ideological shifts apparent among most other classes of the European intelligentsia. The more strictly modernist equation—"abstraction equals spirituality"—was, for instance, early drawn by Paul Gauguin. In a letter sent from Pont Aven in 1888, he simply stated in an oracular fashion that "art is an abstraction." From this postulate it apparently directly follows that, according to Gauguin, "creating, like our Divine Master, is the only way of rising toward God."[63]

In sum, in the voluminous critical and aesthetic debate that surrounds Symbolist innovations, it is always the traditional vocabulary of the esoteric tradition that best defines the "new" aspirations. Accordingly, key phrases in the standard lexicon of Symbolist art theory include such provocative terminology as the artist-priest, the infinite, the transcendent, high consciousness, metaphysical insight, correspondences, synaesthesia, and so forth. Art is, therefore, for the Symbolist artist-theoretician functionally a *religious* art, and the visual sign of the specifically pseudoreligious intention is "abstraction."

Ironically, the New Age art mode deemed most appropriate for what we have called "extraterrestrial portraiture" is anything but abstract; typically its mode is "idealization" (e.g., fig. 15). Idealization is just like the way that Raphael chose to depict a famous celestial sighting reported around 1516 of the Virgin and Child with ET-like cuddly angels, now called the *Sistine Madonna* (fig. 34).[64] We also recall that Raphael's famous contemporary, Leonardo da Vinci, had observed how "the painter has the power to inflame men to love," and he does so by placing "before the lover's eyes the very image of the beloved object, and the lover often engages with it [the portrait], embracing it, and talking with it" (see fig. 35).[65] Around 1502, Leonardo also executed a famous portrait of an idealized female love object presently called the *Mona Lisa*; with slight postmodernist pictorial adjustments, the idealized result looks amazingly like the otherworldly being depicted on Whitley Strieber's "nonfiction" best-seller recounting his spiritual "communion" with the extraterrestrials (fig. 4). But we digress.

Obviously, the significant new means and themes of *l'abstraction* are themselves representative of distinctive *modernist* ideas. As is less obvious, all of these distinctly modernist ideas are encountered in, and presumably even often directly derived from, contemporary occultist publications. One of those was Papus's *Traité élémentaire de Science Occulte* (1897), where he—like the rest of the esoteric coterie—affirmed that, "whereas the employment of Analogy is most characteristic of Occultism, it certainly also has its applications in our contemporary kind of ['real'] Science, and it likewise is used for our particularly modern notions of Art," and, likewise, "the principal methodology belonging to Occult Science is Analogy. We know for a fact that there exists a constant linkage between the Sign and the Idea which it represents, and that signifies the connection between the Visible and the Indivisible."[66]

Those other, mutually shared Symbolist-occultist preoccupations included concern for the loss of quality in earthly life, a deeply felt need for spiritual wholeness, a fundamental mistrust of material values and, therefore, the unanimous rejection of materialist appearances in general. A century later, such notions also exactly correspond to supposed New Age wisdom. There was, additionally, a frequently stated thirst by Symbolists for universal knowledge. Symbolist *gnosis* was to be attained by passage (or "initiation") through ascending perceptual stages, all steadily rising toward higher and more elevated states of "spiritual enlightenment." As is revealed by a careful analysis of the pertinent cultural documents, these spiritualist concerns far transcend the narrow chronological limits usually granted the Symbolist movement, the period of a definitive synthesis of these diverse concerns. In fact, such sweeping metaphysical concerns can be discerned, to a greater or lesser degree, throughout the entire panorama of twentieth-century culture and art.

Something very similar had been conceived during the Symbolist era, which has been acutely observed to be a period fascinated by "hermetic languages," by a thinker with, however, no particular artistic and/or occultist inclinations, the Swiss linguist Ferdinand de Saussure (1857–1913).[67] He stated that any successful attempt to communicate ideas requires a "system of conventions," by which means what was originally mere "noise" for the listener (or just a colored blob for the painter's viewers) becomes intelligible as part of an agreed-upon system of signs, or culturally preestablished relationships. Saussure's "sign" represents the culturally conventionalized union between *signifiant* (signifier) and the *signifié* (signified [idea]); both only coexist as symbiotic components of the Saussurian Sign. In retrospect, this, too, represents another implied attack on positivism, as positivists distinguished between an *objective* or physical reality of objects and events and an opposing individual or *subjective* perception of reality. Saussure and his contemporaries in the emerging social sciences (for instance, Sigmund Freud and Emile Durkheim) bridged this gap.

According to the new linguistic perception initially advocated by Saussure, there is only a social reality of perception, and that is wholly *conventionalized* as it only represents a system of collective norms which organize essentially subjective perceptions, "representations," of the world and which give meaning to disparate communicative acts (be those noise or blobs). Saussure's evolving theories led him to postulate the future existence of a "science of signs," one which, long afterward, would become emblematic of postmodernist thought, Semiology. As was only briefly suggested in Saussure's posthumously published *Cours de linguistique générale* (1916), he had earlier received the first glimmerings of "a science which would study the life of signs within society. . . . We call it *Semiology*, from the Greek *semeion* ('sign'). . . . This procedure will not only clarify the problems of linguistics, but rituals, customs, etc. [thus also 'art' for postmodernists], will, we believe, appear in a new light if they are studied as signs."[68]

Saussure was just one contemporary who was advocating new "systems of relations," that is, an expression of interactive formal strategies by which a whole series of disciplines, from physics to painting, radically transformed themselves at the crucial *fin-de-siècle*, a liminal moment between the *mentalités* of the nineteenth and twentieth centuries.[69] In effect, what transpired was a significant shift in focus, from objects to relationships. An erudite contemporary's retrospective summation of what seemed to be ensuing is found in Alfred North Whitehead's *Science and the Modern World* (1925). Looking back over what seemed to constitute a newly entrenched modernist perception of the world around him, Whitehead recognized that "this new tinge to modern minds is a vehement and passionate interest in the relation of general principles to irreducible and stubborn facts [now] absorbed in the weaving of general principles. It is this union of passionate interest in the detailed facts with equal devotion to *abstract generalization* which forms the novelty in our present society." One clear symptom of the new mentality was "that the adequacy of scientific materialism as a scheme of thought for the use of science was endangered [and particularly] the notion of *mass* was losing its unique preeminence [in favor of] the notion of *energy* being fundamental. . . . But energy is merely the name for the quantitative aspect of a structure of [dynamic] happenings."[70]

In this topsy-turvy world, exclaims Whitehead in reviewing the new theory of relativity, "Heaven knows what seeming nonsense may not tomorrow become demonstrated truth!" Beginning with the Symbolists we find ever more prominence given to abstract art. As defined by Whitehead, who was of course not addressing any particularly modern notion of art, "to be abstract is to transcend particular concrete occasions of actual happening [involving] consideration of the nature of things antecedently to any special investigation into their details. Such a standpoint is termed 'metaphysical.'" Overall, Whitehead concludes that all "the old phraseology is at variance with the psychology of modern civilizations. This change in psychology is largely due to science, and it is one of the chief ways in which the advance of science has weakened the hold of the old religious forms of expression."[71]

Regarding our current fascination with extraterrestrial visitors (e.g., fig. 4), apparitions unheard of in 1921, Whitehead would have found another instance of "nonsense" represented as "demonstrated truth."

SWEDENBORG REVISITED BY THE MODERNS

Anna Balakian, a notable student of the chronologically successive Symbolist and Surrealist cultures in France, has made explicit the immediate, published source of most of these antimaterialist ideas. As she observes, "The Symbolists and their international coterie agreed on accepting *a common origin in the philosophy of Swedenborg* [even though] the manners of transmission have been multiple and simultaneous, as Swedenborgism became associated [first] with the Romantic tradition."[72] *Nihil sub sole novum est*: there is rarely, if ever, anything new under the sun in the esoteric tradition—and we have already pointed out (in chapter 10) that Swedenborg in effect had invented the idea of earthling close encounters with the extraterrestrials.

Accordingly, Balakian stresses that the Swedish seer, a *"voyant,"* was himself just the synthesizer of much earlier forms of the *philosophia perennis*. "It was not the originality of Swedenborg's theories that made it such an attractive cult," Balakian recognizes, "but rather Swedenborg's ability to sum up and popularize so many parallel mystical notions that were inherent in the cabalistic and hermetic cults. . . . Not a single new truth was discovered by Swedenborg: his precepts had all been conceived earlier; his philosophy was a synthesis of all the occult philosophies of the past. In turn, the translations of Swedenborg—into English, French, and German—were so numerous that his ideas became common property and underwent the distortions that generally occur in the indiscriminate handling of abstractions by those who need the concrete example of the thought."[73]

Trained as a civil engineer, Emanuel Swedenborg (1688–1772) framed his esoterica as a comprehensive system. In contrast to most of

the other, strictly modern spokesmen of the esoteric tradition, Swedenborg proceeded from a "traditional" biblical context. To the contrary, the
"moderns" typically tend to draw upon sources outside of the Christian
and European tradition. Typically, New Age fountains of wisdom flow
from the Far East (Zen, et al.), or even from prehistorical sources
(Shamanism, et al.), perhaps, according to the UFO experience postulated since around 1972, even from outer space. Elaborating upon scriptural precedent in the traditional, medieval, and exegetical occidental,
mode, Swedenborg concluded that what is "spirit" in man already pre-
exists in natural form, but needs further redefinition in terms of existence in the afterlife (the *au-delà* of French esotericism).

Thus Swedenborg pioneered a typically modern, postbiblical and
metaliturgical, notion, "Spiritualism." Trained in the scientific methodology of his time, Swedenborg sought the "proofs" of life after death. This
proof was found in the imagination, in the inner consciousness of spiritual sensations, which he treated as being distinct from sensual perceptions. Thus, for Swedenborgians every natural, physical vision had its
penumbra of spiritual recognition; as Swedenborg put it, a dead person "is
simply separated from the physical component. . . . When someone dies,
he simply crosses from one world into another."[74] The Heaven's Gate
UFO cult engineered their own crossing from one world into the next.

The recognition of ongoing life "beyond" (*au-delà*) was to be practically achieved through the enlightened perception of symbols. Swedenborgian *symbola* are phenomena in the physical world that have a dual
meaning, either to the earthly perceptions or to the spiritual organs of
man, where "*such things exist as the ear has never heard, nor the eye
seen.*"[75] The mind (and the imagination) live on forever, even after the
corruption of the earthly body. According to Swedenborg, "It was ignorance to believe that in this heavenly kingdom intelligence died at the
departure and dormancy of material things. . . . To the extent that a
mind can be led away from the sensory matters in the outer person or
the body, it is raised to spiritual and celestial matter."[76]

Tied to these obsessive spiritualist concerns is an omnipresent single
leitmotif, or overriding symbol, which is that of the "correspondences."
John Senior puts this famous doctrine into its true perspective,
remarking how, had Swedenborg instead called his doctrine "allegories,"
then "there would have been little theological dispute. But, like a true
Occultist, he called them 'facts.'"[77] So do the UFOlogists.

Be that as it may, as Swedenborg himself put it in his most influential publication, *Heaven and Hell* (1758):

> The nature of correspondence is unknown nowadays; this occurs for several reasons. The foremost reason is . . . love of self and love of the world. [One who] focuses on worldly things only, since those appeal to his outward senses and gratify his inclinations, he does not focus on spiritual things since these appear to the inner senses and gratify the mind. . . . The ancient people behaved differently. As far as they were concerned, a knowledge of correspondences was the finest of all knowledges.[78]

Presently, it is a commonplace belief among European esotericists that the "ancient people" were sensitives. Erich von Däniken says they got that way with help from the sky-descending ETs (see chapter 10). This is to say, in short, that "ancient people" were *clairvoyants*, and that, equally obviously, modern folks are *not*.

This invidious comparison, one which is monotonously drawn even today between precivilized, superior cosmic-consciousness and modern, inferior "materialism," is an ubiquitous New Age idea. Although generally little discussed as such, it has its most easily documentable roots in Swedenborgism, once, during the nineteenth century, a widely accepted philosophy with a patently occultist character. Long after the demise of the popularity of Swedenborgism, the same belief in the intellectual and ethical superiority of vaguely stated "ancient doctrines" becomes an essential component of a recognized mainstay of modern art, "primitivism." Although the primitivist factor largely determining the "look" of most modern art, from Gauguin up to the present day, has been widely studied by a host of art historians, the strictly occultist parallels to, perhaps even direct origins of, many modernist-primitivist notions still tend to be overlooked. In spite of this unwarranted omission in the standard explanations of modernism, the esoteric background does constitute an essential, and literally "ancient," chapter in the story of the genesis of modern art, particularly the "primitive" kind.[79]

In the event, back in the mid–eighteenth century, the occult "wisdom of the ancients" (*philosophia perennis*) was a topic of lesser interest to Swedenborg, if only because he completely took it for granted. To reiterate, Swedenborg's primary contribution of the esoteric tradition was the theory of the *correspondences*, in which, as he repeatedly stated, "the whole natural world corresponds to the spiritual world—not just the natural world in general, but actually in details. So anything in the natural world that occurs from the spiritual world is called a correspondent. . . . The natural world means all the expanse under the sun, receiving warmth and light from it. All the entities that are maintained from this source belong to that world. The spiritual world, in contrast, is heaven." And the folks that dwell in heaven are called "angels," and we have already made the point (in chapter 10) that Swedenborgian angels function, and even look, like post-modernist ETs (cf. fig. 4). Corresponding precociously to New Age doctrine, the Swedenborgian conclusion was a given: "Since man is both a heaven and an earth in smallest form [a microcosm], on the model of the greatest, he has a spiritual world and a natural world within him."[80]

By this kind of dialectical reasoning, Swedenborg's conclusions regarding an animistic universe, pulsing with hidden life-rhythms, are foregone:

> Things above the earth, like the sun, the moon, and the stars, and things in the atmospheres, like clouds, storms, rain, lightning, and thunder, are correspondences too. . . . In short, all the things that occur in nature, from the smallest to the greatest, are correspondences. Their being correspondences stems from the fact that the natural world and everything in it emerges and persists from the spiritual world, with both worlds emerging and persisting from the Divine.[81]

Besides modernist "primitivism," representing in part the *philosophia perennis* and the post-Swedenborgian correspondences, another frequently commented upon aspect of modern art is technically characterized by its now commonplace look of abstraction. One obvious feature of modernist abstraction is its outright renunciation of Renaissance perspective schemes. The obvious functional result is a perception of "spacelessness" in abstract art. This, too, is another important idea, for which a *locus classicus* may perhaps be found in Swedenborg's *Heaven and Hell*, even granted that the notion of "spacelessness" is indeed ubiquitous in *all* kinds of European mystical literature. Here, in speaking of "Space in Heaven," the clairvoyant Swede pointed out how (as perhaps you did not know)

> angels have no concept or idea of place or space. As this can only look like a paradox, I should like to bring it out into the light, for it has a major bearing. All journeys in the spiritual world occur by means of changes of the state of more inward things, to the point that journeys are simply changes of state. . . . This is how angels travel. So they do not have any spatial intervals, and without spatial intervals, there are no spaces. Instead, there are states and changes of state. Since this is how journeys occur, nearnesses are clearly similarities, and distances dissimilarities, in the state of more inward elements. . . . There are no spaces in heaven, except outward states corresponding to inner ones.[82]

Likewise, and just as any certified UFOlogist will eagerly tell you, our postmodernist ETs "have no concept or idea of place or space." We know this to be fact because amateur artiste Betty Andreasson (among others) saw the ETs, which she also likened to "angels," and which she drew walking through walls (fig. 22).

These fairly extensive quotations from Swedenborg's obviously influential publication may be justified on two grounds. On the one hand, the text of *Heaven and Hell* is quintessential esotericism that incorporates most of the themes and motifs we have analyzed in relation to the timeless occultist condition. These same ideas will appear over and over again in further esoteric (and even in many strictly *art*-theoretical) texts. As becomes readily apparent, the basic occultist pattern repeats itself, regardless of supposed doctrinal differences or dates of appearance of an awesome corpus of ever-proliferating publications. On the other hand, Swedenborgism is acknowledged by historians to have been an all-pervasive factor in early modernist cultural life in France. This is a point easily demonstrated. In a passage from Gérard de Nerval's *Aurélia*, the pre-Symbolist poet speaks of "dreams," and points out how "*Swedenborg appélait ces visions* Memorabilia." As Nerval further explains, such Swedenborgian "memorabilia" are specifically related to reveries or dreams: "*Il les dévait à la réverie plus souvent qu'au sommeil*," that is, "He ascribes them to revery more than to sleep."[83]

Nerval knew what he was talking about, and it seems Swedenborg did not. As we shall see later (in chapter 14), the postmodernist "alien abduction" is recently explained by scientists (not UFOlogists) as constituting a "hypnogogic episode," meaning something arising from the initial slumber-state, not real life. Similar is the "hypnopompic hallucination," the kind that occurs just before waking up. I have myself experienced many such episodes, especially in the course of writing this book. I vividly "experience" writing page after page of awe-inspiring prose; however, when I try to save it onto my hard drive, I never can seem to find the save button belonging to my mental computer keyboard. Drat! I lost it all. Needless to say, at such times, ETs were also very much on my mind. No matter; never mind.

In Nerval's interpolation, itself a quintessential example of hypnopompic Symbolist imagery *avant la lettre*, "Dreaming is a second life . . . that separates us from the invisible world. It is an underground wave that gradually enlightens as one is removed little by little from the shadows and from the pale and mutely static figures who inhabit the realm of limbo. The world of the Spirits is opening up for us."[84] As did all his contemporaries, whether directly attributing this idea to Swedenborg or not, Nerval believed in the indestructibility of the Spirit. For him (and also for many other artists), this is an enduring "fact." As such, the imperishable Spirit may be usefully contrasted to the deceitful mutability of earthly matter, changing according to Good or Evil impulses: "*La matière ne peut pas plus périr que l'esprit, mais elle peut se modifier selon le bien et selon le mal.*"[85] Much the same thing is said (in English) by UFOlogists concerning the stuff of outer space: "Matter can no more perish than can the Spirit, but it can be modified by Good or Evil."

Whereas one could perhaps endlessly cite oblique references to Swedenborg in French literature, without doubt the most widely known (and comprehensive) statement was that found in Honoré de Balzac's "mystic novel" *Seraphita* (1835). Seraphita is a combined hero/heroine who is an *androgyne*, a kind of genderized "correspondence" between male and female. As such, he/she illustrates the perennial wisdom of the ancient Hermeticists' *desideratum* to reconcile the opposites, an esoteric action known as the *coniunctio oppositorum* (joining of the opposites). In the third chapter of *Seraphita* one reads that "to poets and writers, [Swedenborgism] is infinitely marvelous; to seers, it is all absolute truth." In *Seraphita*, the whole world could have read how the reconciliation of the opposites was to be realized: "By learning *the correspondences*, by which worlds are made to concur with the heavens, one comes to know about those correspondences which do exist between these visible and tangible things of this terrestrial world and those invisible and unfathomable things belonging to the spiritual world. This perception is what Swedenborg had called a *celestial arcanum.*"[86]

Balzac proposed a specific motif to symbolize his desideratum of "spiritual correspondence," the *Androgyne*.[87] This is a mythic figure that was to become of capital importance to the UFO experience; ETs are commonly described (as in chapters 2 and 5) as "sexless," or unsexed beings. Among others, the Heaven's Gate UFO cult had pin-up pictures of androgynous ETs (fig. 5), even made themselves into androgynes (nonetheless, as it may be believed, none of them had ever read *Seraphita*).

WELCOME TO THE AGE OF THE IRRATIONAL!

A general appraisal of the evolution of modern culture after the French Revolution would have it that after the Age of Reason there came (and still thrives) the "Age of the Irrational." This Age of the Irrational is still very much with us, even though the current (and quite misinformed) appellation refers to a "new age." This is a misnomer; after all, there is literally nothing at all "new" in the occultists' "ancient wisdom." In a more specific sense, after the Age of Reason (which probably was only "reasonable" in certain, aristocratic quarters), there came the Industrial Revolution, presenting its own painful paradoxes. As man advanced to greater mastery of the physical world, so, too, did his always precarious hold upon the more intangible aspects of his relationship with the universe begin to slip. Security—mental, physical, financial, and, especially, spiritual—seemed menaced on every side by analytical positivism and the social unrest brought about by the new economic systems. Romanticism, the cultural matrix of the period after 1800, aggravated the situation further. On the one hand, there was a widespread taste for the dramatic and unreal *"vie des rêves."* On the other, there was an obsessive, homocentric concentration upon the self. This emotional individualism typically manifested a heightened, and often even hysterical, insistence upon the overwhelming importance of the individual's every action.

Whether by the historian or by the anthropologist, it is universally accepted that in circumstances of anxiety and uncertainty, *superstition* (however it chooses to call itself) is likely to make a prominent showing. Once crude superstition becomes spiritually elevated by means of thick publications verbosely explaining the particular sect's purported doctrinal novelties, meaning their complex theories, then it becomes occultism. Having stated some commonplace generalizations, we may now proceed to examine the historical evidence attesting to the wide diffusion of these esoteric ideas, superstitions resurfacing under many pseudoscholarly guises, which sought to close the gap between man and the intangible. The manifestations of modern occultism are truly hydra-headed. They presently include an overstocked paperback library of stories recounting dire episodes of alien abduction.

Under a widely misunderstood heading, "New Age," representing the secular spirituality of the modern epoch, there shelter an astonishing range of strange, unorthodox obsessions and fallacies, always couched in semireligious terminology. The specifically modernist manifestations of timeless esoterica (to name but a few that come immediately to mind) include hypnotism, magic, astrology, mental telepathy and clairvoyance, water-dowsing and crystal-gazing, lost continents, pyramidology, witches, poltergeists, vampires, reincarnation, water-diets and vegetarianism, geomancy, phrenology, homeopathy, chiropractic and osteopathy, graphology and physiognomy, palmistry, allopathy, parapsychology and (some of) psychiatry, cryptozoology, supermen and super-races, and, last but not least, flying saucers and UFOs. It makes for quite a formidable listing.

One of the important early contributions to the evolving proliferation of modernist esoterica surfaced in the so-called Age of Enlightenment. This was "Mesmerism," named after its founder Franz Anton Mesmer (1734–1815). Mesmer practiced what we would today call hypnotism at well-attended séances. Whatever its scientific basis today, in the early Romantic period hypnosis would have seemed a kind of white magic, offering a proof for the existence of the soul, of a hereafter, clairvoyance, and all forms of prophetic, or mentally superior, "vision." Thus, as a bridge between science and esotericism, hypnosis in part fostered the modern occult revival, and its popularity in the Symbolist period is attested to by some 1,200 bibliographic references.[88] Its popularity today is documented in the abundant literature of alien abductions. In their written form, Mesmer's largely esoteric "hypnotic" doctrines especially showed themselves to be clearly akin to the Swedenborgian "correspondences."

Mesmerism postulated the existence of a subtle fluid pervading all bodies and manifesting itself, for instance, in the motions of the planets, in tidal and atmospheric changes, and so forth. Mesmerism additionally had a particular therapeutic application: when the natural ebb and flow of this fluid within the human body is put out of harmony with the universal rhythm, then nervous or mental disorders result. The specific remedy for such spiritual disharmonies was "harmony," a prophylactic still prescribed by New Age therapists. In the Mesmeric application, the old esotericist call for spiritual harmony was to be achieved by magnets attached to the body and redirecting the vital fluids. Mesmer explained in his *Mémoire sur la découverte du magnétisme animal* that

> animal magnetism is a fluid universally diffused; it is the medium of a mutual influence between the heavenly bodies, the earth, and animated bodies; it is everywhere continuous, so as to leave no void. Its subtlety admits of no comparison; it is capable of receiving, propagating, communicating all the impressions of motions. . . . The actions and the virtues of animal magnetism may be communicated from one body to another, animate and inanimate. . . . In animal magnetism, nature presents a universal method of healing and preserving mankind.[89]

Swedenborgism and Mesmerism, as pseudoscientific doctrines, paved the psychological way in Europe for "Spiritualism," an American export to the entire world dating from the late 1840s.[90] The initial outburst, framed as a religious revival, displayed definitely antiaristocratic phenomena: convulsions, glossolalia, trances, visions, table-rappings, men barking like dogs, and all the *outré* rest. America, for all of its much-vaunted diversity, was (and perhaps still is) a sprawling and raw land ruled by what has often been called the "Protestant mentality," characterized by a bewildering tendency to ideological fragmentation. As the historical evidence painfully attests, besides its enviably fertile industrial production, America is also ever ready to manufacture ever more heterogeneous cults and sects, allowing ever more points of view (some quite bizarre) to raise momentarily their seductive Medusa-heads. As with the strictly occultist sects, there were two broad paths along which the new Protestant sects could journey. There was either the road to some kind of compromise with the reigning scientific rationalism, or there was that twisted track which doubled back in time to a fresh assertion of timeless truths, the *philosophia perennis*.

Initially wholly American, Spiritualism briskly crossed the Atlantic, became hugely popular in France, and thereby it acquired a more European, traditional, or scripturally ritualized character. By the 1850s, a leading proponent was, for example, Allan Kardec, who proposed a doctrine that is unabashedly Swedenborgian in his *Livre des Esprits* (1857). Kardeckian "spirits," *les esprits*, evolve through different grades as they acquire higher moral and intellectual qualities. All these various esoteric doctrines and influences (and many more of the like could be easily mentioned) finally culminated in the foremost figure of the nineteenth-century occultist revival, the one who synthesized all that had historically preceded him within the esoteric tradition, Éliphas Lévi.[91] In Lévi's two fundamental, often reprinted studies, *Dogme et Rituel de la Haute Magie* (1856) and *L'Histoire de la Magie* (1860), we find the ultimate resolution of *philosophia perennis*. It is no coincidence that such ancient wisdom happens to appear on the chronological threshold of the age of early modernism.

Lévi's newly whipped-up ancient wisdom incorporated into one grand fabric esotericist strands as diverse as Swedenborgism, the Cabala, Zoroastrian Manicheanism, Satanic worship, Mesmerism, witchcraft, Pythagorean number mysticism, and the Hermetic tradition, which has always been physically expressed through alchemy. For Lévi and his countless followers, hidden/occult wisdom is all one and the same. "Behind the veil of all the hieratic and mystical allegories of Ancient Doctrines," affirms Lévi, "there are found indications of a [secret] Doctrine, which is everywhere the same and everywhere carefully concealed."[92] The capital importance of the pseudonymous Lévi for the development of the modern esoteric tradition is perhaps nearly incalculable; as John Senior tersely announces, "He is the single greatest occult influence on Symbolism. Baudelaire, Rimbaud, Villiers, Mallarmé, and Yeats [among many others!] read his works."[93]

In his major treatise, *L'Histoire de la Magie*, Lévi took as his opening statement the familiar idea that occultism was the embodiment of hidden, primitive wisdom, the *philosophia perennis*: "Magic is the science of the ancient magi." Ancient wisdom is, therefore, something that considerably antedates, as a profound "science" that is "outside" (in effect, "*aliéné*"), the traditions of European civilization. Also literally *aliénés* from the scientific traditions of Western civilization are those "aliens" so beloved of the UFOlogists. Considered as primitivism, what Lévi has called "the Science of the Ancient Magi" is, of course, the fundamental equivalent of such non-European and magical artifacts—just as were the African and Oceanic ritual "primitive" artworks that later (circa 1910) were to so fascinate the early modernist artists. One of the earliest to be so fascinated was, however, Paul Gauguin, who stated, flat out, that "unquestionably, the Primitive is superior to us—*le sauvage est meilleur que nous*." His next premise was that "we are about to 'ascend' in art to an age of spiritual derangement [*d'égarement*] caused by the physical sciences, mechanical chemistry and the investigation of Nature. Artists have lost all of their *sauvagerie*, now having no instincts at all, which is to say no Imagination at all."[94]

As all these primitivizing vanguard artists—from the Symbolists to the Cubists, and beyond to the present day—knew in unison, the "childish" primitivist artwork, produced by operations that they so often mimicked, had been derived from "high magical practices"—*la Haute Magie*—and that it had been fabricated to serve these magical ends. Had they bothered to read Lévi (and one suspects that they often must have), then they would have also known that "magic, therefore, combines in a single science that which is most certain in Philosophy, which is eternal and infallible in Religion. It reconciles perfectly and incontestably those two terms, so opposed on the first view, Faith and Reason, Science and Belief, Authority and Liberty. It furnishes the human mind with an instrument of philosophical and religious certitude as exact as Mathematics."[95] For Lévi and his many readers, *la Haute Magie* additionally represented

> the memory of this scientific and religious Absolute, a souvenir of this "Doctrine" summarized in a word, of this world alternately lost and recovered, which was transmitted to the Elect of all antique Initiations. . . . The Key of Science has been thrown to children; as might have been expected, it is now, therefore, mislaid and practically lost.[96]

Besides announcing the fact of the accessibility of the secret doctrine to the naive minds of children—"purity of heart therefore purifies intelligence"—Lévi typically inveighs against contemporary materialism.

"We [wrongly] call ourselves strong-minded," he states, "when we are indifferent to everything except material advantages, as, for example, money. Given ignorance, wealth furnishes only destroying weapons."[97] At that point, Lévi introduces his own, stridently antimaterialist remedy for the ills of the contemporary world. The solution for Lévi is the perception of a hidden, universal life force. This new spiritualist and animistic vision is what he calls that

> Composite Agent, a natural and Divine Agent, at once corporeal and spiritual, an Universal Plastic Mediator, a common receptacle for vibrations of movement and images of Form, a fluid and a force which may be called, in a sense at least, the Imagination of Nature. By the mediation of this Force, every nervous apparatus is in secret communication together; hence come Sympathy and Antipathy, hence dreams, hence the phenomena of second sight and extra-natural vision.[98]

Lévi had a name for this wonder-working phenomenon, "Astral Light," a term still used a century and a half later by UFOlogists and other enlightenment-seeking New Age deep-thinkers. By these occult visionary means, states Lévi,

> sight is turned inward, instead of outward; night falls on the external and real world, while fantastic brilliance shines on the world of dreams; even the physical eyes experience a slight quivering and turn up inside the lids. The soul then perceives, by means of images, the reflection of its impressions and thoughts. . . . It is the Universal Imagination, of which each of us appropriates a lesser or greater part according to our grade of sensibility and memory. Therein is the source of all apparitions, all extraordinary visions, and all the intuitive phenomena peculiar to madness or ecstasy.[99]

We have perhaps taken a somewhat unusual tack here by defining Lévi's importance for the central figures of the evolving Symbolist aesthetic. But what was Lévi's significance for the history of occultism itself? For Christopher McIntosh, the answer is perfectly clear:

> It is this: Lévi helped to change the *popular* concept of magic. Whereas magic had hitherto been regarded by most people as a means of manipulating the forces of nature and by many as a dangerous superstition, Lévi presented it as a way of drawing the will through certain channels and turning the magician into a more fully realized human being. . . . Lévi was [certainly] not the first to express it in writing, but he was [certainly] the first to popularize it on a large scale.[100]

MYSTICISM AND MODERN ART THEORY

Modern occultism, a *"popular* concept of magic" particularly when it is of the Éliphas Lévi type, was unquestionably amalgamated into Symbolist artistic thinking, particularly the kind that refers to the strictly visual arts. As is already apparent, unquestionably the more "advanced" visual arts were inevitably evolving toward "abstraction" by the end of the Symbolist era.

Also unquestionable is that, following the Symbolist epoch, the original, essentially "occultist" postulates of Symbolist art became completely standard in early modernist art theory. And they still are to this very day. In this case, one looks for the evidence of a shared conceptual vocabulary, for this is what really best indicates a clear-cut community of fundamental beliefs existing between occultists and Symbolists. The key terms identifying the underlying contributions of the esoteric tradition to modernist art concepts, likewise contemporary New Age jargon, include the following, constantly reiterated buzzwords: "analogy," "intuition," "memory," "ancient wisdom," "harmony," "imagination," "the dream," "correspondences," "suggestion," "the symbol," "manipulation of matter," "essences," "will," "hidden energies," "vitalism," and so on.

For the pursuit of these largely linguistic linkages between esoteric sectarian scriptures and avant-garde artistic expression, our best guide will be the writings of Gabriel-Albert Aurier (1865–1892).[101] Aurier is a critic whom we have already seen to have formulated the most clear and certain formulation of the art theory of his period, Symbolism. As was so common to the "anarchistic" tendencies of his period (as well as the avant-garde in general), from 1890 to his premature death two years later, Aurier began by taking up an emphatically "antimaterialist" stance. Aurier's antimaterialism (just like that of so many of his artistic contemporaries) defied the mainstream attitudes of his time. This was a historical moment when, he says, the establishment "tried to introduce science everywhere, even where it is least concerned." For Aurier, these positivist natural sciences "are, by definition, not able to come to absolute solutions." By his reckoning, such materialist (actually meaning scientific) thinking "must, therefore, be accused of having made this society lose faith, become earth-bound."[102]

The widely accepted positivist attitudes of the physical scientists account, as Aurier believes, "for the poorness of our art, which they have assigned exclusively to the domain of imitation, the only quality that can be established by [their] experimental methods." Alas, "by means of positive science, we shall have returned to animality, pure and simple. We must react."[103] And what, then, is the answer, the means of reaction, the ready-made solution, the way out? According to the boldface conclusion of Aurier (and to so many others of his generation), "It is mysticism alone that can save our society from brutalization, sensualism, and utilitarianism."[104]

In an article published in 1891, in which Aurier discussed the art of Gauguin, the French critic attributed to this renowned Symbolist artist "the clairvoyance of that inner eye of man on which Swedenborg speaks." As such, for Aurier and his readers, Gauguin's art is "the representative materialization of what is the highest and the most truly divine in the world, of what is, in the last analysis, the only thing existent: the Idea." Resorting to the authority of an old neo-Platonic chestnut beloved of the esoteric tradition, "the poor stupid prisoners of the allegorical cavern," who "fool themselves in contemplating the shadows that they take for reality," Aurier concludes that "the normal and final end of painting, as well of the other arts, can never be the direct representation of objects. Its aim is to express Ideas, by translating them into a special language."[105]

Even though one must doubt that Ferdinand de Saussure had ever read any of Aurier's art criticism, a general functional alignment between the two thinkers seems unquestionable. The common glue is Symbolist culture. According to the new terms of his "special language," Aurier proposes that "objects cannot have value more than objects as such; they can only appear to him [that is, to the *clairvoyant*] as *signs*." As a nearly inevitable result, the Symbolist artist must resort to abstraction. According to Aurier, "The task of the artist, whose eye is able to distinguish essences from tangible objects, . . . is *a necessary simplification in the vocabulary of the sign*." In short, for Aurier, and also for a great many later modernists, "objects are nothing but the revealers of the appearances of these ideas and, by consequence, have importance only as signs of Ideas." These ideational signs manifest themselves on the artist's canvas, revealing his uniquely privileged "insight into the Symbolic correspondences." In properly Symbolist painting, according to Aurier, "every detail is, in fact, really nothing but a partial symbol, most often unnecessary for the total significance of the object."[106] As "signs" and "simulcara," such has now become postmodernist theory.

To achieve his goals, the Symbolist artist resorts to the pictorial equivalent of the *philosophia perennis*. According to Aurier, the visionary and modernist artist "has thus, in the last analysis, returned to the formula of art that is simple, spontaneous and primordial." "*L'art primordial*" means, of course, what we call (with the benefit of art-historical hindsight), "primitivist imagery." In the event, to be a primitivist you certainly need not merely ape tribal art ransacked from the French colonies. Aurier is taking about the *idea* of the primordial, or *primitivist attitudes*, and not necessarily about any particular art-historical formal solutions. Therefore, Aurier affirms that "all primeval revelations" are, "without any doubt, the true and absolute art, fundamentally identical with primitive art, to art as it was divined by the instinctive geniuses of the first ages of humanity." By deliberate means, the modern primitivist artist, uniquely endowed with psychic gifts, "finds himself confronted with nature, knowing how to read in every object its abstract significance, the primordial idea that goes beyond it." And just what is it that lies beyond (*au-delà*) this abstract significance? Obviously, it is that ancient wisdom that has always been made available to the uniquely enlightened. Now, in 1892 (and immediately afterward), that gift is particularly the province of the visual artists and, Aurier concludes, "thanks to this gift, art which is complete, perfect, absolute, exists at last."[107]

As a direct consequence, Kandinsky's supposedly "original" call in 1912 for "the great epoch of the Spiritual" was, in effect, already a foregone conclusion by 1890. Kandinsky's apparently novel *"geistige"* or spiritualist leitmotif is largely a paraphrase of numerous preexistent, published, and widely discussed Symbolist texts. Those in turn had themselves an unmistakable functional affinity with widely read apocalyptic texts composed by the likes of Éliphas Lévi. For the historian of culture, the immediate result is that one can easily cite the French antecedents of such clarion calls for a wholly spiritual and abstract art to answer the needs of the coming epoch. For example, we have yet another precedent in Paul Adam's preface to Georges Vanor's *L'Art Symboliste* (1889). As Adam then claimed, "The Age is evidently preparing itself for a new period, a period of force, one of a Science of the Consciousness and of a general felicity. The coming epoch is bound to be mystical, abstract in its imaginative reveries."[108] Or, similarly, we again have the case of Albert Aurier, who wrote (in 1892) how the future age *"sera un siècle de l'Art . . . succédant au siècle de la Science, de la désespérance, du mensonge."* In the forthcoming "Century of Art," says Aurier, which is the one succeeding a despicably positivist "Century of Science" (and that, by his definition, only led to desperation and lies), collectively we shall find ourselves entering into *"un art nouveau, idéaliste et mystique."*[109]

In short, any number of artists, mostly however belonging to what we would now call the beleaguered avant-garde, collectively believed, and quite often themselves published, statements to the effect that a wholly "new art" was bound to transpire as one senescent century merged into a bright new one. The year 1900 was obviously rife with all sorts of utopian and millenarian promise. Specifically, the promise then was the "idealist and mystical new art," for which the most appropriate language was the dematerialized rhetoric of ethically "pure abstraction," *l'abstraction pure.* Now, in the twenty-first century, again self-designated as a "new age," we really *must* cope with those malign alien-abductors, or so we are told. So informed, a few commercial artists are hired to depict ETs and, paradoxically, they portray the otherworldly visitors in that old-fashioned art style called "idealization" (see figs. 1, 4, 5, 15–22, 29). *Nomen est omen.*

NOTES

1. Nat Freedland, *The Occult Explosion* (New York: Putnam, 1972), pp. 33–34.

2. Walter Anderson, *Reality Isn't What It Used to Be* (San Francisco: Harper, 1990), pp. 107–108.

3. Ibid., p. 219.

4. For these, see J. Vankin and J. Whalen, *Sixty Greatest Conspiracies of All Times: History's Biggest Mysteries, Coverups, and Cabals* (Secaucus, N.J.: Citadel, 1996); Robert Anton Wilson, *Everything Is under Control: Conspiracies, Cults, and Cover-Ups* (New York: HarperPerennial, 1998); and, specifically, Jodi Dean, *Aliens in America: Conspiracy Cultures from Outerspace to Cyberspace* (Ithaca, N.Y.: Cornell University Press, 1998).

5. See the works cited above as well as (especially amusing) John Sladek, *The New Apocrypha: A Guide to Strange Sciences and Occult Beliefs* (London: Granada, 1978).

6. For a discussion of Theosophy and its direct offshoot, Anthroposophy, see J. F. Moffitt, *Occultism in Avant-Garde Art: The Case of Joseph Beuys* (Ann Arbor: University of Michigan Press, 1986), pp. 72 ff.

7. R. M. Levine, *Bad Blood: A Family Murder in Marin County* (New York: Bantam, 1982), p. 117.

8. For a detailed, semischolarly, examination of the wide range of such neopaganism, see Margot Adler, *Drawing Down the Moon: Witches, Druids, Goddess-Worshippers, and Other Pagans in America Today* (Boston: Beacon, 1986).

9. D. Murray, "Anthropology, Fiction, and the Occult: The Case of Carlos Castaneda," in *Literature of the Occult: A Collection of Critical Essays*, ed. B. Messent (Englewood Cliffs, N.J.: Prentice-Hall, 1981), pp. 171–82.

10. Freedland, *Occult Explosion*, p. 92.

11. For complementary evidence, see Bergen Evans, *The Natural History of Nonsense* (New York: Vintage, 1958), a classic, pre-ET study of American credulity.

12. W. Kendrick, *The Thrill of Fear: 250 Years of Scary Entertainment* (New York: Grove Weidenfeld, 1991), p. 251.

13. George F. Will, in *Newsweek*, 15 September 1997, p. 84.

14. Éliphas Lévi, *The History of Magic, Including a Clear and Precise Exposition of Its Procedure, Its Rites, and Its Mysteries* (reprint, London: Rider, 1982), p. 358.

15. For this contemporary terminology, and much more, see Robert Jensen, *Marketing Modernism in Fin-de-Siècle Europe* (Princeton: Princeton University Press, 1994).

16. To date, the most comprehensive scholarly investigation of the real background of the many ideological complexities of Symbolist artistic culture, especially useful for exposing in detail its important occultist component, is by F. E. Burhan, *Vision and Visionaries: Nineteenth-Century Psychological Theory, the Occult Sciences, and the Formation of the Symbolist Aesthetic in France* (Ph.D. diss., Princeton University, 1979). For the theoretical contexts of Symbolism, see H. R. Rookmaaker, *Gauguin and Nineteenth-Century Art Theory* (Amsterdam: Swets & Zeitlinger, 1972); and for some of the more important primary documents, see Henri Dorra, ed., *Symbolist Art Theories: A Critical Anthology* (Berkeley: University of California Press, 1994). There is still much scholarly work needed for a better view of this period's artistic accomplishment; for example, for a recent, and quite novel, attempt to define a specifically Symbolist kind of *architectural* expression, see J. F. Moffitt, "Architecture as Primeval Expression: Antonio Gaudí in the Context of the European Symbolist Movement," in *Icon to Cartoon: A Tribute to Sixten Ringbom*, ed. A. Ringbom (Helsinki: Helsingfors, 1995), pp. 161–92.

17. John Willet, *Expressionism* (New York: McGraw Hill, 1978), pp. 13 ff.

18. One particularly useful art-historical treatment of the subject again deserves mention here: Juan Antonio Ramírez's *Medios de masas e historia del arte* (Madrid: Cátedra, 1981).

19. For one's necessary historical grounding in modern occultism, a serious subject unfortunately rarely studied by serious art historians, see James Webb, *The Occult Establishment* (LaSalle, Ill.: Open Court, 1988); *The Occult Underground* (LaSalle, Ill.: Open Court, 1988); see also other useful studies listed here referring to occultism.

20. Willet, *Expressionism*, p. 14.

21. Leon Surette, *The Birth of Modernism: Ezra Pound, T. S. Eliot, W. B. Yeats, and the Occult* (Montreal: McGill-Queens University Press, 1994), pp. 8–9, 94, 207.

22. For this approach, see E. A. Tiryakian, *On the Margin of the Visible: Sociology, the Esoteric, and the Occult* (New York: Dutton, 1974).

23. For what immediately follows, my main source is R. Galbreath, "Explaining Modern Occultism," in *The Occult in America: New Historical Perspectives*, ed. H. Kerr and C. L. Crow (Urbana: University of Illinois Press, 1986), pp. 11–37.

24. Ibid., p. 17.

25. Ibid., p. 18.

26. Ibid., pp. 18–19.

27. Ibid., p. 30.

28. John Senior, *The Way Down and Out: The Occult in Symbolist Literature* (New York: Greenwood, 1968), pp. 39 ff.

29. For this important historical figure, see C. McIntosh, *Éliphas Lévi and the French Occult Revival* (New York: Weiser, 1972). Oddly, Lévi is only briefly mentioned by Leon Surette in his otherwise exhausive study of the occult roots of *The Birth of Modernism*; see Senior, *The Way Down and Out*, pp. 23–24, 129.

30. Lévi, *History of Magic*, p. 60.

31. Ibid., p. 61.

32. Ibid., p. 366.

33. Ibid., p. 221.

34. Ibid., p. 358.

35. Ibid., p. 361.

36. Ibid., pp. 363–64.

37. Ibid., p. 110.

38. Ibid., p. 226.

39. Éliphas Lévi, *Transcendental Magic, Its Doctrine and Ritual* (reprint, London: Rider, 1968), p. 195.

40. Lévi, *History of Magic*, p. 358.

41. Philip J. Klass, *UFO-Abductions: A Dangerous Game* (Amherst, N.Y.: Prometheus Books, 1989), p. 215, with extensive references to Hopkins and his indefatigable abductive mission given in chap. 7–9, 17.

42. J. Webb, *Occult Underground*.

43. Ibid., pp. 281–83. For more historical analyses of this now-commonplace staple of avant-garde conviction, see D. M. Kosinski, *Orpheus in Nineteenth-Century Symbolism* (Ann Arbor: University of Michigan Press, 1989), pp. 63 ff., "Mysticism and the Symbolist Aesthetic: Art as Religion." Kosinski does not, however, cite (as I do here) some earlier statements of Éliphas Lévi to exactly the same emphatic effect. In any event, the equation "Artist as Magician" is truly ancient; see E. Kris and O. Kurz, *Die Legende vom Künstler: Ein geschichtlicher Versuch* (Vienna: Krystall, 1934), pp. 69 ff., "Der Kunstler als Magier."

44. Surette, *Birth of Modernism*, p. 281.

45. Donald Kuspit, *The Cult of the Avant-Garde Artist* (Cambridge: Cambridge University Press, 1993), pp. 1–14. For a detailed analysis of these "belief-system" phenomena, presented in the forensic format of a case study focused upon a single, much lionized, avant-garde artist, Joseph Beuys, see Moffitt, *Occultism in Avant-Garde Art*.

46. Kuspit, *Cult of the Avant-Garde Artist*, pp. 1–14.

47. Ibid., and citing (p. 2) Marc Galanter's four-part definition of "cults."

48. Apollinaire, as quoted in Hershel B. Chipp, ed., *Theories of Modern Art: A Source Book by Artists and Critics* (Berkeley: University of California Press, 1969), p. 224.

49. Franz Marc, as quoted in ibid., pp. 180–81.

50. Paul Klee, as quoted in ibid., p. 186.

51. Wassily Kandinsky, as quoted in ibid., p. 157.

52. Apollinaire, as quoted in ibid., p. 225.

53. Daniel-Henry Kahnweiler, as quoted in ibid., pp. 252–53, 259.

54. Gabriel-Desiré Laverdant, as quoted in Renato Poggioli, *The Theory of the Avant-Garde* (New York: Harper, 1968), p. 9.

55. Paul Gauguin, in Chipp, *Theories*, p. 60.

56. Gilbert-Albert Aurier, as quoted in L. Nochlin, ed., *Impressionism and Post-Impressionism, 1874–1904: Sources and Documents in the History of Art* (Englewood Cliffs, N.J.: Prentice-Hall, 1966), pp. 136–37.

57. Webb, *Occult Establishment*, p. 421 (my emphasis).

58. Ibid.

59. For an exhaustive and many-faceted approach to the problem of the complex relationships finally recognized as having existed between *fin-de-siècle* occultism and early modern art, see the various art-historical essays assembled in M. Tuchman, ed., *The Spiritual in Art, Abstract Painting, 1890–1985* (Los Angeles: Los Angeles County Museum of Art, 1986); V. Loers, ed., *Okkultismus und Avantgarde: Von Munch bis Mondrian, 1900–1915* (Frankfurt: Kunsthalle, 1995).

60. Maurice Denis, as quoted in Chipp, *Theories*, p. 94.

61. Ibid., p. 105.

62. Ibid., p. 107 (my emphasis).

63. Gauguin, as quoted in ibid., p. 60.

64. For a more rational (*"kunstwissenschaftliche"*) approach to this famous image, see D. de Chapeaurouge, *Raffael: Sixtinische Madonna* (Frankfurt: Fischer, 1993).

65. Richter, *The Literary Works of Leonardo da Vinci* (Oxford: Oxford University Press, 1939), vol. 1, p. 64.

66. Papus, *Traité élémentaire de Science Occulte, mettant chacun à même de comprendre et d'expliquer les théories et les symboles employés par les anciens, par les alchimistes, les astrologues, les kabbalistes* (Paris, 1897; facs. ed., St Jean de Braye, 1979), p. 4: "L'emploi de l'analogie, méthode caractéristique de l'Occultisme, a son application à nos sciences contemporaines ou à nos conceptions modernes de l'Art"; p. 28: "La méthode principale de la Science occulte c'est l'Analogie. Nous savons qu'il existe un rapport constant entre le signe et l'idée qu'il représente, c'est-à-dire entre le visible et l'invisible."

67. For what immediately follows, see J. Culler, *Saussure* (London: Faber, 1976). For cogent observations about the Symbolists' obsession with "hermetic languages," see N. Staller, "Babel: Hermetic Languages, Universal Languages, and Anti-Languages in Fin-de-Siècle Parisian Culture," *Art Bulletin* 76 (1994): 331–54.

68. Quoted in Culler, *Saussure*, p. 90.

69. For much more detail on these crucial perceptual shifts, and their direct physical manifestations, see Steven Kern, *The Culture of Space and Time, 1880–1918* (Cambridge: Harvard University Press, 1983).

70. Alfred N. Whitehead, *Science and the Modern World* (reprint, New York: New American Library, 1960), pp. 10, 96.

71. Ibid., pp. 105, 142–43, 171.

72. Anna Balakian, *The Symbolist Movement: A Critical Appraisal* (New

York: Vintage, 1967), p. 11 (my emphasis).

73. Ibid., p. 13.

74. Swedenborg, *Heaven and Hell*, p. 344.

75. Ibid., p. 136.

76. Ibid., p. 368.

77. Senior, *Way Down and Out*, p. 34.

78. Swedenborg, *Heaven and Hell*, p. 80.

79. On the modern art-historical phenomenon, see R. Goldwater, *Primitivism in Modern Art* (New York: Vintage, 1967); W. Rubin, ed., *"Primitivism" in Twentieth-Century Art: Affinity of the Tribal and the Modern* (New York: Abrams, 1984); C. Rhodes, *Primitivism and Modern Art* (London: Thames & Hudson, 1994); for the current situation of Primitivism in the "developed world," largely an expression of cultural snobbery, see S. Price, *Primitive Art in Civilized Places* (Chicago: University of Chicago Press, 1989).

80. Emanuel Swedenborg, *Heaven and Hell*, ed. G. F. Dole (New York: Swedenborg Foundation, 1984), p. 81.

81. Ibid., p. 89.

82. Ibid., p. 145.

83. Gérard de Nerval, as quoted in Senior, *Way Down and Out*.

84. Ibid., p. 77: "La Rêve est une seconde vie . . . qui nous séparent du monde invisible. . . . C'est un souterrain vague qui s'éclaire peu à peu, et ou se dégagent de l'ombre et de la nuit les pàles figures gravement immobilés que habitent le séjour des limbes. . . . Le monde des Ésprits s'ouvre pour nous."

85. Nerval, as quoted in ibid., p. 79.

86. Honoré de Balzac, as quoted in Burhan, *Vision and Visionaries*, p. 213: "En apprenant LES CORRESPONDENCES par lesquelles les mondes concordent avec les cieux [et] savoir les correspondences qui existent entre les choses visibles et pondérables du monde terrestre et les choses invisibles et impondérables du monde spirituel . . . ce que Swedenborg appelle un ARCANE CELESTE."

87. For what immediately follows on the Androgyne, from Balzac to Breton, see Whitney Chadwick, *Myth in Surrealist Painting, 1929–1939* (Ann Arbor: University of Michigan Press, 1980), pp. 30–31.

88. For more on these quasi-occultist appraisals of hypnotism in the Symbolist period, see Burhan, *Vision and Visionaries*, pp. 38ff.; see also Henri Ellenberger, *The Discovery of the Unconscious: The History and Evolution of Dynamic Psychiatry* (New York: BasicBooks, 1979).

89. Anton Mesmer, as quoted in McIntosh, *Éliphas Lévi*, p. 33.

90. For a vivid, anecdotal account of the phenomenon, see Slater Brown, *The Heyday of Spiritualism* (New York: Pocket Books, 1972).

91. Besides McIntosh, *Éliphas Lévi*, see also P. Chacornac, *Éliphas Lévi, rénovateur de l'occultisme en France* (Paris: Nizet, 1926); A. Mercier, *Éliphas Lévi et la pensée magique au XIXe siècle* (Paris: Nizet, 1974).

92. E. Lévi, *Transcendental Magic, Its Doctrine and Ritual* (reprint, London: Rider, 1968), p. 1.

93. Senior, *Way Down and Out*, p. 36.

94. Gauguin, as quoted in Burhan, *Vision and Visionaries*, p. 201.

95. Lévi, *History of Magic*, p. 29.

96. Ibid., p. 32.

97. Ibid., p. 37.

98. Ibid., p. 39.

99. Ibid., p. 40.

100. McIntosh, *Éliphas Lévi*, p. 152.

101. On this influential art critic, see P. Townley Mathews, *Aurier's Symbolist Art Criticism and Theory* (Ann Arbor: University of Michigan Press, 1986).

102. Gabriel-Albert Aurier, as quoted in Chipp, *Theories*, p. 87.

103. Ibid., p. 88.

104. Ibid.

105. Ibid., pp. 88, 89.

106. Ibid., pp. 90, 91.

107. Ibid., pp. 92–93.

108. Paul Adam, as quoted in Burhan, *Vision and Visionaries*, p. 170: "Le Siècle prépare évidemment la période nouvelle; la période de force, de Science consciente et de bonheur. *L'époche à venir sera mystique et abstraite dans les rêves imaginatifs*" (emphasis mine).

109. Aurier, as quoted in ibid.

Chapter 13

An Etiology of the Modernist Experience

THE POWER OF IMAGES AND THE MODERNIST MASS SPECTACLE

For the alert art historian, the apocryphal case of postmodernist ET portraiture, especially its media-charged epiphany at Roswell, demonstrates the enduring need in the human psyche for concrete imagery. By looking at the way we collectively acquire imagery, we now may embark upon a larger etiology of the modern experience, including its occultist accretions. Such an *aetiologia*—from the Greek *aitía*, cause, and *logos*, reasoned description—contextually enhances, as it were, our attempt at a comprehensive ETiology (pardon the pun).

As was explained in great detail by David Freedberg, particularly in Western culture there *is* an inherent "power of images." Moreover, this "prophylactic or amuletic function" (as he calls it) is much more efficacious in "low" art, which is addressed to the masses, than it is in the so-called beaux-arts, catering to a supposedly more intellectually nimble audience culture. Most important, states Freedberg, "Belief becomes belief because of the sheer force of [pictorial] convention," and "the votive archetype swiftly generates [more] votive reproductions, and efficacy spreads contagiously from like to identified like." In all such cases, "Certainly it was not the things themselves that the faithful worshipped; it was what they represented."[1]

Gregorius Magnus said the same thing long before: "What Scripture is to the educated, images are to the ignorant, who see through them what they must accept; they read in them what they cannot read in books."[2] The same holds true with ET votive-portraiture (figs. 1, 4, 5, 15–22), even if there is still little consensus on what *they* represent, if anything. No matter; somehow the public knows "what they must accept." Nonetheless, according to John Damascene, since "the honor shown to the image is transferred to the prototype, whoever honors an image [therefore] honors the person represented by it."[3] Furthermore, granted that visual illustration does reinforce religious devotion, then all the more reason for publishing this investigation, showing when and how a now ubiquitous ET *eikon* actually began (see figs. 16–18).

Things have changed since John Damascene's era, especially the technological means for reproducing votive imagery. Now we live in the postmodernist "age of electronic media," and Margot Lovejoy (the author of a book so titled) explains how, since the 1960s and due specifically to *television*,

> assumptions of coherence vanished in the new cultural infrastructure. . . . Television became the arena of confusion, a melting pot of forms, concepts, and banalities which acted as the crucible for a postmodern consciousness [sponsoring] pastiche as a strategy, creating an aesthetic of quotation, appropriation and incorporation of traditional styles to provide a recollection of the past as part of a de-centered structure of associations. . . . Use of compressed, intensified images and messages, with their edited forced sequences and shock value, have [*sic*] now become part of the customary visual vernacular. Television's image flow has created a visual cultural phenomenon surpassing, and subsuming, the influence of the printed word, also radio and cinema. . . . A mass audience of millions participating collectively in powerful moments in real time, watching the same images—the historic Moonwalk, the Gulf War, a World Cup Soccer final [and UFOs and ETs]—before the perfectly regulated circuitry of TV, is a major new perceptual experience. . . . But that same public, distracted by the TV, loses sight of political and commercial manipulation going on around them, while feeling they are in control through their remote-control options.[4]

Back in 1967, the now trendy French philosopher–cultural critic Jean Baudrillard called the now universal postmodernist effects "simulation," a mental copy of the real, which is now taken to be better—for being much more entertaining—than is the (merely) real. Such simulacra—among which we must now include the postmodernist ETs—represent generation by models of a real without origin or real: a hyper-real. . . . The real is produced from miniaturized units—from matrices, memory banks, and command models—and with these it can be reproduced an indefinite number of times. And since it is no longer measured against some ideal or negative instance, it no longer has to be rational. It is nothing more than operational. In fact, since it is no longer enveloped by an imaginary context, it is no longer real at all. It [including the "reality" of ETs] is hyper-real: the product of an irradiating synthesis of combinatory models in hyper [or outer]-space without atmosphere.[5]

Now, besides the mass media simulacra, we have the mass spectacle, itself often televised. This is the means by which perhaps originally individual modernist minds have been dramatically reshaped, *en masse*. Some of these mass spectacles are relatively benign, like most rock concerts, but others are decidedly pernicious, particularly the kind designed to mold collective political opinion and action. Since there are those who would call the currently commonplace extraterrestrial phenomenon a mass aberration, we must review the most frightening precedent for a collective acceptance of irrationality in recent history. Collective mental manipulation has its own minihistory. It begins in what we have called (in chapter 8) "emotional fascism."

The official line in German *Kultur* between 1933 and 1945 was largely the product of the fertile, but mostly perverse, mind of Adolf Hitler (fig. 7). Few of his policies, including his dictates on the functions of German art, evolved any further after 1933. In fact, most of these had already been laid out years before, in his autobiographical *Mein Kampf* ("My Struggle," 1927). Needless to say, at least something of its contents was made known to *every* German alive during this period. As a former grammar school student recalled, "*Mein Kampf* became the textbook for our history lessons . . . and when we had finished it, we started again from the beginning."[6] As Hitler made clear in his pseudoscriptures, the primary task "begins in education [*Bildung*]." The primary task of Hitlerian *Bildung* was to arrest "all these symptoms of decay, the consequences of the absences of a definite, uniformly acknowledged philosophy," and for want of proper *Bildung*, "humanitarian bilge becomes stylish."[7] In general, education is, alas, to be directed "primarily to . . . the breeding of absolutely healthy bodies. The training of mental abilities is only secondary."[8]

Specifically, the new program designed by Hitler was to educate the folk into the national myth: "The question of the 'nationalization' of a people is, among other things, primarily a question of creating healthy social conditions as a foundation for the possibility of educating the individual. For only those who, through school and upbringing, learn to know the cultural, economic, but above all, political greatness of their own Fatherland can, and will, achieve the inner pride in the privilege of being a member of such a people."[9] One way of emotionally binding the mass audience was sport, itself emblematic of, besides orchestrated collective emotional expression, those supposedly "healthy social conditions" employed for "educating the individual," apprising him and her of "the privilege of being a member of such a people."

Sport is also an essential, and very lucrative, component of the postmodernist infotainment industry. Viewed in informed retrospect, the desired result of the Fascist athletic mass spectacle was—besides "the breeding of absolutely healthy bodies"—to turn passive individual spectators into a cheering crowd, excited but compliant cogs within the tribal war machine. In case anyone doubts the efficacy of *der Sport* as an essential tool of Nazi propaganda, one need only view the artful cinematic treatment of orchestrated mass hysteria depicted by Leni Riefenstahl in her *Olympiad: Fest der Völker* (1938). Its unabashedly political counterpart, another "people's festival" depicting induced mass hysteria, is the hypnotic, triumphant, and dreadful rendition of a Hitlerian *Triumph des Willens* (1936). Here film becomes an authoritative pseudo-event in its own right, a literal "Triumph of the Will."

The artful tool of *Hitlerzeit* education now becomes *völkisch* propaganda, blurring the divisions between lies and realities. Informed critics of postmodernist social phenomena recognize the same symptoms in our culture, but typically fail to give Adolf Hitler, as yet unsung as an *Urpostmoderniste*, the proper credit. Besides acknowledged to be manipulative—and nothing but—Fascist *völkisch Propaganda* is also labeled as "popular art," *völkisch Kunst*. It represents the collectivized modernist experience par excellence. According to the Führer-Messiah, it is primarily visual, and "adjusted to the most limited intelligence," just like television (with which, of course, Hitler was unfamiliar):

> The function of propaganda [is] calling the masses' attention to certain facts, processes, necessities, etc., whose significance is thus for the first time placed within their field of vision. The whole art consists in doing this so skillfully that everyone will be convinced that the fact is real, the process necessary, the necessity correct, etc. . . . All propaganda must be popular [*völkisch*] and its intellectual level must be adjusted to the most limited intelligence among those to whom it is addressed. . . . The art of propaganda lies in understanding the emotional ideas of the great masses and finding, through a psychologically correct form, the way to their attention and, thence, to the heart of the broad masses. . . . All

effective propaganda must be limited to a very few points, and must harp on these, in slogans and until the last member of the public understands. . . . Thus we see that propaganda must follow a simple line and, correspondingly, the basic tactics must be psychologically sound.[10]

Just to squelch those smug smirks I imagine are about to appear on postmodernist, and righteously non-German, faces, I may now pronounce the current English term for Hitler's "propaganda": *advertising*. (And Spaniards, perhaps less naive than we are, often call their commercial advertising *propaganda*.) You—yes, YOU—have also been seduced by it, particularly as it is continually beamed at you from that damned TV set you always have on. And, yes, it has worked upon *you*, and precisely because, to paraphrase the great modern master of mass manipulation, it has been carefully "adjusted to the most limited intelligence among those to whom it is addressed." Likewise, besides being primarily visual, effective commercial advertising is presently "limited to a very few points, and it must harp on these, in slogans and until the last member of the public understands." The same principle works in the infotainment industry, the postmodernist enterprise that brings us innumerable, carefully recreated pictorializations of the UFO experience (figs. 9–15, 17–19).

Things were different in the 1930s, an orthodox-modernist era: then art, like politics, was deadly serious. Whereas then politics had few commercial applications, such as they do presently (as in "the selling of the president," among lesser political aspirants), then, between 1933 and 1945, they had some literally lethal consequences. Now, in a "postmodernist" era, it's all become quite different. Now the issue is not really "culture," at least not as Joseph Beuys (for example) understood *Kultur*. Instead, now the point is *mass marketing:* of politics, movies, sports, books, education and/or entertainment, religion and/or entertainment, and especially art. All these constitute the post–Cold War weapons of mass distraction. But why go on? You already knew all this.

As we further learn from Hitler's *Mein Kampf*, although on a much grander scale, Nazi propaganda art functions rather like postmodernist performance art. Obviously, every German was exposed to these staged spectacles, one way or another. And the Nazi spectacle was skillfully orchestrated; it was "live," intensely visual and oral—in short, it, too, was a messianic, didactic, and highly theatrical artform. If you doubt that, take another look at Leni Riefenstahl's brilliantly constructed films. This propagandistic performance art likewise requires a mass audience, whose emotions and spirits are to be magically manipulated and transformed by the unquestionably talented and charismatic director-artist. It is also the primary instrument for the inculcation of the new beliefs sustaining a new mass religion based upon "lofty and noble great ideas." As was explained by the great German pioneer in designing this kind of titanic and emotionally engaging, modernist artwork,

> Particularly the great masses of the people can be moved only by the power of speech. And all great movements are popular [*völkisch*] movements, volcanic eruptions of human passions and emotional sentiments. . . . A movement with great aims must therefore be anxiously on its guard not to lose contact with the broad masses. . . . It must, furthermore, avoid everything which might diminish, or even weaken, its ability to move the masses, not for "demagogic" reasons, but in the simple knowledge that, without the mighty force of the mass of a people, no great idea, however lofty and noble it may seem, can be realized. . . . The masses, it is true, need superior minds to set them into motion in a given direction, but then, like a flywheel, the masses themselves lend momentum and uniform persistence to the force of the attack.[11]

That last statement calls for reiteration: "The masses need superior minds to set them into motion," just like cattle prodded into the *Schlachthaus*. Journalist testimony, and rather breathless at that, describing just one of these proliferating pseudoreligious political spectacles tells us today just how effective they really were in practice, way back then, *damals*. As one might have read on September 12, 1936, in the *Niederelbisches Tageblatt*:

> We have witnessed many great march-pasts and ceremonies, but none of them was more thrilling and at the same time more inspiring than yesterday's. . . . Twilight covers the Zeppelin Meadow [near Nuremberg] as we enter the grandstand and see that a sea of light envelops the wall formed by the flags of the [Nationalist Socialist] Movement extending and shining for miles into the dark evening. . . . Innumerable swastika flags flutter in the light evening breezes, torn from the darkness by the floodlights and providing a sharp contrast to the pitch black, nocturnal sky. . . . A distant roar becomes stronger and comes even closer. The Führer is there! . . . The surprise is still too great. Nothing like it has ever been seen before. The wide field resembles a powerful Gothic cathedral made of light. Bluish-violet shine the floodlights and between their cones of light hangs the dark cloth of night. One-hundred-forty-thousand people—for it must be that many who are assembled here—cannot tear their eyes away from the sight. Are we dreaming, or is it real? Is it possible to imagine a thing like that? A cathedral of light?
>
> They do not have much time to pursue such thoughts for a new

spectacle is awaiting them. It is perhaps even more beautiful and compelling for those whose senses can embrace it. . . . Then they emerge from the black night—over there, on the southern edge: seven columns of flags pour into the spaces between the ranks. You cannot see the people; you do not recognize the bearers of the flags. All you see is an undulating stream, red and broad, its surface sparkling with gold and silver, which slowly comes closer, like fiery lava. . . . These are sacred symbols: twenty-five thousand flags. . . . The song that contains the oath rises up into the infinite cone of light. . . . It is like a great devotion, for which we are all gathered here, to collect new strength. Yes, that is what it is. A devotional hour of the Movement is being celebrated here, is protected by a sea of light against the [metaphorical] darkness outside.[12]

Well, there's your historical evidence: unquestionably, Nazi performance art worked upon the hearts and minds of the True Believers. It was absolutely effective in its *Bildung* purposes. As such, its "emotional Fascism" provided the authoritative model for all future mental manipulators, even the kind that thrive in democratic societies.

Seventy years ago, the pioneering political gurus of totalitarianism treated the mass spectacle as another weapon in their mass media arsenal, the function of which, then and now, is to collectively mold (*bilden*) hearts and minds. Germans were psychologically shaped by cultist ritual and ceremony. So formed and reformed, ordinary Germans (not necessarily "Nazis") did horrible, truly unspeakable, things to other human beings. They did so because they had been collectively *brainwashed*, programmed for collective hallucinations and mass psychosis. Although on a much reduced scale, likewise the members of such distinctly American and strictly occultist cults, most notoriously the Branch Davidians and Heaven's Gate, were exhorted by *their* charismatic leaders to make their own self-inflicted holocaust. Do you doubt that more are forthcoming?

Whatever the scale and whatever the generic ends—political and/or occultist—the psychological mechanisms of brainwashing are well understood by scientists, psychologists in this case. As they know, it doesn't matter whether you are German or American, or anybody else; under certain circumstances, we are *all* potentially susceptible to collective hypnotic suggestibility. According to psychologist William Sargant:

The whole history of hypnotism [about two centuries long] demonstrates that the people most susceptible to hypnotic states are *normal* people. Hypnotism has never been very successful in treating the severely mentally ill, who have in fact been remarkably unresponsive to all the efforts of Mesmer, Charcot and succeeding generations of hypnotists. When patients develop schizophrenia, severe depression, severe anxiety states, obsessional neuroses and the like, they become far less amenable to hypnotic techniques. *They have generally become much less open to suggestion than normal people. . . .*

It is not the mentally ill but ordinary, normal people who are most susceptible to "[political] brainwashing," "[religious] conversion," "[spirit] possession," "the [individual] crisis," or whatever you wish to call it, and who in their hundreds, or thousands, or millions fall readily under the spell of the demagogue or the revivalist, the witch-doctor [or shaman] or the pop group, the priest or the psychiatrist, or even, in less extreme ways, the propagandist or the advertiser. At the root of this all-too-common human experience is a state of heightened suggestibility, of openness to ideas and exhortation, which is characteristic of subjects under hypnosis.[13]

Fortunately, it presently suits the international masters of the mass media to channel our collective postmodernist mental energies toward materialist consumerism, not self-immolation or, even, genocide. They even offer us chilling diversions like the extraterrestrials (figs. 1, 4, 5, 15–22), that can easily be ignored by people whose intellectual interests are elsewhere occupied. Unfortunately, the Heaven's Gate tribe took them seriously, and they died for doing so. However, if the masters of the mass media ever decide to change their collective minds about sticking mostly with mere consumerism, watch out.

The postmodernist infotainment industry owes more than it would wish to acknowledge to the German pioneers of mass mental manipulation. As we additionally learn from looking at the daily schedules of secondary schools in the Third Reich, German youth had been specifically indoctrinated in *"Aktionen,"* a term used to describe the organized expression of "meaningful customs" through group celebrations. These *Feierstunden* (ceremonial hours) were based upon action, speech, and music, just like Joseph Beuys's performance artworks later also called *Aktionen*. As was explained in a 1941 report, "In school celebrations, the incorporation of the school into the great *Volk* community is most strikingly expressed." The expressed context is that "specific celebrations should he held if they grow organically out of the life of the school and its links with the great *völkisch* events. Since it is the purpose of these celebrations to serve as climaxes, they should be held only infrequently. . . . Action, speech, and music are the pillars upon which the great national celebrations rest. Music serves to prepare the celebrants. Speech opens bridges to their hearts. *Aktion* creates meaningful customs."[14] Something similar happens today at rock concerts, sit-ins, demonstrations, and other kinds of explicitly politicized get-togethers.

Alas, the term *Aktion* later acquired much more sinister implications. Beginning in October 1939, "Aktion T4" was being prepared; this dealt with the systematic liquidation of mentally ill patients in Germany (*die Tötung Geisteskranker in Deutschland*). It was followed, in spring 1941, by "Aktion 14 F 13," designed to "comb out" physically and socially undesirable elements held in domestic concentration camps; some 20,000 people were so eliminated.[15] Initiated in March 1942, "Aktion Reinhard" largely succeeded in its mission: to make Nazi occupied Poland *judenrein* ("cleansed of Jews"). Millions perished.[16] *Aktionen* had become weapons of mass destruction of targeted human "outsiders," the *alieni*.

Hitler had also made clear that the new doctrine—propaganda serving as a "visibly better substitute"—must take on both the moral force and the liturgical power and trappings formerly reserved to orthodox religion. Just like the Symbolist-era theorists, Hitler also put art at the service of religion, and vice versa, but his theology, National Socialism, was the most poisonous occultist creed yet known, at least on that kind of a scale. As the great political showman remarked:

> The great masses of people do not consist of philosophers; precisely for the masses, faith is often the sole foundation of a moral attitude. . . . If religious doctrine and faith are really to embrace the broad masses, the unconditional authority of the content of this faith is the foundation of all efficacy. . . . For the political man, the value of a religion must be estimated less by its deficiencies than by the virtue of a visibly better substitute.[17]

After Hitler's demise, New Age fads provide other kinds of specifically "visibly better substitutes," and these are even more popular than was the Fascist-Nazi sort. Again the key—the concrete link between ecstatic religion and the new secular belief system—is the ubiquitous term *völkisch*, "popular." Hitler conscientiously explained that

> the designation "religious" [*religiöse*] only becomes tangibly conceivable in the moment when it becomes connected with a definitely outlined form of its practice. Then it can even convey a definite, more or less sharp, picture of that soul-state leading to that efficacy which arises from religious inner-longing in the moment when, from the purely metaphysical, infinite world of ideas, a clearly delimited faith forms. Assuredly, this is not the end in itself, but only a means to the end. . . . By helping to raise man above the level of bestial vegetation, faith contributes in reality to the securing and safeguarding of his existence. . . . By abolishing religious education, but without replacing it by an equiv-

alent [i.e., political devotion], the result will be a grave shock to the foundations of existence. . . . Higher ideals provide the premise for man's existence. Thus the circle closes. . . . The situation with the term *völkisch* is similar to that with the term *"religiöse."*[18]

Adolf Hitler thought "art" was especially important to these pragmatic ends, although for rather different reasons than our readers might entertain. As he tells it, "At the early age of twelve—how it happened, I myself do not know—but one day it became clear to me that I would become a painter, an artist."[19] Yes, Hitler always fancied himself an artist, an especially noble and self-sacrificing one who generously lent his creative talents and energies to rectify the moral health of his adopted nation, Germany. "Yet, strange as it may seem, with the passing years, I became more and more interested in architecture. At that time, I regarded this as a natural complement to my gift as a painter, and only rejoiced inwardly at the extension of my artistic scope. I did not suspect that things would turn out differently."[20] Even though his own artistic predilections "turned out differently," Hitler had decreed that *Kunst* should be properly included in the new *völkisch* educational curriculum:

> Important as the type of physical and mental education will be in the *völkisch Staat*, equally important will be the human selection as such. . . . Presently, questions of [intrinsic] talent play a subordinate role. . . . Nevertheless, a peasant boy [as Hitler had been] can possess far more talents than the child of parents enjoying an elevated position in life. . . . If the talented peasant boy had, from his early years, likewise grown up in such an environment, then his intellectual ability would have been quite different.

The emphatic conclusion is that: "today, perhaps, *there is a single field in which origins are really less decisive than the individual's native talent: the field of art*."[21] Not only is art the only really democratic area in the *völkisch* educational curriculum, but it is also the only one where the student need not demonstrate acquired knowledge: hidden, native talent at once overcomes both academic demands and inherited privilege. Moreover, adds Hitler, our failure to realize this obvious fact is a mark of our current spiritual impoverishment: we cannot see that art is the real mark of *all* human intelligence. As he explains, "art" is a unique sector, an innately privileged place,

> *where a man cannot merely "learn," but everything has to be originally innate.* . . . Money and wealth of the parents are almost irrelevant. . . . The greatest artists arise not seldom from the poorest houses. . . . It

does not exactly argue great depth of thought in our time that this realization is not applied to our whole spiritual life. . . . Creative achievements can only arise when ability and knowledge are wedded. . . . Here too the *völkisch Staat* will some day have to intervene by education. Its task is not to preserve the decisive influence of an existing social class, [but instead] to pick the most capable kinds from the sum of all the national comrades and bring them to office and dignity [by] opening the gates of higher state educational institutions to *all talent, absolutely regardless of from what circle it may originate.*[22]

It may be added at this point that Hitler's feigned antiaristocratic attitudes—opening universities "to all talent"—have their clear-cut functional analogues in (for instance) Joseph Beuys's famously repeated statements that "every man is [or should be] an artist"—*Jeder Mensch ist ein Künstler*. Consequently, he, too, opened his own unquestionably popular (*völkisch*) and well-attended art classes "to all talent." No matter; American public universities will now typically admit *any*body into their art programs. If they do not do so strictly for the sake of utopian democracy, then certainly the educational bureaucrats do enjoy the tuition fees the thronging art students diligently fork over.

Hitler's concern for the educative functions and didactic uses of art was to reappear in the writings of the later, lesser propagandists of the Third Reich.[23] Nazi culture was as iconic as was medieval Byzantine culture: it, too, hypnotized itself with imagery, especially that kind depicting the otherworldly *Pantokrator* (figs. 2, 3, 7). The common leaven between one culture and the other, medieval versus modern, is *ideology*. That ideology, whether specifically Byzantine or Nazi, is best drummed into the mass mind by means of icons depicting otherworldly, but inevitably anthropomorphized, divinities (figs. 1, 4, 5, 15–22). The secularized, even pagan, modern revival of icon-magic by Nazi fiat is easily documented. For instance, describing one's properly ecstatic contemplation of the Führer's portrait (fig. 7) upon the national feast day celebrating the new messiah's joyous epiphany upon this weary planet (April 20, 1889), in 1939 an anonymous contributor to *Das Schwarze Korps*, the SS weekly magazine, exclaimed:

Mein Führer! Thus, on this day, I step before your picture. This picture is super-dimensional and nearly limitless. It is powerful, hard, beautiful, and sublime. It is [also] so simple, kind, modest, and warm. Yea, it is father, mother, and brother, all in one, and yet it is more. It carries within it the greatest years of my life. It embraces the quiet hours of reflection, the days full of worries and fears, the sun of faith and fulfillment, the victory which is forever the beginning of new duties and new fields. The more I attempt to comprehend it, the larger, brighter, and more endless it becomes—yet without once feeling strange or distant.[24]

Again, we now know that similar modernist effects are typically wrought upon the True Believers by extraterrestrial portraiture (figs. 1, 4, 5, 15–22). The alien scriptures so industriously assembled by Budd Hopkins, David Jacobs, John Mack, and the others prove that devotional point, likewise proving the ongoing effectiveness of *psychic fascism*.

Additionally, so stated Hitler, art is the single field in which the lone individual's "native talent is decisive." Art, moreover, is not "learned," being instead implicitly innate: *Jeder Mensch ist ein Künstler*. Yet another offshoot of Hitler's skillfully conceived arts of propaganda were visual performances, *Aktionen*, adjusted to the most limited intelligence. In an ostensibly democratic, certainly capitalistic culture, that is the way television works today, especially the kind copiously celebrating alien visitations (figs. 17, 18). Whatever the IQ level of the audience, all such orchestrated visual presentations parallel the great works Hitler called "a *visibly* better substitute." Some visual substitutes even duplicate religious rituals, being "metaphysical" events helping the witnesses "to rise above the level of bestial vegetation." All such organized multimedia mass spectacles express "higher ideas for the premise of man's existence." Consequently, just as Hitler claimed, the term "'*völkisch*' is similar to 'religious.'"[25] And the populist American art of extraterrestrial portraiture certainly smacks of the *religiöse* (as is explained in chapter 11).

In short, as was learned by an entire nation many decades ago, art, rather than being learned, must be popular and mystical and made accessible to all men. Were that goal proclaimed today, you could even believe that it was really an expression of democracy in action, the kind with decidedly New Age overtones. And, better yet, today all good bourgeois citizens, especially the decent, democratic American kind, believe that art is *good* for you, that it *heals* bleakly modernist souls.[26] And there are many people who even hold to the belief that extraterrestrials have descended upon the earth to heal postmodernist souls shriveled by agnosticism and/or atheism (or homosexuality or communism, or what have you). In short, what we have here is not a narrowed political phenomenon that we can blame on one person, even upon an entire nation. A mainly image-driven, manipulative culture of mass persuasion is, I fear, a typically postmodernist condition, our so-called visual culture.[27]

As we must also admit, all art, whether genuinely exalted or merely ersatz, is a thing of the mundane human mind. The complementary conclusion reached by the professional art historian is that all imagery produced by the artistic earthling brain is conditioned by the formal conventions belonging to the artist's historical period and an essentially mundane audience culture (so making another timely reference to currently practiced "reception theory"). That comment certainly pertains to that anomaly we have called extraterrestrial portraiture (figs. 1, 4, 5, 15–22). As E. H. Gombrich has observed, "If art were only, or mainly, an expression of personal vision, there could be no history of art. . . . Art is born of art, not of nature [so explaining] the tenacity of conventions, the role of types and stereotypes in art. . . . You cannot create a faithful image [or 'portrait'] out of nothing. You must have learned the trick, if only from other pictures you have seen."[28] Appearing in ever greater proliferation since 1966 (fig. 16), especially as initially televised in 1975 (figs. 17, 18), our conventionally rendered ETs likewise superbly exemplify what Richard Brilliant called "the established or invented schema" of any given portraiture, even the kind opportunely concocted by earthlings to depict extraterrestrial aliens, whom (we may presume) they have never really seen.[29] Such is evidently the case with the *Virgen de Guadalupe* (fig. 6), another kind of airborne apparition that has unquestionably captivated the popular imagination.

MYSTICISM AND THE POWER OF MODERNIST MUSIC

Superficial structural analogies aside, we need observe the fact of a radical mental difference between the function and spirit of the Renaissance art practice (figs. 33–35) and its modern offshoots, even including lower-class extraterrestrial portraiture (figs. 1, 4, 5, 15–22). This break with tradition needs to be examined in detail. We may do so by briefly mentioning an odd connection existing between mysticism, which we have repeatedly tied to the ET phenomenon (especially in chapter 11), and the power of modernist (versus "classical") music. One reason to do so is because, as it may be assumed, most witnesses of self-described encounters with extraterrestrials have inevitably experienced modern music, particularly the mass-produced popular kind. Aptly calling itself "rock 'n' roll," mainly it is propelled (eponymously) by *rhythm*. Rock music (now including the repugnant "hip-hop" and "rap" offshoots) is—like sport—a major component of the infotainment industry; being very "popular," it is also immensely profitable. Viewed in a broader historical perspective, although the phenomenon is obviously impervious to quantification, modern *rhythms*, like none other known in world history, have obviously shaped the modernist consciousness to make it somehow unlike its historical precedents. Again, the specifically modernist contribution is a now depoliticized, but still emotional, fascism.

In the most obvious sense, this caesura has to do with a basic idea of modernism itself. This is a commonplace notion which has been summed up by at least one writer as representing "the idea of a radical rupture with European artistic tradition."[30] Another fundamental notion underlying the concept of the avant-garde is, according to Renato Poggioli, the major historian of principles of vanguard thought, the expression of "activism." Activism, both psychic and kinetic, is obviously a prerequisite for an ubiquitous kind of activity-based musical performance, in short, a rock concert. Poggioli has, for instance, observed how "activism" also describes "a precise formal tendency within German Expressionism . . . elevating psychological revolt to the level of practical and social reform," and he also notes the provocative titles of two quintessential Expressionist publications, *Der Sturm* and *Die Aktion.* Nevertheless, this tendency nearly inevitably leads to a seemingly opposed result: "the idea of a blind, gratuitous activity, the cult of the act."[31]

Other key, distinctly modernist ideas separating the intentions and formulation of the late-to-postmodernist artworks from their supposed Renaissance predecessors are the complementary notions of "synaesthesia" and "simultaneism." For our purposes, *synaesthesia* refers to the overlap among sense perceptions and *simultaneism* signifies a manifestation of the totality of experience.[32] One can trace these synthetic, specifically modernist effects in turn to their own immediate artistic-historical prototype: the *Gesamtkunstwerk* of the German composer Richard Wagner (1813–1883). The Wagnerian *Gesamtkunstwerk* is what the German musicologist H. H. Stuckenschmidt calls "a 'total' work of art involving both eye and ear."[33] Stuckenschmidt also calls our attention to a much larger Wagnerian psychological effect: "a cult of suffering, finding sanctuary in the idea of redemption. . . . Not merely agony, but the ability to give expression to it in its most intensified form, became the paramount aim in the aesthetic hierarchy of the age. . . . Wagner signified the beginning of a new era in which there would be an end to harmonic and tonal tradition."[34] Although customarily unrecognized as such, as opposed to artworks patronized by upper-class opera-goers, a rock concert is a Wagnerian *Gesamtkunstwerk* designed for consumption by the proletariat. That sort of *Gesamtkunstwerk* belongs to pop culture; so does ET.

Thus, Wagner's highly popular performance pieces—incorporating music, painting, poetry, drama, dance, and lush, overripe emotionality— had first introduced the typically modernist subjectivist concept of the "total theater" to *mass* audiences in both Europe and the Americas. The excitement attendant upon these performances was brilliantly conveyed by Charles Baudelaire in an article published in 1861.[35] According to his well-informed, eyewitness account: "Wagner's concerts promised to be a veritable battle of doctrines, like one of those solemn crises in art, one of those confused scrimmages into which critics, artists and public have the habit of flinging all their passions." As an example, Baudelaire decided to "quote the following passage from an article by M. [Héctor] Berlioz (9 February 1860): 'The foyer of the Théatre-Italien was a curious sight to see on the night of the first concert. It was nothing but angry shouts and arguments which always seemed on the point of ending in blows. . . . In our country at least, when it is a matter of appreciating a type of music different from the normal run, passion and prejudice alone are vocal, preventing good sense and good taste from getting a word in.'"[36]

Having drawn for us (with the help of Berlioz) a vivid picture of the typical avant-garde context of raucous doctrinal strife surrounding Wagner's overwhelming performance piece, Baudelaire then sets about to convey its actual psychological effect. The perceptual-conceptual significance of what he had just witnessed turns out to be uniquely mystical-sensual-emotional—in short, *synesthesiac*. From this it becomes clear that, at least for this hypersensitive witness, "total" theater leads to a truly "total" experience, that is, "simultaneity." As told by Baudelaire, the as yet unnamed experience of *simultaneité* inevitably leads to nothing less than a revelation of the "reciprocal analogies," here meaning the "oneness" of all of god's creations! According to Baudelaire's excited recitation:

> By means of the innumerable combinations of sound, the tumults of the human soul, Richard Wagner was the equal of the most exalted, and certainly was as great as the greatest. I have often heard the opinion expressed that music could not claim to convey anything with precision, as words or painting do. That is true to a certain extent, but it is not wholly true. Music conveys things in its own way and by means peculiar to itself. . . . The only really surprising thing would be that sound could not suggest color, that colors could not give the idea of melody, and that both sound and color together were unsuitable as media for ideas; [this must be so] since *all things always have been expressed by reciprocal analogies*, ever since the day when *God created the world as a complex, indivisible totality*.[37]

Also reminding one of Swedenborg's visionary revelations, Baudelaire thus thoughtfully acknowledged the transcendental nature of his performance-induced cosmic revelation. With even more spectacular eloquence, he then proceeds to relate to us the exact nature of this revelation's sensual, earthbound equivalencies:

> I felt freed from the constraint of weight, and recaptured the memory of the rare joy that dwells in high places. . . . Then, involuntarily, I evoked the delectable state of a man possessed by a profound reverie in total solitude, but a solitude with vast horizons and bathed in a diffused light; immensity without other decor than itself. Soon I became aware of a heightened brightness, of a light growing in intensity so quickly that the shades of meaning provided by a dictionary would not suffice to express this constant increase of burning whiteness. Then I achieved a full apprehension of a soul floating in light, of an ecstasy compounded of joy and insight, hovering above and far removed from the natural world.[38]

Baudelaire correctly, indeed almost clinically, concluded that, so enlightened, literally, he "had undergone, or so at least it seemed to me, *a spiritual operation, a revelation.*" A trendy New Age acolyte might instead say that he had experienced an "out-of-body experience" (OBE). To these striking observations by Baudelaire, there may now be added another, pointing out a much larger historical context for his other-worldly experiences. In short, his account both sets the rapturous tone and has the transcendental content found in all the greatest mystic writers belonging to the esoteric tradition including, of course, Swedenborg. As one now wonders, are these not the same marvelous and soul-transforming results sought by all *modern* performance artists, especially the ones who perform at rock concerts?

But what precisely was in Richard Wagner's mind 140 years ago? To answer these questions, again our best source seems Charles Baudelaire, a most eloquent spokesman for a new kind of psychically susceptible *mass*-audience culture. Besides wonderfully conveying *his* state of mind, the excited Frenchman, unquestionably endowed with a most discerning mind, quoted some statements written by "the master himself." In these, Wagner got right to the heart of the significance and purposes of his multimedia, rhythmic and emotionally convulsive, performance art. As transcribed by Baudelaire, the German composer had stated that

> the only picture of human life that may be called 'poetic' is the one where all motivations, that [used to] have meaning only for the abstract intelligence, [now] give way to purely human motives rooted in the heart. This tendency—the one relating to the invention of the poetic subject—is the sovereign law that governs the poetic form and repre-

sentation. . . . From this stage, I say that I was inevitably being led to point to the *Myth* as the ideal material for the poet.

As Wagner further claimed:

> The myth is the primitive and anonymous poetry of the People [*das Volk*], and we find it taken up again in every age, remodeled constantly by the great poets of cultivated ages. In the myth, indeed, human relations discard almost completely their conventional form, which is intelligible only to abstract reason. They show what is really human in life, what can be understood in any age, and they show it in that concrete form, exclusive of all imitation, that confers upon all true myths their individual character, which is recognizable at the first glance. . . . I abandoned once and for all the domain of [factual] history, and established myself in that of legend. Whatever the epoch or nation it belongs to, legend [meaning "myth"] has the advantage of incorporating exclusively what is purely human in the given epoch or nation, of presenting it in an original and very striking form, thus intelligible at the first glance.

Wagner's concluding statement is especially telling: "The nature of the scene and the whole tone of the legend combine to *transport the mind* to a dream-state—quickly *carrying it on to perfect clairvoyance*—and the mind then discovers a different concatenation of phenomena, which the eyes could not perceive in the normal state of waking."[39] We have already explored the conventional mystical significance accorded to the term "transport" (in chapter 6), and *clairvoyance* merely represents a nineteenth-century accretion from Spiritism, pure occultism. Likewise, postmodernist ETs are not creatures "the eyes could not perceive in the normal state of waking"; for that experience, if not put under hypnosis, you need to find yourself in either a hypnopompic or a hypnagogic sleep-state (as explained in chapter 14).

Wagner's analyses of the literally "clairvoyant" raison d'être of his own multimedia performance art functionally share numerous ideas with those expressed much later by individuals said to be experiencing close encounters with extraterrestrial beings. These common reference points would include the following issues. As Wagner said at the outset, there exists in such self-designated modern art an understood opposition between "abstract intelligence" and the irrational profundities of the poetic instinct, "rooted in the heart." *Myth* (or legend) is the proper vehicle for poetic expression. Why? Above all, because it is *"primitive,"* rooted in the "anonymous poetry of the People." Such *völkisch* materials are timeless, "taken up again in every age, remodeled constantly." These eternal (*ewige*) themes are the antithesis of "conventional form, intelligible only to abstract reason." Nevertheless, they are "recognizable at the first glance." So, evidently, are the ETs (figs. 16, 21, 22), likewise the Blessed Virgin Mary (figs. 6, 33, 34).

Another statement by Wagner provides apparently convincing evidence for the composer's involvement with contemporary occultist beliefs, specifically the Theosophical kind (as discussed in chapter 10). As Wagner affirmed:

> I am convinced that there are universal currents of Divine Thought, vibrating in the ether everywhere, and that anyone who can feel those vibrations is inspired, provided he is conscious of the process. . . . I believe, first of all, that it is this universal vibrating energy that binds the soul of man to the Almighty central power, from which emanates the Life-Principle to which we all owe our existence. This energy links us to the Supreme Force of the Universe, of which we are all a part. . . . In that trance-like condition, which is the prerequisite of all true creative effort, I feel that I am one with this vibrating Force, and that it is omniscient, and that I can draw upon it to an extent that is limited only by my own capacity to do so. . . . Imagination is the creative force, and this is true, I find, not only of musical creations but also of external circumstances. . . . Believe me, imagination creates "reality" [*die Fantasie schafft die Wirklichkeit*]. This is a great cosmic law.[40]

So much for the content of the Wagnerian *Gesamtkunstwerk*, a distinctly totalized, "trance-like" and self-referential "artwork"—so designated *Kunstwerk*—where only *"die Fantasie schafft die Wirklichkeit."* If this is its avowed purpose, then what seems to be its central formal principle? In a word, this is *rhythm*. This is the means by which the performance artist is led "to the extreme limit of his art." As for the audience culture, what does rhythm *do* to it and, specifically, what are the desirable psychological effects of rhythm as such? As Wagner repeatedly states, rhythm is powerful; it captivates its audience; it governs their emotional states; it works a spell; *it transports the mind*. Most of us have experienced those hypnotic and/or intellect-numbing effects, but mainly at the Joe Sixpack audience-cultural level: at a rock concert! And recognizing that participation, however reluctantly as ivory tower elitists, we come full circle, all the way back to the ecstatic mysteries of primitive Greek Dionysian religion (fig. 23).

We also come back to the modernist subject of imposed psychological cohesion en masse. The Branch Davidians were led by David Koresh (aka Vernon Howell). At his instigation, eighty-six of them underwent a collective immolation by fire, a mass suicide, in April 1993. Koresh spiritually inflamed his eventually cremated cult with fiery sermons, some lasting up to twelve hours. He would then conclude his ritualistic harangues with a jumped-up rock concert (and some of his rock 'n' roll performances survive on tape). Mass performances of loud and frenzied gospel music is also a propelling force for those who subscribe to Pentecostal religion. We recall that Betty Andreasson, famed for her close encounters with ETs (figs. 21, 22), was one such. Pentecostalists believe that the Holy Spirit descends upon each and every one of them; its arrival makes them speak in tongues and have visions. So possessed, they hop, twist, and dance in the aisles; then song gives way to a string of "oooohs" and "waaahs" and "la-la-lahs." The role of music in inflaming this particularly proletarian branch of evangelical revelation is easily confirmed: just go to the nearest Pentecostal temple in your neighborhood.

Everybody knows, even including otherwise wholly autistic teenagers, that the bottom-line experience at a rock concert is *rhythm*. As just a word, that, too, is nothing new; it comes from the ancient Greek, *rhythmos*. As you will probably be surprised to learn, it was none other than Aristotle who made the physical basis of "rock 'n' roll"—*rhythmos*—into a component of "fine art." As we should already know, Aristotle had defined (in *Poetics* 6. 2–3) the proper social function of the most sublime of all kinds of classical dramatic expression—"tragedy"—as being the release of *katharsis*: "effecting the proper purgation [*katharsis*] of the emotions of pity and fear."[41] The actual formal characteristic distinguishing classical *tragodía* was, he said, "language embellished with each kind of artistic ornament," and that embellishment represents the specific means for achieving that needful emotion laxative, *katharsis*.[42] Aristotle specifically adds that we are not talking about words, rather: "rhythm, harmony and song"—*rhythmòn kaì harmonían kaì mélos*[43]—meaning the very stuff of proletarian rock 'n' roll as concocted well over two thousand years later!

Without making specific reference to Aristotle and his theory of an emotionally therapeutic *katharsis*, mythologist Joseph Campbell made the very same functional connection:

> Rock music has never seemed that interesting to me. But when you see a room with 8,000 young people going through it for five hours to the beat of these boys [e.g., the rock band "The Grateful Dead"], and when you see those 8,000 kids all going up in the air together: Listen, this is powerful stuff! And what is it? The first thing I thought of was the Dionysian festivals [fig. 23], of course. This energy and these terrific instruments, with electric things that zoom in: This is more than music! It turns something on in here, in the heart. And what it turns on is life-energy. *This is Dionysus talking* through these kids. . . . And when the

great beam of light would go over the crowd, you'd see these marvelous young faces all in utter rapture—for five hours! This is a wonderful, fervent loss of self in the larger self of a homogeneous community. This is what it's all really about. . . . It doesn't matter what the name of the god is, or whether it's a rock group or a clergy. It's somehow hitting that chord of realization of the unity of God in us all. That's a terrific thing, and it just blows the rest away![44]

In sum, all those new artistic effects so carefully engineered by Richard Wagner and mostly rhythm-driven were, just as he said, calculated to alter consciousness, leading it "to a dream-state, that quickly carries it on to perfect clairvoyance—and the mind then discovers a different concatenation of phenomena, which the eyes could not perceive in the 'normal' state."[45] Adolf Hitler *loved* Wagner's performance art, and he took its emotionally manipulative message to heart. In short, that is the strictly *modernist* audience cultural experience: *mass* psychic response, a *mass* catharsis leading to *mass* passivity and compliance: a kind of collective dumbness, a *dementia* ("de-braining"). This is the kind now commonly achieved by a now knowing, meaning willed and skilled, use of *mass* psychic manipulation. And that includes, among a diversity of other mind-boggling postmodernist mental events, the UFO experience and the extraterrestrial phenomenon.

As should by now be perfectly obvious, as specifically explained by Richard Wagner, this is also pure mysticism! The ideas expressed by him so long ago are nothing less than the familiar arguments of the esoteric tradition, a phenomenon whose documents date back at least to the Hellenistic period. In short, other than in its "aesthetic" explanation, this is wholly conventional stuff. The modernist take on the psychological characteristics of such a state of purely "mystical transport" (see chapter 6) were described in 1902 by William James in his classic study on *The Varieties of Religious Experience*:

> Mystical states are more like states of feeling than like states of intellect. . . . Mystical states [nevertheless] seem, to those who experience them, to be also states of knowledge. They are states or insight into depths of truth unplumbed by the discursive intellect. They are illuminations, revelations, full of [apparent] significance and importance, all inarticulate though they remain. When the characteristic sort of consciousness once has set in, the mystic feels as if his own will were in abeyance, and indeed sometimes as if he were grasped and held by a superior power.[46]

In the terminology of modern occultism, the kind of psychic state so vividly described by both Wagner and Baudelaire—in this case, *art-*

induced psychosis!—is properly called, at least by the New Age True Believers, "cosmic consciousness." The *old* name for it (see chapter 6) was *ecstasy, enthusiasm, transport*, even *inspiration*. A century ago, all this was explained according to the new terminology by the influential Canadian occultist Richard M. Bucke in his aptly titled study celebrating a *Cosmic Consciousness* (1901). According to Mr. Bucke:

> The prime characteristic of cosmic consciousness is a consciousness . . . of the life and order of the universe. Along with [this] there occurs an intellectual enlightenment which alone would place the individual on a new plane of existence—which would make him almost a member of a new species. To this is added a state of moral exaltation, an inde-scribable feeling of elevation, elation, and joyousness, and a quickening of the moral sense, which is fully as striking, and more important than is the enhanced intellectual power. With these come what may be called a sense of immortality, a consciousness of eternal life.[47]

Whatever his putative occultist inclinations, Richard Wagner was of course quintessentially "Germanic." The significance of this ethno-graphic attribute of the composer was also recognized by a German scholar, Hans Kohn. In his important study of *The Mind of Germany* (1960), Kohn pointed out how this awesome figure, so centrally placed in the modern consciousness of Germany (Adolf Hitler's, too),

> bore a message of specific Germanic values, an interpretation of history and society, based upon the incomparable preeminence of Wagner's art and of German folkdom. Wagner saw himself not only as a musician of genius but also as a prophet and savior. All of his creative work was infused with, and serves, this avocation . . . protesting against the nine-teenth-century bourgeois world, against men without myth, passion and greatness. . . . [His was] the realm of primitive, pre-Christian myth. . . . These Nordic-Wagnerian myths were rediscovered and adapted in the age of nationalism for nationalistic purposes. . . . Wagner proclaimed it is necessary to found a true community of life (*Lebensgemeinschaft*), which cannot be achieved by political means, but only through art. . . . His artwork will restore the loving union of all arts, and thus set the example of a true folk-community. Alone in Europe, the Germans pos-sess the particular talent of becoming impassioned with what they take as abstract truth, without considering its practical consequences.[48]

Translated into a distinctively American idiom, the same kind of *Lebensgemeinschaft* now operates at your neighborhood rock concert. If you have ever participated in such a highly emotionalized cultural transaction, you know this observation to be correct. Moreover, now the fans are often called "ravers," and they achieve their Maenad-like state by ingesting an aptly named by illegal drug, "ecstacy."

Let us quickly review the contents of this catalogue of self-induced *Irrsinn* (irrationality) produced by the basic elements making up the precedent-setting Wagnerian *Gesamtkunstwerk*. The essential components include primitivism, *völkisch* myth and legend, irrationality at odds with abstract reason, spiritualist revelations, strivings for an indivisible totality, antibourgeois social alienation, titanic rhythmic unity, audience manipulative techniques, the rule of instinct, consciousness-altering effects, paranormal clairvoyance, and the will toward mass psychological manipulation and collective social transformation. This catalogue is part and parcel of the New Age spiritual quest. Accordingly, these factors all apply in equal measure to the mass media–propelled extraterrestrial phenomenon (figs. 1, 4, 5, 15–22). And we may call the common link *psychic fascism*.

Since that represents modernism in its most aberrant mode, let us momentarily retreat to blander subject matter, the broader issues pertaining to art history and their particular mode of perception and expression unique within a modern context. Due to strictly technological innovations, we all now have perceptions like none known to earlier humans. We will now examine in greater detail the actual historical setting, physical and cultural, for the concepts of "synaesthesia" and "simultaneity." These are two notions critical to the early self-definition of modernism—but both were already implicit in the convulsively perceived Wagnerian *Gesamtkunstwerk*. They also help explain a strictly modernist *mentalité* that was eventually to dote on a specialized subgenre: alien close encounters.

MODERNIST SIMULTANEITY IN TIME AND SPACE

The physical setting of the *fin-de-siècle* seemed in fact to demand a universally heightened consciousness of *synaesthesia*, an effect (as yet unnamed)[49] already popularized by the awesome transemotional effects of the Wagnerian showpiece, a phenomenon significant in European culture since 1860. Synaesthesia, along with simultaneity, was also alluded to by Baudelaire in his famous poem "Les Correspondances" (circa 1861). As Baudelaire put it in this acclaimed sonnet: "Every sign expresses both a thought and all forms beneath the heavens: it is a figure sketched by the mysterious thinker"—*"Tout signe exprime une pensée / Et toute forme sous les cieux / Est une figure tracée / Par le penseur mystérieux."*[50]

As it turns out, Baudelaire's poem was heavily influenced by the writings of the prominent modern occultist Éliphas Lévi (see chapter 11), who in 1851 had written a verse by the same name. In fact, adds Filiz Burhan, "Lévi's *Correspondences* presented virtually every element of that mystical theory [of the correspondences] which was involved in the construction of the Symbolist aesthetic attributing genuine perception, or clairvoyance to the 'sacred instinct of genius.'"[51] Certainly Baudelaire was a major source for the complicated intellectual issues informing Symbolism, from which, it may be argued (as in chapter 11), all the major ideas of early modernism ultimately stemmed.[52] *Clairvoyance*, by the way, is the kind of privileged "clear sight" that enables mystics to perceive otherworldly apparitions—the kind you and I can't see. Most likely, neither you nor I have ever seen an ET, but that is due to our lack of clairvoyance, and so the reported "fact" of an alien abduction uniquely belongs to other people more privileged than us to regard such visionary apparitions. They have that spiritual "clear vision" which our earthling opticians seem unable to provide for us.

Simultaneity, however, has largely technological, rather than narrowly artistic, origins. In our revisionist view, strictly material facts explain the emotional gulf separating the two cultures of the nineteenth and twentieth centuries. Some sources of the new modes of perception are decidedly banal. For one thing, until about 1850, all furniture was hand carved; by 1920, it was almost entirely industrially carved. Not long after the Armistice of 1918, virtually all handcrafted articles had vanished from everyday life. The most prestigious, and pricey, exception has since become the "unique" work of "fine art," a free market cultural commodity now lacking the traditional patron dictating to the artist its visual appearance, narrative content, and social function. By the late 1920s, modern art initially became very fashionable, particularly in Paris and Berlin. At that time, even mass culture began to look modern: more reductive, abstract, even occasionally nonfigurative. An omnipresent industrial precursor, in place as early as 1912, was the Ford assembly line, itself as much a model for simplified modern design as was contemporary, but then rarely seen, Cubist art.

In the particular case of *simultaneity*, we have another crucial modernist but wholly psychic event. We are dealing with new, fundamentally altered, cultural apprehensions of the very nature of *time* and *space*.[53] This phenomenon merits investigation, especially given the common recognition that "modernism in the arts [also in real life] is a master code about dislocation, disjunction, loss of a linear sense of time, about sudden forgetfulness."[54] This is also modernism in life itself, and such perceptions have their material roots in the defining modernist situation, capitalism, an economic system fundamentally transforming terrestrial minds in ways never before imagined, not even by the divine mentalities ascribed to God, Yahweh, Allah, Buddha, and all the rest. The great prophet of the modernist mind-set was Karl Marx, and it has all come to pass just as he predicted in the *Manifest der Kommunistischen Partei* (1848):

> Constant revolutionizing of production, uninterrupted disturbance of all social conditions, everlasting uncertainty and agitation distinguish the bourgeois epoch from all earlier ones. All fixed, fast-frozen relations, with their train of ancient and venerable prejudices and opinions are swept away; all new-formed ones become antiquated before they can ossify. All that is solid melts into air.[55]

Another strictly modernist phenomenon—which Marx would have abhorred—is the idea of alien abductions, producing narrations likewise containing recurrent and stereotyped motifs, all of which are expressive of "dislocation, disjunction, loss of a linear sense of time, about sudden forgetfulness." Nonetheless, we may ascribe the timely apparition of the postmodernist ETs to, as Marx put it, "uninterrupted disturbance of all social conditions, everlasting uncertainty and agitation." As the demographics so clearly indicate (see chapter 11), ET experiencers are also wholly "bourgeois."

Moderns (and postmodernists, too), think in different ways from their historical earthling predecessors. Since the late medieval invention of the mechanical clock,[56] the single most momentous development in the history of a uniform cultural grasp of time was the gradual introduction at the end of the nineteenth century of a "world standard time." That innovation supplanted "natural" notions of day and night—and whatever else might fit in between. The natural divisions between day and night had already been blurred by Edison's invention of the electric lamp in 1879. Then the invention of the telegraph made it necessary to impose this preternaturally unnatural time scheme worldwide. Particularly the creation of swift, international railway networks emphasized the need, as much political as economic, for organized, simultaneous worldwide time zones. The next, inevitable, development was the wireless telegraph, which the U.S. Navy had employed as early as 1905. By July 1913 the first time signal had been sent around the globe, transmitted from the Eiffel Tower, itself the architectural emblem of modernism.

On the literal level, electrical impulses were traveling around the world at the dizzying speed of light itself. In a larger sense, traditional heterogeneous time and space had been displaced by a homogeneous continuum. The result was that all human activity had become a construction of measurable, interchangeable time-bits floating in continuous flux in a world now seeming without apparent physical distance. In 1905, in his "Special Theory of Relativity," Albert Einstein concluded that "every reference body has its own particular time."[57] Newton's conventional vision of an atomistic time, a sum of infinitesimally small but discrete units, was now replaced by a theory of flux and continuity, in short, by simultaneity. The new, wholly physical, arena for such theoretical insights was the very real world of the modern metropolis. This materially represented a social setting staged largely among strangers in an atmosphere of intensified psychic stimulation; this became a microcosmic habitat stressed by competition and nurturing intensified individuality, a quickened world ruled by money and largely anonymous commodity exchange. It is not surprising that modern mankind commonly feels itself to be "alienated." Such a perception perhaps naturally leads to encounters with other aliens, even those with extraterrestrial zip codes (figs. 1, 4, 5, 15–22); their speciality is "missing time."

Another banal, but significant, observation deals with the bicycle. Space as well as time became further compressed with the general acceptance of the bicycle, essentially made possible by the introduction of a pneumatic tire in 1890. This was a mundane but timely invention comfortably speeding the rounds of ordinary people up to four times the velocity of walking. Besides being an instrument of social equality—everyone, rich and poor, men and women, came to ride them—the bicycle also expanded the radius of accessible social contacts, from three to five kilometers to some fifteen to thirty. The automobile, of course, compresses space and time yet more. There were only three thousand of them in France in 1900, but already thirteen thousand by 1913. With the invention of the electric clock in 1916, the world became familiar with a visual model for the notion of time as inexorable flux, an operation as significant for Paris as it was for Patagonia. In 1896 there was the first public exhibition of the cinema, an artistic medium that broke up time into discrete, movable parts.[58] This was a technological, also quintessential modernist, art expression which was additionally public and democratic par excellence. It provides, presently, the major vehicle by which to propel the ETs into our collective consciousness (figs. 9–15, 17–19).

Soon the artistic possibilities inherent in the new pictorial-theatrical medium were stretched. Pioneering cinematographers commonly played with the reigning strictures on the irreversibility of near and far—both in time and space—through editing techniques, *montage*. These were compositional devices both contemporary and functionally analogous to the Cubists' *collages*. As a sculptural concept, this simultaneist combinatory technique became known as *assemblage*. The cheap, popular press—*les journaux* and *die Zeitungen*—similarly created a simultaneous collage-montage perception of events; accordingly, the Cubists put scraps of newspapers into their simultaneous collages. Phenomena were all presented ("reported") without much pretense to hierarchical ranking; the trivial and the anecdotal rubbed shoulders with the momentous and the portentous. In the daily papers, every man's universal informational experience, the ominous distant rumblings of *Realpolitik* competed with the fashionable gossip of the inner-city *salons*. Such were the transient disposable "facts" of daily existence in the newly created modernist global village based on wired simultaneity. That is how all of us, simultaneously, get to hear about, and also *see*, the extraterrestrials lurking in our midst (figs. 1, 4, 5, 15–22).

Even before the cinematographers, however, the Impressionist painters had already invented the distinctively modernist idea of an artistic depiction of time, and even space, as a transient fluid medium. As Claude Monet explained, "One does not paint a landscape, a seascape, a figure; [instead] one paints an *impression* of an hour of the day."[59] Paul Cézanne also spoke of the subjective fragmentation of space, as well as time, in a letter of 1906: "The same subject [motif], seen from a different angle, gives a subject for study. . . . [It is potentially] so varied that I think I could be occupied for months without changing my place, simply bending more to the right or left."[60] In 1910 art critic Léon Werth told the public that Picasso's Cubist constructions depicted "the sensations and reflections which we experience with the passage of time."[61] A Cubist painter, Jean Metzinger, went even further, claiming that his colleagues "have allowed themselves to move [in space] around the object, in order to give a concrete representation of it, made of several successive aspects [in time]. *Formerly, a picture took possession of space—now [art] reigns also in time*."[62]

In 1884, for the first time, the term "stream of thought" appeared, in an essay by William James.[63] In 1890 this author added that "consciousness does not appear to itself chopped up in bits. . . . In speaking of it hereafter, let us call it the stream of thought, of consciousness."[64] Such simultaneist notions quickly became universal, and when Henri Bergson contemplated his inner self, he encountered "a continuous flux, a succession of states." Thus he explained our existence in a spaceless time, that elastic, all-encompassing ether he called "duration," *la durée*.[65] As he affirmed in *L'Évolution créatrice* (Creative Evolution,

1907), mentally alert people all "see the material world melt back into a single flux, a continuity of flowing, a becoming."[66] One need not have read Bergson to grasp such ideas; they were "in the air." Virginia Woolf quoted Thomas Hardy's lament to the effect that contemporary writers had "changed everything now. We used to think there was a beginning and a middle and an end. We [of the older generation] believed in the Aristotelian theory."[67] The world was beginning to get more than a bit confusing; living in modern society was becoming so stressful that it made desirable a move to some "elsewhere," if not of geography than within the mind. The more stressed out now even voyage to other worlds, often get themselves abducted by aliens.

This new, technologically induced and universally perceived sense of time—immediate and constant—overturned and nearly destroyed the concept of history as something locked in the past, and thus left discrete and removed. Due to the myriad new technological innovations, the more alert modern artists soon recognized themselves to be inhabiting a world, newly made, that was as fragmented as that artificially composed by them upon their Cubist canvases. With unusual awareness and articulation, the self-consciously modernist issue was analyzed in 1914 by the painter Fernand Léger in a newspaper article appearing in *Les Soirées de Paris*:

> Contemporary achievements in painting are the result of the modern mentality and are therefore closely bound up with the visual aspect of external things which are creative and necessary for the painter. Before tackling the purely technical [painterly] questions, I am going to try to explain why contemporary [Cubist] painting is representative, in the modern sense of the word, of *the new visual state imposed by the evolution of the new means of production*. A work of art must be significant in its own time, like any other intellectual manifestation. Because painting is visual, it is necessarily the reflection of external rather than of psychological conditions. Every pictorial work must possess this momentary and external value; that is what enables it to endure beyond the epoch of its creation.
>
> *If pictorial expression has changed, it is because modern life has required it.* The existence of modern creative people is much more intense and more complex than that of people in earlier centuries. The thing that is imagined is less fixed, the object exposes itself less than it did formerly. When one crosses a landscape by automobile or express train, it becomes fragmented; it loses in descriptive value but gains in synthetic value. The view through the door of the railroad car or through the automobile windshield, in combination with the vehicle's speed, has altered the habitual look of things. A modern man registers a hundred

times more sensory impression than an eighteenth-century artist; so much so that even our language, for example, is full of diminutives and abbreviations. The compression of the modern picture, its variety, its breaking up of forms, are the direct result of all this [modernist] velocity.

It is certain that the evolution of the [mechanical] means of loco-motion and their speed have a great deal to do with the new [artistic] way of seeing. . . . A painter who calls himself "modern" rightly con-siders perspective and sentimental value to be negative methods; he must be able to replace them in his pictures with something other than, for instance, an unending harmony of pure tones, substituting for them instead contrast, which equals dissonance, and hence a maximum expressive effect. . . . I do not know what is an ancient or a modern sub-ject [for art]; all I know is what is a new interpretation. But locomotives, automobiles and, if you insist, advertising billboards, are all good for the application of a form of movements. *All this research comes, as I have said, from the modern environment.*[68]

Accordingly, the burning issues of sequence versus simultaneity were also hotly debated—and employed—by numerous modernist artists. By then, the concept had a name, and thus it became an artistic technique; the futurist Tommaso Marinetti called it "*la simultaneità.*" But ultimately, as Stephen Kern recognized,

The model for the simultaneous art and poetry was music. . . . In [Wag-nerian] opera two or more voices might sing different words at the same time to intensify the urgency of their encounter. . . . Richard Strauss combined two keys at the same time in *Also Sprach Zarathusa* (1896), as did Debussy in parts of *Pelléas et Mélisande* (1902). In the first of the *Fourteen Bagatelles* of 1908, Bela Bartok produced two simultaneously sounding melodic parts written in different keys. Prokofiev had such bi-tonal passages in *Sarcasmes* (1911), and Stravinsky made extensive use of tri-tone harmonies in *Le Sacre du Printemps* (1913). While there were precedents to poly-rhythm and poly-meter in counterpoint and classical symphonic music, there was a striking concentration of them in twen-tieth-century music, beginning with Charles Ives's combination of two marches in different tempi in *Three Places in New England* (1904).[69]

Whatever the technical means, whether vanguard or wholly conven-tional, and whatever the targeted audience, elitist or proletariat, the larger etiology of a distinctively modern experience embraces simul-taneity, emotional satiation, and psychic manipulation. Above all, the fact of mass audiences of millions now simultaneously participating via TV in emotionally charged moments in real time is a major new perceptual experience. Never before had there been a universal visual culture seizing everyone's eyeballs and emotions at the same moment. The power of communally shared imagery is essential to the modernist mass spectacle, be that the broadcasting of a world-historical event—like the pioneering exploration of Mars, the next version of the Gulf War, civil unrest and genocide in the Third World, the assassination of the president—or just another rock concert, then more and more "documentaries" on UFOs and ETs. Without the mass media, there would have been *no* mass audience, no mesmerized subscribers for any of that momentous stuff. People would have instead found some local occurrence to relieve their boredom, might even have read a book, just like they used to do in the other millennia.

NOTES

1. David Freedberg, *The Power of Images: Studies in the History and Theory of Response* (Chicago: University of Chicago Press, 1989), pp. 112, 145, 402.

2. Gregorius Magnus, as quoted in C. Davis-Weyer, ed., *Early Medieval Art, 300–1150* (Englewood Cliffs, N.J.: Prentice-Hall, 1971), p. 48.

3. John of Damascus, as in Sixton Ringbom, *Icon to Narrative: The Rise of the Dramatic Close-Up in Fifteenth-Century Devotional Painting* (Doornspijk: Davnaco, 1984), p. 12.

4. Margot Lovejoy, *Postmodernist Currents: Art and Artists in the Age of Electronic Media* (Englewood Cliffs, N.J.: Prentice-Hall, 1997), pp. 68–69, 83, 112–13.

5. Jean Baudrillard, *Selected Writings* (Stanford, Calif.: Stanford University Press, 1988), p. 167.

6. Ilse McKee, *Tomorrow the World* (London: Dent, 1960), p. 11; the author, who later married an Englishman, wrote her book from that enlightened perspective.

7. Adolf Hitler, *Mein Kampf*, ed. R. Mannheim (Boston: Houghton-Mifflin, 1971), p. 266.

8. Ibid., p. 408.

9. Ibid., pp. 33–34.

10. Ibid., pp. 179–81.

11. Ibid., pp. 107–108.

12. Anonymous journalist, in Joachim Remak, *The Nazi Years: A Documentary History* (Englewood Cliffs, N.J.: Spectrum, 1969), pp. 79–80.

13. William Sargant, *The Mind Possessed: A Physiology of Possession, Mysticism, and Faith Healing* (New York: Penguin, 1975), p. 31 (emphasis in original).

14. Hermann Klauss, *Feierstunden der deutschen Schule*, as quoted in George L. Mosse, ed., *Nazi Culture: Intellectual, Cultural, and Social Life in the Third Reich* (New York: Grossett & Dunlap, 1968), pp. 127–29.

15. For documents on Aktionen T4 and 14 F 13, see Remak, *Nazi Years*, pp. 134–43.

16. For Aktion Reinhard, see Daniel J. Goldhagen, *Hitler's Willing Executioners: Ordinary Germans and the Holocaust* (New York: Vintage, 1997), pp. 194 ff.

17. Hitler, *Mein Kampf*, p. 276.

18. Ibid., pp. 379–80.

19. Ibid., p. 9.

20. Ibid., p. 17.

21. Ibid., pp. 428–29 (my emphasis).

22. Ibid., pp. 429–31 (my emphasis).

23. See Hildegard Brenner, ed., *Kunstpolitik des Nationalsozialismus* (Reinbek: Rowohlt, 1966); Joseph Wulf, ed., *Die bildenden Künste im Dritten Reich. Eine Dokumentation* (Reinbek: Rowohlt, 1966).

24. Anonymous SS celebrant, as in Remak, *Nazi Years*, p. 49.

25. Hitler, *Mein Kampf*, p. 380.

26. For a cogent, and properly acerbic, discussion of this particularly flacid fallacy, see Robert Hughes, *Culture of Complaint: The Flaying of America* (New York: Oxford University Press), pp. 153 ff., "Moral in Itself: Art and the Therapeutic Fallacy."

27. See again Nicholas Mirzoeff, *An Introduction to Visual Culture* (London and New York: Routledge, 1999).

28. E. H. Gombrich, *Art and Illusion: A Study in the Psychology of Pictorial Representation* (Princeton: Princeton University Press, 1960), pp. 4, 24, 83.

29. Richard Brilliant, *Portraiture* (Cambridge: Harvard University Press, 1991), p. 8.

30. I. B. Leavens, *From "291" to Zurich: The Birth of Dada* (Ann Arbor: University of Michigan Research Press, 1983), p. 52.

31. Renato Poggioli, *The Theory of the Avant-Garde* (New York: Harper, 1968), pp. 27–29.

32. For these two fundamental concepts in modern art thinking, appearing in many different contexts, see M. Tuchman, ed., *The Spiritual in Art, Abstract Painting, 1890–1985* (Los Angeles: Los Angeles County Museum of Art, 1986); these are also discussed in a specifically Dadaist context in Leavens, *From "291" to Zurich*.

33. H. H. Stuckenschmidt, *Twentieth-Century Music* (London: Weidenfeld, 1969), p. 17.

34. Ibid., pp. 7, 24.

35. Charles Baudelaire, "Richard Wagner et Tannhäuser à Paris," in *Baudelaire: Selected Writings on Art and Artists* (Harmondsworth, U.K.: Penguin, 1972), pp. 325–57.

36. Ibid., pp. 326–27.

37. Ibid., pp. 327–31 (my emphasis).

38. Ibid., pp. 331–32.

39. Richard Wagner, as quoted in ibid., pp. 338–40.

40. Wagner, as quoted in Joscelyn Godwin, ed., *Music, Mysticism, and Magic: A Sourcebook* (London: Routledge & Kegan Paul, 1986), p. 238; as Godwin concludes from this statement, Wagner's "beliefs had come to resemble those being publicized at the same time [1880] by the Theosophical Society," founded by Madame Blavatsky five years earlier. Another scholar goes further, showing Wagner's importance in disseminating an occultist mind-set among early avant-garde innovators, see Leon Surette, *Birth of Modernism: Ezra Pound, T. S. Eliot, W. B. Yeats, and the Occult* (Montreal: McGill-Queens University Press, 1994), chap. 3, "Nietzsche, Wagner, and Myth."

41. S. H. Butler, ed., *Aristotle's Theory of Poetry and Fine Art* (New York: Dover, 1951), p. 23.

42. For an extensive analysis of this term, see the commentary by the modern editor, S. H. Butcher, to *Aristotle's Theory of Poetry and Fine Art* (reprint, New York: Dover, 1951), pp. 242 ff.

43. Aristotle, in ibid., pp. 22–23 (with Greek text).

44. Joseph Campbell, as in Jerilyn Lee Brandelius, *Grateful Dead Family Album* (New York: Warner, 1989), p. 234 (my emphasis).

45. Wagner, as quoted in Baudelaire, *Selected Writings*, p. 340.

46. William James, *Varieties of Religious Experience* (New York: Mentor, 1958), p. 293.

47. R. M. Bucke, *Cosmic Consciousness: A Study in the Evolution of the Human Mind* (Philadelphia: Innes, 1902), p. 2.

48. Hans Kohn, *The Mind of Germany: The Education of a Nation* (New York: Harper & Row, 1965), pp. 190–204.

49. According to the *Oxford English Dictionary*, the first reference to the word "synesthesia" appeared in *The Century Dictionary* (1889–1891).

50. For the complete text of "Correspondences," see F. E. Burhan, *Vision and Visionaries: Nineteenth-Century Psychological Theory, the Occult Sciences, and the Formation of the Symbolist Aesthetic in France* (Ph.D. diss., Princeton University, 1979), p. 216.

51. Ibid., p. 139.

52. For the essential source-documents, see Henri Dorra, ed., *Symbolist Art Theories: A Critical Anthology* (Berkeley: University of California Press, 1994).

53. For what follows, I am very much in the debt of Steven Kern's magnificent contextual study, *The Culture of Time and Space, 1880–1918* (Cambridge: Harvard University Press, 1983); also useful are the ideas (and details) found in W. S. Heckscher, "Die Genesis der Ikonologie," in E. Kaemmerling, ed., *Ikonographie und Ikonologie* (Cologne: DuMont, 1979), pp. 112–64.

54. Jonathan Hertz and Norman Klein, eds., *Twentieth-Century Art Theory: Urbanism, Politics, and Mass Culture* (Englewood Cliffs, N.J.: Prentice-Hall, 1990), p. 5.

55. Karl Marx and Friedrich Engels, *The Communist Manifesto* (New York: Washington Square Press, 1967), p. 63.

56. For a contextual study of the significance of the discovery of measured "Time" (and similar issues derived from a history of practical inventions), see the

fascinating analysis by Daniel J. Boorstin, *The Discoverers* (New York: Random House, 1983), pp. 4–78, "Time."

57. Albert Einstein and L. Infeld, *The Evolution of Physics* (New York: Simon & Schuster, 1938), p. 181.

58. These statistics are given in Kern, *Culture of Time and Space*, passim. For an iconological study of the consequences of cinematic techniques and thought patterns, see the path-breaking 1934 essay by Erwin Panofsky, "Style and Medium in the Motion Pictures," in his *Three Essays on Style* (Cambridge: MIT Press, 1997), pp. 91–128.

59. Monet, as cited in G. H. Hamilton, "Cézanne, Bergson, and the Image of Time," *College Art Journal* 16, no. 3 (1956): 2–12.

60. Paul Cézanne, *Letters*, ed. John Rewald (Oxford: Oxford University Press, 1946), p. 262.

61. Léon Werth, "Picasso," in *Cubism*, ed. Edward F. Fry (London: Thames & Hudson, 1966), pp. 57–58.

62. Jean Metzinger, "Cubism and Tradition," in ibid., pp. 66–67 (my emphasis).

63. William James, "On Some Omissions of Introspective Psychology," *Mind* (January 1884): 2.

64. William James, *Principles of Psychology* (New York: Holt, 1890), pp. l, 239.

65. Henri Bergson, *An Introduction to Metaphysics* (New York: Liberal Arts, 1955), pp. 23–26.

66. Henri Bergson, *Creative Evolution* (New York: Modern Library, 1944), p. 72.

67. Virginia Woolf, *A Writer's Diary* (New York: Harcourt Brace, 1954), p. 93.

68. Fernand Léger, in Charles Harrison and Peter Woods, eds., *Art in Theory 1900–1990: An Anthology of Changing Ideas* (Oxford: Blackwell, 1992), pp. 157–59 (my emphasis).

69. Kern, *Culture of Time and Space*, p. 75.

Chapter 14

More Strictly Mundane Contexts for ETs, and Some Conclusions

REPORTED TRUTH AND THE LEGAL INTERPRETATION OF CREDIBILITY

In the particular case of the ETs, as we must again insist, the "evidence" is *all* anecdotal, meaning just a corpus of verbal affirmations made after the fact by those troubled individuals who say it "really happened" to them. Worse, these distinctive narratives are nearly always produced as the result of emotional stimulus applied by a "researcher" who only pursues these kinds of fabulous stories. Worse yet, typically the specific stimuli are hypnotic. As was earlier concluded, although admittedly successful in the capitalist-postmodernist mass media marketplace, none of the prolix testimony now attesting to the validity of these sightings would—needless to say—pass muster in any proper court of law.

Pursuing the legal argument further (a forensic procedure which perhaps should be applied to the speculative production of nearly all postmodernist culture mongers), we find two major components pertinent to what constitutes materials likely to convince a jury. Without these, the final verdict must be "not proven." These are, first, the *substance* of the evidence actually presented and, second, the *credibility* of the witnesses attesting to the validity of their experiences. This is a problem that has long since plagued UFOlogy—even before the timely (and more profitable) invention of the alien-abduction experience, now made easily available to you as a paperback book and a made-for-TV and/or blockbuster summer movie. Back in 1969, the patriarch of the UFO experience, J. Allen Hynek, observed that minimal "credibility is to be assigned one-witness cases." Those discarded—and with them apparently the bulk of all ET close-encounter stories—then these are the questions which must be (but rarely are) asked and accurately answered. According to Hynek's ideal interrogation:

> If there are several witnesses, what is their collective objectivity? How well do they respond to tests of their ability to judge and report phenomena? How good is their eyesight? What technical training have they had? What is their general reputation in the community? What is their occupation, and how much responsibility does it involve? What is their reputation for veracity? Are they known for publicity-seeking?[1]

Donald H. Menzel added the two most important questions which have been omitted in standard UFO sighting questionnaires: "What natural phenomenon did your sighting most resemble? Why do you feel that your UFO was not this phenomenon?" His conclusion: "When UFOs [or ETs] are in the news, people look for them and see them. As the publicity subsides, the reports subside."[2]

It is necessary to make clear one's understanding of just what constitutes valid "evidence" as such—and in the strictly legal (forensic) sense. If perchance you are not a devoted follower of the popular *Law and Order* TV series, and so have missed its crash course in standard judicial procedures, then it will be useful to cite the remarks of a former justice of the New York State Supreme Court. Addressing himself to a figurative jury, as well as to opposing attorneys representing both prosecution and defense, Judge Louis B. Heller reminds all concerned parties that "evidence, in the strict sense, includes all the means by which an alleged matter of fact in dispute in a given case is either established or disproved." We must also be made aware that there are three categories of admissible evidence: Judge Heller states that the first is called "*relevant*, if it has the legal capacity to prove or to disprove a principal fact in dispute. It is [secondly] *material*, if it has a direct, effective bearing or influence on one or more pertinent facts at issue in the case on trial. And it is [thirdly] *competent*, if it is given in the form of testimony by a properly qualified person, or if it was produced by such a person."[3]

All three kinds of evidence need to be exhibited in order to establish credibility for the idea of those lucratively published and ubiquitously broadcast tales of extraterrestrial visitations and, especially, those endlessly replayed "abductions" of terrestrials by the outer-space waif folk (see figs. 1, 4, 5, 15–22). Speaking of evidence, as one may now wonder, why is it, with all the 35mm autofocus cameras and handheld video cameras that multitudes of American citizens now possess, there are still no clear and convincing photographs of UFOs, much less of the ETs which pilot the craft while they busy themselves in their daily rounds of alien abductions? Since the physical evidence is either not there or—worse—has frequently been shown by disinterested and qualified observers to have been faked, then the next matter to be addressed obviously concerns the very credibility of the witnesses themselves, those self-proclaimed abductees.

Judge Heller has, as one might expect, some useful observations regarding "the treachery of human memory." Although he never himself needed (for reasons perfectly obvious) to address the egregiously ballooning problem of extraterrestrial abductions, he spoke of the fallibility of the well-intended eyewitness: "Thus, in spite of the best of intentions and an excellent memory, he had yielded to misleading suggestions, had drawn erroneous conclusions, confused his perceptions, forgotten details, and had been deluded by misconceptions." Quoting an observation of Otto Munsterberg, it was also Heller's professional experience that

> in a thousand courts at a thousand places all over the world, witnesses every day affirm by oath in exactly the same way much worse mixtures of truth and untruth, combinations of memory and of illusion, of knowledge and of suggestion, of experience and wrong conclusions. . . . Everyday errors creep into the work of justice through wrong evidence which has the outer marks of truth and trustworthiness. . . . Not every sworn statement is [to be] accepted as absolute reality [and] the instinctive doubt refers primarily to veracity. The public in the main suspects that the witness lies, while taking for granted that if he is normal and conscious of responsibility he may forget a thing, but it would not believe that he could remember the wrong thing. The confidence in the reliability of memory is so general that the suspicion of memory illusions evidently plays a small role in the mind of the juryman, and even the cross-examining lawyer is mostly dominated by the idea that a false statement is the product of intentional falsehood.[4]

So, even with the best of intentions, eyewitnesses frequently get their facts wrong. Heller also cites the results of an experiment pioneered by a professor of criminology long ago in Germany at the University of Berlin. This test of Teutonic veracity has long since become a staple feature in introductory courses to psychology offered in most American colleges. The purpose of the familiar gambit is "to study the exactitude of observation and recollection." As Heller explains:

Unknown to the rest of the class, three students under the professor's direction carefully rehearsed a little scene of violence, lasting less than a minute, which they later suddenly acted out before their astonished classmates in the midst of a lecture: a brief, heated exchange of words, a threat, the drawing of a revolver, an attempt to restrain the hothead, and, in the midst of a general uproar, the firing of the weapon. After the professor had restored order and explained the purpose of the little drama he had written, he asked a part of the class to write at once an exact account of all that had occurred. Other students were to write their reports the next day or, in some cases, a week later. Still others were to give oral depositions under cross-examination.

The actual performance, consisting of both words and actions, was divided, for the purpose of the experiment, into fourteen parts. Any deviation from these—whether an alteration or omission—in a student's report was counted as a mistake. The results proved to be most instructive. In regard to the words spoken during the incident, even the most accurate report was 26 percent mistaken, with the poorest account running as high as 80 percent in error. The reports with reference to the second half of the performance, which was more strongly emotional, gave an average of 15 percent more mistakes than those of the first half. Words were put into the mouths of men who had been silent spectators during the whole short episode; actions were attributed to the chief participants—of which not the slightest trace existed; and essential parts of the tragi-comedy were completely eliminated from the memory of a number of witnesses.[5]

Especially significant here is the finding, since verified by many other researchers,[6] that at times when the context for the witness's perception "was more strongly emotional," then the minimum error factor became at least 40 percent—at best. In the case of the "documented" cases of alien abductions, several of which have already been quoted here, *all* of these turn out to be strongly emotional, in fact often nearly hysterical. Consequently, we may automatically assume the presence of, at best, an inherent error factor that automatically makes questionable any, or all, of the given testimony—regardless of its purported "facts." Another classic series of mnemonic tests, later performed at the University of Göttingen, essentially substantiated the findings of the first experiment. This one took place in at a meeting of jurists, psychologists, and physicians—all, therefore, professionals, the kind well trained in careful observation. As was explained by Professor Munsterberg:

Somewhere in the same street there was that evening a public festivity of the carnival. Suddenly, in the midst of the scholarly meeting, the doors open, a clown in highly colored costume rushes in with mad excitement, and a Negro with a revolver in hand follows him. In the middle of the hall first the one, then the other, shouts wild phrases; then the one falls to the ground, the other jumps on him; then a shot and, suddenly, both are out of the room. The whole affair took less than twenty seconds. All present were completely taken by surprise, and no one, with the exception of the president, had the slightest idea that every word and action had been rehearsed beforehand, or that photographs had been taken of the scene. It seemed most natural that the president should beg the members to write down individually an exact report, inasmuch as he felt sure that the matter would come before the courts.

Of the forty reports handed in, there was only one whose omissions were calculated as amounting to *less* than 20 percent; fourteen had 20 to 40 percent of the facts omitted; twelve omitted 40 to 50 percent, and thirteen still more than 50 percent omissions. But besides the omissions, there were only six among the forty which did not contain positively wrong statements; in twenty-four papers, up to 10 percent of the statements were free inventions, and in ten answers—that is, in one-fourth of the papers—more than 10 percent of *the statements were absolutely false, in spite of the fact that they all came from scientifically trained observers*. Only four persons, for instance, among forty, noticed that the Negro had nothing on his head; the others gave him a derby or a high hat, and so on. In addition to this, a red suit, a brown one, a striped one, a coffee-colored jacket, shirt sleeves, and similar costumes were invented for him. In reality, he wore white trousers and a black jacket with a large red necktie.

The scientific commission which reported the details of the inquiry came to the general conclusion that *the majority of the observers omitted or falsified* about half of the processes which occurred completely within their field of vision. As was to be expected, the judgment as to the time duration of the act varied between a few seconds and several minutes.[7]

Notwithstanding the fact that the mass-produced paperback revelations of extraterrestrial infestations consistently label their contents "nonfiction," such unquestionably successful commercial products would still probably be judged "omitted or falsified" information in a properly run courtroom. Moreover, and just as we have repeatedly seen, since the often genuinely terrified folks claiming to have been kidnapped by extraterrestrials rarely qualify as scientifically trained observers, how much credibility should we grant *them*? Even worse, why should any testimony appearing under hypnosis enjoy any claim to veracity?

Although neither solicitor nor barrister, science author Philip J.

Klass has created a useful list of ten "UFOlogical principles" that illuminate the dangers of accepting on face value accounts of close encounters
with either UFOs or their ET crews. They read as follows:

Principle 1: "Basically honest and intelligent persons who are suddenly exposed to a brief, unexpected event, especially one that involves
an unfamiliar object, may be grossly inaccurate in trying to describe
precisely what they have seen."

Principle 2: "Despite the intrinsic limitations of human perception
when exposed to brief, unexpected and unusual events, some details
recalled by the observer may be reasonably accurate. The problem then
facing the UFO investigator is to try to distinguish between those details
that are accurate and those that are grossly inaccurate. This may prove
impossible, until the true identity of the UFO can be determined, so
that in some cases this poses an insoluble problem."

Principle 3: "If a person observing an unusual or unfamiliar object
concludes that it *is* probably a spaceship from another world, he can then
readily adduce that the object is reacting to *his* presence or actions—
when, in reality, there is absolutely no cause-effect relationship."

Principle 4: "Newspapers that give great prominence to a UFO
report when it is first received subsequently devote little, if any, space
or time to reporting a prosaic explanation for the case when all the facts
are uncovered."

Principle 5: "No human observer, including experienced flight
crews, can accurately estimate either the distance, altitude or the size
of an unfamiliar object in the sky—unless it is in very close proximity
to a familiar object whose altitude or size is known."

Principle 6: "Once news media coverage leads the public to believe
that UFOs may be in the vicinity, there are numerous natural and man-
made objects which, especially when seen at night, can take on unusual
characteristics in the minds of hopeful viewers. Their UFO reports, in
turn, add to the mass excitement—which encourages still more
observers to watch for UFOs. This situation feeds upon itself, until such
time as the news media lose interest in the subjects, and then the 'flap'
quickly runs out of steam."

Principle 7: "In attempting to determine whether a UFO report is a
hoax, an investigator should rely on physical evidence, or the lack of it
where evidence *should* exist, and should not depend on character
endorsements of the principals involved."

Principle 8: "The inability of even experienced investigators to fully
and positively explain a UFO report for lack of sufficient information,
even after a rigorous effort, does not really provide any evidence to support the hypothesis that spaceships from other worlds are visiting Earth."

Principle 9: "Whenever a light is sighted in the night skies that is believed to be a UFO, and when this is reported to a radar operator, who is then asked to search his scope for an unknown target, almost invariably an 'unknown' target *will* be found. Conversely, if an unusual target is spotted on a radarscope at night that is suspected of being a UFO, and an observer is dispatched or asked to search for a light in the night sky, almost invariably a visual sighting will be made."

Principle 10: "Many UFO cases seem puzzling and unexplainable simply because case investigators have failed to devote a sufficiently rigorous effort to the investigation."[8]

Another dedicated student of UFOlogy, who also certainly does not qualify as a trial lawyer, is Jacques Vallée; in fact, he often sounds suspiciously like another True Believer. We read, for instance, how he even grants the possibility of "the existence of a genuine technology pursuing its own hidden agenda," and so he proposed "to regard the UFO phenomenon as a physical manifestation of a form of consciousness that is alien to humans but is able to coexist with us on the earth."[9] Nonetheless, everybody is entitled to their own "hidden agenda." When not pursuing that, as we said before, Vallée does often succeed in raising some significant questions about the True Believers' affirmations. One must above all question, he says, the following points: Do the "witnesses" actually exist? Is the actual site known? Did an abnormal event really happen? As based upon his own, perhaps just a bit credulous but unquestionably energetic research, he has observed some glaring problems particularly associated with the abundant reports of alien abductions:

The scientific experts I consulted, when I showed them the current UFO literature, were amazed and upset at the superficial conditions under which UFO investigators used hypnosis. Unanimously, they considered it unethical for anyone who had already reached a strong personal conclusion about UFOs to interrogate a witness under hypnosis. Yet one is forced to admit that of the leading abduction researchers I have mentioned, *none* has a medical degree, *none* has professional knowledge of psycho-pathology, and *all* have extremely strong personal conclusions regarding the UFO phenomenon and its cultural or religious meaning. In other words, in every case there is much more than scientific curiosity involved: although working with the best intentions, the hypnotist is already committed to a particular conclusion and is trying to verify it.[10]

Thanks to Vallée's Cartesian education (he is, after all, French), he is enabled to see the inherent silliness in the current presentation of the ET hypothesis:

The lessons are clear: one must not only pursue every possible lead but keep an open mind about the whole pattern. For every case [of reported ETs and UFOs] it is useful to follow the same systematic, step-by-step approach: obtaining maps at different scales; writing to the weather bureau to check the temperature, the cloud cover, the wind. If nothing else, this information enables an investigator to assess the validity and the accuracy of the recall by witnesses, and to ground the case in physical reality. Perhaps the most important point to remember is to separate the physical parameters of the sighting from the testimony itself, and the psycho-sociological characteristics of the witness and the environment. Each of these factors needs to be assessed independently of the others. Otherwise, the resulting synthesis is often invalid.

Another important lesson from this experience concerns the uselessness of Occam's razor. This expression is applied to a rule of thinking in science that states that one should never invoke a complex hypothesis when a simple one will fit. It all depends, of course, on what one means by "simple." The theory of a spherical earth spinning around the universe with over fourteen different motions is incredibly complex when compared to the elegant theory of a flat, motionless earth, with the sun and the celestial bodies as simple lamps carried around by angels. Occam must have had a beard.[11]

Also to be considered is the strictly "poetic" explanation. First we have a UFO sighting as reported by bearded author William Shakespeare (speaking through a character named Richard), who saw:

> Three glorious suns, each a perfect sun,
> Not separated with the racking clouds,
> But server'd in a pale clear-shining sky.
> See, see! They join, embrace and seem to kiss,
> As if they vowed some league inviolable:
> Now are they one lamp, one light, one sun,
> In this the heaven figures some event.[12]

But perhaps, after all, it is not really a UFO; perhaps it is but a figment of the overheated human imagination; as put another way by the bearded Bard of Avon:

> And, as imagination bodies forth
> The form of things unknown, the poet's pen
> Turns them to shapes, and gives to airy nothing
> A local habitation and a name . . .
> How easy is a bush suppos'd a bear![13]

Also needed to be considered by the postmodernist deep thinker is the strictly comedic interpretation. Let us imagine the standard ET abduction scenario as it would have been reconstructed by American comedian Bob Newhart, in the format of one of his celebrated ersatz interviews with the archetypal man (or woman) on the street:

> Now, let me see if I've got this straight, Mrs. Credula. First: you were *floated* by three small Gray Beings, next *drawn out* through your window. Then: you went *up a beam of light*, and then into a, a. . . Ah, I see: a hovering alien *spacecraft*. Uh, *huh*. And, in this spacecraft, these Beings did *what*? They *stole your eggs*?!? Uh, why do you think they would want to do a thing like that, Mrs. Credula? Uh, huh; I see. Because they wanted to *breed* with you.[14]

Here is another genre transposition, as recently suggested by psychologist George Howard:

> Imagine that in the near future [Professor Howard] finds himself riding on a horse from Jerusalem to Damascus in order to torture and murder some poor alien abductees if they are unwilling to admit that UFOs do not exist. Suddenly the skies darken, and I say, "Whoa! This don't look so good." A bolt of lightning then knocks me off the horse, and I think, No big deal! People get struck by lightning all the time—I'm just glad to be able to interpret the experience.
>
> But when a booming voice from out of the heavens says, "George, George, why doest thou persecute righteous UFO abductees so?"— that's when it becomes a non-natural experience for me. The voice orders, "You are no longer to be called George; henceforth you are to be known as 'Stupid.'" "I've always thought stupidity was an under-appreciated trait in humans," I reply. "I'm thrilled to be known as 'Stupid.' By the way, Lord, how do your friends address *you*?"
>
> If the voice says, "Yahweh," I'm suddenly Jewish. If God says, "Allah," then I believe in Islam. If "Buddha," I'm a Buddhist. If "Jesus," a Christian. If the voice says, "Zarathustra," I'm momentarily confused. But so great is my commitment to empiricism, even in the religion domain, that eventually I'd be thrilled to be known as "Stupid the Zoroastrian"! Or imagine that the lightning bolt had been a laser-beam, and that the booming voice replied, "I am Jaopg from the planet Rooze." Suddenly this experience would have nothing to do with God and religion. I would immediately believe completely in the "reality" of alien contact.[15]

But such bantering will have little positive effect; the advocates of the alien-abduction thesis are a humorless lot. No matter: as I have already suggested, much of the UFO/ET problem—and the abundant paperback publications which celebrate it—would be obviated with a mere change of title: "MFO" (misidentified fugitive observations). *Nomen est omen . . .*

"RETRIEVED MEMORIES" AND A BALONEY KIT

My conclusion: the best explanation for the postmodernist myth of "alien abductions" as specifically "relived" under hypnosis is—according to the title of an excellent monograph treating a now-omnipresent syndrome—"The Myth of Repressed Memory."[16] Most likely, other than the welcome income enjoyed by opportunistic pulp publishers and television producers, in the end, it is all just an "airy nothing." No matter; according to my research, there are three historical stages in the modernist evolution of ET ekphrastic artworks. Our current model, the iconographic canon established in the testimony of Budd Hopkins's, David Jacobs's, and John Mack's hypnotized eyewitnesses, is, as Patrick Huyghe observes, "the short Gray entity, [which] although ubiquitous today, was largely absent from the UFO scene prior to the 1960s."[17] As has not been done previously, I will again narrowly specify the date of its appearance in this definitive form as being late in 1966, with an even wider (paperback) *divulgation* occurring a year later, and then the inevitable cinematic recreation (figs. 16–19).

Similarly forgotten today, a more diversified verbal model for previous ET formal heterogeneity was initially published by a once widely read European visionary author around 1760, and his ekphrasis was further embroidered by an imaginative American follower in 1847, and many other complementary accounts followed in due course (as was recounted in chapter 10). Nonetheless, these authors were themselves only embroidering upon a truly ancient literary genre reporting ubiquitous extraterrestrial contacts. All such apocryphal legends culminate in the Hill *apocalypsis-revelatio* (figs. 16–19), wrought when Lyndon Johnson was embroiling us all in a cultural meltdown called Vietnam. And at every stage of a somewhat hysterical historical evolution it seems there was an ekphrastic artist-illustrator ready and able to lend his vocational talents to a vivid visualization of the initially verbalized ET (figs. 1, 4, 5, 15–22).

UFOlogists typically tell us that their investigations "challenge science." Their claims also mightily strain credibility, and blaming it all on a government conspiracy really doesn't advance their cause—except among themselves. As is well known (in certain quarters that is), it does prove fairly easy to refute all those esoteric claims about the kind of physical phenomena whose appearance "challenges science." That is, if one ever takes the time to do so (for some strictly UFOlogical misinterpretations, see chapters 5 and 8). In fact, fortunately there exist any number of scientific, some strictly psychological, published appraisals of the bases for all those physical claims for varied paranormal phenomena, including (*inter alia*) karma and rebirth, etheric and astral bodies, stigmata, poltergeists, séances, telepathy and ESP, dowsing, visions and out-of-body experiences, levitation, cryptozoology, automatic writing, and psychic auras. (Et cetera.) According to their authors, the kind that are *not* card-carrying True Believers in New Age wisdom, the reasonable conclusion (instead) is to show them all to be products of the over-imaginative human mind, delusions as it were.[18]

Let me provide one example, standing for all the diverse rest. In this case, we are dealing with an instance of "spontaneous" recollection of a close encounter with an ET, not that increasingly disparaged kind that arises out of hypnotic instigation. Being spontaneously recovered, of course, *that* kind of retrieved memory is naturally and automatically taken to be authentic. The example referred to we have already examined in some detail: Whitley Strieber's million-dollar best-seller, *Communion: A True Story* (see fig. 4). Either it is what Whitley says it represents—another nasty close encounter with those ever-pesky aliens (as recounted in chapter 5)—or it is not. Not so, says psychologist Robert A. Baker, one of those pesky party poopers (perhaps himself even an extraterrestrial coconspirator). Dr. Baker rudely dismissed Strieber's colorful encounters with the ETs back in 1987 as constituting just another tiresome instance of "sleep-related phenomena"—but who wants to read that *boring* scientific literature? In any event, according to Baker's published rebuttal:

In Strieber's *Communion* is a classic, textbook description of a hypnopompic hallucination, complete with the awakening from a sound sleep, the strong sense of reality and of being awake, the paralysis (due to the fact that the body's neural circuits keep our muscles relaxed and help preserve our sleep), and the encounter with strange beings. Following the encounter, instead of jumping out of bed and going in search of the strangers he has seen, Strieber typically goes back to sleep. He even reports that the burglar alarm was still working—proof again that the intruders were mental rather than physical. Strieber also reports an occasion when he awakes and believes that the roof of his house is on fire and that the aliens are threatening his family. Yet his only response to this was to go peacefully back to sleep. Again, clear evidence of a hypnopompic dream. Strieber, of course, is convinced of the reality of these experiences. This, too, is expected. If he was not convinced of their reality, then the experience would not be hypnopompic or hallucinatory [and certainly not publishable].[19]

Oh my, that *is* distressing news—like hearing for the first time that Santa Claus and the Tooth Fairy do not really exist (but which I thought I had proven to exist, as in chapter 2). Oh, well, we shall just have to learn to live with such embarrassing revelations—with others forthcoming below.

Like their unacknowledged occultist brethren, UFOlogists have made a great many "scientific" claims. That's what they call them; alas, scientists call them "pseudoscientific." The nice thing about grandiose theories is that they have often brought spiritual benefit to their many spiritually needy followers; if not, the sheep and goats drop out of that particular program. No matter; there is always another fascinating fallacy lurking in the mass media neighborhood. Regarding their various pseudoscientific assertions, and likewise nearly all other "otherworldly" claims generated by any other occultist gurus you would care to mention, past and present, there is a simple way of dealing with them—that is, should one ever bother, or even care, to do so.

The late Carl Sagan, a scientist in the proper sense, invented his own "baloney detection kit," so designed to be applied toward rectifying most New Age beliefs: UFOs and ETs, also telepathy and ESP, dowsing, visions and out-of-body experiences, levitation, cryptozoology, psychic auras, karma and spiritual rebirth (metempsychosis), etheric and astral bodies, and so on. District attorneys and police detectives, likewise art historians, will find this deconstructive equipment useful; although reluctantly, likewise postmodernist literary theorists, maybe even avant-garde art critics, will benefit from such mental prophylaxis. However you may wish to apply them, Sagan's conceptual remedies for pseudoscientific irrationality go like this (and I quote):

- Whenever possible there must be independent confirmation of the "facts."
- Encourage substantive debate on the evidence by knowledgeable proponents of all points of view.
- Arguments from authority carry little weight—"authorities" have made mistakes in the past. They will do so again in the future. Perhaps a better way to say it is that in science there are no authorities; at most there are experts.
- Spin more than one hypothesis. If there's something to be explained, think of *all* the different ways in which it *could* be explained. Then think of tests by which you might systematically disprove each of the

alternatives. What survives, the hypothesis that resists disproof in this Darwinian selection among "multiple working hypotheses," has a much better chance of being the right answer than if you had simply run with the first idea that caught your fancy.

- Try not to get overly attached to a hypothesis just because it's yours. It's only a way station in the pursuit of knowledge. Ask yourself why you like the idea. Compare it fairly with the alternatives. See if you can find reasons for rejecting it. If you don't, others will.
- Quantify. If whatever it is you're explaining has some measure, some numerical quantity attached to it, you'll be much better able to discriminate among competing hypotheses. What is vague and qualitative is open to many explanations. Of course there are truths to be sought in the many qualitative issues we are obliged to confront, but finding *them* is more challenging.
- If there's a chain of argument, *every* link in the chain must work (including the premise)—not just most of them.
- Occam's Razor. This convenient rule-of-thumb urges us when faced with two hypotheses that explain the data *equally well* to choose the simpler [less esoteric] one.
- Always ask whether the hypothesis can be, at least in principle, falsified. Propositions that are untestable, unfalsifiable are not worth much. You must be able to check assertions out. Inveterate skeptics must be given the chance to follow your reasoning, to duplicate your experiments and see if they get the same result.
- In sum, extraordinary claims require extraordinary evidence, that is, real proof.[20]

THE TELEVISIONED POSTMODERNIST AUDIENCE CULTURE FOR EXTRATERRESTRIAL ESOTERICA

If we grant the general acceptance (at least in certain quarters) of often-subtle occultist thought patterns, a particularly shaped expression of the general irrationality characterizing much modernist cultural expression (as discussed in chapters 12 and 13), then we need to seek another explanation for it. What psychological *needs* does it answer? As one author has recognized, such widespread contemporary occult activities and beliefs mainly "appeal to those disillusioned with the apparent failure of traditional values and systems. Seeking beliefs and ideas, the individual is beckoned by the occult and pseudosciences. The latter also serve as vehicles for 'outsiders,' those whom the Establishment has not, or cannot absorb. Perhaps the natural tendency is a by-product of adolescent rebellion [hence] younger people are [most often] the customers."[21] In the particular case of pseudoscience, that essential component of modern occultism, Martin Gardner points out that "the average fan may well be a chap in his teens, with a smattering of 'scientific' knowledge—culled however mainly from science fiction [an oxymoron], enormously gullible, with a strong bent toward occultism, no real understanding of the scientific method, and a basic insecurity, for which he compensates by fantasies of scientific 'power.'"[22] While valid, these conclusions are still rather generalized.

Besides "enormously gullible, with no real understanding of the scientific method," what is a modern person "with a strong bent toward occultism" actually like? In this case, some initial scholarly research (some already cited in chapter 11) has been done specifically on the psychological traits distinguishing the present-day adherents to various kinds of self-styled "occult sciences," among which I include UFOlogy. One among many of these distinctively modernist movements ("cults") is the one called "Anthroposophy," and Geoffrey Ahern appears to be the only scholar ever to have bothered to explore in a methodical way the pointed question of "who is most likely to be convened to Anthroposophy." (One of those was, by the way, the celebrated vanguard artist Joseph Beuys.)[23] Based on extensive interviews, Ahern finds that eleven psychological traits characterize the Anthroposophical convert. Ironically, the results of Dr. Ahern's investigations into the psychological makeup of Rudolf Steiner's current followers of Anthroposophy may also remind one of the characteristics of most New Age adherents, that is, should you have actually lived and worked with them. According to Ahern:

1. Such people tend to come from middle-class backgrounds.
2. "Many described themselves as unhappy as children."
3. Instead of worldliness, there tends to be in these devotees a "rather quaint earnestness," leading to "a removed quality, which could become strange and disturbing."
4. There is among them "considerable criticism of their mothers," and "nearly all reacted against their fathers."
5. Most had been accepted for traditional university courses, which most had then "rejected as meaningless."
6. For such people, "conventional work-roles were seen as an imprisonment."
7. There is also a "strong tendency towards vegetarianism."
8. All these people "basically deplored a wage-mentality."
9. "Almost all the members were white."
10. Most followers "come from cold and broken pasts, that often lacked satisfactory social contacts."

11. Finally, and above all, "Anthroposophists strive to leave materialism and individualism behind, and to develop spiritual individuality instead."[24]

The same syndrome also must correspond to much of the audience culture voluntarily supporting the extraterrestrial legend. This audience culture must be, if only for chronological reasons, considered thoroughly "postmodernist" in its *mentalité* (as just described in chapter 13). For all the oceans of ink that have been spilled, by lionized French deep thinkers and trendy American academic wannabes, in defining this omnipresent syndrome, "postmodernism," the bottom line is that postmodernists represent the first ever audience culture reared on, and mentally shaped by, television.

Pullulating at the lower rung of the (chronological) postmodernist audience culture are those bio-organisms who merely consume *any* sort of television, also patronizing rock concerts, blockbuster movies, and mass sports events, all essentially just "to kill time." These people, of which there are millions and millions, are to be found swarming at the bottom of the postmodernist cultural pond, essentially because this inferior siting seems to be their social, economic, and/or educational, birthright. In no way genetic, all cultural tastes and biases (including ET obsession) are obviously *acquired*, and cultural acquisition seems mostly predictable by identifiable social locations: up, down, in the middle. Conversely, at the truly elite levels of postmodernist audience cultures, one finds a much smaller bunch, the superior minority, including those who support, patronize, even produce vanguard art. They *abhor* television—at least, so they say.

Because of its distinctive packaging and unique content, television represents the quintessential postmodernist cultural product. It is also the actual means by which most people, me too, have actually *seen* the extraterrestrials (figs. 9–15, 17–19). In order to illustrate the physical nature of this distinctive television experience, I will cite the "Three Commandments" media analyst Neil Postman found "observable in every type of television programming," from the lowest "entertaining" types to the most noble "educational" and "documentary" efforts. As defined by Postman, the Three Commandments of All Television Programming, representing pure "democracy" in its most ubiquitous application, are these:

> *Thou shalt have no prerequisites*. Every television program must be a complete package in itself. No previous knowledge is to be required.

There must not be even a hint that learning is hierarchical, that it is an edifice constructed on a foundation. The learner must be allowed to enter at any point without prejudice. This is why you shall never hear or see a television program begin with the caution that if the viewer has not seen the previous programs, this one will be meaningless. Television is a non-graded curriculum and excludes no viewer for any reason, at any time. In other words, in doing away with the idea of sequence and continuity in education, television undermines the idea that sequence and continuity have anything to do with thought itself.

Thou shalt induce no perplexity. In television teaching, perplexity is a superhighway to low ratings. A perplexed learner is a learner who will turn to another station. This means that there must be nothing that has to be remembered, studied, applied or, worst of all, endured. It is assumed that any information, story or idea can be made immediately accessible, since the contentment, not the growth, of the learner is paramount.

Thou shalt avoid exposition like the ten plagues visited upon Egypt. Of all the enemies of television-teaching, including continuity and perplexity, none is more formidable than exposition. Arguments, hypotheses, discussions, reasons, refutation or any of the traditional instruments of reasoned discourse turn television into radio or, worse, third-rate printed matter. Thus, television-teaching always takes the form of storytelling, conducted through dynamic images and supported by music. This is as characteristic of *Star Trek* as it is *Nova*, of commercials as of *Sesame Street*. Nothing will be taught on television that cannot be both visualized and placed in a theatrical context.

The final conclusion to be drawn is self-evident:

The name we may properly give to an "education" without prerequisites, perplexity and exposition is *entertainment*. . . . The consequences of this reorientation toward learning are to be observed not only in the decline of the potency of the classroom but, paradoxically, in the refashioning of the classroom into a place where both teaching and learning are intended to be vastly amusing activities. . . . Whereas in a classroom, one may ask a teacher questions, one can ask nothing of a television screen. Whereas school is centered on the development of language, television demands attention to *images*. . . . And this style of learning is, by its nature, hostile to what has been called book-learning or its hand-maiden, school-learning.[25]

In any event, various scientific studies now prove that *none* of this bounty of televised "education," meaning "infotainment," really does—after all is said and done—"significantly increase learning."[26]

This same "educational" definition also broadly applies to a strictly occultist kind of performance art invented by Rudolf Steiner in 1912 and called "eurythmy." Steiner, the founder of Anthroposophy, did not demand that the audiences for his esoteric eurythmic performances be apprised of their deeper, occult significance; for him, it was sufficient that the enthralled spectators passively appreciate "art." Like the better sort of television, Steiner's eurythmic occultist performances also represented a specifically didactic and rhetorical, in short educational, medium; likewise, they were additionally meant to become "an expression of life itself." To make my rhetorical point, I will interpolate key terms, in this case "television" or "television performer," in brackets. According to Steiner, writing well over a half-century before television became universally imposed upon a compliant postmodernist audience culture:

> In every branch of eurythmic [television] activity, it is above all necessary that the personality, the whole human being of the eurythmist [television performer] should be brought into play, so that the eurythmist [television performer] may become an expression of life itself. This cannot be achieved unless one enters into the spirit of Eurythmy [Television], feeling it actually as visible speech. As in the case of all artistic appreciation, it is quite possible for anyone to enjoy Eurythmy [Television], as a spectator, without having acquired any knowledge of its essential basis, just as it is quite unnecessary to have studied harmony or counterpoint in order to be able to appreciate music.[27]

As this suggests, there was a certain kind of audience culture, occultists, which partook of the television mentality long before that now ubiquitous technology was physically invented. Once invented, it was then to be brought into the daily lives of the whole world, even those people with no understanding of, or even much sympathy for, self-identified occultism.

Another name for postmodernists, at least the younger American sort, is "Generation-X"; the older ones are called "boomers." For both these generations, especially the more recently minted, television proved to be the fundamental "learning" experience. These X-people were born in and around the year 1973, by which time we had Watergate, proving that the president *was* "a crook," and therefore [*sic*] that all governments and institutions were, still are, probably likewise corrupt. Such perceptions are, besides paranoid, also conspiratorial.[28] By 1973, 50,000 American youths had expired in Vietnam, being put there due mainly to their inferior economic and/or educational birthright.

Besides that, we *lost*; even John Wayne was discredited. From 1973 on, we additionally had the OPEC experience, finally showing everybody living within the capitalist economies how conventional Cold War ideologies (godless commies versus freedom fighters) were not really the essential issue. As we then learned en masse, instead, the real point is who gets to distribute indispensable material necessities: they get the profits and *you* have no control over any of it. Then came Reagan and the Yuppies, who you and I were *not*. By now, nearly everyone realized that in mass media–driven "democracy" your vote, cast as an individual, essentially meant nothing—unless it was cast *en bloc*, as a market index or demographic figure, meaning within a namable subtribal collectivity.

In short, by 1975 nearly everybody began to feel like marionettes, with their psychic strings being jerked around by unseen powers. Differing degrees of awareness of one's coglike manipulation and political impotence mostly inspired apathy and/or cynicism. Another effect, of great profit to the infotainment industry, is the Conspiracy, especially if its loathsome workings can be reduced to a largely pictorial language; *The X-Files* does that very well. We now entertain ourselves with many conspiracies, most of which do get televised.[29] Dramatized "sightings" of extraterrestrials and their UFOs do make for wonderful television experiences (figs. 9–15, 17–19); these can be easily visualized, in fact, more easily than can so many other "paranormal" sensations also appealing to the postmodernist masses. I myself happily subscribe to the Great Conspiracy Theory; however, rather than saying that it is engineered by the government, "trying to cover up the truth about Roswell," I'd say instead that it is the work of the infotainment industry, "trying to make a buck from Roswell."

At the bottom of the gene pool, Joe Sixpack gets paranoid, maybe goes on maneuvers in the woods with his local militia buddies or, if he gets really inspired, he just might see a UFO and have a close encounter with its bug-eyed crew. That is just what happened to Travis Walton and the sweaty woodchoppers working with bumbling Mike Rogers (fig. 20). At the far upper end of the social-educational scale, these alarming postmodernist real-world perceptions—including the Three Commandments of All Television Programming, which brought everybody vivid images symbolizing this mass manipulation—have psychologically shaped a new audience culture. This *foule postmoderniste* also includes the admittedly elitist audience culture for unabashedly subjective, overtly emotionalized, polemical, and didacticized avant-garde artistic self-expression, most prominently TV-like "performance art" with a stridently political platform. On a lower rung, you have all those hyperdecibel pulsating rock concerts broadcast on MTV and the like. Nonetheless, shared by all parties is a universal exposure to the warped (and warping) psychic world of television.

It is now well documented that scary movies and television shows treating themes of the supernatural or the paranormal—ghosts or ETs—can work adverse effects on children. Such cinematic concoctions have been shown in controlled experiments to dramatically elevate levels of physiological arousal and to induce a variety of negative postviewing effects, such as bad dreams, haunting images, fear of being alone, and the fear of going into certain places, for example, basement or attic, in the child's home.[30] As we have repeatedly seen, skeptics (a beleaguered minority) insist upon rigorous empirical investigations in order to establish any and all declarations concerning paranormal phenomena, ETs included. Nonetheless, there had been few published studies that actually provided empirical evidence supporting the skeptics' claims of media impact, especially TV, in the propagation of such postmodernist apocrypha. Until recently, it seems the skeptics simply did not bother to provide the evidence actually substantiating their dire conclusions. However, Glenn G. Sparks, of Purdue University, has published several articles reporting his controlled experiments substantiating those allegations regarding the crucial role of television in both supporting and actively propagating paranormal beliefs.[31]

A typical example of the material Sparks has surveyed is the series *Unsolved Mysteries* (Lifetime channel), routinely depicting in the most graphic way people's "real" encounters with UFOs, space aliens, even ghosts. Similar offerings are *Beyond Belief: Fact or Fiction?* (on the Fox channel), *Mysteries of the Unexplained* (Discovery channel), and so on. Besides some regularly appearing series, there are also many specials or documentaries frequently appearing on TV which purvey the same tired repertoire of paranormal materials. In such programs, viewers are typically supplied with dramatic recreations of the alleged events and close encounters. Remember: TV is a *visual* medium. These stories typically contain colorful flying saucers and other strange craft, also bug-eyed ETs, that look very convincing (see figs. 18, 19). Nonetheless, in these instances, the narrators do *not* call attention to the fact that the wonderful things shown are merely human artifacts.

Looking oh-so-very real, for much attention is paid to the creation of convincing special effects (F/X), they naturally tend to capture the audience's imagination, even to work upon their belief systems. Also, these TV simulations typically include a prefatory "reality" tag: "The following story of paranormal activity [type A, B, or C] is based on reported incidents." Needless to say, since no meaningful distinction is ever drawn between the merely "reported" and the thoroughly confirmed event, "reported" is generally (and erroneously) taken to be synonymous with fact. In short, Sparks's experiments, correctly using double-blind controls, do establish that such video displays, especially the kind with the reality tag disclaimer, did work upon the passive viewers and that they have actually "increased their UFO beliefs significantly. . . . A relationship did emerge between exposure to the paranormal programs and paranormal beliefs."[32] While we are glad that at last a properly trained researcher has repeatedly bothered to design and execute the needed experiments, then to publish the results in reputable scientific journals, his findings only confirm what we already knew from our own empirical observations.

A typical college teacher of Gen-X types, Peter Sacks (a pseudonym, so he won't get fired), has exhumed the appalling mental furniture of this television-shaped postmodernist generation—and, *nota bene*, he is only referring to the kind with a "higher" education! Besides recognizing the obvious, that "GenXers are creatures of popular culture," he also acknowledges a detrimental cultural legacy from their boomer-elders: the irrational thought processes institutionalized by New Age beliefs, in short, modern occultism. Says Sacks, "GenXers appear to be no less inclined to harbor beliefs in such phenomena as angels and near-death experiences as many of their New Age parents, aunts, and uncles." And then he cites the objectively gathered evidence (that is, as gathered by even older scholars) proving this point, namely, "Nearly six in ten students agreed, or were unsure, that UFOs 'are actual spacecraft from other planets.' Half the students believed that some people have psychic power to accurately predict the future. Almost half agreed, or were unsure, that time travel into the past was possible. Some 56 percent believed that 'séances can communicate with the dead.'"[33]

Want more? Sacks also records, properly appalled, the actual "exhibits" produced by that omnipresent "postmodernist pop-culture" currently shaping the malleable minds of his mostly apathetic college students, supposedly the future intellectual elite of the nation:

> *Exhibit 1*: On the *New York Times* paperback best-seller list, two books about near-death experiences are among the top ten most popular books, one (*Embraced by the Light*) having been a best-seller for 29 weeks.
> *Exhibit 2*: For $4.95, you can buy the premier copy of the magazine *Unexplained Universe*, whose colorful, glossy cover of space aliens and werewolves shouts: NEW EVIDENCE: ANGELS ARE REAL! PHOTOGRAPHIC PROOF THAT AN ANCIENT RACE EXISTED ON THE MOON! BEWARE, THE LIVING WEREWOLF! 1995 UFO ENCOUNTERS.
> *Exhibit 3*: The December 1994 issue of *Ladies Home Journal*,

whose cover is adorned with two darling young girls, angels floating in white lace through the clouds. Read the cover story, titled, "Joy to the World: Perfect Angels and Other Stories of Real-Life Miracles."

Exhibit 4: A cornucopia of TV shows, all about the paranormal and the pseudoscientific. Many hold themselves up to be fact-based documentaries, and they are called *Sightings, The Extraordinary, The Other Side, Encounters: The Hidden Truth, National Geographic Explorer's Mysteries of the Afterlife,* and *Unsolved Mysteries.*

Exhibit 5: An entire issue of *TV Guide* devoted to "TV's New Supernatural Craze."

Exhibit 6: A *Time* magazine survey that shows almost seven in every ten American adults believe angels exist; that nearly one in two people think they have their own angel guarding over them; that Harvard and Boston College offer between them three courses about angels.

Exhibit 7: Sophy Burnham, author of the best-selling *A Book of Angels*, says that "my own angel is helping me write this, telling me only as much information as I really need to know."[34]

One of Sacks's main tasks is to document exactly how his college bosses (academic administrators) coerced him into making college teaching, and everything else that now passes for "higher" education, "entertaining like television." Sacks ends up by putting all this audience culture mental manipulation where it rightly belongs, into the real-world workings of postmodernist culture. Given his experiences, his conclusion (mine, too) is that "Generation X is arguably the first fully *post*-modern cohort of Americans, and they are the product of their culture and of their place in history." As we all should recognize by now, postmodernism represents "a debilitating cynicism toward established authorities and power structures of modernity, as well as a flowering of anti-rational beliefs in such things as guardian angels, satanic cults, and the paranormal." Even if not mentioned by the official French deep thinkers, Sacks recognizes (just as I do) that "a defining characteristic of postmodernity is that the culture appears to be returning to pre-Enlightenment states of mind, when such notions as witches, devils, satanic cults, angels, UFOs, and other unprovable explanations held so much power over people."[35]

A poignant observation by one of Sacks's brighter students sums up the real source of all this cultural malaise and theoretically empowered irrationality: "If there's a unifying force of our generation, it's TV. We're a society that has grown up watching TV, going for the fast laugh, the quick entertainment. It's rare to find somebody who just sits and reads. . . . With media it's so impersonal. We don't want to be personal any more with anybody." In short, passive cynicism and functional illiteracy are the most easily observed mental markers of present-day consumers of what passes for "higher" education. Sacks's sympathetic conclusion: "Indeed, the powerful contradiction between unreal images of the amusement culture and the reality of diminishing economic prospects would become the basis of great fear and uncertainty for much of Generation-X."[36] I'll take that explanation over all the others offered previously by the prestigious (or just trendy) likes of Jean Baudrillard, Guy Debord, Gilles Deleuze, Julia Kristeva, Luce Irigaray, Jacques Lacan, Bruno Latour, Jean-François Lyotard, and, of course, Michel Foucault: *je m'en fou(cault)*![37]

But let us mention one other opinion, that of John Walker in his *Art in the Age of Mass Media* (1994). He explains that educators in particular commonly criticize the ubiquitous media according to the following criteria:

> The mass media, it is argued, reproduce dominant ideologies and are thus a conservative or counter-revolutionary force; they encourage passivity, apathy, and a sense of powerlessness; power is concentrated in the hands of a few people who are motivated by self-interest, private profit and/or social control; the culture associated with the mass media tends to be of low quality, bland, escapist, stereotyped, standardized, conformist and trivial. In short, [postmodernist] mass culture is seen as an "opium of the people," a means by which the laboring classes are manipulated and diverted during their leisure hours in preparation for their daily toil in offices and factories, or as a compensation for the misery of unemployment.[38]

From this jeremiad, the art historian retrieves a question relevant to his academic discipline: in short, what is the future of elitist art? In any event, since our culture routinely grants the premise that vanguard artists are uniquely sensitive to the *Zeitgeist*, that they are "the forerunners and revealers of our times," then it seems only fitting that they would sensitively respond to such collective spiritual malaise. At its best, their future avant-garde art will be truly provocative, intellectually challenging, emotionally transcendent. At its worse, it will only be like the culture surrounding the artists: "of low quality, bland, escapist, stereotyped, standardized, conformist, and trivial." Who knows, maybe the only growth industry in future artistic production will be extraterrestrial portraiture, particularly the kinetic kind you see on the telly. Made with specific reference to the pioneering ETs first incarnated in order to be televised in the 1975 TV movie *The UFO Incident* (figs. 17, 18), Michael Shermer's conclusion parallels mine:

> The alien abduction phenomenon is the product of an unusual altered state of consciousness interpreted in a cultural context replete with

films, television programs, and science fiction literature about aliens and UFOs. . . . Driven by mass media that revel in such tabloid-type stories, the alien abduction phenomenon is now in a positive feedback loop. The more people who have had these unusual mental experiences see and read about others who have interpreted similar incidents as abduction by aliens, the more likely that it is that they will convert their own stories into their own alien abduction. The feedback loop was given a strong boost in late 1975 after millions watched NBC's *The UFO Incident*, a movie about Betty and Barney Hill's abduction dreams. The stereotypical alien with a large, bald head, elongated eyes, reported by so many abductees since 1975, was created by NBC artists for this program.[39]

THE MODERNIST CINEMATIC CONSCIOUSNESS

If it was not on television, then most likely your most vivid close encounter with extraterrestrial portraiture was at the cineplex (figs. 9–15, 19). Besides birthing television in an almost inevitable fashion, the movies have shaped the modern consciousness in fundamental ways. So basic and so far-reaching are these effects that they often go unmentioned by those who chronicle the wonders of our modern age; omnipresent, they seem to become almost invisible—like the very air we breathe.

No matter; the art historian feels obliged both to emphasize their significance and to explain the exact nature of the unique contributions of this intensely visual medium. Just as Gutenberg's invention (the printed book) transformed the medieval world, so has cinematic consciousness made a new mentality for the modern world. Hand in hand with those physical signs designating a radically different and often materially threatening technological environment encroaching upon the early modernist cityscape, there came, as we have already seen, two other important, essentially psychological, cultural readjustments: "synaesthesia" and "simultaneity." Synaesthesia and simultaneity (as historically situated in chapter 13) represent the essence of the cinematic experience and, like the lowly ETs, the movie syndrome also has its art-historical sources and contexts.

Both of these uniquely modernist psychological situations, synaesthesia and simultaneity, were soon to be translated into conspicuously visual, patently modernist, artistic techniques. First came cinematic montage (circa 1903), and then came (circa 1910) the elitist painters' collage, and both are combinatory techniques. Incidentally, the medieval alchemist, an occultist, had a name for the shared end results, *ars combinatoria*. What initially arose, almost unconsciously, out of a mechanized, quintessential modernist *folk art* entertainment—the movies with their synesthesiac and simultaneous montage-collage technique—soon evolved into an elitist, avant-garde determination. Translated into the strictly sculptural terms of avant-garde expression, these originally "cinematic" techniques became known as *assemblage*. Given that originally the movies were an easily dismissed by-product of the rudely democratic and urbanized, *lumpenproletariater Volksgeist*, it of course took some time before their intrinsic artistic potential would become routinely recognized by savants placed outside of the cinematic industry. By 1934 however, the year Riefenstahl's *Sieg des Willens* celebrating Nazi pseudoreligious ritual was produced, even its potential political applications were fully realized.

The first (and probably still the best) comprehensive art-historical analysis of "Style and Medium in the Motion Pictures" was published in 1934 by Erwin Panofsky, an expatriated European art historian who had "witnessed its development from the very beginnings."[40] Panofsky was well aware of both the mundane (and largely accidental) mechanical origins of his subject. He also recognized its real psychological implications as a sign of the times (*Zeitgeist*). Even in 1934, Panofsky was able to recognize that cinema "was a technical invention that gave rise to the discovery and gradual perfection of a new art." With almost archaeological hindsight, Panofsky also recognized that "the films produced between 1900 and 1910 preestablish the subject matter and methods of the moving picture as we know it today." As a wholly "new art," pre-Cubist era cinema already presented "unique and specific possibilities [which] can be defined as dynamization of space and, accordingly, spatialization of time."

New physical modes of expression engender new ways of thinking, of conception itself; therefore, Panofsky saw how "a hitherto unknown language was forced [after 1900] upon a public not yet capable of reading it, but the more proficient the public became, the more refinement could develop in that language." Cinema's traditional corollary was the theater, where space is static and, Panofsky observed, "the spectator cannot leave his seat, and the setting of the stage cannot change." Quite to the contrary, "with the movies the situation is reversed." As Panofsky concluded, in the ubiquitous cinematic medium,

> not only do bodies move in space, but space itself does, approaching, receding, turning, dissolving and re-crystallizing, as space appears through the controlled locomotion and focusing of the camera and through the cutting and editing of the various shots, not to mention such special effects as visions, transformations, disappearances, slow-

motion and fast-motion shots, reversals and trick films. This opens up a world of possibilities, of which the stage can never dream.[41]

At about the same time, yet another, still essentially unknown, émigré German scholar, Walter Benjamin, recognized the fundamental cultural importance, and even some aesthetic potential, inherent to the proletarian movies. In that now widely read essay, "The Work of Art in the Age of Mechanical Reproduction," first published in 1936, Benjamin noted that whereas the traditional mode of conceptual vision belonging to

> the painter is a total one, that of the cameraman consists of multiple fragments which are assembled under a new law. Therefore, for contemporary man the [fragmentary] representation of reality by the cinema is incomparably more significant than is the vision of the painter since it offers, precisely because of the complete permeation of reality with mechanical equipment, an aspect of reality which is [perceived] free of all equipment.[42]

Benjamin implies (and I would agree with him) that easel painting has become inherently obsolescent due to its traditional conceptual convictions, thus its inherent limitations. To the contrary, the cinema, due to its untraditional, still uncodified, and wholly mechanical operations, is pure modernism. As we should do now, Benjamin saw those fundamental conceptual operations, referred to here as representing "simultaneity" or what he called "multiple fragments assembled under a new law," as being central to a functional definition of modernism, particularly its most favored mass medium, now including TV. But all this, especially the wholly manipulative effect, was recognized even earlier by an anguished writer, Franz Kafka:

> The cinema disturbs one's vision. The speed of the movements and the rapid change of images force men to look continually from one to another. Sight does not master the picture, *it is the pictures which master one's sight*. They flood one's consciousness. The cinema involves putting the eye into uniform, when before it was naked. *Films are iron shutters*.[43]

As Benjamin put it in 1936, as it had been traditionally conceived, "painting is simply in no position to present an object for simultaneous collective experience, as was possible for architecture at all times, for the epic poem in the past, and [uniquely] for the movie today." As he broadly observes, according to his Marxist convictions, "art will tackle the most difficult and important tasks where it is able to mobilize the masses. Today, it does so [i.e., represents 'simultaneous collective experience'] best in the film." This mobilization of the masses—in effect their psychological manipulation—will happen mainly because their "reception in a state of distraction, which is increasing noticeably in all fields of art and which is symptomatic of profound [cultural] changes in perception, finds in the film its true means of exercise."[44]

Benjamin also made an extremely cogent (especially for an observation made in 1936) art-historical reference to Dadaism to illustrate what we might call the all-pervasive "cinematic mentality" of the advanced modernist audience culture. As he recalled the intentions of what was then a relatively recent art movement, "Dadaism attempted to create by pictorial and literary means the effects which the public today seeks in the movies." As Benjamin adds, "Dadaism sacrificed the market values which are so characteristic of the [commercial] film in favor of higher ambitions[:] what they intended, and what they achieved was a relentless destruction of the aura of their creations, which they branded as reproductions with the very means of production."[45] More specifically,

> The work of art made by the Dadaists became an instrument of ballistics. It hit the spectator like a bullet; it happened to him, thus acquiring a tactile quality. It paralleled a [contemporaneous] demand for film, the distracting element of which is also primarily tactile, being based on changes of place and focus which periodically assail the spectator. Let us compare the screen on which a movie unfolds with the canvas of a painting. The painting invites the spectator to [leisurely] contemplation; placed before it, the spectator can abandon himself to his associations. Before the movie frame, he cannot do so. No sooner has his eye grasped a scene than it is already changed. It cannot be arrested. . . . The spectator's process of association in view of these images is indeed interrupted by their constant, sudden change. This constitutes the shock effect of film, which, like all shocks, should be cushioned by heightened presence of mind. By means of its technical structure, [even commercial] film has taken the physical shock effect out of the wrappers in which Dadaism had, as it were, kept inside the moral shock effect.[46]

Panofsky and Benjamin seem rather precocious in their wholly intellectual grasp of the world-historical significance of cinematic expression, a premonition then still largely *in potentia*. Nonetheless, pervasive effects of the ubiquitous techniques of cinema could be found everywhere in contemporary modernist expression, even if they were not always literally referred to as "cinematic." For example, while musing in her journals during the 1930s, Anaïs Nin realized that her ideal of a "swift new novel" must match "our modern life in speed, rhythms, condensation, abstraction, miniaturization, X rays of our secrets, [and become] a subjective gauge of external events."[47] We also saw how Virginia Woolf, born in 1882, quoted Thomas Hardy's lament to the effect that contemporary writers had "changed everything now. We used to think there was a beginning and a middle and an end. We [of the older generation] believed in the Aristotelian theory."[48] Perhaps depressed by her cultural insights, Woolf committed suicide in 1941.

A theoretical position notoriously avoided in avant-garde expression, especially in its performance art, are fixed narrative sequences, from "beginning," to "middle," to "end." Panofsky had however found these conventions still maintained in 1934, and precisely in the most popular art form of his time, the movies. In the commercial cinema, says Panofsky, there was still to be found "observance of the Aristotelian rule, that the story must have a beginning, a middle, and an ending, a rule the abrogation of which has done so much to estrange the general public from the more elevated spheres of modern [art and] writing."[49] However, this anachronism had, and still has, an easily understood economic motive. Commercial cinema, in order to realize a profit by selling its mechanically reproduced product to a mass market, must necessarily remain "old-fashioned." In that way, the market, a cloddish and vulgar "general public," is not alienated by unfamiliar narrative expositions. Nevertheless, strictly cinematic techniques have long since become standard tools of avant-garde expression in wholly different media. Likewise, they have proved essential to the propagation of the postmodernist extraterrestrials so eagerly consumed by the proletariat masses (figs. 9–15, 17–19).

The movies, crassly commercial products notoriously catering to the wholly undeveloped aesthetic taste typifying a *lumpenproletariat* mass audience, are notoriously ignored in the formalistic prognostications produced by progressive art critics who appoint themselves guardians of the eternal flame of the avant-garde. For them, typically "real" art is only represented exclusively by the works of self-conscious painters and sculptors, "plastic" artists, the kind who might even produce performance art. Nonetheless, the popular and largely mechanized movies—and not all those esoteric and elitist avant-garde performance-events and multimedia installations—represent the authentically "modern" form of artistic expression. On the most basic level, the unique technology of the cinema, for actually being wholly unprecedented *technology*, is inherently "modern." And so, centuries hence, when all the rest reverts to mere dust and dead sound and fury, most likely only the movies, maybe television also, will be remembered by the art-historical argonauts of the future, most likely themselves extraterrestrials descended from on high.

As these future astronaut scholars will recognize, as in cinema, so too in elitist or nonpopular, modernist literature: "near" and "far," beginning and end, are typically telescoped or reversed, if not discarded outright. This kind of timeless and spaceless reconstruction of a specifically modernist universe also establishes the environmental context for those extraterrestrial creatures that are always said to live beyond earthly time and space. In a way, they are much more truly "modern" than are their merely earthling counterparts, inexorably grounded in time and space by the banal need to earn a living and to tend to their nuclear families. Nonetheless, all the major effects of this accumulating technological input, without however actually listing any technical innovations specifically wrought by the cinema, were clearly recognized by Fernand Léger, a Cubist painter, as early as 1913:

> Photography requires fewer sittings than does portrait painting, captures a likeness more faithfully, and costs less. The portrait painter is dying out, and the genre scenes and historical paintings will die out also; not by a natural death, but killed off by their historical period. . . .
> I maintain that modern mechanical achievements, such as color *photography, the motion-picture camera,* the profusion of more or less popular novels, and the popularizations of cabaret theaters have effectively replaced, and henceforth rendered superfluous, the development of sentimental pictorial representations and of popular subject matter in pictorial art. I earnestly ask myself how all those more or less historical or dramatic pictures once shown in the French Salon can compete with the screen of any *cinema. Visual realism has never before been so intensely captured.*

Now Léger must relate these technological advances, including the cinematic challenge, to a new demand for narrow specialization in "abstraction." This is a visual consequence which, he suggests, itself arises from the contemporary myth of the *Zeitgeist:*

> Each art is isolating itself and limiting itself to its own domain. Specialization is a modern characteristic, and pictorial art, like all other manifestations of human genius, must submit to its law. It is logical, for by limiting each discipline to its own purpose, it enables achievements to be intensified. In this way pictorial art gains in [social] realism. The modern conception is not simply a passing abstraction, only valid for a few initiates. It instead represents the total expression of a new generation whose need it shares and whose aspirations it answers.[50]

In short, it was the cinema that first visually taught both the general public and modernist artists alike systematically how to destroy space and time. So doing, it taught the world how to be modern. It also taught that beyond this world there must be many others, the kind beyond space and time. When vanguard painters chose to depict these "other worlds," they usually resorted to an artistic technique they called "the fourth dimension."[51] Whatever it called itself, this new, largely technologically induced and universally exhibited, "cinematic" sense of time—immediate and constant—overturned and nearly destroyed the traditional concept of "history." Previously, history had been objectively perceived as something locked in "the past." As a metaphorical prisoner of time and space, history was thus left discrete and removed from immediate emotional experience. In the cinematic/TV modern era, history is hot and *now*. So are the ETs, the futuristic kind arising from zip codes beyond space and time.

Given their ubiquity some ninety years ago, the burning issues of "sequence" versus "simultaneity" were also hotly debated by numerous artists. The avant-garde lost no time in embodying these essentially polemical, and probably largely cinema-based, theoretical positions into their artworks. After 1910, the predominant artistic mind-set had even gotten itself an impressive name, and thus it became much more employable as a visual technique: this was "*la simultaneità*" of futuristic expression. But chronology alone suggests that they did so, and then named it, only *after* they had all gone to the movies, a modernist medium which everybody could afford to attend and experience. The analogous techniques, representing historically novel mind-sets and expressed in narrative fragmentation and spatial and temporal reversals, were most likely informally absorbed first while comfortably seated in cheap seats in the local *cinéma* or *Kino*. In retrospect, it appears much less likely that the process was initially triggered by any imagery officially displayed in the austere and convention-bound halls of the Alte Pinakothek, Museo del Prado, or the Trocadéro. Just like the ETs, modern artistic perception and reported experience really began in real-life, in nonelitist universal world of the mass media (see figs. 1, 4, 5, 9–15, 17–19).

Just as abstract art appeared in response to the drastic professional challenge posed by economically accessible photographic materials (as scholars do recognize), so, too, must that modernist cultural anomaly called "the avant-garde" be viewed in the art-historical context of the movies (as scholars apparently do not recognize). Much, if not all, the pioneering abstract art of the orthodox modernist sort proved visually unappealing to the uninitiated masses, for it was antithetical to their uneducated taste for realism and easy sentimentality. Likewise, beginning with the Futurists and the Dadaists, so, too, was much of typically vanguard "performance art" made stridently unentertaining, unreal and unsentimental, meaning specifically antithetical to the form and content of the modernist popular art form par excellence, the movies. From the cinematic angle, one could rewrite the history of modern art, that is, as action and reaction, all as centered in the neighborhood *kino*.

Of specific bearing to our ongoing subject—the present-day "picturing of extraterrestrials," themselves inevitably treated as generic "monsters"—is the decisive contribution made by the movies to the creation of an international "culture of horror." Happily, this topic has been discussed at length (and with considerable wit) by David Skal.[52] He observes that "horror has always had a certain affinity for modern art movements," and it appears that "at a root level, they are both inspired by similar cultural anxiety." The strictly populist literary genre of outerspace fiction is credited with being inaugurated in 1927 with the founding of the pulp magazine called *Amazing Stories* by Hugo Gernsback, who also coined the term "science fiction" in 1929.[53] Soon after, as Skal observes, "the most lasting and influential invention of 1931 would be the modern horror film"; that was the year that *Dracula* premiered. The macabre antihero is, of course, a vampire, a nocturnal alien-infester who toys with terrified humans and sucks up their vital fluids— just as do the vampirelike ETs popularized much later by Budd Hopkins, Whitley Strieber, David Jacobs, and John Mack, among many others.

Dracula premiered in 1931, the year in which the Austrian national bank failed, triggering the economic collapse of Europe. What ensued was a period in which "untold millions had been left with the feeling that modern life—and death—was nothing but an anonymous, crushing assembly line," and a corollary result was that "the massive shared hardship of the Depression galvanized motion pictures as a dominant form of cultural expression."[54] The year 1931 was also the *annus mirabilis* (*horribilis*) that saw the premiere of *Frankenstein*, a semihuman, hulking creature wrought by perverse technology. Just two years after the cinematic debut of Dracula and Frankenstein, the world witnessed the official installation of the monster of the century; Adolf Hitler was elected German chancellor in January 1933. Many, many more cinematic monsters followed. In sum, a cinematic convention of what Skal calls "dread and circuses" had been permanently installed in the popular modernist consciousness.

The next significant cinematic step in universal horrification was attained in the 1950s, following World War II, which "had introduced two radical new forms of mechanized death—the atomic bomb and the extermination camp." Obsessed with such "necro-technology," Americans were also consumed with what Skal calls "invasion/annihilation anxieties," and these found particularly vivid expression in a sudden outbreak of UFO hysteria. As documented in the movies, "monsters came in two basic shapes in the fifties: gigantic, stomping mutations, explicitly the product of atomic testing; and alien invaders, sometimes overgrown themselves, but usually intent on some kind of brainwashing or ideological control." Again, so, too, operate the *fin-de-millénium* ETs popularized by Hopkins, Jacobs, Strieber, Mack, and all the other postmodernist horror hucksters. Beginning with *Godzilla* (1954—a monster who needed commercial rebirth in 1998, then earning his meretricious makers $471.8 million!), Skal lists dozens more Hollywood creations, including many where "ideological otherness went extraterrestrial."[55]

Then, as now—when the problem is narrowly called "alien abduction"—the conventions of the monstrous science fictional genre presented "the vision of an all-encompassing *conspiracy*, understood only by disbelieved and persecuted protagonists." In point of fact, dire perceptions of "grandiose conspiracies and takeover *first* flourished as a stock element of fifties horror films." Back then was when we (also a then-youthful David Jacobs, Budd Hopkins, Whitley Strieber, John Mack, etc.) were first treated to "repeated images of bulging eyes and—especially—bulging brains," also "heads shaped like gargantuan light bulbs, their bugging eyes the size of baseballs," as accompanied by a general "withering and atrophy in the body." The egregious hydrocephalic motif was then illustrated in such cinematic gems as *Donovan's Brain* (1953), *This Island Earth* (1955), *The Beast with a Million Eyes* (1955), *The Brain from the Planet Arous* (1957), *Invasion of the Saucer Men* (1957), *The Cyclops* (1957), *The Crawling Eye* (1958), and so forth. Also explaining our present situation, Skal observes that "the fifties *first* saw teenagers become a market segment unto themselves"; by 1958, adolescents comprised 72 percent of the movie-going public.[56] If anything, the attendance figures (and attendees) have only gotten worse.

As previously shown by our careful transcriptions of the alien-abduction scenarios first published in the 1980s, a newly favored motif then introduced concerns the micro-abduction of ova and sperm; the dysfunctional reproductive literary motif is still popular in the early third millennium. Skal also puts this into its cultural context. In 1960, the birth control pill was first legally introduced; henceforth, "women could now 'control' their sex lives, or at least separate sex from reproduction."

Alas, a contemporary phenomenon was thalidomide, a mild tranquilizer which, unexpectedly, produced a wave of birth defects, and thus the 1960s was treated to "the spectacle of monstrous birth." Hollywood took heed. In 1968, "Rosemary's Baby" was thrown in the public's face. That misbegotten offspring looked like a thalidomide horror, but the specific cause of this twisted fetus was a conspiracy of devil worshippers.

In 1968, *2001: A Space Odyssey* also fueled the public's growing fascination with uncanny embryos, now however firmly placing their source in outer space. Other pop cultural icons based on gynecological horror images included *The Exorcist* (1973), *It's Alive* (1974), *Eraserhead* (1976), *It Lives Again* (1978), *The Brood* (1979), *Gremlins* (1984), *Child's Play* (1988), and so on. As never before, the public was treated "to images of reproductive nightmares," the kind where "externalized aggression become homicidal dwarves." In an age of (real-world) AIDS, herpes hysteria, anorexia and bulimia, Tylenol poisoning, carcinogenic food additives, dioxin, toxic waste dumps, seeping radon gas, radiation disasters, obligatory urine testing, and so forth, the wider result was a recurrent "evocation of reproduction as unnatural parasitism," further postulating that "reproduction was a kind of death, a devastating insult to the body and personal autonomy."[57] Hence, the dysfunctional gynecological imagery of countless, always invasive and insulting, contemporaneous alien-abduction experiments so luridly performed in print by Jacobs, Hopkins, Strieber, Mack, and so on.

The movies, as both "form" and "content," also represent the quintessential expression of postmodernist pop culture, whatever its chosen medium or (mostly dreadful) thematic materials. Postmodernism *is* international mass culture, and British artist Richard Hamilton (born 1922) identified the characteristics ("11 Commandments") of that universal phenomenon way back in 1957: "1. popular (designed for mass audiences); 2. transient (short-term solution); 3. expendable (easily forgotten); 4. low cost; 5. mass produced; 6. young (aimed principally at youth); 7. witty; 8. sexy; 9. gimmicky; 10. glamorous; 11. big business."[58] Not so ironically, Hamilton's own vanguard "Pop" artworks, like those of all his professional peers, were/are *not* mass produced and, above all, they were *not* aimed at a mass audience. To the contrary, all "art" depicting extraterrestrials—ranging from the crude graphic materials in the tabloids to the flashy and emotionally riveting, multimillion-dollar Hollywood space operas (figs. 5, 9–15, 19)—is most certainly aimed at a mass audience. It even has its own literary sector, the cheap, typically illustrated, mass-produced paperback (figs. 1, 4, 16, 21, 22). The abundant apocryphal postmodernist portraiture of ETs defines the art-historical line drawn between elitist and populist audience cultures.

Because these are all material, and so thoroughly mundane, facts, they are usually perceived as being of no direct relationship to the otherworldly or hermetically sealed spirit world routinely attributed to the modern vanguard artist. Certainly, he (or she) will *not* traffic in extraterrestrial vulgarities: heaven forbid! But our hypothetical Everyman Modernist Artist lived, and still thrives in this same, intensely physical and increasingly violent, cinematic world. Now it has become *Mondo Televizione*. Accordingly, these were the kind of facts about world events and innovations which were being endlessly reported to Everyman Modernist Artist by the newly ubiquitous mass media, particularly and most vividly by its kinetic photography.

For pioneer avant-garde artists who were working on the esoteric fringes of modern mechanized civilization immediately before the First World War, the cumulative effect of this mechanized sense-input was to bring about a new kind of collective psychology, a set of shared assumptions: *us* (vanguard creators) versus *them* (the uncreative masses). And this perception of exclusivity is what they set about to translate into various, mostly unprecedented, kinds of pictorial languages, some of which eventually became "machinelike," literally "mechanized."[59] What were once pioneering insights have, however, long since become thoroughly conventionalized routines; just look into any postmodernist art school curriculum. Similarly, wholly conventionalized are widely disseminated, and egregiously dramatized, stories of close encounters with the extraterrestrials. Encounters with them represent uniquely privileged experiences to those who perceive them, just like the vanguard artist's close encounters with his hermetic muse.

Contextually viewed, not surprisingly the "look" of modern art represents a strictly visualized expression of attitudes unique to our modern, and so typically mechanized and cinematic, culture. In the immediate historical situation of the pre–World War I decades, even the defiantly antimechanical technique of creating abstract art "by chance" essentially is just another material product of the Modern Age, just as are its antitheses: mechanical artifacts like the wireless radio and the motorcar and cine-camera. But modernist pictorial abstraction is also, so we are often told, a highly individualized product of the human mind; as such, avant-garde pictorial abstraction is often taken emblematically to express currently coveted "spiritual values" of one sort or another.[60] Much the same is said about all those postmodernist close encounters with the extraterrestrials. Having put them into a broad modernist cultural context, we may now address a narrower issue. In short, what is truly distinctive about the *mentalité* that has welcomed them, even shaped them out of Shakespeare's "airy nothing"?

THE MASS-HYSTERIA HYPOTHESIS:
A POSTMODERNIST MENTAL MELTDOWN?

According to Dr. John E. Mack, one of its most prestigious apostles, the UFO experience is "of obvious scientific interest." I agree; no question about *that*. But I now need to ask which kind of "scientist" has the proper professional training and the right sort of diagnostic tools needed to define the real nature of the UFO experience. Surely not the physicists, for they must work with physical evidence, the kind that is so conspicuous by its very absence—even after a half-century of increasingly zealous pursuit of UFOs and ETs. The "evidence" presented by the UFOlogists in dogged defense of their beloved tales of alien abduction is, at bottom, all verbal: just talk. In the form of carefully transcribed transcripts, that talk has already been entered into the records of this ongoing trial (see chapters 2 and 5). Talk is a product of the human imagination. And the only kind of scientists qualified to deal with this surprising fertile productive agent, viz. the human mind, are psychologists. Alas, even their "science" is not perfect, as (hopefully) Dr. Mack would himself be the first to admit.

Elaine Showalter, a distinguished student of literature and a historian of modern psychological theory, particularly the kind dealing with hysteria, published a book in 1997 with a provocative title: *Hystories: Hysterical Epidemics and Modern Media*. It succeeded in immediately offending mobs of sensitive souls. She was deluged with hate mail and warned of imminent assassination. Her editors at Columbia University Press were unkindly called "cunt-sucking maggots to let this one slither through."[61] Why? In short, she had the temerity to label as "hysterical epidemics" such typically postmodernist mass maladies as chronic fatigue syndrome, Gulf War syndrome, recovered memory, satanic ritual abuse, multiple personality disorder, and—last but not least—alien abduction. Among all these diverse contemporary malaises, the art historian recognizes that the alien-abduction legend is—by far—the best (or most abundantly) *illustrated* (see figs. 1, 4, 5, 15–22, among hundreds of pictures not reproduced here). As such, the UFO experience most strongly appeals to the "phantasmatic factor"—the creative imagination, in Greek, *phantasmata*—recognized as useful to human indoctrination since the medieval era (see chapter 11).

For all of these mass hysterical syndromes signaled by Professor Showalter, there is a homegrown, historical-hysterical precedent. The mass madness that is of greatest interest to defining the American Mass Hysterical Experience (AMHE) is represented in the celebrated Salem witch trials.[62] The delusion was triggered way back in 1692 by a group of Puritan teenagers who had been listening to altogether too many tales of West Indian sorcery, voodoo rites, witchery, and other such black and un-Christian arts. They had heard the stories from Tituba, a black kitchen slave who, ironically enough, was employed in the rectory of the village minister, the Reverend Samuel Parris. Tituba, with the innocence then attributed to the stereotypical noble savage, undertook to entertain the young white ladies during long winter evenings with tales from her colorful Caribbean childhood. But the girls, finding that they could attract considerable attention by feigning hysterical fits—which they attributed to the work of "witches"—succeeded in deluding their more credulous elders. Their winter voodoo sessions served them in good stead; they put on a performance that would have done credit to the Prince Beelzebub described in the *Malleus Maleficarum* (see chapter 7). They screamed, claimed they were being bitten, choked, pricked, strangled, and stabbed. They rolled their eyeballs and were convulsed with racking pains. They conversed with unseen apparitions, presumably those of their demonic tormentors; they smelled brimstone; they saw "familiars" or witches' imps. Or, if the evil spirits moved them otherwise, they became pale as death, with muscles relaxed, as though victims of catalepsy.

The effect of this demonic theater of the absurd upon a Puritan community—which already believed implicitly in Satan, witchcraft, and the imminence of doomsday—can readily be imagined. Only a few doubted the reality of the girls' demonized performance art. Eventually the madness spread to surrounding villages and, as a consequence, dozens of citizens, mostly elderly women, were thrown into jails, tried as witches, and twenty were eventually hanged. While the hysteria lasted, the girls acted in a role similar to that belonging to much later, Cold War era, congressional committees investigating "communist infiltration"; well over two centuries later, those zealous politicians would themselves be called the instigators of "witch hunts." Two hundred and fifty years before, the collusive New England teenagers succeeded in getting innocent persons "identified" as witches by confessed ex-witches who, of course, found it expedient to get on the side of right thinking and political correctness. They made their accusations stick by putting on fearful courtroom demonstrations of bewitchment for the benefit of the credulous judges. Eventually their accusations became so fantastic that they ceased to be credible even to the most hell-and-brimstone Puritan Divines—but not until incalculable damage had already been done.

Long before the timely postmodernist invention of the trendy *folies postmodernistes du jour*—namely chronic fatigue syndrome, Gulf War syndrome, recovered memory, satanic ritual abuse, multiple personality disorder, and the alien-abduction legends—similar historical examples of mass hysteria were documented and neatly analyzed in a fascinating, but a long out of print, publication (evidently missed by Professor Showalter) authored by J. P. Chaplin and entitled *Rumor, Fear, and the Madness of Crowds* (1959). His homegrown American follies included the end of the world scare, as predicted by one William Miller back in 1831, the great airship craze of 1897 (see chapter 8), the Red Scare of 1919–1920, the riotous funeral orgies following the earthly demise of actor Rudolf Valentino in 1926, the Martian invasion broadcast by Orson Welles in 1938 (see chapter 8), the Mattoon (Illinois) mad gasser attacks of 1944, the flying saucer craze inaugurated in 1947 (see chapter 8), the Red Scare beginning in 1950, the reincarnation of Bridey Murphy published in 1956 (see chapter 11), and so forth. Long before, these repetitious outbreaks had been labeled "moral epidemics" by Charles Mackay in his classic monograph titled *Extraordinary Popular Delusions and the Madness of Crowds* (1841).

According to the comprehensive definition given back in 1959 by Chaplin, also nicely applying two-score years later to various *folies du jour* enhancing the pseudomillenarian year 2000 C.E.:

> Mass hysteria is a loosely used term which may refer to anything from mere excitement brought about by a disturbing rumor to true mass outbreaks of individual hysteria, such as those which took place in Salem at the witch trials. . . . In cases of true mass hysteria, individuals become so disturbed that they may see or hear things that do not exist or suffer severe bodily disturbances, such as choking, vomiting, convulsions, and the like. The term is used here in its broadest sense. That is, we shall find all degrees of hysterical manifestations, ranging from transitory instances of wild excitement to severe delusions accompanied by violent mental and bodily disturbances. However, irrespective of the form of the outbreak, all hysterical manifestations have one outstanding characteristic which links them together: they occur as the result of suggestion in highly suggestible individuals. Just as [Pierre] Janet could suggest an anesthesia in his patients, so can a sincere but credulous bearer of tales, a faith healer, a propagandist or a rumormonger implant strange beliefs or generate wild excitement in the hyper-suggestive.[63]

It is not surprising, in view of the prevalence of hysteria, that it had been a subject of study long before our day. Its history is a fascinating story in itself. It was recognized as a disease by the ancient Greeks. Mistakenly attributed to a derangement of the υστερα (uterus or womb), it was eponymously called "hysteria." Since it is readily observable that the male half of the population is also commonly prone to hysterical disorders (for instance, Whitley Strieber, as shown in chapter 5), it is odd that the Greeks, with all their celebrated wisdom and knowledge, should so limit the disease to women. Perhaps it is not so surprising after all; according to postmodernist standards of political correctness, they represented the first significant group of "dead, white, European males." Either way, the authority of the Hellenes in such matters remained uncontested; in the nineteenth century hysteria was unilaterally dubbed the "female malady."[64] Back then, were the patient a male (a *hysteric* male), he was merely called "neurasthenic" by the (male) doctor, who likely came from the same social class as did his stressed-out patient.

Another contemporary name for neurasthenia was "nervous exhaustion"; a hundred years ago—as is the case presently—exhaustion caused by the often irreconcilable demands of work, family, and leisure was/is a badge of successes. Presently, your mental breakdown—now often diagnosed as chronic fatigue syndrome—represents the circumstantial evidence attesting to your heroic struggle for social position, economic power, *prestige.* Now, even though the symptoms are unquestionably "real," and the patients *do* suffer, a skeptical postmodernist might relabel the Victorian (and postmodernist) male neurasthenics as "testerics." Whereas the symptoms of chronic fatigue syndrome (CFS) are essentially subjective—the patients state they "feel" the effects of this or that malaise—what can be actually quantified are the sufferers themselves: more than 90 percent are white, and women actually do outnumber men, by three or four to one.[65] Obviously, CFS is not an equal opportunity employer. Nevertheless, the classic misogynist misconception *still* finds sanction in contemporary speech, for such exhibitions of wild excitement and mental disturbance—in short, all extremes of emotionality—are still, in the popular mind at least, considered an exclusive prerogative of the "weaker sex."

That traditional notion, a typical display of male chauvinism and patriarchal prejudice, should have at least been discarded since World War I and the lessons it supplied regarding "shell shock," an exclusively *male* "hysterical" ailment—and for obvious reasons. In 1916, it was reported that shell shock cases accounted for as much as 40 percent of all casualties in the fighting zones. Shell shock displayed all the classic physical symptoms of hysteria, the kind formerly exclusively attributed to female neurotics: psychosomatic paralysis, blindness, deafness, mutism or autism, limping, heart palpitations, dizziness, loss of appetite (anorexia), bizarre body postures and facial grimaces, epilectoid seizures and fainting, vomiting and choking, spontaneous fits of sobbing and laughter, glossolalia, nightmares and insomnia, disorientation and depression.[66] According to a recent professional appraisal, hysteria is "primarily a pathological personality structure resulting from inner psychic conflict."[67]

Now, to the contrary, we should all admit that hysteria is an equal opportunity assailant for postmodernist men *and* women. We especially know this since men are often abducted by ETs, or at least so we are told by best-selling authors like Whitley Strieber. Elaine Showalter calls him a "classic hysteric," and she has the professional credentials to make the label stick. As she characterizes his best-selling autobiographical account of alien abduction (see also chapter 5):

> Indeed, what Strieber describes in *Communion* is a life history of false memories, invented tales, and bizarre behavior. As a student at the University of Texas in the late 1960s, he had longer and longer experiences of what appear to be fugue states [i.e., epileptic automatism followed by amnesia], ranging from a few hours to six weeks. Strieber tells us that he invented a number of narratives to account for his whereabouts during these times and to explain his anxiety and need to escape. In January 1968, he got a loan to study film at the London School of Film Technique. After a frightening incident, in which he found himself inexplicably on the roof of a friend's flat, Strieber felt an urgent need to flee.
>
> He set out for Europe on a six-week odyssey but says he remembers virtually nothing about it. He thinks he was in Florence, Strasbourg, and Barcelona, where he "holed up in a back room in a hotel on the Ramblas . . . like a fugitive, never wanting to be alone, haunting the Ramblas, grateful for the unceasing crowds. The rest of the memory is a jumbled mess." For eighteen years after the trip—that is, until writing the book—he told people that he had spent six weeks in Florence. For a while, then, he told a story that he actually went to Russia and then to France for the [student] uprising of May 1968, although he knew full well that "they ended two months before I crossed France." "*Why did I need those absurd stories?*" Strieber asks himself. "They are not lies; when I tell them, I myself believe them. I don't lie. Perhaps I tell them to myself when I tell them to others, so that I can hide from myself whatever has made me a refugee in my own life."[68]

Psychologist Robert Baker gives us the strictly professional, and quite succinct, appraisal of this exceptionally well paid abductee-author:

> Strieber is a classic example of the fantasy-prone syndrome: he is easily hypnotized; he is amnesiac; he has vivid memories of his early life; reports body immobility and rigidity; a very religious background; a

very active fantasy life; he is a writer of occult and highly imaginative novels; he has unusually strong sensory experiences—particularly smells and sounds—and vivid dreams. . . . [He weaves] elaborate fantasies woven in fine cloth from the now universally familiar UFO-abduction fable—a fable known to every man, woman, and child newspaper reader or movie-goer in the nation.[69]

As the rest of us might ask, why do any of us "need those absurd stories," the kind already "known to every man, woman, and child" in the nation, perhaps the whole world? The apparent answer is this: it is not what we need, rather what benefits the paperback publishers, movie producers, and other money-grubbing profiteers managing the infotainment industry. Showalter makes another disturbing observation: "Alien-abduction scenarios closely resemble women's *pornography* [catering to] desires for touch, gazing, penetration"[70] (a conclusion amply documented by the stories quoted in chapter 2). My own observation is that similar impulses spark the complementary publishing phenomenon of "vampire abductions" (e.g., the phenomenal best-sellers by Anne Rice, including *Interview with the Vampire*, 1976, with many more following in the same neck-sucking vein).

But alien abductions are but a small component of a larger syndrome, a sort of collective postmodernist mental meltdown. In short, what we have found are the shared features of a pan-cultural symptomology of anxiety and stress; *hysteria*, forthcoming in its accepted narrative variations, mimics culturally permissible expressions of distress. Hysteria needs to be redefined as a universal (non–gender specific) response to emotional conflict. As Showalter explains:

In the 1990s the United States has become the hot zone of psychogenic diseases, new and mutating forms of *hysteria* amplified by modern communications and *fin de siècle* anxiety. . . . In the interaction between 1990s millennial panic, new psychotherapies, religious fundamentalism, and American political paranoia, we can see the crucible of virulent hysterias in our own time. The heroes and heroines of 1990s hysterias call themselves traumatists and UFOlogists, experiencers and abductees, survivors and survivalists. . . . As the panic reaches epidemic proportions, hysteria seeks out scapegoats and enemies—from unsympathetic doctors, abusive fathers, and working mothers to devil-worshipping sadists, curious extraterrestrials, and evil governments.

Hysteria not only survives in the 1990s, it is more contagious than in the past. Infectious diseases are currently spread by ecological change, modern technology, urbanization, jet travel, and human interaction. Infectious epidemics of hysteria are spread by stories circulated through self-help books, articles in newspapers and magazines, TV talk shows and series, films, the Internet, and even literary criticism. The cultural narratives of hysteria, which I call *hystories*, multiply rapidly and uncontrollably in the ear of mass media, telecommunication, and e-mail. . . . Like all narratives, hystories have their own conventions, stereotypes, and structures. Writers inherit common themes, structures, characters, and images; critics call these common elements *intertextuality*. We need not assume that patients are either describing an organic disorder or else lying when they present similar narratives of symptoms. Instead, patients learn about diseases from the media, unconsciously develop the symptoms, and then attract media attention in an endless cycle. The human imagination is not infinite, and we are all bombarded by these plot lines every day. Inevitably, we all live out the social stories of our time.[71]

As she also points out (as have others), modern hysterical epidemics require at least three components: (1) vulnerable and suggestive patients; (2) therapist-enthusiasts and "expert" theorists; and (3) supportive cultural environments. Even a century ago, some physicians had learned that hysteria could be *iatrogenic*, something new created by the interaction between doctor and patient. Essentially, through a verbal definition, the iatrogenic malady is initially invented by the therapist-enthusiasts, whose role is to play the comforting friend supporting and endorsing the patient's narrative. At the next stage, the emergent iatrogenic tale becomes popularized by the authoritative theorists. Empirical experience (scientific research, too) proves that telling the story to an approving audience fixes it ever more firmly in the teller's belief system. The role of the pathetic patient in all this is rather like a novice actor obeying the commands of the imperious stage director working from an unwritten script. The literary model was set in place by dark-eyed Svengali's mind control over the compliant Trilby. That unseen script is there however; hence the eventual uniformity of the various hysterical performances.

Functionally so close to the alien-abduction syndrome—and especially to the specific procedures used to document its existence (see above, chapters 2 and 5)—as to become a near exact sibling is the postmodernist recovered memory gig. It works in practice just like multiple personality disorder, so brilliantly (and profitably) pioneered by Bridey Murphy (see chapter 11).[72] If either can boast of something like a scientific pedigree, then that is the familiar Freudian concept of "repression," hypothesizing the existence of dreadful "repressed memories." These only the skilled likes of Dr. Freud can extrude from the pathetic patient's subconscious. Unfortunately, well over sixty years after Sigmund Freud advanced his fundamental—and very influential—hypothesis, experimental research conducted by accredited professionals has yet to find any credible evidence to support its prestigious existence.[73] Nonetheless, we have all heard about the characteristically lurid tales of repressed experiences of childhood sexual abuse: how could we miss them? The mass media *loves* these stories, and for all the obvious reasons. Amazingly, the traumatic originals had remained wholly lost to the victim—until they were opportunely *retrieved by hypnosis.*

Besides the best-selling alien-abduction books we have already studied, other hugely profitable publications grounded in the same postmodernist repression myth include (also citing the publishers responsible for their propagation): Flora Schreiber's *Sybil* (Henry Regnery, 1973; the inevitable, 1976, movie is now cited as being "largely responsible for popularizing multiple-personality disorder"), Ralph Allison's *Minds in Many Pieces* (Rawson-Wade, 1980), Michelle Smith and Louis Padzer's *Michelle Remembers* (Congdon and Lathes, 1980), Daniel Keyes's *The Minds of Billy Milligan* (Random House, 1981), Ellen Bass and Laura Davis's *The Courage to Heal* (Harper and Row, 1988), Lauren Stafford's *Satan's Underground* (Harvest House, 1988), Judith Spencer's *Suffer the Child* (Pocket Books, 1989), Pamela Hudson's *Ritual Child Abuse* (R and E Publishers, 1991), Judith Herman's *Trauma and Recovery* (BasicBooks, 1992), Gail Feldman's *Lessons in Evil, Lessons from the Light* (Crown, 1993), Margaret Smith's *Ritual Abuse* (Harper San Francisco, 1993), and there are (of course) many more forthcoming.[74]

In effect, the therapist and the patient work together in order to construct a memory story, a "confabulation." This iatrogenic disorder created in recovered memory (RM) therapy allows for the creation of a new dramatized identity: impotent victim for the patient; omniscient healer for the therapist. As psychologist Robert Baker reports, "Confabulation, the tendency of ordinary, sane individuals to confuse fact with fiction and to report fantasized events as actual occurrences, shows up without fail in nearly every context in which hypnosis is employed, including the forensic area."[75] Elaine Showalter has a disturbing global view of the phenomenon: "Recovered memory is primarily a white woman's phenomenon."[76] The statistics are pretty clear on that point; RM is typically not an equal opportunity employer.

Yes, childhood sexual abuse is real, terrifyingly so—but the *real* victims do remember it, all too well, and they certainly do not require hypnosis years later in order to recall it. However, for female Euro-American professionals reporting RM, often these opportunely retrieved *tableaux noirs* of childhood sexual abuse, suggests Showalter, "could explain many of the disappointments and failures in her professional life." Put otherwise, "It isn't *my* fault." Showalter's position is emphatically stated: "My quarrel in this book is not with the realities of child abuse, or the vigorous investigations of *children's* complaints, but with the ideologies of recovered memory and process of accusation based on *adult* therapy."[77]

As for her opinion on the current alien-abduction hystory, offering us all "a satisfying blend of techno-futurism, religion, and a spiritual quest," we may just refer to her dismissal of another contemporary favorite, "satanic ritual abuse," which—as witchcraft (fig. 26)—we recognize to be anything but new. In this case, Showalter observes that

> advocates defend the consistency of the narrative but seem not to understand the power of literary conventions, the morphology of folk tales, the repetitions of rumors and, above all, the way that suggestion works to produce confabulations. . . . Novels and movies create popular imagery, but [these] stories can't flourish unless therapists are willing to stake their reputations on the cases. . . . An inverse relation of logic pertains, which I'll call Showalter's Law: As the hystories get more bizarre, the experts get more impressive.[78]

To complement this *Grundbegriff* (a "basic principle" referring contextually to likes of "experts" like Dr. John E. Mack), we now have "Moffitt's Law," the one referring to the self-fulfilling fallacy. This admittedly jaundiced viewpoint is supported by the observations of psychologist Robert Baker:

> When "hypnosis" is used on people and they are "regressed," i.e., asked to imagine some past period of their life, and this suggestion is followed up with additional social demands and psychological pressures to comply with the hypnotist's biases and convictions—you will elicit anything and everything but the truth. Reports of being raped, of eating baby's hearts and eyeballs, reports of torture, murder, orgies and sexual molestation, incest—anything that is feared or fearful—are common.
>
> The clinician/hypnotist can readily produce *Twilight Zone* or *X-Files* tales and nightmares, and anything his client has ever read [or seen on TV] or imagined or feared may emerge as an actual event or occurrence. Over eight years experience in the laboratory, with over five hundred students and community volunteers, looking at hypnosis and memory, past-lives regressions, future-lives progressions, and other relaxation effects, can be convincing of the fact that it is, indeed, quite easy to persuade people that things that never happened really did happen. Moreover, if the regressers and progressers take the time and trouble or make a sincere effort to account for the sources of their dreams, visions, and imagined scenarios, they usually have little difficulty in doing so.[79]

Another interesting bit of published data specifically referring to the satanic ritual routine (not provided by Showalter) makes a direct comparison between the picturesque motifs associated with this postmodernist revival of witchcraft and the celebrated postmodernist encounters with the extraterrestrial neo-incubi. In short, what both kinds of dreadfully close encounters share is *a common iconography*. The comparison, worked out in tabular form by Gwen Dean, a California therapist,[80] looks like this:

Alien Abduction Accounts		*Ritual Satanic Abuse Accounts*
examining table	vs.	altar table
forced intercourse	vs.	ritual rape
scary eyes	vs.	scary eyes
babies important	vs.	babies important
out-of-body experience	vs.	out-of-body experience
wounds, scars, bruises	vs.	wounds, scars, bruises
amnesia	vs.	amnesia
voyeur observers	vs.	voyeur observers
fear of hypnosis	vs.	fear of hypnosis
forced against will	vs.	forced against will
feels like being drugged	vs.	feels like being drugged
told you are special	vs.	told you are special
isolated from other humans	vs.	isolated from other humans
abducted at young ages	vs.	abducted at young ages

Henry Fuseli would have delighted in the comparison (see chapter 7). Perhaps what seems called for now is a revised version of the Miranda Rule: "You have *the right* to an abduction experience, but . . ."

No matter; all this, and with specific reference to the "UFO experience" (so called since 1972), was effectively related to mass hysteria back in 1959 by Carl Jung:

> But if we want to understand a mass rumor [or mass hysteria] which, it appears, is even accomplished by collective visions, we must not remain satisfied with all too rational and superficially obvious motives. The cause must strike at the roots of our existence if it is to explain such an extraordinary phenomenon as the UFOs [later birthing the ETs]. Although they were observed as rare curiosities in earlier centuries, they merely gave rise to the usual local rumors. The universal mass rumor was reserved for our enlightened, rationalistic age.
>
> The widespread fantasy about the destruction of the world at the

end of the first millennium was metaphysical in origin and needed no UFOs in order to appear rational. Heaven's intervention was quite consistent with the *Weltanschauung* of that age. But, nowadays, public opinion would hardly be inclined to resort to the hypothesis of a metaphysical act, otherwise innumerable persons would already have been preaching about the warning signs in heaven. Our *Weltanschauung* does not expect anything of this sort [but the Heaven's Gate UFO cult did so in 1997: fig. 5]. We would be much more inclined to think of the possibility of psychic disturbances and interventions, especially as our psychic equilibrium has become something of a problem since the last [or second] World War. In this respect, there is increasing uncertainty. . . .

Psychologists who are conscious of their responsibilities should not he dissuaded from critically examining a mass [hysterical] phenomenon like the UFOs, since the apparent impossibility of the reports suggests to common sense that the most likely explanation lies in a psychic disturbance. . . . The present [1959, likewise 2001] world situation is calculated as never before to arouse expectations of a redeeming, supernatural event. If these expectations have not dared to show themselves very clearly, this is simply because no one is deeply rooted enough in the tradition of earlier centuries to consider an intervention from heaven as a matter of course. We have indeed strayed far from the metaphysical certainties of the Middle Ages, but not so far that our historical and psychological background is empty of all metaphysical hope. Consciously, however, rationalistic enlightenment predominates, and this abhors [back in 1959] all leanings towards the "occult."[81]

Now, in 2003 C.E., those once abhorrent "leanings towards the occult" are called "New Age"—and the swarming masses seem to find them not in the least abhorrent. Among significant exemplars widely televised recently, think of David Koresh and his Branch Davidians. Now think of Herff ("Do") Applewhite and his Heaven's Gaters, voluntarily sped away to the Other Side on their very own UFO. Now think of all those industrious UFOlogists lurking in our midst. How many of *them* are there? Their teeming ranks probably correspond to the "statistics" quoted by UFOlogists Budd Hopkins, David Jacobs, and John Mack to establish the number of alien encounters supposedly experienced by stunted Americans: "From several hundred thousand to *several million Americans* may have had abduction or abduction-related experiences."[82] These guys have got it right for once: a holocaust is coming! But, please note Budd, David, and John, *this is a mental holocaust*, a side effect of a universal cultural infestation, an AIDS-like epidemic of the postmodernist mass mind.

SOME CONCLUSIONS, MOSTLY DREARY

The human mind is a wonderfully ingenious instrument. Autonomous and ambitious, it constantly seeks answers and explanations; it frantically strives to connect all the dots. One mental phenomenon, wholly unique to humans, explains most of the frantic dot-connecting. Among all terrestrial biological entities, only *Homo sapiens* is cognizant of a personally appointed *death*, one's inevitable corporeal extinction. This unique psychic revelation thus leads fearful humans to postulate, as all other earthly species cannot, an "afterlife." Although absolutely unsupported to date by any scientific evidence, this singular surmise gave birth to two further hypotheses—"heaven" and "hell"—equally ungrounded in verifiable physical (geographical) fact. Another characteristically human manifestation is the phenomenon we have relabeled MFOs, all that anomalous stuff opportunely seen "up there"; that also called for imaginative hypotheses, an endless stream of them. Similarly ungrounded are the ETs, said to regularly descend to earth via UFOs from (the) heaven(s). The rational explanation for MFOs—forget it: it is either eyestrain or misidentified natural phenomena—is *boring*. The alternative, really weird option—an intervention by genetically supernatural, divine, and/or extraterrestrial, entities—is *exciting*. Given the two choices, ennui or titillation, which would *you* prefer?

We have reviewed in detail the various reasons why one may particularly doubt the authenticity of the omnipresent alien-abduction legend. Nonetheless, it is a significant, even literally illustrative, feature of our postmodernist culture, and that is now best called a posttextual visual culture.[83] As such, the alien-abduction legend deserves our rapt attention, like "the drug problem," "child abuse," "acid rain," "urban decay," "global warming," and "the coming plague." As shown here, there are abundant reasons for doubting the validity of the ET experience, meaning such as it is specifically labeled—"nonfiction"—and reported by its professed adherents. Nonetheless, the phenomenon does unquestionably exist—that is, however, as *a mass-hysterical syndrome*. Besides the skepticism of the art historian, also to be considered is the Occam's razor applied by anthropologists, historians of religion, clinical psychologists, accredited scientists, and, especially, the experienced trial judge and district attorney. To the contrary, UFOlogists have their own interpretation of the Occamite principle: focus on what is not known, and ignore what is known; emphasize data that fit, and ignore the kind that does not; pick out what suits the alien-abduction theory and dismiss (or avoid outright) all the rest.

The UFOlogists should all know that, most likely, it is all little more than "baloney" (but we can think of a better b-word). However, if the media moguls, especially the television producers and the paperback publishers, also are aware of the evidently thoroughly bogus nature characterizing so many of their commercial products, clearly they are not sharing their insider knowledge with us. Unquestionably, they will keep pumping it out—and will rake in the returns (*$$*)—because someone you know *will* buy it. I will now however confess my willingness to cooperate with the infotainment industry. Here is my magnanimous offer. For a mere half-million-dollar advance on my forthcoming royalties—up front, please—I will let you publish my own book-length, wonderfully detailed and extremely lurid, exposé of my very own, deliciously gauche, close encounters with the ETs. Moreover, if you don't like the first draft, I will adjust it to include other otherworldly details more to your liking (including fugitive sightings of cherry-red pubic hair). Can we do lunch?[84]

In sum, you now recognize how even an earthling art historian can, and should, prescribe a needful postmodernist cultural mammogram. To do so, you often have to read a lot of rubbish. It's dirty work, but someone has to do it. Another who did so, centuries before, was Hercules. The stables of Augeas, king of Elis, held three thousand oxen; they fed—and they excreted, copiously. Their stalls had not been cleaned out for thirty years. Hercules performed the needful hygienic task in one day by diverting river waters to flush out the barn. The people of Elis were grateful; environmental pollution was markedly reduced in their neighborhood. Now they could happily set about inventing many new kinds of crap.

Alas, this particular cultural mammogram will do no good, even if correctly read. I admit that my targets will not be blasted by any bolt of lightning descending from the Great Beyond, neither from heaven nor from hell. Earlier (in chapter 9) we reviewed an unquestionably useful historical study of the UFO experience composed back in 1982 by Professor David M. Jacobs. Then he made repeated reference to the "UFOlogist belief structure," the kind postulated upon the "extraterrestrial hypothesis." As is documented by the thrust of Dr. Jacobs's subsequent publications, like so many other postmodernist ET/UFO champions, he now enthusiastically subscribes to the same "belief structure." Using other terminology, it is all just a matter of opinion.

Jacobs has one; you have one; I have my own opinion. Since we all have an *opinion*, let us define the term. According to *Webster's Collegiate Dictionary*, it is "that which is opined; a belief or sentiment, with reference to something which involves one's *feelings*." In short, "an opinion, in ordinary usage, is what one believes about anything." Put your sentient opinions together and—*voilà!*—you get a "belief structure." If there is any sure thing about *opinion*—something actually known about the phenomenon, its kernel of objective fact, the observable, repeatable and verifiable data associated with *opinion*—it is simply this: *mine* will not change *yours*, and vice versa. Democritus also had an opinion: "Nothing exists except atoms and empty space; everything else is opinion."

Let us expand the definition process, so exposing, perhaps even deflating, a hidden but intractable emotional component. Religion is another way of saying "belief structure"; nobody would argue that point. One or the other, such things are taken very seriously by their subscribers. The fundamental distinction between all the wonderfully diverse varieties of religious beliefs in the world is simply this: there are yours, mine, and *theirs*. Either way, in any form, its ideological basis is *opinion*, as defined above. Noah Webster said that *religion* represents "the outward act or form by which men [and women] indicate recognition of a god or gods, to whom obedience and honor are due; the feeling or expression of human love, fear, or awe of some superhuman or overruling power; a system of faith." Which reminds me of the concept of the Almighty, as expressed by Mel Brooks and Carl Reiner in their memorable comedy routine called "The 2,000 Year-Old Man":

> Even before the All Mighty I believed in a superior being. His name was Phil. Out of respect we called him Philip. Philip was big and strong like an ox. He had a big red beard, a chest like a barrel, and arms the size of two oak trees. Nobody was as powerful as Philip. If he wanted, he could kill you. As a result we revered him and we prayed to him. "Ooooh, Philip, please don't hurt us. Don't pinch us. Please don't take our eyes out." But one day Phil was hit by a bolt of lightning. All of a sudden we looked up in the sky and said, "There's something bigger than Phil!"

Substitute "extraterrestrial" for "Philip," or "ET" for "Phil," and you see what I mean.

To the contrary of *opinion*, generally taken to be singular in its source, *religion* is necessarily a collective experience. Religion is nearly universally recognized to be a good thing; it brings a sense of fellowship ("belonging") and (even) spiritual comfort to its adherents. That is why they will stick with it, typically tenaciously. The typically disparaged act of rejection of the canonized mass belief system is called *apostasy*, literally meaning (in Greek) a conscious decision to "stand apart." When religions rule over a society, in extreme cases (as history has repeatedly shown) your egregious apostasy can get you burned at the stake or, the more modern way, left standing apart at a bullet-pocket wall with your terminal jolt of nicotine.

As our survey of the historical documents shows, UFOlogy should be granted the status of a New Age pseudoreligion. My point, a terminal one, is this. It is most unlikely, and this a statistically grounded conclusion, also a historical paradigm, that people will ever voluntarily change or renounce outright their religious affiliations. This is especially implausible because religious beliefs (collectively held *opinions*) typically define, even name, the very identity, also the psychology of the individual subscriber. Current psychic identity kits include "Christian," "Mormon," "Jew," "Muslim," "Buddhist," also "UFOlogist" and "abductee." Similarly, one will not adopt a position of *apostasy* in regard to one's previously published statements of determined allegiance to any given "belief structure"—no matter if someone else can clearly show that to be naught but mere *opinion*.

Given this fact, and having reached the finale of my appointed task, I must recognize that this book, upon which I have expended so much labor and love, will produce no effect whatsoever. To think otherwise is to stand exposed as being as naïve as are committed UFOlogists. UFOlogists will—of course!—doggedly continue to adhere to their quirky belief system, shown here to represent naught but mere *opinion*. Moreover, TV and movie producers will continue to market their visually seductive UFOlogical wares as long as public demand persists. Obviously so; no surprise there: *demand* produces *supply*, which in turn generates *money* for the opportunistic purveyors. And, particularly, the commercial publishers seem to have a vested interest in maintaining the status quo, in vending their entertaining, hence profitable, paranoia: "alienophobia," as it were. These paperback vendors seem scarcely interested in exposing the fallacies of ET apocrypha; to the contrary, they continue to pour fuel on the emotional bonfires of alienophobia.[85] As the historian knows, the classical-era terms for such vendors of spurious delights were: (male) *amans, nurus, paelex-pellax, zelotypus*; (female) *amica, concubina, domina, hera, meretrix, nupta,* and so forth.

If indeed "the truth is out there," then the *truth* is simply, merely that we live in a capitalist society, and here—no surprise this—all that matters is *supply* (theirs) and *demand* (ours). In sum, when it's not just about emotional stimulus for the postmodernist American masses— cheap thrills and paranoid chills—then mostly it's all about money, great sums of it. And, trust me, the demand for alien thrills and chills will persist. But if—God (ET) forbid!—it does not, then always lurking behind the postmodernist scenery are a thronging host of new mental aberrations, novel weapons of mass distraction: *panem et circences* for the *hoi polloi*, demanding exploitation by the more nimble-witted proprietors of the postmodernist Augean psychic stables. The result is what I call "Toxic Pop.Culture Exposure Syndrome" (TPCES).

In that sense, of course, I have wasted a lot of my time, perhaps also the reader's. No matter; never mind. I could have wasted my time in other, much more commonplace, ways: playing golf (aka "kólfr"), doing crossword puzzles, stroking crystals, watching a soccer match, smoking pot, painting watercolors, masturbation, chanting mantras, plucking at a lute, composing blank verse, and so on and so forth. Conversely, one might even devise a handy how-to-do-it book for the mass composition of avant-garde blank verse.[86] Alternatively, one even might strenuously research and write a book like this: a how-to-do-it book for potential "abductees," also helpfully citing the publishers and television producers who are most likely to buy—literally—your forthcoming "nonfiction" story.[87]

Doing those other things—humping golf bags, solving crossword puzzles, kicking balls around, painting watercolors, playing the guitar, chanting mantras and fondling crystals, dabbling in onanism, and composing reams of intractably blank verse—are all ways of killing time, of independently diverting oneself, of concocting autonomous means of self-expression. All these alternate diversions represent diverse, essentially harmless and ecologically sound, activist alternatives to passive surrender to the mesmerizing bewitchments provided in such unchecked abundance by the postmodernist infotainment industry.

A final observation has it that our time—the Modern Age—has been, above all, the Age of Mass Delusions. Viewed in the context of all *other* historical periods, ours is uniquely the Age of Mass Delusions—and how could it have been otherwise? Never before were there what we now call the "mass media," and these have now been made immediately accessible to all potential consumers inhabiting a now wholly wired global village. Among other effects, mostly baleful, by so vigorously vending their cheap thrills,[88] the mass media have also produced a worldwide infection of ETs and UFOs. And what's next? God only knows . . .

Ite; missa est.

POSTSCRIPT

Indeed, "God only knows." As this book was going to press, a transfiguring event occurred. After September 11, 2001—a date that will truly live in infamy—previously ambiguous American perceptions of "alien invasion" became stark reality.

Now, "ET" means an earthling terrorist. Now, as we all know, indeed these postmillenarian ETs do dwell among us, as "sleepers." Now, their "UFO" turns out to be a hijacked airliner, one made into a deadly guided missile. This time, however, their UFOs were photographed (no hoax this time, alas); then they were immediately shown on television to millions of stunned viewers around the world. We all saw the cinematic debut of the twenty-first-century UFOs and authentic portraits of their inhumane ET pilots.

After September 11, 2001, the material and, above all, the psychological conditions of life in America have been drastically altered, perhaps forever. So have all the old, twentieth-century definitions of "alien invasion."

NOTES

1. J. Allen Hynek, as quoted in Carl Sagan, *UFOs: A Scientific Debate* (New York: Barnes & Noble, 1996), pp. 42–43.

2. Donald H. Menzel, in ibid., p. 144.

3. Louis B. Heller, *Do You Solemnly Swear?* (New York: Curtis, 1968), p. 262.

4. Otto Munsterberg, as quoted in ibid., p. 439.

5. Heller, as quoted in ibid., p. 440.

6. See, among others, E. M. Borchard, *Convicting the Innocent: Errors of Criminal Justice* (New Haven: Yale University Press, 1932); Elizabeth F. Loftus, *Eyewitness Testimony* (Cambridge: Harvard University Press, 1979); E. F. Loftus and K. Ketcham, *Witness for the Defense* (New York: St. Martin's, 1991); D. F. Ross et al., *Adult Eyewitness Testimony: Current Trends and Developments* (Cambridge: Cambridge University Press, 1994).

7. Munsterberg, in Heller, *Do You Solemnly Swear?*, pp. 440–41 (my emphasis).

8. See Philip Klass, *UFOs Explained* (New York: Random House, 1974).

9. J. Vallée, *Confrontations: A Scientist's Search for Alien Contact* (New York: Ballantine, 1990), pp. 13, 131.

10. Ibid., p. 156.

11. Ibid., p. 85.

12. Shakespeare, *King Henry VI*, III.ii.

13. *A Midsummer Night's Dream*, V.i.

14. Imaginary comic routine, as in C. D. B. Bryant, *Close Encounters of the Fourth Kind: Alien Abductions, UFOs, and the Conference at M.I.T.* (New York: Knopf, 1995), p. 92; among us UFOlogists, the understood reference is to Budd Hopkins's much-applauded account of "The Linda Cortile Abduction Case."

15. R. E. Bartholomew and G. S. Howard, *UFOs and Alien Contact: Two Centuries of Mystery* (Amherst, N.Y.: Prometheus Books, 1998), pp. 245–46.

16. Elizabeth Loftus, *The Myth of Repressed Memory: False Memories and Allegations of Sexual Abuse* (New York: St. Martin's, 1996); see also H. Wakefield and R. Underwager, *Return of the Furies: An Investigation into Recovered Memory Therapy* (Chicago: Open Court, 1994).

17. Patrick Huyghe, *The Field Guide to Extraterrestrials* (New York: Avon, 1996), p. 129.

18. Particularly good at showing the actual mental mechanics of a heap of trendy New Age delusions (even though written before the term "New Age" was coined!) is D. H. Rawcliffe, *Occult and Supernatural Phenomena* (New York: Dover, 1960); for some further, strictly physical, deconstruction, see Terence Hines, *Pseudoscience and the Paranormal: A Critical Examination of the Evidence* (Amherst, N.Y.: Prometheus Books, 1994); Joe Nickell, *Mysterious Realms: Probing Paranormal, Historical, and Forensic Enigmas* (Amherst, N.Y.: Prometheus Books, 1993); Joe Nickell, ed., *The Outer Edge: Classic Investigations of the Paranormal* (Amherst, N.Y.: CSICOP, 1996).

19. Robert A. Baker, "The Aliens among Us: Hypnotic Regression Revisited," *Skeptical Inquirer* 12, no. 2 (1987): 157; see also S. Blackmore, "Abduction by Aliens or Sleep Paralysis," *Skeptical Inquirer* 22, no. 3 (1998): 23–28.

20. Carl Sagan, *The Demon-Haunted World: Science as a Candle in the Dark* (New York: Ballantine, 1997), pp. 210–11.

21. N. Goran, *Fact, Fraud, and Fantasy: The Occult and Pseudosciences* (Totowa, N.J.: Littlefield, Adams, 1979), pp. 170–71.

22. Martin Gardner, *Fads and Fallacies in the Name of Science* (New York: Dover, 1957), p. 348.

23. See John F. Moffitt, *Occultism in Avant-Garde Art: The Case of Joseph Beuys* (Ann Arbor: University of Michigan Research Press, 1986).

24. For more details, see Geoffrey Ahern, *Sun at Midnight: The Rudolf Steiner Movement and the Western Esoteric Tradition* (Wellingborough, U.K.: Thorsons, 1984), pp. 21–30.

25. Neil Postman, *Amusing Ourselves to Death: Public Discourse in the Age of Show Business* (New York: Penguin, 1986), pp. 143–44, 147–48.

26. Studies cited in ibid., pp. 170–71.

27. Rudolf Steiner, *Eurythmy as Visible Speech: Fifteen Lectures* (London: Steiner Press, 1984), p. 21.

28. For the postmodernist "cultures of conspiracy," particularly the kind supporting the ET legends, see Jodi Dean, *Aliens in America: Conspiracy Cultures from Outerspace to Cyberspace* (Ithaca, N.Y.: Cornell University Press, 1998).

29. See J. Vankin and J. Whalen, *Sixty Greatest Conspiracies of All Time: History's Biggest Mysteries, Coverups, and Cabals* (Secaucus, N.J.: Citadel, 1996); Robert Anton Wilson, *Everything Is under Control: Conspiracies, Cults, and Cover-Ups* (New York: Harper Perennial, 1998); and, specifically, Dean, *Aliens in America*.

30. J. Cantor, "Fright Reactions to Mass Media," in *Media Effects: Advances in Theory and Research*, ed. J. Bryant and D. Zillman (Hillsdale, N.J.: Lawrence Erlbaum, 1994), pp. 40–46.

31. G. G. Sparks, "Paranormal Depictions in the Media: How Do They Affect What People Believe? " *Skeptical Inquirer* (July/August 1998): 35–39 (citing 7 previous publications).

32. Ibid.

33. Peter Sacks, *Generation-X Goes to College: An Eye-Opening Account of Teaching in Postmodern America* (Chicago: Open Court, 1996), pp. 138–39.

34. Ibid., p. 131.

35. Ibid., pp. 110, 133, 135.

36. Ibid., pp. 144–45, 157.

37. For a witty deconstruction (in French!) of this lot, see Alan Sokol and Jean Bricmont, *Impostures intellectuelles* (Paris: Editions Odile Jacob, 1997) for another approach, parody, see H. M. S. Phake-Potter, *Postmodernist Deconstruction for Dummies: A Survivor's Guide to Building Your Academic Career*, ed. J. F. Moffitt (Philadelphia: Xlibris, 2002).

38. John A. Walker, *Art in the Age of Mass Media* (Boulder, Colo.: Westview, 1994), p. 12.

39. Michael Shermer, *Why People Believe Weird Things: Pseudoscience, Superstition, and Other Confusions of Our Time* (New York: Freeman, 1997), p. 95.

40. E. Panofsky, "Style and Medium in the Motion Pictures," reprinted in *Three Essays on Style* (Cambridge: MIT Press, 1997), pp. 93–123. For a broader historical viewpoint, see Arnold Hauser, *The Social History of Art* (New York: Vintage, 1960), IV, 226ff., "The Film Age."

41. Panofsky, "Style and Medium," pp. 96–98.

42. Walter Benjamin, *Illuminations* (London: Tiranti, 1970), pp. 231–49.

43. Franz Kafka, in Jonathan Hertz and Norman Klein, *Twentieth-Century Art Theory: Urbanism, Politics, and Mass Culture* (Englewood Cliffs, N.J.: Prentice-Hall, 1990), pp. 253–54 (my emphasis).

44. Benjamin, *Illuminations*, p. 234.

45. Ibid., p. 236.

46. Ibid., pp. 237–38.

47. Anaïs Nin, *The Novel of the Future* (New York: Holt, 1972), p. 19.

48. Virginia Woolf, *A Writer's Diary* (New York: Harcourt Brace, 1954), p. 93.

49. Panofsky, "Style and Medium," p. 113.

50. Fernand Léger, as in Charles Harrison and Peter Woods, eds., *Art in Theory, 1900–1990: An Anthology of Changing Ideas* (Oxford: Blackwell, 1992), p. 199 (my emphasis).

51. On this technique, see Linda D. Henderson, *The Fourth Dimension and Non-Euclidean Geometry in Modern Art* (Princeton: Princeton University Press, 1983).

52. David J. Skal, *Monster Show: A Cultural History of Horror* (New York: Penguin, 1994).

53. Karl S. Guthke, *The Last Frontier: Imaging Other Worlds, from the Copernican Revolution to Modern Science Fiction* (Ithaca, N.Y.: Cornell University Press, 1990), pp. 24, 34.

54. Skal, *Monster Show*, pp. 55, 114, 115, 135 (also noting, on p. 211, that "one of Adolf Hitler's favorite movies was *King Kong*").

55. Ibid., pp. 229–30, 247–53, 255.

56. Ibid.

57. Ibid., pp. 288, 290, 298, 300–301; for another complementary phenomenon, Stephan King, see ibid., chap. 13, "The Dance of Death." (Skal, however, does not ever refer to the influential *published* ET scenarios that I have carefully transcribed.)

58. Richard Hamilton, in Walker, *Art in the Age of Mass Media*, pp. 26–27.

59. For an art-historical survey of this distinctly modernist imagery, see K. G. Pontus Hultén, *The Machine as Seen at the End of the Mechanical Age* (New York: Museum of Modern Art, 1968).

60. See the various essays in M. Tuchman, ed., *The Spiritual in Art, Abstract Painting, 1890–1985* (Los Angeles: Los Angeles County Museum of Art, 1986).

61. Elaine Showalter, preface, *Hystories: Hysterical Epidemics and Modern Media*, 2d ed. (New York: Columbia University Press, 1997), p. 10.

62. On this antique episode, also usefully stressing a modern "hysterical" explanation, see C. L. Alderman, *The Devil's Shadow: The Story of Witchcraft in Massachusetts* (New York: Archway, 1970).

63. J. P. Chaplin, *Rumor, Fear, and the Madness of Crowds* (New York: Ballantine, 1959), p. 11.

64. See E. Showalter, *The Female Malady: Women, Madness, and English Culture, 1830–1980* (New York: Penguin, 1987), recording many contemporary opinions.

65. For CFS, see Showalter, *Hystories*, chap. 8 (with further bibliography).

66. See Showalter, *The Female Malady*, chap. 7, "Male Hysteria."

67. Martha N. Evans, *Fits and Starts: A Genealogy of Hysteria in Modern France* (Ithaca, N.Y.: Cornell University Press, 1991), p. 2.

68. Showalter, *Hystories*, p. 197.

69. Robert A. Baker, in Kendrick Frazer, ed., *The UFO Invasion: The Roswell Incident, Alien Abductions, and Government Coverups* (Amherst, N.Y.: Prometheus Books, 1997), p. 217.

70. Showalter, *Hystories*, p. 196.

71. Ibid., pp. 4–6.

72. For a timely deconstruction of this postmodern malady, see ibid., chap. 11, "Multiple Personality Disorder."

73. David S. Holmes, "The Evidence for Repression: An Examination of Sixty Years of Research," in *Repression and Dissociation: Implications for Personality, Theory, Psychopathology, and Health*, ed. J. Singer (Chicago: University of Chicago Press, 1990), pp. 85–102.

74. Titles cited in Frazer, *The UFO Invasion*, pp. 249–50; for the vulgar

Sybil movie's role in "popularizing multiple-personality disorder," see *Newsweek*, 25 January 1999, pp. 66–68.

75. Baker, "Aliens among Us," pp. 147–62.

76. Showalter, *Hystories*, p. 151.

77. Ibid., pp. 152, 158 (in chap. 10, "Recovered Memory"); for more deconstrutive details, see also Wakefield and Underwager, *Return of the Furies*.

78. Showalter, *Hystories*, pp. 180–81, 189; see esp. chap. 13, "Alien Abductions."

79. Baker, in Frazer, *The UFO Invasion*, p. 251.

80. Gwen Dean data, in Bryan, *Close Encounters of the Fourth Kind*, p. 138.

81. Carl Jung, as in Jay David, *Flying Saucer Reader* (New York: Signet, 1967), pp. 135, 137.

82. John E. Mack, *Abduction: Human Encounters with Aliens* (New York: Scribner's, 1994), p. 448.

83. See Nicholas Mirzoeff, *An Introduction to Visual Culture* (London and New York: Routledge, 1999).

84. Just for the historical record, here is a list of commercial American publishers, most of whom have manufactured those books, typically issued as nonfiction, which deal with those New Age aberrations which have been consistently treated here as "fiction." However, this particular list only includes publishers to whom a literary agent I had hired actually sent a prospectus of the present book, mine; all those listed refused to publish it, the routine defense being "not right for our list," and, as one senior editor even admitted outright, "the market is too limited to satisfy X-Corp's sales goals." Arranged alphabetically, the *salon des refusés (ou refuseurs)* includes: Avon; BasicBooks; Citadel (Carol Publishing Group); Dutton-Plume; M. Evans; Farrar, Straus & Giroux; Free Press; W. H. Freeman; Frome International; HarperCollins; Llewellyn; Wm. Morrow; Plenum; Random House; Routledge; Scribner's; Simon & Schuster; Times Books; Westview Press. My apologies to any rejecters whom I may have missed, and no hurt feelings: one now recognizes the capitalist exigencies of the postmodern infotainment marketplace.

85. Among endless others, here is a quintessential paperback example of paranormal apocrypha—435 pages, with loads of pictures and a wholly credulous text—recently created by mass media experts (Time/Life), and as marketed to a mass captive audience (Book-of-the-Month Club): Editors of Time/Life Books, *Mysteries of the Unknown* (New York: Book-of-the-Month Club, 1997).

86. For some examples of the latter diversion, "composing blank verse"— with specific instructions telling *you* exactly how to make (even publish) your very own angst-ridden poetic productions, and with versification here treated (finally) as an endeavor perhaps comparable to (just) solving crossword puzzles, see H. M. S. Phake-Potter, *Poetic Inspiration for Dummies: How to Create Modern Verse, For Better or Worse*, ed. J. F. Moffitt (Philadelphia: Xlibris, 2002).

87. For the most likely publishers for your preferably eroticized confabulations, see note 84.

88. All the preceeding now serves to update (into the twenty-first century) the data gathered in Les Daniels, *Living in Fear: A History of Horror in the Mass Media* (New York: Scribner's, 1975).

Bibliography of Cited Publications

Achenbach, Joel. *Captured by Aliens: The Search for Life and Truth in a Very Large Universe.* New York: Simon & Schuster, 1999.

Adamski, George. *Flying Saucers Have Landed.* New York: British Book Centre, 1953.

———. *Inside the Flying Saucers.* New York: Paperback Library, 1967.

Adler, Margot. *Drawing Down the Moon: Witches, Druids, Goddess-Worshippers, and Other Pagans in America Today.* Boston: Beacon, 1986.

Ahern, Geoffrey. *Sun at Midnight: The Rudolf Steiner Movement and the Western Esoteric Tradition.* Wellingborough, U.K.: Thorsons, 1984.

Alderman, C. L. *The Devil's Shadow: The Story of Witchcraft in Massachusetts.* New York: Archway, 1970.

Andersen, Kurt. "The Origin of Alien Species." *New Yorker* (14 July 1997): 38–39.

Anderson, Walter. *Reality Isn't What It Used to Be.* San Francisco: Harper, 1990.

Andrews, G. C. *Extra-Terrestrials among Us.* St. Paul, Minn.: Fate/Llewelyn, 1993.

Apocryphal Gospels. *Los Evangelios Apócrifos.* Edited by A. de Santos Otero. Madrid: Biblioteca de Autores Cristianos, 1963.

Aristotle. *Aristotle's Theory of Poetry and Fine Art.* Edited by S. H. Butcher. New York: Dover, 1951.

Auerbach, Erich. *Mimesis: The Representation of Reality in Western Literature.* Garden City, N.Y.: Anchor, 1957.

Baker, Robert A. "The Aliens among Us: Hypnotic Regression Revisited." *Skeptical Inquirer* 12, no. 2 (1987): 147–62.

Balakian, Anna. *The Symbolist Movement: A Critical Appraisal*. New York: Vintage, 1967.

Barasch, Moshe. *Icon: Studies in the History of an Idea*. New York: New York University Press, 1992.

———. *Imago Hominis: Studies in the Language of Art*. New York: New York University Press, 1994.

Barlowe, Wayne D. *Barlowe's Guide to Extraterrestrials: Great Aliens from Science Fiction Literature*. New York: Workman, 1987.

Barry, Bill. *Ultimate Encounter: The True Story of a UFO Kidnapping*. New York: Bantam, 1978.

Bartholomew, Robert E., and G. S. Howard. *UFOs and Alien Contact: Two Centuries of Mystery*. Amherst, N.Y.: Prometheus Books, 1998.

Baudelaire, Charles. *Selected Writings on Art and Artists*. Harmondsworth, U.K.: Penguin, 1972.

Baudrillard, Jean. *Selected Writings*. Stanford: Stanford University Press, 1988.

Begley, Sharon. "Religion and the Brain." *Newsweek,* 7 May 2001, pp. 51–57.

Belting, Hans. *Likeness and Presence: A History of the Image before the Era of Art*. Chicago: University of Chicago Press, 1996.

Benjamin, Walter. *Illuminations*. London: Tiranti, 1970.

Bergier, Jacques. *Les Extra-Terrestres dans l'Histoire*. Paris: J'ai Lu, 1970; *Extraterrestrial Visitations from Prehistoric Time to the Present*. New York: Signet, 1974.

Bergson, Henri. *Creative Evolution*. New York: Modern Library, 1944.

———. *An Introduction to Metaphysics*. New York: Liberal Arts, 1955.

Berlitz, Charles, and Bill Moore. *The Roswell Incident*. New York: Berkley, 1980.

Bernheimer, Richard. *Wild Men in the Middle Ages: A Study in Art, Sentiment, and Demonology*. New York: Octogon, 1970.

Bernstein, Morey. *The Search for Bridey Murphy*. New York: Pocket Books, 1956.

Bird, S. Elizabeth. *Dressing in Feathers: The Construction of the Indian in American Popular Culture*. Boulder, Colo.: Westview, 1996.

Blackmore, S. "Abduction by Aliens or Sleep Paralysis?" *Skeptical Inquirer* 22, no. 3 (1998): 23–28.

Bloom, Harold. *Omens of Millennium: The Gnosis of Angels, Dreams, and Resurrection*. New York: Riverhead, 1997.

Boethius. *The Consolation of Philosophy*. Edited by I. Edman. New York: Modern Library, 1943.

Boorstin, Daniel J. *The Image: A Guide to Pseudo-Events in America*. New York: Colophon, 1964.

———. *The Discoverers*. New York: Random House, 1983.

Borchard, E. M. *Convicting the Innocent: Errors of Criminal Justice*. New Haven: Yale University Press, 1932.

Brady, J. D., ed., *A Manual of Exorcism, Very Useful for Priests and Ministers of the Church*. New York: Hispanic Society, 1975.

Brandelius, Jerilyn Lee. *Grateful Dead Family Album*. New York: Warner, 1989.

Brandon, Ruth. *The Spiritualists: The Passion for the Occult in the Nineteenth and Twentieth Centuries*. London: Weidenfeld & Nicolson, 1983.

Brenner, Hildegard, ed. *Kunstpolitik des Nationalsozialismus.* Reinbek: Rowohlt, 1966.

Brilliant, Richard. *Portraiture.* Cambridge: Harvard University Press, 1991.

Brodie, Fawn M. *No Man Knows My History: The Life of Joseph Smith, the Mormon Prophet.* New York: Knopf, 1957.

Brosnan, John. *Future Tense: The Cinema of Science Fiction.* New York: St. Martin's, 1979.

Brown, Peter. *Madame Blavatsky's Baboon: A History of the Mystics, Mediums, and Misfits Who Brought Spiritualism to America.* New York: Schocken, 1995.

Brown, Slater. *The Heyday of Spiritualism.* New York: Pocket Books, 1972.

Brunvand, Jan H. *The Vanishing Hitchhiker: American Urban Legends and Their Meanings.* New York: Norton, 1981.

Bryan, C. D. B. *Close Encounters of the Fourth Kind: Alien Abduction, UFOs, and the Conference at M.I.T.* New York: Knopf, 1995.

Bryant, J., and D. Zillman, eds. *Media Effects: Advances in Theory and Research.* Hillsdale, N.J.: Lawrence Erlbaum, 1994.

Bucke, R. M. *Cosmic Consciousness: A Study in the Evolution of the Human Mind.* Philadelphia: Innes, 1902.

Buckley, Christopher. *Little Green Men.* New York: HarperPerennial, 1999.

Buddensieg, T., and H. Rogge. *Industriekultur: Peter Behrens and the AEG.* Cambridge: Harvard University Press, 1984.

Bullard, Thomas E. *UFO Abductions: The Measure of a Mystery.* Vol. 1: *Comparative Study of Abduction Reports.* Bloomington, Ind.: Fund for UFO Research, 1987.

Burhan, F. E. *Vision and Visionaries: Nineteenth-Century Psychological Theory, the Occult Sciences, and the Formation of the Symbolist Aesthetic in France.* Unpubl. Ph.D. diss. Princeton University, 1979.

Burton, Richard, *The Anatomy of Melancholy.* Edited by H. Jackson. London: Dell, 1932.

Callistratus. *Descriptions.* Edited by A. Fairbanks. London: Loeb, 1969.

Campbell, Hannah. *Why Did They Name It . . . ?* New York: Ace, 1964.

Cantor, J. "Fright Reactions to Mass Media." In *Media Effects: Advances in Theory and Research.* Edited by J. Bryant and D. Zillman, 40–46. Hillsdale, N.J.: Lawrence Erlbaum, 1994.

Cantril, H. *The Invasion from Mars: A Study in the Psychology of Panic.* Princeton: Princeton University Press, 1940.

Carducho, Vicente. *Diálogos de la Pintura: Su defensa, origen, esencia, definición, modos y diferencias.* Edited by F. Calvo Serraller. Madrid: Cátedra, 1979.

Carnegie, Dale. *How to Win Friends and Influence People.* New York: Pocket Books, 1977.

Carpenter, T. H. *Art and Myth in Ancient Greece.* London: Thames & Hudson, 1991.

Carus, Paul. *The History of the Devil and the Idea of Evil.* LaSalle Ill.: Open Court, 1990.

Catechism of the Council of Trent for Parish Priests. Rockford, Ill.: TAN Books, 1982.

Cézanne, Paul. *Letters.* Edited by John Rewald. Oxford: Oxford University Press, 1946.

Chacornac, P. *Éliphas Lévi, rénovateur de l'occultisme en France.* Paris: Alcan, 1926.

Chadwick, Whitney. *Myth in Surrealist Painting, 1929–1939.* Ann Arbor: University of Michigan Press, 1980.

Chambers, Frank. *The History of Taste: An Account of the Revolutions of Art Criticism and Theory in Europe.* New York: Columbia University Press, 1932.

Chapeaurouge, Donat de. *Raffael: Sixtinische Madonna, Begegnung von Cäsaren-Papst und Künstler-König.* Frankfurt a/M: Fischer, 1993.

Chaplin, J. P. *Rumor, Fear, and the Madness of Crowds.* New York: Ballantine, 1959.

Chipp, Hershel B., ed. *Theories of Modern Art: A Source Book by Artists and Critics.* Berkeley: University of California Press, 1969.

Christian, William. *Apparitions in Late Medieval and Renaissance Spain.* Princeton: Princeton University Press, 1981.

Cohn, Norman. *The Pursuit of the Millennium.* London: Secker & Warburg, 1957.

———. *Europe's Inner Demons: An Enquiry Inspired by the Great Witch-Hunt.* New York: New American Library, 1975.

Coke, Van Deren. *The Painter and the Photograph.* Albuquerque: University of New Mexico Press, 1972.

Conway, Flo, and Jim Siegelman. *Snapping: America's Epidemic of Sudden Personality Change.* New York: Delta, 1979.

Corliss, William R. *Handbook of Unusual Natural Phenomena.* New York: Arlington House, 1983.

Cormack, Robin. *Painting the Soul: Icons, Death Masks, and Shrouds.* London: Reaktion, 1997.

Crews, Frederick. "The Mindsnatchers." *New York Review of Books* (June 25, 1998): 14–19.

Crowe, Michael J. *The Extraterrestrial Life Debate, 1750–1900.* Mineola, N.Y.: Dover, 1999.

Culler, J. *Saussure.* London: Faber, 1976.

Curtius, E. R. *European Literature and the Latin Middle Ages.* New York: Torchbooks, 1963.

Daniels, Les. *Living in Fear: A History of Horror in the Mass Media.* New York: Scribner's, 1975.

Däniken, Erich von. *Chariots of the Gods? Unsolved Mysteries of the Past.* New York: Bantam, 1971.

———. *Gods from Outer Space: Return to the Stars, or Evidence for the Impossible.* New York: Bantam, 1972.

Darlington, David. *Area 51—The Dreamland Chronicles: The Legend of America's Most Secret Military Base.* New York: Holt, 1997.

David, Jay, ed. *The Fying Saucer Reader.* New York: Signet, 1967.

Da Vinci, Leonardo. *The Literary Works of Leonardo da Vinci.* Edited by J. P. Richter. Oxford: Oxford University Press, 1939.

Davis-Weyer, C., ed. *Early Medieval Art, 300–1150.* Englewood Cliffs, N.J.: Prentice-Hall, 1971.

Dean, Jodi. *Aliens in America: Conspiracy Cultures from Outerspace to Cyberspace.* Ithaca: Cornell University Press, 1998.

Debord, Guy. *La Société du Spectacle.* Paris: Gallimard, 1992.

Deonna, Walter. *De la Planète Mars en Terre Sainte: Art et Subconscient. Un Médium peintre: Hélène Smith.* Paris: De Boccard, 1932.

Dick, Steven J. *Plurality of Worlds: The Origins of the Extraterrestrial Life Debate from Democritus to Kant.* Cambridge: Cambridge University Press, 1982.

Dione, R. L. *God Drives a Flying Saucer.* New York: Bantam, 1978.

Dodds, E. R. *The Greeks and the Irrational.* Berkeley: University of California Press, 1971.

Dorra, Henri, ed. *Symbolist Art Theories: A Critical Anthology.* Berkeley: University of California Press, 1994.

Downing, Barry H. *The Bible and Flying Saucers.* Philadelphia: Lippincott, 1968.

Dresden, Sem. *Humanism in the Renaissance.* New York: McGraw-Hill, 1968.

Drimmer, Frederick, ed. *Captured by the Indians: Fifteen Firsthand Accounts, 1750–1870.* New York: Dover, 1985.

Duby, Georges. *L'An Mil.* Paris: Gallimard, 1980.

Durwood, Thomas, ed. *Close Encounters of the Third Kind: A Document of the Film.* New York: Ballantine, 1978.

Eberhart, George M., ed. *UFOs and the Extraterrestrial Contact Movement: A Bibliography.* Metuchen, N.J.: Scarecrow Press, 1986.

Einstein, Albert, and L. Infeld. *The Evolution of Physics.* New York: Simon & Schuster, 1938.

Ellenberger, Henri F. *The Discovery of the Unconscious: The History and Evolution of Dynamic Psychiatry.* New York: BasicBooks, 1979.

Elsworthy, Frederick T. *The Evil Eye: The Origins and Practices of Superstition.* New York: Collier, 1970.

Erdoes, Richard. *A.D. 1000: Living on the Brink of Apocalypse.* New York: Harper, 1988.

Erickson, C. *The Medievial Vision: Essays in History and Perception.* Oxford: Oxford University Press, 1976.

Evans, Bergen. *The Natural History of Nonsense.* New York: Vintage, 1958.

Evans, Hilary, and J. Spencer, eds. *UFOs, 1947–1987: The Forty Year Search for an Explanation.* London: Fortean Press, 1987.

Evans, Martha N. *Fits and Starts: A Genealogy of Hysteria in Modern France.* Ithaca, N.Y.: Cornell University Press, 1991.

Ewen, Stuart. *All-Consuming Images: The Politics of Style in Contemporary Culture.* New York: BasicBooks, 1988.

Faulkner, William. *The Sound and the Fury.* New York: Vintage, 1956.

Fielding, W. J. *Strange Superstitions and Magical Practices.* New York: Doubleday, 1945.

Fischer, Helmut. *Die Ikone: Ursprung, Sinn, Gestalt.* Freiburg: Herder, 1995.

Flournoy, Théodore. *From India to the Planet Mars: A Case of Multiple Personality and Imaginary Languages.* Princeton: Princeton University Press, 1994.

Fort, Charles. *New Lands.* New York: Ace, 1968.

———. *The Book of the Damned.* New York: Ace, 1972.

Fowler, Ronald E. *The Andreasson Affair.* New York: Bantam, 1980 (hardback ed., Englewood Cliffs, N.J.: Prentice-Hall, 1979).

———. *The Andreasson Affair, Phase Two.* Englewood Cliffs, N.J.: Prentice-Hall, 1982.

———. *The Watchers: The Secret Design Behind UFO Abduction.* New York: Bantam, 1990.

———. *The Allagash Abductions.* Tigard, Ore.: Wild Flower Press, 1993.

Frascina, Francis, and J. Harris, eds. *Art in Modern Culture: An Anthology of Critical Texts.* London: Phaidon, 1992.

Frazer, Kendrick, ed. *The UFO Invasion: The Roswell Incident, Alien Abductions, and Government Coverups.* Amherst, N.Y.: Prometheus Books, 1997.

——— . *Encounters with the Paranormal: Science, Knowledge, and Belief.* Amherst, N.Y.: Prometheus Books, 1998.

Freedberg, David. *The Power of Images: Studies in the History and Theory of Response.* Chicago: University of Chicago Press, 1989.

Freedland, Nat. *The Occult Explosion.* New York: Berkley, 1972.

Freud, Sigmund. *The Interpretation of Dreams.* Edited by J. Strachey. New York: Avon, 1965.

Friedman, J. B. *The Monstrous Races in Medieval Art and Thought.* Cambridge: Harvard University Press, 1981.

Friend, A. M. "The Portraits of the Evangelists in Greek and Latin Manuscripts." *Art Studies* 5 (1927): 115–47; 7 (1929): 3–29.

Fry, Edward F., ed. *Cubism.* London: Thames & Hudson, 1966.

Fuller, Curtis, ed. *Proceedings of the First International UFO Congress.* New York: Warner, 1980.

Fuller, John G. *The Interrupted Journey: Two Lost Hours "Aboard a Flying Saucer."* New York: Dell, 1967.

Fussell, Paul. *Bad or, The Dumbing of America.* New York: Touchstone, 1991.

Gablik, Suzi. *Has Modernism Failed?* New York: Thames & Hudson, 1985.

Gandolfo, F. *Il "Dolce Tempo": Mistica, Ermetismo e Sogno nel Cinquecento.* Rome: Bulzoni, 1978.

Gardiner, Eileen, ed. *Visions of Heaven and Hell before Dante.* New York: Italica, 1989.

Gardner, Martin. *Fads and Fallacies in the Name of Science.* New York: Dover, 1957.

———. *Science: Good, Bad, and Bogus.* New York: Avon, 1983.

———. *The New Age: Notes of a Fringe Watcher.* Amherst, N.Y.: Prometheus Books, 1988.

Garrett, Laurie. *The Coming Plague: New Emerging Diseases in a World out of Balance.* New York: Penguin, 1995.

Godwin, Joscelyn, ed. *Music, Mysticism, and Magic: A Sourcebook.* London: Routledge & Kegan Paul, 1986.

Goldhagen, Daniel J. *Hitler's Willing Executioners: Ordinary Germans and the Holocaust.* New York: Vintage, 1997.

Goldwater, Robert. *Primitivism in Modern Art.* New York: Vintage, 1967.

Gombrich, E. H. *Art and Illusion: A Study in the Psychology of Pictorial Representation.* Princeton: Princeton University Press, 1969.

Goran, Morris. *Fact, Fraud, and Fantasy: The Occult and Pseudosciences.* Totowa, N.J.: Littlefield, Adams, 1979.

Gordon, Henry. *Channeling into the New Age: The "Teachings" of Shirley MacLaine and Other Such Gurus.* Amherst, N.Y.: Prometheus Books, 1988.

Greenblatt, Stephan. *Renaissance Self-Fashioning: From More to Shakespeare.* Chicago: University of Chicago Press, 1980.

Grubb, Nancy. *Angels in Art.* New York: Abbeville, 1995.

Grun, Bernard. *The Timetables of History: A Horizontal Linkage of People and Events.* New York: Touchstone, 1982.

Guazzo, Francesco Maria. *Compendium Maleficarum.* Edited by Montague Summers. New York: Dover, 1988.

Guerra, Manuel. *Simbología Románica.* Madrid: Fundación Universitaria Española, 1986.

Guthke, Karl S. *The Last Frontier: Imagining Other Worlds, from the Copernican Revolution to Modern Science Fiction.* Ithaca, N.Y.: Cornell University Press, 1990.

Halberstam, David. *The Fifties.* New York: Villard Books, 1993.

Halbey, Marianne. *66 Hexen: Kult und Verdammung.* Dortmund: Harenberg, 1987.

Hamilton, G. H. "Cézanne, Bergson, and the Image of Time." *College Art Journal* 16, no. 3 (1956): 2–12.

Happold, F. C., ed. *Mysticism: A Study and an Anthology.* Harmondsworth, U.K.: Penguin, 1971.

Harpur, Patrick. *Daimonic Reality: A Field Guide to the Otherworld.* London: Arkana/Penguin, 1995.

Harrison, Charles, and Peter Wood, eds. *Art in Theory, 1900–1990: An Anthology of Changing Ideas.* Oxford: Blackwell, 1992.

Hauser, Arnold. *The Social History of Art.* New York: Vintage, 1960.

Haywood, Ian. *Faking It: Art and Politics of Forgery.* New York: St. Martin's, 1987.

Heller, Louis B. *Do You Solemnly Swear?* New York: Curtis, 1968.

Heller, Reinhold. *Edvard Munch: The Scream.* New York: Viking, 1972.

Henderson, Linda D. *The Fourth Dimension and Non-Euclidean Geometry in Modern Art.* Princeton: Princeton University Press, 1983.

Herrmann, Joachim. *Das falsche Weltbild: Astronomie und Aberglaube.* Munich: DTV, 1973.

Hertz, Jonathan, and Norman Klein, eds. *Twentieth-Century Art Theory: Urbanism, Politics, and Mass Culture*. Englewood Cliffs, N.J.: Prentice-Hall, 1990.

Hertz, Richard, ed. *Theories of Contemporary Art*. Englewood Cliffs, N.J.: Prentice-Hall, 1985; 2d ed. (with different essays), 1993.

Hesiod. *Homeric Hymns and Homerica*. Edited by H. G. Evelyn-White. London: Loeb, 1964.

Hess, John, and Karen Hess. *The Taste of America*. New York: Penguin, 1977.

Hess, Thomas B., and Linda Nochlin, eds. *Woman as Sex Object: Studies in Erotic Art*. New York: Newsweek, 1972.

Hines, Terence. *Pseudoscience and the Paranormal: A Critical Examination of the Evidence*. Amherst, N.Y.: Prometheus Books, 1994.

Hinz, Berthold. *Die Malerei im deutschen Faschismus*. Munich: Hanser Verlag, 1974.

Hite, Shere. *The Hite Report: A Nationwide Study of Female Sexuality*. New York: Dell, 1977.

Hitler, Adolf. *Mein Kampf*. Edited by R. Mannheim. Boston: Houghton-Mifflin, 1971.

Hoffer, Eric. *The True Believer: Thoughts on the Nature of Mass Movements*. New York: Perennial Library, 1966.

Hofstadter, Richard. *The Paranoid Style in American Politics and Other Essays*. Cambridge: Harvard University Press, 1996.

Hopkins, Budd. *Missing Time*. New York: Berkley, 1983.

———. *Intruders: The Incredible Visitations at Copley Woods*. New York: Ballantine, 1988.

Hughes, Robert. *Culture of Complaint: The Fraying of America*. New York: Oxford University Press, 1993.

Huyghe, Patrick. *The Field Guide to Extraterrestrials*. New York: Avon, 1996.

Hynek, J. Allen. *The UFO Experience: A Scientific Inquiry*. New York: Ballantine, 1974.

Ioakimidis, Demétre, ed. *Histoires d'extraterrestres*. Paris: Livre de Poche, 1974.

Ishakower, Otto. "A Contribution to the Psychopathology of Phenomena Associated with Falling Asleep." *International Journal of Psycho-Analysis* 19 (1938): 331–45.

Jacobs, David M. *The UFO Controversy in America*. Bloomington: Indiana University Press, 1975.

———. *Secret Life: Firsthand Documented Accounts of UFO Abductions*. New York: Fireside, 1993.

———. *The Threat*. New York: Simon & Schuster, 1998.

James, William. *Principles of Psychology*. New York: Holt, 1890.

———. *The Varieties of Religious Experience*. New York: Mentor, 1958.

Janson, H. W. *Sixteen Studies*. New York: Abrams, 1973.

Jenkins, Mariana. *The State-Portrait: Its Origin and Evolution*. New York: College Art Association, 1947.

Jensen, Robert. *Marketing Modernism in Fin-de-Siècle Europe*. Princeton: Princeton University Press, 1994.

Jessup, M. K. *The Case for the UFOs: Unidentified Flying Objects*. New York: Bantam, 1955.

Johnson, William, ed. *Focus on the Science Fiction Film*. Englewood Cliffs, N.J.: Prentice-Hall, 1972.

Jung, Carl Gustav. *Flying Saucers: A Modern Myth of Things Seen in the Sky*. Princeton: Princeton University Press, 1973.

Kaemmerling, Ekkehard, ed. *Ikonographie und Ikonologie: Theorien—Entwicklung—Probleme*. Cologne: DuMont, 1979.

Kamen, Henry. *The Spanish Inquisition*. New York: Mentor, 1965.

Kanon, Gregory N. *The Great UFO Hoax*. Lakeville, Minn.: Galde Press, 1997.

Kempe, Margery. *The Book of Margery Kempe*. Edited by W. Butler-Bowdon. Oxford: Oxford University Press, 1954.

Kendrick, Walter. *The Thrill of Fear: 250 Years of Scary Entertainment*. New York: Grove Weidenfeld, 1991.

Kern, Steven. *The Culture of Space and Time, 1880–1918*. Cambridge: Harvard University Press, 1983.

Kerr, H., and C. L. Crow, eds. *The Occult in America: New Historical Perspectives*. Urbana: Illinois University Press, 1986.

Kingman, Mark. *Dreams of the Millennium: Report from a Culture on the Brink*. London: Faber & Faber, 1996.

Klass, Philip J. *UFOs Explained*. New York: Random House, 1974.

———. *UFOs: The Public Deceived*. Amherst, N.Y.: Prometheus Books, 1983.

———. *UFO-Abductions: A Dangerous Game*. Amherst, N.Y.: Prometheus Books, 1989.

———. *The Real Roswell Crashed Saucer Coverup*. Amherst, N.Y.: Prometheus Books, 1997.

Klingender, Francis D. *Art and the Industrial Revolution*. London: Paladin, 1972.

Koch, Howard. *The Panic Broadcast: Portrait of an Event*. New York: Avon, 1971.

Kohn, Hans. *The Mind of Germany: The Education of a Nation*. New York: Harper & Row, 1965.

Korff, Kal K. "What Really Happened at Roswell." *Skeptical Inquirer* 21, no. 3 (July/August 1997): 24–31.

———. *The Roswell UFO Crash: What They Don't Want You to Know*. New York: Dell, 2000.

Kors, A. C., and E. Peters, eds. *Witchcraft in Europe, 1100–1700: A Documentary History*. College Park: Pennsylvania State University Press, 1986.

Kosinski, D. M. *Orpheus in Nineteenth-Century Symbolism*. Ann Arbor: University of Michigan Press, 1989.

Kramer, Heinrich, and James Sprenger. *The Malleus Maleficarum*. Edited by Montague Summers. New York: Dover, 1971.

Kris, Ernst, and Otto Kurz. *Die Legende vom Künstler: Ein geschichtlicher Versuch*. Vienna: Krystall, 1934.

Kurtz, Paul, ed. *A Skeptic's Handbook of Parapsychology*. Amherst, N.Y.: Prometheus Books, 1992.

———. "UFO Mythology: The Escape to Oblivion." *Skeptical Inquirer* 21, no. 3 (July/August 1997): 12–14.

Kusche, L. D. *The Bermuda Triangle Mystery—Solved.* New York: Warners, 1975.

Kuspit, Donald. *The Cult of the Avant-Garde Artist.* Cambridge: Cambridge University Press, 1993.

Lears, T. J. J. *Fables of Abundance: A Critical History of Advertising in America.* New York: BasicBooks, 1994.

Leavens, I. B. *From "291" to Zurich: The Birth of Dada.* Ann Arbor: University of Michigan Research Press, 1983.

Le Bon, Gustave. *Psychologies des foules.* Paris: Alcan, 1895; *The Psychology of Peoples.* New York: Macmillan, 1898.

Lee, Renasselaer W. *Ut Pictura Poesis: The Humanistic Theory of Painting.* New York: Norton, 1967.

Levenstein, Harvey A. *Paradox of Plenty: A Social History of Eating in Modern America.* Oxford: Oxford University Press, 1993.

Lévi, Eliphas. *Transcendental Magic, Its Doctrine and Ritual.* London: Rider, 1968.

———. *The History of Magic, Including a Clear and Precise Exposition of Its Procedure, Its Rites, and Its Mysteries.* London: Rider, 1982.

Levine, R. M. *Bad Blood: A Family Murder in Marin County.* New York: Bantam, 1982.

Lewis, I. M. *Ecstatic Religion: An Anthropological Study of Spirit Possession and Shamanism.* Harmondsworth, U.K.: Penguin, 1971 (rev. ed., London: Routledge, 1989).

Lewis, James R., ed. *The Gods Have Landed: New Religions from Other Worlds.* Albany: State University of New York Press, 1995.

Lewis, Jon E., ed. *The Permanent Book of the Twentieth Century: Eye-Witness Accounts of the Moments That Shaped Our Century.* New York: Carroll & Graf, 1994.

Lindner, Robert. *The Fifty-Minute Hour: A Collection of True Psychoanalytic Tales.* New York: Bantam, 1966.

Lledó, Joaquín. *Los Milenarismos.* Madrid: Acento, 1999.

Loers, V., ed. *Okkultismus und Avantgarde: Von Munch bis Mondrian, 1900–1915.* Frankfort: Kunsthalle, 1995.

Loftus, Elizabeth F. *Eyewitness Testimony.* Cambridge: Harvard University Press, 1979.

———. *The Myth of Repressed Memory: False Memories and Allegations of Sexual Abuse.* New York: St. Martin's, 1996.

Loftus, Elizabeth F., and K Ketcham. *Witness for the Defense.* New York: St. Martin's, 1991.

Lomazzo, Gian Paolo. *Scritti sulle arti.* Edited by R. P. Ciardi. Florence: Centro Di, 1974.

L'Orange, H. P. *Apotheosis in Ancient Portraiture.* New Rochellem, N.Y.: Caratzas, 1982.

Lorenzen, Coral. *Flying Saucers: The Startling Evidence of the Invasion from Outer Space.* New York: Signet, 1966.

Lorenzen, Coral, and Jim Lorenzen. *The Flying Saucer Occupants.* New York: Signet, 1967.

Lovejoy, Margot. *Postmodernist Currents: Art and Artists in the Age of Electronic Media.* Englewood Cliffs, N.J.: Prentice-Hall, 1997.

Luck, Georg, ed. *Arcana Mundi: Magic and the Occult in the Greek and Roman World.* Baltimore: Johns Hopkins University Press, 1985.

Lynes, Russell. *The Tastemakers.* New York: Universal Library, 1954.

MacDougall, Curtis. *Hoaxes.* New York: Dover, 1958.

———. *Superstition and the Press.* Amherst, N.Y.: Prometheus Books, 1983.

Mack, John E. *Abduction: Human Encounters with Aliens.* New York: Ballantine, 1995.

Mackay, Charles. *Extraordinary Popular Delusions and the Madness of Crowds.* New York: Page, 1932.

MacKenzie, J. L. *Dictionary of the Bible.* New York: Dutton, 1965.

Macrobius. *Commentary on the Dream of Scipio.* Edited by W. H. Stahl. New York: Columbia University Press, 1990.

Maguire, Henry. *Art and Eloquence in Byzantium.* Princeton: Princeton University Press, 1981.

Mango, Cyril, ed. *The Art of the Byzantine Empire, 312–1453.* Englewood Cliffs, N.J.: Prentice-Hall, 1972.

Maritain, Jacques. *Creative Intuition in Art and Poetry.* New York: Vintage, 1958.

Marling, Karel Ann. *As Seen on TV: The Visual Culture of Everyday Life in the 1950s.* Cambridge: Harvard University Press, 1994.

Marx, Karl, and Friedrich Engels. *The Communist Manifesto.* New York: Washington Square Press, 1967.

Masters, R. E. L. *Eros and Evil: The Sexual Psychopathology of Witchcraft.* Baltimore: Penguin, 1974.

Matheson, Terry. *Alien Abductions: Creating a Modern Phenomenon.* Amherst, N.Y.: Prometheus Books, 1998.

Mathews, Patricia T. *Aurier's Symbolist Art Criticism and Theory.* Ann Arbor: University of Michigan Press, 1986.

McAndrew, James. *The Roswell Report: Case Closed.* New York: Barnes & Noble, 1997.

McDannell, C., and B. Lang. *Heaven: A History.* New York: Vintage, 1990.

McIntosh, Christopher. *Éliphas Lévi and the French Occult Revival.* New York: Weiser, 1972.

McKee, Ilse. *Tomorrow the World.* London: Dent, 1960.

Menzel, Donald H., and Lyle G. Boyd. *The World of Flying Saucers.* New York: Doubleday, 1963.

Mercier, A. *Éliphas Lévi et la pensée magique au XIXe siècle.* Paris: Alcan, 1974.

Messent, B., ed. *Literature of the Occult: A Collection of Critical Essays.* Englewood Cliffs, N.J.: Prentice-Hall, 1981.

Michel, Aimé. "The Strange Case of Dr. X." *Flying Saucer Review* (1972): 11–32.

Miller, Mary E. *The Art of Mesoamerica, from Olmec to Aztec.* London: Thames & Hudson, 1986.

Mirzoeff, Nicholas. *An Introduction to Visual Culture.* London and New York: Routledge, 1999.

Moffitt, John F. "Who Is the 'Old Man in a Golden Helmet'?" *Art Bulletin* 46, no. 3 (1984): 417–27.

———. *Occultism in Avant-Garde Art: The Case of Joseph Beuys.* Ann Arbor: University of Michigan Research Press, 1986.

———. "Malleus Maleficarum: A Literary Context for Fuseli's Nightmare." *Gazette des Beaux Arts* 114 (1990): 1–7.

———. "The Meaning of 'Christ after the Flagellation' in Siglo de Oro Sevillian Painting." *Wallraf-Richartz Jahrbuch* 53 (1992): 139–54.

———. "Architecture as Primeval Expression: Antonio Gaudí in the Context of the European Symbolist Movement." In *Icon to Cartoon: A Tribute to Sixten Ringbom*, 161–92. Edited by A. Ringbom. Helsinki: Helsingfors, 1995.

———. *Art Forgery: The Case of the Lady of Elche.* Gainesville: Florida University Press, 1995 (*El caso de la Dama de Elche: Crónica de una leyenda.* Barcelona: Destino, 1997).

———. "The Palestrina Mosaic with a 'Nile Scene': Philostratus and Ekphrasis; Ptolemy and Chorographia." *Zeitschrift für Kunstgeschichte* 60, no. 2 (1997): 227–47.

———. "Balaam or Isaiah in the Catacomb of Priscilla." *Konsthistorisk Tidskrift* 66, no. 3 (1997): 77–87.

———. *The Arts in Spain.* London: Thames & Hudson, 1998.

———. "The Extraterrestrials among Us: An Eye-Witness Report of a Close Encounter with 'Kólfr.'" *Journal of Irreproducible Results* 64, no.1 (March/April 1999): 3–5.

———. "The Native American 'Savage' as Pictured by French Romantic Artists and Writers." *Gazette des Beaux-Arts* 123, no. 3 (September 1999): 117–30.

———. "Modern Extraterrestrial Portraiture: An Art-Historical Inquest." In *Mélanges Antoine Faivre* (Gnostica 3), 623–46. Edited by J. Godwin. Leuven: Peeters, 2001.

———. "A Pictorial Counterpart to 'Gothick' Literature: 'Daemonialitas' and the Haunting 'Incubus' in Henry Fuseli's *Nightmare.*" *Mosaic* 34, no. 3 (September 2001): 1–22.

———. *Alchemist of the Avant-Garde: The Case of Marcel Duchamp.* Albany: State University of New York Press, 2003 (in press).

———. [H. M. S. Phake-Potter, pseud.]. *Postmodernist Deconstruction for Dummies: A Survivor's Guide to Building Your Academic Career.* Philadelphia: Xlibris, 2002.

———. [H.M.S. Phake-Potter, pseud.]. *Poetic Inspirations for Dummies: How to Create Modern Verse, For Better or Worse.* Philadelphia: Xlibris, 2002.

Moffitt, John F. and Santiago Sebastián. *O Brave New People: The European Invention of the American Indian.* Albuquerque: University of New Mexico Press, 1996.

Montgomery, Ruth. *Aliens among Us.* New York: Putnam, 1985.

Morgan, David, ed. *Icons of American Protestantism: The Art of Warner Sallman.* New Haven: Yale University Press, 1996.

Mosse, George L., ed. *Nazi Culture: Intellectual, Cultural, and Social Life in the Third Reich.* New York: Grossett & Dunlap, 1968.

Mulvey-Roberts, Marie. *Handbook to Gothic Literature.* New York: New York University Press, 1998.

National Enquirer UFO Report. New York: Pocket Books, 1985.

Newberg, Andrew. *Why God Won't Go Away: Brain Science and the Biology of Belief.* New York: Ballantine, 2001.

New York Post Staff. *Heaven's Gate: Cult Suicide in San Diego.* New York: HarperCollins, 1997.

Nickell, Joe. "A Fantasy Assessment Biography." *Skeptical Inquirer* 21, no. 4 (July/August 1997): 15–16.

———. "Extraterrestrial Iconography." *Skeptical Inquirer* 21, no. 5 (September/October 1997): 18–19.

———. *Looking for a Miracle: Weeping Icons, Relics, Stigmata, Visions, and Healing Cures.* Amherst, N.Y.: Prometheus Books, 1998.

———. "Exorcism! Driving Out the Nonsense," *Skeptical Inquirer* 25, no. 1 (January/February 2001): 20–24.

———. ed. *Mysterious Realms: Probing Paranormal, Historical, and Forensic Enigmas.* Amherst, N.Y.: Prometheus Books, 1993.

———, ed. *The Outer Edge: Classic Investigations of the Paranormal.* Amherst, N.Y.: CSICOP, 1996.

Nin, Anaïs. *The Novel of the Future.* New York: Holt, 1972.

Nochlin, Linda, ed. *Impressionism and Post-Impressionism, 1874–1904* (Sources and Documents in the History of Art). Englewood Cliffs, N.J.: Prentice-Hall, 1966.

Nordau, Max. *Degeneration.* Lincoln: Nebraska University Press, 1993.

Ober, William B. *Bottoms Up! A Pathologist's Essays on Medicine and the Humanities.* New York: Perennial, 1988.

Pacheco, Francisco. *El arte de la pintura.* Edited by B. Bassegoda i Hugas. Madrid: Cátedra, 1990.

Panati, Charles. *Panati's Extraordinary Origins of Everyday Things.* New York: Harper, 1987.

———. *Panati's Parade of Fads, Follies, and Manias. The Origins of Our Most Cherished Obsessions.* New York: Harper, 1991.

Panofsky, Erwin. *Three Essays on Style.* Cambridge: MIT Press, 1997.

Papus. *Traité élémentaire de Science Occulte, mettant chacun à même de comprendre et d'expliquer les théories et les symboles employés par les anciens, par les alchimistes, les astrologues, les kabbalistes.* Paris, 1897 [facs. ed., St Jean de Braye, 1979].

Patristic Authors. *The Ante-Nicene Fathers: Translations of the Writings of the Fathers Down to* A.D. 325. Edited by. A. Roberts and J. Donaldson. Grand Rapids, Mich.: Tanner, 1963.

Peebles, Curtis. *Watch the Skies! A Chronicle of the Flying Saucer Myth.* Washington D.C.: Smithsonian, 1994.

Peters, Harry T. *Currier & Ives, Printmakers to the American People*. Garden City, N.Y.: Anchor, 1942.

Philostratus the Younger/the Elder. *Imagines*. Edited by A. Fairbanks. London: Loeb, 1969.

Plato. *Great Dialogues of Plato*. Edited by W. H. D. Rouse. New York: Mentor, 1956.

———. *Phaedrus and Letters VII and VIII*. Edited by W. Hamilton. Harmondsworth, U.K.: Penguin, 1973.

Poggioli, Renato. *The Theory of the Avant-Garde*. New York: Harper, 1968.

Pollitt, J. J., ed. *The Art of Greece, 1400–31 B.C.* Englewood Cliffs, N.J.: Prentice-Hall, 1965.

Pontus Hultén, K. G., ed. *The Machine as Seen at the End of the Mechanical Age*. New York: Museum of Modern Art, 1968.

Poole, Stafford. *Our Lady of Guadalupe: The Origins and Sources of a Mexican National Symbol, 1531–1797*. Tucson: Arizona University Press, 1996.

Postman, Neil. *Amusing Ourselves to Death: Public Discourse in the Age of Show Business*. New York: Penguin, 1986.

Potter, Charles E. *Days of Shame*. New York: Signet, 1971.

Powell, Nicolas. *Fuseli: The Nightmare*. New York: Viking, 1973.

Price, Sally. *Primitive Art in Civilized Places*. Chicago: University of Chicago Press, 1989.

Progoff, J., ed. *The Cloud of Unknowing*. New York: Columbia University Press, 1957.

Pulos, Arthur J. *American Design Ethic: A History of Industrial Design to 1940*. Cambridge: Harvard University Press, 1983.

Ramírez, Juan Antonio. *Medios de masas e historia del arte*. Madrid: Cátedra, 1981.

Randi, James. *Flim-Flam! Psychics, ESP, Unicorns, and Other Delusions*. Amherst, N.Y.: Prometheus Books, 1986.

Randles, Jenny. *UFO Study*. London: Robert Hale, 1981.

———. *The UFO Conspiracy: The First Forty Years*. London: Javelin, 1988.

———. *Alien Contacts and Abductions*. New York: Sterling, 1994.

Rawcliffe, D. H. *The Psychology of the Occult*. London: Ridgway, 1952; rpt. *Occult and Supernatural Phenomena*. New York: Dover, 1960.

Redfern, N. *The FBI Files: The FBI's UFO Top Secrets Exposed*. London: Pocket Books, 1998.

Reed, G. *The Psychology of Anomalous Experiences*. Amherst, N.Y.: Prometheus Books, 1988.

Remak, Joachim, ed. *The Nazi Years: A Documentary History*. Englewood Cliffs, N.J.: Spectrum, 1969.

Reston, James. *The Last Apocalypse: Europe at the Year 1000 A.D.* New York: Doubleday, 1997.

Rhodes, Colin. *Primitivism and Modern Art*. London: Thames & Hudson, 1994.

Ringbom, Sixten. *Icon to Narrative: The Rise of the Dramatic Close-Up in Fifteenth-Century Devotional Painting*, Doornspijk: Davaco, 1984.

———. *Les images de dévotion (XIIe–XVe siècle)*. Paris: Monfort, 1995.

Rookmaaker, H. R. *Gauguin and Nineteenth-Century Art Theory.* Amsterdam: Swets & Zeitlinger, 1972.

Root, Deborah. *Cannibal Culture: Art, Appropriation, and the Commodification of Difference.* Boulder, Colo.: Westview, 1996.

Rosenblum, Robert. *Transformations in Late Eighteenth-Century Art.* Princeton: Princeton University Press, 1970.

Ross, D. F., et al. *Adult Eyewitness Testimony: Current Trends and Developments.* Cambridge: Cambridge University Press, 1994.

Rubin, William, ed. *"Primitivism" in Twentieth-Century Art: Affinity of the Tribal and the Modern.* New York: Abrams, 1984.

Ruthven, Martin. *The Divine Supermarket.* London: Chatto & Windus, 1989.

Sacks, Peter. *Generation-X Goes to College: An Eye-Opening Account of Teaching in Postmodern America.* Chicago: Open Court, 1996.

Sagan, Carl. *The Demon-Haunted World: Science as a Candle in the Dark.* New York: Ballantine, 1997.

Sagan, Carl, and T. Page, eds. *UFO's: A Scientific Debate.* New York: Barnes & Noble, 1996.

Saliba, John A., ed. *Flying Saucer Contactees: A Sociopsychological Perspective.* Detroit: Apogee, 1990.

Sander, Ralph. *Das Star Trek Universum. Das erste deutsche Handbuch zur erfolgreichsten Multimedia-SF-Serie der Welt.* Munich: Heyne, 1989–1995 (3 vols.).

Sargant, William. *The Mind Possessed: A Physiology of Possession, Mysticism, and Faith Healing.* New York: Penguin, 1975.

Sass, Louis A. *Madness and Modernism: Insanity in the Light of Modern Art, Literature, and Thought.* New York: BasicBooks, 1992.

Scharf, Aaron. *Art and Photography.* Harmondsworth, U.K.: Penguin, 1974.

Schiff, Gert, et al. *Henry Fuseli, 1741–1825.* London: Phaidon, 1975.

Schow, David J., and J. Frentzen. *The Outer Limits: The Official Companion.* New York: Ace, 1986.

Schreyer, Lothar, ed. *Bildnis der Engel: Ein Schaubuch und Lesebuch.* Freiburg i. B.: Herder, 1940.

Schwartz, Hillel. *Century's End: A Cultural History of the Fin de Siècle from the 990s through the 1990s.* New York: Doubleday, 1990.

Scot, Reginald. *The Discoverie of Witchcraft.* New York: Dover, 1989.

Senior, John. *The Way Down and Out: The Occult in Symbolist Literature.* New York: Greenwood, 1968.

Sheaffer, Robert. *The UFO Verdict.* Amherst, N.Y.: Prometheus Books, 1981.

———. *UFO Sighting—The Evidence.* Amherst, N.Y.: Prometheus Books, 1998.

Shearman, John. *Only Connect . . . Art and the Spectator in the Italian Renaissance.* Princeton: Princeton University Press, 1992.

Sheikh, A. A., ed. *Imagery: Current Theory, Research, and Applications.* New York: Wiley, 1983.

Shermer, Michael. *Why People Believe Weird Things: Pseudoscience, Superstition, and Other Confusions of Our Time.* New York, Freeman, 1997.

Showalter, Elaine. *The Female Malady: Women, Madness, and English Culture, 1830–1980.* New York: Penguin, 1987.

———. *Hystories: Hysterical Epidemics and Modern Media.* New York: Columbia University Press, 1997.

Siegel, Ronald. *Fire in the Brain: Clinical Tales of Hallucination.* New York: Dutton, 1992.

Silverman, Deborah L. *Art Nouveau in Fin-de-Siècle France: Politics, Psychology, and Style.* Berkeley: University of California Press, 1989.

Singer, J., ed. *Repression and Dissociation: Implications for Personality, Theory, Psychopathology, and Health.* Chicago: University of Chicago Press, 1990.

Sinistrari, Lodovico Maria. *Demoniality.* Edited by Montague Summers. New York: Dover, 1989.

Skal, David J. *The Monster Show: A Cultural History of Terror.* New York: Penguin, 1994.

Sladek, John. *The New Apocrypha: A Guide to Strange Sciences and Occult Beliefs.* London: Granada, 1978.

Smith, Toby. *Little Gray Men: Roswell and the Rise of a Popular Culture.* Albuquerque: University of New Mexico Press, 2000.

Snyder, James. *Medieval Art: Painting, Sculpture, Architecture, Fourth–Fourteenth Century.* New York: Abrams, 1989.

Sobchack, Vivian. *Screening Space: The American Science Fiction Film.* New York: Ungar, 1993.

Sokal, Alan, and Jean Bricmont. *Impostures Intellectuelles.* Paris: Editions Odile Jacob, 1997.

Sparks, G. G. "Paranormal Depictions in the Media: How Do They Affect What People Believe?" *Skeptical Inquirer* 22, no. 3 (July/August 1998): 35–39.

Staller, Natalie. "Babel: Hermetic Languages, Universal Languages, and Anti-Languages in Fin-de-Siècle Parisian Culture." *Art Bulletin* 76 (1994): 331–54.

Steiger, Brad, and H. Hewes. *UFO Missionaries Extraordinary.* New York: Pocket Books, 1976.

———. *The UFO Abductors.* New York: Berkley, 1988.

Steiner, Rudolf. *Eurythmy as Visible Speech: Fifteen Lectures.* London: Steiner Press, 1984.

Stoichita, Victor, *Visionary Experience in the Golden Age of Spanish Art.* London: Reaktion, 1995.

Story, Ronald. *The Space Gods Revealed: A Close Look at the Theories of Erich von Däniken.* London: New English Library, 1978.

———. *Guardians of the Universe?* New York: St. Martin's, 1980.

———, ed. *Encyclopedia of UFOs.* New York: New American Library, 1980.

———, ed. *Encyclopedia of Extraterrestrial Encounters.* New York: New American Library, 2001.

"The Story of Betty Crocker." Minneapolis: General Mills, 1997 (a 6-page feuilleton).

Strick, Philip. *Science Fiction Movies.* London: Octopus, 1976.

Strieber, Whitley. *Communion: A True Story.* New York: Bantam, 1987.

————. *Breakthrough: The Next Step.* New York: HarperCollins, 1995.

————. *Confirmation: The Hard Evidence of Aliens among Us.* New York: St. Martin's, 1998.

Stubblebine, James, ed. *Giotto: The Arena Chapel Frescoes.* New York: Norton, 1969.

Stuckenschmidt, H. H. *Twentieth-Century Music.* London: Weidenfeld, 1969.

Stupple, David. "Mahatmas and Space Brothers: The Ideology of an Alleged Contract with Extraterrestrials." *Journal of American Culture* 7 (1984): 131–39.

Suerbaum, Ulrich, with Ulrich Broich and Raimund Borgmeier. *Science Fiction: Theorie und Geschichte, Themen und Typen, Form und Weltbild.* Stuttgart: Reclam, 1981.

Surette, Leon. *The Birth of Modernism: Ezra Pound, T. S. Eliot, W. B. Yeats, and the Occult.* Montreal: McGill-Queens University Press, 1994.

Swedenborg, Emanuel. *Miscellaneous Theological Works.* New York: Swedenborg Publishing Society, 1905.

————. *Heaven and Hell.* Edited by G. F. Dole. New York: Swedenborg Foundation, 1984.

Teresa of Avila, Saint. *The Life of Saint Teresa.* Edited by J. M. Cohen. Harmondsworth, U.K.: Penguin, 1957.

————. *Libro de su Vida.* México: Porrúa, 1972.

Thompson, Keith. *Angels and Aliens: UFOs and the Mythic Imagination.* New York: Ballantine, 1993.

Time/Life Books. *Mysteries of the Unknown.* New York: Book-of-the-Month Club, 1997.

Tiryakian, E. A. *On the Margin of the Visible: Sociology, the Esoteric, and the Occult.* New York: Dutton, 1974.

Tomory, P. A. *The Life and Art of Henry Fuseli.* London: Phaidon, 1972.

Tono Martínez, J., ed. *La Polémica de la Posmodernidad.* Madrid: Ed. Libertarias, 1986.

Tuchman, Maurice , ed. *The Spiritual in Art, Abstract Painting, 1890–1985.* Los Angeles: Los Angeles County Museum of Art, 1986.

Turner, Alice K. *The History of Hell.* New York: Harvest, 1995.

Twitchell, James B. *Adcult USA: The Triumph of Advertising in American Culture.* New York: Columbia University Press, 1996.

Tyrrell, G. N. M. *Apparitions.* New York: Collier, 1963.

Umlauf, Hana, et al. *The World Almanac Book of the Strange.* New York: Signet, 1977.

Vallée, Jacques. *Anatomy of a Phenomenon: UFOs in Space—A Scientific Appraisal.* New York: Ballantine, 1972.

————. *Confrontation: A Scientist's Search for Alien Contact.* New York: Ballantine, 1990.

————. *Revelations: Alien Contact and Human Deception.* New York: Ballantine, 1993.

Vankin, J., and J. Whalen. *Sixty Greatest Conspiracies of All Times: History's Biggest Mysteries, Coverups, and Cabals.* Secaucus, N.J.: Citadel, 1996.

Völker, Klaus, ed. *Künstliche Menschen: Dichtungen und Dokumente über Golems, Homunculi, Androiden und liebende Statuen.* Munich: DTV, 1971.

Wakefield, H., and R. Underwager. *Return of the Furies: An Investigation into Recovered Memory Therapy.* Chicago: Open Court, 1994.

Walker, John A. *Art in the Age of Mass Media.* Boulder, Colo.: Westview, 1994.

Walters, Ed. *The Gulf Breeze Sightings: The Most Astounding Multiple Sightings of UFOs in U.S. History.* New York: Avon, 1991.

Walton, Travis. *The Walton Experience.* New York: Berkley, 1978.

Walton, Travis, with John White. *Fire in the Sky: The Travis Walton Experience.* New York: Marlowe, 1995.

Webb, James. *The Harmonious Circle: The Lives and Work of G. I. Gurdjieff, D. P. Ouspensky, and Their Followers.* LaSalle, Ill: Open Court, 1987.

———. *The Occult Establishment.* LaSalle, Ill: Open Court, 1988.

———. *The Occult Underground.* LaSalle, Ill.: Open Court, 1988.

Weldon, John, and Zola Levitt. *UFOs: What on Earth Is Happening?* Irvine, Calif.: Harvest House, 1975.

Whitehead, Alfred N. *Science and the Modern World.* New York: New American Library, 1960.

Willet, John. *Expressionism.* New York: McGraw Hill, 1978.

Wilson, Colin. *The Mammoth Book of the Supernatural.* New York: Carroll and Graf, 1991.

Wilson, Robert Anton. *Everything Is under Control: Conspiracies, Cults, and Cover-Ups.* New York: HarperPerennial, 1998.

Wilson, Sheryl C., and Theodore X. Barber. "The Fantasy-Prone Personality: Implications for Understanding Imagery, Hypnosis, and Parapsychological Phenomena." In *Imagery: Current Theory, Research, and Applications,* 340–90. Edited by A. A. Sheikh. New York: Wiley, 1983.

Wimsatt, W. K. *Literary Criticism: A Short History.* New York: Vintage, 1957.

Woolf, Virginia. *A Writer's Diary.* New York: Harcourt Brace, 1954.

Wulf, Joseph, ed. *Die bildenden Künste im Dritten Reich. Eine Dokumentation.* Reinbek: Rowohlt, 1966.

Zilsel, Edgar. *Die Entstehung des Geniebegriffes: Ein Beitrag zur Ideengeschichte der Antike und des Frühkapitalismus.* Tübingen: Mohr, 1926.

Index

(note: *passim* indicates topics and/or contexts reiterated throughout the text)